Street by Street

KT-408-555

GLASGOW

CLYDEBANK, COATBRIDGE, EAST KILBRIDE, HAMILTON, PAISLEY

Airdrie, Barrhead, Cambuslang, Cumbernauld, Dumbarton, Erskine, Johnstone, Kirkintilloch, Milngavie, Motherwell, Newton Mearns, Renfrew, Rutherglen, Uddingston, Wishaw

2nd edition September 2004
© Automobile Association Developments Limited 2004

Original edition printed May 2001

Ordnance Survey® This product includes map data licensed from Ordnance Survey ® with the permission of the Controller of Her Majesty's Stationery Office. © Crown copyright 2004. All rights reserved. Licence number 399221.

Published by AA Publishing (a trading name of Automobile Association Developments Limited, whose registered office is Millstream, Maidenhead Road, Windsor, Berkshire SL4 5GD. Registered number 1878835).

Mapping produced by the Cartography Department of The Automobile Association. (A02087)

A CIP Catalogue record for this book is available from the British Library.

Printed by GRAFIASA S.A., Porto, Portugal

Ref: ML070z

Key to map pages	ii-iii
Key to map symbols	iv–1
Enlarged map pages	2-3
Main map pages	4-181
Index – towns & villages	182
Index – streets	183-210
Index – featured places	210-214
Acknowledgements	214

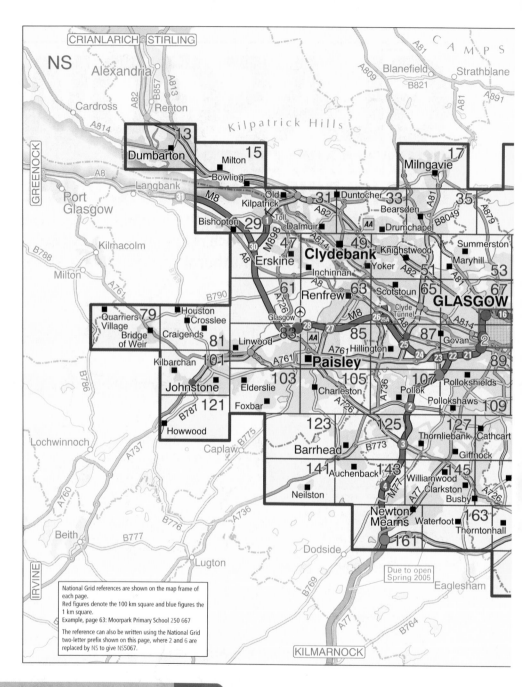

National Grid references are shown on the map frame of each page.
Red figures denote the 100 km square and blue figures the 1 km square.
Example, page 63: Moorpark Primary School 250 667

The reference can also be written using the National Grid two-letter prefix shown on this page, where 2 and 6 are replaced by NS to give NS5067.

Scale of enlarged map pages 1:10,000   6.3 inches to 1 mile

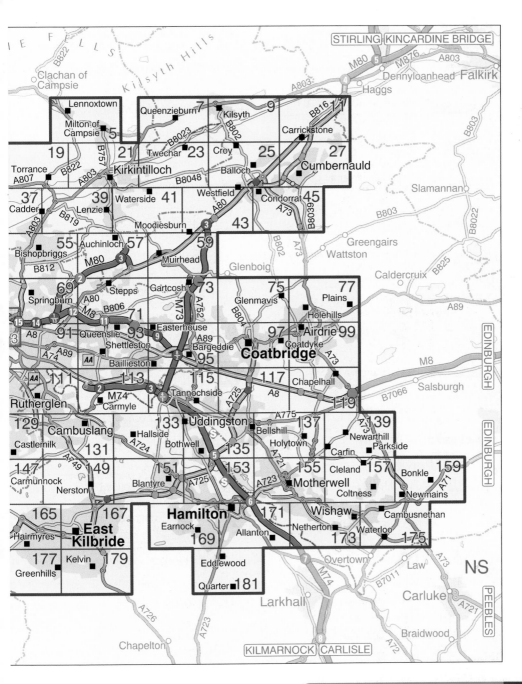

4.2 inches to 1 mile

Scale of main map pages 1:15,000

Junction 9	Motorway & junction	⊖	Underground station
Services	Motorway service area	⊖	Light railway & station
	Primary road single/dual carriageway	+++++++++	Preserved private railway
Services	Primary road service area	*LC*	Level crossing
	A road single/dual carriageway	•—•—•—•	Tramway
	B road single/dual carriageway	- - - - - -	Ferry route
	Other road single/dual carriageway	....	Airport runway
	Minor/private road, access may be restricted	– · – · – ·	County, administrative boundary
← ←	One-way street	▼▼▼▼▼▼	Mounds
	Pedestrian area	**17**	Page continuation 1:15,000
============	Track or footpath	**3**	Page continuation to enlarged scale 1:10,000
▪▪▪▪▪▪▪	Road under construction		River/canal, lake
[– – –]	Road tunnel		Aqueduct, lock, weir
AA	AA Service Centre	465 ▲ Winter Hill	Peak (with height in metres)
P	Parking		Beach
P+	Park & Ride		Woodland
	Bus/coach station		Park
	Railway & main railway station		Cemetery
	Railway & minor railway station		Built-up area

Featured building			Abbey, cathedral or priory	
City wall			Castle	
Hospital with 24-hour A&E department			Historic house or building	
Post Office			Dirleton Castle NTS — National Trust for Scotland property	
Public library			Museum or art gallery	
Tourist Information Centre			Roman antiquity	
Seasonal Tourist Information Centre			Ancient site, battlefield or monument	
Petrol station, 24-hour — Major suppliers only			Industrial interest	
Church/chapel			Garden	
Public toilets			Garden Centre — Garden Centre Association Member	
Toilet with disabled facilities			Farm or animal centre	
Public house — AA recommended			Zoological or wildlife collection	
Restaurant — AA inspected			Bird collection	
Madeira Hotel — Hotel — AA inspected			Nature reserve	
Theatre or performing arts centre			Aquarium	
Cinema			Visitor or heritage centre	
Golf course			Country park	
Camping — AA inspected			Cave	
Caravan site — AA inspected			Windmill	
Camping & caravan site — AA inspected			Distillery, brewery or vineyard	
Theme park				

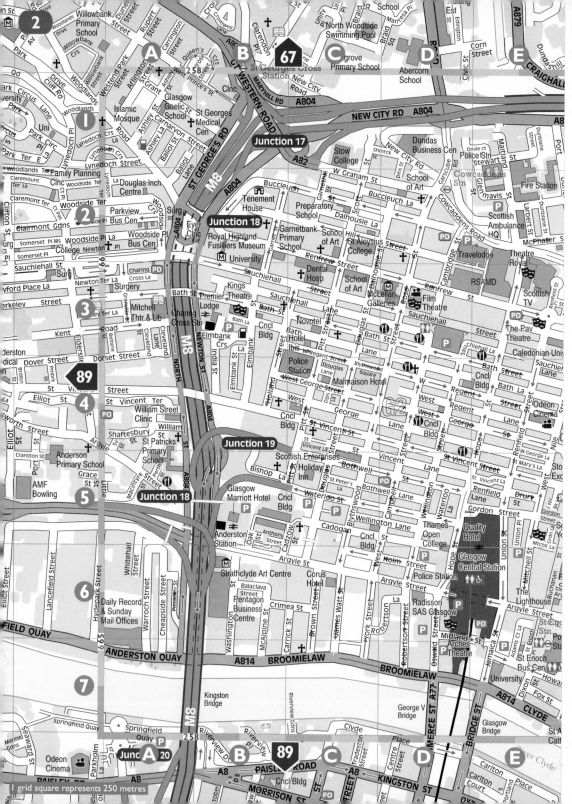

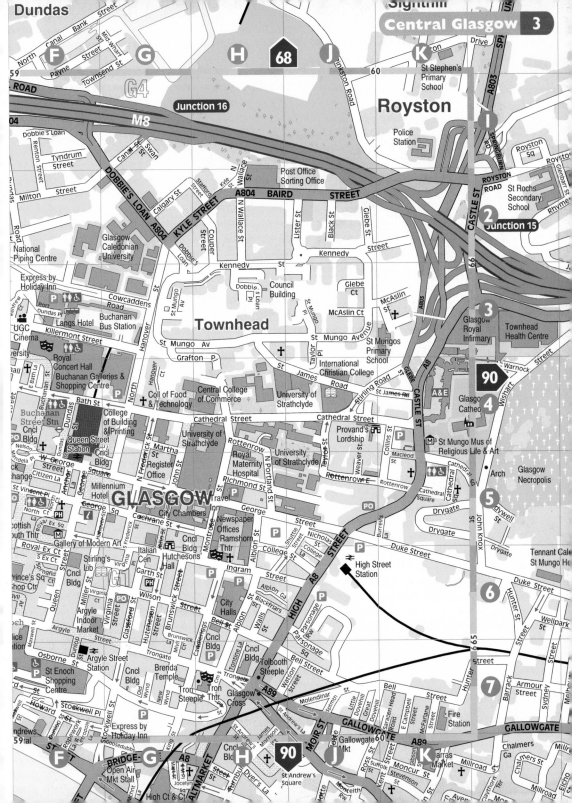

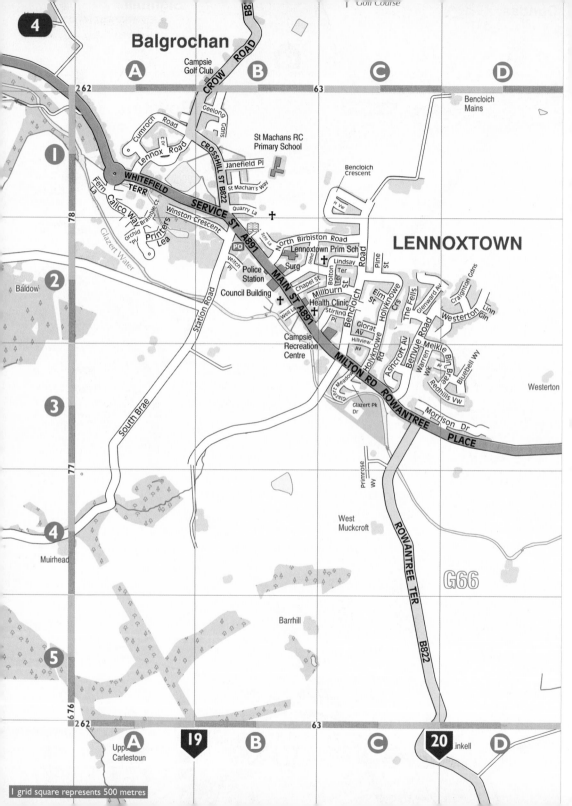

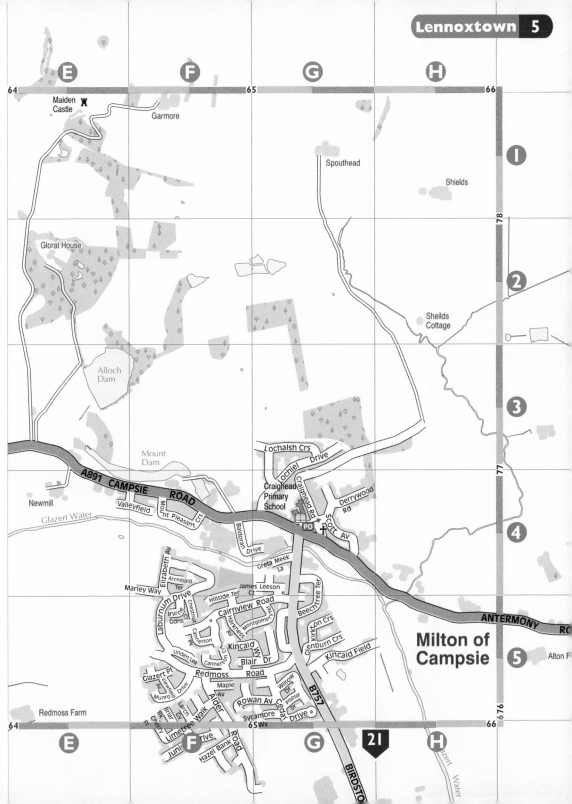

E F G H

64 65 66

I

Maiden Castle
Garmore

Spouthead

Shields

Glorat House

78

Alloch Dam

Sheilds Cottage

Mount Dam

Lochalsh Crs

Lochiel Drive

A891 CAMPSIE ROAD

Newmill

Glazert Water

Valleyfield

Mount Pleasant Crs

Craighead Primary School

Craighead Rd

Derrywood Rd

PO

Scott Av

77

Baldoran Drive

Greta Meek La

Elizabeth Av

Archibald Ter

Marley Way

Laburnum Drive

Chestnut

Irvine Gdns

James Leeson Ct

Hillside Ter

Cairnview Road

Beechtree Ter

Harkness

Montgomery

Camerton Pk

Kirkton Crs

Linden Lea

Cannerton Pk

Kincaid Wy

Blair Dr

Glenburn Crs

Kincaid Field

ANTERMONY RD

Milton of Campsie

Alton P

Glazert Pl

Viewfield Av

Munro

Briar Bk

Cherry Pl

Redmoss Road

Maple Av

Larch

Alder

Juniper

Limetree Walk

Drive

Rowan Av

Sycamore

Cedar

Willow Dr

Poplar

Drive

B757

Redmoss Farm

Hazel Bank Road

BIRDSTO

21

Glazert Water

676

64 65 66

E F G H

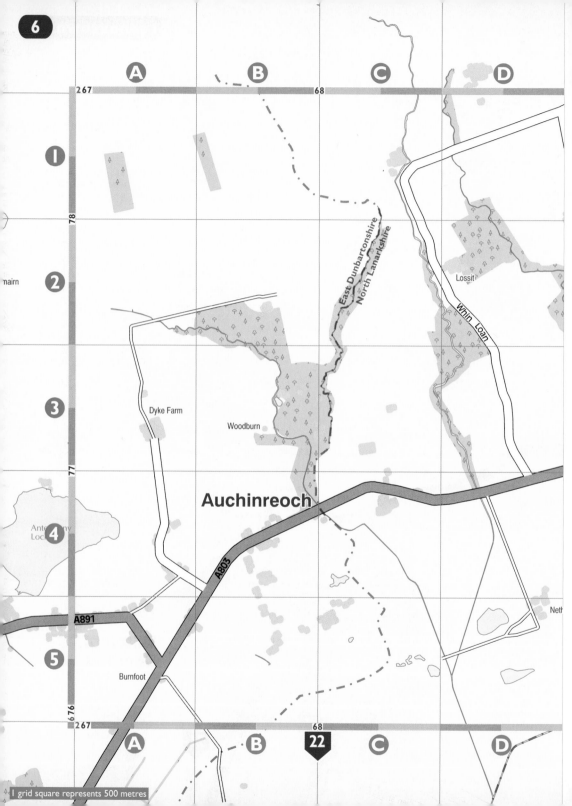

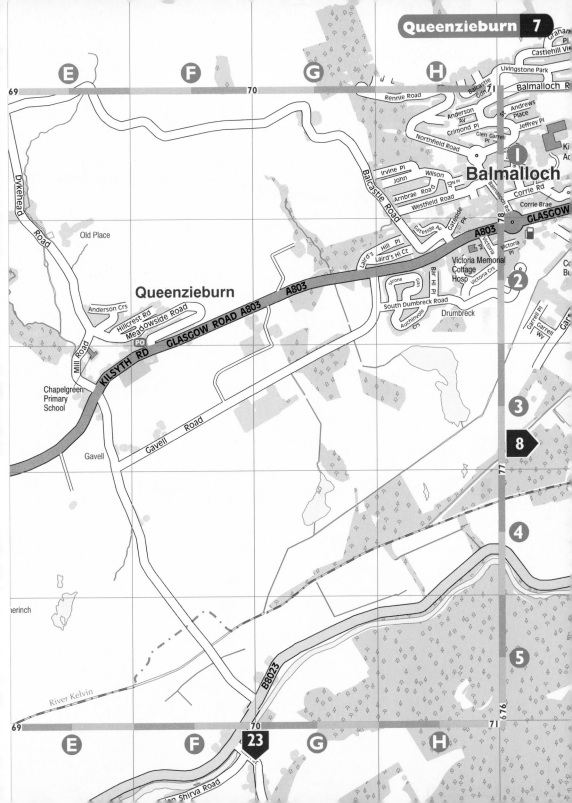

Balmalloch

Queenzieburn

GLASGOW

A803

KILSYTH RD

GLASGOW ROAD A803

A803

Dykehead Road

Old Place

Anderson Crs

Hillcrest Rd

Meadowside Road

PO

Mill Road

Chapelgreen
Primary
School

Gavell

Gavell   Road

River Kelvin

merinch

Rennie Road

Balcastle Road

Irvine Pl

John

Wilson

Arnbrae Road

Westfield Road

Gateside

Gateside Av

Gateside PK

Laird's Hill Pl

Laird's Hill Ct

S.rone

Gdn

Bar Hill Pl

Bar Hl Pl

South Dumbreck Road

Auchinvole
Crs

Drumbreck

Victoria Memorial
Cottage
Hosp

Victoria Crs

Victoria

Victoria

PK

Balmalloch Rd

Balcastle
Gdn

71

Anderson
AV

Crimond Pl

Glen Garrell
Pl

Northfield Road

St Andrews
Place

Jeffrey Pl

Livingstone Park

Castlehill Vie

Granham
Pl

Balmalloch R

Corrie Rd

Corrie Brae

Garrell Pl

Garrell
Wy

Car

Ki
Ad

Co
Bu

E   F   G   H   I

69   70   71

78

77

676

23

8

2

3

4

5

E   F   G   H

69   70   71

an Shirva Road

B8023

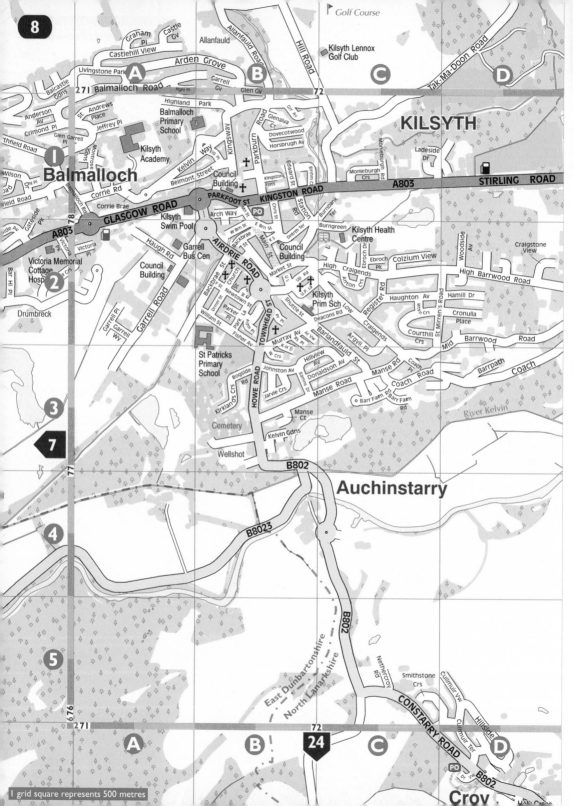

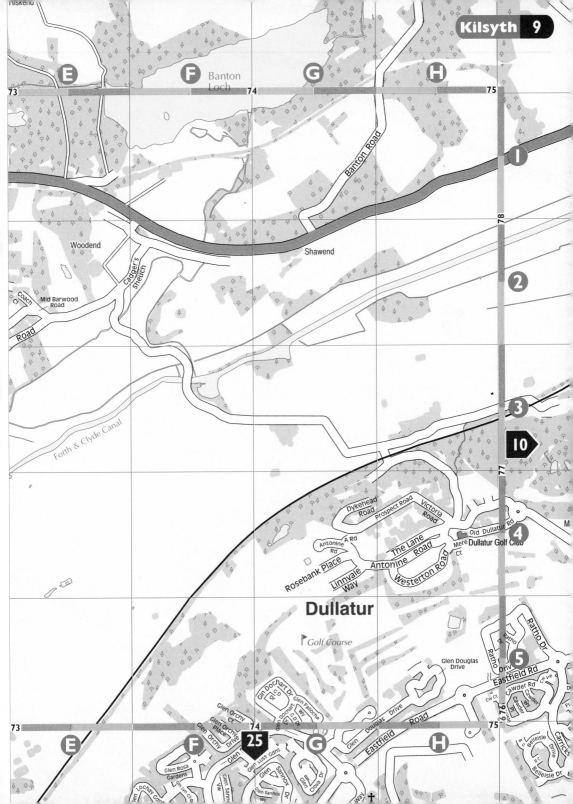

E F Banton Loch G H

73 74 75

1

78

2

Banton Road

Woodend

Shawend

Cadger's Sheuch

Coach Cl

Mid Barwood Road

Road

Forth & Clyde Canal

3

10

77

4

M

Dykehead Road

Prospect Road

Victoria Road

Old Dullatur Rd

Dullatur Golf Club

Mere Ct

A Rd

Antonine Rd

The Lane

Antonine Road

Westerton Road

Rosebank Place

Linnvale Way

Dullatur

Golf Course

Glen Douglas Drive

Ratho Dr

Ratho

Ratho Pl

5

Eastfield Rd

Cawder Rd

Crowder Wy

Cawder Wy

Cw Ct

76

Glen Dochart Dr

C D Dr

Glen Falloch

Glen Dochart Wy

C D Dr

Glen Orchy Ct

Glen Orchy Place

Glen Orchy Drive

Glen

Glen Douglas Drive

Eastfield Road

Carrick

Belleisle Drive

B Cl

Belleisle Dr

73 74 75

E F **25** G H

Glen Rosa Gardens

Glen Lochay Gdns

Glen un Cre

Glen Luss Gdns

Glen Sannox Vw

Glen Sannox Dr

Glen Clova Dr

Way

A · B · 76 · C · D

275

A803

1

78

Forth & Clyde Canal

2

3

9

77

Westerwood

Duncan M

Edenside

The Links

Victoria Road

Muirhead

King's Drive

Ladybank

Carnoustie Way

Birkdale Crs

Golf Course

St Andrews Drive

The Westerwood Hotel

4

Dullatur Rd

Mere Dullatur Golf Club

Ct

Queens Drive

King's View

Gt Crs

Troon Gdns

Mainhead Farm

Rosemount

Gleneagles Av

Muirfield Road

n Road

Ratho Dr

Ratho

Ratho Drive

Cowder Rd

C.Vw

Turnberry Gdns

Tr G

Rigghead Av

Roadside

5

Glen Doug Drive

Eastfield Rd

Cowder Wd

Cowder

Darley Rd

Fullarton Rd

Cathkin Crs

Portland Rd

Carrickstone Rd

Gailes Rd

N Br

M Com

Eastfield Road

Dornoch Wy

Grange

Southerness Dr

Smithwends

Surg

Roadside

The Wynd

676

Belleisle

Cowder

Pamurly Dr

Nairn Wy

The Auld Rd

Kirkwall

PO

Main St

275

Belleisle Cres

Belleisle Dr

Belleisle Gdns

A rickstone Road

Hayston Rd

Callander Rd

Callander Ct

Lansdowne

Letham

Carrickstone

26

A80

The Auld Rd

Baronhill

Glasgow Road

Springfield Road

Cumbernauld Primary School

Wigtoun Pl

Stirling St

Longwill

A8011

A · B · 76 · C · D

I grid square represents 500 metres

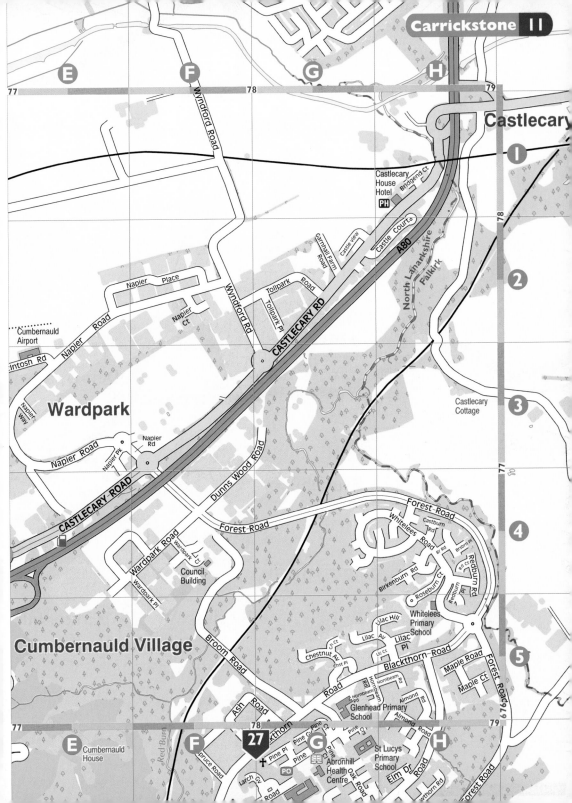

Castlecary

E   F   G   H

77   78   79

1

2

Castlecary
House
Hotel
PH

Bridgend Ct

Castle view

Castle Court

A80

North Lanarkshire

Falkirk

78

Cumbernauld
Airport

Napier   Place

Napier
Ct

Carnhall Farm
Road

Tollpark   Road

Tollpark Pl

Tollpark Rd

Wyndford Road

Wyndford Rd

CASTLECARY RD

3

Intosh Rd

Napier   Road

Wardpark

Napier
Way

Napier Road

Napier Pk

Napier
Rd

CASTLECARY ROAD

Dunns Wood Road

Forest Road

Castlecary
Cottage

77

Forest Road

Whitelees Road

Castburn
Rd

Br Rd

Brborn Rd

Redburn Rd

4

Cumbernauld Village

Wardpark Road

Wardpark Ct

Wardpark Pl

Council
Building

Broom Road

Birkenburn Rd

Roseburn Ct

Redburn

Rd Ct

Lilac Hill

Lilac Av

Lilac
Pl

Chestnut AV

Chst Pl

Lc Ct

Blackthorn Road

Whitelees
Primary
School

Maple Road

Maple Ct

Forest Road 619

5

Ash   Road

Blackthorn   Road

Hornbeam
Rd

Hornbeam

Almond
Rd

Almond
Road

Glenhead Primary
School

St Lucys
Primary
School

77   78   79

E   Cumbernauld
House

F

27

Bruce Road

Pine Pl

Pine

Pine Ct

Pine

Pine Cr

G

Abronhill
Health
Centre

PO

Larch Gv

Oak Road

St Lucys
Primary
School

H

Elm Dr

wthorn Rd

Forest Road

Red Burn

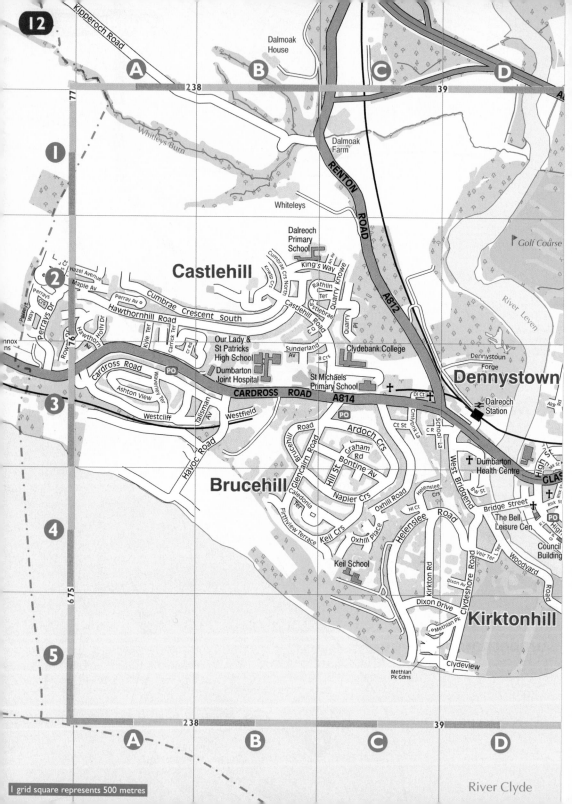

Kipperoch Road

A 238 **B** **C** 39 **D** A

1

Dalmoak House

77

Whiteleys Burn

Dalmoak Farm

Whiteleys

RENTON ROAD

Golf Course

River Leven

Dalreoch Primary School

Castlehill

King's Way

An Av

Cumbrae Crs North

Lomond Crs

Rathlin Ter

Castlebrae

Quarry Knowe

A812

Hazel Avenue

Maple Av

2

Perrays

Perrays Dr

Way

Perray Av

Cumbrae Crescent South

Castlehill Road Co

Quarry Pl

76

Hawthornhill Road

Rowan Dr

Hawthorn Av

Holly Dr

Kyle Ter

Carrick Ter

Cr Rd

Our Lady & St Patricks High School

Sunderland AV

B Crs

Clydebank College

Dennystoun

Dennystown

Lennox ns

Cardross Road

PO

Ashton View

Waverley Ter

Dumbarton Joint Hospital

St Michaels Primary School

DI Ct

Dalreoch Station

3

Westcliff

Tallsman Av

Westfield

CARDROSS ROAD A814

Ct St

Chirynk La

School La

High St

Alc

Havoc Road

PO

Bruce Cairn Road

Road

Ardoch Crs

Graham Rd

Bontine Av

Hill St

C R

Mk St

Dumbarton Health Centre

675

Brucehill

Glencairn Ter

Caledonia Ter

Napier Crs

Oxhill Road

West Bridgend

Helenslee Crs

W St

RISK St

High St

GLAS

PO

High

4

Firthview Terrace

Kell Crs

Oxhill Place

Hl Ct

Helenslee Road

Bridge Street

The Bell Leisure Cen

Council Building

Woodyard

Road

Keil School

Kirkton Rd

Dixon Av

Clydeshore Road

Veir Ter

5

Dixon Drive

Methlan Pk

Kirktonhill

Clydeview

Methlan Pk Gdns

238 **A** **B** 39 **C** **D**

River Clyde

1 grid square represents 500 metres

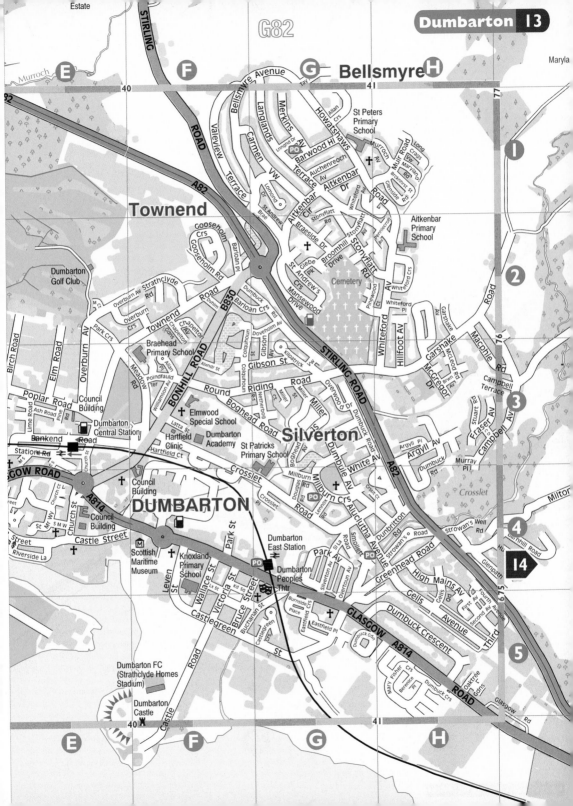

14

A   242   B   Overtoun   C   43   D

Carsnake Av
McGregor Dr
Macphie Rd
McLeod Rd
Brwn Av
Campbell Terrace
Fraser Av
Campbell Avenue
Road
Murray Pl
Dumbuck Rd
ll Av

1

Barnhill

13

Strowan
Milton Brae
Barnhill Road
Hunter's Av
Glenpath

2

Loch Bowie

Milton Brae

Middleton

Mains Av
Cells
First Av
Fourth Avenue
Second Av
Third
Avenue
Crescent
Oaktree Gdns
umbuck Crs

3

ROAD
Glasgow Rd
A82
A814

Dumbuck

Milton Brae

Lennox Rd
Colquhoun
Crannog Rd
Road
Milton Court
Milton Primary School
Hill Ww
Milton Hill
PO

Milton

4

Travelodge

674

Milton Island

5

West Dunbartonshire
Renfrewshire

A82

A   242   B   **28**   C   43   D

River Clyde

1 grid square represents 500 metres

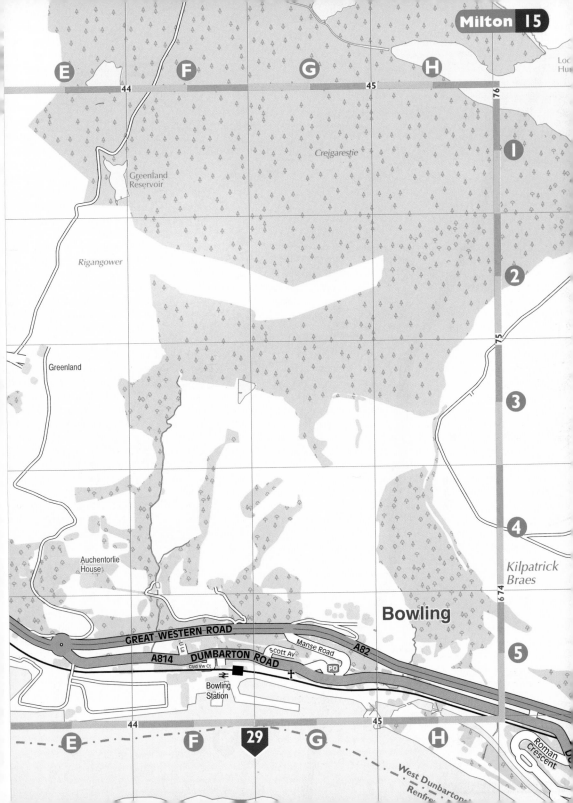

E 44 F G 45 H

76

I

Creigarestie

2

Greenland
Reservoir

75

Rigangower

3

Greenland

4

Auchentorlie
House

Kilpatrick
Braes

674

Bowling

5

GREAT WESTERN ROAD

Manse Road

A82

A814   DUMBARTON ROAD

Scott Av

Clyd Vw Ct

PO

Bowling
Station

E 44 F **29** G 45 H

Roman
Crescent

West Dunbarton

Renfre

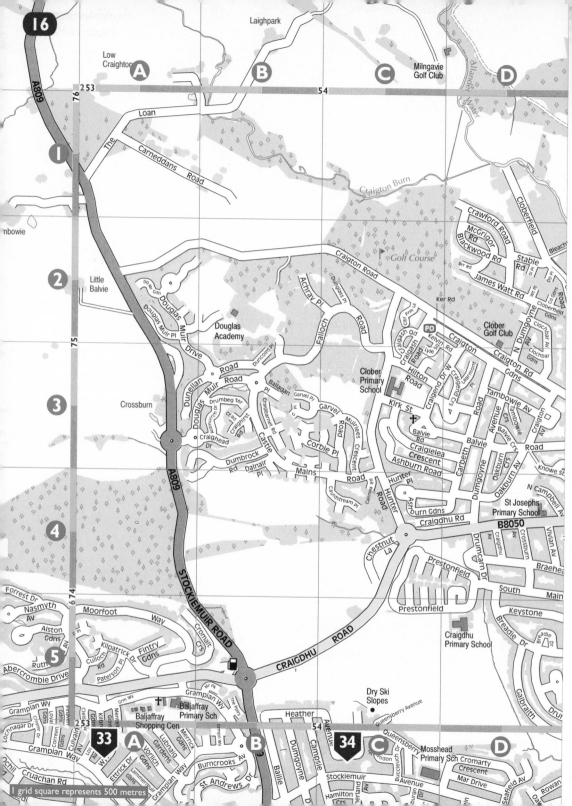

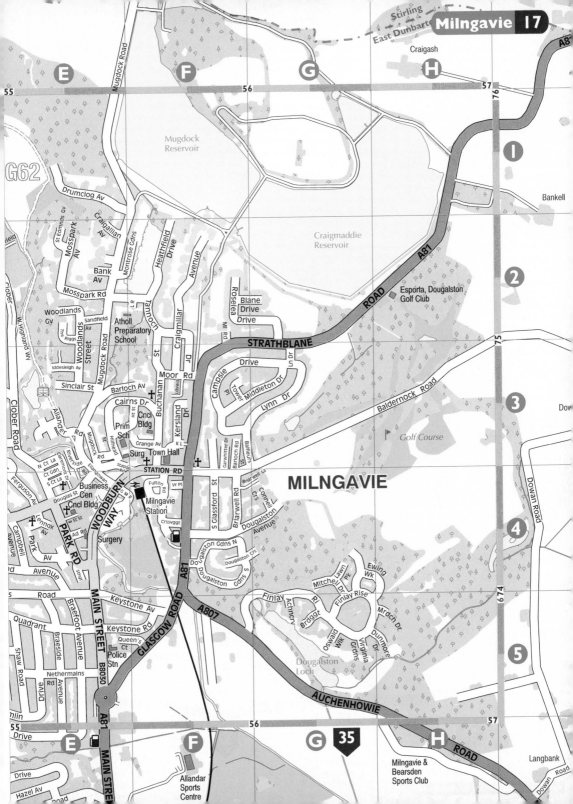

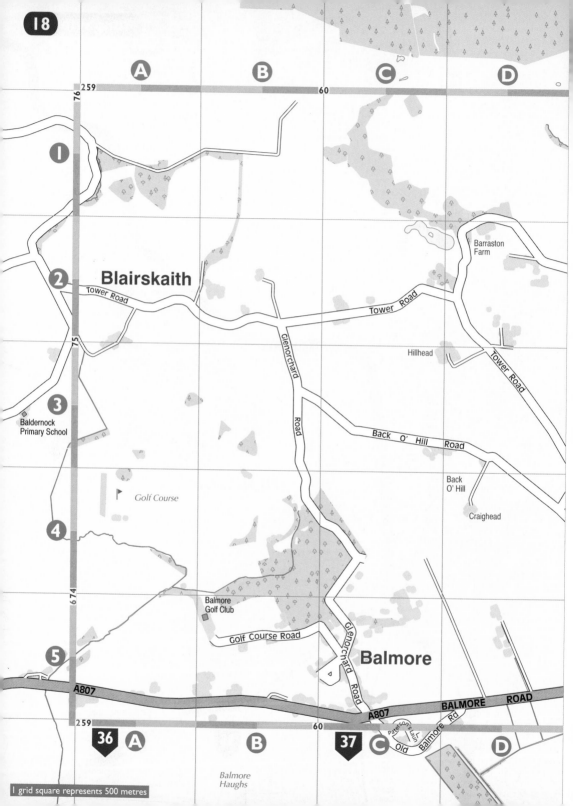

E F G 4 H

4

61 62 63 76

I

Upper
Carlestoun

2

75

Langshot
Farm

Acre Valley
House

3 Carlston

CAMPSIE ROAD

20

Barraston Road

Acre Valley Road

Balgrochan

Wardend Rd

W Balgrochan Road

Nevis Dr

Blair Gdns

Campbell Pl

Maitland Drive

Buchanan Pl

Moray Pl

Atholl Av

Kings Pk

School Road

Mill Crs

Park Crs

4

674

Torrance
Primary
School

West Rd

Woodmill Dr

Torrance

Dalriada Dr

Cormack Av

McHl McPr Dr

Hawthorn St

Guthrie

Viola Pl

Rosehill

Kelvin Vw

River Ke

Tower Road

Smeaton Av

Dundas Av

Charlotte Av

Clyde Av

Crgmdd Gdns

Forth Road

Allander Dr

Craigmarloch

MAIN ST

B822

PO

Firbank Av

Queens Vw

Firbank Av

Rosehill Road

5

River Kelvin

E F G 38 H

61 62 63

TORRANCE

Bogton

RO

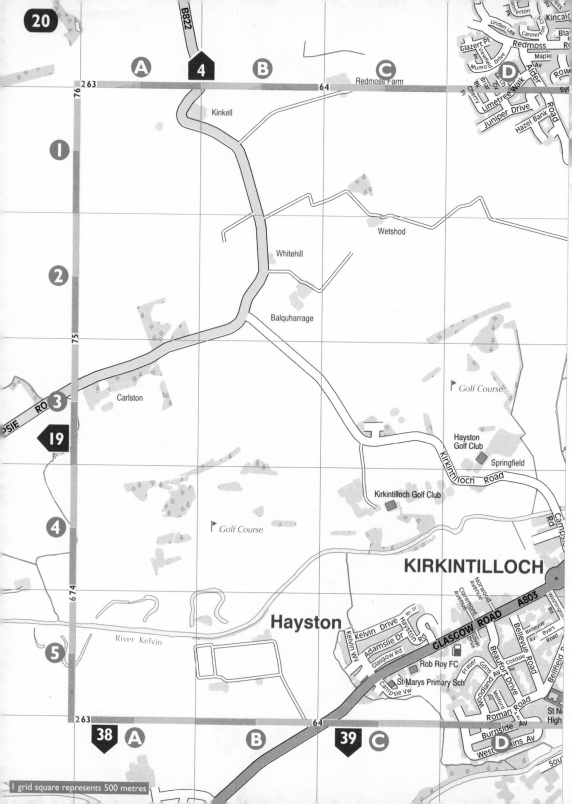

20

A   **4**   **B**   **C**   **D**

263   76   64   Redmoss Farm

Kinkell

1

Wetshod

2

Whitehill

Balquharrage

75

Golf Course

3

Carlston

19

Hayston
Golf Club

Springfield

Kirkintilloch Golf Club

Kirkintilloch Road

4

Golf Course

KIRKINTILLOCH

Campsie Rd

674

Hayston

Kelvin Drive

Adamslie Dr

Kelvin Vw

Glasgow Rd

River Kelvin

GLASGOW ROAD   A803

Washington Rd

Claremont Avenue

Norwood Avenue

Bellevue Av

Byars Rd

Bellevue Road

Rob Roy FC

Beaufort Drive

Coxdale

Fraser Gdns

Campsie Vw

St Marys Primary Sch

Woodland Av

Melford Rd

Roman Road

Burnside Av

West Nins Av

Bellfield Rd

St Ni High

St Ni

38   **A**   **B**   **39**   **C**   **D**

263   64

I grid square represents 500 metres

22

Burnfoot

A   B   **6**   C   D

76 267   68

I

North Lanarkshire
East Dunbartonshire

2

B8023

Auchendavie
Forth & Clyde Canal
St Flanan

3
Alloway Dr
Ellisland Dr   Ellisland
Drum.hill   Tintock Road
Alloway   Drive   Kingsway   Antonine   Eastermains   St Flanan Road
21   Carrick   Ct   Tintock
Allow   Alloway Gdns   Mauchline   Av   Clarinda   **Harestanes**
Burns Dr   Crs   Strathearn Cv
Doon Wy   Harestanes   Kintyre   Gdns
Mossgiel   Doon   Primary Sch   Rannoch Drive   Glenelg   Kinkell Gdns
Fell s View Av   Loch Ct   Crt   Crs
Afton   Doon   Road   Armour   Armour   Cowal   Crs   Applecross   Road   Badenoch Road   Loch Pl
Vw   Burns   Harestanes   Ct   Road
4   Langmuir Road   Gdns   Moray Pl   Moidart Gdns   **Solsgirth**
Merkland Sch   Fossil Grove
PO   Merkland
St Flannans   Pl   David Gray
Primary   Dr
School

674   Merkland

5   Woodstock   Avenue   Drive
Lammermoor Rd   Avvert's Crs   BG Ytts
Lammermoor Crs   Barrhill Ct   **Rosebank**   Kirkintilloch Road
Quarry   Drive   Barrhill Road   staffa Dr   Bute Rd   KIRKINTILLOCH ROAD
Briar Road   Muirside   Avenue   Ulst   Iona   Way   Gartconner Av   Gartconner   Wester
PO   Blackburn   Islay Road   St   Primary School   Gartshore
Oxgang   Crs   ROAD   St Agathas
Primary   Primary School
Sch
Kirkintilloch   267
High School
B8048   **40**   A   SIDE   B   **41**   C   D
68
Cairn Av   Moss Rd   **Waterside**
Bankhead   Alexander
PO

I grid square represents 500 metres

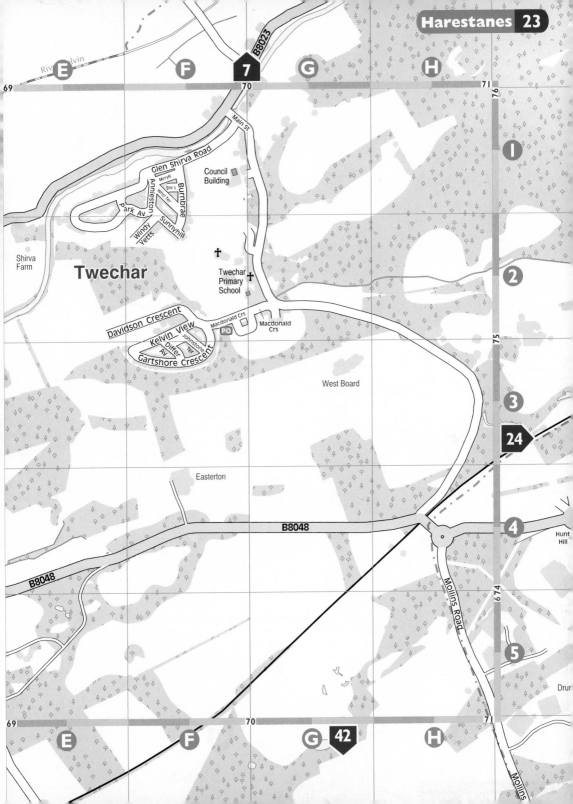

Riv **E** lvin

E **F** **7** **G** **H**

B8023

I

Main St

Glen Shirva Road

Council Building

Mrryfi
Shr L
Wnd Ter
Annieston
Burnbrae
Park Av
Windy Yetts
Sunnyhill

Shirva Farm

Twechar

Twechar Primary School

2

Davidson Crescent

Kelvin View
Johnstone
Differ
Av
Gartshore Crescent

Macdonald Crs
PO
Macdonald Crs

West Board

3

24

Easterton

B8048

4

Hunt Hill

B8048

Mollins Road

674

5

Drur

E **F** **G** **42** **H**

Mollins

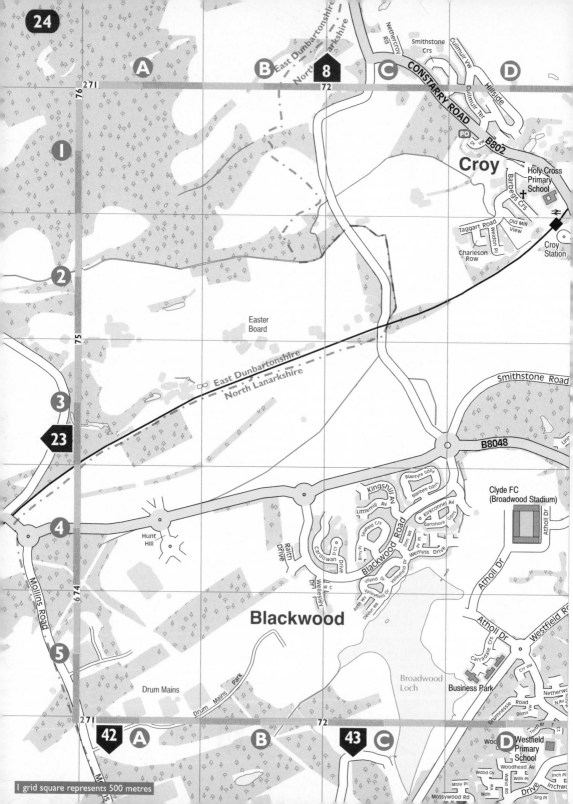

24

A B C D

271 76 72

8

Nethercroy Rd

Smithstone Crs

Cullmuir Vw

CONSTARRY ROAD

East Dunbartonshire
North Lanarkshire

Cullmuir Ter

Hillside

B802

PO

Croy

Holy Cross
Primary
School

Croy Station

Barbegs Crs

Taggart Road

Weldon Pl

Old Mill
View

Charleson
Row

1

2

Easter
Board

East Dunbartonshire
North Lanarkshire

75

Smithstone Road

3

23

B8048

Linn

4

Hunt
Hill

Kingshill Av

Littlemill Av

Blantyre Gdns
Blantyre Gdns

Clyde FC
(Broadwood Stadium)

Atholl Dr

Kirkconnel Av

Cardowan Drive

Raith
Drive

Seafield Crs

Birny Pl

Crs

Dixn Wk

Gartshore Gdns

Wemyss Drive

Yallerfield Dr

Cnts

Atholl Dr

Wellesley
Dr

V C

Villyrd Dr

Airth Wy

Devon Wk

Yallerfield Dr

Blackwood

Westfield Rd

Atholl Dr

Mollins Road

674

5

Drum Mains

Drum Mains Park

Broadwood
Loch

Business Park

Carradale Crs

Crr Vw

Netherw

Road

Drummessie

Westfield
Primary
School

271 72

42 A B **43** C D

Woodhead Av

Woodmill Rd

Wdhd Gv

Wdhd
Pl

Wdhd Rd

Inch Pl

Mssy Pl

Inchwd

Grg Pl

Drive

Mossywood Rd

I grid square represents 500 metres

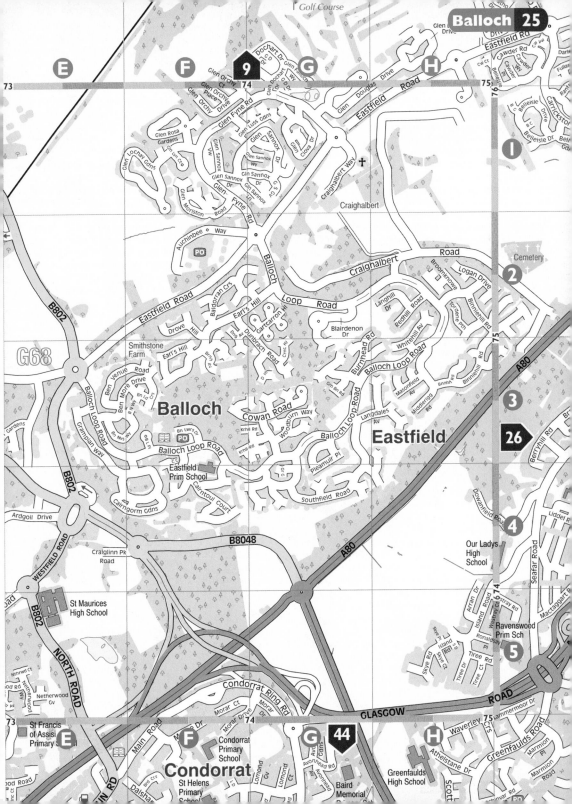

Cumbernauld Village

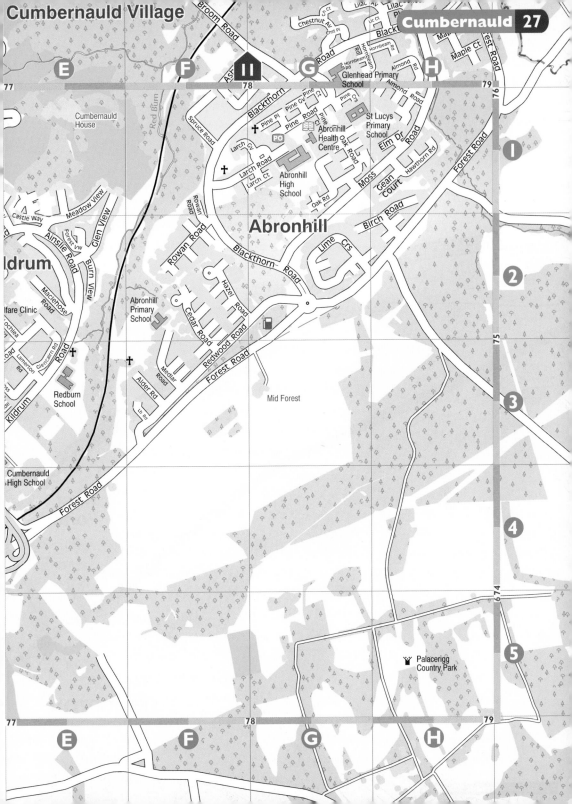

E F **II** G H

77 78 79

76

Broom Road

chestnut Av

Lilac Av

Lilac Ct

Blackt

Maple Ct

rest Road

Maple

Cumbernauld House

Red Burn

Ash

Blackthorn

Spruce Road

Pine Pl Pine Gv Pine

Pine Road

Pine Road

Chestnut Rd

Hornbeam

Hornbeam Rd

Glenhead Primary School

Almond

Almond Rd

Almond Road

St Lucys Primary School

Elm Dr

Forest Road

I

PO

Larch Gv

Larch Road

Larch Ct

Abronhill Health Centre

Oak Road

Oak Rd

Moss

Elm Dr

Road

Hawthorn Rd

Abronhill High School

Oak Rd

Cean court

Birch Road

Rowan Road

Rowan Road

Kildrum

Castle Way

Meadow View

Glen View

Forest Vw

Ainslie Road

Burn View

Abronhill

Blackthorn Road

Lime Crs

2

75

Maclehose Road

Welfare Clinic

ochlea

Glencairn Rd

Road

Lamberton Rd

Kildrum

Abronhill Primary School

Hazel Road

Cedar Road

Redwood Road

Medlar Road

Alder Rd

LD Rd

Blackthorn Road

Forest Road

3

Redburn School

Mid Forest

74

Cumbernauld High School

Forest Road

4

Palacerigg Country Park

5

77 78 79

E F G H

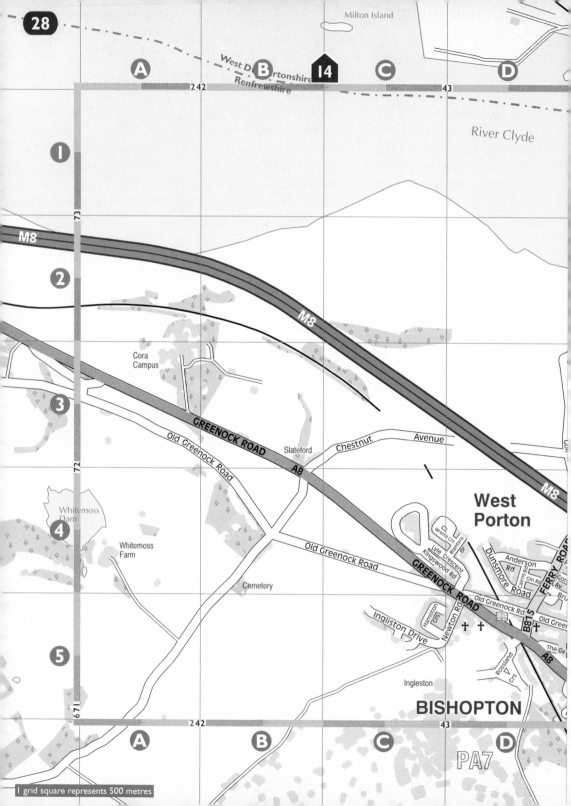

28

A **242** B **14** C **43** D

Milton Island

West D...rtonshire
Renfrewshire

River Clyde

1

73

M8

2

M8

3

Cora
Campus

GREENOCK ROAD

Old Greenock Road

Slateford

A8

Chestnut   Avenue

**West
Porton**

72

Whitemoss
Dam

4

Whitemoss
Farm

Old Greenock Road

Wraith Crs
Ct
Blantyre
Dr

Lyle Crescent

Kingswood Rd

GREENOCK ROAD

Cairns Rd
Gln Rd

Anderson
Rd

Cor...
Av

FERRY ROAD

Bru...

Old Green...

Dunsmore Road

B815

Cemetery

Old Greenock Rd

Hamilton
Crs

Newton Rd

† †

†

Ingliston Drive

The Gv

5

Rossland
Crs

A8

Ingleston

671

BISHOPTON

A **242** B C **43** D

PA7

1 grid square represents 500 metres

GREAT WESTERN ROAD

Manse Road

A82

A814 DUMBARTON ROAD

Scott Av

Clyd Vw Ct

PO

Bowling Station

E   **F**   **15**   **G**   **H**

44   45

Roman Crescent

I

West Dunbartonshire
Renfrewshire

River Clyde

73

2

Erskine Home Farm

Golf Course

3

Erskine Golf Club

Erskine Hospital

72

30

Princes Park

Cemetery

B815

Kirkton

Nursery Av

Shilton Lane

A898

4   Junction

B815

Road

North Porton

Kingston Road

Toll

Ba

Campbell Av

Buchanan Av

Fraser Av

Stuart

Cameron Av

Queens Drive

Wallace Av

Leslie

Lennox

Mill Av

Shaw Av

Redwood

Road

Laighpark

Drumcross Road

Drumcross

M8

5

Sempill Av

Aytoun Drive

Bargarran

Holms Crs

Bishopton Prim Sch

Renshaw Road

Brisbane

Fleming Rd

Churchill Drive

Maxwell Rd

Dargavel Av

Kingston

Lamont Gdn

Chisholm

Camphill Gdn

Camphill Crs

Hay Av

Dunglass Rd

Devon Dr

Old Greenock Road

Castle Crs

Cawdor

Morar Crs

Carrick Road

Tweton

Almond Crs

Yarrow

Ettrick Cr

Craigh

44   45

E   **F**   **46**   **G**   **H**

Bishopton Health Centre

Poplar

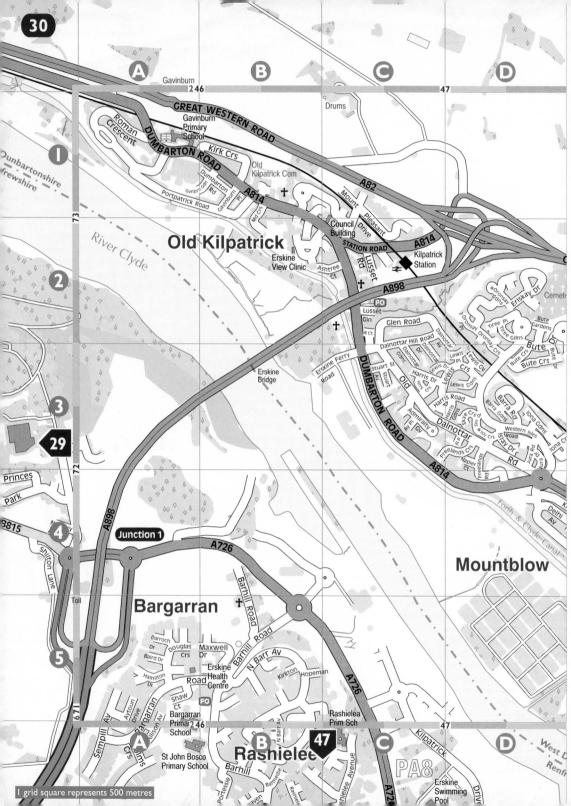

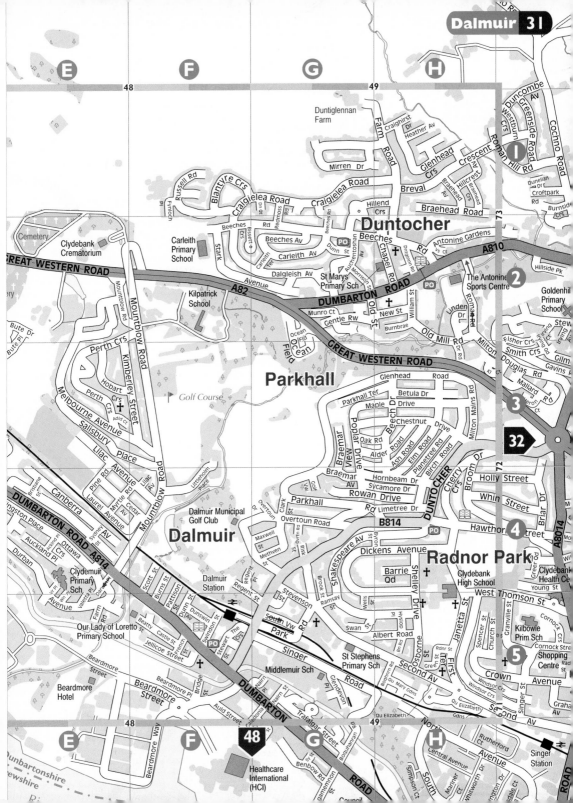

E F G H

48 49

I

Duncombe Av
Greenside Road
Westburn
Cochno Road
Roman Hill Rd
Dunellan Dr
Croftpark Rd
Burnside Crs

Duntiglennan Farm

Heather Av
Craighirst Dr
Farm Road
Glenhead Crs
Crescent
Hillcrest
Braehead
Breval
Braehead Road

Mirren Dr
Hillend

Russell Rd
Blantyre Crs
Craigielea Road
Redmoss
Craigielea Road

Fyfloch
Id
Dn Cr

2
A810
Hillside Pk

Cemetery
Clydebank Crematorium

GREAT WESTERN ROAD

Carleith Primary School
Beeches Av
Carleith Av
Carleith Ter
Stark
Bissett
Beeches
Dunn
PO
Chapel Rd
Antonine Gardens
The Antonine Sports Centre

Duntocher

Avenue
A82
DUMBARTON ROAD
Dalgleish Av
St Marys Primary Sch
Auchentoshan
Morrison St
Old St
William St
New St
Linden Dr
Roman Rd
PO
Goldenhill Primary School

Kilpatrick School

Mountblow Rd

Munro Ct
Gentle Rw
Ocean Field
Ocean Field
Burnbrae
Old Mill Rd
Milton
Fisher Crs
Irving St
Smith Crs
Gavins
Gilm
Stew

Bute Dr
Bute Pl

GREAT WESTERN ROAD

Douglas Rd
Mallard Rd

Perth Crs
Kimberley Street
Hobart
Perth Crs
Cedar
Golf Course

Parkhall

Glenhead Road
Betula Dr
Parkhall Ter
Drive
Maple
Chestnut
Poplar
Oak Rd
Beech Road
Ash Road
Elm Road
Planetree Rd
Birch Road
Milton Mains Rd

3
A8014
32

Melbourne Avenue
Salisbury Place
Lilac Avenue
Pine Rd
Myrtle
Laurel Av
Cedar
Littleholm Place

Braemar View
Braemar Av
Hornbeam Dr
Sycamore Dr
Rowan Drive
Cherry Crs
Broom Dr
Holly Street
Whin Street
Mallard
Ct

DUMBARTON ROAD A814
Canberra Av
Ottawa
Auckland Pl
Durtan
Brisbane
Sydney Av
Clark
Overtoun
Golf
Parkhall
Overtoun Road
Limetree Dr
B814
Hawthorn Street
PO
4
Briar Dr
Clydebank Health Ce

Dalmuir Municipal Golf Club

Dalmuir

Kingston Place
Clydemuir Primary Sch
Farm Rd
Avenue
Our Lady of Loretto Primary School

Scott St
Burns St
Pattison St
Dunswin Av
Dalmuir Station
Regent St
Maxwell St
Methven St
Risk St
South Vw Rd
Shakespeare Av
Dickens Avenue
Shelley Drive
Barrie Qd
Osborne St

Radnor Park

Clydebank High School
Janetta St
Spencer St
Church St
Granville St
Kilbowie Prim Sch
Cornock St
5
Shopping Centre

Beattie St
Castle St
Jellicoe Street
Bridge
Swinton
Stewart
PO
The
Singer
Stevenson
Ramsay St
Wells St
Hyslop St
Swan St
Albert Road
St Stephens Primary Sch
Second Av
First Ter
Green
Crown
Windsor Crs
Graha
Second Av

Beardmore Hotel
Beardmore Street
Beardmore Pl
Beardmore Pl
Middlemuir Sch
Trafalgar Street
Glenlevon Road
Second Road
Du Mary Gdns
Du Elizabeth
Du Elizabeth Gdns
North
West Thomson St
Young St
West Thomson St
Rutherford
Avenue
Central Avenue
Singer Station

E F 48 G H

48 49

DUMBARTON ROAD
Auld Street
Nairn St
Caledonia St
Benbow Rd
Gannennon
Baughanbrahan St

Healthcare International (HCI)

Dunbartonshire
Renfrewshire
Ri

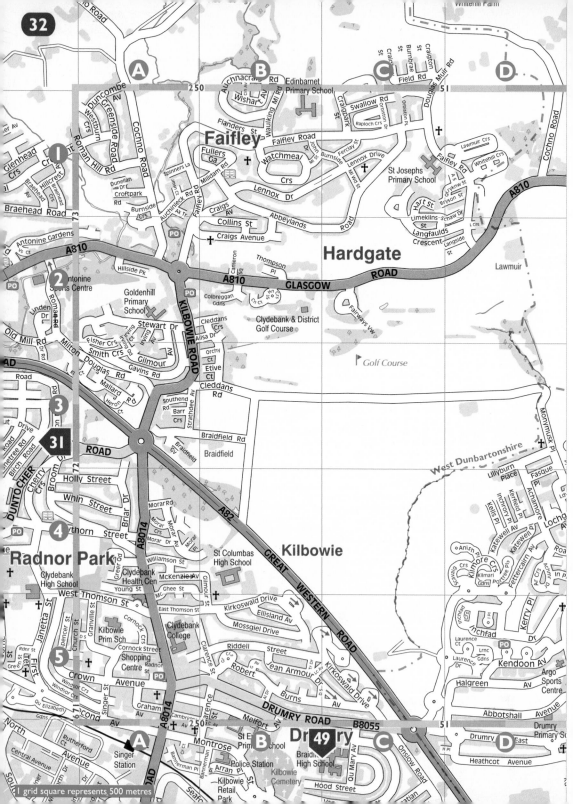

Law

Windyhill

Windyhill
Golf Club

E

F

G

H

16

Baljaffray
Primary Sch

Abercrombie Drive

Rutherford Av

Culloch
Rd

Kilpa

Paterson

Grampian Wy

Grampian Wy

The Pk

Mr Pk

A809

Cemetery

52

ROAD

B8050

BALJAFFRAY

Grampian Wy

Lochnagar Dr

Correen

Finwen

Loyal
Gdns

53

Clisti Av

Gdns

Menteith

Merrick

Lubnaig
Gdns

Burncrooks

St Andrews Dr

Grampian Way

Ochil
Rd

Cruachan Rd

Drive

Wyvis Av

Ettrick Dr

Lammermuir Gdns

Vorlich

Gardens

Grampian Way

I

Ledi

Craigmore
Rd

Pentland
Pl

Lawers
Dr

Burnside

Br

Achn Ct

University
of Glasgow

73

Nevis

Sidlaw Road

St Andrews
Primary School

Cairngorm
Crs

Tinto Road

Bonnaughton Rd

DUNTOCHER ROAD A810

DRYMEN

2

Castlehill

Rd

Surgery

Kn Ct

Whitehurst

Stirling

Drive

T Gdn

Lw Gdn

Sk Gdn

Rosslyn

Dryburgh Rd

PO

Nithsdale Crs

Iain

Road

Castlehill
Primary School

Abbotsford

Scott Dr

Iain

Laurence

Antonine Rd

Eagle Crs

Milverton Avenue

Fairway

Southview

Westbourne Crs

Ballaig
Av

Park
Crs

Golfview

Westbou

Drive

3

Glen Road

East Dunbartonshire
City of Glasgow

Peel Gln
Gdns

Golf Course

Bearsden
Golf Club

Upr Glenburn Rd

34

Thorn

Road

Overbrae Pl

Foswell
Dr

Ladyloan Avenue

Springside
Gdns

Summerhill
Primary School

Camstradden Dr W

Scotus
College

72

Ldyln
Gdns

Overbrae
Gdns

Kilcloy Av

Springside Pl

Crogarry

Backmuir Rd

Saddell

Drummore

Road

Drummore
School

Camstradden Dr E

High School
of Glasgow

4

Lochgoin
Primary School

Cncl Bldg

Kinfauns Drive

St Clare's
Prim Sch

Police
Station

St Pius
Primary School

Summerhill

Pitmilly

Summrh Pl

Drummore Rd

Chesters

Road

Ledmore
Drive

Invercanny

Invercanny Drive

Ar Pl

Drumchapel
High School

Ryedale
Place

Rayne
Rd

Pilton

Northmuir

Summerhill Dr

Summerhill Gdns

Drummore Rd

Station

Pinewood
Primary School

5

Dunkenny
Road

Ledmore
Av

Langfaulds
Primary
School

Harrow Pl

Cally
Av

Bayfield
Av

Barkmill Av

Blackcraig
Av

Sherwood
Pl

Kinfauns Drive

Conon Avenue

Doon Crs

Tweed Drive

Pell

Ha/beath Av

Howgate Av

Kinfauns Drive

Linkwood

Drive

Linkwood
Crs

Bayfield

Kinclaven Av

Mernton Av

Jedworth Av

Goyle
Av

Tallant Ter

Teith

Annan Drive

Colquhoun Park
Primary School

Cncl Bldg

Hecla Av

Indoor
Market

PO

Drumchapel Health
Cen

Southdeen
Rd

Tallant

Carolside Drive

Road

Carron Crs

Annick

Castlesburn Road

Forth Rd

Eskdale

Road

Hecla Pl

Cncl Bldg

Hecla
Sq

Drumchapel

G15

Linkwood
Gardens

Southdeen

Avenue

Kinglas Rd

Falloch
Rd

Spey

52

Donald Dewar
Leisure Centre

E

E

F

50

G

Stone
Primary School

Cloan Avenue

H

PO

Deveron Road

Cairnsmore

Drumchapel
Pool

Drum

Garscadden

Duntreath Road

Belsyde Av

Dipple

Stonedyke

Essenside

Boon Dr

Dalsetter

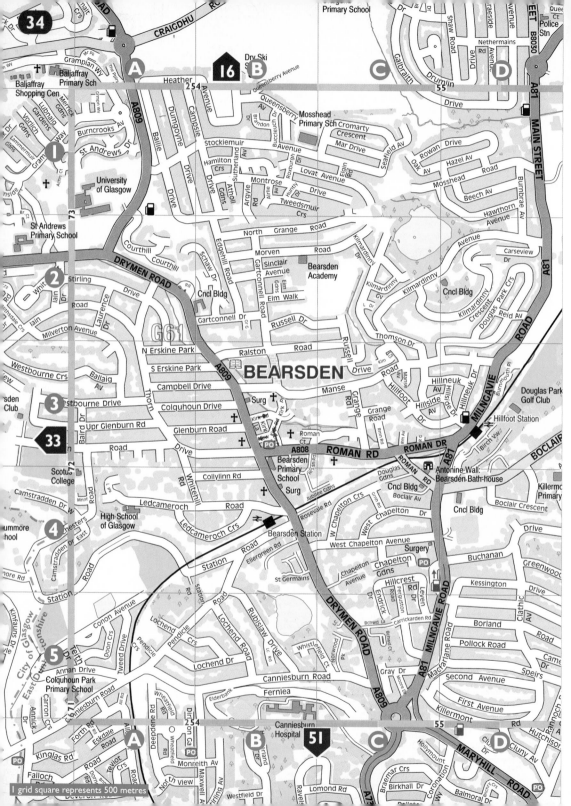

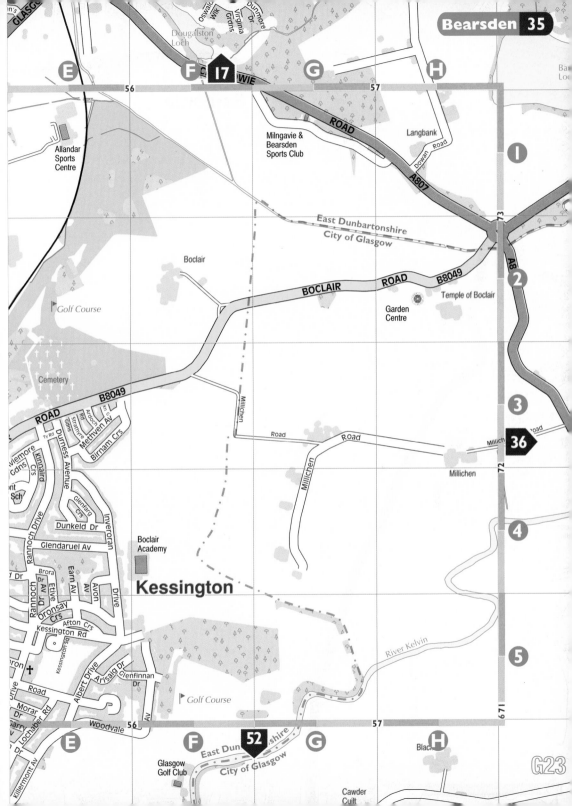

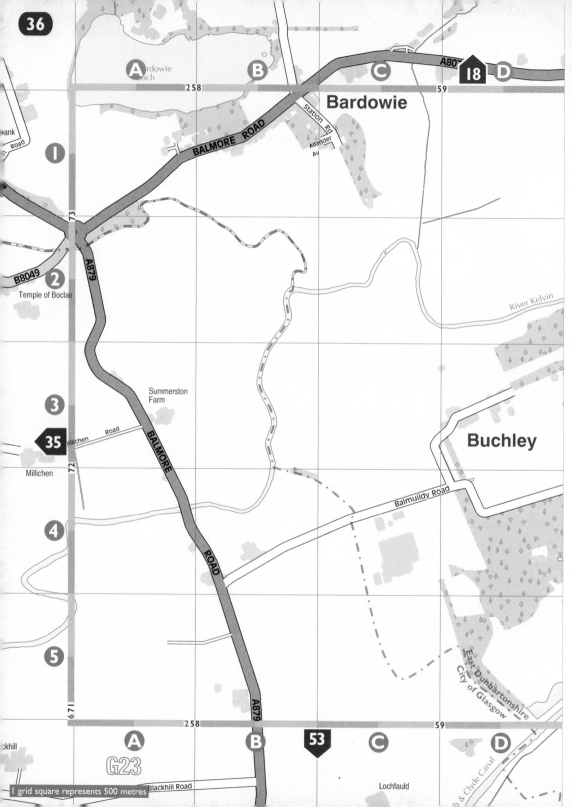

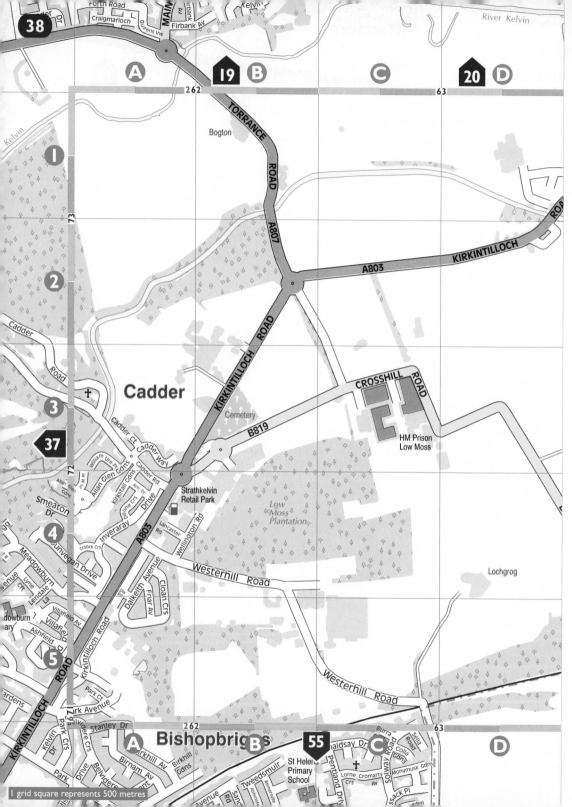

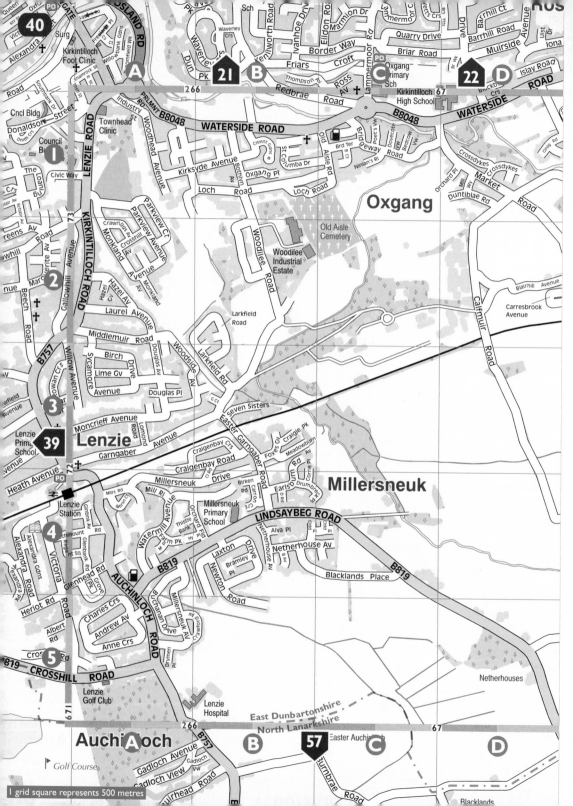

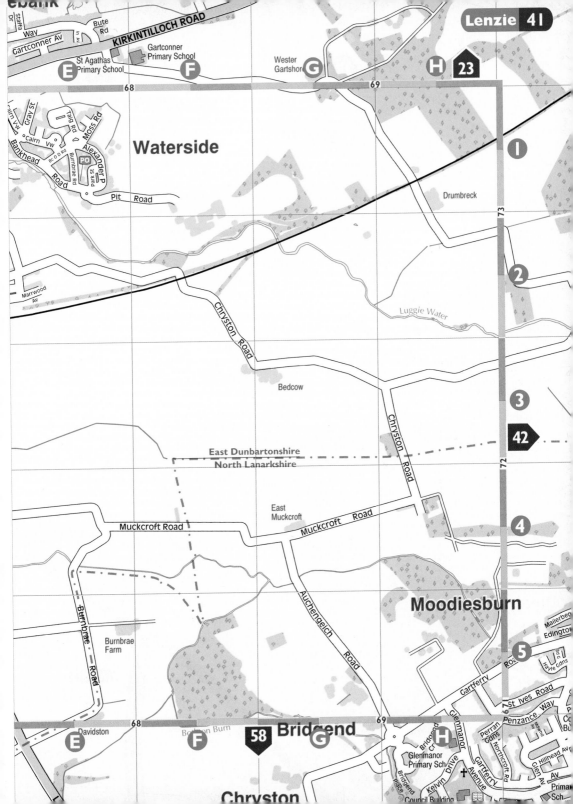

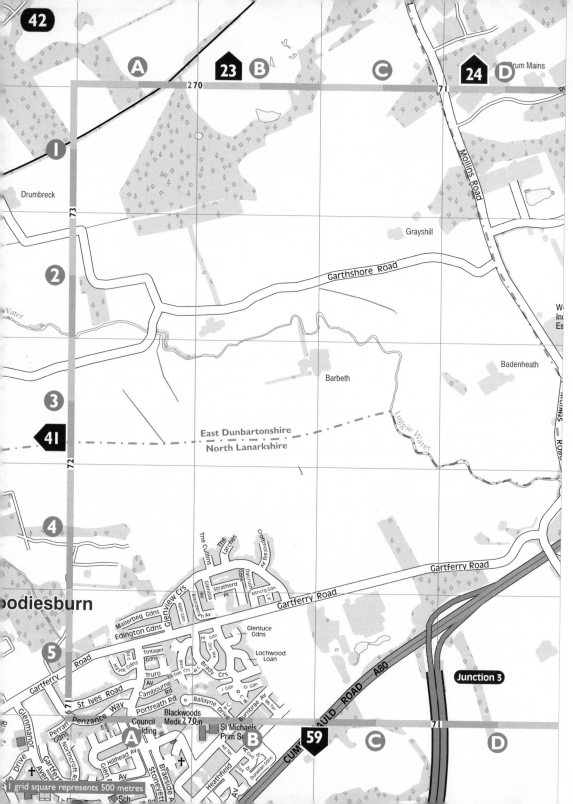

42

A **23** B C **24** D Drum Mains

270 71

1

Drumbreck

73

Grayshill

2

Water

Garthshore Road

3

Badenheath

Barbeth

Luggie Water

41

72

East Dunbartonshire
North Lanarkshire

4

The Cuillins
The Larches
Croftmoraig Av
Glenisla Av
Dalcruin Gdns
Strathord Pl
Aitncrg Gdn

Gartferry Road

Gartferry Road

oodiesburn

Glenview Crs

Mallerbeg Gdns
Edington Gdns
Adel Gdns
Blairden's Av
Glenluce Gdns

Tintagel Gdns
Road
Hl Te Gdns
Truro Av
Cambourne Rd
Whit Gdns Crs
Brady Crs
Hr Gdn
Ch Te Wk
Kls Gdn
Lochwood Loan

A80

5

Gartferry

St Ives Road
Perran Gdns
Penzance Way
Portreath Rd

Ballayne Drive
Burnbrae Av
Mawldd
Glenmanor

Junction 3

Glenmanor
Cartferry
Hillhead Av
Glen Av
Braeside A
Stoneyett
Northcroft A
Heathfield
Av

Blackwoods
Council
Building
Medic...on
270

A B **59** C D

St Michaels
Prim Sc

CUM...AULD ROAD 71

1 grid square represents 500 metres

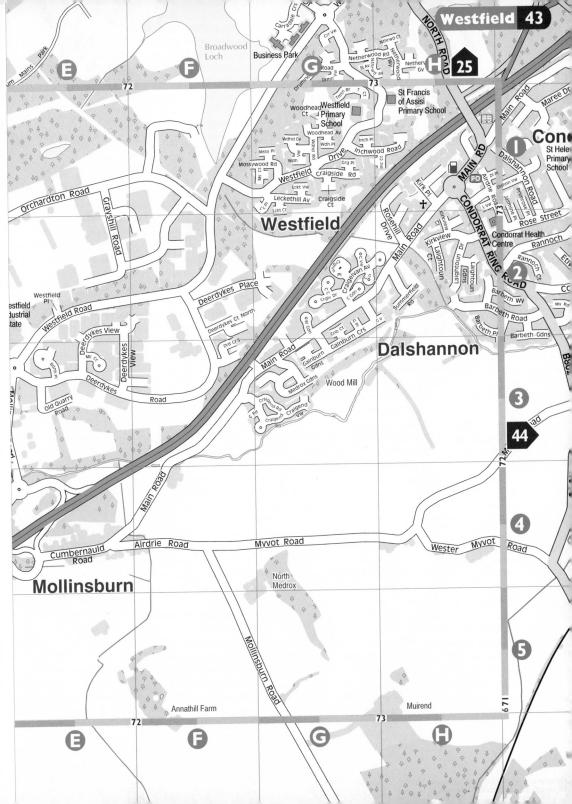

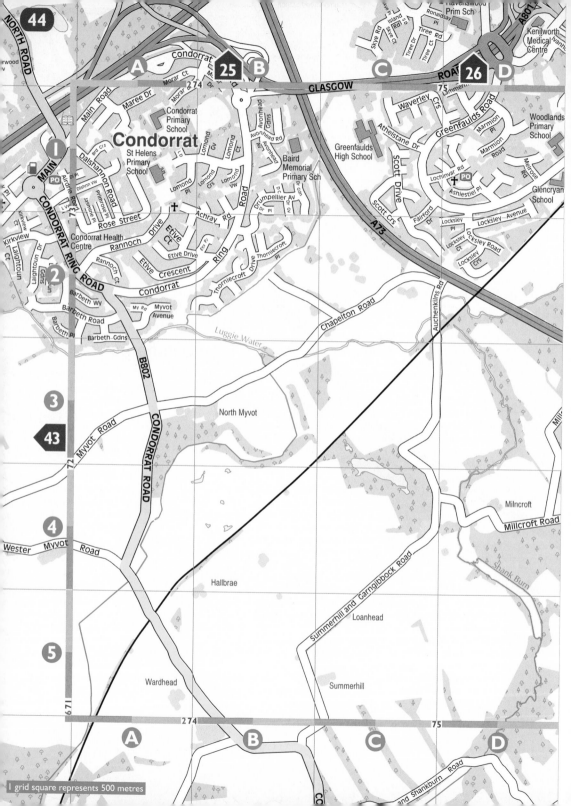

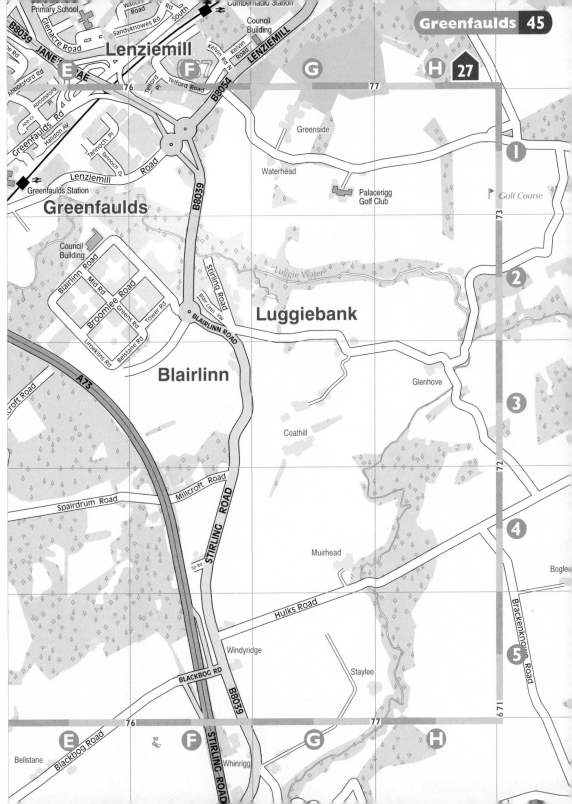

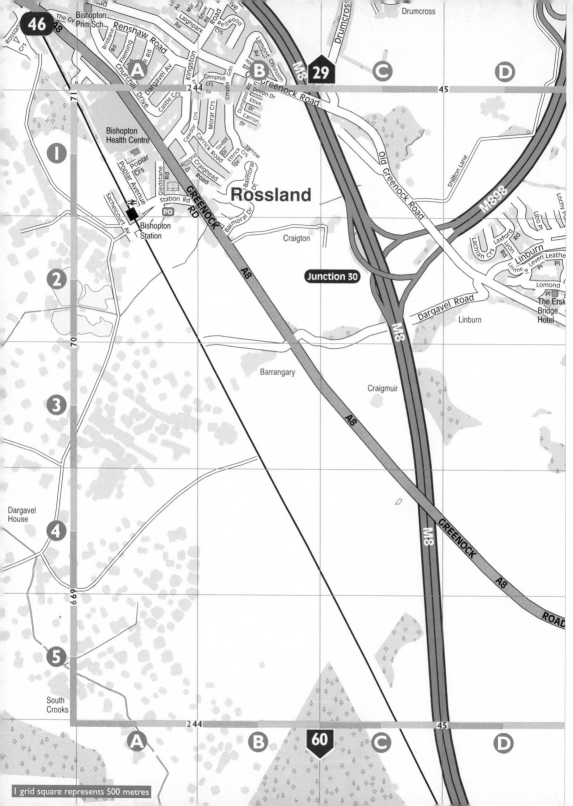

46

A8

The Gv

Rossland

Bishopton Prim Sch

Renshaw Road

Laighpark Av

Brisbane Rd

Fleming Rd

Churchill Drive

Dargavel Av

Kingston

Camphill Gdn

Cmphill Crs

Cmphill GV

B

29 M8

Drumcross

Drumcross

C

D

2 44

45

Bishopton Health Centre

Poplar Crs

Poplar Avenue

Gledstane Rd

Sachelcourt Av

Station Rd

GREENOCK RD

PO

Bishopton Station

Castle Crs

Cavidor Crs

Carrick Road

Morar Crs

Trevlor

Craighead Road

Almond Crs

Ettrick Crs

Etrick Rd

Balmoral Crs

Devon Dr

Dungtas Rd

Etive

Carron

Yarrow

Old Greenock Road

Snitton Lane

M898

Lochry Place

Ubo Pl

Laxford

Rd

Lachlan Crs

Lyon

Lonne P

Linburn

Leven Leather

Pl

1

Bishopton Station

Craighead

Balmoral Dr

Craigton

Rossland

Lomond

Pl

The Erskine

2

70

Junction 30

Dargavel Road

Linburn

The Erskine Bridge Hotel

M8

3

Barrangary

Craigmuir

A8

4

Dargavel House

M8

699

GREENOCK

ROAD

A8

5

South Crooks

A

2 44

B

60

C

45

D

1 grid square represents 500 metres

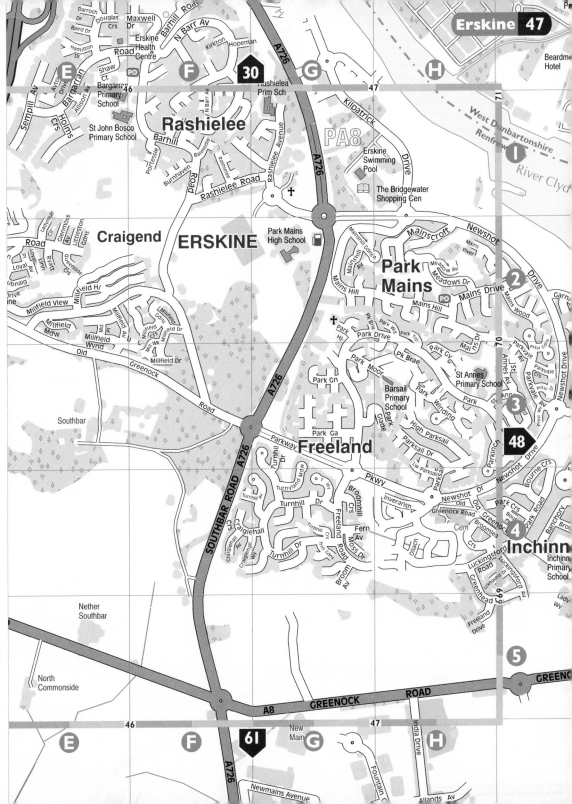

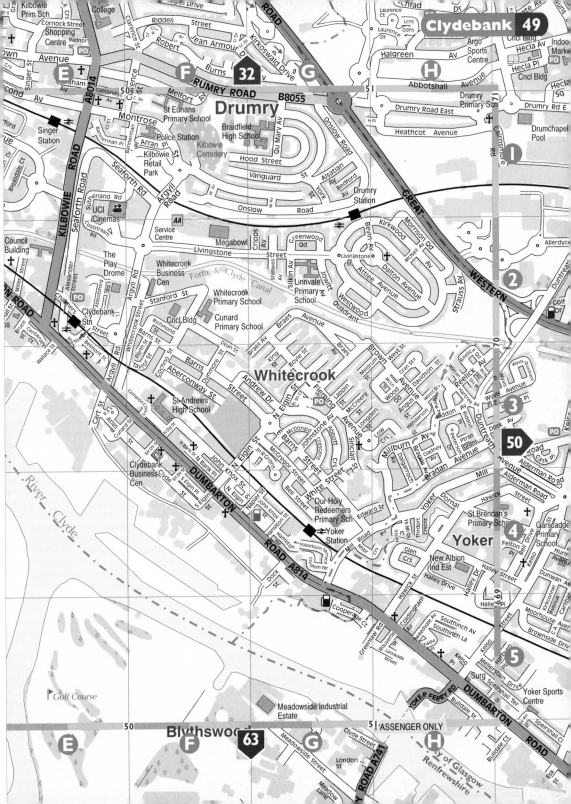

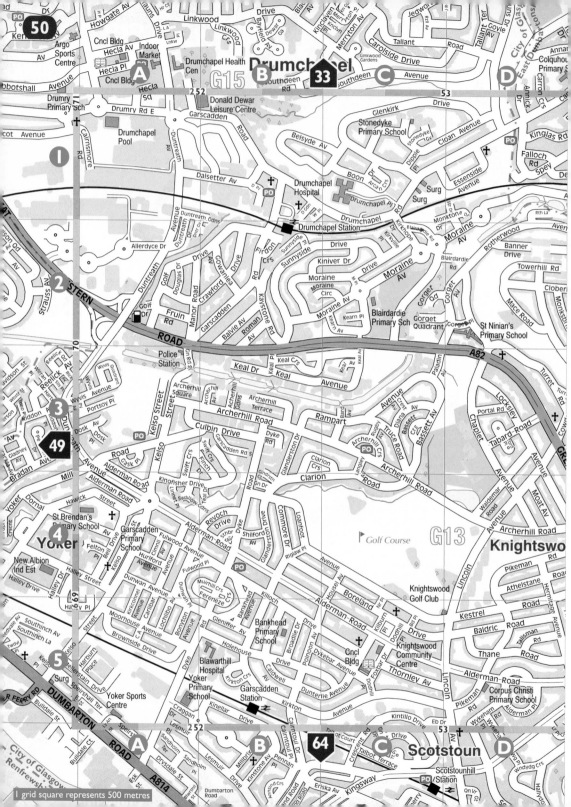

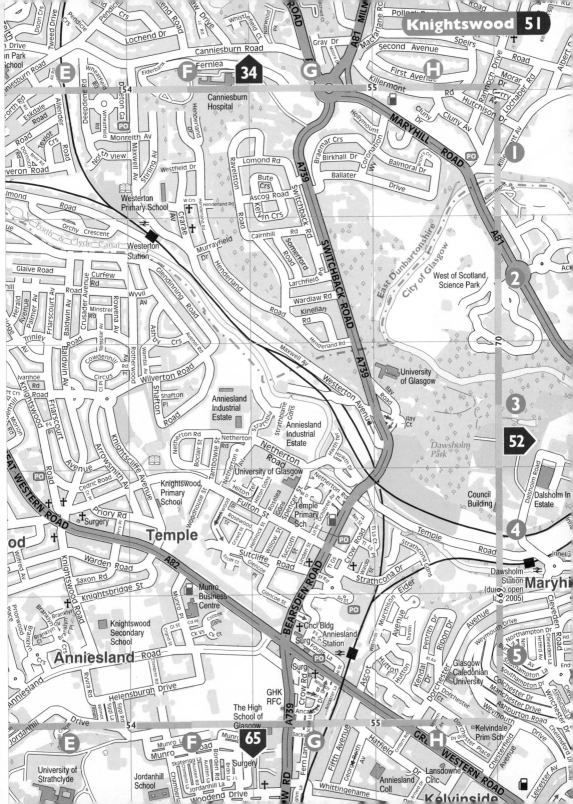

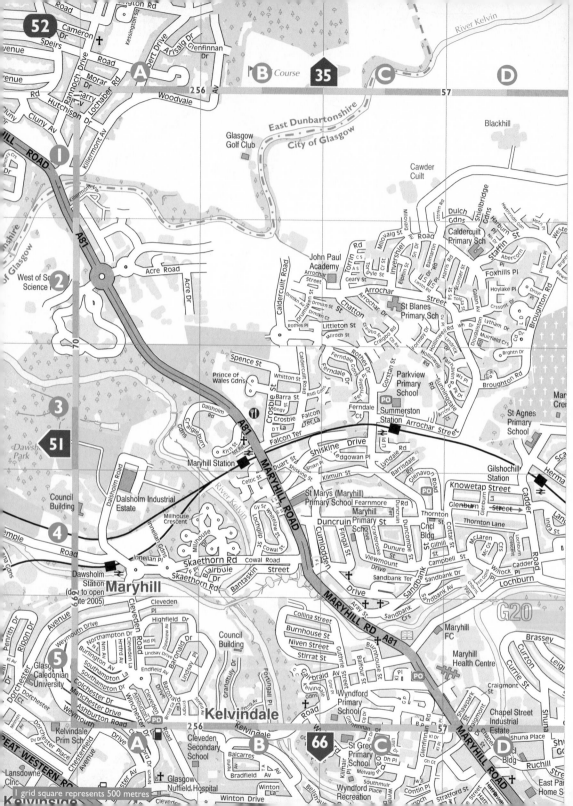

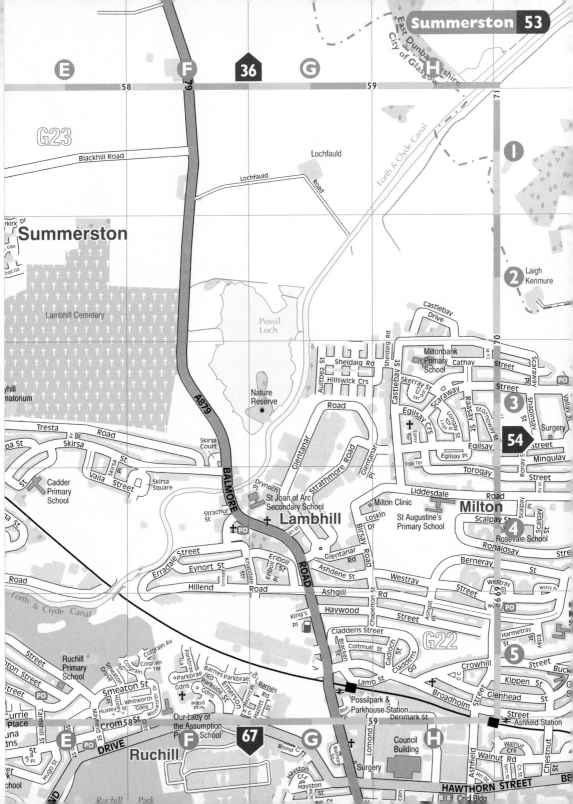

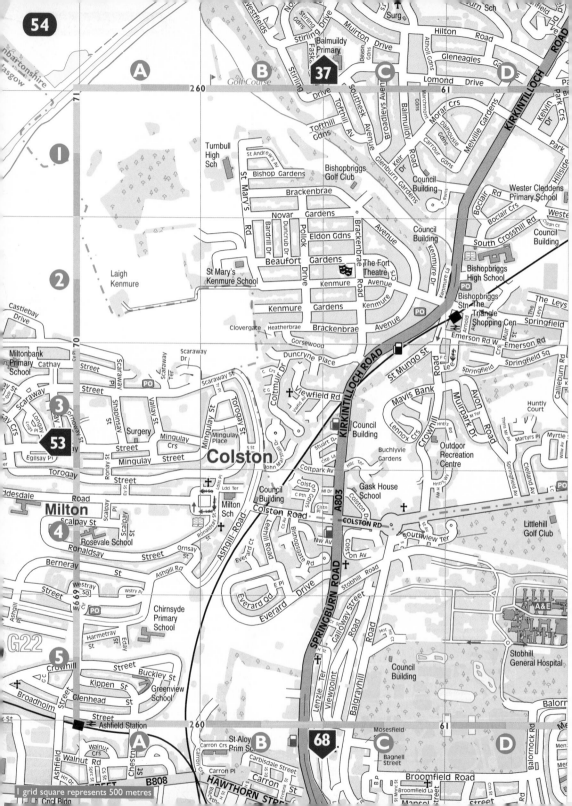

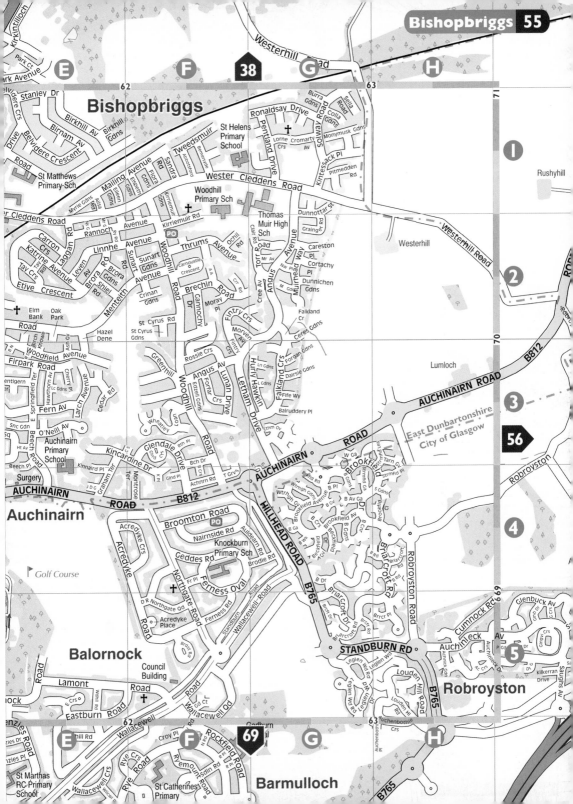

56

A 264 **B** **39** **C** Gadloch 65 **D**

Loch Farm

B819 CROSSHILL

Crosshill Rd

I

B812

Parkhillhead

Golf

Rushyhill

ROBROYSTON ROAD

Westerhill Road

2

Robroyston Rd

70

Langmuir

Lumloch

B812 AUCHINAIRN ROAD

3

st Dunbartonshire

City of C

55

Road

Langmuirhead Road

Cardyke Farm

Robroyston

4

Auchinleck Road

Auchinleck

North Lanarkshire
City of Glasgow

M80

Cumnock Rd

Glenbuck Av

Saughs Drive

Saughs Road

5

Auchinleck

Saughs Rd

Saughs Road

Bogside Rd

Robroyston

B765

Hill Road

A 264 **B** Road **70** **C** **D** **Stepps**

Junction 2

Dunalastair Drive St Flians

Ballalg Crs

sneuk Crescent

neuk Av

Road

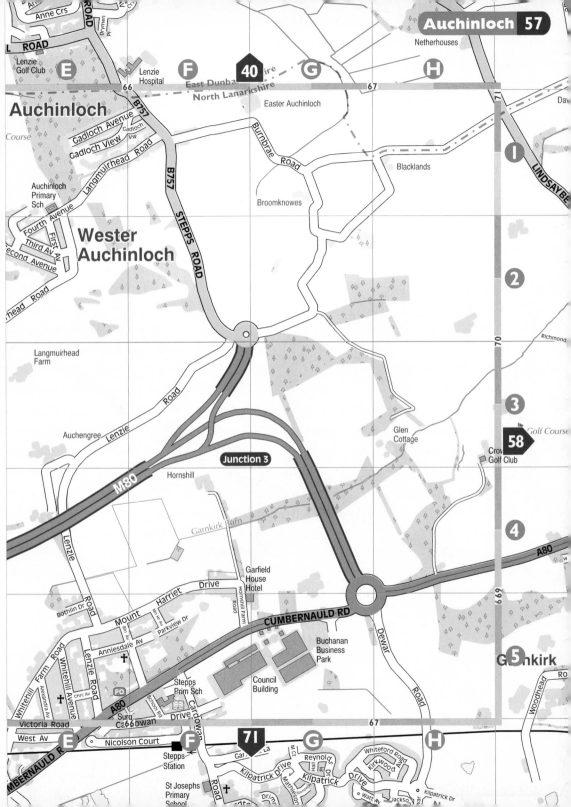

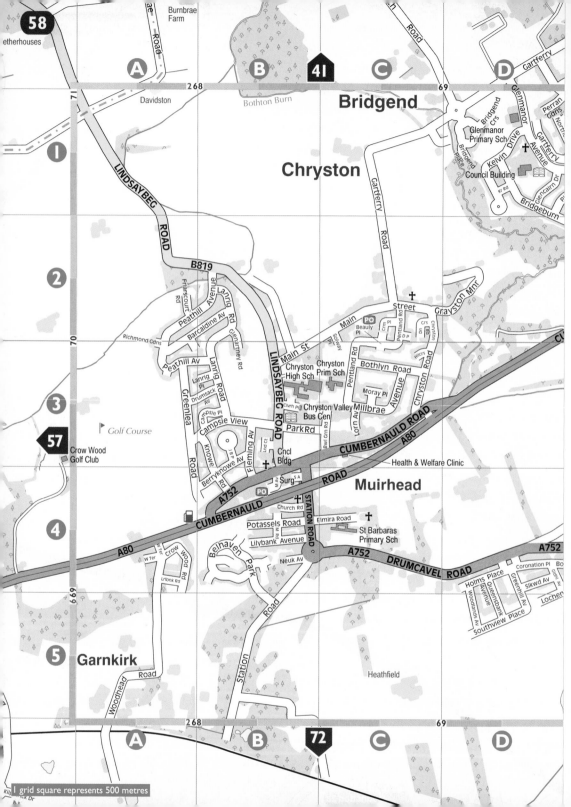

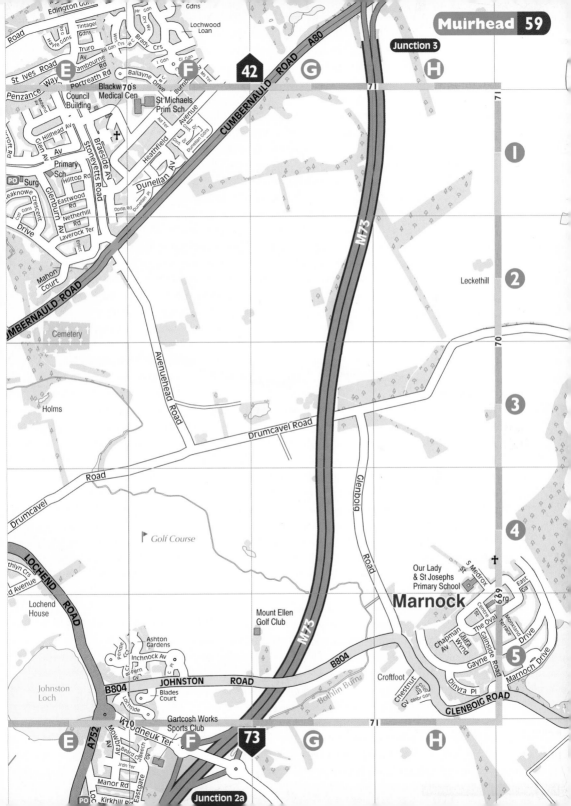

60

South Crooks

A 244 B **46** C D 45

M8

1

68

2

HOUSTON ROAD

Netherfield

Selvieland

3

Moss Road

Fulwood

67

Birkenhead

4

Knowes Auchans Road

81

5

666

Moss Cottage

244 A Moss Road B **82** C 45 D

I grid square represents 500 metres

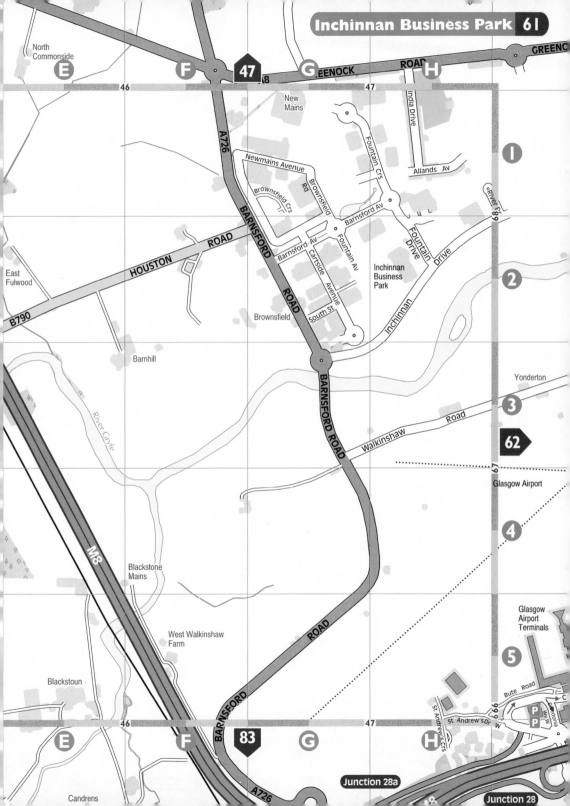

North Commonside

E

F

47

GEENOCK ROAD **H**

GREENC

46

47

I

New Mains

India Drive

Fountain Crs

Allands Av

A726

Newmains Avenue

Brownsfield Crs

Rd

Brownsfield

Barnsford AV

river Gr

River Gr

Barnsford

HOUSTON ROAD

East Fulwood

B790

ROAD

Barnsford Av

Cartside

Fountain Av

Avenue

South St

Fountain Av

Fountain Drive

Inchinnan Drive

Inchinnan Business Park

2

Brownsfield

Barnhill

Inchinnan

River Gryfe

M8

BARNSFORD ROAD

Walkinshaw Road

Yonderton

3

62

97

Glasgow Airport

4

Blackstone Mains

West Walkinshaw Farm

ROAD

Blackstoun

Glasgow Airport Terminals

5

Bute Road

St Andrew's Cr

St Andrew's Dr

WV

W

999

W

P P

C

E

F

83

G

H

BARNSFORD ROAD

46

47

A726

Candrens

Junction 28a

Junction 28

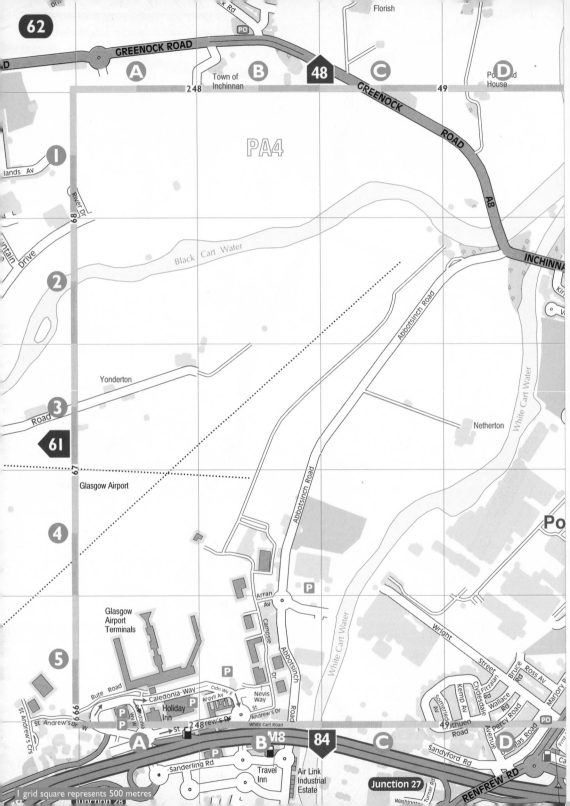

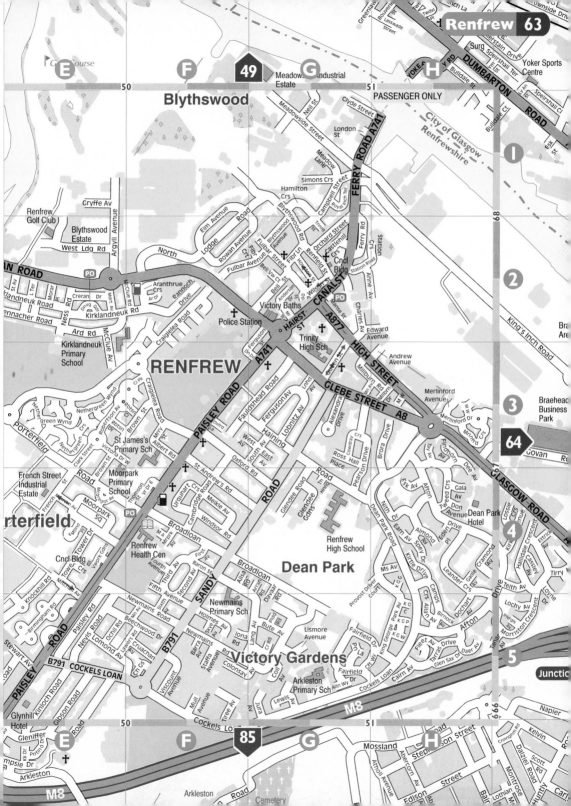

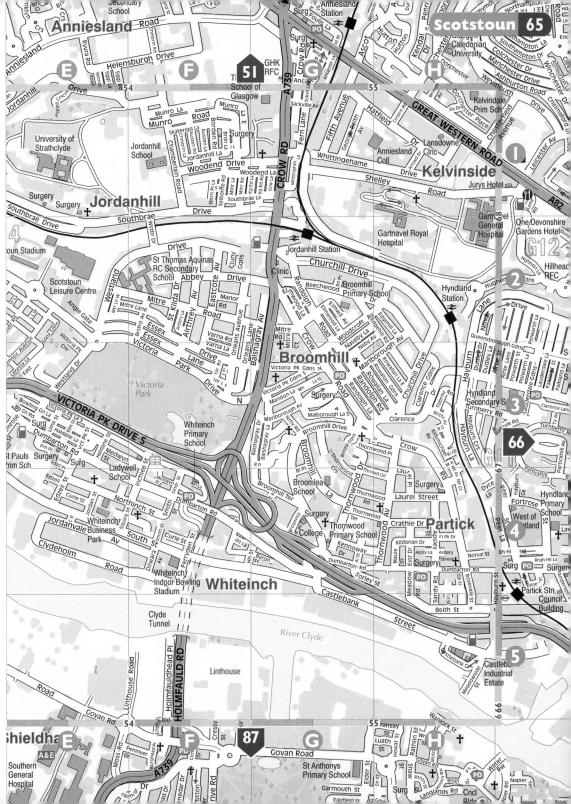

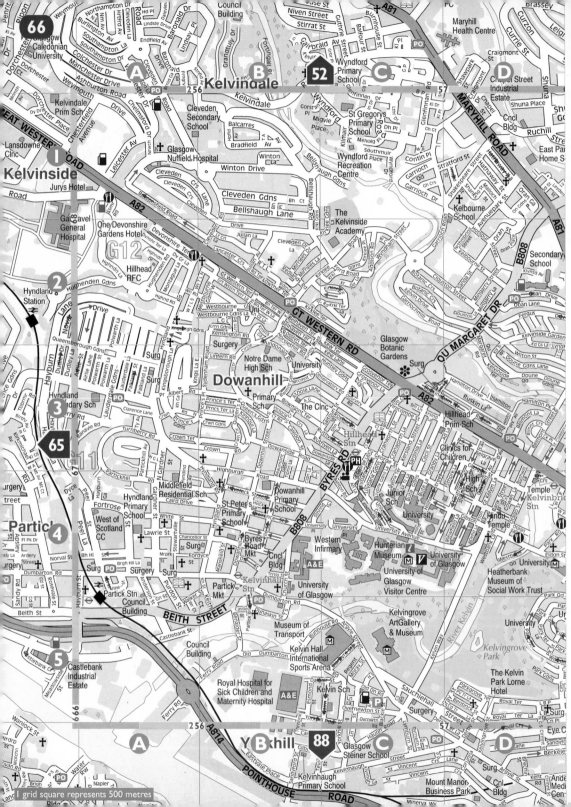

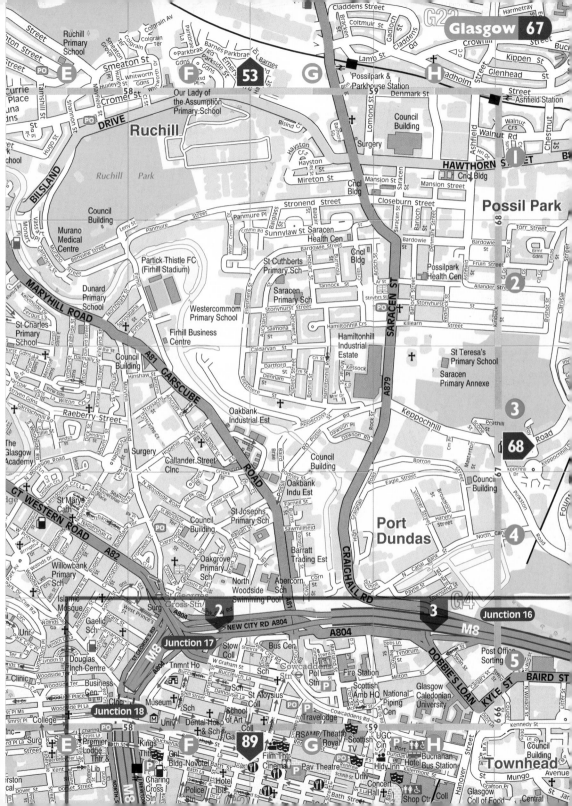

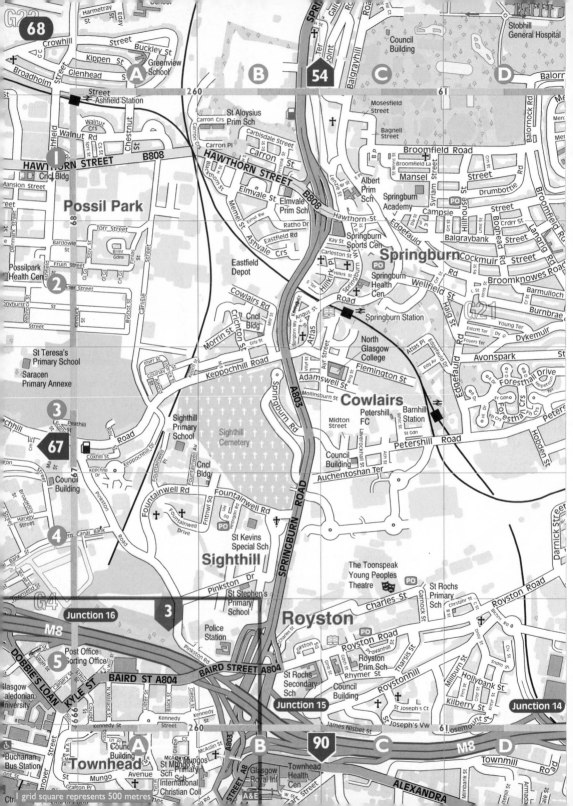

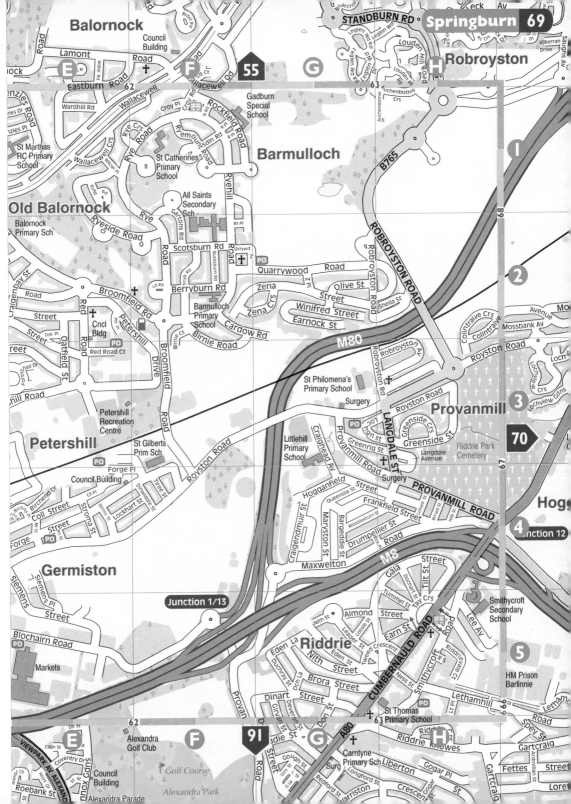

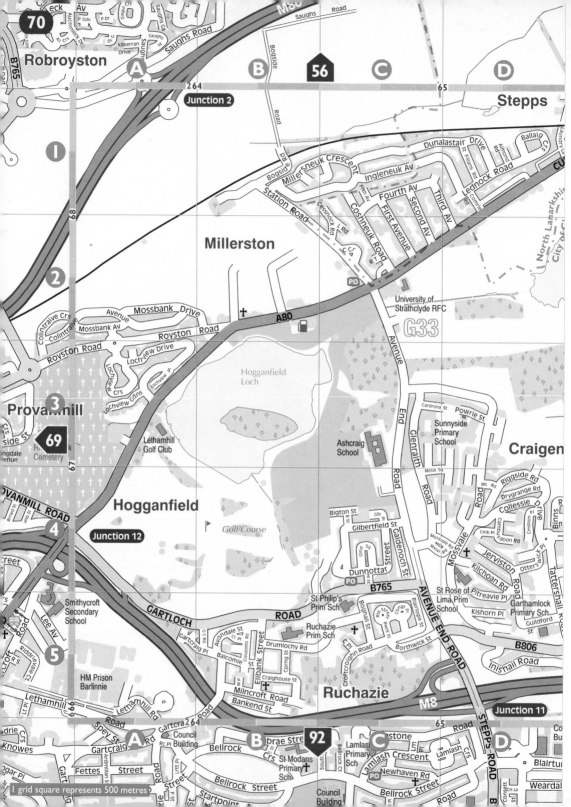

Robroyston

Stepps

70

56

B765

Junction 2

I

Millersneuk Crescent

Dunalastair Drive

Ballaig Crs

Inglenuek Av

Fourth Av

Third Av

Lednock Road

North Lanarkshire

City of

First Avenue

Second Av

Station Road

Millerston

PO

University of Strathclyde RFC

G33

2

Mossbank Drive

Colintrave Crs

Colintrave

Mossbank Av

Avenue

Royston Road

A80

Hogganfield Loch

Avenue

Lochview Drive

Lochview Crs

Lochview Gdns

Royston Road

Powrie St

Cardrona St

Provanmill

3

69

Cemetery

Lethamhill Golf Club

Ashcraig School

Sunnyside Primary School

Craigen

Glenraith

Road

Mssvl

Riggside Rd

Drygrange Rd

Hogganfield

Golf Course

Bigton St

Gilbertfield St

Collessie Drive

Mossvale

Road

4

Junction 12

Caldenoch St

Jerviston

Kilchoan Rd

Pitreavie Pl

Dunnottar St

St Rose of Lima Prim School

Garthamlock Primary Sch

Kishorn Pl

Guildford

PROVANMILL ROAD

St Philip's Prim Sch

PO

B765

Ruchazie Prim Sch

Boghall St

Smithycroft Secondary School

5

Lee Av

GARTLOCH ROAD

Borthwick St

B806

Inishail Road

Avondale St

Ellbank Street

Drumlochy Rd

Riddrie

Craighouse St

AVENUE END ROAD

STEPPS ROAD

HM Prison Barlinnie

Milncroft Road

Bankend St

Ruchazie

M8

Junction 11

Lethamhill Rd

Gartcraig

A

92

B

C

D

Bellrock

Council Building

Brae Street

St Modans Primary Sch

Lamlash Primary Sch

Lamlash Crescent

Lamlash Crs

Gartcraig

Fettes Street

Bellrock Street

PO

Newhaven Rd

Council Building

Bellrock Street

I grid square represents 500 metres

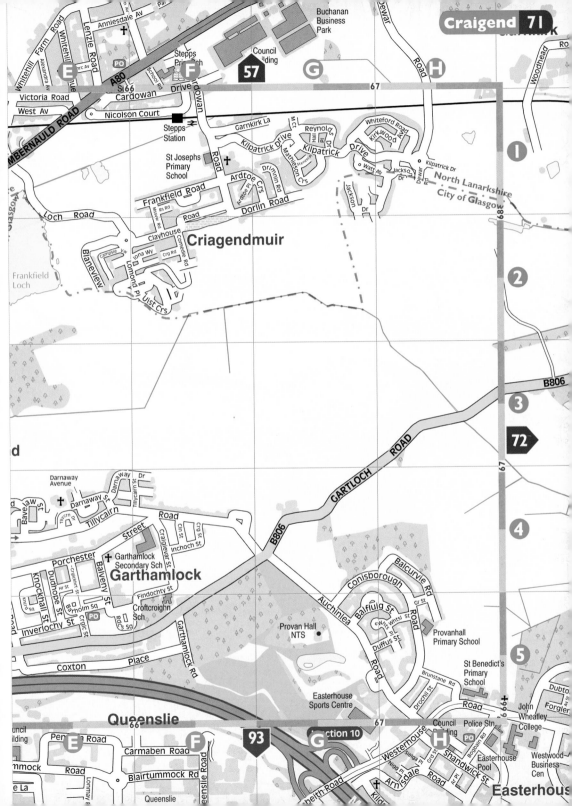

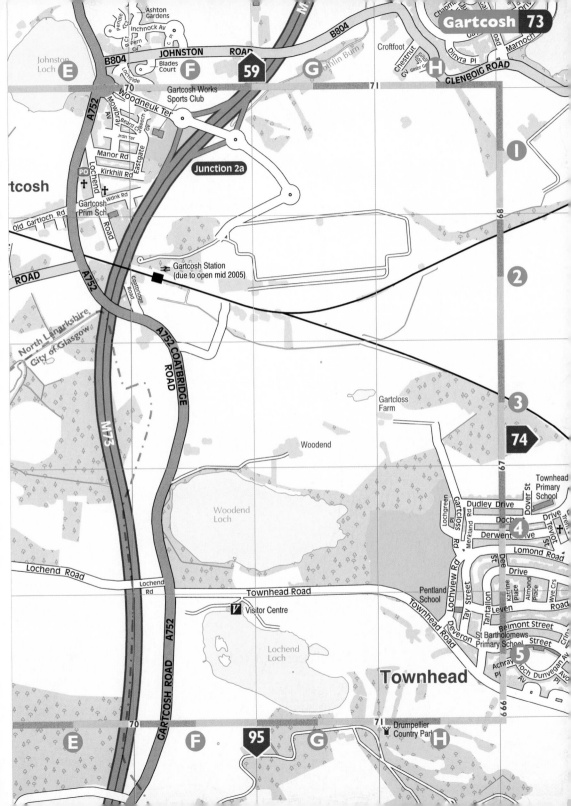

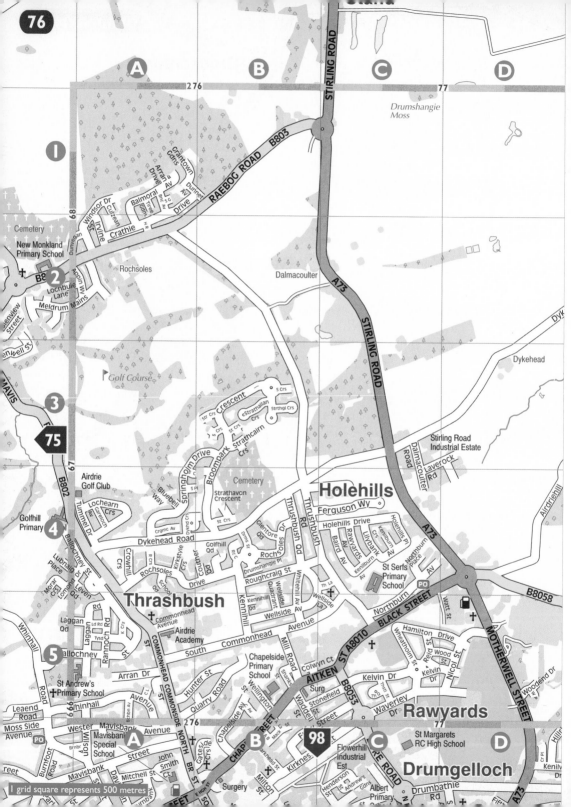

Drumshangie

Darngavil R...

E F G H

78 79

I

Arbu...

2

Bal...

Ballochney Road

...ehead Road

Arbuckle

3

Road

Airdriehill

Ballochney Road

Springbank AV
Silverdale Ter
Arindale Rd
Achleca Gdns
Craiglea Ter
Kintyre Crescent
Affric AV
Meadow View
Ballochney East
Meadow View

Plains

Arkaig AV
Aberfeldy AV
West AV
Bellos Pl
Livingston Drive
Bruce Street
Moffat View

Annieshill View

Wallace St

Jarvie AV
Nth St
Station Road
Brownle...
Avenue
A89

Victor St
Arden St
Stanning St

PO

MAIN STR 4

Plains
Primary
School

St David's
Primary School

STREET A89 AIRDRIE ROAD

Plains
Country Park

5

BURNHEAD ROAD

B8058

St Philips
School

Easter Mof...
Golf Club

CONNOR ST

Church
Crs

Kirk Crs

FORREST

Clarkston

78 79

Drumgelloch Street
99 AV

Colliertree Clebe
Crs

Craighead Street

Springhillg Rd

Rosebank

Forrest St

TOWE...

E F **99** G H

...worth ...ive

McAllister Avenue

Clarkston
Primary

Katherine

Grahamshill...

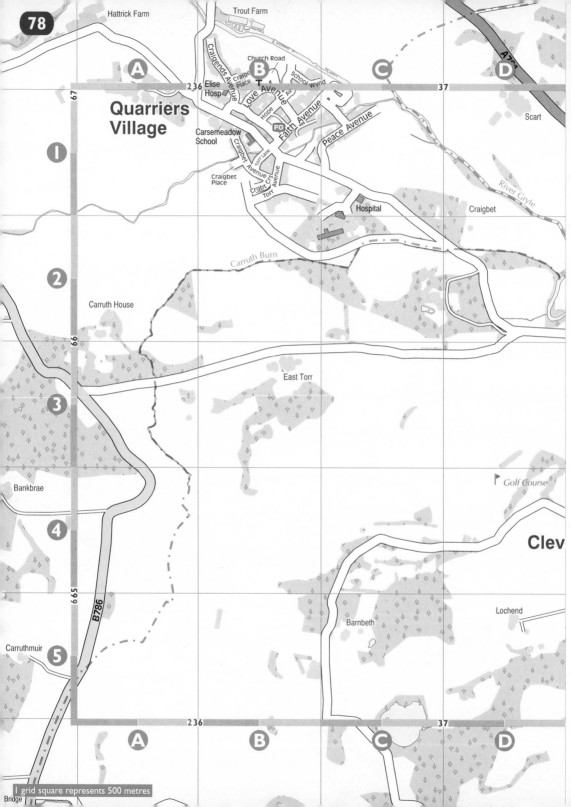

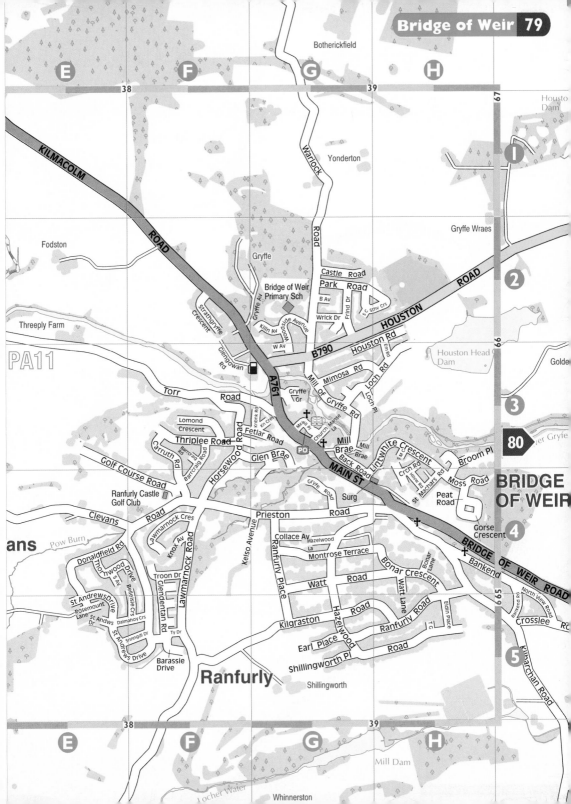

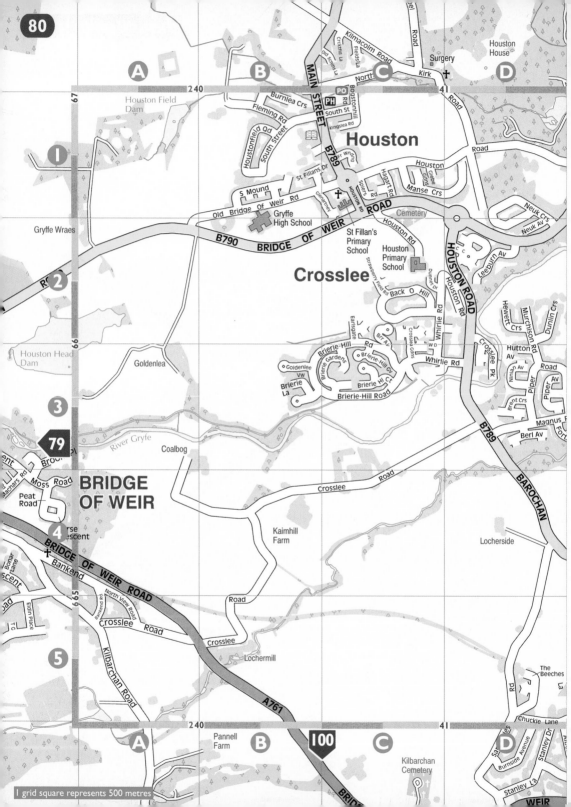

A   B   C   D

240   67   41

I

Houston Field Dam

Burnlea Crs

Fleming Rd

Houstonfield Qd

South Street

South St

Kingslea Rd

St Fillans Dr

MAIN STREET

B789

PH PO

Kilmacolm Road

Old Schls La

Crichton La

Fieldsla

North

Kirk

Surgery

Houston House

Houston

Houston Road

Houston Cotts

Houston Rd

Manse Crs

Neuk Crs

Neuk Av

2

Gryffe Wraes

Rd

S Mound

Old Bridge Of Weir Rd

Gryffe High School

B790   BRIDGE OF WEIR ROAD

Clearmnt

Hagart Rd

Spiers Rd

Houston Rd

Cemetery

St Fillan's Primary School

Houston Primary School

Houston Rd

Crosslee

Strawberry Field Rd

Back O Hill

Dunnet Dr

Whirlie Rd

Whirlie Rd

Leepurn Av

Houston Cotts

Crosslee Pk

Hewett Crs

Murchison Rd

Dunlin Crs

Hutton Av

Piper Rd

Piper Av

Brent Crs

Magnus

Berl Av

Fort

3

Houston Head Dam

Goldenlea

Earlsgate

Brr Av

Crosslee Cotts

W D

Brierie-Hill Gardens

Brierie-Hill

Rd

Brierie-Hill Gv

Goldenlee Vw

Brierie La

Brierie Hl Ct

Brierie-Hill Road

River Gryfe

Coalbog

B789

BAROCHAN

79

Bro

Vachars Rd

Moss Road

Peat Road

BRIDGE OF WEIR

Crosslee   Road

Kaimhill Farm

Locherside

The Beeches

4

rse escent

BRIDGE OF WEIR ROAD

Bankend

Bonar hane

Eldin Place

Bankend Rd

North View Road

Crosslee   Road

Road

Crosslee

Lochermill

Rd

5

Crescent

Tc

Kilbarchan Road

A761

240

41

A   B   **100**   C   D

Pannell Farm

BRID

Kilbarchan Cemetery

Stanley Dr

Burnside Avenue

Chuckie Lane

Stanley La

WEIR

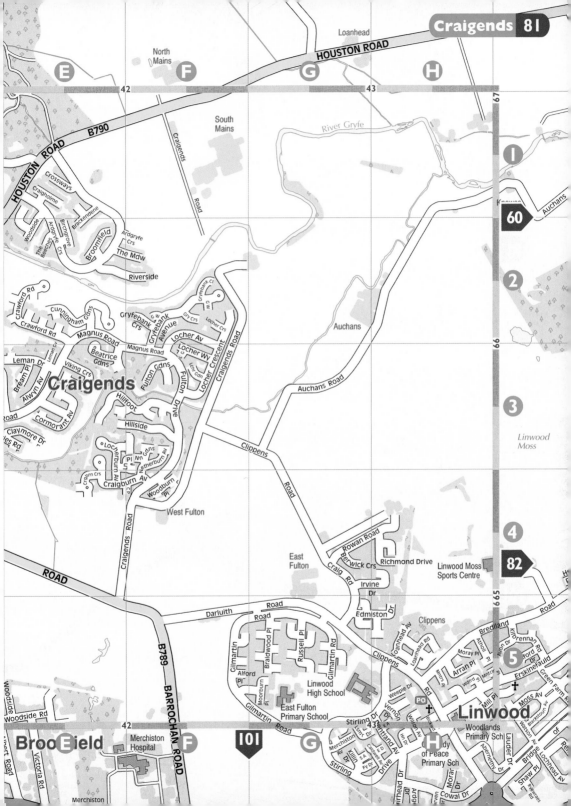

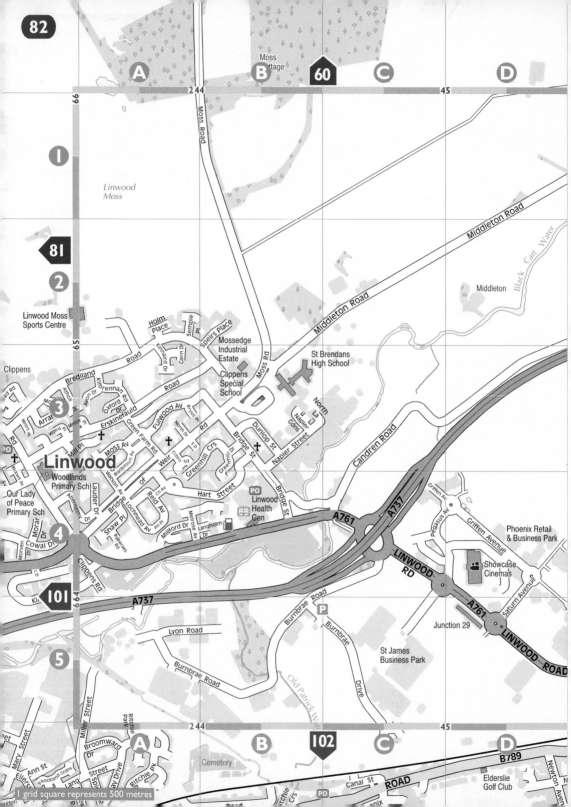

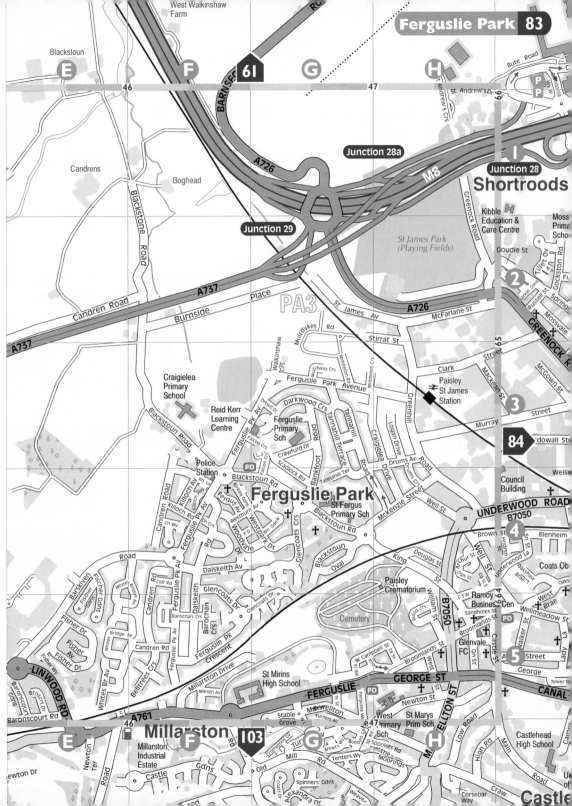

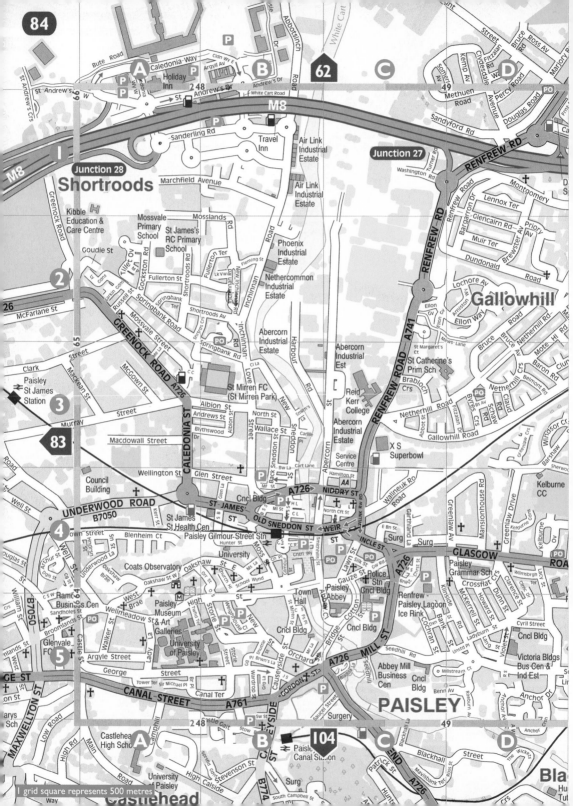

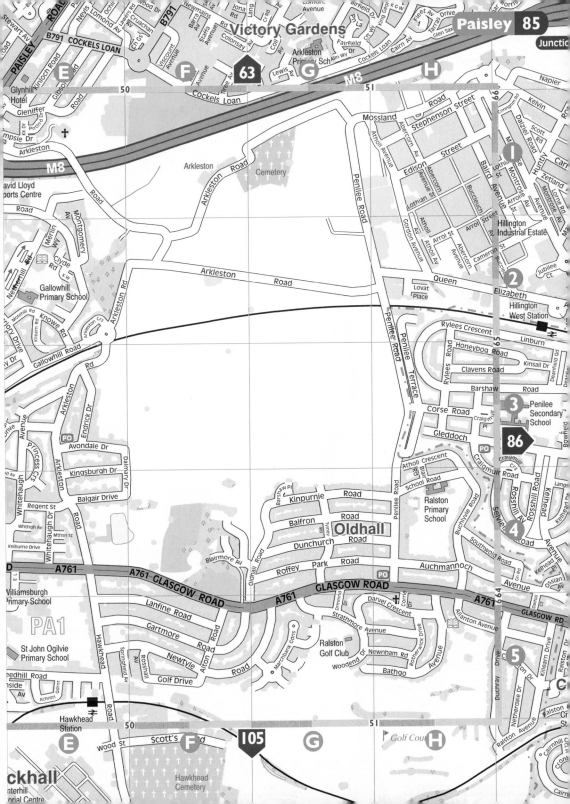

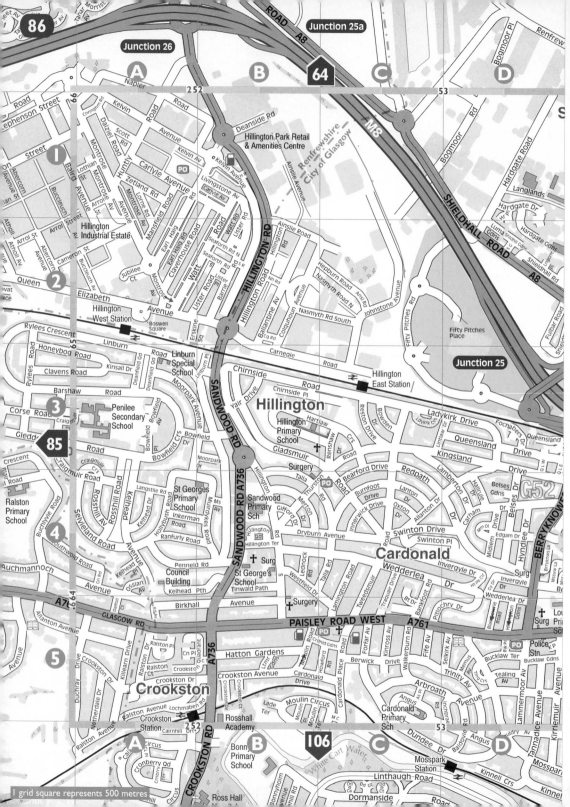

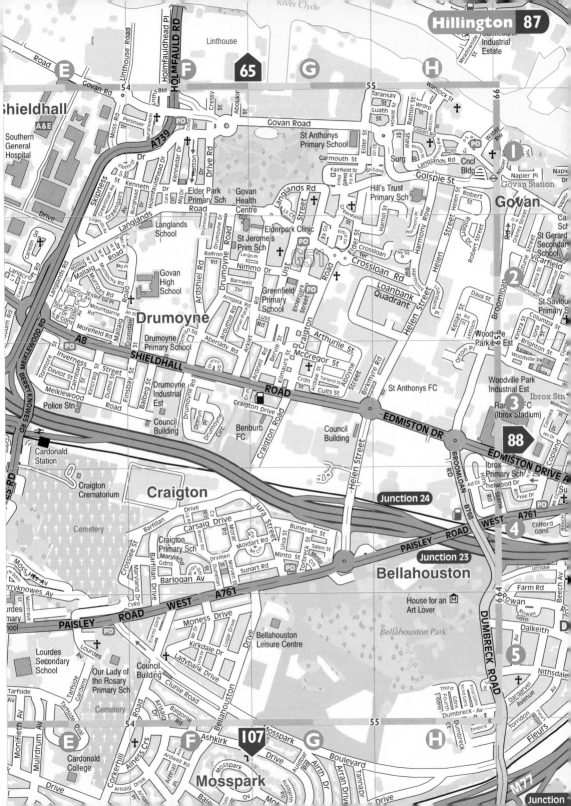

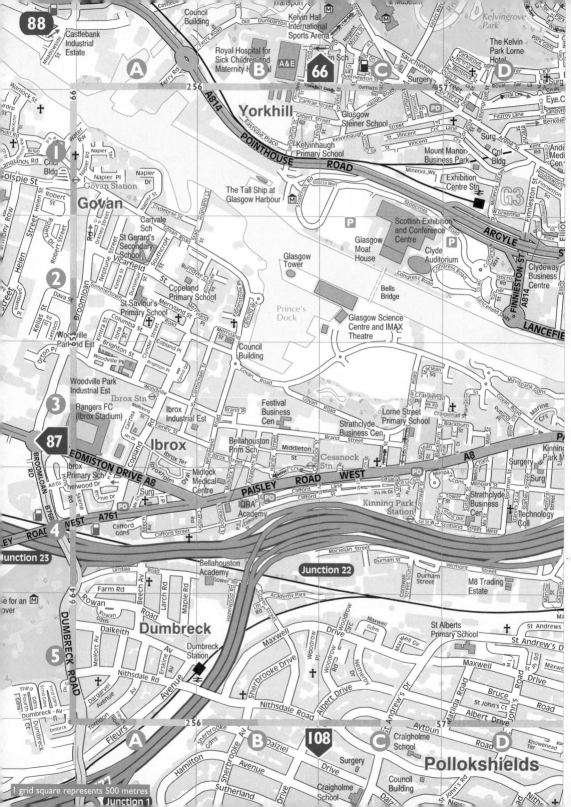

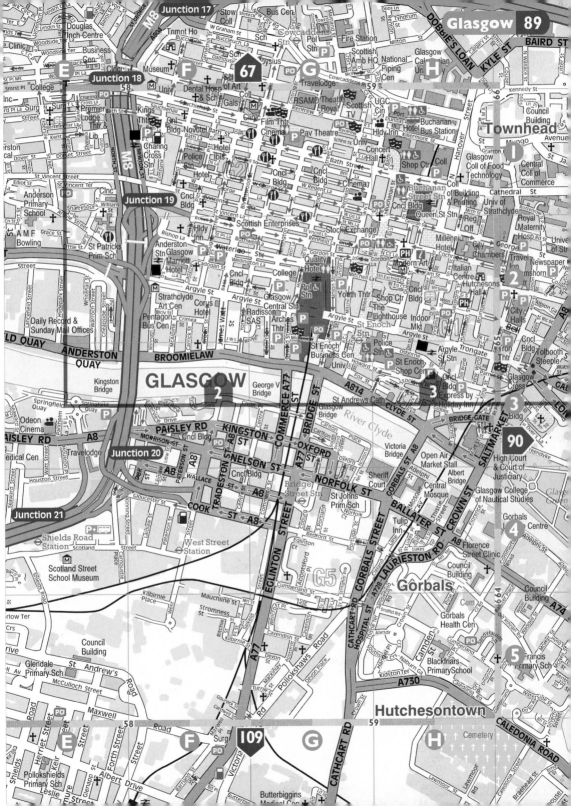

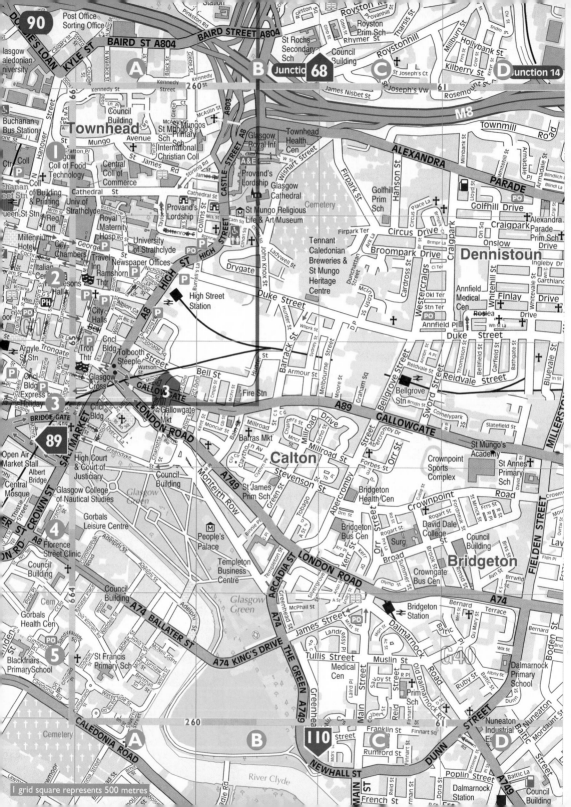

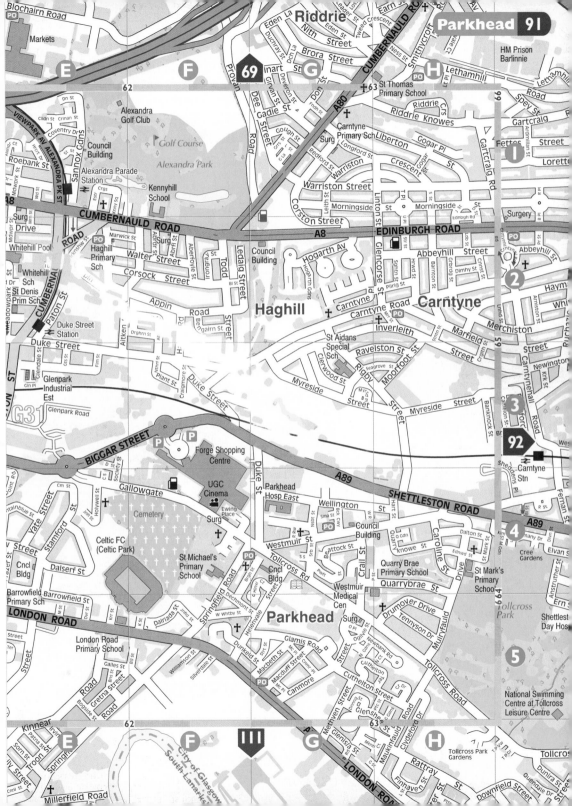

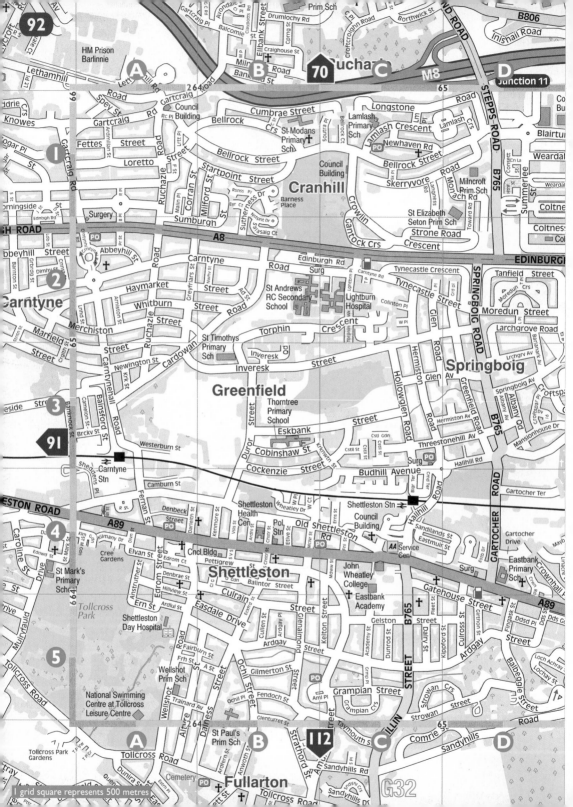

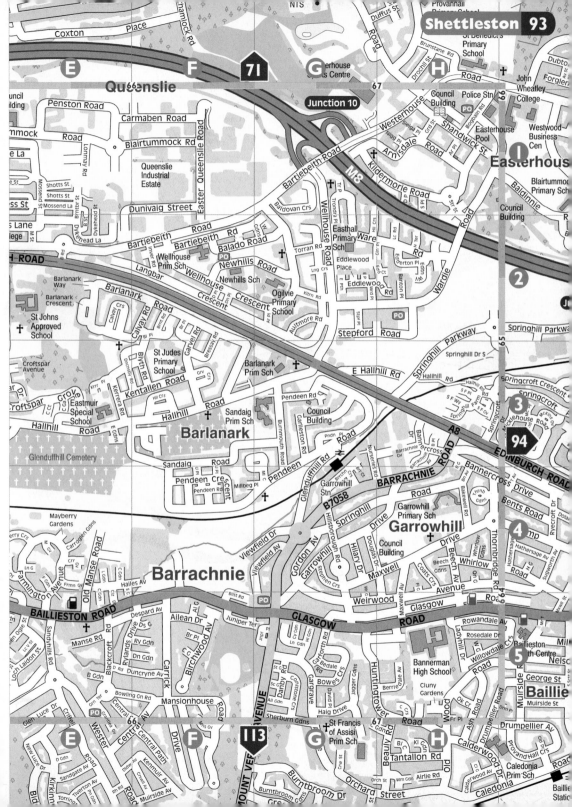

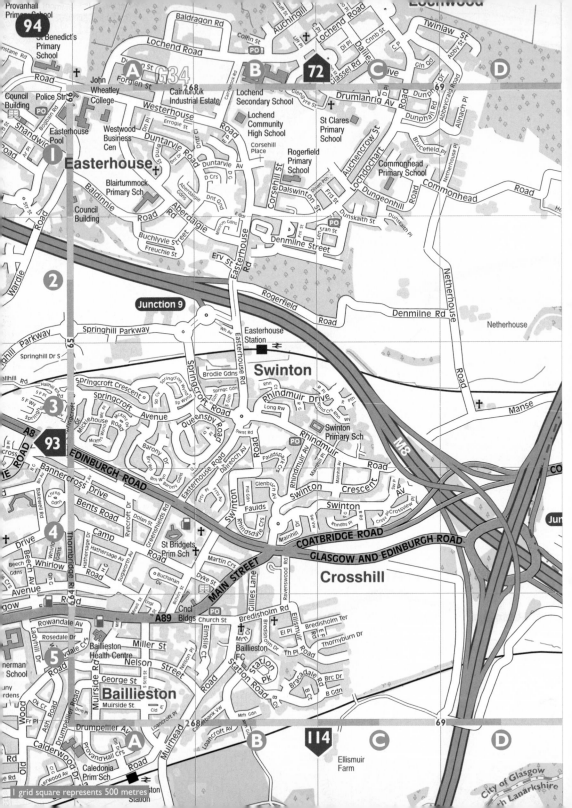

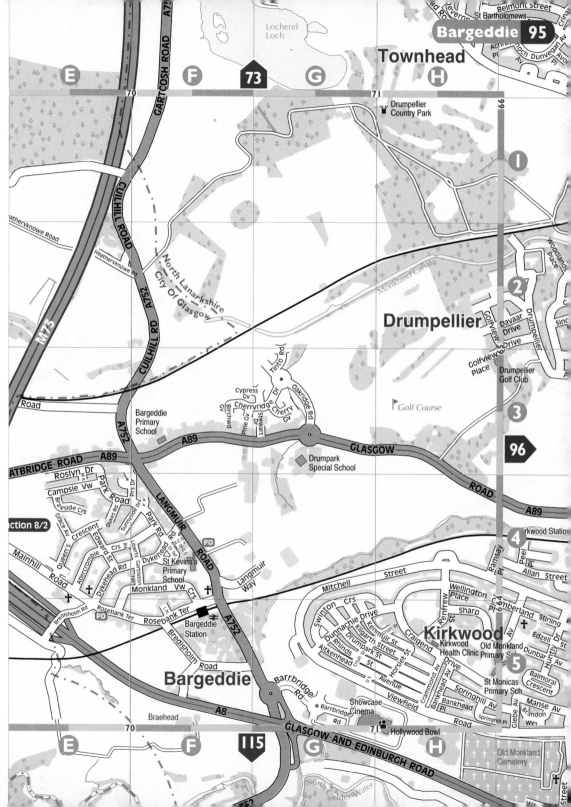

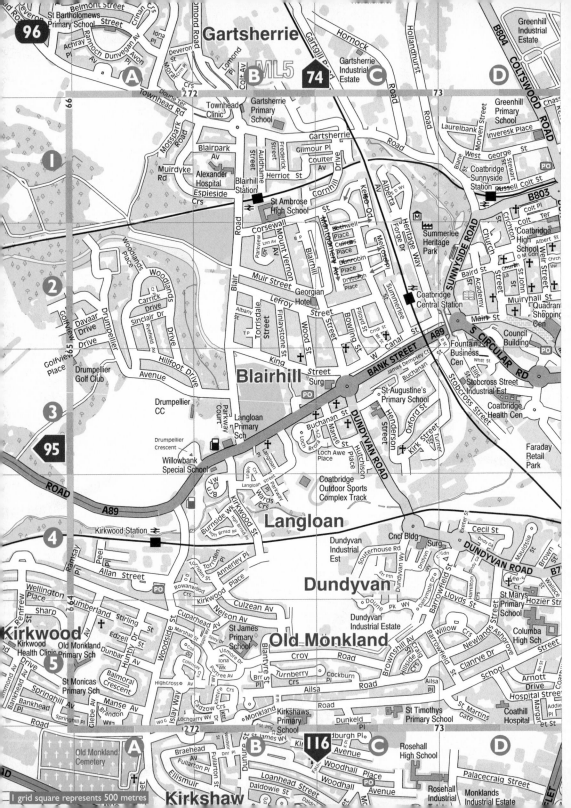

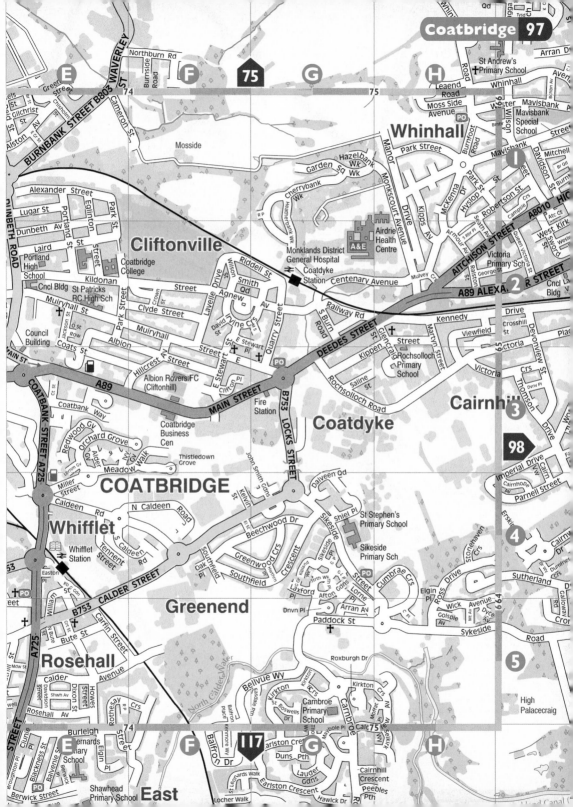

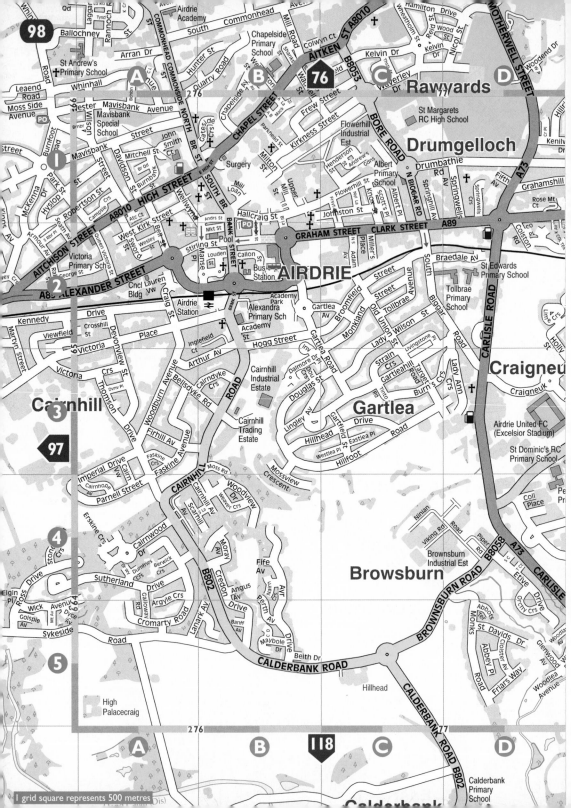

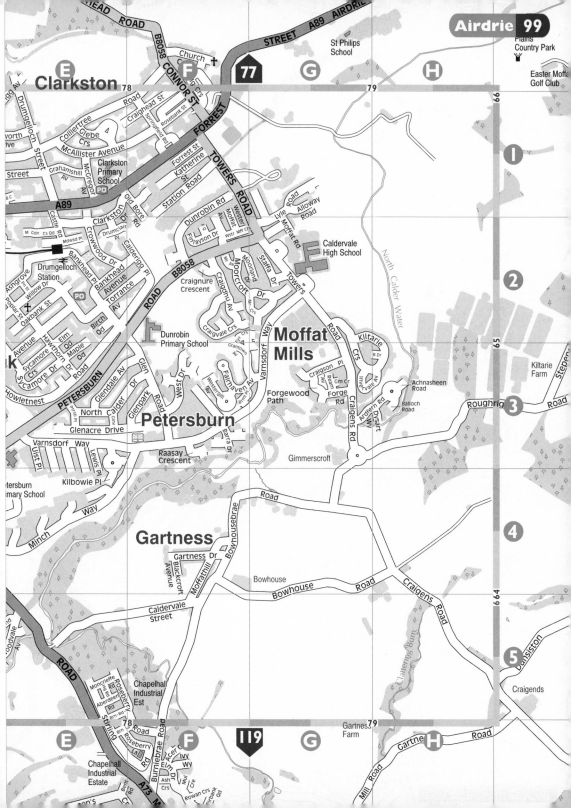

Plains Country Park

Easter Moffat Golf Club

St Philips School

E Clarkston 78

F Church

77

G

H

I

2

3

4

5

B8058 CONNOR ST

FORREST

STREET A89 AIRDRIE

HEAD ROAD

Road

Colliertree Crs

Craighead St

Rosebank st

Springfield Rd

McAllister Avenue

Clarkston Glebe

Clarkston Primary School PO

Grahamshill Av

McGregor St

Forrest St

Katherine St

Station Road

TOWERS ROAD

Dunrobin Rd

Westerl

Finlayson Dr

Moffat Av

Wstr Mff Crs

Lyle Road

Alloway Road

Moffat Rd

Caldervale High School

North Calder Water

A89

Street

Castle

M Gdn Cs Rd

Mdwsd Pl

Clarkston Dr

Old Bore Rd

Drumclair Pl

Crowwood Dr

Calderigg Pl

B8058

Staffa Dr

Moorland

Moorcroft

Towers

Kiltarie Crs

Kiltarie Farm

Stepp

Road

Drumgelloch Station

Ashgrove

Willow Dr

Bankhead Pl

Bankhead Avenue

Torrance Av

Craignure Crescent

Craignur Av

Craigvale Crs

Crantown Av

Mr Crs

Dr

Craigson Pl

Ream

Gm Crs

Inver Vale

B Dr

Achnasheen Road

Kiltarie Farm

Oakbank St

Oaknark St

Birch Qd

Dunrobin Primary School

Fairhaven

Westergill Av

Forgewood Path

Forge Rd

Craigens Rd

Ardfern Rd Dysart Wy

Balloch Road

Roughrig Road

Sycamore Dr

Hawthorn Dr

Elm Qd

Maple Qd

Road

PETERSBURN

Glendale Av

Glen Dr

Glenpark Road

West Dr

Fairhaven Dr

Brm Dr

Varnsdorf Way

Moffat Mills

Roughrig Road

Sycamore Av

North Calder

Glenacre Drive

Petersburn

Barra Dr

Raasay Crescent

Gimmerscroft

Howletnest

Uist Pl

Varnsdorf Way

Lewis Pl

Kilbowie Pl

Road

Road

tersburn imary School

Minch

Way

Gartness

Gartness Dr

Bowhousebrae

Blackcroft Avenue

Morfathill

Bowhouse

Bowhouse Road

Craigens Road

Caldervale Street

Moncrieffe Roseberry Aberdeen Rd

Chapelhall Industrial Est

Clattering Burn

Dunsiston

Craigends

ROAD

Stirling

Brn Rd

Burnliebrae Road

Roseberry La

Acer Cr

Ivy Wy

Elm Dr

Mull Cre

Ash Dr

Rowan Crs

E

F

119

G

Gartness Farm

Gartnes 79

Mill Road

GARTNE **H** Road

Chapelhall Industrial Estate

A73

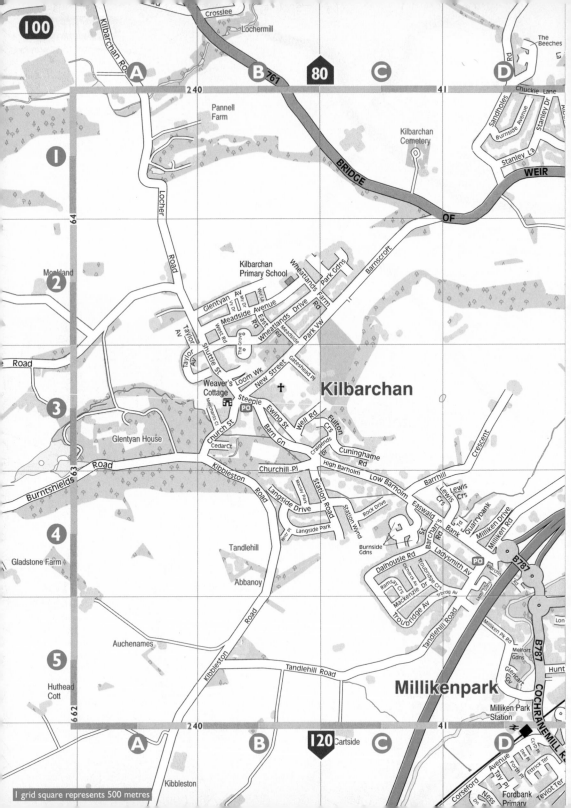

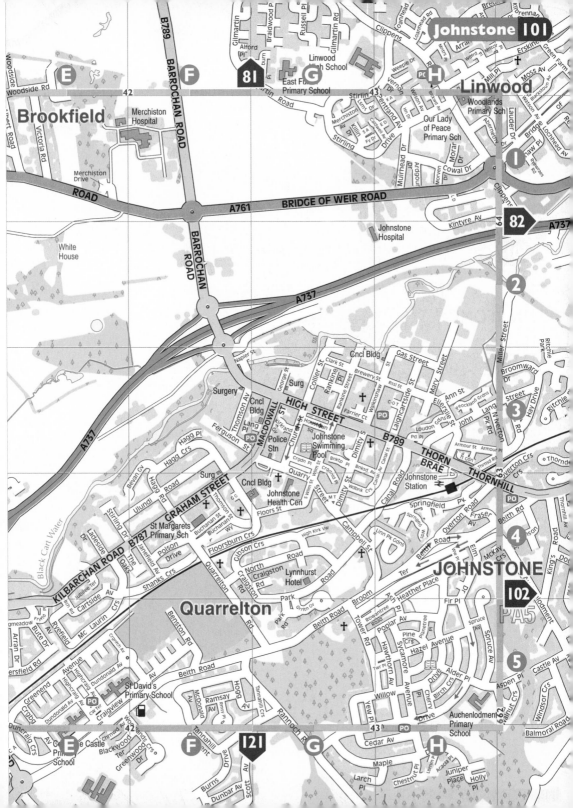

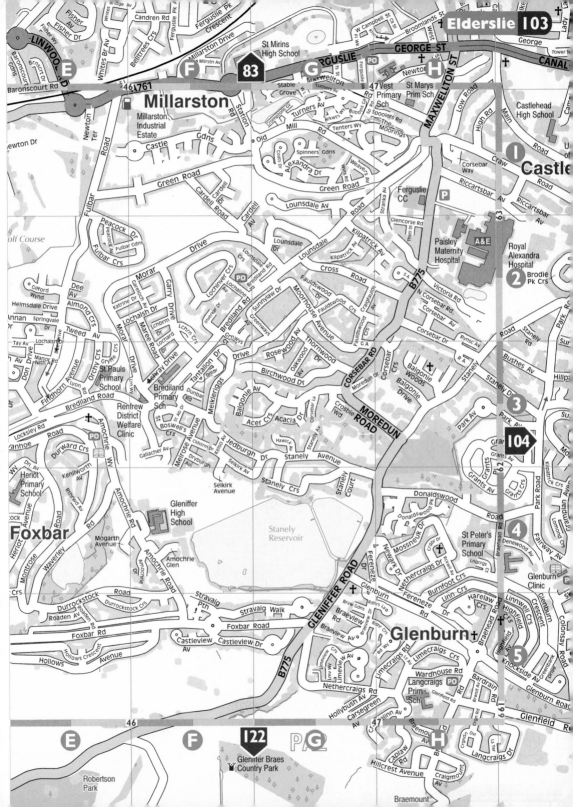

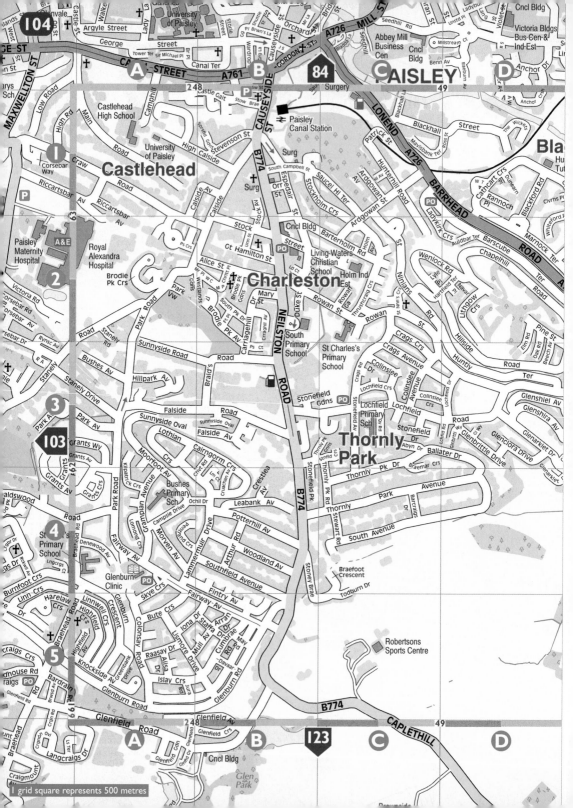

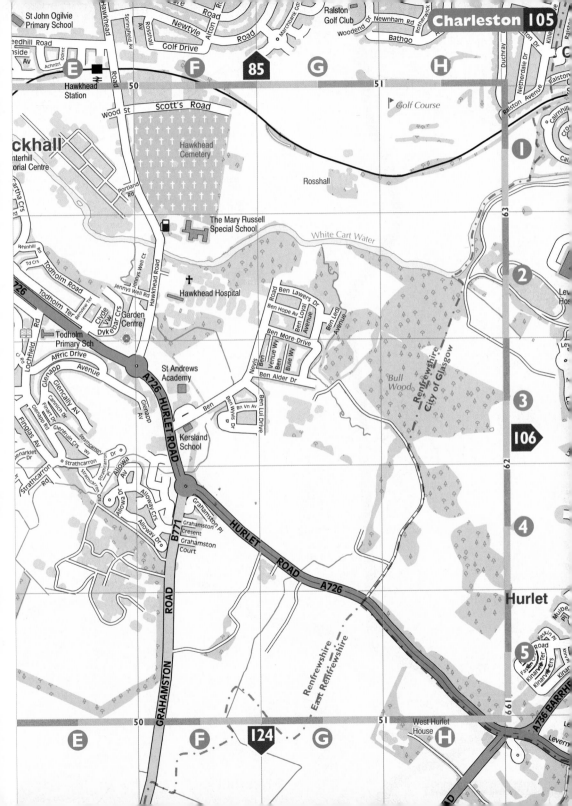

St John Ogilvie
Primary School

Hawkhead

Newtyle
Rosshall
Golf Drive
Alton
Road

Springfield Av
Marchbank Gdns

Ralston
Golf Club
Newnham Rd
Woodend Dr
Bathgo

Duchray
Netherdale Dr
Rotherwick
Killee

reedhill Road

nside
Av

Achntri

E

Hawkhead
Station

F

85

50

G

51

H

Ralston Avenue

Carmlrhl

Ralston

ctor

Cal

I

Wood St

Scott's Road

Golf Course

interhill
orial Centre

ckhall

Hawkhead
Cemetery

Rosshall

2

Portland Rd

B726
Todholm Road

Whinhill Rd
Td Crs

Todholm Ter

Birkview Ter

Hawkhead Road

Jennys Weil Rd

Jennys Weil Ct

The Mary Russell
Special School

White Cart Water

Clyde
Vw
Dyke
Cedar Crs

Garden
Centre

Hawkhead Hospital

Road

Ben Lawers Dr

Ben Hope Av

Ben Loyal
Avenue

Ben Ledi
Avenue

Lev
Hos

Todholm
Primary Sch

Lochfield

C
Rd

Affric Drive

St Andrews
Academy

Ben More Drive

News

Venue Wy

Ben
Bule Wy

3

Glenapp
Avenue

Glencally Av

Carnlich Dr

Finart Dr
Glenfruin Crs

Glenarklet
Dr

Strathcarron Wy

Strathcarron Pl

Ben Alder Dr

Ben

Renfrewshire
City of Glasgow

Bull
Wood

106

Finglas Av

Glenapp
Av

A726 HURLET ROAD

Kersland
School

Ben Wyvis Dr

Ben Lui Drive

Ben Bn Vn Av

Strathcarron
Rd

Allowa
Av

Allowa Dr

Allowa Crs

4

B771 GRAHAMSTON ROAD

Grahamston Pl

Grahamston
Cresent

Grahamston
Court

HURLET

ROAD

A726

Hurlet

Mulbe

Faskin Pl

5

Faskin
Rd

Kinarve Ter

Kinarve Crs

Kinar

A736 BARRH

50

Renfrewshire

East Renfrewshire

51

West Hurlet
House

E

F

124

G

H

Leven

A736 BARRH

Leven

661

GRAHAMSTON ROAD

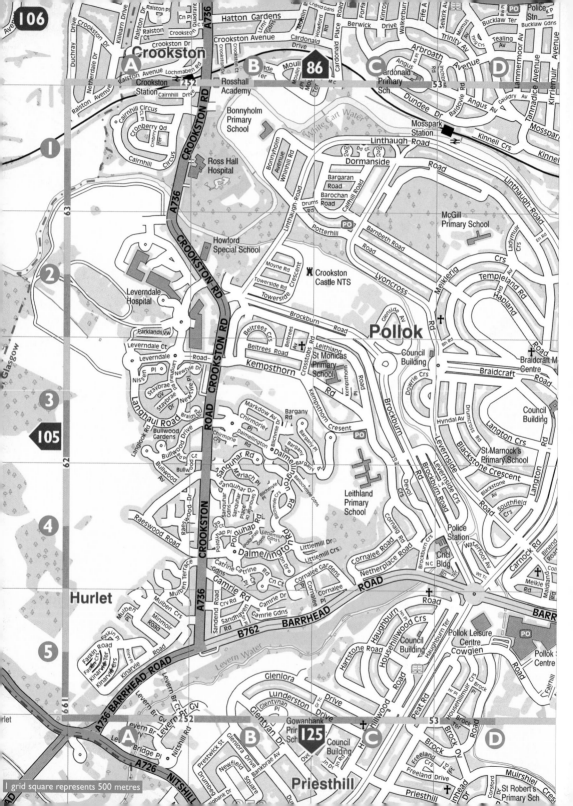

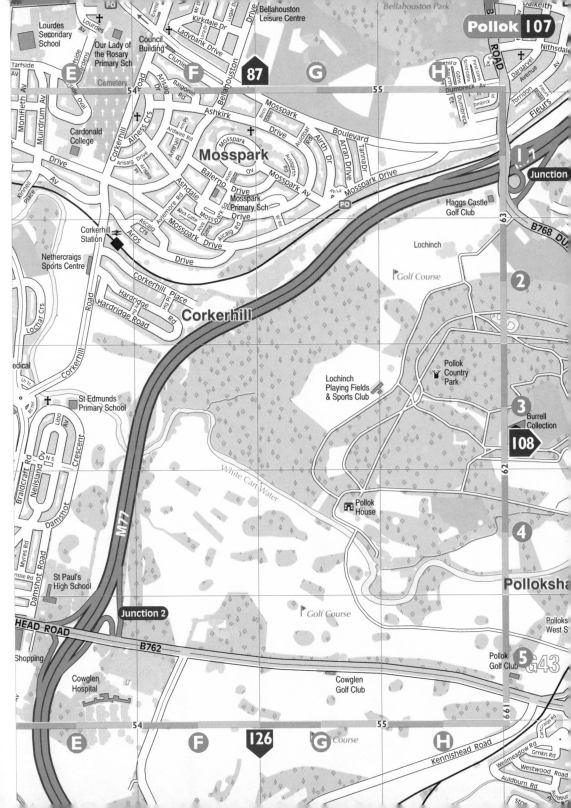

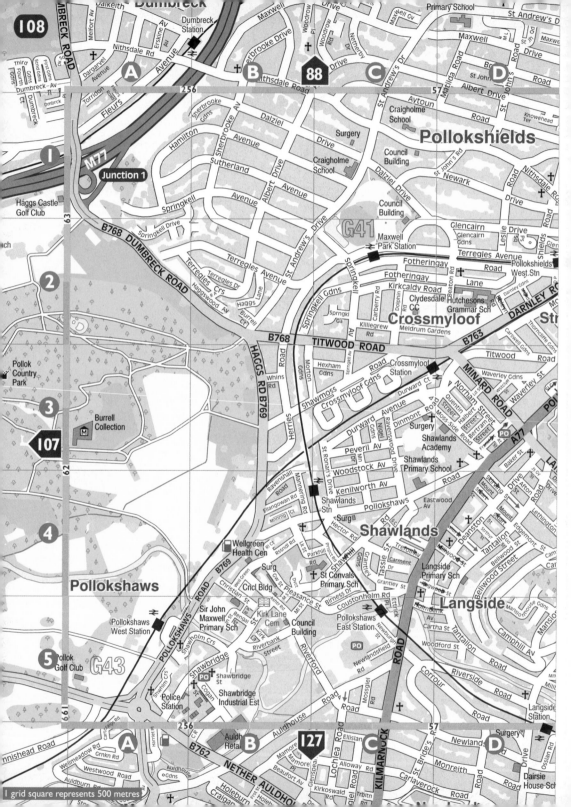

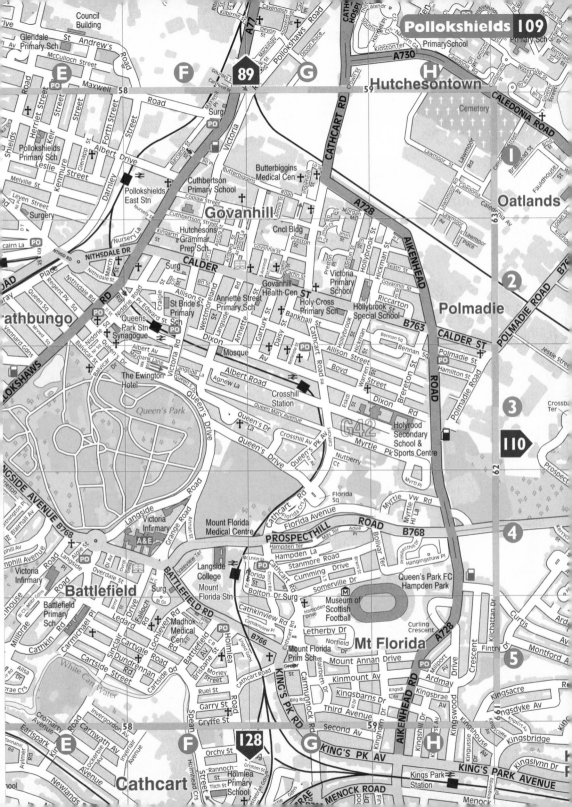

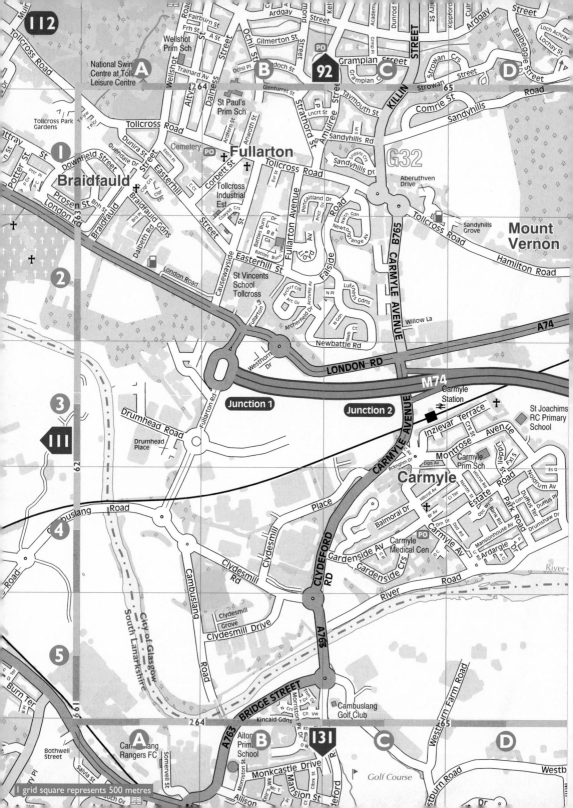

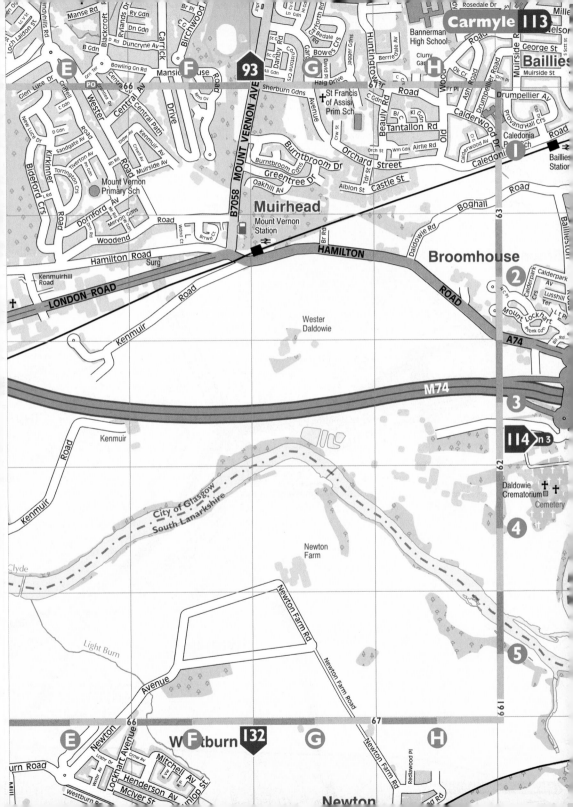

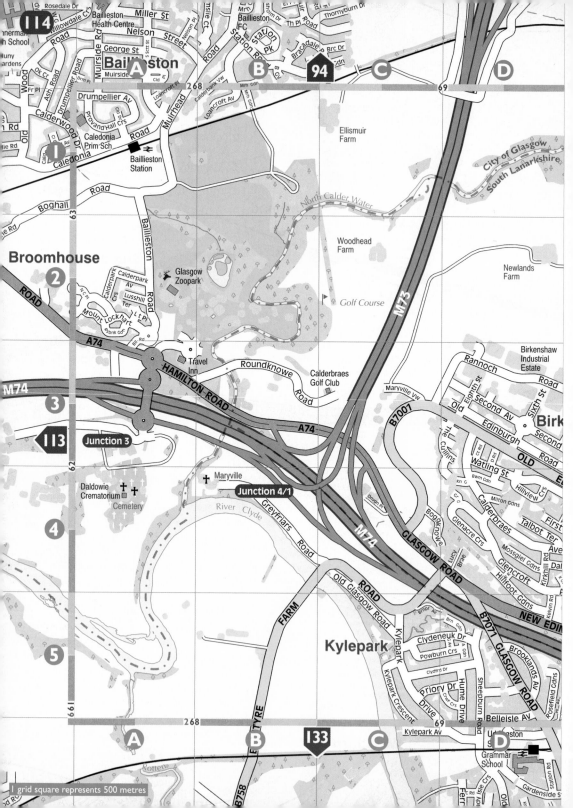

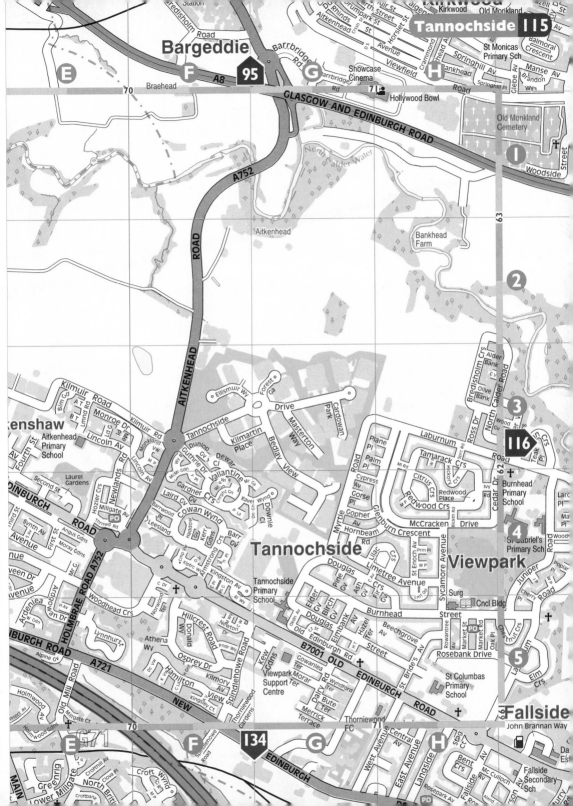

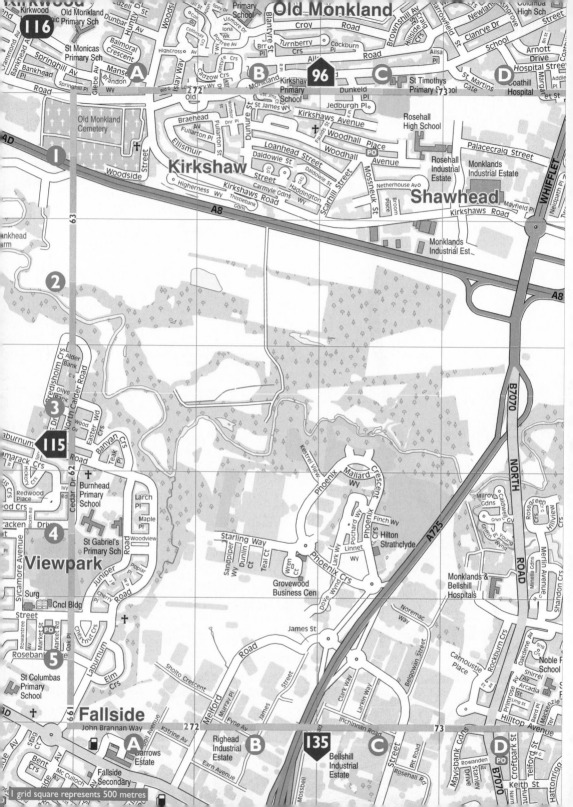

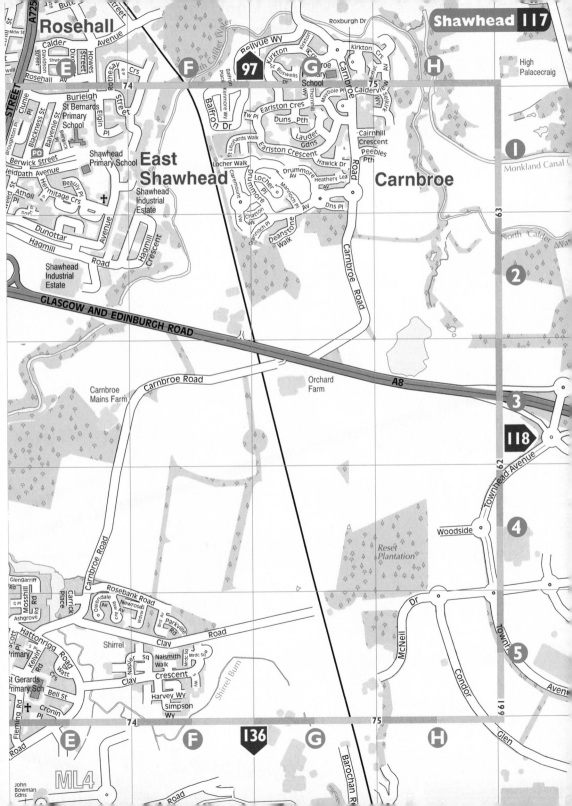

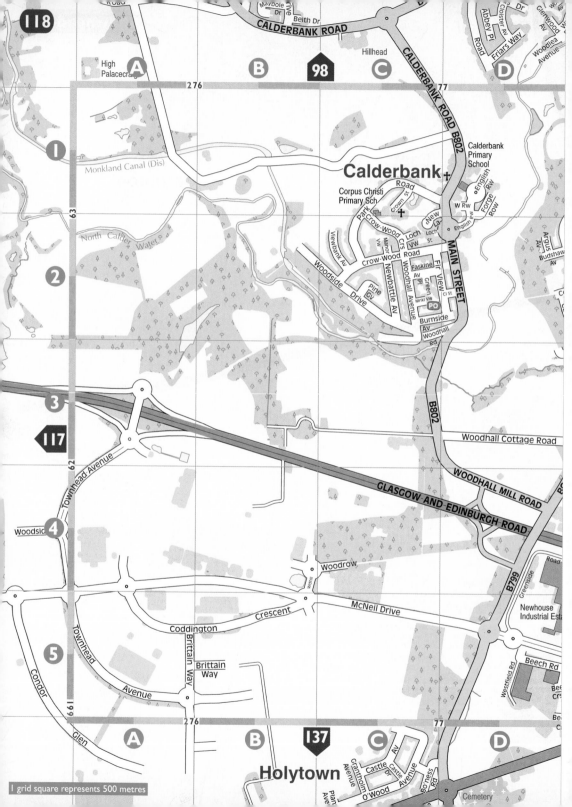

120

Auchenames

Huthead
Cott

A

240

62

B

100

Cartside

C

Millikenpark

D

COCHRANEMILL RD

B787

Hunt

Melfort
Gdns

Glencart
Gv

41

Millerton Park
Station

Avenue

Corseford

Tweed
Pl

Ness Av

Tay Pl

Forth Pl

Ettrick Ter

Teviot Ter

Spey Pl

Annan Pl

Fordbank
Primary
School

Churchill
Avenue

Palme

Pl

1

Kibbleston

Faulds

Kibbleston
Road

2

Drygate

Thirdpart
Hall

Kibbleston
Road

A737

Black Cart Water

BEITH

Corseford
School

Meikle
Corseford

ROAD

St Cuthberts
High School

St Anthonys
Primary School

Midton Road

Hallhill

Walpole Pl

Swan Rd

Linnet Av

Martlet
Dr

Plover
Pl

Curlew

PO

3

Station

Howwood
Station

Drygait

Torbracken

B787

Midton Road

Road

4

Earlshill Drive

Krim Wy

Elliston Crescent

Mayfield Crescent

Mayfield Drive

New Avenue

Station Av

Hallside St

Md Ct

PO

Elliston Rd

Elliston Pl

George Street

Howwood
Primary
School

MAIN STREET

Kirk Wynd

Ulister Crescent

Elliston

B787

BOWFIELD RD

Bowfield
Way

B776

Semple View

Hill Road

Hillfoot Drive

Carsewood
Avenue

Howwood

Tor
Bracken

5

B7

B776
999

A

240

B

PA9

Skiff Wood

C

41

D

North
Muirdykes

North

1 grid square represents 500 metres

E
F
101
G
H
I
102
2
3
4
5

Millersfield Rd
Greenend
Avenue
Hincraig
Highcraig
Dundonald Av
Beith Road
Rd
Hawthorn Av
Twr
Sycamore Avenue
Avenue
Aspen Pl
Craigbo
Dundor
Craigview
St David's
Primary School
Ramsay
Rannoch Road
Willow
Elm
Walnut Crs
Windsor Crs
Balmoral Road

Cochrane Castle
Primary
School
Blackwood
Greenwood Crs
Tannahill
Crescent
Burns
Drive
Dunbar Av
Scott Av
Bruce Av
Cedar Av
PO
Maple
Larch
Chestnut Pl
Juniper
Place
Holly
Pl
Auchenlodment
Primary
School

Johnston
High School

Cochrane Castle
Golf Club

Auchengreoch Av
Auchengreoch Rd
Stateston
Rd
Finch
Pl
Heron Pl
Falcon Rd
Kestrel Pl
Tern Pl
Wren Pl
Sanderling Pl
Sheldrake Pl
Stateston Road

Golf Course

Craigenfeoch

Hallhill

Auchengreoch Road

Craigmuir

Mountop

High Burnside

Bent

42
43

E
F
G
H

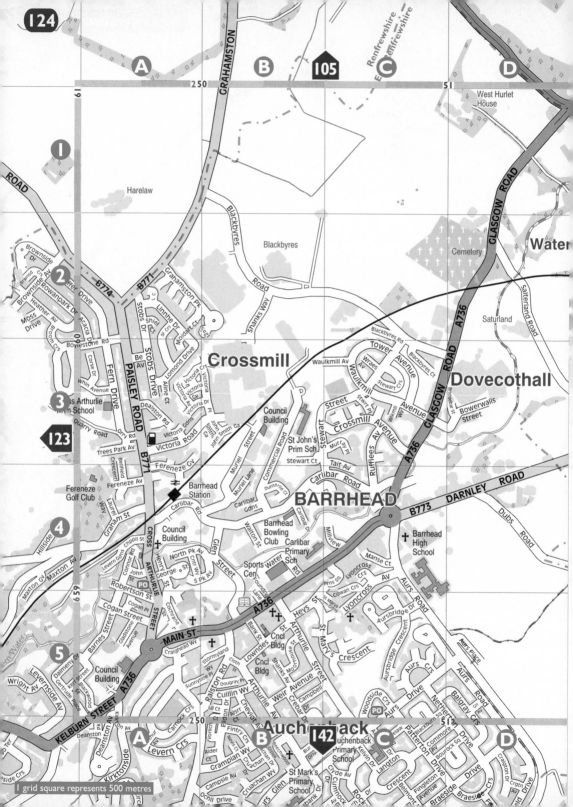

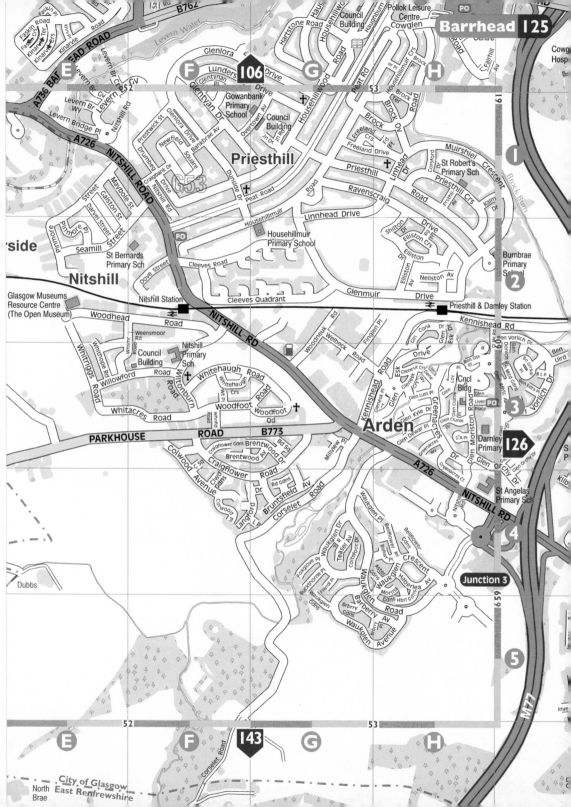

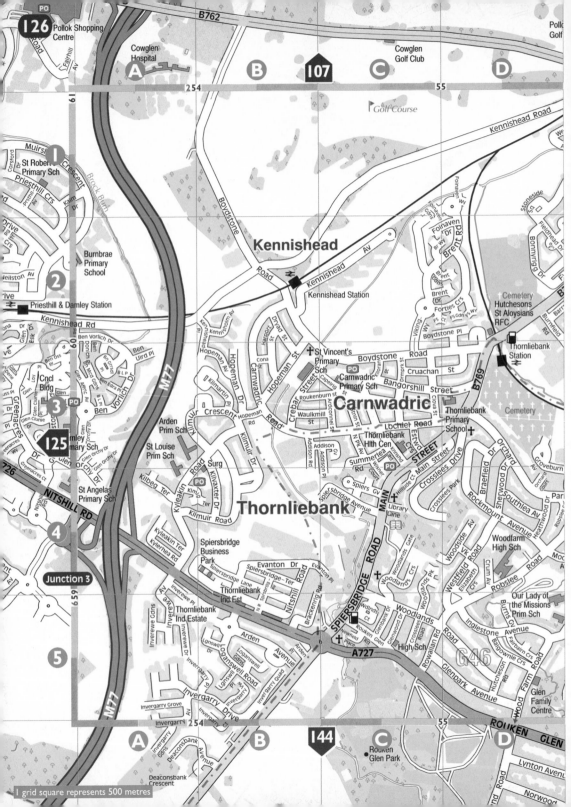

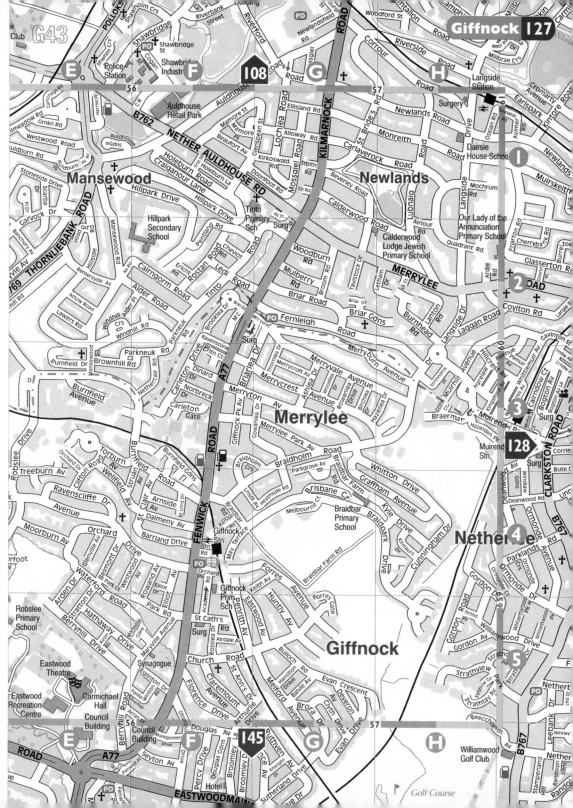

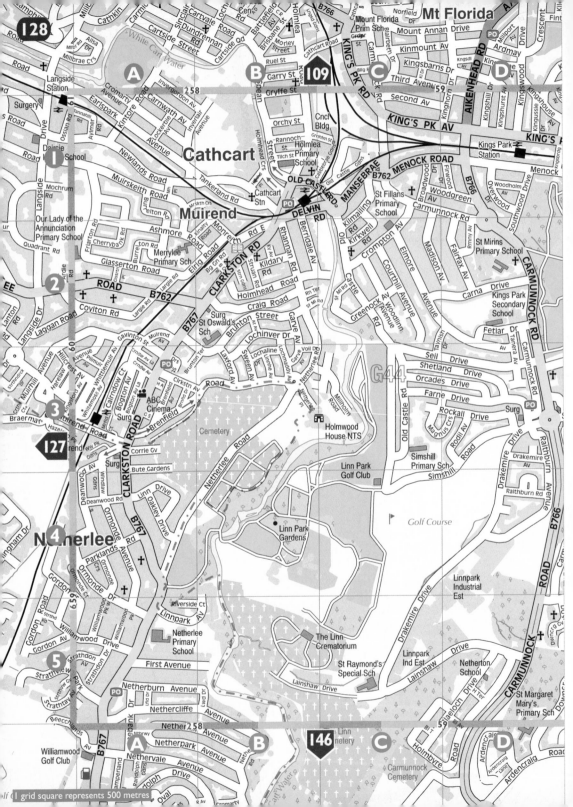

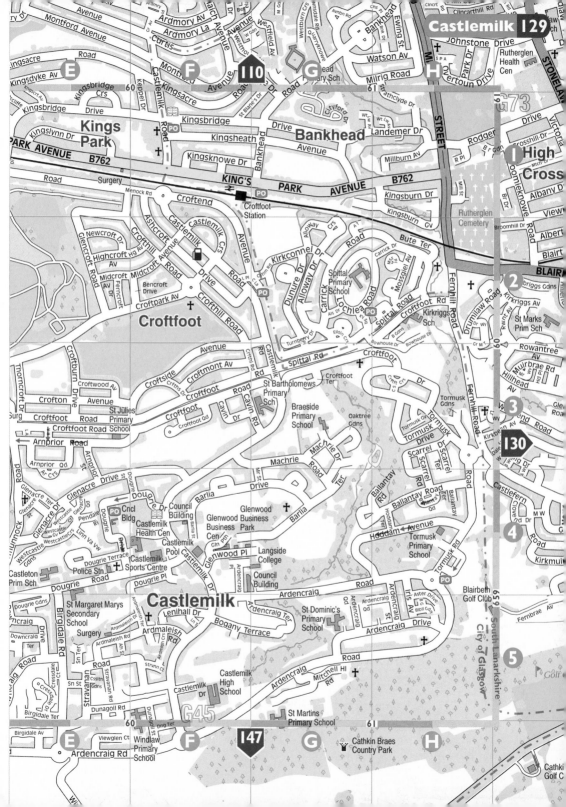

Kings Park

Bankhead

High Cross

Croftfoot

Castlemilk

King's Park Avenue B762

Montford Avenue

Kingsacre Road

Kingsbridge Drive

Kingsheath Avenue

Kingsknowe Dr

Landemer Dr

Millburn Av

Kingsburn Dr

Kingsburn Gv

Rutherglen Cemetery

Rutherglen Health Cen

Johnstone Drive

Overtoun Drive

Croftend Avenue

Croftfoot Station

Castlemilk Avenue

Croftfoot Road

Croftfoot Road

Spittal Rd

Croftfoot Road

Spittal Primary School

Kirkriggs Sch

St Marks Prim Sch

Rowantree

Muirbrae Rd

Hillhead Av

Tormusk Gdns

Tormusk Drive

Scarrel Dr

Ballantay Rd

Ballantay Road

Hoddam Avenue

Tormusk Primary School

St Bartholomews Primary Sch

Braeside Primary School

Oaktree Gdns

Croftfoot Road Primary School

Arnprior Road

Glenacre Drive

Council Building

Glenwood Business Park

Glenwood Business Cen

Langside College

Council Building

Ardencraig Road

St Dominic's Primary School

Castlemilk Health Cen

Castlemilk Pool

Castlemilk Sports Centre

Police Stn

Castleton Prim Sch

Dougrie Road

St Margaret Marys Secondary School

Castlemilk

Lenihall Dr

Bogany Terrace

Ardmaleish Rd

Castlemilk High School

Castlemilk Dr

Ardencraig Road

Blairbeth Golf Club

City of Glasgow

South Lanarkshire

St Martins Primary School

Windlaw Primary School

Ardencraig Rd

Cathkin Braes Country Park

Cathki Golf C

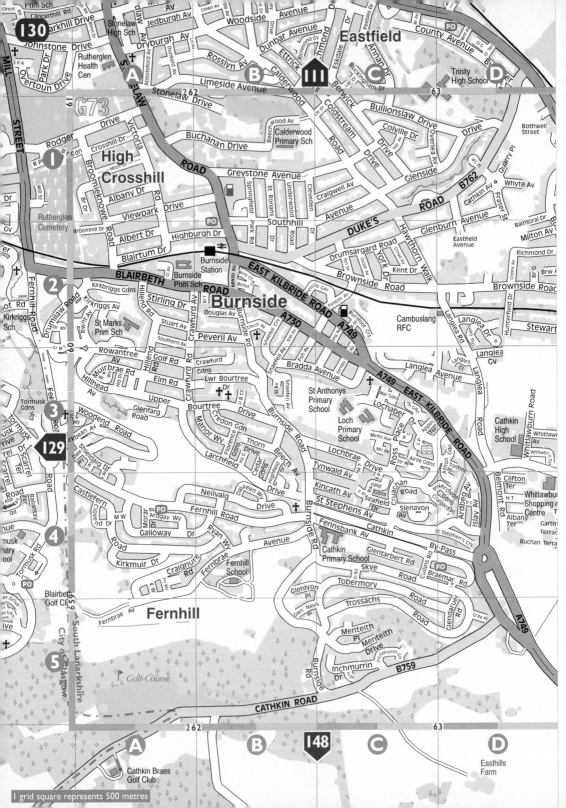

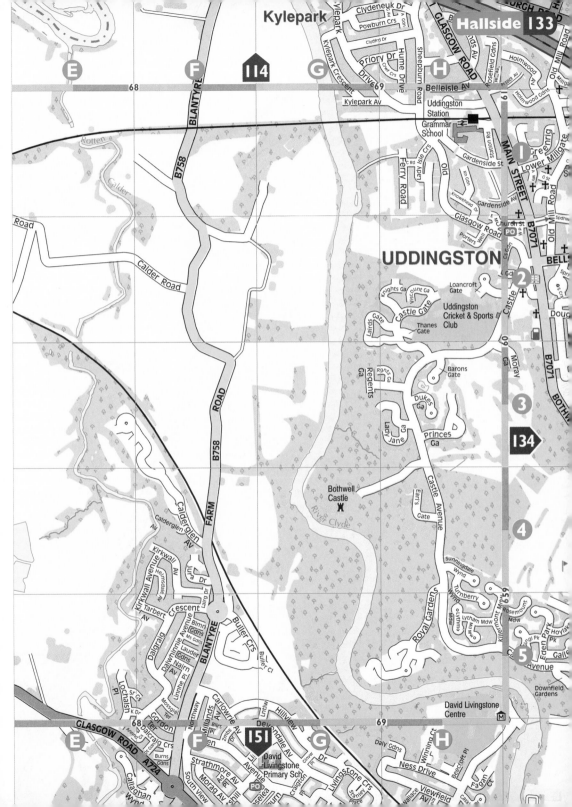

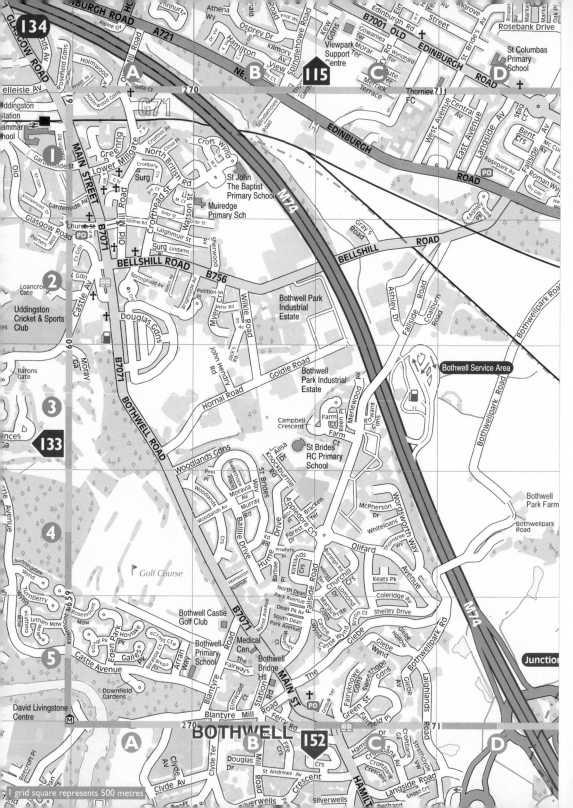

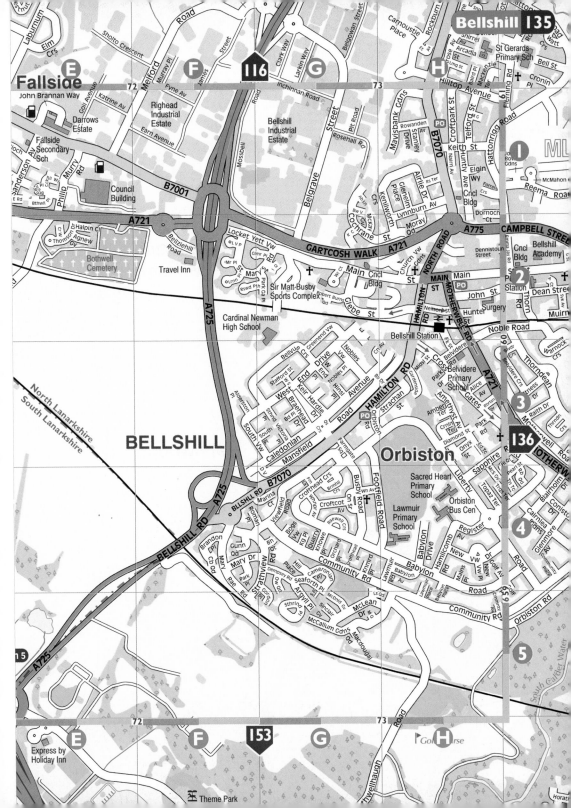

Fallside

E

F

116

G

H

I

72

73

John Brannan Way

Laburnum Crs

Elm Crs

Sholto Crescent

Melford

Murray Pl

Fyne Av

James Street

Clark Way

Larkin Way

Inchinnan Road

Carnoustie Place

Rockburn

Snirrel Av

Arcadia

Watt

St Gerards Primary Sch

Bell St

Cronin

Coll Avenue

Katrine Av

Righead Industrial Estate

Earn Avenue

Bellshill Industrial Estate

Rosehall Rd

Pl Road

Belgowan Street

Mavisbank Gdns

Rowanden

Stanley Drive

Telford St

Croftpark St

Keith St

Cncl Bldg

McMahon

Reema Rd

Darrows Estate

Fallside Secondary Sch

Anderson Av

Philip Murry Rd

B7001

Mossbell Road

Belgrave Street

Glenairn Place

Airlie Dr

Kenilworth

Lynnburn Av

Moray

Rs Ter

Nairn Av

Huntly Ave

Elgin Wy

Forrest Crs

Dornoch Ct

Cncl Bldg

Jim Bowie Gdns

ML

Council Building

A721

Locket Yett Vw

Cochrane St

Mckay

GARTCOSH WALK

A721

A775

CAMPBELL STREET

Bothwell Cemetery

Travel Inn

Bellziehill Road

Mary

Park Gd Pl

Glmr Pl

Main St

Cncl Bldg

Church Vw

Gdns

NORTH ROAD

MAIN ST

HAMILTON RD

Main St

Dennistoun Street

Cncl Bldg

Bellshill Academy

Dean Street

Sir Matt Busby Sports Complex

Robert Burns Rd

Glebe St

PO

John St

2

Station

Thorn Rd

Muirn

Cardinal Newman High School

A725

Greenend Vw

Nobles Vw

Cr Av

Bellshill Station

MOTHERWELL RD

Noble Road

Belvidere

Belvidere Primary School

Thorndean

Warnock Crs

BellVue Crs

Stafford St

West End Drive

Kelf

Hardie

Nobles Pl

Hirst

Cross

Park

Belvidere Crs

Alice

AV

3

Raith Dr

BELLSHILL

North Lanarkshire

South Lanarkshire

West Braehead

Strand

Bd P Pl

Road

Avenue

HAMILTON RD

Strachan St

Amethyst Ter

Crnlin Ter

Diamond St

Onyx Rd

Park Rd

Crmn Dr

A721

Ironness Crs

MOTHERWELL RD

136

MOTHERWELL ROAD

South Vw

Caledonian

Mansfield

PO Rd

Farmgate

Busby Road

Sapphire

Topaz Ter

Liberty

Sacred Heart Primary School

Orbiston Bus Cen

Blairholm Dr

Cairnies Road

Glenmore

4

BELLSHILL RD

B7070

Marina

Crofthead Crs

Brmill

Croftcot Av

Orn St

Orchard

Foot field Rd

Lawmuir Primary School

Register

Hamilcomb

New

Conisto Dr

Brandon Ct Qd

Gunn Qd

Mary Dr

Viewfield Road

Roman Pl

Bogs Vw

Kg Pl

Quarry

Knowe

Gaewell Rd

Greenhead

Babylon

Babylon Drive

Mains

Babylon Road

BELLSHILL RD

A725

Strathview

Park Rae Rd

Hill Place

Seaforth Pl

Cameron Rd

Community Rd

Lawmuir

Babylon AV

5

A725

Brandon

Dempsey Rd

Argyll Pl

Sinclair

McMnld

McLean Dr

Community Rd

Orbiston Road

South Calder Water

sthring

McCallum Gdns

Macdougall

Macdougall Rd

E

F

153

G

H

72

73

Express by Holiday Inn

Golf Horse

Theme Park

Inchwellhaugh

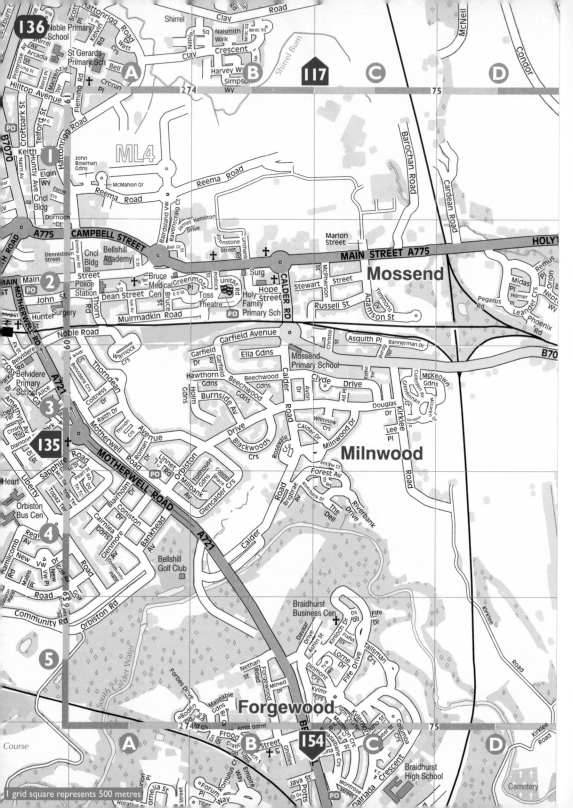

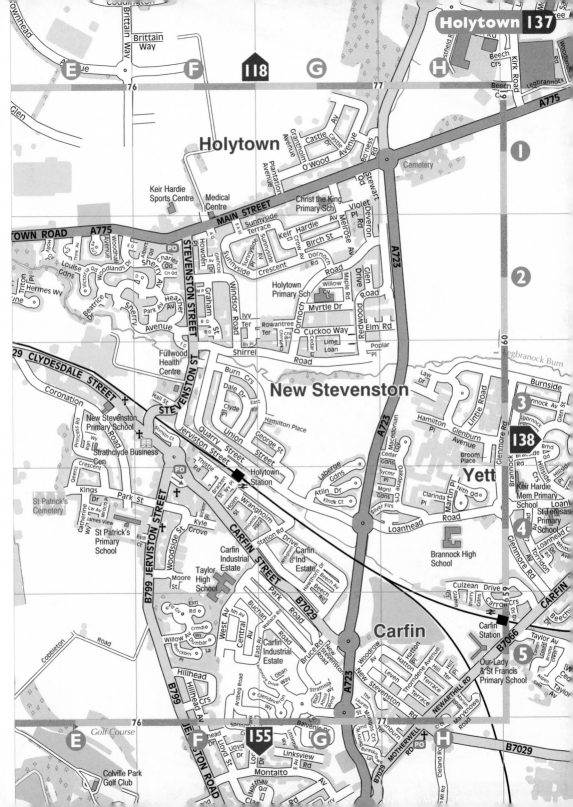

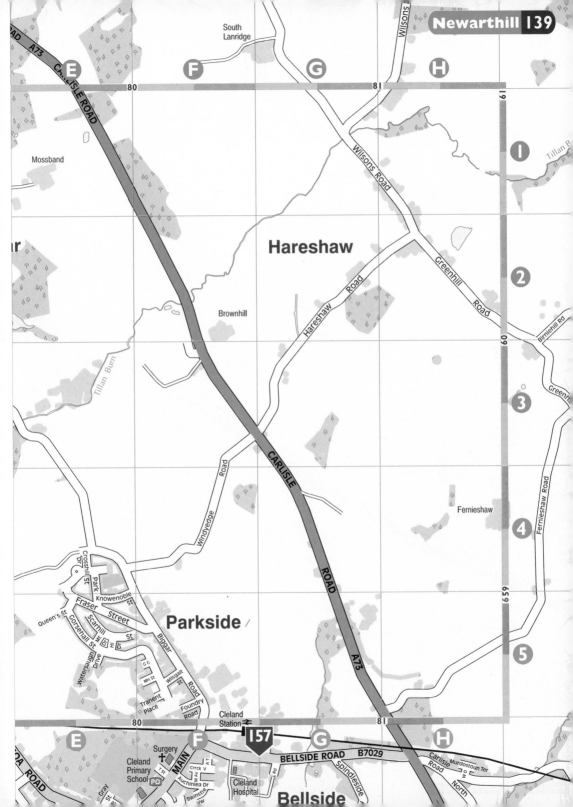

A 246 **B** **122** **C** 47 **D**

Mossneuk Farm

Capellie Fm

Greenfieldmuir

1

58

Killoch Water

2

Foreside

Station Brae

Ferneze Road

Crofthead Industrial Estate

3

57

Milnthird

G78

Mdws

Millview Ter

Holehouse Brae

Broad

Millview Ter
Matheny Ter
Hths
Mill Ter
Orr Ter
Brig Co
Limmill Ter
The
Alexander Ter

Holehouse

Pattiston

4

A736 **LOCHLIBO ROAD**

Levern Water

Glenlivet Rd
Glenorrin Wy
Glen Creran Crs
Glen Roy Dr
Glen Doll Rd
Gln Finlet Road
Glen Mark Rd
Gln Crn
Glen Muir Rd
Lyon Rd
Glen Tarbert
Glenshee Av
Glen Isla Av

Uplawmoor Road

Crumyards

5

656

Kilburn

King's

A 246 Jaapston **B** **C** 47 **D**

Craig of Neilston

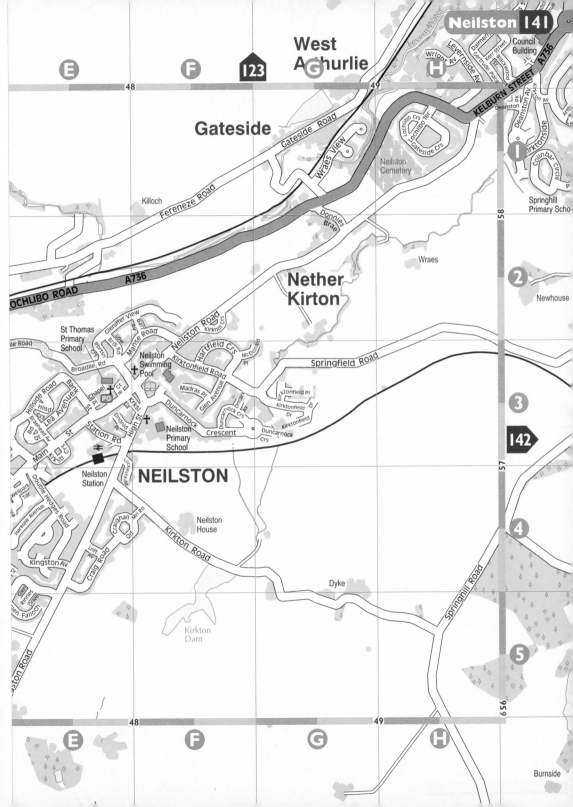

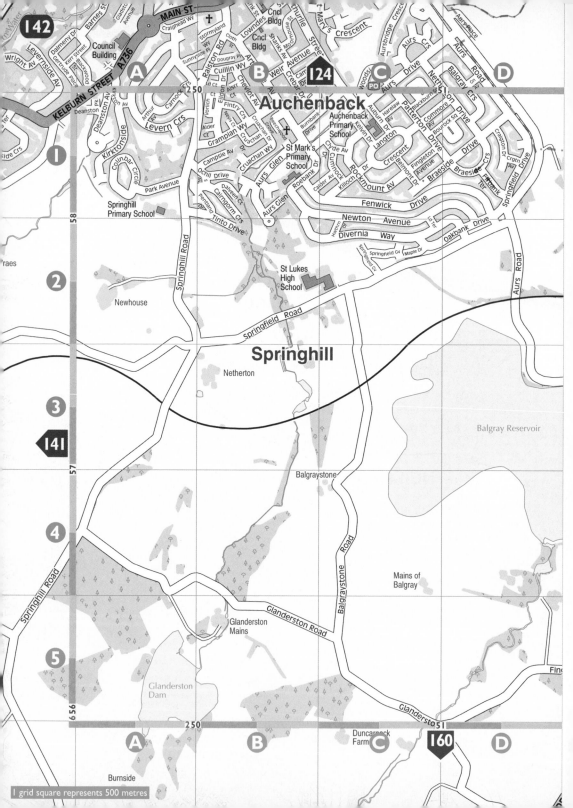

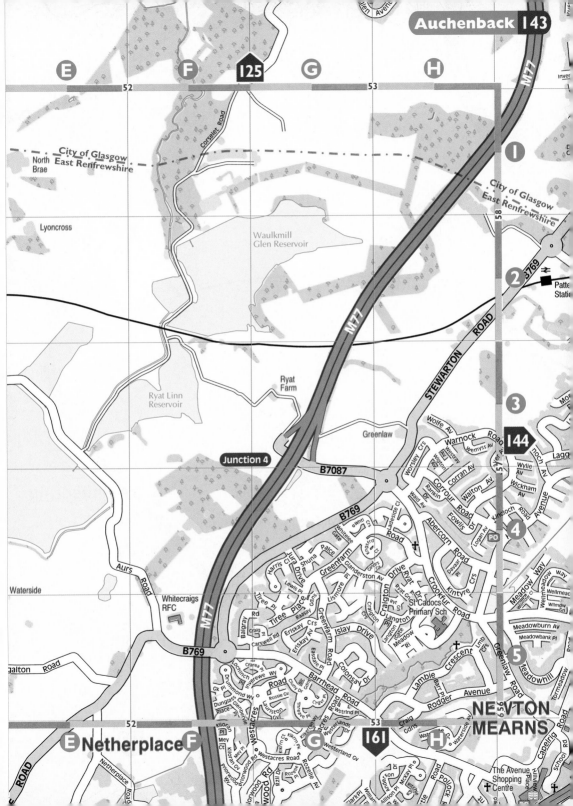

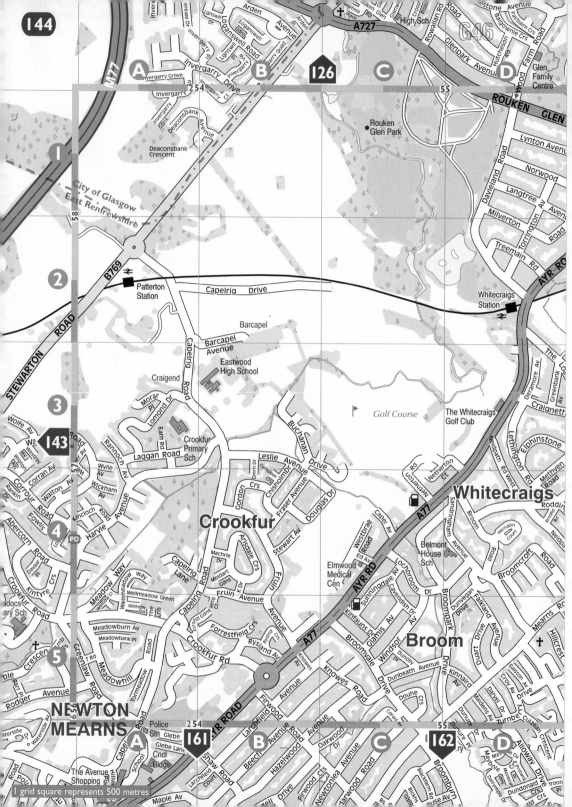

144

G46

A · 254 · B · **126** · C · 55 · D

Invergarry Grove
Invergarry
Invergarry Drive
Invergarry Gdns
Invergarry Ct

Barra Quad

ROUKEN GLEN

Glen Family Centre

Lynton Avenue

Deaconsbank Crescent

Deaconsbank Avenue

Rouken Glen Park

Norwood

Langtree Av

Milverton

Treemain Rd

Tortington Av

Daveland Road

AYR ROAD

I

City of Glasgow
East Renfrewshire

58

2

B769

Patterton Station

Capelrig   Drive

Whitecraigs Station

STEWARTON   ROAD

Capelrig Road

Barcapel

Barcapel Avenue

Eastwood High School

Golf Course

The Whitecraigs Golf Club

Deramore Av

Greenbank Av

Craigneth

The

3

Craigend

Morar Pl

Lomond Dr

Wolfe Av

W2

Westray

Wigton Pl

Crookfur Primary Sch

Buchanan   Drive

Netherton Rd

Lethington Rd West

Elphinstone

Craigneth

Methven Road

143

57

Rannoch Rd

Laggan Road

Earn Rd

Wylie Av

Wickham Av

Leslie   Avenue

Gordon Crs

Cmm II Crs

Campbell

Chisholm Dr

Fraser Avenue

Douglas Dr

Sanringham

Broom

Roddinc

Netherton Ct

Netherton Rd

Corran Av

Corrour Road

Fowlis

Walton Av

Kincloch Road

Avenue

Harvie

Crookfur

Arisdale Crs

Machrie Dr

Moldart Gdns

Stewart Av

Fruin   Avenue

A77

AYR RD

Westbrae Road

Capel Av

Ed Av

Whitecraigs

Belmont House Sch

Herndon Court

Broomcroft Road

Broompark

4

PO

Abercorn Road

Dayaar

Crs

Kintyre

Capelrig Lane

Wellmeadow Way

Wellmeadow Green

Wilmdw Gn

Fruin   Avenue

Hrtg Gdns

Fld Gdns

Elmwood Medical Cen

Sunningdale Av

Lochbroom Dr

Cavendish Dr

Glamis Av

Dunolly

Windsor

Broom

Dunvegan Drive

Falkland Avenue

Mearns Rd

Hillcrest

5

Crookfur Road

ary Sch

Meadow Way

Meadowburn Av

Meadowbank Pl

Crookfur Rd

Forrestfield Crs

Rysland Av

Broomvale Drive

Kinfauns Dr

Dunbeath Avenue

Kinnaird Av

Dunure

Trent

Croy Av

Daniel Av

Maidens Av

Turnbe

Culzean Crescent

Rodger   Avenue

Greenlaw Road

Meadowhill Road

Tormeadow Road

AYR ROAD

Larchfield

Firwood

Larchfield Court

Knowes   Road

Knowes Road

Caldon

Doune Crs

Maybole

Alloway Drive

NEWTON MEARNS

Police Stn

Glebe

Cncl Bldgs

Glebe Lane

School Rd

Capel Rd

A · 254 · **161** · B · Beech Avenue · Hazelwood Road · C · 55 · **162** · D

Larnshaw Road

Firwood Drive

Newtonlea Avenue

Oakwood Dr

Larwood Road

Broomburn Dr

Dundonald

| I grid square represents 500 metres

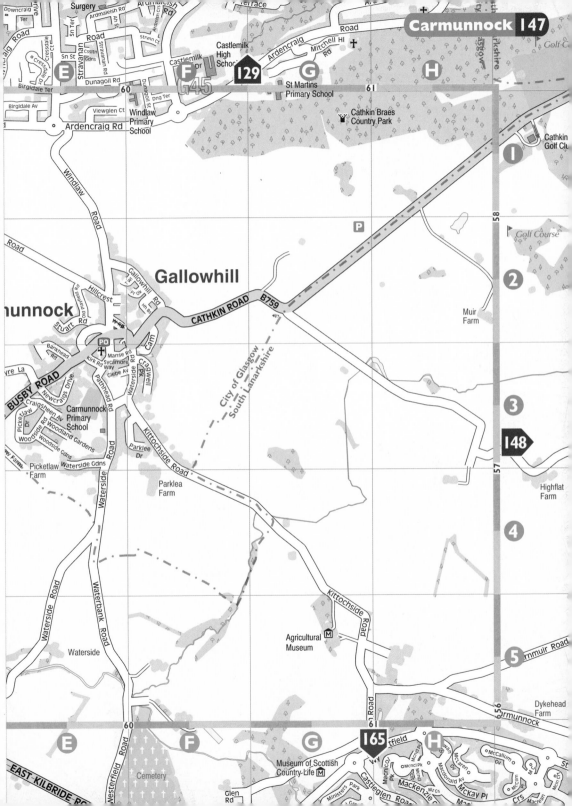

148

130

Golf Course

CATHKIN RO

262

63

B759

Burnside Rd

Menteith
Drive

Inchmurrin
Dr

Inchmurrin Ct

Pl

A

B

C

D

Cathkin Braes
Golf Club

Easthills
Farm

1

58

South Cathkin
Farm

Golf Course

2

Muir
Farm

3

147

57

Highflat
Farm

Cairnmuir Road

Nerston Road

4

Cairnmuir Road

Nerston Road

Cairnmuir Road

Rogerton

Markethill

Mains

5

Cairnmuir Road

656

Carmunnock

Dykehead
Farm

Quarry Road

262

James Hamilton
Heritage Park

63

Stewart

A

Road

165

B

Stewartfield

C

166

D

McEwan
Gdns

McCallum
Gv

McCaren
Pl

Macdonald Av

Stewartfield Way

Stewartfield Way

Stewartfield Way

Esmry Pl

1 grid square represents 500 metres

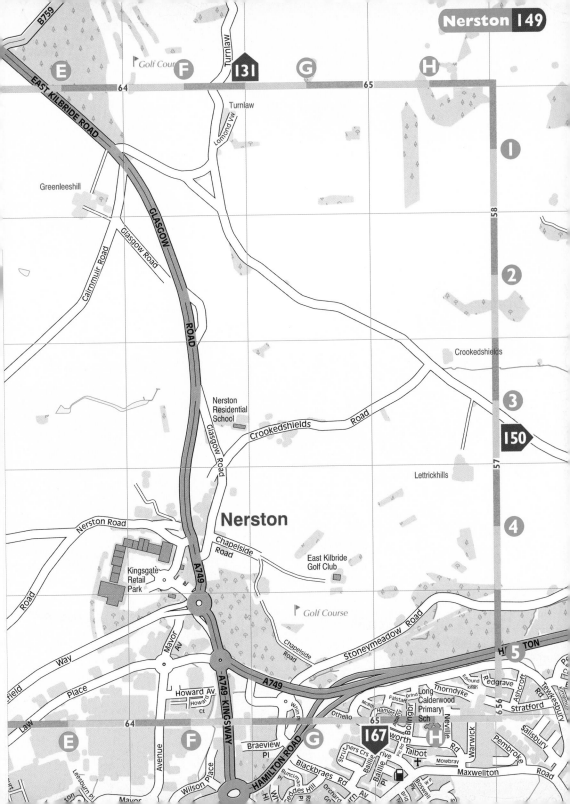

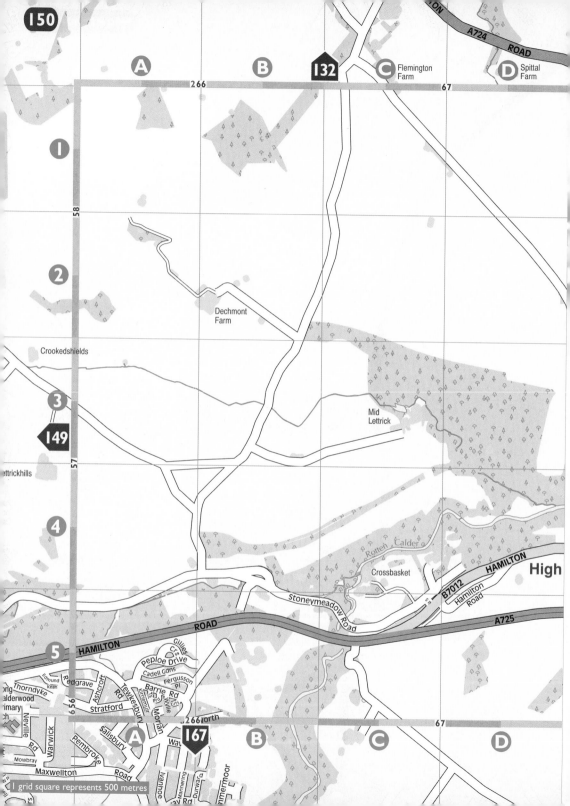

150

A B **132** C Flemington Farm D Spittal Farm

A724 ROAD

I

266 67

58

2

Dechmont Farm

Crookedshields

3

149

57

Mid Lettrick

Lettrickhills

4

Rotten Calder

Crossbasket

HAMILTON

High

B7012

Hamilton Road

5

HAMILTON ROAD

Stoneymeadow Road

A725

Gillies Crs

Peploe Drive

Cadell Gdns

Fergusson Pl

Redgrave

Thorndyke Rd

Edmund Kean

Ashcroft

Tewkesbury Rd

Barrie Rd

Stratford

Wylie

Moran

alderwood

rimary

Neville Rd

Warwick

Salisbury

266 67

Pembroke Road

Mowbray

Maxwellton

A **167** B C D

Wav

Ivanhoe

Mannering

Durward

59

1 grid square represents 500 metres

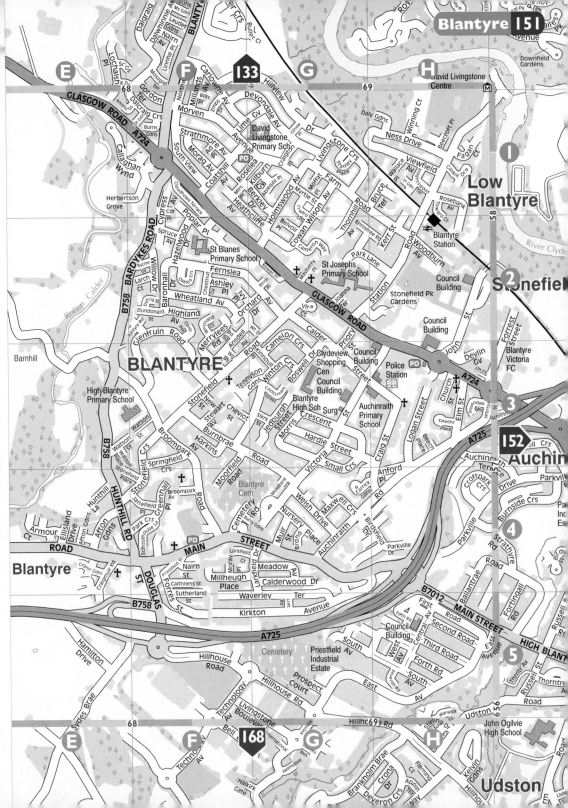

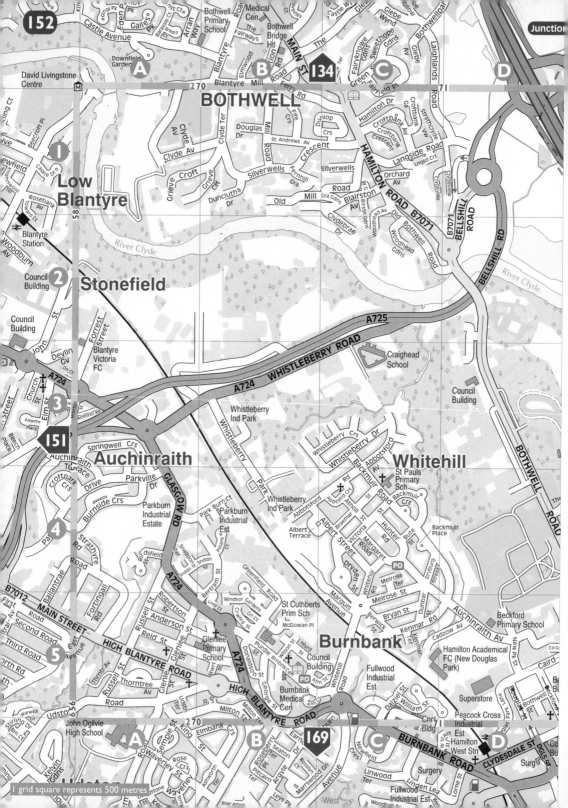

Junction

134

151

169

BOTHWELL

Low Blantyre

Stonefield

Auchinraith

Whitehill

Burnbank

David Livingstone Centre

Blantyre Station

Council Building

Council Building

Blantyre Victoria FC

Craighead School

Council Building

Whistleberry Ind Park

Whistleberry Ind Park

Parkburn Industrial Estate

Parkburn Industrial Est

St Pauls Primary Sch

Glenlee Primary School

St Cuthberts Prim Sch

Council Building

Burnbank Medical Cen

Hamilton Academical FC (New Douglas Park)

Beckford Primary School

Fullwood Industrial Est

Superstore

Peacock Cross Industrial

John Ogilvie High School

River Clyde

River Clyde

A725

A724

WHISTLEBERRY ROAD

HAMILTON ROAD B7071

BELLSHILL RD

BOTHWELL ROAD

GLASGOW RD

A724

HIGH BLANTYRE ROAD

MAIN STREET

BURNBANK ROAD

CLYDESDALE ST

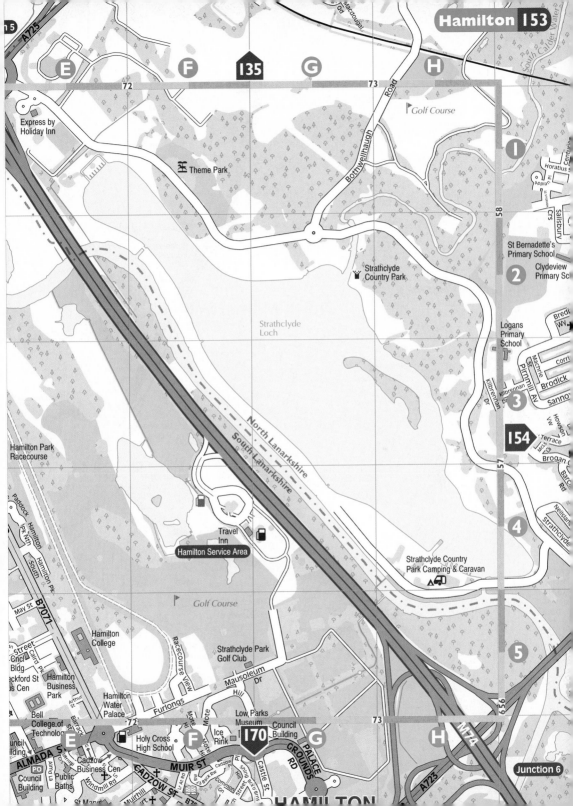

E F **135** G H

72 73

I

58

2

3

154

57

4

56

5

E F **170** G H

72 73

Express by
Holiday Inn

Theme Park

Golf Course

Bothwellhaugh Road

Strathclyde
Country Park

Strathclyde
Loch

St Bernadette's
Primary School

Clydeview
Primary Sc

Logans
Primary
School

Horatius
Lp

Salisbury

CP5

Bredi
WY

Machrie St

Pirnmill AV

Kilbrennan

Corri

Brodick

Sanno

Howson

McGs

Terrace

Brogan

Neilsland

Strathclyde

Strathclyde

Barcla
Rd

Hamilton Park
Racecourse

North Lanarkshire
South Lanarkshire

Travel
Inn

Hamilton Service Area

Strathclyde Country
Park Camping & Caravan

Paddock

Hamilton
Pk Nth

Hamilton
Pk
South

May St

B7071

Golf Course

Hamilton
College

Strathclyde Park
Golf Club

Racecourse View

Mausoleum
Dr

Hill

Hamilton
Water
Palace

Hamilton
Business
Park

Furlongs

More
Hill

More
Hill

Low Parks
Museum

Council
Building

Bell
College of
Technolog

ALMADA ST

PO
Council
Building

Council
Bldg

eckford St
us Cen

Holy Cross
High School

Cadzow
Business Cen

MUIR ST

Ice
Rink

PALACE
GROUNDS
RD

Castle St

M74

A723

HAMILTON

A725

15

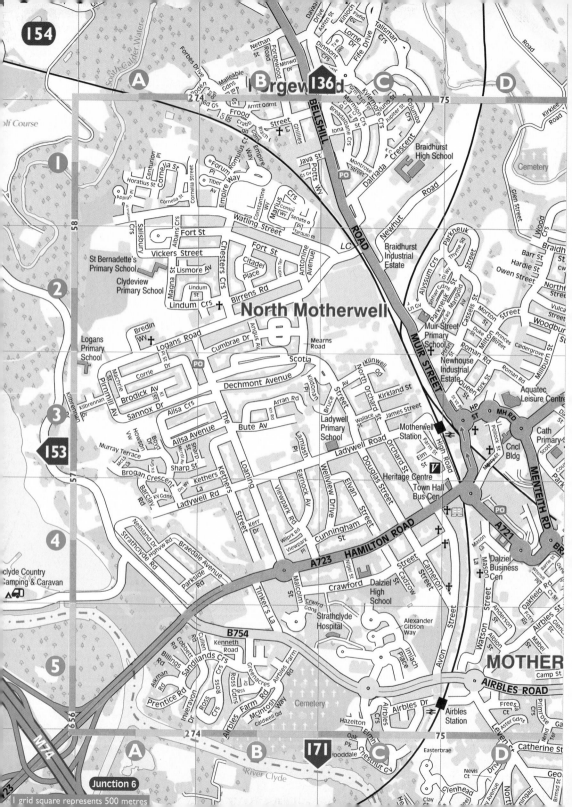

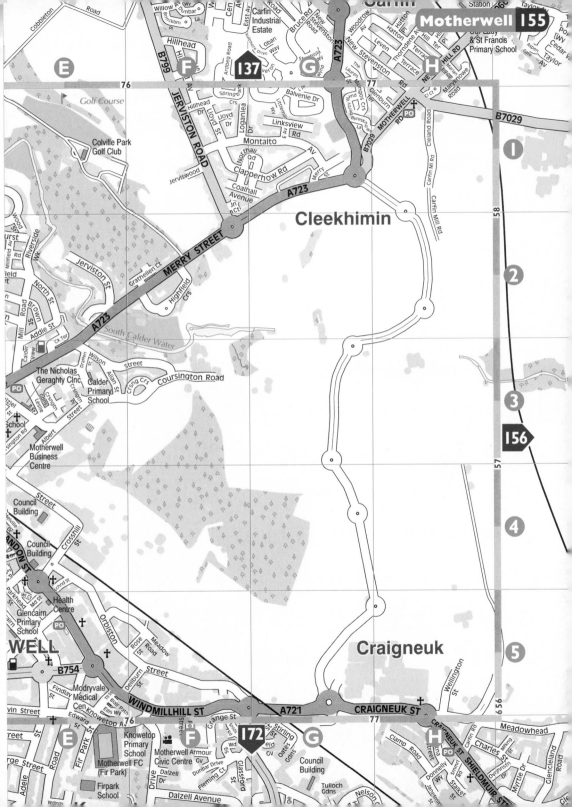

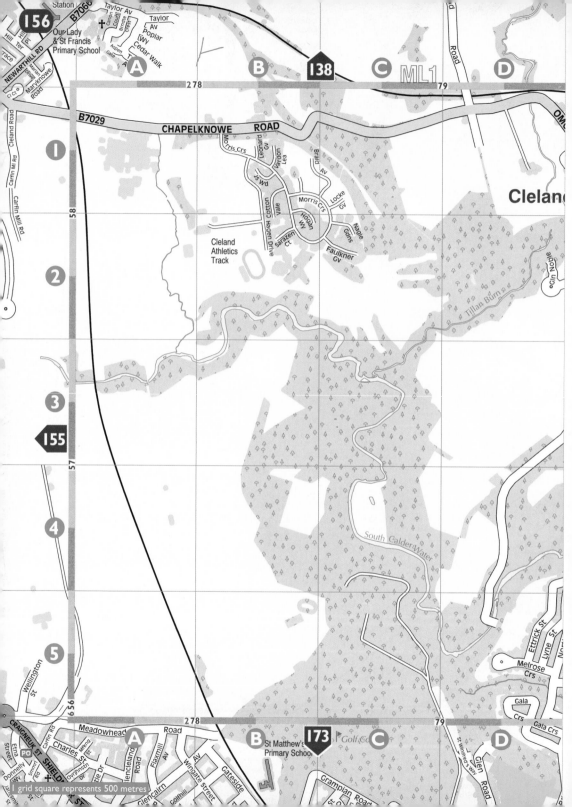

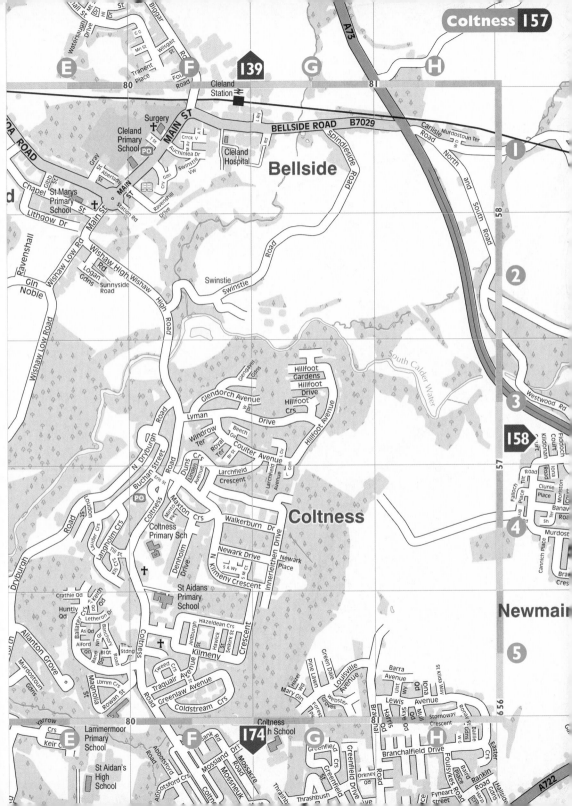

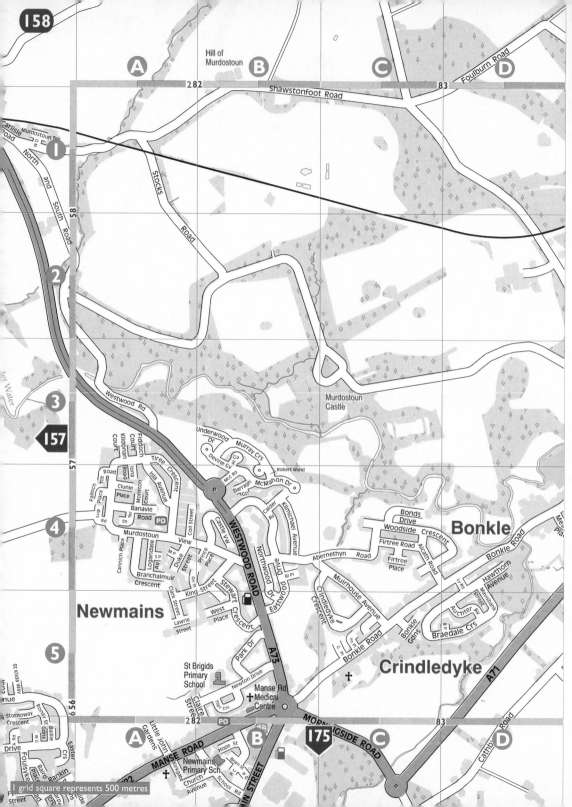

158

A B C D

Hill of Murdostoun

282 83 Foulburn Road

Shawstonfoot Road

Carlisle Road
Murdostoun Ter
North and South Road

1

Stocks Road

2

3

Westwood Rd

Murdostoun Castle

157

Underwood Dr
Murray Crs
Devine Gv
Robert Wynd
McMahon Dr
Darragh Gdn
Calder Av
McC Rd

Fiddoch Court
Kildonan Court
Iona Road
Tiree Crescent
Isla Avenue

Falloch Tilt
Clunie Place
Moriston Court
Banavie Road
PO

Cannich Place
Murdostoun View
Coll Street
Duke Street
Prince Street

Logandale
Branchalmuir Crescent

Clark Street
King Street
Lawrie Street

West Place
Stewart Crescent

Bonds Drive
Woodside Crescent
Firtree Road
Firtree Place
Alcath Road

Bonkle

Abernethyn Road

Kilmichael Avenue
Northwood Dr
Eastwood Dr

Muirhouse Avenue
Crindledyke Crescent

Bonkle Road

Hawthorn Avenue
Auchter Av
Braedale Crs

Bonkle Gdns

Newmains

4

Crindledyke

5

A71

St Brigids Primary School

Park Dr
Newton Drive
Claire Street

Manse Rd
Medical Centre

A73

Stornoway Crescent
Baillie
St Kilda Way

282 PO 83

175

A B C D

MORNINGSIDE ROAD

Cathb Road

MANSE ROAD

Little John Gardens
Hope St
Newmains Primary Sch
Church

MAIN STREET

I grid square represents 500 metres

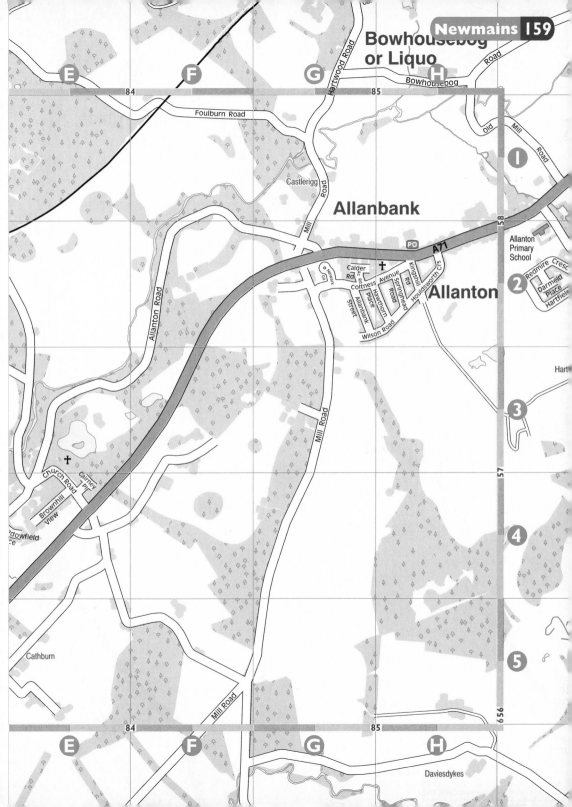

Bowhousebog or Liquo

Allanbank

Allanton

Castlerigg

Allanton Primary School

Allanton Road

Foulburn Road

Hartwood Road

Bowhousebog

Old Mill Road

Mill Road

Calder Rd

Coltness Place

Hawthorn

Springhead Road

Kingshill Rd

Houldsworth Crs

Avenue

Wilson Road

Allanbank Street

Newark

PO

A71

Redmire Cresc

Darmeld Place

Hartfield

Hartf

Church Road

Cairney Pl

Brownhill View

Mill Road

Mill Road

Brownhill View

adowfield

ce

Cathburn

Daviesdykes

E

F

G

H

I

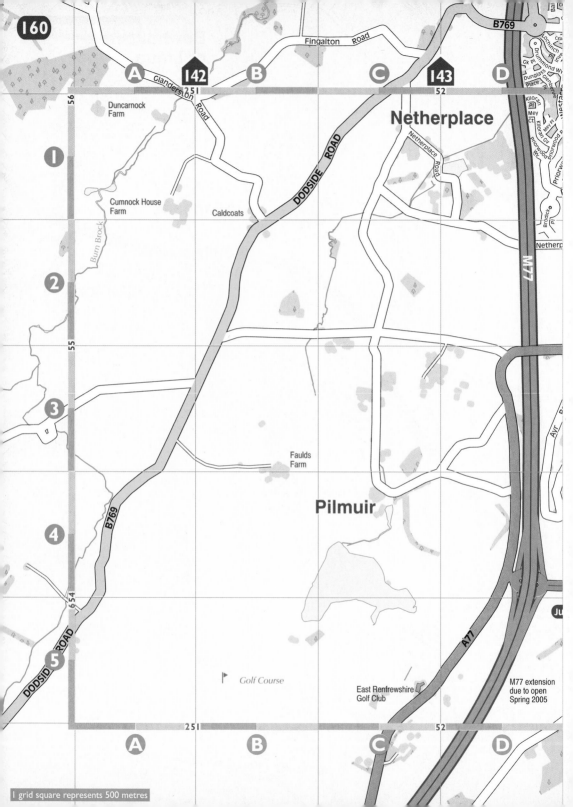

A · Glanderston Road · 142 · 251 · B · Fingalton Road · C · 143 · 52 · D · B769

Duncarnock Farm

Netherplace

Netherplace Road

Kilgoran Pl
Mev Pl
Kilgoran Ct
Gleneview
Dunglass
Priorwood
Priorwood Wy
Priorwood

1

Cumnock House Farm

Caldcoats

DODSIDE ROAD

Brocklehill

Netherpl

Burn Brock

2

55

3

654

DODSIDE ROAD

B769

Faulds Farm

4

Pilmuir

A77

M77

Ju

5

Golf Course

East Renfrewshire Golf Club

M77 extension due to open Spring 2005

251 · A · B · C · 52 · D

I grid square represents 500 metres

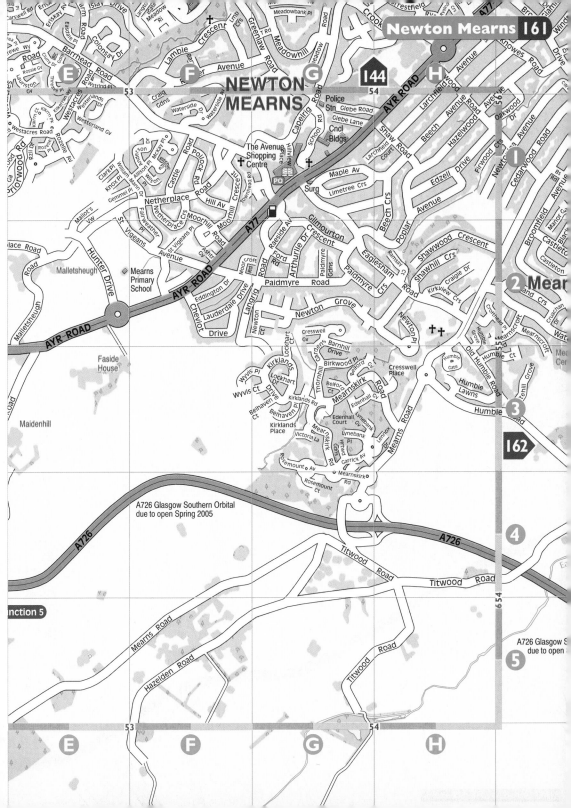

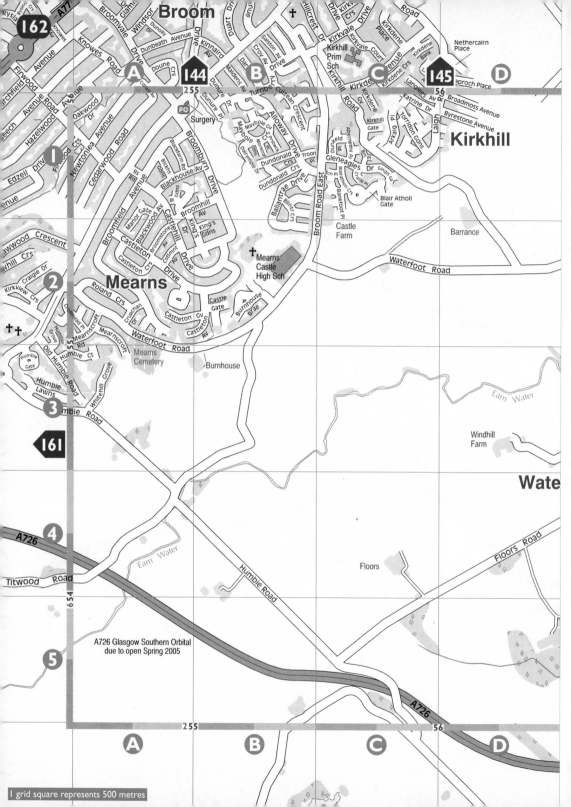

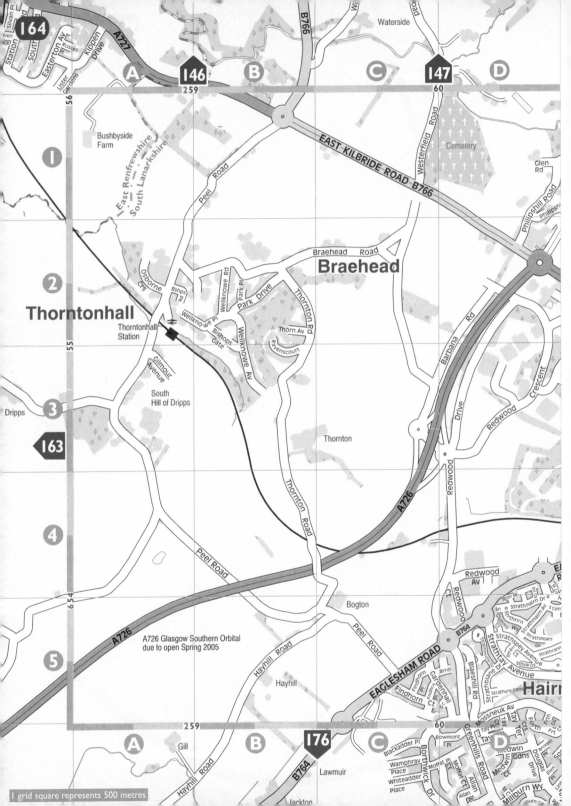

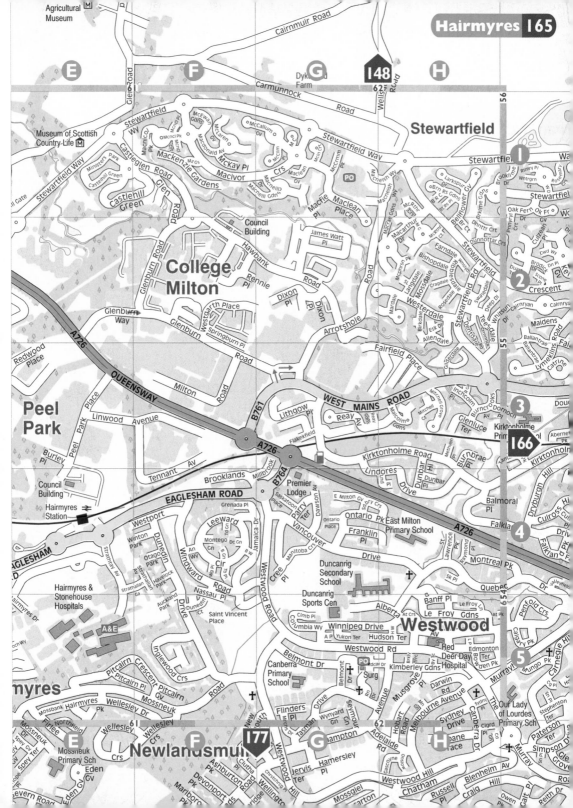

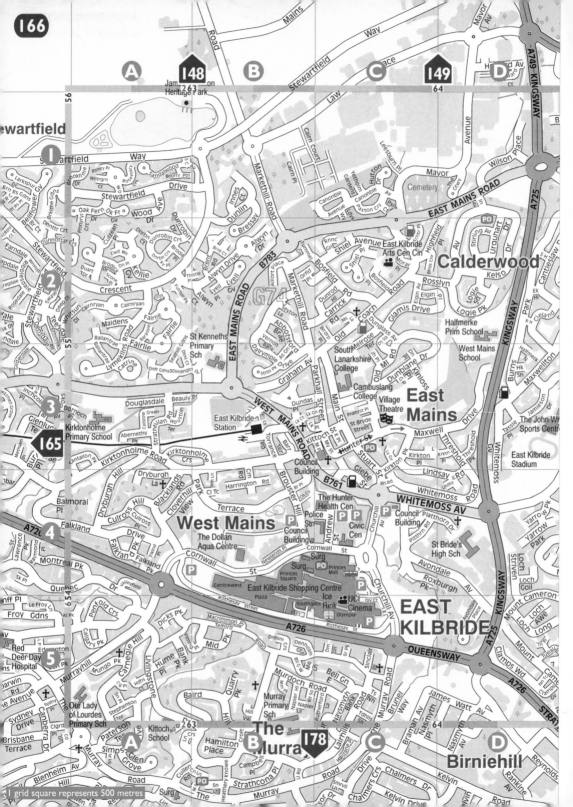

A **148** 263 B C **149** D

Stewartfield

Jam...on Heritage Park

East Mains Road

Calderwood

East Kilbride Arts Cen Cin

East Mains

St Kenneths Primary Sch

South Lanarkshire College

Halfmerke Prim School

West Mains School

Kirktonholme Primary School

165

East Kilbride Station

WEST MAINS ROAD

Cambuslang College

Village Theatre

East Kilbride Stadium

The John Wr Sports Centre

West Mains

The Dollan Aqua Centre

The Hunter Health Cen

Police Str

Council Building

Civic Cen

Council Building

St Bride's High Sch

Centrewest

East Kilbride Shopping Centre

Princes Mall

Princes Square

Ice Rink

Cinema

Olympia

UCI

EAST KILBRIDE

QUEENSWAY

A726

Red Deer Day Hospital

Murrayhill

Our Lady of Lourdes Primary Sch

Murray Primary Sch

Kittoch School

Hamilton Place

The Murray

178

Birniehill

A 263 B **178** C D

WHITEMOSS AV

1 grid square represents 500 metres

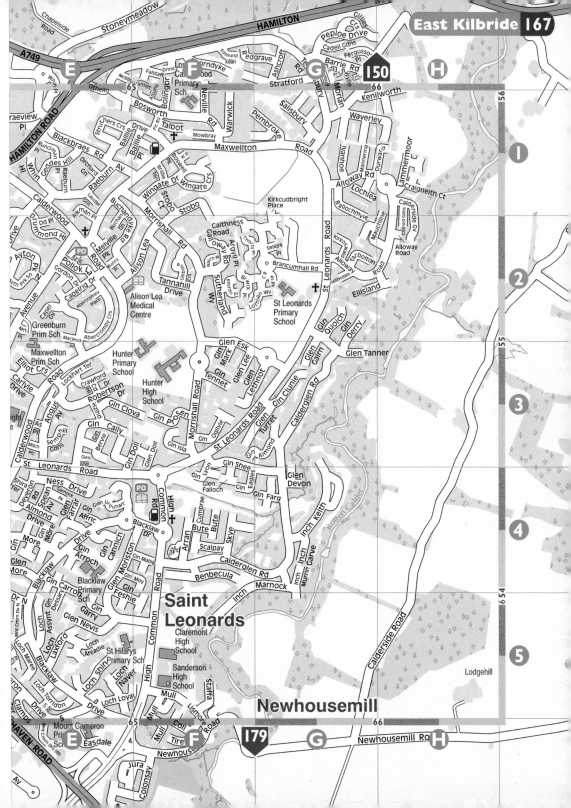

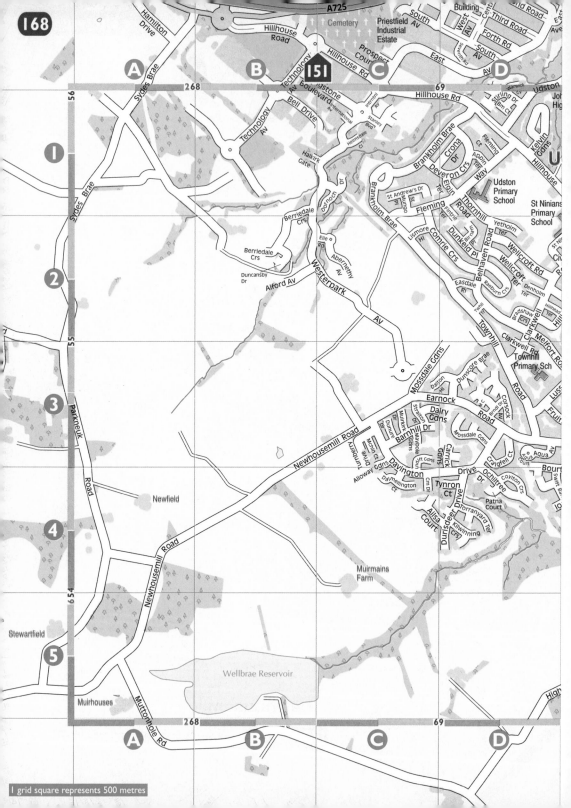

151

A725

Hamilton Drive

Hillhouse Road

Cemetery

Priestfield Industrial Estate

Building

South Av

Third Road

West Av

Forth Rd

South Av

East

Hillhouse Rd

Technology Boulevard

Technology Av

Bell Drive

Prospect Court

Hillhouse Rd

Stirling Dr

Udston

Kelvin Gdns

Hillhouse

Technology Av

Halkirk Gate

Brankholm Brae

Crona Dr

Deveron Crs

Apoin Way

Fleming Ter

Thornhill

Udston Primary School

St Ninians Primary School

Berriedale Crs

Dornoch Dr

St Andrew's Dr

Fleming

Dunkeld Pl

Wellcroft Rd

Wellcroft

Berriedale Crs

Elie Rd

Abernethy Av

Lismore Hl

Comrie Crs

Belhaven Road

Easdale Ri

Yetholm Ter

Denholm Ter

Duncansby Dr

Alford Av

Westerpark Av

Townhill

Raeburn Crs

Bradshaw Crs

Melfort Rd

Clarkwell Rd

Townhill Primary Sch

Sydes Brae

Parkneuk Road

Mossdale Gdns

Dunscore Brae

Dalton

Earnock Road

Corsock

Townhill Road

Newhousemill Road

Murkirk

Stratton

Dairy Gdns

Mossdale Gdns

Craigfell Ct

Aqua

Newfield

Turnberry Drive

Mohin Ct

Dunlop

Barnhill Dr

Maybole Gdns

Carrick Gdns

Alloway Gdns

Dalmellington

Mt Gdns

Davington

Drive

Tynron Ct

Ochilfree

Coviton Crs

Bour

Newhousemill Road

Alisa Court

Kilsyth

Kilwinning Crs

Torranyard Ter

Patna Court

Muirmains Farm

Stewartfield

Wellbrae Reservoir

High

Muirhouses

Muttonhole Rd

A 268 B C 69 D

1 grid square represents 500 metres

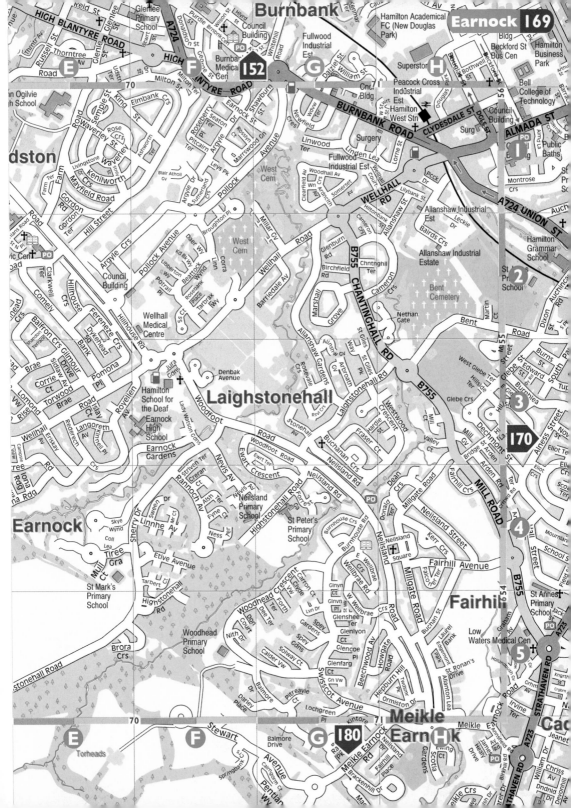

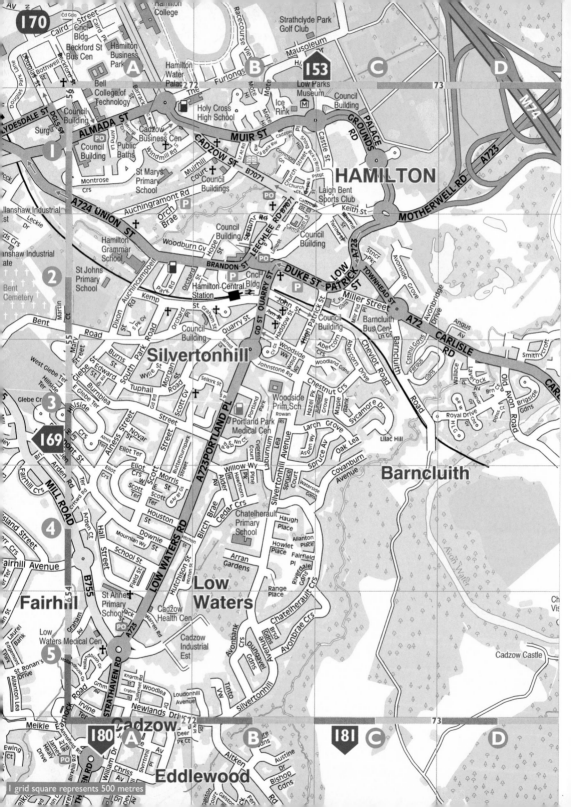

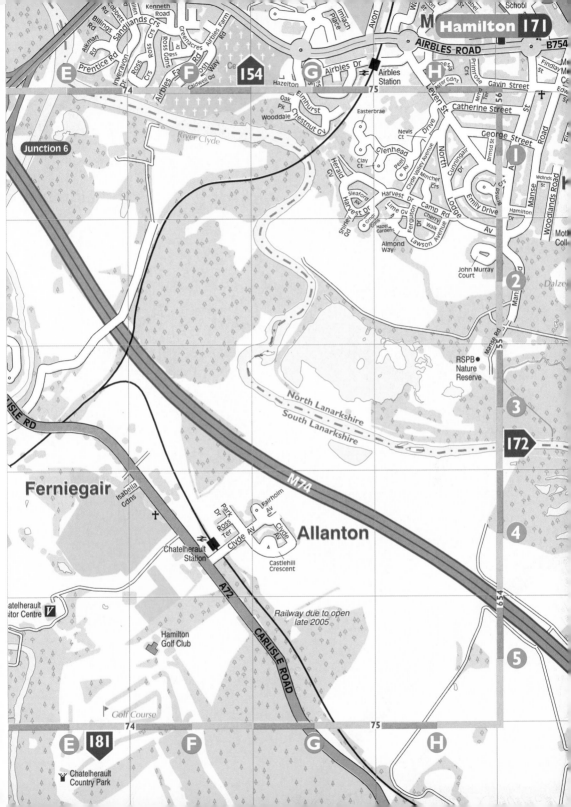

Kenneth Road
Imlach Place
Avon
School
AIRBLES ROAD
B754

E

Cobbett Rd
Billings Rd
Aikman Rd
Alkman Rd
Sandlands Crs
Ross Crs
Ross Gdns
Ross Crs
Inveravon Dr
Prentice Rd

F
Greenacres
Airbles Farm Rd
Ash Way
Caldwell Rd
Airbles Farm Dr

154

Hazelton
Oak Pk
Elmhurst
Chestnut Gv
Wooddale
Elmhurst Gv

G
Airbles Dr

Airbles Station

Airbles Dr

Aster Gdns
Primrose Crs
Primrose St
Findlay St

H

Gavin Street

I

Catherine Street

George Street

Easterbrae

Nevis Ct
Clay Ct
Pearl Av
Glenhead
Clyde Valley Avenue
Mincher Crs
Cunningair Dr
North Lodge
Camp Rd
Emily Drive
Manse St
Brms St
Woodlands Road

Herald Gv
Harvest Dr
Harvest Rd
Shirley Rd
Sleaford
Grndr Gdns
Lime Gv
Hazel Gardens
Ferguson
Cherry Walk
Lawson Avenue
Almond Way
Camp Rd
Lodge Av

John Murray Court

Hamilton Dr

Manse Rd
56
55

Mot...
Coll...

Dalze...

RSPB ●
Nature
Reserve

2

River Clyde

Junction 6

North Lanarkshire
South Lanarkshire

M74

3

172

4

Ferniegair

Isabella Gdns

Park Dr
Ross Ter
Clyde Av
Fairholm Av
Clyde Av

Allanton

Castlehill Crescent

Chatelherault Station

atelherault
sitor Centre V

Hamilton Golf Club

Railway due to open late 2005

CARLISLE ROAD

A72

CARLISLE RD

Golf Course

5

54

654

74
75

E **181**
F
G
H

Chatelherault Country Park

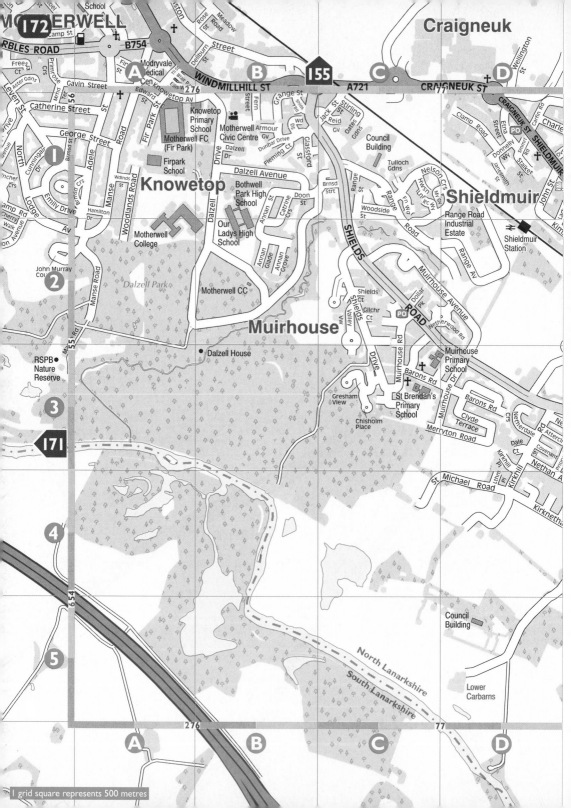

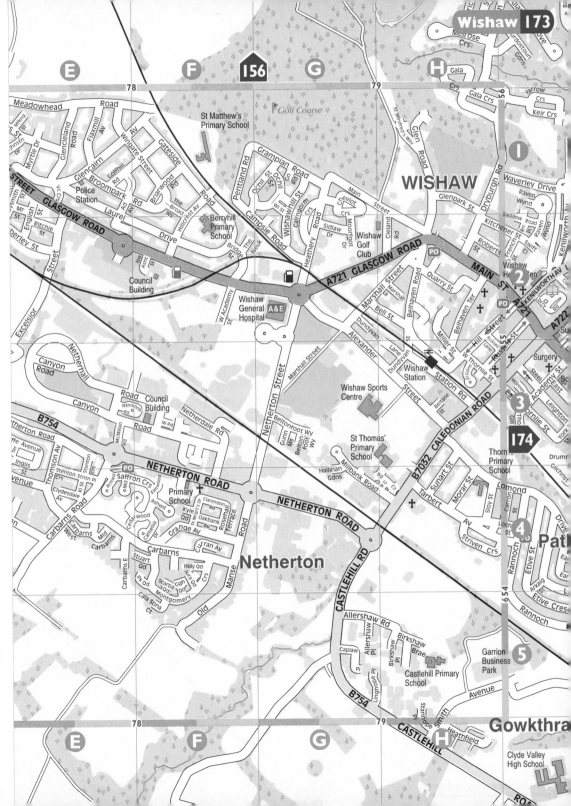

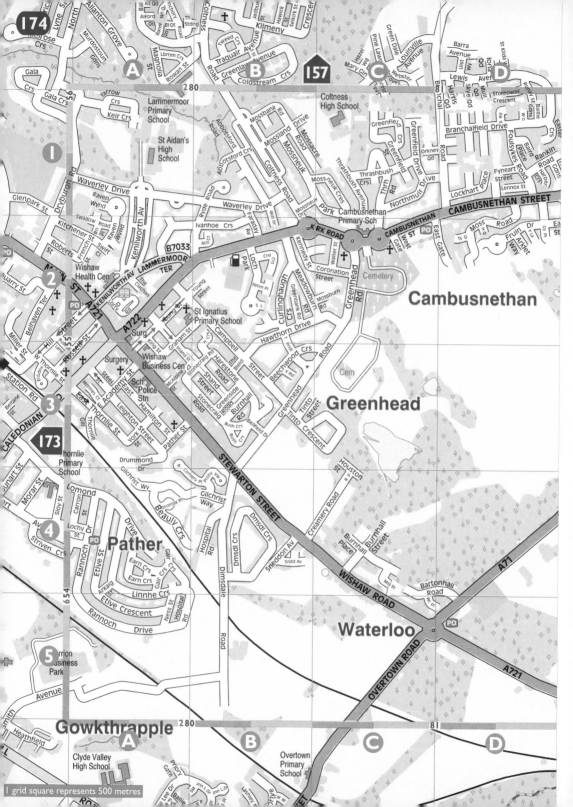

174

A   **B**   **157**   **C**   **D**

Gala Crs
Gala Cres

Melrose Crs

North
Lyne
Allanton Grove
Muirostoun Gdns

Magnolia St
Rowan St

Lbrnm Crs
Traquair Avenue
Greenland Avenue
Coldstream Crs
Kilmeny

Tweed Crs

Jedbur
Hawick
Selkirk St
Coltness Crescent

Th Stdng

Bal
Alford
Banff

Green Dale
Louisville Avenue
Pine Lawn
Mary Gln
Webster Groves

Barra Avenue

St Kilda St
Iona Od
Mill
Skye Od
Aver

Lewis St
Harris St
Stornoway Crescent

I

Lammermoor
Primary School

St Aidan's
High
School

Coltness High School

Greenfield Crs
Greenfield St
Greenfield Drive
Thrashbush
Thrashbush Road

Branchalfield Drive
Orkney Qd
Foulsykes Road
Baird
Rankin Road
Lennox St

Lockhart Place
Fyneart Street

Waverley Drive

Dryburgh Rd

Glenpark st

Raven Wynd
Swallow Road

Kitchener St
Roberts St

Mossbank Rd
Abbotsford Road
Mossland Road

Mossacre
Mossneuk
Coltness Road

Moss-neuk Cres
Mossneuk Drive

Mossneuk Park
Cambusnethan Primary-Sch

Thin Rd
Northmuir Drive

CAMBUSNETHAN STREET

Moss Road
Fruln Dr
Arket Way

2

Wishaw
Health Cen

Kenilworth Av
Lammermoor Ter
B7033

French
Swift
Raven Wynd

Waverley Drive
Ryde Road
Ivanhoe Crs
Faraday Av

Young Street
Loch Road

Webb St
Ach

KIRK ROAD
Kennedy St
Walter St
Coronation Street

Cambusnethan
Primary-Sch
West Gate
East Gate
PO

Cambusnethan

3

Belhaven Ter
PO
A721

Hill Street
Russell Street
W

Steel
King St
Graham St
McAhone

St Ignatius Primary School

Surg
Wishaw
Business Cen

Campbell Street
Hardstone
Shand Street
Greenside Road
Stonecraig Road
Burnhall

Curlinghaugh
Greenpark Rd
Hawthorn Drive
Beechwood Crs
Bell field Dr
Bush Rd

Meadowburn Rd
Mossburn

Greenhead Rd
Greenhead Road
Tinto Street
Tinto Crescent

Cem

Greenhead

Houston St

173

Station Rd
CALEDONIAN
Thornlie St

Thornlie Gill
York St
Pather St
Hamilton
Leighton Street

Academy St
Police Stn

Thornlie
Primary
School

Drummond Dr
Gilchrist Wy
Gilchrist Way

Beauly Crs
Coronry Pl
Prlory Vw

STEWARTON STREET

Creamery Road

4

Morar St
PO
Lomond St
Carron St
Lochy Dr
Sloy St

Rannoch St
Etive St
Arkaig
Earn Crs
Earn Crs
Linnhe Crs
Ness St

Pather

Gair Crs
Gair Crs
Hospital Road

Dmsdl Crs
Dimsdale Road

Sneddon Av
Sndd Av

Burnhall Place
Burnhall Street
Bartonhall Road

A71

5

Striven Crs
Lochy Dr

rrion
Business
Park

Rannoch Drive
Etive Crescent

Avenue

Waterloo

PO

A721

WISHAW ROAD

OVERTOWN ROAD

A   **B**   **C**   **D**

Gowkthrapple

Heathfield

Clyde Valley
High School

Overtown
Primary
School

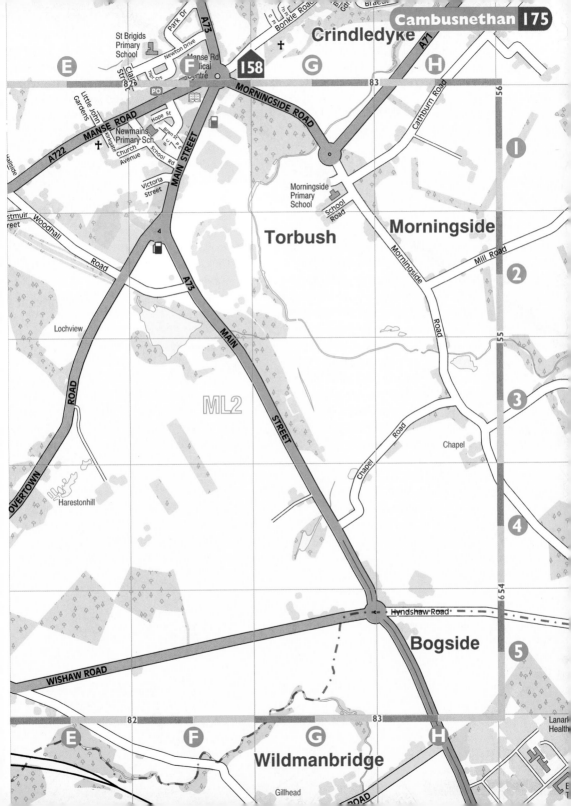

E
F
158
G
H

St Brigids
Primary
School

Park Dr

A73

Bonkle Road

Crindledyke

A71

Newton Drive

Manse Rd

Medical
Centre

Morningside Road

83

Cathburn Road

Clarke Street

Thirl Crs

PO

Little John
Gardens

MANSE ROAD

Hope St

Brown St

Newmains
Primary Sch

MAIN STREET

I

A722

Church
Avenue

School Rd

Victoria
Street

Morningside
Primary
School

Morningside

Mill Road

2

Woodhall

Road

A73

Torbush

Morningside

Road

55

Lochview

ML2

MAIN STREET

Chapel

Road

Chapel

3

OVERTOWN

Harestonhill

Chapel

Road

4

654

Hyndshaw Road

Bogside

5

WISHAW ROAD

82

83

Lanark
Health

E
F
G
H

Wildmanbridge

Gillhead

ROAD

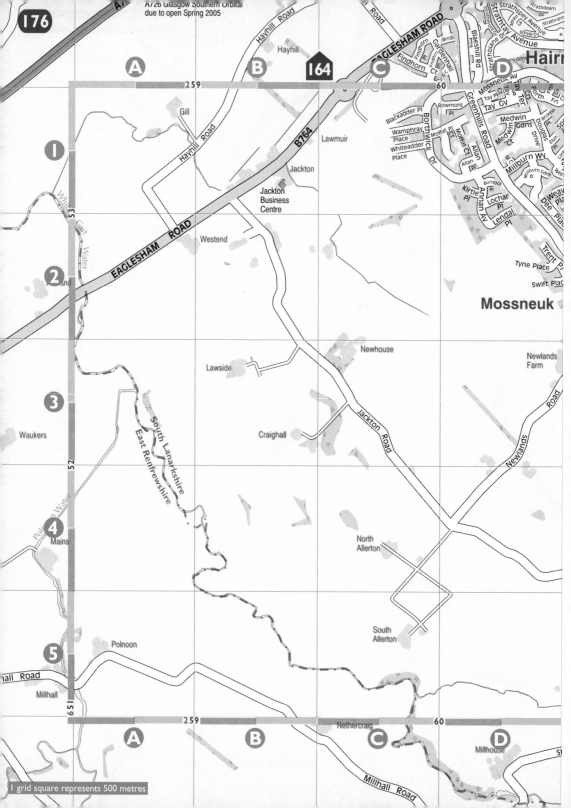

1 grid square represents 500 metres

167 ewhousemill

Lodgehill

Calderside

Newhousemill Road

St Hilarys Primary Sch

Claremont High School

Sanderson High School

Loch Maree

Loch Laxford

Loch Meadie

Loch Shin

Loch Naver

Loch Loyal

Blacklaw

Loch Torridon

High Con

Mull

Staffa

Mull

Coll

Tiree

Newhousemill Road

Mount Cameron Primary School

Clamps Drive

Mint Cmn Dri sth

Easdale

Jura

Colonsay

Colonsay

Edge Farm

E

F

G

H

I

Colvilles Pl

Colvilles Pl

Colvilles Place

Calderglen Country Park

East Kilbride Sports Club

Torrance House Golf Club

Rotten Burn

2

3

STRATHAVEN ROAD

STRAVEN ROAD

Young Pl

Young Place

Golf Course

Calder Water

Crutherland Farm

4

A726

5

65

66

53

52

651

E

F

G

H

Quarry

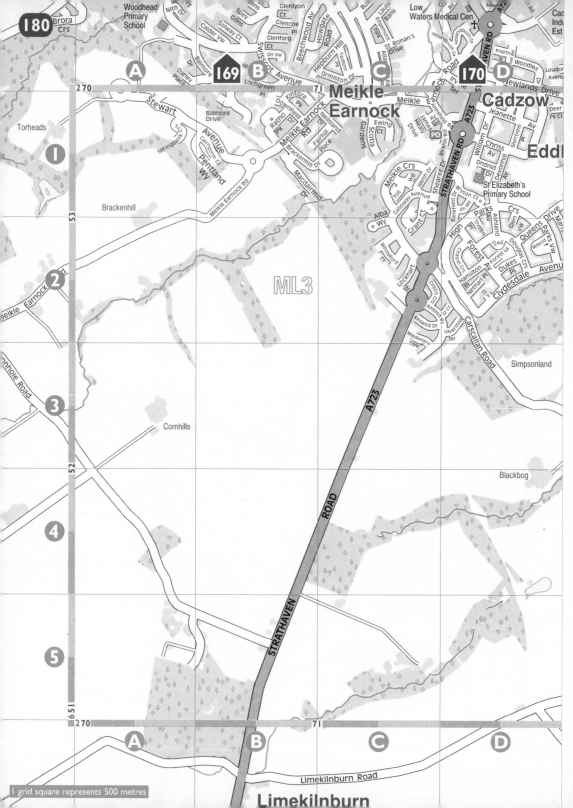

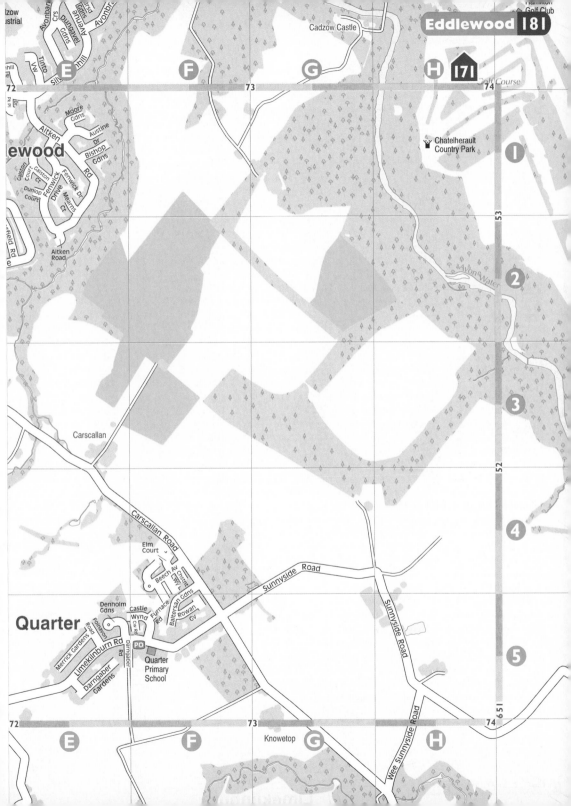

171

Avonbank Industrial

Tinto VW

Avonhead Gdns

Avonhead Avenue

Avonbr...

E

Cadzow Castle

F

G

H

I

72

73

74

Moore Gdns

Aitken Rd

Austine Dr

Bishop Gdns

lewood

Galston Court

Galston Ct

Fenwick Drive

Fenwick Dr

Mearns Ct

Dunlop Court

...field Rd

Aitken Road

Chatelherault Country Park

Avon Water

53

2

3

52

Carscallan

Carscallan Road

4

Elm Court

Beech Av

Chestnut CW L

Sunnyside Road

Denholm Gdns

Furnace Rd

Battersan Gdns

Rowan CV

Quarter

Merrick Gardens

Panavon Road

Castle Wynd

CW Rd

Limekilnburn Rd

Darngaber Rd

PO

Quarter Primary School

Darngaber Gardens

Sunnyside Road

5

65 1

72

73

74

E

F

Knowetop

G

Wee Sunnyside Road

H

Abronhill	27	C2
Airdrie	98	B2
Allanbank	159	C1
Allanton	159	H2
Allanton	171	G4
Anniesland	51	E5
Arden	125	G3
Auchenback	142	B1
Auchinairn	55	E4
Auchinloch	57	E1
Auchinrairth	152	A3
Auchinreoch	6	B4
Auchinstarry	8	C4
Baillieston	94	A5
Balloch	25	F5
Balmalloch	7	H1
Balmore	18	C5
Balornock	55	E5
Bankhead	129	G1
Bardowie	36	C1
Bargarran	30	A5
Bargeddie	95	F5
Barlanark	93	F3
Barmulloch	69	G1
Barncluith	170	C4
Barrachnie	93	F4
Barrhead	124	B4
Battlefield	109	F4
Bearsden	34	B5
Bellahouston	87	H4
Bellshill	135	E3
Bellside	157	G1
Bellsmyre	13	G1
Biggar Road	138	D2
Birdston	21	E2
Birkenshaw	114	D3
Birniehill	178	D1
Bishopbriggs	55	E1
Bishopton	28	C5
Blackhall	104	D1
Blackwood	163	G5
Blairhill	96	B5
Blairlinn	45	F3
Blairskaith	18	A2
Blantyre	151	E3
Blythswood	63	F1
Bogside	175	H5
Bonkle	158	D4
Bothwell	152	A1
Bowling	15	H5
Braehead	164	C2
Braidfauld	111	H1
Bridgend	58	C1
Bridge of Weir	80	A4
Bridgeton	90	D4
Brookfield	78	A1
Broom	144	C5
Broomhill	65	G5
Broomhouse	113	H2
Browsburn	98	C4
Brucehill	12	B4
Buchley	36	D5
Burnbank	152	C5
Burnfoot	75	H4
Burnside	130	B2
Busby	146	A5
Cadder	38	A3
Cadzow	180	D1
Cairnhill	97	H3
Calderbank	118	C1
Calderwood	166	C2
Calton	90	C3
Cambuslang	131	F3
Cambusnethan	174	C2
Carbrain	26	C4
Cardonald	86	C4
Carfin	137	G5
Carmunnock	146	D2
Carmyle	112	C4
Carnbroe	117	H1
Carntyne	91	H2
Carnwadric	126	C3
Carrickstone	10	B5
Castlecary	11	H1
Castlehead	104	A1
Castlehill	12	A2
Castlemilk	129	F5
Cathcart	128	A1
Chapelhall	119	F3
Charleston	104	B2
Chryston	58	B1
Clarkston	77	E5
Clarkston	145	G3
Cleekhimin	155	G2
Cleland	156	D1
Clevans	78	D4
Cliftonville	97	H2
Clydebank	48	D2
Coatbridge	97	E4
Coatdyke	97	G3
College Milton	165	F2
Colston	54	B3
Coltness	157	G4
Condorrat	44	A1
Corkerhill	107	F2
Cowlairs	68	C3
Craigend	47	E2
Craigend	70	D3
Craigends	81	E3
Craigneuk	138	C4
Craigneuk	155	G5
Craigton	87	F4
Cranhill	92	B1
Cragendmuir	71	F2
Crindledyke	158	C5
Croftfoot	129	F2
Crookfur	144	A4
Crookston	86	A5
Crosshill	94	C4
Crosslee	80	B2
Crossmill	124	B3
Crossmyloof	108	C2
Croy	24	D1
Cumbernauld	26	B4
Cumbernauld Village	11	E5
Dalmarnock	110	D1
Dalmuir	31	F4
Dalshannon	43	H5
Dalton	132	D5
Dean Park	63	G4
Dennistoun	90	D2
Dennystown	12	D3
Dovecothall	124	D3
Downhill	66	B5
Drumchapel	33	F5
Drumgeloch	98	C1
Drumpellier	95	H2
Drumry	49	F1
Dullatur	9	G5
Dumbarton	13	F4
Dumbreck	88	A5
Dundyvan	96	B4
Duntocher	31	G2
Earnock	169	E4
Easterhouse	93	H1
Eastfield	25	G3
Eastfield	111	G5
East Kilbride	166	C5
East Mains	166	C5
East Shawhead	117	F1
Eddlewood	180	D1
Elderslie	102	B2
Erskine	47	H3
Faifley	32	B1
Fairhill	169	H5
Fallside	116	A5
Ferguslie Park	83	F4
Fernhill	130	A5
Ferniegair	171	E4
Flemington	131	H4
Forgewood	136	B5
Foxbar	103	E4
Freeland	47	G3
Fullarton	112	B1
Gallowhill	84	D2
Gallowhill	147	F2
Garnkirk	58	A5
Garrowhill	93	H4
Gartcosh	72	D1
Garthamlock	71	E4
Gartlea	98	C3
Gartloch	72	B3
Gartness	99	F4
Gartsherrie	74	B5
Gateside	141	H1
Germiston	69	E4
Giffnock	127	G5
Glasgow	3	G5
Glenburn	103	H5
Glennavis	75	G2
Gorbals	89	H4
Govan	88	A1
Govanhill	109	F1
Greenend	97	F5
Greenfaulds	45	E1
Greenfield	92	B5
Greenhead	174	C3
Greenhills	178	A2
Haghill	91	G2
Hairmyres	164	D5
Hailside	132	B2
Hamilton	170	C1
Hardgate	32	C2
Hareshaw	139	G2
Harestanes	22	C3
Hayston	150	D4
High Blantyre	150	D4
High Crosshill	130	A1
High Gallowhill	39	F2
Hillington	86	B3
Hogganfield	70	A4
Holehills	76	C4
Holehouse	140	C4
Holytown	137	F1
Houston	80	C1
Howwood	120	B4
Hurlet	106	A5
Hutchesontown	89	H5
Ibrox	88	A3
Inchinnan	48	A4
Johnstone	101	H4
Jordanhill	65	E1
Kelvin	178	D3
Kelvindale	52	B5
Kelvinside	65	H1
Kennishead	126	B2
Kessington	35	F4
Kilbarchan	100	B3
Kilbowie	32	B4
Kildrum	26	D2
Kilsyth	8	C1
Kings Park	129	E1
Kirkhill	162	D1
Kirkintilloch	20	C4
Kirkshaw	116	A1
Kirktonhill	12	D5
Kirkwood	95	H5
Knightswood	50	D4
Knowetop	98	C3
Kylepark	114	C5
Laighstonehall	169	F5
Lambhill	53	G4
Langloan	96	B4
Langside	108	D5
Lennoxtown	4	C2
Lenzie	40	A3
Lenziemill	26	D5
Linwood	101	H3
Lochwood	72	C5
Low Blantyre	151	H1
Low Waters	170	B4
Luggiebank	45	G2
Mansewood	127	E1
Marnock	59	H5
Maryhill	52	A4
Mearns	162	A2
Meikle Earnock	180	C1
Merrylee	127	G3
Millarston	103	F1
Millersneuk	40	C4
Millerston	70	B2
Milikenpark	100	C5
Milngavie	17	G4
Milnwood	136	C3
Milton	14	C4
Milton	53	H4
Milton of Campsie	5	H5
Moffat Mills	99	G2
Mollinsburn	43	E4
Moodiesburn	41	H5
Morningside	175	H2
Mossend	136	C2
Mossneuk	176	D2
Mosspark	107	F1
Motherwell	154	D5
Mountblow	30	D4
Mount Florida	109	G5
Mount Vernon	112	D2
Muirend	128	A1
Muirhead	58	C4
Muirhead	113	G1
Muirhouse	172	B2
The Murray	178	B1
Neilston	141	F4
Nerston	149	F4
Nether Kirton	141	G2
Netherlee	127	H4
Netherplace	160	C1
Netherton	173	E4
Newarthill	138	C3
Newhousemill	167	G5
Newlands	127	G1
Newlandsmuir	177	E1
Newmains	158	A5
New Stevenston	137	F1
Newton	132	C1
Newton Mearns	143	H5
Nitshill	125	E2
North Motherwell	154	B2
Oatlands	110	A1
Old Balornock	69	E1
Oldhall	85	G4
Old Kilpatrick	30	A2
Old Monkland	96	B5
Orbiston	135	G3
Oxgang	40	C1
Paisley	84	C5
Parkhall	31	G3
Parkhead	91	G5
Park Mains	47	H2
Parkside	139	F5
Partick	65	H4
Pather	174	A4
Peel Park	165	E3
Petersburn	99	F3
Petershill	69	E3
Pilmuir	160	B4
Pollok	106	C2
Pollokshaws	108	A4
Pollokshields	108	C2
Polmadie	109	H2
Port Dundas	67	H4
Porterfield	62	D4
Possil Park	67	H1
Priesthill	125	F1
Provanmill	69	H3
Quarrelton	101	F5
Quarriers Village	78	A1
Quarter	181	E5
Queenslie	93	E1
Queenzieburn	7	F2
Radnor Park	31	H3
Ranfurly	79	F5
Rashielee	47	F1
Rawyards	76	C5
Renfrew	63	F3
Riddrie	69	G5
Robroyston	55	H5
Rogerton	148	C4
Rosebank	22	A5
Rosehall	97	E5
Rossland	46	B1
Royston	68	B5
Ruchazie	70	C5
Ruchill	67	F1
Rutherglen	110	B3
Saint Leonards	167	F5
Scotstoun	64	C1
Seafar	26	A4
Shawhead	116	C1
Shawlands	108	C4
Sheddens	146	A5
Shettleston	92	B4
Shieldhall	86	D1
Shieldmuir	172	D1
Shortroods	83	H1
Sighthill	68	B4
Silverton	13	G3
Silvertonhill	170	A3
Solsgirth	22	B4
Springboig	92	D3
Springburn	68	C2
Springhill	142	B3
Stamperland	146	A2
Stepps	70	D1
Stewartfield	165	H1
Stonefield	152	A2
Strathbungo	108	D2
Summerston	53	E2
Swinton	94	B3
Tannochside	115	F4
Temple	51	F4
Thorniebank	126	B4
Thornly Park	104	C3
Thorntonhall	163	H2
Thrashbush	76	A5
Torbush	175	G2
Torrance	19	F4
Townend	13	F2
Townhead	2	H3
Townhead	73	H5
Twechar	23	E2
Uddingston	133	H2
Udston	168	D1
Victory Gardens	63	F5
Viewpark	115	H4
Wardpark	11	E3
Waterfoot	162	D4
Waterloo	174	C5
Waterside	41	F1
Waterside	124	D2
West Arthurlie	123	G5
Westburn	132	B1
West Drumoyne	87	F2
Wester Auchinloch	57	E2
Westfield	45	G2
West Mains	166	A4
West Porton	28	D4
Westwood	165	H5
Whifflet	97	E4
Whinhall	97	H1
Whitecraigs	144	D4
Whitecrook	49	G5
Whitehill	173	E5
Whitehills	178	C5
Whiteinch	65	F4
Williamwood	145	E2
Wishaw	173	H1
Yett	137	H4
Yoker	48	B1
Yorkhill	88	B1

USING THE STREET INDEX

Street names are listed alphabetically. Each street name is followed by its postal town or area locality, the Postcode District, the page number, and the reference to the square in which the name is found.

Standard index entries are shown as follows:

Abbey Cl *PSLY* PA1 ....**84** B4

Street names and selected addresses not shown on the map due to scale restrictions are shown in the index with an asterisk:

Barty's Rd *BLSH* ML4 * **136** B2

GENERAL ABBREVIATIONS

ACC	ACCESS	CON	CONVENT	FK	FORK
ALY	ALLEY	COT	COTTAGE	FLD	FIELD
AP	APPROACH	COTS	COTTAGES	FLDS	FIELDS
AR	ARCADE	CP	CAPE	FLS	FALLS
ASS	ASSOCIATION	CPS	COPSE	FM	FARM
AV	AVENUE	CR	CREEK	FT	FORT
BCH	BEACH	CREM	CREMATORIUM	FWY	FREEWAY
BLDS	BUILDINGS	CRS	CRESCENT	FY	FERRY
BND	BEND	CSWY	CAUSEWAY	GA	GATE
BNK	BANK	CT	COURT	GAL	GALLERY
BR	BRIDGE	CTRL	CENTRAL	GDN	GARDEN
BRK	BROOK	CTS	COURTS	GDNS	GARDENS
BTM	BOTTOM	CTYD	COURTYARD	GLD	GLADE
BUS	BUSINESS	CUTT	CUTTINGS	GLN	GLEN
BVD	BOULEVARD	CV	COVE	GN	GREEN
BY	BYPASS	CYN	CANYON	GND	GROUND
CATH	CATHEDRAL	DEPT	DEPARTMENT	GRA	GRANGE
CEM	CEMETERY	DL	DALE	GRG	GARAGE
CEN	CENTRE	DM	DAM	GT	GREAT
CFT	CROFT	DR	DRIVE	GTWY	GATEWAY
CH	CHURCH	DRO	DROVE	GV	GROVE
CHA	CHASE	DRY	DRIVEWAY	HGR	HIGHER
CHYD	CHURCHYARD	DWGS	DWELLINGS	HL	HILL
CIR	CIRCLE	E	EAST	HLS	HILLS
CIRC	CIRCUS	EMB	EMBANKMENT	HO	HOUSE
CL	CLOSE	EMBY	EMBASSY	HOL	HOLLOW
CLFS	CLIFFS	ESP	ESPLANADE	HOSP	HOSPITAL
CMP	CAMP	EST	ESTATE	HRB	HARBOUR
CNR	CORNER	EX	EXCHANGE	HTH	HEATH
CO	COUNTY	EXPY	EXPRESSWAY	HTS	HEIGHTS
COLL	COLLEGE	EXT	EXTENSION	HVN	HAVEN
COM	COMMON	F/O	FLYOVER	HWY	HIGHWAY
COMM	COMMISSION	FC	FOOTBALL CLUB		

IMP	IMPERIAL	MTN	MOUNTAIN		
IN	INLET	MTS	MOUNTAINS		
IND EST	INDUSTRIAL ESTATE	MUS	MUSEUM		
INF	INFIRMARY	MWY	MOTORWAY		
INFO	INFORMATION	N	NORTH		
INT	INTERCHANGE	NE	NORTH EAST		
IS	ISLAND	NW	NORTH WEST		
JCT	JUNCTION	O/P	OVERPASS		
JTY	JETTY	OFF	OFFICE		
KG	KING	ORCH	ORCHARD		
KNL	KNOLL	OV	OVAL		
L	LAKE	PAL	PALACE		
LA	LANE	PAS	PASSAGE		
LDG	LODGE	PAV	PAVILION		
LGT	LIGHT	PDE	PARADE		
LK	LOCK	PH	PUBLIC HOUSE		
LKS	LAKES	PK	PARK		
LNDG	LANDING	PKWY	PARKWAY		
LTL	LITTLE	PL	PLACE		
LWR	LOWER	PLN	PLAIN		
MAG	MAGISTRATE	PLNS	PLAINS		
MAN	MANSIONS	PLZ	PLAZA		
MD	MEAD	POL	POLICE STATION		
MDW	MEADOWS	PR	PRINCE		
MEM	MEMORIAL	PREC	PRECINCT		
MKT	MARKET	PREP	PREPARATORY		
MKTS	MARKETS	PRIM	PRIMARY		
ML	MALL	PROM	PROMENADE		
ML	MILL	PRS	PRINCESS		
MNR	MANOR	PT	PORT		
MS	MEWS	PTH	PATH		
MSN	MISSION	PZ	PIAZZA		
MT	MOUNT				

QD QUADRANT
QU QUEEN
QY QUAY
R RIVER
RBT ROUNDABOUT
RD ROAD
RDG RIDGE
REP REPUBLIC
RES RESERVOIR
RFC RUGBY FOOTBALL CLUB
RI RISE
RP RAMP
RW ROW
S SOUTH
SCH SCHOOL
SE SOUTH EAST
SER SERVICE AREA
SH SHORE
SHOP SHOPPING
SKWY SKYWAY
SMT SUMMIT
SOC SOCIETY
SP SPUR
SPR SPRING
SQ SQUARE
ST STREET
STN STATION
STR STREAM
STRD STRAND
SW SOUTH WEST
TDG TRADING
TER TERRACE
THWY THROUGHWAY
TNL TUNNEL
TOLL TOLLWAY
TPK TURNPIKE
TR TRACK
TRL TRAIL
TWR TOWER
U/P UNDERPASS
UNI UNIVERSITY
UPR UPPER
V VALE
VA VALLEY
VIAD VIADUCT
VIL VILLA
VIS VISTA
VLG VILLAGE
VLS VILLAS
VW VIEW
W WEST
WD WOOD
WHF WHARF
WK WALK
WKS WALKS
WLS WELLS
WY WAY
YD YARD
YHA YOUTH HOSTEL

POSTCODE TOWNS AND AREA ABBREVIATIONS

AIRDRIE Airdrie
BAIL/MDB/MHD Baillieston/Moodiesburn/Muirhead
BALLOCH Balloch
BLSH Bellshill
BLTYR/CAMB Blantyre/Cambuslang
BNYBR/BNK Bonnybridge/Banknock
BRHD/NEIL Barrhead/Neilston
BRWEIR Bridge of Weir
BSDN Bearsden
BSHPBGS Bishopbriggs
BSHPTN Bishopton
CAR/SHTL Carmyle/Shettleston
CARD/HILL/MSPK Cardonald/Hillington/Mosspark
CARLUKE Carluke
CGLE Central Glasgow east
CGLW Central Glasgow west
CLYDBK Clydebank
COWCAD Cowcaddens
CRG/CRSL/HOU Craigends/Crosslee/Houston
CRMNK/CLK/EAG Carmunnock/Clarkston/Eaglesham
CSMK Castlemilk
CTBR Coatbridge
CUMB Cumbernauld
DEN/PKHD Dennistoun/Parkhead
DMBTN Dumbarton
DMNK/BRGTN Dalmarnock/Bridgeton
DRUM Drumchapel
EKILN East Kilbride north
EKILS East Kilbride south
ERSK Erskine
ESTRH Easterhouse
GBLS Gorbals
GIF/THBK Giffnock/Thornliebank
GOV/IBX Govan/Ibrox
GVH/MTFL Govanhill/Mount Florida
HMLTN Hamilton
HWWD Howwood
JNSTN Johnstone
KKNTL Kirkintilloch
KLBCH Kilbarchan
KLMCLM Kilmacolm
KNTSWD Knightswood
KSYTH Kilsyth
KVD/HLHD Kelvindale/Hillhead
KVGV Kelvingrove
LNPK/KPK Linn Park/King's Park
LRKH Larkhall
MLNGV Milngavie
MRYH/FIRH Maryhill/Firhill
MTHW Motherwell
NMRNS Newton Mearns
OLDK Old Kilpatrick
PLK/PH/NH Pollock/Priesthill/Nitshill
PLKSD/SHW Pollockshields/Shawlands
PLKSW/MSWD Pollockshaws/Mansewood
PPK/MIL Possil Park/Milton
PSLY Paisley
PSLYN/LNWD Paisley north/Linwood
PSLYS Paisley south
PTCK Partick
RNFRW Renfrew
RUTH Rutherglen
SCOT Scotstoun
SHOTTS Shotts
SMSTN Summerston
SPRGB/BLRNK Springburn/Balornock
STPS/GTHM/RID Stepps/Garthamlock/Riddrie
STRHV Strathaven
UD/BTH/TAN Uddingston/Bothwell/Tannochside
WISHAW Wishaw

Index - streets

Abb - And

A

Abbey Cl *PSLY* PA1 84 B4
Abbeycraig Rd *ESTRH* G34 94 D1
Abbey Dr *SCOT* G14 65 F2
Abbeygreen St *ESTRH* G34 72 D5
Abbeyhill St *CAR/SHTL* G32 91 H2
Abbeylands Rd *CLYDBK* G81 32 B2
Abbey Pl *AIRDRIE* ML6 98 D5
Abbey Rd *JNSTN* PA5 102 A2
Abbotsford *BSHPBGS* G64 55 F1
Abbotsford Av *HMLTN* ML3 152 C3
RUTH G73 111 E5
Abbotsford Brae *EKILN* G74 166 B2
Abbotsford Ct *CUMB* G67 45 E1
Abbotsford Crs *HMLTN* ML3 152 C4
PSLYS PA2 102 C5
WISHAW ML2 174 B1
Abbotsford La *BLSH* ML4 135 G1
Abbotsford Pl *CUMB* G67 45 E1
GBLS G5 89 G5
Abbotsford Rd *AIRDRIE* ML6 119 F3
BSDN G61 33 H2
CLYDBK G81 49 E2
CUMB G67 45 E1
HMLTN ML3 152 B4
WISHAW ML2 174 B1
Abbotshall Av *DRUM* G15 32 D5
Abbotsinch Rd
PSLYN/LNWD PA3 62 B5
Abbots Ter *AIRDRIE* ML6 98 D5
Abbot St *PLKSD/SHW* G41 108 D3
PSLYN/LNWD PA3 84 C3
Abbott Crs *CLYDBK* G81 49 G3
Aberconway St *CLYDBK* G81 49 F3
Abercorn Av
CARD/HILL/MSPK G52 85 H2
Abercorn Crs *HMLTN* ML3 170 C3
Abercorn Dr *HMLTN* ML3 170 C2
Abercorn Pl *SMSTN* G23 52 D2
Abercorn Rd *NMRNS* G77 143 H4
Abercorn St *CLYDBK* G81 32 D1
PSLYN/LNWD PA3 84 C4
Abercrombie Crs
BAIL/MDB/MHD G69 95 E4
Abercromby Crs *EKILN* G74 167 E2
Abercromby Dr
DMNK/BRGTN G40 90 C3
Abercromby Pl *EKILN* G74 167 E2
Abercromby St
DMNK/BRGTN G40 90 C4
Aberdalgie Gdns *ESTRH* G34 94 A1
Aberdalgie Rd *ESTRH* G34 94 A1
Aberdeen Rd *AIRDRIE* ML6 99 E5
Aberdour St *DEN/PKHD* G31 91 F2
Aberfeldy Av *AIRDRIE* ML6 77 G3
Aberfeldy St *DEN/PKHD* G31 91 F2
Aberfoyle St *DEN/PKHD* G31 91 F2
Aberlady Rd *GOV/IBX* G51 87 F2
Aberlady St *MTHW* ML1 157 E1
Abernethy Av *HMLTN* ML3 168 C2
Abernethy Dr
PSLYN/LNWD PA3 101 H1
Abernethyn Rd *WISHAW* ML2 158 B4
Abernethy Pk *EKILN* G74 166 A3
Abernethy Pl *NMRNS* G77 162 C1
Abernethy St *DEN/PKHD* G31 91 F2
Aberuthven Dr *CAR/SHTL* G32 112 C1
Abiegail Pl *BLTYR/CAMB* G72 151 G1
Aboukir St *GOV/IBX* G51 87 F1
Aboyne Dr *PSLYS* PA2 104 C3
Aboyne St *GOV/IBX* G51 87 G3
Acacia Dr *BRHD/NEIL* G78 123 H2
PSLYS PA2 103 G3
Acacia Pl *JNSTN* PA5 121 H1
Acacia Wy *BLTYR/CAMB* G72 132 B2
Academy Pk *AIRDRIE* ML6 98 B2
PLKSD/SHW G41 88 B5
Academy Rd *GIF/THBK* G46 127 F5
Academy St *AIRDRIE* ML6 98 B2
CAR/SHTL G32 92 C5
CTBR ML5 96 D2
Academy Ter *BLSH* ML4 136 A2
Acer Crs *PSLYS* PA2 103 F3
Acer Gv *AIRDRIE* ML6 119 F1
Achamore Crs *DRUM* G15 32 D4
Achamore Dr *DRUM* G15 32 D4
Achamore Rd *DRUM* G15 32 D4
Acherhill Gdns *KNTSWD* G13 50 B3
Achnasheen Rd *AIRDRIE* ML6 99 H3
Achray Dr *PSLYS* PA2 103 F3
Achray Pl *CTBR* ML5 73 H5
MLNGV G62 16 B2
Achray Rd *CUMB* G67 44 A2
Acorn St *DMNK/BRGTN* G40 90 C5
Acre Dr *MRYH/FIRH* G20 52 A2
Acredyke Crs
SPRGB/BLRNK G21 55 E4
Acredyke Pl *SPRGB/BLRNK* G21 55 F5
Acredyke Rd *RUTH* G73 110 C4
SPRGB/BLRNK G21 55 E4
Acre Rd *MRYH/FIRH* G20 52 A2
Acre Valley Rd *BSHPBGS* G64 19 F3
Adam Av *AIRDRIE* ML6 98 C2
Adams Court La *CGLE* G1 2 E7
Adamsliedrive *KKNTL* G66 20 C5
Adamson St *BLSH* ML4 136 C2
Adams Pl *KSYTH* G65 8 B2
Adamswell St
SPRGB/BLRNK G21 68 B3
Adamswell Ter
BAIL/MDB/MHD G69 59 F1
Addie St *MTHW* ML1 155 E2
Addiewell Pl *CTBR* ML5 96 D5
Addiewell St *CAR/SHTL* G32 92 B2
Addison Gv *GIF/THBK* G46 126 B3
Addison Pl *GIF/THBK* G46 126 B3
Addison Rd *GIF/THBK* G46 126 B3
KVD/HLHD G12 66 C2
Adelaide Ct *CLYDBK* G81 31 E3
Adelaide Rd *EKILS* G75 177 G1
Adele St *MTHW* ML1 172 A1
Adelphi St *GBLS* G5 89 H4
Admiral St *PLKSD/SHW* G41 88 D4
Admiralty Gv *OLDK* G60 30 C3
Admiralty Pl *OLDK* G60 30 C3
Advie Pl *GVH/MTFL* G42 109 G4
Affric Av *AIRDRIE* ML6 77 H3
Affric Dr *PSLYS* PA2 105 E3
Afton Crs *BSDN* G61 35 E5
Afton Dr *RNFRW* PA4 63 H4
Afton Gdns *BLTYR/CAMB* G72 151 E4
CTBR ML5 97 G4
Afton Rd *CUMB* G67 26 D2
Afton St *PLKSD/SHW* G41 108 D4
Afton Vw *KKNTL* G66 21 H4
Agamemnon St *CLYDBK* G81 48 C1
Agnew Av *CTBR* ML5 97 F2
Agnew Gv *UD/BTH/TAN* G71 135 E2
Agnew La *GVH/MTFL* G42 109 F3
Aikenhead Rd *GVH/MTFL* G42 109 H2
LNPK/KPK G44 128 D1
Aikman Pl *EKILN* G74 167 E2
Aikman Rd *MTHW* ML1 154 A5
Ailean Dr *CAR/SHTL* G32 93 F5
Ailean Gdns *CAR/SHTL* G32 93 F5
Aillort Pl *EKILN* G74 166 B2
Ailort Av *LNPK/KPK* G44 128 B2
Ailsa Av *MTHW* ML1 154 A3
Ailsa Ct *HMLTN* ML3 168 C4
Ailsa Crs *MTHW* ML1 154 A3
Ailsa Dr *CLYDBK* G81 32 A2
GIF/THBK G46 145 F2
GVH/MTFL G42 109 E5
KKNTL G66 21 H3
PSLYS PA2 104 A5
RUTH G73 129 G2
UD/BTH/TAN G71 134 B3
Ailsa Pl *CTBR* ML5 96 C5
Ailsa Rd *BSHPBGS* G64 55 E1
CTBR ML5 96 B5
RNFRW PA4 63 F4
Ainslie Av *CARD/HILL/MSPK* G52 86 B1
Ainslie Rd *CARD/HILL/MSPK* G52 86 B2
CUMB G67 27 E2
Airbles Crs *MTHW* ML1 154 C5
Airbles Dr *MTHW* ML1 154 C5
Airbles Farm Rd *MTHW* ML1 154 B5
Airbles Rd *MTHW* ML1 154 B5
Airbles St *MTHW* ML1 154 D5
Airdale Av *GIF/THBK* G46 127 F5
Airdriehill Rd *AIRDRIE* ML6 76 D4
Airdrie Rd *AIRDRIE* ML6 77 G5
CUMB G67 43 F4
KSYTH G65 8 B2
Airgold Dr *DRUM* G15 33 E4
Airlie Av *BSDN* G61 34 B1
Airlie Dr *BLSH* ML4 135 H1
Airlie Gdns *RUTH* G73 130 C3
Airlie La *KVD/HLHD* G12 66 A3
Airlie Rd *BAIL/MDB/MHD* G69 113 H1
Airlie St *KVD/HLHD* G12 66 A3
Airlour Rd *PLKSW/MSWD* G43 127 H2
Airth Dr *CARD/HILL/MSPK* G52 107 G1
Airth La *CARD/HILL/MSPK* G52 107 G1
Airthrey Av *SCOT* G14 65 F2
Airthrey La *SCOT* G14 65 F2
Airth Wy *BALLOCH* G68 24 C5
Aitchison Ct *AIRDRIE* ML6 98 A1
Aitchison St *AIRDRIE* ML6 97 H2
Aitkenbar Cir *DMBTN* G82 13 G2
Aitkenbar Dr *DMBTN* G82 13 G2
Aitken Cl *WISHAW* ML2 158 B3
Aitkenhead Av *CTBR* ML5 95 G5
Aitkenhead Rd *AIRDRIE* ML6 119 E2
UD/BTH/TAN G71 115 F3
Aitken Rd *HMLTN* ML3 181 E2
Aitken St *AIRDRIE* ML6 76 B5
DEN/PKHD G31 91 E3
Alasdair Ct *BRHD/NEIL* G78 124 B5
Albans Crs *MTHW* ML1 154 A2
Albany *EKILN* G74 167 F1
Albany Av *CAR/SHTL* G32 92 D3
Albany Dr *RUTH* G73 130 A1
Albany Qd *CAR/SHTL* G32 92 D3
Albany Rd *HMLTN* ML3 180 C1
Albany St *CTBR* ML5 96 B2
DMNK/BRGTN G40 90 D5
Albany Ter *BLTYR/CAMB* G72 130 D4
Alba Wy *HMLTN* ML3 180 C2
Alberta Av *CTBR* ML5 96 C1
EKILS G75 165 G5
Alberta Crs *EKILS* G75 165 H5
Alberta Pk *EKILS* G75 165 H5
Albert Av *GVH/MTFL* G42 109 F3
Albert Br *GBLS* G5 89 H4
Albert Dr *BSDN* G61 35 E5
PLKSD/SHW G41 88 D5
RUTH G73 130 A2
Albert Pl *AIRDRIE* ML6 98 C1
Albert Qd *MTHW* ML1 137 F2
Albert Rd *CLYDBK* G81 31 G5
GVH/MTFL G42 109 F3
JNSTN PA5 100 D1
KKNTL G66 39 H5
RNFRW PA4 63 F5
Albert St *CTBR* ML5 96 D2
HMLTN ML3 152 C4
MTHW ML1 155 E3
Albert Ter *HMLTN* ML3 152 B4
Albion Ga *CGLE* G1 3 H6
Albion St *BAIL/MDB/MHD* G69 113 G1
CGLE G1 3 H6
CTBR ML5 97 E2
MTHW ML1 154 D5
PSLYN/LNWD PA3 84 B3
Albion Wy *EKILS* G75 178 C3
Alcaig Rd
CARD/HILL/MSPK G52 107 F2
Alcath Rd *WISHAW* ML2 158 C4
Alder Av *HMLTN* ML3 170 B4
KKNTL G66 39 G3
Alder Bank *UD/BTH/TAN* G71 115 H3
Alder Ct *BRHD/NEIL* G78 142 B1
EKILS G75 177 H3
Alder Crs *EKILS* G75 177 H3
Alder Ga *BLTYR/CAMB* G72 132 B2
Alder Gv *CTBR* ML5 97 E3
Alderman Pl *KNTSWD* G13 50 D5
Alderman Rd *KNTSWD* G13 50 A4
Alder Pl *EKILS* G75 177 H3
JNSTN PA5 101 H5
PLKSW/MSWD G43 127 E2
Alder Rd *CLYDBK* G81 31 G3
CUMB G67 27 F3
DMBTN G82 12 D3
KKNTL G66 5 F5
PLKSW/MSWD G43 127 F2
Alderside Av *WISHAW* ML2 173 E1
Alderside Gdns
UD/BTH/TAN G71 114 D5
Alderstocks *EKILS* G75 178 B3
Alderston Pl *BLSH* ML4 135 F3
Aldersyde Pl *BLTYR/CAMB* G72 151 F1
Aldersyde Ter *MTHW* ML1 157 F1
Alexander Av
UD/BTH/TAN G71 134 D1
Alexander Balfour Gdns
HMLTN ML3 170 A4
Alexander Crs *GBLS* G5 89 H5
Alexander Gdns *HMLTN* ML3 170 D3
Alexander Gibson Wy
MTHW ML1 154 C5
Alexander Pl *KKNTL* G66 41 E1
Alexander St *AIRDRIE* ML6 97 H2
CLYDBK G81 49 E2
CTBR ML5 97 E1
DMBTN G82 13 F3
WISHAW ML2 173 G2
Alexander Ter *BRHD/NEIL* G78 140 D4
Alexandra Av
STPS/GTHM/RID G33 57 E5
Alexandra Ct *DEN/PKHD* G31 91 E1
Alexandra Dr *PSLY* PA1 103 G1
RNFRW PA4 63 G3
Alexandra Gdns *KKNTL* G66 39 H4
Alexandra Pde *DEN/PKHD* G31 90 C1
Alexandra Pk *KKNTL* G66 39 H4
Alexandra Park St
DEN/PKHD G31 91 E1
Alexandra Rd *KKNTL* G66 39 H4
Alexandra St *KKNTL* G66 21 E5
Alexandria Qd *MTHW* ML1 137 F2
Alford Av *BLTYR/CAMB* G72 168 B2
KKNTL G66 20 D5
Alford Pl *PSLYN/LNWD* PA3 81 F5
Alford Qd *WISHAW* ML2 157 E5
Alford St *SPRGB/BLRNK* G21 68 A3
Alfred La *KVD/HLHD* G12 66 D3
Algie St *PLKSD/SHW* G41 109 E4
Algoma Pl *EKILS* G75 165 G5
Alice Av *BLSH* ML4 135 H3
Alice St *PSLYS* PA2 104 B2
Aline Ct *BRHD/NEIL* G78 124 A3
Alison Lea *EKILN* G74 167 F2
Allan Av *RNFRW* PA4 63 H5
Allanbank St *SHOTTS* ML7 159 G2
Allan Ct *EKILS* G75 176 D1
Allan Crs *DMBTN* G82 13 G1
Allandale Av *MTHW* ML1 138 C2
Allander Av *MLNGV* G62 36 B1
Allander Dr *BSHPBGS* G64 19 E5
Allander Gdns *BSHPBGS* G64 37 G4
Allander Rd *MLNGV* G62 17 E3
Allander St *PPK/MIL* G22 67 H2
Allands Av *RNFRW* PA4 61 H1
Allanfauld Rd *CUMB* G67 26 B3
Allan Glen Gdns *BSHPBGS* G64 37 H4
Allan Pl *DMBTN* G82 13 F3
DMNK/BRGTN G40 111 E1
EKILS G75 176 D1
Allanshaw Gdns *HMLTN* ML3 169 G2
Allanshaw Gv *HMLTN* ML3 169 G3
Allanshaw St *HMLTN* ML3 169 H2
Allan St *CTBR* ML5 96 A4
DMNK/BRGTN G40 111 E2
MTHW ML1 155 E3
Allanton Av *PSLY* PA1 85 H5
Allanton Dr
CARD/HILL/MSPK G52 86 C4
Allanton Gv *WISHAW* ML2 157 E5
Allanton Lea *HMLTN* ML3 169 H5
Allanton Pl *HMLTN* ML3 170 B4
Allanton Rd *WISHAW* ML2 159 F2
Allbany Crs *BLSH* ML4 137 E2
Allendale *EKILN* G74 165 H2
Allender Rd *BSDN* G61 34 A5
Allen Wy *RNFRW* PA4 63 G5
Allerdyce Dr *DRUM* G15 50 A2
Allershaw Pl *WISHAW* ML2 173 G5
Allershaw Rd *WISHAW* ML2 173 G5
Allerton Gdns *CAR/SHTL* G32 93 G5
Alleysbank Rd *RUTH* G73 110 D3
Allison Av *ERSK* PA8 47 E1
Allison Dr *BLTYR/CAMB* G72 131 F1
Allison Pl *BAIL/MDB/MHD* G69 72 D2
NMRNS G77 161 F1
Allison St *GVH/MTFL* G42 109 F2
Allnach Pl *ESTRH* G34 94 D1
Alloway Av *PSLYS* PA2 105 E4
Alloway Ct *KKNTL* G66 22 A3
Alloway Crs *PSLYS* PA2 105 F4
RUTH G73 129 G2
Alloway Dr *CLYDBK* G81 32 B5
KKNTL G66 22 A3
NMRNS G77 162 B1
PSLYS PA2 105 F4
RUTH G73 129 G2
Alloway Gdns *HMLTN* ML3 168 C4
KKNTL G66 22 A3
Alloway Gv *KKNTL* G66 21 H3
Alloway Rd *AIRDRIE* ML6 99 G1
EKILN G74 167 H2
PLKSW/MSWD G43 127 G1
Alloway Ter *KKNTL* G66 21 H3
Almada La *HMLTN* ML3 170 A1
Almada St *HMLTN* ML3 170 A1
Almond Av *RNFRW* PA4 63 H4
Almond Crs *PSLYS* PA2 103 E2
Almond Dr *BSHPTN* PA7 46 A1
EKILN G74 167 E4
KKNTL G66 39 G3
Almond Pl *CTBR* ML5 74 A5
Almond Rd *BSDN* G61 50 D1
CUMB G67 11 H5
STPS/GTHM/RID G33 70 D1
Almond St *STPS/GTHM/RID* G33 69 G5
Almond V *UD/BTH/TAN* G71 115 F5
Almond Wy *MTHW* ML1 171 H2
Alness Crs
CARD/HILL/MSPK G52 107 E1
Alness St *HMLTN* ML3 170 A3
Alness Ter *HMLTN* ML3 170 A3
Alpine Gv *UD/BTH/TAN* G71 115 E5
Alsatian Av *CLYDBK* G81 49 G1
Alsh Ter *HMLTN* ML3 169 F4
Alston Av *CTBR* ML5 97 E1
Altnacreag Gdns
BAIL/MDB/MHD G69 42 B5
Alton Rd *PSLY* PA1 85 F5
Altpatrick Gdns *JNSTN* PA5 102 A1
Altyre St *CAR/SHTL* G32 112 A1
Aluclutha Av *DMBTN* G82 13 G4
Alva Gdns
CARD/HILL/MSPK G52 107 F2
Alva Ga *CARD/HILL/MSPK* G52 107 F1
Alva Pl *KKNTL* G66 40 B4
Alwyn Av *CRG/CRSL/HOU* PA6 81 E3
Alwyn Ct *EKILN* G74 166 B2
Alwyn Dr *EKILN* G74 166 B2
Alyssum Crs *MTHW* ML1 154 C2
Alyth Crs *CRMNK/CLK/EAG* G76 146 B2
Alyth Gdns
CARD/HILL/MSPK G52 107 F1
CRMNK/CLK/EAG G76 146 B2
Amber Ter *BLSH* ML4 135 H3
Ambleside *EKILS* G75 177 E2
Ambleside Ri *HMLTN* ML3 180 C2
Amethyst Av *BLSH* ML4 135 H3
Amisfield St *MRYH/FIRH* G20 66 D1
Amochrie Dr *PSLYS* PA2 103 F4
Amochrie Gln *PSLYS* PA2 103 F4
Amochrie Rd *PSLYS* PA2 103 F4
Amochrie Wy *PSLYS* PA2 103 E3
Amulree Pl *CAR/SHTL* G32 92 B5
Amulree St *CAR/SHTL* G32 112 B1
Ancaster Dr *KNTSWD* G13 51 G5
Ancaster La *KNTSWD* G13 51 G5
Anchor Av *PSLY* PA1 84 D5
Anchor Crs *PSLY* PA1 104 D1
Anchor Dr *PSLY* PA1 84 D5
Anchor La *CGLE* G1 3 F5
Anchor Wynd *PSLY* PA1 104 D1
Ancroft St *MRYH/FIRH* G20 67 F3
Andersen Ct *EKILS* G75 178 B2
Anderside *EKILS* G75 178 B3
Anderson Av *KSYTH* G65 7 H1
Anderson Ct *BLSH* ML4 136 A2
Anderson Crs *KSYTH* G65 7 E2
Anderson Dr *NMRNS* G77 161 F1
RNFRW PA4 63 G2
Anderson La *AIRDRIE* ML6 98 B1
Anderson Rd *BSHPTN* PA7 28 D4
Anderson St *AIRDRIE* ML6 98 B1
HMLTN ML3 152 A5
MTHW ML1 154 D5
PTCK G11 66 A4

Anderston Quay KVGV G3 ....2 A7
Andrew Av KKNTL G66 ....40 A5
Andrew RFW PA4 ....63 H3
Andrew Dr CLYDBK G81 ....49 F3
Andrew Sillars Av
  BLTYR/CAMB G72 ....131 H2
Andrews St PSLYN/LNWD PA3 ....84 A3
Andrew St EKILN G74 ....166 C4
Anford Pl BLTYR/CAMB G72 ....151 H4
Angela Wy UD/BTH/TAN G71 ....134 B4
Angle Ga SCOT G14 ....65 E2
Angus Av AIRDRIE ML6 ....98 B4
  BSHPBGS G64 ....55 G2
  CARD/HILL/MSPK G52 ....106 C3
  EKILN G74 ....167 E3
  HMLTN ML3 ....170 D2
  MTHW ML1 ....154 B2
Angus Gdns UD/BTH/TAN G71 ....115 E4
Angus Ov CARD/HILL/MSPK G52 ....86 C5
Angus Pl CARD/HILL/MSPK G52 ....86 C5
  EKILN G74 ....167 E3
  SPRGB/BLRNK G21 ....49 H3
Anish Pl PLK/PH/NH G53 ....32 D4
Annan Av EKILS G75 ....176 D1
Annan Crs AIRDRIE ML6 ....119 E3
Annandale St GVH/MTFL G42 ....109 G3
Annan Dr BSDN G61 ....33 H5
  PSLYS PA2 ....102 D2
  RUTH G73 ....111 G5
Annan Gln MTHW ML1 ....172 B2
Annan Gv MTHW ML1 ....172 B2
Annan Pl JNSTN PA5 ....120 C1
Annan St GVH/MTFL G42 ....109 F4
  MTHW ML1 ....172 B2
Annbank Pl DEN/PKHD G31 ....90 C3
Annbank St DEN/PKHD G31 ....90 C3
Ann Ct HMLTN ML3 ....152 B5
Ann Dr RNFRW PA4 ....63 H4
Anne Crs KKNTL G66 ....40 A5
Annerley Pl CTBR ML5 ....96 B4
Annes Ct DMNK/BRGTN G40 ....90 B5
Annette St GVH/MTFL G42 ....109 F2
Annfield Gdns
  BLTYR/CAMB G72 ....151 E1
Annfield Pl DEN/PKHD G31 ....90 C2
Annick Dr BSDN G61 ....33 H5
Annick St BLTYR/CAMB G72 ....132 A2
Anniesdale Av
  STPS/GTHM/RID G33 ....57 E5
Annieshill Vw AIRDRIE ML6 ....77 H4
Anniesland Crs SCOT G14 ....64 B1
Anniesland Rd KNTSWD G13 ....51 E5
  SCOT G14 ....64 B1
Annieston KSYTH G65 ....23 F1
Anniversary Av EKILS G75 ....177 F3
Annsfield Rd HMLTN ML3 ....180 C1
Ann St HMLTN ML3 ....152 B5
  JNSTN PA5 ....101 H3
Ansdell Av BLTYR/CAMB G72 ....151 F3
Anson St DMNK/BRGTN G40 ....90 C5
Anstruther St CAR/SHTL G32 ....92 A5
Antermony Rd KKNTL G66 ....22 C1
Anthony St CCLW G2 ....2 B5
Antigua Wy EKILS G75 ....165 F4
Anton Crs KSYTH G65 ....8 C2
Antonine AIRDRIE ML6 ....76 B3
Antonine Av MTHW ML1 ....154 B1
Antonine Gdns CLYDBK G81 ....31 H2
Antonine Rd BSDN G61 ....9 C4
  BSDN G61 ....33 G2
Anwoth St CAR/SHTL G32 ....112 B1
Appin Crs DEN/PKHD G31 ....91 E2
Appin Rd DEN/PKHD G31 ....91 F2
Appin Ter HMLTN ML3 ....168 D2
  RUTH G73 ....130 B3
Appin Wy AIRDRIE ML6 ....75 H2
  CTBR ML5 ....96 B5
Appleby Cl EKILS G75 ....177 E2
Appleby St PPK/MIL G22 ....67 G3
Applecross Gdns
  BAIL/MDB/MHD G69 ....42 A5
Applecross Rd KKNTL G66 ....22 B4
Applecross St MRYH/FIRH G20 ....67 H3
Appledore Crs
  UD/BTH/TAN G71 ....134 B4
Appleyla PTCK G11 ....65 H4
Appley St PTCK G11 ....65 H4
Aqua Av HMLTN ML3 ....168 D3
Aqua Ct HMLTN ML3 ....168 D3
Araburn Dr EKILS G75 ....178 B3
Aranthrue Crs RNFRW PA4 ....63 F2
Aranthrue Dr RNFRW PA4 ....63 F2
Aray St MRYH/FIRH G20 ....52 C5
Arbroath Av
  CARD/HILL/MSPK G52 ....86 C5
Arbroath Gv HMLTN ML3 ....169 G3
Arbuckle Pl AIRDRIE ML6 ....77 H3
Arcadia St BLSH ML4 ....116 D5
  DMNK/BRGTN G40 ....90 B5
Arcan Crs DRUM G15 ....50 C1
Archerfield Av CAR/SHTL G32 ....112 B2
Archerfield Crs CAR/SHTL G32 ....112 B2
Archerfield Dr CAR/SHTL G32 ....112 B2
Archerfield Gv CAR/SHTL G32 ....112 B2
Archerhill Av KNTSWD G13 ....50 B3
Archerhill Rd KNTSWD G13 ....50 A3
Archerhill Crs KNTSWD G13 ....50 A3
Archerhill Ter KNTSWD G13 ....50 A3
Archibald Ter KKNTL G66 ....5 F4
Archiebald Pl BLSH ML4 ....117 G1
Arch Wy KSYTH G65 ....8 B1
Ardargie Dr CAR/SHTL G32 ....112 D4
Ardargie Gv CAR/SHTL G32 ....112 D4
Ardargie Pl CAR/SHTL G32 ....112 D4
Ardbeg Av BSHPBGS G64 ....37 H5
  RUTH G73 ....130 D4
Ardbeg La GVH/MTFL G42 ....109 F2
Ardbeg Rd MTHW ML1 ....137 H5
Ardconnel St GIF/THBK G46 ....126 B3
Arden Av GIF/THBK G46 ....126 B5
Ardenclutha Av HMLTN ML3 ....169 F1
Arden Ct HMLTN ML3 ....170 A4
Ardencraig Crs CSMK G45 ....146 D1
Ardencraig Dr CSMK G45 ....129 G5
Ardencraig Gdns CSMK G45 ....129 G5
Ardencraig La CSMK G45 ....146 D1
Ardencraig Pl CSMK G45 ....129 G5
Ardencraig Qd CSMK G45 ....129 H5
Ardencraig Rd CSMK G45 ....129 G5
Ardencraig St CSMK G45 ....130 A5
Ardencraig Ter CSMK G45 ....129 H5
Arden Dr GIF/THBK G46 ....127 E5
Ardenlea UD/BTH/TAN G71 ....115 E5

Ardenlea St DMNK/BRGTN G40 ....111 E1
Arden Pl GIF/THBK G46 ....126 B5
Arden Rd HMLTN ML3 ....169 H3
Arden St AIRDRIE ML6 ....77 H4
Arden Ter HMLTN ML3 ....169 H3
Ardery St PTCK G11 ....65 H4
Ardessie St SMSTN G23 ....52 C2
Ardfern Rd AIRDRIE ML6 ....99 G3
Ardfern St CAR/SHTL G32 ....112 B1
Ardgay Pl CAR/SHTL G32 ....92 B5
Ardgay St CAR/SHTL G32 ....92 B5
Ardgay Wy RUTH G73 ....130 A4
Ardgoil Dr BALLOCH G68 ....25 H2
Ardgour Dr PSLYN/LNWD PA3 ....101 H1
Ardgowan Av PSLYS PA2 ....104 C1
Ardgowan Dr
  UD/BTH/TAN G71 ....115 E4
Ardgowan St PSLYS PA2 ....104 C2
Ardgryfe Crs
  CRG/CRSL/HOU PA6 ....81 G3
Ardholm St CAR/SHTL G32 ....92 B4
Ardhu Pl DRUM G15 ....33 E4
Ardlaw St GOV/IBX G51 ....87 G3
Ardle Rd PLKSW/MSWD G43 ....142 A2
Ardlui St CAR/SHTL G32 ....92 A5
Ardmaleish Crs CSMK G45 ....129 F5
Ardmaleish Dr CSMK G45 ....129 F5
Ardmaleish Rd CSMK G45 ....129 F5
Ardmaleish St CSMK G45 ....129 F5
Ardmaleish Ter CSMK G45 ....129 F5
Ardmillan St
  STPS/GTHM/RID G33 ....92 A1
Ardmory Av GVH/MTFL G42 ....110 B5
Ardmory La RUTH G73 ....110 B5
Ardmory Pl GVH/MTFL G42 ....110 B5
Ardnahoe Av GVH/MTFL G42 ....110 A4
Ardnahoe Pl GVH/MTFL G42 ....110 A4
Ardneil Rd GOV/IBX G51 ....87 G3
Ardnish St GOV/IBX G51 ....87 F2
Ardoch Crs DMBTN G82 ....12 C3
Ardoch Gv BLTYR/CAMB G72 ....131 H2
Ardochrig EKILS G75 ....178 B3
Ardoch Rd BSDN G61 ....35 E3
Ardoch St PPK/MIL G22 ....67 H2
Ardo Gdns RNFRW PA4 ....63 G1
Ardshiel Rd GOV/IBX G51 ....87 F2
Ardsloy Pl SCOT G14 ....64 B2
Ard St CAR/SHTL G32 ....92 B5
Ardtoe Crs STPS/GTHM/RID G33 ....57 F5
Ardtoe Pl STPS/GTHM/RID G33 ....71 F1
Arduthie Rd GOV/IBX G51 ....87 F2
Ardwell Rd
  CARD/HILL/MSPK G52 ....107 F1
Argus Av AIRDRIE ML6 ....118 D2
Argyle Crs AIRDRIE ML6 ....119 E2
  HMLTN ML3 ....169 F2
Argyle Gdns KKNTL G66 ....40 B3
Argyle Rd BSDN G61 ....34 B1
Argyle St CCLW G2 ....2 D6
  KVGV G3 ....66 C5
  PSLY PA1 ....84 A5
Argyll Ar CGLE G1 ....3 K6
Argyll Av DMBTN G82 ....13 H4
  PSLYN/LNWD PA3 ....62 B5
  RNFRW PA4 ....63 E2
Argyll Pl BLSH ML4 ....135 C4
  DMBTN G82 ....13 H4
  EKILN G74 ....167 F2
  KSYTH G65 ....8 B2
Argyll Rd CLYDBK G81 ....49 F2
Arisaig Dr BSDN G61 ....35 E5
  CARD/HILL/MSPK G52 ....107 E1
Arisaig Pl
  CARD/HILL/MSPK G52 ....107 E1
Aristotle Crs NMRNS G77 ....144 B4
Arkaig Av AIRDRIE ML6 ....77 G3
Arkaig Pl NMRNS G77 ....162 C1
Arkaig St WISHAW ML2 ....173 H4
Ark La DEN/PKHD G31 ....90 B3
Arkleston Crs PSLYN/LNWD PA3 ....85 E2
Arkleston Rd PSLY PA1 ....85 E3
Ark Ter BLTYR/CAMB G72 ....130 D4
Arklet Rd GOV/IBX G51 ....87 F3
Arklet Wy WISHAW ML2 ....174 D2
Arkwrights Wy PSLY PA1 ....103 G1
Armadale Ct DEN/PKHD G31 ....90 D1
Armadale Pl DEN/PKHD G31 ....90 D1
Armour Av AIRDRIE ML6 ....97 H2
Armour Ct BLTYR/CAMB G72 ....151 F4
  KKNTL G66 ....22 A4
Armour Dr KKNTL G66 ....22 A4
Armour Gv MTHW ML1 ....172 B1
Armour Pl JNSTN PA5 ....101 H3
Armour St COWCAD G4 ....90 B3
  JNSTN PA5 ....101 H3
Armstrong Crs
  UD/BTH/TAN G71 ....115 F4
Armstrong Gv EKILS G75 ....178 A1
Arnbrae Rd KSYTH G65 ....8 A1
Arngask Rd GOV/IBX G51 ....87 F2
Arnhall Pl
  CARD/HILL/MSPK G52 ....107 F1
Arnhem St BLTYR/CAMB G72 ....132 A2
Arnholm Pl
  CARD/HILL/MSPK G52 ....107 F1
Arnisdale Pl ESTRH G34 ....93 H1
Arnisdale Rd ESTRH G34 ....93 H1
Arnisdale Wy RUTH G73 ....130 A4
Arniston St CAR/SHTL G32 ....92 B2
Arniston Wy PSLYN/LNWD PA3 ....84 D2
Arnold Av BSHPBGS G64 ....54 D2
Arnol Pl STPS/GTHM/RID G33 ....93 H3
Arnott Dr CTBR ML5 ....96 D5
Arnott Wy BLTYR/CAMB G72 ....131 H1
Arnprior Crs CSMK G45 ....129 E5
Arnprior Qd CSMK G45 ....129 E5
Arnprior Rd CSMK G45 ....129 E5
Arnprior St CSMK G45 ....129 E5
Arnside Av GIF/THBK G46 ....127 E5
Arnwood Dr KVD/HLHD G12 ....65 H1
Arondale Rd AIRDRIE ML6 ....99 E2
Aron Ter BLTYR/CAMB G72 ....131 H3
Aros Dr CARD/HILL/MSPK G52 ....107 E2
Aros La CARD/HILL/MSPK G52 ....107 E2
Arran AIRDRIE ML6 ....76 A3
Arran Av CTBR ML5 ....97 G5
  DMBTN G82 ....13 E2
  PSLYN/LNWD PA3 ....61 H4
Arran Dr AIRDRIE ML6 ....76 A1
  CARD/HILL/MSPK G52 ....107 E1
  CUMB G67 ....26 C2
  GIF/THBK G46 ....127 E5

JNSTN PA5 ....101 E5
  KKNTL G66 ....21 G4
  PSLYS PA2 ....104 B5
Arran Gdns HMLTN ML3 ....170 B4
Arran Pl CLYDBK G81 ....49 F1
  CTBR ML5 ....97 G5
  PSLYN/LNWD PA3 ....84 D3
Arran Rd MTHW ML1 ....154 B3
  RNFRW PA4 ....63 G4
Arran Ter RUTH G73 ....129 G3
Arran Vw KSYTH G65 ....8 C1
Arranview St AIRDRIE ML6 ....119 F3
Arran Wy UD/BTH/TAN G71 ....134 A5
Arrochar Ct SMSTN G23 ....52 C3
Arrochar Dr SMSTN G23 ....52 C2
Arrochar St SMSTN G23 ....52 C3
Arrol Pl DMNK/BRGTN G40 ....91 E4
Arrol St CARD/HILL/MSPK G52 ....85 H2
Arrotshole Rd EKILN G74 ....165 G2
Arrowsmith Av KNTSWD G13 ....51 E3
Arthur Av AIRDRIE ML6 ....98 A3
  BRHD/NEIL G78 ....142 A1
Arthurlie Av BRHD/NEIL G78 ....124 B5
Arthurlie Dr GIF/THBK G46 ....145 F1
  NMRNS G77 ....161 G2
Arthurlie St BRHD/NEIL G78 ....124 B5
  GOV/IBX G51 ....87 H2
Arthur Rd PSLYS PA2 ....104 B4
Arthur St CRMNK/CLK/EAG G76 ....145 H4
  HMLTN ML3 ....153 E5
  KVGV G3 ....66 B5
  PSLY PA1 ....83 H4
Arundel Dr BSHPBGS G64 ....38 A4
  GVH/MTFL G42 ....109 F5
Ascaig Crs
  CARD/HILL/MSPK G52 ....107 F2
Ascog Rd BSDN G61 ....51 G1
Ascog St GVH/MTFL G42 ....109 F2
Ascot Av KVD/HLHD G12 ....65 E1
Ascot Ct KVD/HLHD G12 ....65 F1
Ashbank Crs AIRDRIE ML6 ....119 F1
Ashburn Gdns MLNGV G62 ....16 C4
Ashburn Rd MLNGV G62 ....16 C3
Ashburton La KVD/HLHD G12 ....52 A5
Ashburton Pk EKILS G75 ....177 F1
Ashburton Rd KVD/HLHD G12 ....51 H5
Ashby Crs KNTSWD G13 ....51 F2
Ashcroft EKILN G74 ....150 A5
Ashcroft Av KKNTL G66 ....4 C3
Ashcroft Dr LNPK/KPK G44 ....129 F1
Ashdale Dr
  CARD/HILL/MSPK G52 ....107 F1
Ashdene St PPK/MIL G22 ....53 G4
Asher Rd AIRDRIE ML6 ....119 F2
Ashfield BSHPBGS G64 ....37 H5
Ashfield Rd
  CRMNK/CLK/EAG G76 ....145 H4
  MLNGV G62 ....17 E4
Ashfield St PPK/MIL G22 ....67 H2
Ashgill Pl PPK/MIL G22 ....53 H5
Ashgill Rd PPK/MIL G22 ....53 G5
Ash Gv BSHPBGS G64 ....55 E3
  KKNTL G66 ....39 G4
  UD/BTH/TAN G71 ....115 G4
Ashgrove AIRDRIE ML6 ....99 E2
  CTBR ML5 ....96 D5
Ashgrove St
  DMNK/BRGTN G40 ....110 D2
Ashiestiel Pl CUMB G67 ....44 D1
Ashkirk Dr
  CARD/HILL/MSPK G52 ....107 F1
Ashland Av HMLTN ML3 ....180 D1
Ashlea Dr GIF/THBK G46 ....127 G3
Ashlea Gdns AIRDRIE ML6 ....77 G3
Ashley La UD/BTH/TAN G71 ....134 D1
Ashley Pk UD/BTH/TAN G71 ....134 D1
Ashley Pl BLTYR/CAMB G72 ....151 F2
Ashley St KVGV G3 ....2 A1
Ashmore Rd
  PLKSW/MSWD G43 ....128 A2
Ash Pl EKILS G75 ....177 H2
Ash Rd BAIL/MDB/MHD G69 ....113 H1
  CLYDBK G81 ....31 G2
  CUMB G67 ....11 F5
  DMBTN G82 ....13 E3
Ashton Gn EKILN G74 ....166 B3
Ashton La KVD/HLHD G12 ....66 C4
Ashton Rd KVD/HLHD G12 ....66 C4
  RUTH G73 ....110 D3
Ashton St MTHW ML1 ....136 B5
Ashton Vw DMBTN G82 ....12 A3
Ashtree Ct OLDK G60 ....30 D3
Ashtree Gv NMRNS G77 ....161 F2
Ashtree Rd PLKSW/MSWD G43 ....108 B5
Ashvale Crs SPRGB/BLRNK G21 ....68 B2
Ashworth Ter HMLTN ML3 ....169 F1
Ash Wynd BLTYR/CAMB G72 ....132 B3
Aspen Dr SPRGB/BLRNK G21 ....68 D2
Aspen Ga MTHW ML1 ....138 A3
Aspen Pl BLTYR/CAMB G72 ....132 A2
  JNSTN PA5 ....101 H5
Aspen Wy HMLTN ML3 ....170 B3
Asquith Pl BLSH ML4 ....117 G1
Aster Dr CSMK G45 ....129 H5
Aster Gdns MTHW ML1 ....154 D5
  PLK/PH/NH G53 ....125 G4
Athelstane Dr CUMB G67 ....44 C1
Athelstane Rd KNTSWD G13 ....51 E5
Athena Wy UD/BTH/TAN G71 ....115 F5
Athole Gdns KVD/HLHD G12 ....66 B3
Athole La KVD/HLHD G12 ....66 B3
Atholl Av CARD/HILL/MSPK G52 ....85 H1
  MLNGV G62 ....17 E4
Atholl Crs PSLY PA1 ....85 H4
Atholl Dr BALLOCH G68 ....24 D5
  GIF/THBK G46 ....145 G2
Atholl Gdns BSDN G61 ....34 B1
  BSHPBGS G64 ....38 A5
  KVD/HLHD G12 ....66 B3
  RUTH G73 ....130 D3
Atholl La BAIL/MDB/MHD G69 ....59 F1
Atholl Pl CTBR ML5 ....117 H1
  PSLYN/LNWD PA3 ....81 H5
Atholl St HMLTN ML3 ....152 C4
Atholl Ter UD/BTH/TAN G71 ....115 E3
Atlas Pl SPRGB/BLRNK G21 ....68 C3
Atlas Rd SPRGB/BLRNK G21 ....68 B3
Atlas St CLYDBK G81 ....49 E3
Atlin Dr MTHW ML1 ....138 C1
Attercliffe Av WISHAW ML2 ....172 D3
Attlee Av CLYDBK G81 ....50 A4
Attow Rd PLKSW/MSWD G43 ....127 G2

Auburn Dr BRHD/NEIL G78 ....142 C1
Auchans Rd
  CRG/CRSL/HOU PA6 ....81 G3
Auchenbothie Crs
  STPS/GTHM/RID G33 ....69 H1
Auchenbothie Pl
  STPS/GTHM/RID G33 ....69 H1
Auchencrow St ESTRH G34 ....94 C1
Auchencruive MLNGV G62 ....17 G5
Auchendavie Rd KKNTL G66 ....22 B3
Auchengeich Rd
  BAIL/MDB/MHD G69 ....41 G4
Auchengilloch EKILS G75 ....178 B3
Auchengreoch Av JNSTN PA5 ....121 E1
Auchengreoch Rd JNSTN PA5 ....121 E1
Auchenhowie Rd MLNGV G62 ....35 E1
Auchenkilns Rd CUMB G67 ....44 C2
Auchenlodment Rd
  JNSTN PA5 ....102 A2
Auchenreoch Av DMBTN G82 ....13 C1
Auchenstewart Ct
  WISHAW ML2 ....174 B2
Auchentorlie Qd PSLY PA1 ....85 E5
Auchentorlie St PTCK G11 ....65 G4
Auchentoshan Av CLYDBK G81 ....31 G2
Auchentoshan Ter
  SPRGB/BLRNK G21 ....68 B4
Auchinairn Rd BSHPBGS G64 ....55 G4
Auchinbee Farm Rd
  BALLOCH G68 * 25 F1
Auchinbee Wy BALLOCH G68 ....25 F1
Auchincampbell Rd
  HMLTN ML3 ....170 A2
Auchinden Ct BSDN G61 ....33 H1
Auchingill Pl ESTRH G34 ....72 C5
Auchingill Rd ESTRH G34 ....72 B5
Auchingramont Rd
  HMLTN ML3 ....170 A2
Auchinlea Dr MTHW ML1 ....157 F1
Auchinlea Rd ESTRH G34 ....71 G5
Auchinleck Av
  STPS/GTHM/RID G33 ....55 H5
Auchinleck Crs
  STPS/GTHM/RID G33 ....55 H5
Auchinleck Gdns
  STPS/GTHM/RID G33 ....55 H5
Auchinleck Rd CLYDBK G81 ....32 A2
  STPS/GTHM/RID G33 ....56 A4
Auchinleck Ter CLYDBK G81 ....32 A1
Auchinloch Rd KKNTL G66 ....40 A4
Auchinloch St
  SPRGB/BLRNK G21 ....68 C3
Auchinraith Av HMLTN ML3 ....151 D5
Auchinraith Rd
  BLTYR/CAMB G72 ....151 G4
Auchinvole Crs KSYTH G65 ....7 H2
Auchmannoch Av PSLY PA1 ....85 H4
Auchnacraig Rd CLYDBK G81 ....32 B1
Auchter Av WISHAW ML2 ....158 C5
Auchterburn Rd SHOTTS ML7 ....174 D1
Auchter Rd WISHAW ML2 ....174 D1
Auckland Pk EKILS G75 ....165 F5
Auckland Pl CLYDBK G81 ....31 E4
Auckland St PPK/MIL G22 ....67 G2
Auldbar Rd
  CARD/HILL/MSPK G52 ....107 G1
Auldbar Ter PSLYS PA2 ....104 D2
Auldburn Pl
  PLKSW/MSWD G43 ....126 D1
Auldburn Rd
  PLKSW/MSWD G43 ....126 D1
Auldgirth Rd
  CARD/HILL/MSPK G52 ....107 G1
Auldhame St CTBR ML5 ....96 B1
Auldhouse Av
  PLKSW/MSWD G43 ....127 F1
Auldhouse Gdns
  PLKSW/MSWD G43 ....127 F1
Auldhouse Rd
  PLKSW/MSWD G43 ....127 E1
Auldhouse Ter
  PLKSW/MSWD G43 ....127 F1
Auld Kirk Rd BLTYR/CAMB G72 ....131 H4
Auldlum St MTHW ML1 ....137 H5
The Auld Rd CUMB G67 ....26 C1
Auld's Brae AIRDRIE ML6 ....98 B1
Auld St CLYDBK G81 ....31 F5
Aultbea St PPK/MIL G22 ....53 G5
Aultmore Dr MTHW ML1 ....137 F5
Aultmore Rd
  STPS/GTHM/RID G33 ....93 G2
Aursbridge Dr BRHD/NEIL G78 ....124 C5
Aursbridge Gv BRHD/NEIL G78 ....124 C5
Aurs Crs BRHD/NEIL G78 ....124 C5
Aurs Dr BRHD/NEIL G78 ....142 C1
Aurs Gln BRHD/NEIL G78 ....142 B1
Aurs Pl BRHD/NEIL G78 ....142 D1
Aurs Rd BRHD/NEIL G78 ....124 D4
  NMRNS G77 ....143 F5
Austen La KNTSWD G13 ....65 F1
Austen Rd KNTSWD G13 ....65 F1
Austine Dr HMLTN ML3 ....181 E1
Avenel Rd KNTSWD G13 ....51 F2
Avenue End Rd
  STPS/GTHM/RID G33 ....70 C2
Avenuehead Rd
  BAIL/MDB/MHD G69 ....59 F3
Avenuepark St MRYH/FIRH G20 ....66 D2
Avenue St DMNK/BRGTN G40 ....90 D4
  RUTH G73 ....111 E3
Aviemore Gdns BSDN G61 ....34 D2
Aviemore Rd
  CARD/HILL/MSPK G52 ....107 F2
Avoch St ESTRH G34 ....72 A4
Avon Av BSDN G61 ....35 E4
Avonbank Crs HMLTN ML3 ....170 B5
Avonbank Rd RUTH G73 ....110 C5
Avonbridge Dr HMLTN ML3 ....170 B4
Avondale Av EKILN G74 ....166 C4
Avondale Dr PSLY PA1 ....85 E4
Avondale Pl EKILN G74 ....166 D3
Avondale St
  STPS/GTHM/RID G33 ....70 C2
Avon Dr BLSH ML4 ....136 B3
  PSLYN/LNWD PA3 ....82 A4
Avonhead Av CUMB G67 ....44 A5
Avonhead Gdns CUMB G67 ....44 A5
Avonhead Pl CUMB G67 ....44 A5
Avonhead Rd CUMB G67 ....44 A5
Avon Pl CTBR ML5 ....96 B5
Avon Rd BSHPBGS G64 ....54 D3

GIF/THBK G46 ....127 E5
Avonside Gv HMLTN ML3 ....170 C2
Avonspark St
  SPRGB/BLRNK G21 ....68 D3
Avon St HMLTN ML3 ....154 C5
Aylmer Rd PLKSW/MSWD G43 ....128 A1
Ayr Rd GIF/THBK G46 ....145 E4
  NMRNS G77 ....160 D3
Ayr St SPRGB/BLRNK G21 ....68 C2
Ayton Pk North EKILN G74 ....166 D2
Ayton Pk South EKILN G74 ....166 D2
Aytoun Dr ERSK PA8 ....48 A1
Aytoun Rd PLKSD/SHW G41 ....108 C1

B

Babylon Av BLSH ML4 ....135 H4
Babylon Dr BLSH ML4 ....135 H5
Babylon Pl BLSH ML4 ....135 H5
Babylon Rd BLSH ML4 ....135 H4
Backbrae St KSYTH G65 ....8 B2
Back Cswy DEN/PKHD G31 ....91 G4
Back O' Barns HMLTN ML3 ....152 C4
Backmuir Pl HMLTN ML3 ....152 C4
Backmuir Rd DRUM G15 ....33 G5
  HMLTN ML3 ....152 C3
Back O' Dykes Rd KKNTL G66 ....41 E1
Back O Hill CRG/CRSL/HOU PA6 ....80 C2
Back O' Hill Rd BSHPBGS G64 ....18 C3
Back Rd BRWEIR PA11 ....79 G3
Back Rw HMLTN ML3 ....170 A2
Back Sneddon St PSLY PA1 ....84 A4
Badenheath Pl BALLOCH G68 ....43 E5
Badenoch Road, KKNTL G66 ....22 D4
Bagnell St SPRGB/BLRNK G21 ....68 C1
Bahamas Wy EKILS G75 ....165 F4
Bailie Dr BSDN G61 ....34 A1
Baillie Dr EKILN G74 ....167 E1
  UD/BTH/TAN G71 ....134 B4
Baillie Pl EKILN G74 ....167 F1
Baillies La AIRDRIE ML6 ....98 B1
Bailliesmuir Pl WISHAW ML2 ....158 B4
Baillieston Rd CAR/SHTL G32 ....92 D5
  UD/BTH/TAN G71 ....114 A3
Baillie Wynd UD/BTH/TAN G71 ....115 F5
Bainsford St CAR/SHTL G32 ....92 A3
Baird Av AIRDRIE ML6 ....76 C4
  CARD/HILL/MSPK G52 ....85 H1
Baird Brae MRYH/FIRH G20 ....67 E3
Baird Ct BSDN G61 ....44 A1
Baird Dr BSDN G61 ....34 A2
  ERSK PA8 ....30 A5
Baird Hl EKILS G75 ....166 A5
Baird Pl BLSH ML4 ....116 A5
  WISHAW ML2 ....174 D1
Bairds Crs HMLTN ML3 ....169 H3
Bairdsland Vw BLSH ML4 ....136 A2
Baird St COWCAD G4 ....3 H2
  SPRGB/BLRNK G21 ....96 ?
Baker St PLKSD/SHW G41 ....108 D3
Bakewell Rd
  BAIL/MDB/MHD G69 ....93 H4
Balaclava St CCLW G2 ....2 D5
Balado Rd STPS/GTHM/RID G33 ....93 F2
Balbeggie St CAR/SHTL G32 ....92 D5
Balbeg St GOV/IBX G51 ....87 F3
Balblair Rd
  CARD/HILL/MSPK G52 ....107 G1
Balcarres Av KVD/HLHD G12 ....66 B1
Balcary Pl AIRDRIE ML6 ....119 F3
Balcastle Gdns KSYTH G65 ....7 H1
Balcastle Rd KSYTH G65 ....7 H1
Balcomie St
  STPS/GTHM/RID G33 ....70 B5
Balcurvie Rd ESTRH G34 ....71 H4
Baldernock Rd MLNGV G62 ....17 H4
Baldinnie Rd ESTRH G34 ....94 A1
Baldoran Dr KKNTL G66 ....4 A2
Baldovan Crs
  STPS/GTHM/RID G33 ....93 G1
Baldovie Rd
  CARD/HILL/MSPK G52 ....106 D1
Baldragon Rd ESTRH G34 ....72 A5
Baldric Rd KNTSWD G13 ....50 D5
Baldwin Av KNTSWD G13 ....51 E2
Balerno Dr
  CARD/HILL/MSPK G52 ....107 F1
Balfleurs St MLNGV G62 ....17 G3
Balfluig St ESTRH G34 ....71 G5
Balfour St MRYH/FIRH G20 ....66 C1
Balfour Ter EKILS G75 ....178 C1
Balfron Crs HMLTN ML3 ....169 E2
Balfron Dr CTBR ML5 ....117 F1
Balfron Rd GOV/IBX G51 ....87 F3
  PSLY PA1 ....85 F4
Balgair Dr PSLY PA1 ....85 E4
Balgair St PPK/MIL G22 ....53 F5
Balgair Ter CAR/SHTL G32 ....92 C4
Balglass St PPK/MIL G22 ....67 G2
Balgonie Av PSLYS PA2 ....103 E3
Balgonie Dr PSLYS PA2 ....103 H3
Balgonie Rd
  CARD/HILL/MSPK G52 ....107 F1
Balgonie Woods PSLYS PA2 ....103 H3
Balgownie Crs GIF/THBK G46 ....126 D5
Balgraybank St
  SPRGB/BLRNK G21 ....68 D2
Balgray Crs BRHD/NEIL G78 ....142 D1
Balgrayhill Rd
  SPRGB/BLRNK G21 ....54 C5
Balgray Rd NMRNS G77 ....143 G5
Balgraystone Rd NMRNS G77 ....142 C5
Balintore St CAR/SHTL G32 ....92 B4
Baliol La KVGV G3 ....2 A1
Baljaffray Rd BSDN G61 ....33 F1
Ballagan Pl MLNGV G62 ....16 B3
Ballaig Av BSDN G61 ....33 H2
Ballaig Crs STPS/GTHM/RID G33 ....70 D1
Ballantay Qd CSMK G45 ....130 A5
Ballantay Rd CSMK G45 ....130 A5
Ballantay Ter CSMK G45 ....130 A5
Ballantine Av
  CARD/HILL/MSPK G52 ....86 B2

Ballantrae EKILN G74 166 A2
Ballantrae Crs NMRNS G77 162 B1
Ballantrae Dr NMRNS G77 162 B1
Ballantrae Rd
BLTYR/CAMB G72 151 H5
Ballater Crs WISHAW ML2 157 E5
Ballater Dr BSDN G61 51 G1
PSLYS PA2 104 C3
RNFRW PA4 48 A4
Ballater Pl GBLS G5 90 A5
Ballater St GBLS G5 89 H4
Ballayne Dr
BAIL/MDB/MHD G69 42 B5
Ballerup Ter EKILS G75 178 B2
Ballindalloch Dr DEN/PKHD G31 90 D1
Ballindalloch La DEN/PKHD G31 90 D1
Balloch Gdns
CARD/HILL/MSPK G52 107 G1
Balloch Loop Rd BALLOCH G68 25 E3
Ballochmill Rd
BLTYR/CAMB G72 111 G4
Ballochmyle EKILN G74 167 G1
Ballochmyle Crs
PLK/PH/NH G53 106 B4
Ballochmyle Dr
PLK/PH/NH G53 106 B3
Ballochmyle Gdns
PLK/PH/NH G53 106 B4
Ballochmyle Pl
PLK/PH/NH G53 106 B4
Ballochney Rd AIRDRIE ML6 77 E2
Ballochney St AIRDRIE ML6 75 H5
Ballochnie Dr AIRDRIE ML6 77 H3
Balloch Rd AIRDRIE ML6 99 H3
Balloch Vw CUMB G67 26 B3
Ballogie Rd LNPK/KPK G44 109 G5
Balmalloch Rd KSYTH G65 7 H1
Balmartin Rd SMSTN G23 52 C2
Balmedie ERSK PA8 47 F1
Balmeg Av GIF/THBK G46 145 F2
Balmoral Av AIRDRIE ML6 76 A1
Balmoral Crs CTBR ML5 96 A5
RNFRW PA4 48 B4
Balmoral Dr BLTYR/CAMB G72 130 D2
BSDN G61 51 H1
BSHPTN PA7 46 B2
CAR/SHTL G32 112 C4
Balmoral Gdns
BLTYR/CAMB G72 133 F5
UD/BTH/TAN G71 115 E3
Balmoral Pl EKILN G74 165 H4
Balmoral Rd JNSTN PA5 102 A4
Balmoral St SCOT G14 64 C3
Balmore Dr HMLTN ML3 169 F5
Balmore Pl PPK/MIL G22 53 G5
Balmore Rd BSHPBGS G64 18 D5
MLNGV G62 36 A1
SMSTN G23 53 F4
Balmore Sq MRYH/FIRH G20 67 G1
Balmuildy Rd BSHPBGS G64 36 C4
Balornock Rd
SPRGB/BLRNK G21 54 D5
Balruddery Pl BSHPBGS G64 55 G3
Balshagray Av PTCK G11 65 G3
Balshagray Crs PTCK G11 65 F4
Balshagray Dr PTCK G11 65 G3
Balshagray La PTCK G11 65 G3
Balshagray Pl PTCK G11 65 G3
Baltersan Gdns HMLTN ML3 181 F5
Baltic Ct DMNK/BRGTN G40 110 D1
Baltic La DMNK/BRGTN G40 110 D1
Baltic Pl DMNK/BRGTN G40 90 C5
Baltic St DMNK/BRGTN G40 90 D5
Balure St DEN/PKHD G31 91 F2
Balvaird Crs RUTH G73 110 D5
Balvaird Dr RUTH G73 110 D5
Balvenie Dr MTHW ML1 155 G1
Balvenie St CTBR ML5 117 E1
Balveny St STPS/GTHM/RID G33 71 E4
Balvicar Dr GVH/MTFL G42 109 E3
Balvicar St GVH/MTFL G42 109 E2
Balvie Av DRUM G15 50 B2
GIF/THBK G46 127 G5
Balvie Crs MLNGV G62 16 D3
Balvie Rd MLNGV G62 16 D3
Banavie Rd PTCK G11 66 A3
WISHAW ML2 158 A4
Banchory Av AIRDRIE ML6 76 A1
PLKSW/MSWD G43 127 E2
RNFRW PA4 48 A4
Banchory Crs BSDN G61 51 H1
Banchory Rd WISHAW ML2 157 E5
Baneberry Pth EKILN G74 166 A1
Banff Av AIRDRIE ML6 98 B5
Banff Pl EKILS G75 165 H5
Banff Qd WISHAW ML2 157 E5
Banff St STPS/GTHM/RID G33 70 C4
Bangorshill St GIF/THBK G46 126 C3
Bank Av MLNGV G62 17 E2
Bankbrae Av PLK/PH/NH G53 125 F1
Bankend BRWEIR PA11 79 H4
Bankend Rd BRWEIR PA11 80 A5
DMBTN G82 13 E3
Bankend St
STPS/GTHM/RID G33 70 B5
Bankfield Dr HMLTN ML3 180 D2
Bankfoot Dr
CARD/HILL/MSPK G52 86 C5
Bankfoot Pl NMRNS G77 162 C1
Bankfoot Rd
CARD/HILL/MSPK G52 86 C5
PSLYN/LNWD PA3 83 G4
Bankglen Rd DRUM G15 33 G4
Bankhall St GVH/MTFL G42 109 G2
Bankhead Av AIRDRIE ML6 99 E2
BLSH ML4 136 A4
CTBR ML5 95 H5
KNTSWD G13 50 B5
Bankhead Dr RUTH G73 110 D5
Bankhead Pl AIRDRIE ML6 99 E2
CTBR ML5 95 H5
Bankhead Rd
CRMNK/CLK/EAG G76 147 E3
KKNTL G66 41 E1
RUTH G73 110 C5
Bankholm Pl
CRMNK/CLK/EAG G76 146 A5
Banknock St CAR/SHTL G32 91 H3
Bank Pk EKILS G75 166 A5
Bank Rd CAR/SHTL G32 112 D4
Bankside Av JNSTN PA5 101 G3
Banks Rd KKNTL G66 21 G4
Bank St AIRDRIE ML6 98 B1
BLTYR/CAMB G72 131 F1
BRHD/NEIL G78 124 B5
BRHD/NEIL G78 141 E3
CTBR ML5 96 C3
KVD/HLHD G12 66 D4
PSLY PA1 84 C5
Banktop Pl JNSTN PA5 101 G3
Bank Vw AIRDRIE ML6 119 E2
Bankview Dr KKNTL G66 20 C5
Bannercross Av
BAIL/MDB/MHD G69 93 H4
Bannercross Dr
BAIL/MDB/MHD G69 93 H3
Bannercross Gdns
BAIL/MDB/MHD G69 93 H4
Banner Dr KNTSWD G13 50 D2
Bannerman Dr BLSH ML4 136 C2
Bannerman Pl CLYDBK G81 49 F1
Banner Rd BSDN G61 51 E1
Bannockburn Pl MTHW ML1 137 F5
Bantaskin St MRYH/FIRH G20 52 B4
Banton Pl STPS/GTHM/RID G33 93 H2
Banton Rd KSYTH G65 9 G1
Banyan Crs UD/BTH/TAN G71 116 A3
Barassie EKILN G74 166 A2
Barassie Ct UD/BTH/TAN G71 134 A5
Barassie Dr BRWEIR PA11 79 F5
Barbados Gn EKILS G75 165 F4
Barbae Pl UD/BTH/TAN G71 134 B4
Barbana Rd EKILN G74 164 D3
Barbegs Crs KSYTH G65 24 D1
Barberry Av PLK/PH/NH G53 125 G5
Barberry Gdns
PLK/PH/NH G53 125 G5
Barberry Pl PLK/PH/NH G53 125 G5
Barbeth Gdns CUMB G67 44 A3
Barbeth Pl CUMB G67 43 H2
Barbeth Rd CUMB G67 43 H2
Barbeth Wy CUMB G67 43 H2
Barbreck Rd GVH/MTFL G42 109 E2
Barcaldine Av
BAIL/MDB/MHD G69 58 A2
Barcapel Av NMRNS G77 144 B3
Barclay Av JNSTN PA5 102 A2
Barclay Ct OLDK G60 30 C2
Barclay Rd MTHW ML1 154 A4
Barclay St SPRGB/BLRNK G21 68 C1
Barcloy Pl AIRDRIE ML6 119 G3
Barcraigs Dr PSLYS PA2 104 C4
Bard Av KNTSWD G13 50 C3
Bardowie St PPK/MIL G22 67 H2
Bardrain Av JNSTN PA5 102 B2
Bardrain Rd PSLYS PA2 103 H5
Bardrill Dr BSHPBGS G64 54 B2
Bardykes Rd BLTYR/CAMB G72 151 F2
Barfillan Dr
CARD/HILL/MSPK G52 87 F4
Bargany Ct PLK/PH/NH G53 106 B3
Bargany Pl PLK/PH/NH G53 106 B4
Bargany Rd PLK/PH/NH G53 106 B3
Bargaran Rd PLK/PH/NH G53 106 C1
Bargarran Rd ERSK PA8 47 E1
Bargarron Dr PSLYN/LNWD PA3 84 D2
Bargeddie St
STPS/GTHM/RID G33 69 G4
Bar Hill Pl KSYTH G65 7 H2
Barhill Rd ERSK PA8 30 B5
Barholm Sq
STPS/GTHM/RID G33 71 E5
Barke Rd CUMB G67 26 C2
Barkly Ter EKILS G75 165 H5
Barlae Av
CRMNK/CLK/EAG G76 163 F5
Barlanark Av CAR/SHTL G32 92 D2
Barlanark Crs CAR/SHTL G32 93 E2
Barlanark Pl
STPS/GTHM/RID G33 93 F2
Barlanark Rd
STPS/GTHM/RID G33 93 E2
Barlanark Wy CAR/SHTL G32 93 E2
Barlandfauld St KSYTH G65 8 B2
Barlia Dr CSMK G45 129 F4
Barlia St CSMK G45 129 F4
Barlia Ter CSMK G45 129 G4
Barloan Crs DMBTN G82 13 F2
Barloan Pl DMBTN G82 13 F2
Barloch Av MLNGV G62 17 E3
Barloch Rd MLNGV G62 17 F3
Barloch St PPK/MIL G22 67 H2
Barlogan Av
CARD/HILL/MSPK G52 87 F4
Barlogan Qd
CARD/HILL/MSPK G52 87 F4
Barmulloch Rd
SPRGB/BLRNK G21 68 D2
Barnbeth Rd PLK/PH/NH G53 106 C2
Barncluith Rd HMLTN ML3 170 C2
Barnes Rd MRYH/FIRH G20 53 G5
Barness Pl STPS/GTHM/RID G33 92 B1
Barnes St BRHD/NEIL G78 124 A5
Barnflat St RUTH G73 111 E3
Barn Gn KLBCH PA10 100 B3
Barnhill Dr HMLTN ML3 168 C3
NMRNS G77 161 G2
SPRGB/BLRNK G21 68 D3
Barnhill Rd DMBTN G82 14 A2
Barnkirk Av DRUM G15 33 F5
Barnscroft KLBCH PA10 100 C2
Barnsford Av RNFRW PA4 61 G2
Barnsford Rd RNFRW PA4 61 G3
Barns St CLYDBK G81 49 F3
Barnton St CAR/SHTL G32 91 H2
Barnwell Ter GOV/IBX G51 87 F2
Barochan Crs PSLYN/LNWD PA3 83 F5
Barochan Rd BLSH ML4 136 C1
CRG/CRSL/HOU PA6 80 D4
PLK/PH/NH G53 106 C1
Baronald Dr KVD/HLHD G12 52 A5
Baronald Ga KVD/HLHD G12 52 A5
Baronald St RUTH G73 111 E3
Baron Ct HMLTN ML3 170 D3
Barone Dr
CRMNK/CLK/EAG G76 145 F2
Baronhall Dr BLTYR/CAMB G72 151 F2
Baronhill CUMB G67 10 C5
Baron Rd PSLYN/LNWD PA3 84 D3
Baronscourt Dr PSLY PA1 83 E5
Baronscourt Gdns
PSLYN/LNWD PA3 83 E5
Baronscourt Rd JNSTN PA5 103 E1
Barons Ga UD/BTH/TAN G71 133 H3
Barons Rd MTHW ML1 172 D3
Baron St RNFRW PA4 63 F4
Barony Dr BAIL/MDB/MHD G69 94 A3
Barony Gdns
BAIL/MDB/MHD G69 94 A4
Barony Pl BALLOCH G68 24 C4
Barony Wynd
BAIL/MDB/MHD G69 94 A4
Barra Av RNFRW PA4 63 F5
WISHAW ML2 157 H5
Barrachnie Av
BAIL/MDB/MHD G69 93 H4
Barrachnie Ct
BAIL/MDB/MHD G69 93 G4
Barrachnie Crs
BAIL/MDB/MHD G69 93 G4
Barrachnie Gv
BAIL/MDB/MHD G69 93 H3
Barrachnie Pl
BAIL/MDB/MHD G69 93 H3
Barrachnie Rd
BAIL/MDB/MHD G69 93 H4
Barrack St COWCAD G4 90 B3
HMLTN ML3 153 E5
Barra Dr AIRDRIE ML6 99 F3
Barra Gdns OLDK G60 30 D3
Barra Pl CTBR ML5 96 B5
Barra Rd OLDK G60 30 D3
Barraston Rd BSHPBGS G64 19 E2
Barra St MRYH/FIRH G20 52 B3
Barr Av BRHD/NEIL G78 141 F2
Barrbridge Rd
BAIL/MDB/MHD G69 95 G5
Barrcraig Rd BRWEIR PA11 79 F4
Barr Crs CLYDBK G81 32 A3
Barr Farm Rd KSYTH G65 8 C3
Barr Gv UD/BTH/TAN G71 115 F4
Barrhead Rd NMRNS G77 143 G5
PLK/PH/NH G53 106 B5
PSLYS PA2 104 C1
Barrhill Ct KKNTL G66 22 A5
Barrhill Crs KLBCH PA10 100 C4
Barrhill Rd KKNTL G66 22 A5
Barriedale Av HMLTN ML3 169 G2
Barrie Qd CLYDBK G81 31 H4
Barrie Rd CARD/HILL/MSPK G52 86 B2
EKILN G74 150 A5
Barrie St MTHW ML1 154 D4
Barrington Dr COWCAD G4 67 E4
Barrisdale Rd MRYH/FIRH G20 52 C4
WISHAW ML2 158 A4
Barrisdale Wy RUTH G73 130 A3
Barrland Dr GIF/THBK G46 127 F4
Barrland St PLKSD/SHW G41 109 F1
Barrmill Rd PLKSW/MSWD G43 126 D2
Barrochan Rd
CRG/CRSL/HOU PA6 81 F5
JNSTN PA5 101 F2
Barrowfield St CTBR ML5 96 C5
DMNK/BRGTN G40 90 D4
Barrpath KSYTH G65 8 D3
Barr Pl NMRNS G77 143 H5
PSLY PA1 84 A5
Barr St MRYH/FIRH G20 67 F3
MTHW ML1 154 D2
Barr Ter EKILN G74 166 B3
Barrwood Pl UD/BTH/TAN G71 115 F4
Barrwood St
STPS/GTHM/RID G33 69 H4
Barry Gdns BLTYR/CAMB G72 151 F4
Barscube Ter PSLYS PA2 104 D2
Barshaw Dr PSLY PA1 84 D3
Barshaw Pl PSLY PA1 85 G4
Barshaw Rd
CARD/HILL/MSPK G52 85 H3
Barskiven Rd PSLYN/LNWD PA3 83 E5
Barterholm Rd PSLYS PA2 104 C2
Bartholomew St
DMNK/BRGTN G40 110 D1
Bartiebeith Rd
STPS/GTHM/RID G33 93 E2
Bartonhall Rd WISHAW ML2 174 C4
Barty's Rd BLSH ML4 * 136 B2
Barwood Hl DMBTN G82 13 G1
Bassett Av KNTSWD G13 50 C3
Bassett Crs KNTSWD G13 50 C3
Bathgate St DEN/PKHD G31 90 D3
Bathgo Av PSLY PA1 85 H5
Bath La CGLW G2 2 C3
Bath St CGLW G2 2 B3
Batson St GVH/MTFL G42 109 G2
Battlefield Av GVH/MTFL G42 109 F5
Battlefield Gdns
GVH/MTFL G42 109 F5
Battlefield Rd GVH/MTFL G42 109 F4
Battles Burn Dr CAR/SHTL G32 112 B2
Battles Burn Ga CAR/SHTL G32 112 B2
Battles Burn Vw
CAR/SHTL G32 112 B2
Bavelaw St
STPS/GTHM/RID G33 71 E4
Bayfield Av DRUM G15 33 F5
Bayfield Ter DRUM G15 33 F5
Bay Willow Ct
BLTYR/CAMB G72 132 C3
Beaconsfield Rd KVD/HLHD G12 66 A1
Beard Crs BAIL/MDB/MHD G69 73 E1
Beardmore Pl CLYDBK G81 31 F5
Beardmore St CLYDBK G81 31 F5
Beardmore Wy CLYDBK G81 48 B1
Bearford Dr
CARD/HILL/MSPK G52 86 C4
Bearsden Rd KNTSWD G13 51 G5
Beaton Rd PLKSD/SHW G41 108 D2
Beatrice Dr MTHW ML1 137 E2
Beatrice Gdns
CRG/CRSL/HOU PA6 81 E3
Beattock St DEN/PKHD G31 91 G4
Beattock Wynd HMLTN ML3 169 F2
Beatty St CLYDBK G81 31 F5
Beaufort Av
PLKSW/MSWD G43 127 F1
Beaufort Dr KKNTL G66 20 D5
Beaufort Gdns BSHPBGS G64 54 B2
Beauly Crs WISHAW ML2 174 A4
Beauly Dr PSLYS PA2 102 D3
Beauly Pl BAIL/MDB/MHD G69 58 C2
CTBR ML5 117 E1
EKILN G74 166 A3
MRYH/FIRH G20 66 C1
MTHW ML1 137 F3
Beauly Rd BAIL/MDB/MHD G69 113 H1
Beaumont Ga KVD/HLHD G12 66 B4
Beckfield Crs
STPS/GTHM/RID G33 55 G4
Beckfield Dr
STPS/GTHM/RID G33 55 G4
Beckfield Ga SPRGB/BLRNK G21 55 G4
Beckfield Gv
STPS/GTHM/RID G33 55 G4
Beckfield Wk
STPS/GTHM/RID G33 55 G4
Beckford St HMLTN ML3 152 D5
Bedale Rd BAIL/MDB/MHD G69 93 G5
Bedcow Vw KKNTL G66 40 C1
Bedford Av CLYDBK G81 49 G1
Bedford La GBLS G5 89 G4
Bedford St GBLS G5 89 G4
Bedlay Ct BAIL/MDB/MHD G69 42 B5
Bedlay Vw UD/BTH/TAN G71 115 G3
Beech Av BAIL/MDB/MHD G69 93 H4
BLTYR/CAMB G72 131 E1
BRWEIR PA11 79 G2
BSDN G61 34 D1
GOV/IBX G51 88 A4
HMLTN ML3 181 F4
JNSTN PA5 102 B2
MTHW ML1 137 G4
NMRNS G77 161 H1
PSLYS PA2 104 D3
RUTH G73 130 B3
Beechbank Av AIRDRIE ML6 98 A1
Beech Crs BLTYR/CAMB G72 132 B3
MTHW ML1 118 D5
NMRNS G77 161 H2
Beech Dr CLYDBK G81 31 H3
Beeches Av CLYDBK G81 31 G2
Beeches Rd CLYDBK G81 31 G2
The Beeches
CRG/CRSL/HOU PA6 81 E2
JNSTN PA5 80 D5
Beech Gdns
BAIL/MDB/MHD G69 93 H4
Beech Gv BAIL/MDB/MHD G69 73 F1
EKILS G75 177 G2
WISHAW ML2 157 F3
Beechgrove Av
UD/BTH/TAN G71 115 H5
Beechgrove Qd MTHW ML1 137 F2
Beechgrove St
DMNK/BRGTN G40 * 111 E2
Beechlands Av LNPK/KPK G44 127 H5
Beechlands Dr
CRMNK/CLK/EAG G76 145 F4
Beechmount Rd KKNTL G66 39 H4
Beech Pl BLTYR/CAMB G72 151 H3
BSHPBGS G64 55 E3
Beech Rd BSHPBGS G64 55 E3
JNSTN PA5 101 E5
KKNTL G66 39 H2
MTHW ML1 118 D5
Beechtree Ter KKNTL G66 5 G5
Beechwood WISHAW ML2 173 E4
Beechwood Av
CRMNK/CLK/EAG G76 145 F4
HMLTN ML3 169 G5
RUTH G73 130 B1
Beechwood Ct BSDN G61 34 C5
CUMB G67 26 B5
Beechwood Crs WISHAW ML2 174 B3
Beechwood Dr CTBR ML5 97 F4
PTCK G11 65 G2
RNFRW PA4 63 E5
Beechwood Gdns BLSH ML4 136 B3
Beechwood Gv
BRHD/NEIL G78 142 B1
Beechwood La BSDN G61 34 C5
Beechwood Pl PTCK G11 65 G2
Beechwood Rd CUMB G67 26 B4
Beechworth Dr MTHW ML1 138 A5
Beecroft Pl BLTYR/CAMB G72 151 H1
Beil Dr KNTSWD G13 50 A4
Beith Dr AIRDRIE ML6 98 B5
Beith Rd HWWD PA9 120 C3
JNSTN PA5 101 F5
Beith St PTCK G11 65 H5
Belford Ct NMRNS G77 161 G3
Belford Gv NMRNS G77 161 G3
Belgowan St BLSH ML4 116 C5
Belgrave La KVD/HLHD G12 66 D3
Belgrave St BLSH ML4 135 G1
Belhaven Ct NMRNS G77 161 F3
Belhaven Pk
BAIL/MDB/MHD G69 58 B4
Belhaven Pl NMRNS G77 161 G3
Belhaven Rd HMLTN ML3 168 D2
WISHAW ML2 173 H2
Belhaven Ter KVD/HLHD G12 66 B2
WISHAW ML2 173 H2
Belhaven Terrace La
KVD/HLHD G12 66 B2
Belhaven Ter West
KVD/HLHD G12 66 B2
Belhaven Terrace West La
KVD/HLHD G12 66 B2
Bellahouston Dr
CARD/HILL/MSPK G52 107 F1
Bellairs Pl BLTYR/CAMB G72 151 F1
Bellas Pl AIRDRIE ML6 77 H4
Bell Dr BLTYR/CAMB G72 168 B1
Belleisle Av UD/BTH/TAN G71 133 H1
Belleisle Ct BALLOCH G68 26 A1
Belleisle Crs BRWEIR PA11 79 E4
Belleisle Dr BALLOCH G68 26 A1
Belleisle Gdns BALLOCH G68 26 A1
Belleisle Gv BALLOCH G68 10 A5
Belleisle St GVH/MTFL G42 109 G3
Bellevue Av KKNTL G66 20 D5
Bellevue Rd KKNTL G66 20 D5
Bellfield Crs BRHD/NEIL G78 124 A3
Bellfield Dr WISHAW ML2 174 B3
Bellfield Rd KKNTL G66 20 D5
Bellfield St DEN/PKHD G31 90 D3
Bellflower Av PLK/PH/NH G53 125 H4
Bellflower Ct EKILN G74 165 H2
Bellflower Gdns
PLK/PH/NH G53 125 H4
Bellflower Gv EKILN G74 165 H2
Bellflower Pl PLK/PH/NH G53 125 H4
Bell Gn East EKILS G75 166 C5
Bell Gn West EKILS G75 166 B5
Bellgrove St DMNK/BRGTN G40 90 C3
Bellrock Ct STPS/GTHM/RID G33 92 C1
Bellrock Crs
STPS/GTHM/RID G33 92 B1
Bellrock St STPS/GTHM/RID G33 92 B1
Bells Br GOV/IBX G51 88 C2
Bellscroft Av RUTH G73 110 C5
Bellsdyke Rd AIRDRIE ML6 98 A3
Bellshaugh Ct KVD/HLHD G12 66 B1
Bellshaugh Gdns
KVD/HLHD G12 66 B1
Bellshaugh La KVD/HLHD G12 66 B1
Bellshaugh Pl KVD/HLHD G12 66 B1
Bellshaugh Rd KVD/HLHD G12 66 B1
Bellshill Rd BLSH ML4 135 F4
HMLTN ML3 152 D2
MTHW ML1 136 B5
UD/BTH/TAN G71 134 A2
Bellside Rd AIRDRIE ML6 119 G3
MTHW ML1 157 G1
Bellsmyre Av DMBTN G82 13 F1
Bell St AIRDRIE ML6 98 A2
BLSH ML4 117 E5
CGLE G1 3 J7
CLYDBK G81 49 G4
RNFRW PA4 63 G2
WISHAW ML2 173 G2
Belltrees Crs PSLYN/LNWD PA3 83 F5
Bell View Ct RNFRW PA4 63 G2
Bellvue Crs BLSH ML4 135 G3
Bellvue Wy CTBR ML5 97 F5
Bellwood St PLKSD/SHW G41 108 D5
Bellziehill Rd BLSH ML4 135 F2
Belmont Crs KVD/HLHD G12 66 D3
Belmont Dr BRHD/NEIL G78 142 C1
EKILS G75 165 G5
GIF/THBK G46 127 E4
RUTH G73 111 E5
Belmont La KVD/HLHD G12 66 D3
Belmont Rd BLTYR/CAMB G72 130 D4
PSLYN/LNWD PA3 84 D3
Belmont St CLYDBK G81 49 E2
CTBR ML5 73 H5
KSYTH G65 8 A1
KVD/HLHD G12 66 D3
MRYH/FIRH G20 67 E3
Belses Dr CARD/HILL/MSPK G52 86 D4
Belses Gdns
CARD/HILL/MSPK G52 86 D4
Belstane Pl UD/BTH/TAN G71 134 B4
Belstane Rd CUMB G67 45 E3
Belsyde Av DRUM G15 50 B1
Beltane St KVGV G3 2 A3
WISHAW ML2 173 H3
Beltonfoot Wy WISHAW ML2 173 G3
Beltrees Av PLK/PH/NH G53 106 B3
Beltrees Crs PLK/PH/NH G53 106 B2
Beltrees Rd PLK/PH/NH G53 106 B3
Belvidere Crs BLSH ML4 136 A3
BSHPBGS G64 54 D1
Belvidere Rd BLSH ML4 135 H3
Belvoir Pl BLTYR/CAMB G72 151 G2
Bemersyde BSHPBGS G64 55 F1
Bemersyde Av
PLKSW/MSWD G43 127 E2
Bemersyde Rd PSLYS PA2 102 C4
Ben Alder Dr PSLYS PA2 105 G3
Benalder St PTCK G11 66 B5
Benbecula EKILN G74 167 F4
Benbow Rd CLYDBK G81 48 C1
Ben Buie Wy PSLYS PA2 105 G3
Bencloich Crs KKNTL G66 4 C1
Bencloich Rd KKNTL G66 4 C2
Bencroft Dr LNPK/KPK G44 129 F2
Ben Donich Pl PLK/PH/NH G53 126 A2
Ben Edra Pl PLK/PH/NH G53 126 A3
Benford Av MTHW ML1 138 A3
Benford Knowe MTHW ML1 138 A3
Bengairn St DEN/PKHD G31 91 F2
Bengal Pl PLKSW/MSWD G43 108 B5
Bengal St PLKSW/MSWD G43 108 B5
Ben Garrisdale Pl
PLK/PH/NH G53 126 A3
Benhar Pl STPS/GTHM/RID G33 92 A2
Benholm St CAR/SHTL G32 112 A1
Ben Hope Av PSLYS PA2 105 G2
Ben Laga Pl PLK/PH/NH G53 126 A3
Ben Lawers Dr BALLOCH G68 25 F3
PSLYS PA2 105 G2
Ben Ledi Av PSLYS PA2 105 G2
Ben Ledi Crs BALLOCH G68 25 F3
Ben Loyal Av PSLYS PA2 105 G2
Ben Lui Dr PSLYS PA2 105 G3
Ben Lui Pl BALLOCH G68 25 F3
PLK/PH/NH G53 126 A3
Ben Macdui Gdns
PLK/PH/NH G53 126 A3
Ben More Dr BALLOCH G68 25 E3
PSLYS PA2 105 G2
Bennan Pl EKILS G75 177 H4
Bennan Sq GVH/MTFL G42 109 H3
Benn Av PSLY PA1 84 C5
Ben Nevis Rd PSLYS PA2 105 F3
Ben Nevis Wy BALLOCH G68 25 E3
Ben Oss Pl PLK/PH/NH G53 125 H3
Benson St CTBR ML5 96 D5
Benston Rd JNSTN PA5 101 F5
Bent Crs UD/BTH/TAN G71 134 D1
Benthall St GBLS G5 90 A5
Bentinck St KVGV G3 66 D5
Bent Rd AIRDRIE ML6 119 E1
HMLTN ML3 169 H2
Bents Rd BAIL/MDB/MHD G69 94 A4
Ben Uird Pl PLK/PH/NH G53 126 A3
Ben Vane Av PSLYS PA2 105 F3
Ben Venue Rd BALLOCH G68 25 E3
Ben Venue Wy PSLYS PA2 105 G3
Benview Rd
CRMNK/CLK/EAG G76 145 H3
Benview St MRYH/FIRH G20 67 E2
Benview Ter PSLYS PA2 105 E2
Ben Vorlich Dr
PLK/PH/NH G53 126 A3
Benvue Rd KKNTL G66 4 C3
Ben Wyvis Dr PSLYS PA2 105 F3
Berelands Crs RUTH G73 110 B5
Berelands Pl RUTH G73 110 C5
Beresford Av SCOT G14 65 F2
Berkeley St KVGV G3 88 D1
Berkeley Terrace La KVGV G3 89 E1
Berkley Dr BLTYR/CAMB G72 151 F1
Berl Av CRG/CRSL/HOU PA6 80 D3
Bernadette Crs MTHW ML1 138 A5
Bernadette St MTHW ML1 138 A4
Bernard St DMNK/BRGTN G40 90 D5
Bernard Ter DMNK/BRGTN G40 90 D5
Berneray St PPK/MIL G22 53 H4
Berridale Av LNPK/KPK G44 128 B2
Berriedale EKILS G75 164 D5
Berriedale Av
BAIL/MDB/MHD G69 93 H5
Berriedale Crs
BLTYR/CAMB G72 168 B2
Berriedale Qd WISHAW ML2 157 E5
Berryburn Rd
SPRGB/BLRNK G21 69 F2
Berryhill Dr GIF/THBK G46 127 E5
Berryhill Rd CUMB G67 26 A4
GIF/THBK G46 145 E1
Berryknowe Av
BAIL/MDB/MHD G69 58 B4
Berryknowes Av
CARD/HILL/MSPK G52 86 D4
Berryknowes La
CARD/HILL/MSPK G52 86 D4
Berryknowes Rd
CARD/HILL/MSPK G52 86 D4
GOV/IBX G51 87 E3
Bertram St HMLTN ML3 152 B5
PLKSD/SHW G41 108 D3

Bervie St GOV/IBX G51 87 G3
Berwick Crs AIRDRIE ML6 98 A4
PSLYN/LNWD PA3 81 G4
Berwick Dr
CARD/HILL/MSPK G52 86 C5
RUTH G73 111 G5
Berwick Pl CTBR ML5 117 E1
EKILN G74 167 F2
Berwick St CTBR ML5 117 E1
HMLTN ML3 152 C5
Bessemer Dr EKILS G75 178 D3
Bethal La EKILS G75 177 F4
Betula Dr CLYDBK G81 31 H3
Bevan Gv JNSTN PA5 101 F4
Beveridge Ter BLSH ML4 136 C3
Beverley Rd
PLKSW/MSWD G43 127 G1
Bevin Av CLYDBK G81 49 G2
Bideford Crs CAR/SHTL G32 113 E1
The Bield WISHAW ML2 174 B3
Biggar Rd MTHW ML1 138 D2
Biggar St DEN/PKHD G31 91 E3
Bigton St STPS/GTHM/RID G33 70 C4
Billings Rd MTHW ML1 154 A5
Bilsland Ct MRYH/FIRH G20 67 G1
Bilsland Dr MRYH/FIRH G20 67 E1
Binend Rd PLK/PH/NH G53 106 D4
Binniehill Rd BALLOCH G68 25 H3
Binnie Pl DMNK/BRGTN G40 90 B4
Binns Rd STPS/GTHM/RID G33 70 D4
Birch Av CRMNK/CLK/EAG G76 146 A4
Birch Brae HMLTN ML3 170 B4
Birch Crs CRMNK/CLK/EAG G76 145 H4
JNSTN PA5 101 H5
Birch Dr BLTYR/CAMB G72 131 H1
KKNTL G66 40 A3
Birchend Dr SPRGB/BLRNK G21 69 E4
Birchend Pl SPRGB/BLRNK G21 68 D4
Birchfield Dr SCOT G14 64 C2
Birchfield Rd HMLTN ML3 169 G2
Birchgrove CRG/CRSL/HOU PA6 81 E2
Birch Gv UD/BTH/TAN G71 115 G5
Birch Knowe BSHPBGS G64 55 E3
Birchlea Dr GIF/THBK G46 127 G3
Birchmount Ct AIRDRIE ML6 99 E1
Birch Pl BLTYR/CAMB G72 132 C3
BLTYR/CAMB G72 151 G2
Birch Qd AIRDRIE ML6 99 E2
Birch Rd CLYDBK G81 31 H4
CUMB G67 27 G2
DMBTN G82 13 E3
Birch St GBLS G5 110 A1
MTHW ML1 137 G2
Birch Vw BSDN G61 34 D3
Birchview Dr
CRMNK/CLK/EAG G76 146 A5
Birchwood Av CAR/SHTL G32 93 F5
Birchwood Dr PSLYS PA2 103 G3
Birchwood Gv CTBR ML5 95 F3
Birchwood Pl CAR/SHTL G32 93 F5
Birdsfield Dr BLTYR/CAMB G72 151 G4
Birdsfield St HMLTN ML3 152 A4
Birdston Rd KKNTL G66 21 E1
SPRGB/BLRNK G21 55 F5
Birgidale Av CSMK G45 147 E1
Birgidale Rd CSMK G45 129 E5
Birgidale Ter CSMK G45 129 E5
Birkdale EKILN G74 165 H2
Birkdale Ct UD/BTH/TAN G71 134 A5
Birkdale Crs BALLOCH G68 10 B4
Birkenburn Rd CUMB G67 11 H4
Birken Rd KKNTL G66 40 B4
Birkenshaw St DEN/PKHD G31 91 E2
Birkhall Av
CARD/HILL/MSPK G52 86 A5
RNFRW PA4 48 A4
Birkhall Dr BSDN G61 51 G1
Birkhill Av BSHPBGS G64 55 E1
Birkhill Gdns BSHPBGS G64 55 E1
Birkhill Rd HMLTN ML3 180 D1
Birkmyre Rd GOV/IBX G51 87 G3
Birkshaw Brae WISHAW ML2 173 H5
Birkshaw Pl WISHAW ML2 173 H5
Birkwood Pl NMRNS G77 161 G3
Birkwood St
DMNK/BRGTN G40 111 E2
Birmingham Rd RNFRW PA4 63 E5
Birnam Av BSHPBGS G64 55 E1
Birnam Crs BSDN G61 35 E3
Birnam Pl HMLTN ML3 168 D2
NMRNS G77 162 C1
Birnam Rd DEN/PKHD G31 111 G1
Birness Dr PLKSW/MSWD G43 108 C5
Birnie Ct SPRGB/BLRNK G21 69 F3
Birnie Rd SPRGB/BLRNK G21 69 F2
Birnock Av RNFRW PA4 63 H5
Birrell Rd MLNGV G62 16 D2
Birrens Rd MTHW ML1 154 B2
Birsay Rd PPK/MIL G22 53 G4
Bishopdale EKILN G74 165 H2
Bishop Gdns BSHPBGS G64 54 B1
HMLTN ML3 181 E1
Bishop La CGLW G2 2 B5
Bishopmill Pl SPRGB/BLRNK G21 69 F2
Bishops Ga EKILN G74 164 B2
Bishopsgate Rd
SPRGB/BLRNK G21 54 B4
Bishops Pk EKILN G74 164 A2
Bissett Crs CLYDBK G81 31 F2
Blackadder Pl EKILS G75 176 C1
Blackbog Rd CUMB G67 45 F5
Blackbraes Rd EKILN G74 167 E1
Blackburn Crs DMBTN G82 12 C3
KKNTL G66 22 A5
Blackburn Sq BRHD/NEIL G78 142 C1
Blackburn St GOV/IBX G51 88 D3
Blackbyres Ct BRHD/NEIL G78 124 C3
Blackbyres Rd BRHD/NEIL G78 124 C2
Blackcraig Av DRUM G15 33 F5
Blackcroft Av AIRDRIE ML6 99 F4
Blackcroft Gdns CAR/SHTL G32 93 E5
Blackcroft Rd CAR/SHTL G32 93 E5
Blackdyke Rd KKNTL G66 21 G4
Blackfarm Rd NMRNS G77 162 A1
Blackfaulds Rd RUTH G73 110 B4
Blackford Rd PSLYS PA2 104 D1
Blackfriars St CGLE G1 3 H6
Blackhall La PSLY PA1 104 C1
Blackhall St PSLY PA1 104 C1
Blackhill Pl STPS/GTHM/RID G33 69 G4
Blackhill Rd SMSTN G23 53 E1
Blackhouse Av NMRNS G77 162 A1
Blackhouse Gdns NMRNS G77 162 A1
Blackhouse Rd NMRNS G77 162 A1
Blackie St KVGV G3 88 C1
Blacklands Pl KKNTL G66 40 C4
Blacklands Rd EKILN G74 166 A4
Blacklaw Dr EKILN G74 167 E4
Blacklaw La PSLYN/LNWD PA3 84 B4
Blackmoor Pl MTHW ML1 137 F4
Blackmoss Dr BLSH ML4 135 G3
Blackness St CTBR ML5 117 E1
Blackstone Av PLK/PH/NH G53 106 D4
Blackstone Crs
PLK/PH/NH G53 106 D3
Blackstone Rd
PSLYN/LNWD PA3 83 F1
Blackstoun Av
PSLYN/LNWD PA3 82 A4
Blackstoun Ov
PSLYN/LNWD PA3 83 G4
Blackstoun Rd
PSLYN/LNWD PA3 83 G4
Black St AIRDRIE ML6 76 C5
COWCAD G4 3 J2
Blackswell La HMLTN ML3 170 C2
Blackthorn Av KKNTL G66 39 F3
Blackthorn Gv KKNTL G66 39 G3
Blackthorn Rd CUMB G67 27 G1
UD/BTH/TAN G71 115 H4
Blackthorn St PPK/MIL G22 68 B1
Blackwood EKILS G75 178 A3
Blackwood Av NMRNS G77 162 A2
PSLYN/LNWD PA3 81 H5
Blackwood Gdns MTHW ML1 154 B1
Blackwood Rd BALLOCH G68 24 C4
MLNGV G62 16 D2
Blackwoods Crs BLSH ML4 136 B3
Blackwood St BRHD/NEIL G78 123 H5
KNTSWD G13 51 F4
Blackwood Ter JNSTN PA5 121 E1
Bladda La PSLY PA1 84 C5
Blades Ct BAIL/MDB/MHD G69 59 F5
Bladnoch Dr DRUM G15 50 D1
Blaeloch Av CSMK G45 146 D1
Blaeloch Dr CSMK G45 146 D1
Blaeloch Ter CSMK G45 146 C1
Blaeshill Rd EKILS G75 164 D5
Blairatholl Av PTCK G11 65 H3
Blairatholl Crs NMRNS G77 162 C1
Blairatholl Gdns PTCK G11 65 H3
Blair Atholl Ga NMRNS G77 162 C1
Blair Atholl Gv HMLTN ML3 169 F1
Blair Atholl Wynd MTHW ML1 137 G5
Blairbeth Dr LNPK/KPK G44 109 G5
Blairbeth Rd RUTH G73 130 A2
Blairbeth Ter RUTH G73 130 B2
Blairbuie Dr MRYH/FIRH G20 52 B4
Blair Crs BAIL/MDB/MHD G69 113 H1
Blairdardie Rd DRUM G15 50 C2
Blairdenan Av
BAIL/MDB/MHD G69 42 A5
Blairdenon Dr BALLOCH G68 25 G2
Blair Dr KKNTL G66 5 F5
Blair Gdns BSHPBGS G64 19 F4
NMRNS G77 143 G5
Blairgowrie Rd
CARD/HILL/MSPK G52 86 D5
Blairhall Av PLKSD/SHW G41 109 E4
Blairhill Av KKNTL G66 40 D2
Blairhill Pl CTBR ML5 96 B2
Blairhill St CTBR ML5 96 C2
Blairholm Dr BLSH ML4 136 A4
Blairlinn Rd CUMB G67 45 F2
Blair Linn Vw CUMB G67 45 F2
Blairlogie St
STPS/GTHM/RID G33 70 C5
Blairmore Av PSLY PA1 85 F4
Blairpark Av CTBR ML5 96 B1
Blair Pth MTHW ML1 155 E5
Blair Rd CTBR ML5 96 B2
PSLY PA1 85 H3
Blairston Av UD/BTH/TAN G71 152 C1
Blairston Gdns
UD/BTH/TAN G71 152 C1
Blair St CAR/SHTL G32 92 A4
Blairtum Dr RUTH G73 130 A2
Blairtummock Rd
STPS/GTHM/RID G33 92 D1
Blake Rd CUMB G67 26 C3
Blane Dr MLNGV G62 17 F2
Blane St CTBR ML5 96 D1
Blaneview STPS/GTHM/RID G33 71 E2
Blantyre Crs CLYDBK G81 31 F1
Blantyre Dr BSHPTN PA7 28 D4
Blantyre Farm Rd
BLTYR/CAMB G72 133 F5
UD/BTH/TAN G71 133 F1
Blantyre Gdns BALLOCH G68 24 C4
Blantyre Mill Rd
UD/BTH/TAN G71 134 B5
Blantyre Rd UD/BTH/TAN G71 134 B5
Blantyre St CTBR ML5 96 B5
KVGV G3 66 C5
Blaven Ct BAIL/MDB/MHD G69 94 B5
Blawarthill St SCOT G14 64 A1
Bleachfield MLNGV G62 16 D2
Bleasdale Ct CLYDBK G81 49 E1
Blenheim Av EKILS G75 177 H1
STPS/GTHM/RID G33 57 E5
Blenheim Ct KSYTH G65 8 B1
PSLY PA1 84 A4
Blochairn Rd SPRGB/BLRNK G21 68 D5
Bluebell Gdns CSMK G45 129 H5
MTHW ML1 136 B5
Bluebell Wy AIRDRIE ML6 76 A4
KKNTL G66 4 D3
Bluevale St DEN/PKHD G31 90 D3
Blythe Pl STPS/GTHM/RID G33 93 F2
Blyth Rd STPS/GTHM/RID G33 93 F3
Blythswood Av RNFRW PA4 63 G2
Blythswood Dr
PSLYN/LNWD PA3 84 A3
Blythswood Rd RNFRW PA4 63 G1
Blythswood Sq CGLW G2 2 C4
Blythswood St CGLW G2 2 D3
The Boardwalk EKILS G75 178 D2
Bobbins Ga PSLY PA1 103 G1
Boclair Av BSDN G61 34 C4
Boclair Crs BSDN G61 34 D4
BSHPBGS G64 54 D2
Boclair Rd BSDN G61 34 D3
BSHPBGS G64 54 D1
Boclair St KNTSWD G13 51 F3
Bodden Sq MTHW ML1 119 F5
Boden Qd MTHW ML1 136 B5
Boden St DMNK/BRGTN G40 90 D5
Bodmin Gdns
BAIL/MDB/MHD G69 42 A5
Bogany Ter CSMK G45 129 F5
Bogbain Rd ESTRH G34 93 H1
Boggknowe UD/BTH/TAN G71 114 C4
Boghall Rd UD/BTH/TAN G71 113 H1
Boghall St STPS/GTHM/RID G33 70 C5
Boghead Av DMBTN G82 13 G4
Boghead Rd DMBTN G82 13 F3
KKNTL G66 39 F3
SPRGB/BLRNK G21 68 D1
Bogleshole Rd
BLTYR/CAMB G72 111 H5
Bogmoor Pl GOV/IBX G51 64 D5
Bogmoor Rd GOV/IBX G51 86 D1
Bogside Rd KSYTH G65 8 B3
STPS/GTHM/RID G33 56 B5
Bogside St DMNK/BRGTN G40 91 E5
Bogs Vw BLSH ML4 135 G4
Bogton Av LNPK/KPK G44 128 A3
Bogton Avenue La
LNPK/KPK G44 128 A3
Boleyn Rd PLKSD/SHW G41 108 D2
Bolingbroke EKILN G74 167 F1
Bolivar Ter GVH/MTFL G42 109 H4
Bolton Dr GVH/MTFL G42 109 F4
Bolton Ter KKNTL G66 4 C2
Bon Accord Rd
CRMNK/CLK/EAG G76 146 A4
Bon Accord Sq CLYDBK G81 49 E3
Bonar Crs BRWEIR PA11 79 H4
Bonar La BRWEIR PA11 79 H4
Bonawe St MRYH/FIRH G20 67 E3
Bonds Dr WISHAW ML2 158 C4
Bo'ness Rd AIRDRIE ML6 118 D4
MTHW ML1 137 G1
Boness St DMNK/BRGTN G40 91 E5
Bonhill Rd DMBTN G82 13 F3
Bonhill St PPK/MIL G22 67 G3
Bonkle Gdns WISHAW ML2 158 C5
Bonkle Rd WISHAW ML2 158 C5
Bonnar St DMNK/BRGTN G40 110 D1
Bonnaughton Rd BSDN G61 33 G2
Bonnyholm Av
PLK/PH/NH G53 106 B1
Bonnyrigg Dr
PLKSW/MSWD G43 126 D2
Bontine Av DMBTN G82 12 C4
Bonyton Av KNTSWD G13 50 A5
Boon Dr DRUM G15 50 C1
Boquhanran Rd CLYDBK G81 31 H5
Borden La KNTSWD G13 65 F1
Borden Rd KNTSWD G13 65 F1
Border Wy KKNTL G66 21 G5
Boreland Dr HMLTN ML3 168 D3
KNTSWD G13 50 C4
Boreland Pl KNTSWD G13 50 C5
Bore Rd AIRDRIE ML6 98 C1
Borgie Crs BLTYR/CAMB G72 131 F2
Borland Rd BSDN G61 34 D5
Borron St COWCAD G4 67 H3
Borrowdale EKILS G75 177 E3
Borthwick Dr EKILS G75 176 C1
Borthwick St
STPS/GTHM/RID G33 70 C5
Bosfield Cnr EKILN G74 166 C2
Bosfield Pl EKILN G74 166 C2
Bosfield Rd EKILN G74 166 B2
Boswell Ct PLKSD/SHW G41 109 E5
Boswell Dr BLTYR/CAMB G72 151 G3
Boswell Pk EKILN G74 167 F1
Boswell Sq
CARD/HILL/MSPK G52 86 A2
Bosworth Rd EKILN G74 167 F1
Botanic Crs MRYH/FIRH G20 66 C2
Bothlin Dr STPS/GTHM/RID G33 57 E5
Bothlyn Av KKNTL G66 40 B1
Bothlyn Crs
BAIL/MDB/MHD G69 58 D4
Bothlyn Rd BAIL/MDB/MHD G69 58 C3
Bothwellhaugh Qd BLSH ML4 135 G4
Bothwellhaugh Rd BLSH ML4 153 G1
Bothwell La CGLW G2 2 C5
KVD/HLHD G12 66 D4
Bothwellpark Pl
UD/BTH/TAN G71 135 E1
Bothwellpark Rd
UD/BTH/TAN G71 134 C5
Bothwell Pl CTBR ML5 96 C2
PSLYS PA2 102 D4
Bothwell Rd HMLTN ML3 152 D3
UD/BTH/TAN G71 134 A3
Bothwell St BLTYR/CAMB G72 130 D1
CGLW G2 2 C5
HMLTN ML3 152 D5
Bourne Ct RNFRW PA4 48 A4
Bourne Crs RNFRW PA4 48 A4
Bourne St HMLTN ML3 170 C1
Bourock Sq BRHD/NEIL G78 142 C1
Bourtree Rd HMLTN ML3 168 D4
Bouverie St RUTH G73 110 C4
SCOT G14 49 H5
Bowden Dr
CARD/HILL/MSPK G52 86 C3
Bowden Pk EKILS G75 165 H5
Bower St KVD/HLHD G12 66 D3
Bowerwalls St BRHD/NEIL G78 124 D3
Bowes Crs BAIL/MDB/MHD G69 93 G5
Bowfield Av
CARD/HILL/MSPK G52 86 A3
Bowfield Crs
CARD/HILL/MSPK G52 86 A3
Bowfield Dr
CARD/HILL/MSPK G52 86 A3
Bowfield Pl
CARD/HILL/MSPK G52 86 A3
Bowfield Rd HWWD PA9 120 A4
Bowhousebrae Rd AIRDRIE ML6 99 F4
Bowhouse Dr CSMK G45 129 H3
Bowhouse Gdns CSMK G45 129 H2
Bowhouse Rd AIRDRIE ML6 99 G5
Bowie St DMBTN G82 12 D4
Bowling Green La SCOT G14 65 E3
Bowling Green Rd
BAIL/MDB/MHD G69 58 C3
CAR/SHTL G32 93 E5
LNPK/KPK G44 128 B2
SCOT G14 65 E3
Bowling Green St BLSH ML4 136 A2
Bowling Green Vw
BLTYR/CAMB G72 132 C3
Bowling St CTBR ML5 96 C2
Bowman St GVH/MTFL G42 109 F2
Bowmont Pl EKILS G75 176 C1
Bowmont Ter KVD/HLHD G12 66 B3
Bowmore Gdns RUTH G73 130 D4
UD/BTH/TAN G71 114 D4
Bowmore Rd
CARD/HILL/MSPK G52 87 F4
Bowmount Gdns
KVD/HLHD G12 66 B3
Bowyer Vennel BLSH ML4 135 G1
Boyd Dr MTHW ML1 154 A3
Boydstone Pl GIF/THBK G46 126 C2
Boydstone Rd
PLKSW/MSWD G43 126 B1
Boyd St GVH/MTFL G42 109 G3
Boylestone Rd BRHD/NEIL G78 123 H3
Boyle St CLYDBK G81 49 G3
Boyndie St ESTRH G34 94 A1
Brabloch Crs PSLYN/LNWD PA3 84 C3
Bracadale Dr
BAIL/MDB/MHD G69 94 C5
Bracadale Gdns
BAIL/MDB/MHD G69 94 C5
Bracadale Gv
BAIL/MDB/MHD G69 94 B5
Bracadale Rd
BAIL/MDB/MHD G69 94 B5
Brackenbrae Av BSHPBGS G64 54 B1
Brackenbrae Rd BSHPBGS G64 54 C2
Brackendene
CRG/CRSL/HOU PA6 81 E2
Brackenhill Dr HMLTN ML3 180 B1
Brackenhurst St DMBTN G82 13 H1
Brackenrig Crs
CRMNK/CLK/EAG G76 163 F5
Brackenrig Rd GIF/THBK G46 126 B5
Bracken St MTHW ML1 137 F4
PPK/MIL G22 53 G5
Bracken Ter UD/BTH/TAN G71 134 B4
Brackla Av KNTSWD G13 49 H3
Braco Av AIRDRIE ML6 119 E3
Bradan Av KNTSWD G13 49 H4
Bradda Av RUTH G73 130 B3
Bradfield Av KVD/HLHD G12 66 B1
Bradshaw Crs HMLTN ML3 168 D2
Brady Crs BAIL/MDB/MHD G69 42 B5
Braedale Av AIRDRIE ML6 98 C2
MTHW ML1 154 A4
Braedale Crs WISHAW ML2 158 C5
Braedale Pl WISHAW ML2 158 D5
Braeface Rd CUMB G67 26 A3
Braefield Dr GIF/THBK G46 126 D4
Braefoot Av MLNGV G62 17 E5
Braefoot Crs PSLYS PA2 104 C4
Braehead BLTYR/CAMB G72 151 G4
Braehead Av BRHD/NEIL G78 141 E3
CLYDBK G81 31 H1
CTBR ML5 116 A1
MLNGV G62 16 D4
Braehead Crs CLYDBK G81 31 H1
Braehead Dr BLSH ML4 135 G3
Braehead Pl BLSH ML4 135 G3
Braehead Qd BRHD/NEIL G78 141 E3
MTHW ML1 138 A3
Braehead Rd CLYDBK G81 31 H1
CUMB G67 26 D2
EKILN G74 164 B2
PSLYS PA2 122 D2
Braehead St GBLS G5 110 A1
KKNTL G66 21 E4
Braemar Av CLYDBK G81 31 G4
Braemar Ct GIF/THBK G46 127 H3
Braemar Crs BSDN G61 51 G1
PSLYS PA2 104 C3
Braemar Dr JNSTN PA5 102 A3
Braemar Rd RNFRW PA4 48 A4
RUTH G73 130 C4
Braemar St GVH/MTFL G42 109 E5
HMLTN ML3 152 C4
Braemar Vw CLYDBK G81 31 G3
Braemore Gdns PPK/MIL G22 68 A2
Braemount Av PSLYS PA2 122 D1
Braes Av CLYDBK G81 49 G3
Braesburn Pl CUMB G67 11 H4
Braesburn Rd CUMB G67 11 H4
Braeside Av
BAIL/MDB/MHD G69 59 E1
MLNGV G62 17 E5
RUTH G73 111 F5
Braeside Crs
BAIL/MDB/MHD G69 95 E4
BRHD/NEIL G78 142 D1
Braeside Dr BRHD/NEIL G78 142 C1
DMBTN G82 13 G2
Braeside Gdns HMLTN ML3 170 B5
Braeside Pl BLTYR/CAMB G72 131 G3
Braeside Rd MTHW ML1 138 A3
Braeside St MRYH/FIRH G20 67 E3
Braes O' Yetts KKNTL G66 22 A5
Braeview Av PSLYS PA2 103 G5
Braeview Dr PSLYS PA2 103 G5
Braeview Gdns PSLYS PA2 103 G5
Braeview Pl EKILN G74 166 D1
Braeview Rd PSLYS PA2 103 G5
Braid Av MTHW ML1 156 B1
Braidbar Farm Rd
GIF/THBK G46 127 G4
Braidbar Rd GIF/THBK G46 127 F4
Braidcraft Rd PLK/PH/NH G53 106 D3
Braidcraft Ter PLK/PH/NH G53 107 E3
Braidfauld Gdns CAR/SHTL G32 112 A1
Braidfauld Pl CAR/SHTL G32 112 A2
Braidfauld St CAR/SHTL G32 112 A2
Braidfield Gv CLYDBK G81 32 A3
Braidfield Rd CLYDBK G81 32 B3
Braidholm Crs GIF/THBK G46 127 F3
Braidholm Rd GIF/THBK G46 127 G3
Braidhurst St MTHW ML1 154 D2
Braidley Crs EKILS G75 178 B3
Braidpark Dr GIF/THBK G46 127 G4
Braids Dr PLK/PH/NH G53 106 A3
Braid Sq COWCAD G4 67 F4
Braid's Rd PSLYS PA2 104 B3
Braid St COWCAD G4 67 F4
Braidwood Pl PSLYN/LNWD PA3 81 G5
Braidwood St WISHAW ML2 157 F3
Bramah Av EKILS G75 178 C1
Bramble Ct KKNTL G66 4 A2
Brambling Ct WISHAW ML2 173 G4
Bramley Pl AIRDRIE ML6 99 F3
KKNTL G66 40 B4
Brampton EKILS G75 177 E2
Branchalfield Dr WISHAW ML2 174 D1
Branchalmuir Crs
WISHAW ML2 158 A4
Branchal Rd WISHAW ML2 157 G5
Branchock Av
BLTYR/CAMB G72 132 A3
Brancumhall Rd EKILN G74 167 G2
Brandon Dr BSDN G61 34 B1
Brandon Gdns
BLTYR/CAMB G72 130 D2
Brandon Pl BLSH ML4 135 F4
Brandon St DEN/PKHD G31 90 C3
HMLTN ML3 170 B2
MTHW ML1 154 D4
Brandon Wy CTBR ML5 96 A5
Brand Pl GOV/IBX G51 88 B3
Brand St GOV/IBX G51 88 C3
Brankholm Brae HMLTN ML3 168 C1
Branklyn Cl KNTSWD G13 51 E5
Branklyn Crs KNTSWD G13 51 E5
Branklyn Gv KNTSWD G13 51 E5
Branklyn Pl KNTSWD G13 51 E5
Brannock Av MTHW ML1 138 A3
Brannock Pl MTHW ML1 138 A3
Brannock Rd MTHW ML1 138 A4
Brassey St MRYH/FIRH G20 52 D5
Breadalbane Crs MTHW ML1 154 C1
Breadalbane Gdns RUTH G73 130 C3
Breadalbane St KVGV G3 89 E1
Breadie Dr MLNGV G62 16 D5
Breamish Pl EKILS G75 177 E2
Bream Pl CRG/CRSL/HOU PA6 81 E3
Brechin Rd BSHPBGS G64 55 F2
Brechin St KVGV G3 88 D1
Breck Av PSLYS PA2 102 C5
Brediland Rd PSLYN/LNWD PA3 81 H5
PSLYS PA2 102 D5
Bredin Wy MTHW ML1 154 A2
Bredisholm Crs
UD/BTH/TAN G71 115 H3
Bredisholm Dr
BAIL/MDB/MHD G69 94 B5
Bredisholm Rd
BAIL/MDB/MHD G69 94 B5
Bredisholm Ter
BAIL/MDB/MHD G69 94 B5
Brendon Av EKILS G75 177 F4
Brenfield Av LNPK/KPK G44 128 A3
Brenfield Dr LNPK/KPK G44 128 A3
Brenfield Rd LNPK/KPK G44 128 A3
Brent Ct EKILN G74 166 B2
Brent Crs CRG/CRSL/HOU PA6 80 D3
Brent Dr GIF/THBK G46 126 C2
Brent Gdns GIF/THBK G46 126 C2
Brent Rd EKILN G74 166 B2
GIF/THBK G46 126 D2
Brent Wy GIF/THBK G46 126 C2
Brentwood Av
PLK/PH/NH G53 125 F3
Brentwood Dr PLK/PH/NH G53 125 F3
Brentwood Sq
PLK/PH/NH G53 125 G3
Brereton St GVH/MTFL G42 109 H3
Bressay EKILN G74 166 B2
Bressay Rd
STPS/GTHM/RID G33 93 F3
Breval Crs CLYDBK G81 31 H1
Brewery St JNSTN PA5 101 G3
Brewster Av PSLYN/LNWD PA3 84 D2
Briar Bank KKNTL G66 5 F5
Briarcroft Dr SPRGB/BLRNK G21 55 G5
Briarcroft Pl
STPS/GTHM/RID G33 55 H5
Briarcroft Rd
SPRGB/BLRNK G21 55 G5
Briar Dr CLYDBK G81 32 A4
Briar Gdns PLKSW/MSWD G43 127 G2
Briar Gv PLKSW/MSWD G43 127 G2
Briarlea Dr GIF/THBK G46 127 F3
Briar Neuk BSHPBGS G64 55 E3
Briar Rd KKNTL G66 21 H5
PLKSW/MSWD G43 127 G2
Briar Wk KKNTL G66 22 A5
Briarwell La MLNGV G62 17 F4
Briarwell Rd MLNGV G62 17 F4
Briarwood Ct CAR/SHTL G32 113 F2
Briarwood Rd WISHAW ML2 173 F1
Brick La PSLY PA1 84 C4
Bridgebar St BRHD/NEIL G78 124 D3
Bridgeburn Dr
BAIL/MDB/MHD G69 58 D1
Bridgeford Av BLSH ML4 117 F5
Bridgegait MLNGV G62 17 G5
Bridge-Gate CGLE G1 89 H3
Bridgegate Pth CGLE G1 90 A3
Bridgend Ct BALLOCH G68 11 H1
Bridgend Crs
BAIL/MDB/MHD G69 58 D1
Bridgend Pl
BAIL/MDB/MHD G69 58 D1
Bridge of Weir Rd
CRG/CRSL/HOU PA6 80 B2
JNSTN PA5 100 C1
PSLYN/LNWD PA3 82 A4
Bridge St BLTYR/CAMB G72 131 F1
CLYDBK G81 31 F5
DMBTN G82 12 D4
GBLS G5 89 G3
HMLTN ML3 169 H3
PSLY PA1 84 C5
PSLYN/LNWD PA3 82 B4
WISHAW ML2 173 F2
Bridgeway Ct KKNTL G66 40 C1
Bridgeway Rd KKNTL G66 40 C1
Bridgeway Ter KKNTL G66 40 C1
Bridie Ter EKILN G74 167 F1
Brierie Av CRG/CRSL/HOU PA6 80 C2
Brierie Gdns
CRG/CRSL/HOU PA6 80 C3
Brierie Hill Ct
CRG/CRSL/HOU PA6 80 C3
Brierie-Hill Gv
CRG/CRSL/HOU PA6 80 C3
Brierie-Hill Rd
CRG/CRSL/HOU PA6 80 B3
Brierie La CRG/CRSL/HOU PA6 80 B3
Brigbrae Av BLSH ML4 136 B4
Brigham Pl SMSTN G23 52 D3
Brighton Pl GOV/IBX G51 88 A3
Brighton St GOV/IBX G51 88 A3
Brightside Av
UD/BTH/TAN G71 134 A2
Brig O'lea Ter BRHD/NEIL G78 140 D4
Brigside Gdns HMLTN ML3 170 D3
Brisbane Ct GIF/THBK G46 127 G4
Brisbane Rd BSHPTN PA7 29 E5
Brisbane St CLYDBK G81 31 E4
LNPK/KPK G44 109 F5
Brisbane Ter EKILS G75 177 H1
Brittain Wy BLSH ML4 118 A5
Broadford St COWCAD G4 67 H4
Broadholm St PPK/MIL G22 53 H5
Broadleys Av BSHPBGS G64 54 C1
Broadlie Ct BRHD/NEIL G78 141 E3
Broadlie Dr KNTSWD G13 50 B5
Broadlie Rd BRHD/NEIL G78 140 D3
Broadloan RNFRW PA4 63 F4
Broadmoss Av NMRNS G77 162 D1
Broad Sq BLTYR/CAMB G72 151 F2
Broad St DMNK/BRGTN G40 90 C4
The Broad Wy WISHAW ML2 173 F1
Broadwood Dr LNPK/KPK G44 128 C1
Brockburn Crs PLK/PH/NH G53 106 C4
Brockburn Rd PLK/PH/NH G53 106 C3

Brockburn Ter
 PLK/PH/NH G53....106 D4
Brocklinn Pk *EKILS* G75....176 D1
Brock Ov *PLK/PH/NH* G53....125 H1
Brock Pl *PLK/PH/NH* G53....106 D1
Brock Rd *PLK/PH/NH* G53....125 G1
Brock Ter *PLK/PH/NH* G53....125 G1
Brockville St *CAR/SHTL* G32....32 A3
Brodick Av *MTHW* ML1....154 A3
Brodick Dr *EKILN* G74....166 A2
Brodick Pl *NMRNS* G77....160 D2
Brodick St *SPRGB/BLRNK* G21....68 D5
Brodie Gdns
 BAIL/MDB/MHD G69....94 B3
Brodie Park Av *PLYS* G52....104 B2
Brodie Park Crs *PSLYS* PA2....104 B2
Brodie Park Gdns *PSLYS* PA2....104 B2
Brodie Pl *EKILN* G74....166 A2
Brodie Rd *SPRGB/BLRNK* G21....55 F4
Brogan Crs *MTHW* ML1....154 A3
Bron Wy *CUMB* G67....26 C4
Brookfield Av
 STPS/GTHM/RID G33....55 G4
Brookfield Avenue Ga
 STPS/GTHM/RID G33....55 G4
Brookfield Cnr
 STPS/GTHM/RID G33....55 G4
Brookfield Ct
 STPS/GTHM/RID G33....55 H4
Brookfield Gdns
 STPS/GTHM/RID G33....55 G4
Brookfield Rd
 STPS/GTHM/RID G33....55 G4
Brooklands Av
 UD/BTH/TAN G71....114 D5
Brooklea Dr *GIF/THBK* G46....127 F2
Brooklime Dr *EKILN* G74....165 H1
Brooklime Gdns *EKILN* G74....165 H1
Brookside St *DMNK/BRGTN* G40....90 D4
Brook St *CLYDBK* G81....31 G4
 DMNK/BRGTN G40....90 C4
Broom Av *ERSK* PA8....47 G2
Broomburn Dr *NMRNS* G77....162 A1
Broom Crs *BRHD/NEIL* G78....123 H2
 EKILS G75....178 A5
Broomcroft Rd *NMRNS* G77....144 D4
Broom Dr *CLYDBK* G81....31 H4
Broomfield *CRG/CRSL/HOU* PA6....81 F4
Broomfield Av
 BLTYR/CAMB G72....111 G5
 NMRNS G77....162 A2
Broomfield La
 SPRGB/BLRNK G21....68 C1
Broomfield Pl
 SPRGB/BLRNK G21....68 C1
Broomfield Rd *SPRGB/BLRNK* G21....144 D4
 SPRGB/BLRNK G21....68 C2
Broomfield Ter *AIRDRIE* ML6....98 C2
Broomfield Ter
 UD/BTH/TAN G71....115 E3
Broom Gdns *KKNTL* G66....39 G2
Broomhill Av *CAR/SHTL* G32....112 C1
 NMRNS G77....162 A1
 PTCK G11....65 G3
Broomhill Crs *BLSH* ML4....135 G4
 ERSK PA8....47 G4
Broomhill Dr *DMBTN* G82....13 G4
 PTCK G11....65 G3
 RUTH G73....130 A2
Broomhill Farm Ms *KKNTL* G66....21 G4
Broomhill Gdns *NMRNS* G77....162 A1
 PTCK G11....65 G3
Broomhill La *PTCK* G11....65 G3
Broomhill Pl *PTCK* G11....65 G3
Broomhill Rd *PTCK* G11....65 G4
Broomieknowe Av *RUTH* G73....130 A1
Broomieknowe Gdns
 RUTH G73....129 H1
Broomieknowe Rd *RUTH* G73....130 A1
Broomielaw *KVGV* G3....2 D7
Broomknoll St *AIRDRIE* ML6....98 B2
Broomknowe *BALLOCH* G68....25 F3
Broomknowes Rd
 SPRGB/BLRNK G21....68 C2
Broomlands Av *ERSK* PA8....48 A3
Broomlands Crs *ERSK* PA8....48 A3
Broomlands Gdns *ERSK* PA8....48 A3
Broomlands Rd *CUMB* G67....26 C5
Broomlands St *PSLY* PA1....83 H5
Broomlands Wy *ERSK* PA8....48 B3
Broomlea Crs *RNFRW* PA4....47 H4
Broomlee Rd *CUMB* G67....44 C1
Bromley Dr *GIF/THBK* G46....145 F1
Bromley La *GIF/THBK* G46....145 F1
Broom Pk *DEN/PKHD* G31....90 C2
Broompark Av
 BLTYR/CAMB G72....151 F4
Broompark Circ *DEN/PKHD* G31....90 C1
Broompark Crs *AIRDRIE* ML6....98 C2
Broompark Dr *DEN/PKHD* G31....90 C2
 NMRNS G77....144 C4
 RNFRW PA4....48 A4
Broompark La *DEN/PKHD* G31....90 C2
Broompark Rd
 BLTYR/CAMB G72....151 F3
 WISHAW ML2....173 E1
Broom Pl *BRWEIR* PA11....79 H3
 MTHW ML1....137 H5
Broom Rd *CUMB* G67....26 B5
 NMRNS G77....144 D4
 PLKSW/MSWD G43....127 G2
Broom Rd East *NMRNS* G77....162 C2
Broomside St *MTHW* ML1....172 A4
Broomstone Av *NMRNS* G77....162 A2
Broom Ter *JNSTN* PA5....101 G5
Broomton Rd
 SPRGB/BLRNK G21....55 F4
Broomvale Dr *NMRNS* G77....144 D4
Broomward Dr *JNSTN* PA5....102 A1
Brora Crs *HMLTN* ML3....169 E5
Brora Dr *BSDN* G61....34 D5
 GIF/THBK G46....127 G5
 RNFRW PA4....63 H3
Brora Gdns *BSHPBGS* G64....55 F1
Brora Rd *BSHPBGS* G64....55 F1
Brora St *STPS/GTHM/RID* G33....69 G5
Broughton *EKILS* G75....178 B4
Broughton Dr *SMSTN* G23....52 D3
Broughton Gdns *SMSTN* G23....52 D2

Broughton Pl *CTBR* ML5....117 E1
 HMLTN ML3....169 F2
Brougham St *SMSTN* G23....52 D3
Brouster Hl *EKILN* G74....166 B4
Brouster Pl *EKILN* G74....166 B4
Brown Av *CLYDBK* G81....49 G3
 DMBTN G82....13 E5
Brownhill Rd *GIF/THBK* G46....127 E3
Brownhill Vw *WISHAW* ML2....159 E4
Brownieside Pl *AIRDRIE* ML6....77 H3
Brownlie St *GVH/MTFL* G42....109 F4
Brown Pl *BLTYR/CAMB* G72....131 F1
Brown Rd *CUMB* G67....26 B3
Brownsburn Rd *AIRDRIE* ML6....98 C5
Brownsdale Rd *RUTH* G73....110 C5
Brownsfield Crs *RNFRW* PA4....61 C1
Brownsfield Rd *RNFRW* PA4....61 C1
Brownshill Av *CTBR* ML5....96 C5
Brownside Av
 BLTYR/CAMB G72....130 D2
 BRHD/NEIL G78....123 H2
Brownside Crs *BRHD/NEIL* G78....123 H2
 KNTSWD G13....
Brownside Dr *BRHD/NEIL* G78....123 H2
 KNTSWD G13....
Brownside Gv *BRHD/NEIL* G78....123 H2
Brownside Rd *RUTH* G73....130 C2
Brownsland Ct
 BAIL/MDB/MHD G69....59 F5
Brown's La *PSLY* PA1....84 B5
Brown St *CGLW* G2....2 C6
 CTBR ML5....96 D4
 MTHW ML1....155 E2
 PLKSD/SHW G41....88 D5
 PSLY PA1....83 H4
 RNFRW PA4....63 F3
 WISHAW ML2....175 F1
Browside Av *PSLYS* PA2....103 H5
Bruce Av *JNSTN* PA5....121 F4
 MTHW ML1....154 C3
 PSLYN/LNWD PA3....84 D2
Brucefield Pl *ESTRH* G34....94 C1
Brucehill Rd *DMBTN* G82....12 B4
Bruce Pl *EKILS* G75....178 C1
Bruce Rd *BSHPTN* PA7....29 E4
 MTHW ML1....137 C5
 PLKSD/SHW G41....88 D5
 PSLYN/LNWD PA3....84 C2
 RNFRW PA4....62 D5
Bruce St *AIRDRIE* ML6....77 H4
 BLSH ML4....136 A1
 CLYDBK G81....49 G2
 CTBR ML5....97 E1
 DMBTN G82....13 F5
Bruce Ter *BLTYR/CAMB* G72....151 H1
 EKILS G75....178 C1
Brunel Wy *EKILS* G75....166 C5
Brunstane Rd *ESTRH* G34....71 H5
Brunswick La *CGLE* G1....3 G6
Brunswick St *CGLE* G1....3 G6
Brunton St *LNPK/KPK* G44....128 B2
Bruntsfield Av *PLK/PH/NH* G53....125 G4
Bruntsfield Gdns
 PLK/PH/NH G53....125 G4
Bryan St *HMLTN* ML3....169 E2
Bryce Pl *EKILS* G75....177 H2
Brydson Pl *PSLYN/LNWD* PA3....84 A4
Bryon Ct *UD/BTH/TAN* G71....134 C5
Bryson Ct *HMLTN* ML3....180 D1
Bryson St *CLYDBK* G81....32 C1
Buccleuch Av
 CARD/HILL/MSPK G52....85 H1
 CRMNK/CLK/EAG G76....145 G5
Buccleuch Dr *BSDN* G61....34 B1
Buccleuch La *COWCAD* G4....2 B2
Buccleuch St *KVGV* G3....2 B2
Buchanan Av *BSHPTN* PA7....29 E4
Buchanan Crs *BSHPBGS* G64....55 F3
 HMLTN ML3....169 G3
Buchanan Dr
 BLTYR/CAMB G72....130 D1
 BSDN G61....34 D4
 BSHPBGS G64....55 F3
 KKNTL G66....40 A4
 NMRNS G77....144 B5
 RUTH G73....130 A1
Buchanan Gv
 BAIL/MDB/MHD G69....94 A4
Buchanan Pl *BSHPBGS* G64....19 F4
Buchanan St *AIRDRIE* ML6....98 B1
 BAIL/MDB/MHD G69....94 A5
 CGLE G1....3 F4
 DMBTN G82....13 E3
 JNSTN PA5....101 F4
 MLNGV G62....17 F3
Buchandyke Rd *EKILN* G74....167 E1
Buchan Gn *EKILN* G74....167 E2
Buchan Rd *MTHW* ML1....154 C3
Buchan St *WISHAW* ML2....174 D3
Buchan Ter *BLTYR/CAMB* G72....130 D4
Buchlyvie Gdns *BSHPBGS* G64....54 D3
Buchlyvie Rd *PSLY* PA1....85 H4
Buchlyvie St *ESTRH* G34....94 A2
Buckingham Dr *CAR/SHTL* G32....112 C4
 RUTH G73....111 G5
Buckingham St *KVD/HLHD* G12....66 C3
Buckingham Ter
 KVD/HLHD G12....66 C3
Bucklaw Gdns
 CARD/HILL/MSPK G52....86 D5
Bucklaw Pl
 CARD/HILL/MSPK G52....86 D5
Bucklaw Ter
 CARD/HILL/MSPK G52....86 D5
Buckley St *PPK/MIL* G22....54 A5
Bucksburn Rd
 SPRGB/BLRNK G21....69 F2
Buckthorne Pl *PLK/PH/NH* G53....125 G5
Budhill Av *CAR/SHTL* G32....92 D4
Budshaw Av *AIRDRIE* ML6....118 D2
Buildale Ct *SCOT* G14....64 A1
Buildale St *SCOT* G14....64 A1
Buller Cl *BLTYR/CAMB* G72....133 G5
Buller Crs *BLTYR/CAMB* G72....133 G5
Bullionslaw Dr *RUTH* G73....130 C1
Bullin Rd *CRMNK/CLK/EAG* G76....146 A4
Bull Rd *CRMNK/CLK/EAG* G76....146 A4
Bullwood Av *PLK/PH/NH* G53....106 A4
Bullwood Ct *PLK/PH/NH* G53....106 A4
Bullwood Dr *PLK/PH/NH* G53....105 H3
Bullwood Gdns
 PLK/PH/NH G53....106 A3
Bullwood Pl *PLK/PH/NH* G53....106 A3
Bunbury Ter *EKILS* G75....165 H5

Bunessan St
 CARD/HILL/MSPK G52....87 G4
Burghead Dr *GOV/IBX* G51....87 F1
Burghead Pl *GOV/IBX* G51....87 F1
Burgher St *DEN/PKHD* G31....91 F4
Burgh Hall La *PTCK* G11....66 A4
Burgh Hall St *PTCK* G11....66 A4
Burgh La *KVD/HLHD* G12....66 C3
Burleigh Rd *UD/BTH/TAN* G71....134 C4
Burleigh St *CTBR* ML5....117 E1
 GOV/IBX G51....87 H2
Burley Pl *EKILN* G74....165 E3
Burlington Av *KVD/HLHD* G12....52 A5
Burmola St *PPK/MIL* G22....67 G2
Burnacre Gdns
 UD/BTH/TAN G71....114 D5
Burnawn Gdns
 STPS/GTHM/RID G33....55 G4
Burnawn Gv
 STPS/GTHM/RID G33....55 G4
Burnawn Pl
 STPS/GTHM/RID G33....55 G4
Burnbank Centre *HMLTN* ML3....152 B5
Burnbank Dr *BRHD/NEIL* G78....142 B1
Burnbank Gdns
 MRYH/FIRH G20....67 E4
Burnbank Qd *AIRDRIE* ML6....98 A1
Burnbank Rd *HMLTN* ML3....169 G1
Burnbank St *AIRDRIE* ML6....98 A1
 CTBR ML5....97 E1
Burnbank Ter *COWCAD* G4....67 E4
 KSYTH G65....8 C1
Burnblea Gdns *HMLTN* ML3....170 A3
Burnblea St *HMLTN* ML3....170 A3
Burnbrae *CLYDBK* G81....31 H2
Burnbrae Av
 BAIL/MDB/MHD G69....59 F1
 BSDN G61....35 G1
Burnbrae Dr *PSLYN/LNWD* PA3....82 C5
 RUTH G73....130 C2
Burnbrae Rd *BLTYR/CAMB* G72....151 F5
 JNSTN PA5....121 G1
 KKNTL G66....41 E1
 KKNTL G66....57 G1
Burnbrae St *SPRGB/BLRNK* G21....68 D2
Burncleuch Av
 BLTYR/CAMB G72....131 F3
Burn Crs *AIRDRIE* ML6....119 E2
 MTHW ML1....137 F5
Burncrooks Av *BSDN* G61....16 A5
Burndyke Ct *GOV/IBX* G51....88 B2
Burndyke Sq *GOV/IBX* G51....88 B2
Burnet Rose Ct *EKILN* G74....165 H1
Burnet Rose Gdns *EKILN* G74....165 H1
Burnet Rose Pl *EKILN* G74....165 H1
Burnett Rd
 STPS/GTHM/RID G33....93 F2
Burnfield Av *GIF/THBK* G46....127 E3
Burnfield Dr *GIF/THBK* G46....127 E3
Burnfield Gdns *GIF/THBK* G46....127 F3
Burnfield Rd *GIF/THBK* G46....126 D2
Burnfoot Crs *PSLYS* PA2....103 H5
 RUTH G73....130 C2
Burnfoot Dr
 CARD/HILL/MSPK G52....86 C4
Burnfoot Rd *AIRDRIE* ML6....97 H1
Burngreen *KSYTH* G65....8 C2
Burnhall Pl *WISHAW* ML2....174 C4
Burnhall Rd *WISHAW* ML2....174 C4
Burnhall St *WISHAW* ML2....174 C4
Burnham Rd *SCOT* G14....64 B2
Burnhaven *ERSK* PA8....47 F1
Burnhead Rd *AIRDRIE* ML6....77 E5
 BALLOCH G68....25 G5
Burnhead St *UD/BTH/TAN* G71....115 G5
Burnhill Qd *RUTH* G73....110 C4
Burnhill St *RUTH* G73....110 C4
Burnhouse Av *BALLOCH* G68....25 F4
Burnhouse Brae *NMRNS* G77....162 B2
Burnhouse Crs *HMLTN* ML3....169 G4
Burnhouse Rd *HMLTN* ML3....169 G4
Burnhouse St *MRYH/FIRH* G20....52 C5
Burniebrae Rd *AIRDRIE* ML6....119 F1
Burnlea Crs *CRG/CRSL/HOU* PA6....80 B3
Burnlip Rd *CTBR* ML5....74 D2
Burnmouth Pl *BSDN* G61....34 D3
Burnmouth Rd
 STPS/GTHM/RID G33....93 G5
Burnock Pl *EKILS* G75....177 G3
Burnpark Av *UD/BTH/TAN* G71....114 C5
Burn Pl *BLTYR/CAMB* G72....111 H5
Burns Av *BSHPTN* PA7....29 E5
Burns Crs *AIRDRIE* ML6....22 A4
 KKNTL G66....21 F1
Burns Dr *JNSTN* PA5....121 F1
Burns Gdns *BLTYR/CAMB* G72....151 F1
Burns Gv *GIF/THBK* G46....126 D5
Burnside Av *AIRDRIE* ML6....118 C2
 BLSH ML4....136 B5
 BRHD/NEIL G78....124 A4
 KKNTL G66....39 G3
Burnside Ct *BSDN* G61....33 H1
 MTHW ML1....155 H4
Burnside Crs *BLTYR/CAMB* G72....162 A4
Burnside Gdns
 CRMNK/CLK/EAG G76....145 G4
 KLBCH PA10....100 C4
Burnside Ga *RUTH* G73....130 B2
Burnside La *HMLTN* ML3....170 B2
Burnside Pl *DMBTN* G82....13 C5
 PSLYN/LNWD PA3....81 H5
Burnside Rd *CTBR* ML5....75 C5
 GIF/THBK G46....145 G4
 JNSTN PA5....102 B4
 MTHW ML1....138 A3
 RUTH G73....130 B2
Burnside St *DMBTN* G82....13 E2
 MTHW ML1....172 C1
Burnside Vw *CTBR* ML5....96 B4
Burnside Wk *CTBR* ML5....96 B4
Burns Pk *EKILN* G74....166 A4
Burns Rd *AIRDRIE* ML6....119 E1
 CUMB G67....26 C3
 KKNTL G66....21 H4
Burns St *CLYDBK* G81....31 F5

Bunhouse Rd *KVGV* G3....66 C5
 HMLTN ML3....170 A3
Burnthouse Dr
 BAIL/MDB/MHD G69....113 G1
Burntbroom Gdns
 CAR/SHTL G32....113 G1
Burntbroom Rd
 BAIL/MDB/MHD G69....113 G2
Burntbroom St
 STPS/GTHM/RID G33....93 E2
Burn Ter *BLTYR/CAMB* G72....111 H5
Burn Vw *CUMB* G67....27 E2
Burnwood Dr *AIRDRIE* ML6....99 H5
Burra Gdns *BSHPBGS* G64....55 G1
Burrell Ct *PLKSD/SHW* G41....108 B2
Burrell's La *COWCAD* G4....3 K5
Burrelton Rd
 PLKSW/MSWD G43....128 A2
Busby Rd *BLSH* ML4....135 G4
 CRMNK/CLK/EAG G76....146 A3
Bush Crs *WISHAW* ML2....174 D3
Bushes Av *PSLYS* PA2....104 A3
Busheyhill St *BLTYR/CAMB* G72....131 F2
Bute Av *MTHW* ML1....154 B3
 RNFRW PA4....63 G4
Bute Crs *BSDN* G61....51 G1
 OLDK G60....30 D3
 PSLYS PA2....104 A5
Bute Dr *JNSTN* PA5....101 E5
 OLDK G60....30 D3
Bute Gdns *KVD/HLHD* G12....66 C4
 LNPK/KPK G44....128 A4
 OLDK G60....30 D2
Bute La *PSLYN/LNWD* PA3....84 A4
Bute Pl *OLDK* G60....30 D3
Bute Rd *KKNTL* G66....22 B5
Bute St *CTBR* ML5....97 E5
 HMLTN ML3....152 C4
Bute Ter *RUTH* G73....129 H2
 UD/BTH/TAN G71....115 G4
Butterbiggins Rd
 GVH/MTFL G42....109 F1
Butterburnpark St
 HMLTN ML3....170 A4
Butterfield Pl *PLKSD/SHW* G41....109 E1
Buttermere *EKILS* G75....177 E3
Byars Rd *KKNTL* G66....20 D5
Byrebush Rd *PLK/PH/NH* G53....106 D3
Byres Av *PSLYN/LNWD* PA3....84 D3
Byres Crs *PSLYN/LNWD* PA3....84 D3
Byres Rd *JNSTN* PA5....102 C2
 KVD/HLHD G12....66 C4
 OLDK G60....30 B3
Byreston Av *NMRNS* G77....162 D1
Byron Ct *UD/BTH/TAN* G71....134 D1
Byron St *CLYDBK* G81....31 F4
 PTCK G11....65 E4
Byshot St *PPK/MIL* G22....68 A2

C

Cable Depot Rd *CLYDBK* G81....48 C2
Cadder Pl *MRYH/FIRH* G20....52 D4
Cadder Rd *BSHPBGS* G64....37 H2
 MRYH/FIRH G20....52 D4
Cadder Wy *BSHPBGS* G64....38 A3
Cadell Gdns *EKILN* G74....150 A5
Cadger's Sheuch *KSYTH* G65....9 E2
Cadoc St *BLTYR/CAMB* G72....131 G2
Cadogan St *CGLW* G2....2 D6
Cadzow Av *GIF/THBK* G46....145 E2
 HMLTN ML3....152 C5
Cadzow Crs *CTBR* ML5....96 A5
Cadzow Dr *BLTYR/CAMB* G72....131 E2
Cadzow Gn *EKILN* G74....166 A3
Cadzow Pk *HMLTN* ML3....170 B1
Cadzow Rd *HMLTN* ML3....181 E6
Cadzow St *CGLW* G2....2 D6
 HMLTN ML3....170 A2
 MTHW ML1....154 C4
Caird Dr *PTCK* G11....66 A4
Caird Gdns *HMLTN* ML3....152 D5
Caird St *HMLTN* ML3....152 D5
Cairn Av *RNFRW* PA4....63 H5
Cairnban St *GOV/IBX* G51....87 E3
Cairnbrook Rd *ESTRH* G34....94 B1
Cairn Ct *EKILN* G74....166 B1
Cairndow Av *LNPK/KPK* G44....128 A3
Cairndow Avenue La
 LNPK/KPK G44....128 A3
Cairndow Ct *LNPK/KPK* G44....128 A3
Cairn Dr *PSLYN/LNWD* PA3....82 A3
Cairndyke Crs *AIRDRIE* ML6....98 B3
Cairney Pl *WISHAW* ML2....177 G4
Cairngorm Crs *BRHD/NEIL* G78....142 B1
 BSDN G61....33 H1
 PSLYS PA2....104 A3
 WISHAW ML2....173 G2
Cairngorm Gdns *BALLOCH* G68....25 E4
Cairngorm Rd
 PLKSW/MSWD G43....127 F2
Cairnhill Av *AIRDRIE* ML6....98 B4
Cairnhill Circ
 CARD/HILL/MSPK G52....106 A1
Cairnhill Ct *CTBR* ML5....117 G1
Cairnhill Dr
 CARD/HILL/MSPK G52....106 A1
Cairnhill Pl
 CARD/HILL/MSPK G52....106 A1
Cairnhill Rd *AIRDRIE* ML6....98 A4
 BSDN G61....51 G2
Cairnhope Av *AIRDRIE* ML6....98 A4
Cairnlea Dr *GOV/IBX* G51....88 A3
Cairnlea Gdns *BLSH* ML4....136 A3
Cairnlea Rd *MLNGV* G62....16 C4
Cairnmuir Rd *EKILN* G74....148 A5
Cairnoch Hl *BALLOCH* G68....25 E3
Cairnryan *EKILN* G74....166 B2
Cairns Av *BLTYR/CAMB* G72....131 G3
Cairns Dr *MLNGV* G62....17 F2
Cairnsmore Rd *DRUM* G15....50 A1
Cairns Rd *BLTYR/CAMB* G72....131 G4
 BSHPTN PA7....28 D1

Cairn St *SPRGB/BLRNK* G21....54 C5
Cairnswell Av
 BLTYR/CAMB G72....131 H3
Cairnswell Pl *BLTYR/CAMB* G72....131 H3
Cairntoul Ct *BALLOCH* G68....25 F4
Cairntoul Dr *KNTSWD* G13....50 B5
Cairntoul Pl *SCOT* G14....64 B1
Cairn Vw *KKNTL* G66....40 D1
Cairnview Rd *KKNTL* G66....40 D1
Caithness Rd *EKILN* G74....167 G2
Caithness St *BLTYR/CAMB* G72....151 F4
 MRYH/FIRH G20....67 E2
Cala Sona Ct *WISHAW* ML2....173 F5
Calcots Pl *ESTRH* G34....72 C5
Caldarvan St *PPK/MIL* G22....67 G3
Caldeen Rd *CTBR* ML5....97 E4
Calder Av *BRHD/NEIL* G78....142 B1
 WISHAW ML2....158 D4
Calderbank Ter *MTHW* ML1....155 E3
Calderbraes Av
 UD/BTH/TAN G71....114 A1
Caldercuilt Rd *MRYH/FIRH* G20....52 B3
Calder Dr *BLSH* ML4....136 A2
 BLTYR/CAMB G72....131 F2
Calder Ga *BSHPBGS* G64....37 G4
Calderglen Rd *EKILN* G74....167 G4
Caldergrove *MTHW* ML1....154 D2
Calderigg Pl *AIRDRIE* ML6....99 E2
Calder Pl *BAIL/MDB/MHD* G69....114 A2
Calder Rd *BLSH* ML4....135 F3
 PSLYN/LNWD PA3....83 F4
 SHOTTS ML7....159 G2
 UD/BTH/TAN G71....114 A1
Calderside Gv *EKILN* G74....167 H1
Calderside Rd *EKILN* G74....167 H4
 BLTYR/CAMB G72....151 G2
Calder St *CTBR* ML5....97 E5
 GVH/MTFL G42....109 F2
Calderwood Av
 BAIL/MDB/MHD G69....113 H1
Calderwood Dr
 BAIL/MDB/MHD G69....113 H1
Calderwood Gdns
 BAIL/MDB/MHD G69....113 H1
 EKILN G74....167 H2
Calderwood Rd *EKILN* G74....167 G3
 PLKSW/MSWD G43....127 H1
 RUTH G73....111 F5
Caldwell Av *KNTSWD* G13....50 B5
 PSLYN/LNWD PA3....81 H5
Caldwell Gv *BLSH* ML4....116 D4
Caldwell Qd *MTHW* ML1....154 B5
Caledonia Av *GBLS* G5....110 A1
 RUTH G73....111 E3
Caledonia Ct *PSLYN/LNWD* PA3....84 A4
Caledonia Dr
 BAIL/MDB/MHD G69....114 A1
 MTHW ML1....
Caledonian Av *BLSH* ML4....135 G3
Caledonian Crs *KVD/HLHD* G12....66 D4
Caledonian Rd *WISHAW* ML2....173 H4
Caledonia Rd *GBLS* G5....
 UD/BTH/TAN G71....113 H1
Caledonia St *CLYDBK* G81....48 B1
 GBLS G5....110 A1
 PSLYN/LNWD PA3....84 A4
Caledonia Wy East
 PSLYN/LNWD PA3....62 B5
Caledonia Wy West
 PSLYN/LNWD PA3....62 B5
Caledon La *KVD/HLHD* G12....66 B4
Caledon St *KVD/HLHD* G12....66 B4
Calfhill Rd *PLK/PH/NH* G53....106 C1
Calfmuir Rd *KKNTL* G66....40 D2
Calgary Pk *EKILS* G75....166 A5
Calgary St *COWCAD* G4....3 F1
Calico Wy *KKNTL* G66....4 A1
Callaghan Wynd
 BLTYR/CAMB G72....151 E1
Callander Ct *BALLOCH* G68....26 B1
Callander Rd *AIRDRIE* ML6....119 E3
 BALLOCH G68....
Callander St *MRYH/FIRH* G20....67 E2
Callieburn Rd *BSHPBGS* G64....54 D3
Callon St *AIRDRIE* ML6....98 C2
Callside Av *DRUM* G15....50 A2
Calside *PSLYS* PA2....104 A2
Calside Av *PSLYS* PA2....104 A1
Calvay Crs *STPS/GTHM/RID* G33....93 E2
Calvay Rd *STPS/GTHM/RID* G33....93 E2
Cambourne Rd
 BAIL/MDB/MHD G69....42 A5
Cambridge Av *CLYDBK* G81....49 E1
Cambridge Rd *RNFRW* PA4....63 F4
Cambridge St *CGLW* G2....2 E3
Camburn St *CAR/SHTL* G32....92 A4
Cambusdoon Rd
 STPS/GTHM/RID G33....70 D4
Cambuskenneth Gdns
 CAR/SHTL G32....112 D1
Cambus Pl *STPS/GTHM/RID* G33....70 D4
Cambusnethan St
 WISHAW ML2....174 D1
Camden St *GBLS* G5....89 H5
Camelia Dr *WISHAW* ML2....173 G4
Camellon Crs *BLTYR/CAMB* G72....151 G3
Camelon St *CAR/SHTL* G32....92 A3
Cameron Ct *CLYDBK* G81....49 F3
Cameron Crs
 CRMNK/CLK/EAG G76....147 F5
 HMLTN ML3....169 G2
Cameron Dr *BSDN* G61....35 E4
 NMRNS G77....144 B4
 UD/BTH/TAN G71....115 F4
Cameronian Pl *BLSH* ML4....135 G3

Cameron Sq CLYDBK G81 32 B2
Cameron St
CARD/HILL/MSPK G52 85 H2
CTBR ML5 97 E1
MTHW ML1 154 C4
Cameron Wy BLTYR/CAMB G72 151 G2
Camlachie St DEN/PKHD G31 91 E4
DMNK/BRGTN G40 * 90 D4
Campbell Av BSHPTN PA7 29 E4
DMBTN G82 13 H4
MLNGV G62 17 E4
Campbell Crs NMRNS G77 144 B3
UD/BTH/TAN G71 134 B3
Campbell Dr BRHD/NEIL G78 124 B3
BSDN G61 34 A3
DMBTN G82 13 H3
Campbell La HMLTN ML3 170 B2
Campbell Pl BSHPBGS G64 19 F4
EKILS G75 178 B1
Campbell St BLSH ML4 136 A2
HMLTN ML3 170 B1
JNSTN PA5 101 G4
MRYH/FIRH G20 52 C4
RNFRW PA4 63 G2
WISHAW ML2 174 B2
Campbell Ter DMBTN G82 13 H3
Camphill PSLYS PA2 104 A1
Camphill Av KKNTL G66 21 E5
PLKSD/SHW G41 108 D5
Camphill Crs BSHPTN PA7 29 F5
Camphill Gdns BSHPTN PA7 29 F5
Campion Rd MTHW ML1 154 D2
Camp Rd BAIL/MDB/MHD G69 94 A4
MTHW ML1 171 H1
RUTH G73 110 C2
Camps Crs RNFRW PA4 63 H4
Campsie Av BRHD/NEIL G78 142 B1
Campsie Crs AIRDRIE ML6 98 A1
Campsie Dr BSDN G61 34 A1
MLNGV G62 17 F3
PSLYN/LNWD PA3 62 B5
PSLYS PA2 104 A4
Campsie Gdns
CRMNK/CLK/EAG G76 145 F2
Campsie Pl BAIL/MDB/MHD G69 58 B3
Campsie Rd BSHPBGS G64 19 H3
EKILS G75 177 F5
KKNTL G66 5 E4
WISHAW ML2 173 F1
Campsie St SPRGB/BLRNK G21 68 C1
Campsie Vw
BAIL/MDB/MHD G69 58 B3
BAIL/MDB/MHD G69 95 E4
BLTYR/CAMB G72 132 B4
CUMB G67 26 D2
HMLTN ML3 169 E3
KKNTL G66 20 C5
STPS/GTHM/RID G33 71 E2
UD/BTH/TAN G71 115 F4
Campston Pl
STPS/GTHM/RID G33 70 C5
Camp St MTHW ML1 154 D5
Camsbusmore Pl
STPS/GTHM/RID G33 70 D4
Camstradden Dr East
BSDN G61 33 H4
Camstradden Dr West
BSDN G61 33 H4
Camus Pl DRUM G15 33 E4
Canal Av JNSTN PA5 101 H4
Canal La KKNTL G66 21 F4
Canal Rd JNSTN PA5 101 H4
Canal St COWCAD G4 3 G1
JNSTN PA5 101 H3
JNSTN PA5 102 C1
KKNTL G66 21 F4
PSLY PA1 84 A5
RNFRW PA4 63 G2
Canal Ter PSLY PA1 84 A5
Canberra Av CLYDBK G81 31 E4
Canberra Dr EKILS G75 165 H5
Cander Rigg BSHPBGS G64 37 H4
Candleriggs CGLE G1 3 H7
Candren Rd PSLYN/LNWD PA3 82 C3
Candren Wy PSLYN/LNWD PA3 83 F4
Canmore Pl DEN/PKHD G31 91 G5
Canmore St DEN/PKHD G31 91 G5
Cannerton Crs KKNTL G66 5 F5
Cannerton Pk KKNTL G66 5 F5
Cannich Dr PSLYS PA2 105 E3
Cannich Pl WISHAW ML2 158 A4
Canniesburn Rd BSDN G61 50 D1
Canonbie Av EKILN G74 166 C1
Canonbie St ESTRH G34 72 C5
Canon Ct MTHW ML1 138 A5
Canterbury EKILS G75 177 H1
Cantieslaw Dr EKILN G74 166 D2
Canting Wy GOV/IBX G51 88 B2
Canyon Rd WISHAW ML2 173 E3
Capel Av NMRNS G77 144 C4
Capel Gv EKILN G74 167 E2
Capelrig Dr EKILN G74 167 E2
NMRNS G77 144 B2
Capelrig La NMRNS G77 144 A4
Capelrig Rd NMRNS G77 144 A2
Capelrig St GIF/THBK G46 126 B3
Caplaw Pl WISHAW ML2 173 G5
Caplaw Rd PSLYS PA2 122 D1
Caplethill Rd BRHD/NEIL G78 124 A2
PSLYS PA2 123 G1
Caprington St
STPS/GTHM/RID G33 70 B5
Cara Dr GOV/IBX G51 87 F1
Carbarns WISHAW ML2 173 F4
Carbarns East WISHAW ML2 173 E4
Carbarns Rd WISHAW ML2 173 E4
Carbarns West WISHAW ML2 173 E4
Carberry Rd PLKSD/SHW G41 108 C2
Carbeth Rd MLNGV G62 16 D4
Carbeth St PPK/MIL G22 67 G2
Carbisdale St PPK/MIL G22 68 B1
Carbost St SMSTN G23 52 C2
Carbrook St PSLY PA1 83 H5
SPRGB/BLRNK G21 68 D5
Cardarrach St
SPRGB/BLRNK G21 68 D2
Cardean Rd BLSH ML4 136 D1
Cardell Av PSLYS PA2 103 F2
Cardell Crs AIRDRIE ML6 119 E2
Cardell Dr PSLYS PA2 103 F1
Cardell Rd PSLYS PA2 103 F1
Cardonald Dr
CARD/HILL/MSPK G52 86 B5
Cardonald Gdns
CARD/HILL/MSPK G52 86 B5
Cardonald Place Rd
CARD/HILL/MSPK G52 86 C5
Cardowan Dr BALLOCH G68 24 B4
STPS/GTHM/RID G33 71 E1
Cardowan Pk
UD/BTH/TAN G71 115 G3
Cardowan Rd CAR/SHTL G32 92 A3
STPS/GTHM/RID G33 57 F5
Cardow Rd SPRGB/BLRNK G21 69 F2
Cardrona St
STPS/GTHM/RID G33 70 C3
Cardross Rd DMBTN G82 12 B3
Cardross St DEN/PKHD G31 90 C2
Cardwell St PLKSD/SHW G41 89 F5
Cardyke St SPRGB/BLRNK G21 68 D2
Careston Pl BSHPBGS G64 55 G2
Carey Gdns MTHW ML1 157 F1
Carfin Mill Rd MTHW ML1 155 H1
Carfin Rd MTHW ML1 138 A5
WISHAW ML2 172 D1
Carfin St CTBR ML5 97 E5
GVH/MTFL G42 109 G2
MTHW ML1 137 F4
Carfrae St KVGV G3 88 B1
Cargill Sq BSHPBGS G64 55 F3
Carham Dr
CARD/HILL/MSPK G52 86 D4
Carillon Rd GOV/IBX G51 88 B4
Carisbrooke Crs BSHPBGS G64 38 A4
Carlaverock Rd
PLKSW/MSWD G43 127 G1
Carleith Av CLYDBK G81 31 G2
Carleith Qd GOV/IBX G51 87 E2
Carleith Ter CLYDBK G81 31 G2
Carleston St SPRGB/BLRNK G21 68 C2
Carleton Ct GIF/THBK G46 127 F3
Carleton Dr GIF/THBK G46 127 F3
Carleton Ga GIF/THBK G46 127 F3
Carlibar Av KNTSWD G13 50 A5
Carlibar Dr BRHD/NEIL G78 124 B4
Carlibar Gdns BRHD/NEIL G78 124 B4
Carlibar Rd BRHD/NEIL G78 124 B4
Carlile Pl PSLYN/LNWD PA3 84 B3
Carlisle Rd AIRDRIE ML6 98 D4
HMLTN ML3 170 D3
MTHW ML1 139 G3
Carlisle St PPK/MIL G22 68 A2
Carlowrie Av BLTYR/CAMB G72 133 F5
Carlton Ct GBLS G5 89 G3
Carlton Pl GBLS G5 89 G3
Carlyle Av CARD/HILL/MSPK G52 86 B1
Carlyle Dr EKILN G74 167 E3
Carmaben Rd
STPS/GTHM/RID G33 93 E1
Carment Dr PLKSD/SHW G41 108 C4
Carmen Vw DMBTN G82 13 F1
Carmichael Pl GVH/MTFL G42 109 E5
Carmichael St GOV/IBX G51 88 A3
Carmunnock By-Pass
CSMK G45 146 C2
Carmunnock Rd
CRMNK/CLK/EAG G76 146 C4
EKILN G74 147 H5
LNPK/KPK G44 109 G5
Carmyle Av CAR/SHTL G32 112 C2
Carmyle Gdns CTBR ML5 116 B1
Carna Dr LNPK/KPK G44 128 D2
Carnarvon St KVGV G3 2 A1
Carnbroe Rd BLSH ML4 117 E4
Carneddans Rd MLNGV G62 16 A1
Carnegie Hl EKILS G75 166 A5
Carnegie Pl EKILS G75 166 A5
Carnegie Rd
CARD/HILL/MSPK G52 86 B3
Carnoch St SMSTN G23 52 C2
Carnock Crs BRHD/NEIL G78 142 A1
Carnock Rd PLK/PH/NH G53 106 D4
Carnoustie Ct
UD/BTH/TAN G71 134 A5
Carnoustie Crs BSHPBGS G64 55 F2
EKILS G75 177 F2
Carnoustie Pl BLSH ML4 116 D5
GBLS G5 89 E4
Carnoustie St GBLS G5 89 E4
Carnoustie Wy BALLOCH G68 10 B4
Carntynehall Rd CAR/SHTL G32 92 A3
Carntyne Pl CAR/SHTL G32 91 G2
Carntyne Rd CAR/SHTL G32 91 G2
Carnwadric Rd GIF/THBK G46 126 B3
Carnwath Av
PLKSW/MSWD G43 128 A1
Caroline St DEN/PKHD G31 91 H4
Carolside Av
CRMNK/CLK/EAG G76 145 H3
Carolside Dr DRUM G15 33 G5
Carousel Crs WISHAW ML2 174 B2
Carradale Crs BALLOCH G68 24 D5
Carradale St CTBR ML5 96 C2
Carrbridge Dr MRYH/FIRH G20 52 C5
Carresbrook Av KKNTL G66 40 D2
Carriagehill Av PSLYS PA2 104 B2
Carriagehill Dr PSLYS PA2 104 B3
Carrickarden Rd BSDN G61 34 C5
Carrick Ct KKNTL G66 22 A3
Carrick Crs GIF/THBK G46 145 F1
Carrick Dr CAR/SHTL G32 93 F5
CTBR ML5 96 A2
RUTH G73 129 H2
Carrick Gdns BLSH ML4 116 D4
BLTYR/CAMB G72 151 G4
HMLTN ML3 168 D3
Carrick Gv CAR/SHTL G32 93 F5
Carrick Pl BLSH ML4 117 E4
CTBR ML5 74 B1
CTBR ML5 96 A2
Carrick Rd BSHPBGS G64 55 F2
BSHPTN PA7 46 A1
CUMB G67 26 C1
EKILN G74 166 C2
RUTH G73 129 G2
Carrickstone Rd BALLOCH G68 26 A1
Carrickstone Vw BALLOCH G68 10 B5
Carrick St KVGV G3 2 C7
Carrick Ter DMBTN G82 12 A3
Carrick V MTHW ML1 157 F1
Carrington St COWCAD G4 67 E4
Carroglen Gdns CAR/SHTL G32 93 E4
Carroglen Gv CAR/SHTL G32 93 E4
Carroll Crs MTHW ML1 137 H5
Carron Ct HMLTN ML3 169 G4
Carron Crs BSDN G61 33 H5
BSHPBGS G64 55 E2
KKNTL G66 40 B4
SPRGB/BLRNK G21 68 B1
Carron Dr BSHPTN PA7 46 B1
Carron Pl CTBR ML5 74 A5
EKILS G75 178 C3
PPK/MIL G22 68 B1
Carron St PPK/MIL G22 68 B1
WISHAW ML2 174 A4
Carrour Gdns
BSHPBGS G64 54 C1
Carruth Rd BRWEIR PA11 79 F3
Carsaig Dr
CARD/HILL/MSPK G52 87 F4
Carscallan Rd HMLTN ML3 180 D2
Carsegreen Av PSLYS PA2 122 C1
Carseview Dr BSDN G61 34 D2
Carsewood Av HWWD PA9 120 A4
Carstairs St DMNK/BRGTN G40 110 D2
Carswell Gdns PLKSD/SHW G41 108 D2
Carswell Rd NMRNS G77 143 F5
Cartcraigs Rd
PLKSW/MSWD G43 127 E1
Cartha Crs PSLYS PA2 104 D1
Cartha St PLKSD/SHW G41 108 C5
Cart La PSLYN/LNWD PA3 84 B3
Cartsbridge Rd
CRMNK/CLK/EAG G76 145 H4
Cartside Av JNSTN PA5 101 E5
RNFRW PA4 61 G2
Cartside Dr
CRMNK/CLK/EAG G76 146 B4
Cartside Pl
CRMNK/CLK/EAG G76 146 A5
Cartside Qd PLKSW/MSWD G43 109 F5
Cartside Rd
CRMNK/CLK/EAG G76 146 A5
Cartside St GVH/MTFL G42 109 E5
Cart St CLYDBK G81 49 E3
Cartvale La PSLYN/LNWD PA3 84 B3
Cartvale Rd GVH/MTFL G42 109 E5
Cartview Ct
CRMNK/CLK/EAG G76 146 A4
Caskie Dr BLTYR/CAMB G72 151 H1
Cassels Gv MTHW ML1 154 B1
Cassels St MTHW ML1 154 D2
Cassiltoun Gdns CSMK G45 129 E5
Cassley Av RNFRW PA4 64 A4
Castburn Rd CUMB G67 11 H4
Castle Av JNSTN PA5 102 A3
MTHW ML1 137 G1
UD/BTH/TAN G71 133 H4
UD/BTH/TAN G71 134 A2
Castlebank Ct KNTSWD G13 51 F5
Castlebank Crs PTCK G11 65 H5
Castlebank Gdns KNTSWD G13 51 F5
Castlebank St PTCK G11 65 G5
Castlebank Vls KNTSWD G13 51 F5
Castlebay Dr PPK/MIL G22 53 H2
Castlebay Pl PPK/MIL G22 53 H3
Castlebay St PPK/MIL G22 53 H3
Castlebrae DMBTN G82 12 B2
Castlebrae Gdns
LNPK/KPK G44 128 C1
Castlecary Rd CUMB G67 11 E4
Castle Chimmins Av
BLTYR/CAMB G72 132 A3
Castle Chimmins Rd
BLTYR/CAMB G72 132 A4
Castle Ct CUMB G67 11 H2
KKNTL G66 21 F5
Castle Crs BSHPTN PA7 46 A1
Castlecroft Gdns
UD/BTH/TAN G71 134 A2
Castle Dr MTHW ML1 137 G1
Castlefern Rd RUTH G73 129 H4
Castlefield Gdns EKILS G75 177 G3
Castle Gait PSLY PA1 104 B1
Castle Gdns
BAIL/MDB/MHD G69 59 E2
PSLYS PA2 103 F1
Castle Ga NMRNS G77 162 B2
UD/BTH/TAN G71 133 H2
Castleglen Rd EKILN G74 165 E1
Castlegreen Crs DMBTN G82 13 G5
Castlegreen St DMBTN G82 13 F5
Castlehill Crs AIRDRIE ML6 119 G3
HMLTN ML3 171 G4
RNFRW PA4 63 G2
Castlehill Dr NMRNS G77 162 A1
Castlehill Gdns HMLTN ML3 170 C3
Castlehill Gn EKILN G74 165 E1
Castlehill Qd DMBTN G82 12 B3
Castlehill Rd BSDN G61 33 G2
DMBTN G82 12 B2
WISHAW ML2 173 G5
Castlelaw Gdns CAR/SHTL G32 92 C3
Castlelaw St CAR/SHTL G32 92 C3
Castle Mains Rd MLNGV G62 16 B3
Castlemilk Crs LNPK/KPK G44 129 F2
Castlemilk Dr CSMK G45 129 F5
Castlemilk Rd LNPK/KPK G44 110 B5
RUTH G73 129 G3
Castlemount Av NMRNS G77 162 A2
Castle Qd AIRDRIE ML6 99 E2
Castle Rd AIRDRIE ML6 99 E1
BRWEIR PA11 79 G2
JNSTN PA5 102 B1
NMRNS G77 161 F1
Castle St AIRDRIE ML6 118 D2
BAIL/MDB/MHD G69 113 G1
CLYDBK G81 31 F5
COWCAD G4 3 K4
DMBTN G82 13 E4
HMLTN ML3 170 C1
PSLY PA1 83 H5
PTCK G11 66 B5
RUTH G73 111 E4
Castleton Av NMRNS G77 162 A2
SPRGB/BLRNK G21 54 B4
Castleton Crs NMRNS G77 162 A2
Castleton Dr NMRNS G77 162 A2
Castleton Gv NMRNS G77 162 A2
Castleview BALLOCH G68 11 G2
Castle Vw WISHAW ML2 158 B4
Castleview Av PSLYS PA2 103 F5
Castleview Dr PSLYS PA2 103 F5
Castle Wy CUMB G67 27 E2
Castle Wynd HMLTN ML3 181 E5
UD/BTH/TAN G71 134 C5
Cathay St PPK/MIL G22 53 H3
Cathburn Rd WISHAW ML2 175 H1
Cathcart Crs PSLYS PA2 104 D1
Cathcart Pl RUTH G73 110 C5
Cathcart Rd GBLS G5 89 G5
LNPK/KPK G44 109 F5
RUTH G73 110 C5
Cathedral Sq COWCAD G4 3 K5
Cathedral St COWCAD G4 3 H4
Catherine St MTHW ML1 171 H1
Catherine Wy MTHW ML1 137 E4
Cathkin Av BLTYR/CAMB G72 130 D1
RUTH G73 111 F5
Cathkin By-Pass RUTH G73 130 C4
Cathkin Crs BALLOCH G68 10 A5
Cathkin Dr
CRMNK/CLK/EAG G76 145 F2
Cathkin Pl BLTYR/CAMB G72 130 D1
Cathkin Rd
CRMNK/CLK/EAG G76 147 F2
GVH/MTFL G42 109 E5
UD/BTH/TAN G71 114 D3
Cathkinview Pl GVH/MTFL G42 109 F5
Cathkinview Rd
GVH/MTFL G42 109 F5
Catrine EKILN G74 166 A3
Catrine Ct PLK/PH/NH G53 106 B4
Catrine Crs MTHW ML1 172 B1
Catrine Gdns PLK/PH/NH G53 106 B4
Catrine Pl PLK/PH/NH G53 106 B4
Catrine Rd PLK/PH/NH G53 106 B4
Cauldstream Pl MLNGV G62 16 C4
Causewayside Crs
CAR/SHTL G32 112 B2
Causewayside St
CAR/SHTL G32 112 B2
Causeyside St PSLY PA1 84 B5
PSLYS PA2 104 B1
Cavendish Dr NMRNS G77 144 C4
Cavendish Pl GBLS G5 89 G5
Cavendish St GBLS G5 89 G5
Cavin Dr CSMK G45 129 F3
Cavin Rd CSMK G45 129 F3
Cawder Ct BALLOCH G68 9 H5
Cawder Pl BALLOCH G68 10 A5
Cawder Rd BALLOCH G68 10 A5
Cawder Vw BALLOCH G68 10 A5
Cawder Wy BALLOCH G68 10 A5
Cawdor Crs BSHPTN PA7 46 A1
Cawdor Wy EKILN G74 166 A2
Cayton Gdns
BAIL/MDB/MHD G69 93 G5
Cecil St CRMNK/CLK/EAG G76 145 H3
CTBR ML5 96 D4
KVD/HLHD G12 66 C3
Cedar Av CLYDBK G81 31 E4
JNSTN PA5 121 G1
UD/BTH/TAN G71 115 G4
Cedar Ct BLTYR/CAMB G72 132 B3
EKILS G75 177 H3
KLBCH PA10 100 B3
MRYH/FIRH G20 67 F4
Cedar Crs HMLTN ML3 170 B4
Cedar Dr EKILS G75 177 H3
KKNTL G66 5 G5
KKNTL G66 39 H3
UD/BTH/TAN G71 116 A4
Cedar Gdns MTHW ML1 137 H3
RUTH G73 130 B4
Cedar La MTHW ML1 137 G2
Cedar Pl BLTYR/CAMB G72 151 F1
EKILS G75 177 H3
Cedar Rd BSHPBGS G64 55 E3
CUMB G67 27 F2
Cedar St MRYH/FIRH G20 67 F4
Cedar Wk MTHW ML1 138 A5
Cedarwood WISHAW ML2 173 E4
Cedarwood Av NMRNS G77 144 C5
Cedarwood Rd NMRNS G77 162 A1
Cedric Pl KNTSWD G13 51 E4
Cedric Rd KNTSWD G13 51 E4
Celtic St MRYH/FIRH G20 52 B4
Cemetery Rd
BLTYR/CAMB G72 151 F4
CARD/HILL/MSPK G52 87 E5
Centenary Av AIRDRIE ML6 97 G2
Centenary Ct CLYDBK G81 49 E2
Centenary Gdns CTBR ML5 96 C4
HMLTN ML3 170 B3
Centenary Qd MTHW ML1 137 E2
Central Av BLTYR/CAMB G72 131 E1
BLTYR/CAMB G72 151 H5
CAR/SHTL G32 113 E1
CLYDBK G81 48 D1
MTHW ML1 137 E2
MTHW ML1 137 F5
PTCK G11 65 G4
UD/BTH/TAN G71 134 D1
Central Gv CAR/SHTL G32 93 E5
Central Pth CAR/SHTL G32 113 F1
Central Rd PSLY PA1 84 B4
Central Wy CUMB G67 26 A5
PSLY PA1 84 B4
Centre St AIRDRIE ML6 118 D2
CTBR ML5 59 H5
GBLS G5 89 G3
Centre Wy BRHD/NEIL G78 124 A4
Centrewest EKILN G74 166 B4
Centurion Pl MTHW ML1 154 A1
Ceres Gdns BSHPBGS G64 55 G2
Cessnock Rd
STPS/GTHM/RID G33 70 B1
Cessnock St GOV/IBX G51 88 B4
Chalmers Crs EKILS G75 178 C1
Chalmers Dr EKILS G75 178 C1
Chalmers Ga DMNK/BRGTN G40 90 B3
Chalmers St CLYDBK G81 49 E2
DMNK/BRGTN G40 90 B3
Chamberlain La KNTSWD G13 65 F1
Chamberlain Rd KNTSWD G13 51 F5
Chancellor St PTCK G11 66 A4
Chantinghall Rd HMLTN ML3 169 G2
Chantinghall Ter HMLTN ML3 169 G2
Chapel Ct RUTH G73 110 C4
Chapel Crs HMLTN ML3 180 D2
Chapelcross Av AIRDRIE ML6 76 B5
Chapelhill Rd PSLYS PA2 104 D2
Chapelknowe Rd MTHW ML1 156 A1
Chapel Pl BRHD/NEIL G78 141 E3
Chapel Rd CLYDBK G81 31 H2
WISHAW ML2 175 G4
Chapelside Av AIRDRIE ML6 98 B1
Chapelside Rd EKILN G74 149 G5
Chapel St AIRDRIE ML6 98 B1
KKNTL G66 4 B2
MRYH/FIRH G20 66 D1
MTHW ML1 157 E1
RUTH G73 110 C4
Chapelton Av BSDN G61 34 C4
DMBTN G82 13 F3
Chapelton Gdns BSDN G61 34 C4
DMBTN G82 13 F3
Chapelton Rd CUMB G67 44 C2
Chapelton St PPK/MIL G22 53 H5
Chaplet Av KNTSWD G13 50 D3
Chapman Av CTBR ML5 59 H5
Chapman St GVH/MTFL G42 109 F2
Chappell St BRHD/NEIL G78 124 A4
Charing Cross La KVGV G3 2 A3
Charles Av RNFRW PA4 63 G2
Charles Crs KKNTL G66 40 A5
Charleson Rw KSYTH G65 24 D2
Charles Qd MTHW ML1 137 F2
Charles St KSYTH G65 8 B1
SPRGB/BLRNK G21 68 C5
WISHAW ML2 172 D1
Charlotte Av BSHPBGS G64 19 F5
Charlotte Pl PSLYS PA2 104 B2
Charlotte St CGLE G1 90 A3
DMBTN G82 12 C3
Charnwood Av JNSTN PA5 121 E1
Chassels St CTBR ML5 96 D1
Chateau Gv HMLTN ML3 170 D3
Chatelherault Av
BLTYR/CAMB G72 130 D2
Chatelherault Crs HMLTN ML3 170 B5
Chatham EKILS G75 177 H1
Chatton St SMSTN G23 52 C2
Chatton Wk CTBR ML5 117 F2
Cheapside St KVGV G3 2 A6
Chelmsford Dr KVD/HLHD G12 66 A1
Cherry Bank KKNTL G66 39 G3
Cherrybank Rd
PLKSW/MSWD G43 128 A2
Cherrybank Wk CTBR ML5 97 G1
Cherry Crs CLYDBK G81 31 H4
Cherry Gv CTBR ML5 95 G3
Cherry Pl BSHPBGS G64 55 E3
JNSTN PA5 101 H5
KKNTL G66 5 F5
MTHW ML1 137 G3
UD/BTH/TAN G71 116 A4
Cherryridge Dr CTBR ML5 95 F3
Cherrytree Dr
BLTYR/CAMB G72 132 B3
Cherry Wk MTHW ML1 171 H1
Cherrywood Rd JNSTN PA5 102 B2
Chesterfield Av KVD/HLHD G12 65 H1
Chesters Crs MTHW ML1 154 B2
Chesters Pl RUTH G73 110 C5
Chesters Rd BSDN G61 33 H4
Chester St CAR/SHTL G32 92 B4
Chestnut Av BSHPTN PA7 28 C3
CUMB G67 11 G5
Chestnut Ct CUMB G67 11 G5
KKNTL G66 5 F5
Chestnut Crs EKILS G75 177 H2
HMLTN ML3 170 B3
UD/BTH/TAN G71 115 H5
Chestnut Dr CLYDBK G81 31 H3
KKNTL G66 39 G2
Chestnut Gv BLTYR/CAMB G72 151 F2
CTBR ML5 59 H5
MTHW ML1 171 G1
Chestnut La MLNGV G62 16 C4
Chestnut Pl CUMB G67 11 G5
JNSTN PA5 121 H1
Chestnut St PPK/MIL G22 68 A1
Chestnut Wy BLTYR/CAMB G72 132 B3
HMLTN ML3 181 F4
Cheviot Av BRHD/NEIL G78 124 B5
Cheviot Crs EKILS G75 177 F4
WISHAW ML2 173 G1
Cheviot Dr NMRNS G77 161 F2
Cheviot Rd HMLTN ML3 170 C3
PLKSW/MSWD G43 127 F2
PSLYS PA2 104 A4
Cheviot St BLTYR/CAMB G72 151 F3
Chirmorie Crs PLK/PH/NH G53 106 B3
Chirmorie Pl PLK/PH/NH G53 106 B3
Chirnside Pl
CARD/HILL/MSPK G52 86 B3
Chirnside Rd
CARD/HILL/MSPK G52 86 B3
Chisholm Av BSHPTN PA7 29 F5
Chisholm Dr NMRNS G77 144 B4
Chisholm Pl MTHW ML1 172 C3
Chisholm St CTBR ML5 97 E1
Chisolm St CGLE G1 3 H7
Chrighton Gn
UD/BTH/TAN G71 115 F4
Chriss Av HMLTN ML3 180 D1
Christchurch Pl EKILS G75 177 G1
Christian St PLKSW/MSWD G43 108 B4
Christie La PSLY PA1 84 B4
Christie St BLSH ML4 136 C3
PSLY PA1 84 C4
Christopher St
SPRGB/BLRNK G21 68 D5
Chryston Rd
BAIL/MDB/MHD G69 58 C3
KKNTL G66 41 F2
Chuckie La JNSTN PA5 80 D5
Church Av RUTH G73 130 B2
STPS/GTHM/RID G33 57 E5
WISHAW ML2 175 E1
Church Ct DMBTN G82 13 E4
HMLTN ML3 170 B1
Church Crs AIRDRIE ML6 77 F5
Church Hl PSLY PA1 84 B4
Churchill Av EKILN G74 166 C4
JNSTN PA5 120 D1
Churchill Crs UD/BTH/TAN G71 134 C4
Churchill Dr BSHPTN PA7 29 E5
PTCK G11 65 H3
Churchill Pl KLBCH PA10 100 B4
Church La CTBR ML5 96 D2
Church Manse La BRWEIR PA11 79 G3
Church Rd BAIL/MDB/MHD G69 58 B4
BRWEIR PA11 79 H4
CRMNK/CLK/EAG G76 146 A4
GIF/THBK G46 127 F5
WISHAW ML2 159 E4
Church St BAIL/MDB/MHD G69 94 B5
BLTYR/CAMB G72 151 H3
CLYDBK G81 31 H5
CTBR ML5 96 D2
DMBTN G82 13 E4
HMLTN ML3 170 B1
JNSTN PA5 101 G3
KLBCH PA10 100 B3
KSYTH G65 8 B2
MTHW ML1 138 G3
PTCK G11 66 B5
UD/BTH/TAN G71 133 H2
Church Vw BLTYR/CAMB G72 112 B5
CTBR ML5 96 D2
Church View Gdns BLSH ML4 135 H2
Circus Dr DEN/PKHD G31 90 C2
Circus Place La DEN/PKHD G31 90 C2
Citadel Pl MTHW ML1 154 B2
Citizen La CGLE G1 3 F5
Citrus Crs UD/BTH/TAN G71 115 H4
Cityford Dr RUTH G73 129 G1
Civic St COWCAD G4 2 E1
Civic Wy KKNTL G66 39 H1
Clachan Dr GOV/IBX G51 87 F1
The Clachan WISHAW ML2 174 A2
Claddens Pl KKNTL G66 40 C4

Claddens Qd PPK/MIL G22 .....53 H5
Claddens St PPK/MIL G22 .....53 G5
Cladence Gv EKILS G75 .....178 C3
Claire St WISHAW ML2 .....158 A5
Clairmich Gdns RNFRW PA4 .....63 F5
Clairmont Gdns KVGV G3 .....5 J7
Clair Rd BSHPBGS G64 .....55 G2
Clamp Rd WISHAW ML2 .....172 D1
Clamps Ter EKILN G74 .....166 C5
Clamps Vw EKILN G74 .....167 E5
Clamps Wd EKILN G74 .....166 D5
Clanrye Dr CTBR ML5 .....96 D5
Clapperton Rd MTHW ML1 .....155 F1
Claremont Av KKNTL G66 .....20 D6
Claremont Dr MLNGV G62 .....17 E3
Claremont Gdns MLNGV G62 .....17 E4
Claremont Pas KVGV G3 .....67 E5
Claremont Pl KVGV G3 .....67 E5
Claremont St KVGV G3 .....88 D1
Claremont Ter KVGV G3 .....67 E5
Claremont Av GIF/THBK G46 .....127 F5
Claremount Terrace La
 KVGV G3 .....66 D5
Claremount Vw CTBR ML5 .....117 F1
Clarence Dr PSLY PA1 .....84 D4
 PTCK G11 .....65 H5
Clarence Gdns PTCK G11 .....65 H5
Clarence La KVD/HLHD G12 .....66 A3
Clarence St CLYDBK G81 .....32 B5
 PSLY PA1 .....84 D4
Clarendon Pl COWCAD G4 .....67 F4
Clarendon Rd WISHAW ML2 .....173 F4
Clarendon St MRYH/FIRH G20 .....67 F4
Clare St SPRGB/BLRNK G21 .....68 D5
Clarinda Crs KKNTL G66 .....22 A5
Clarinda Pl MTHW ML1 .....137 H4
Clarion Crs KNTSWD G13 .....50 B3
Clarion Rd KNTSWD G13 .....50 B4
Clarkin Av EKILS G75 .....177 F4
Clark Pl NMRNS G77 .....161 E1
Clarkston Av LNPK/KPK G44 .....128 A3
Clarkston Dr AIRDRIE ML6 .....99 E2
Clarkston Rd
 CRMNK/CLK/EAG G76 .....145 H2
 LNPK/KPK G44 .....128 B2
Clark St AIRDRIE ML6 .....98 C1
 CLYDBK G81 .....31 G4
 JNSTN PA5 .....101 G3
 PSLY/LNWD PA3 .....83 H3
 RNFRW PA4 .....63 E3
 WISHAW ML2 .....158 A4
Clark Wy BLSH ML4 .....116 C5
Clarkwell Rd HMLTN ML3 .....168 D2
Clarkwell Ter HMLTN ML3 .....169 E2
Clathic Av BSDN G61 .....34 D5
Claude Av BLTYR/CAMB G72 .....132 B4
Claud Rd PSLY/LNWD PA3 .....84 D3
Clavens Rd
 CARD/HILL/MSPK G52 .....85 H3
Claverhouse Pl PSLYS PA2 .....104 D1
Claverhouse Rd
 CARD/HILL/MSPK G52 .....86 A2
Clavering St East PSLY PA1 .....83 H4
Clavering St West PSLY PA1 .....83 H4
Clay Ct MTHW ML1 .....171 G1
Clay Crs BLSH ML4 .....117 E5
Clayhouse Rd
 STPS/GTHM/RID G33 .....71 F2
Claymore Dr
 CRG/CRSL/HOU PA6 .....81 E3
Claypotts Pl
 STPS/GTHM/RID G33 .....70 B5
Clay Rd BLSH ML4 .....117 F5
Claysiaps Rd KVGV G3 .....66 C5
Claythorn Av DMNK/BRGTN G40 .....90 B3
Claythorn Circ
 DMNK/BRGTN G40 .....90 B3
Claythorn St DMNK/BRGTN G40 .....90 B4
Clayton Ter DEN/PKHD G31 .....90 C2
Clearfield Av HMLTN ML3 .....169 G1
Cleddans Crs CLYDBK G81 .....32 B2
Cleddans Rd CLYDBK G81 .....32 B2
 KKNTL G66 .....21 G4
Cleddans Vw AIRDRIE ML6 .....75 H2
Cleddens Ct BSHPBGS G64 .....54 D2
Cleeves Od PLK/PH/NH G53 .....125 F2
Cleeves Rd PLK/PH/NH G53 .....125 F2
Cleghorn St MRYH/FIRH G20 .....67 G3
Cleish Av BSDN G61 .....16 A5
Cleland La GBLS G5 .....89 H5
Cleland Pl EKILN G74 .....166 D2
Cleland Rd MTHW ML1 .....138 C5
 WISHAW ML2 .....157 H4
Cleland St GBLS G5 .....89 H4
Clelland Av BSHPBGS G64 .....54 D3
Clerwood St CAR/SHTL G32 .....91 G3
Cleuch Gdns
 CRMNK/CLK/EAG G76 .....145 G2
Clevans Rd BRWEIR PA11 .....79 E4
Cleveden Crescent La
 KVD/HLHD G12 .....66 A1
Cleveden Crs KVD/HLHD G12 .....66 A1
 RUTH G73 .....130 B1
Cleveden Dr KVD/HLHD G12 .....66 A2
Cleveden Drive La
 KVD/HLHD G12 .....66 B2
Cleveden Gdns KVD/HLHD G12 .....52 A5
Cleveden La KVD/HLHD G12 .....52 A5
Cleveden Pl KVD/HLHD G12 .....52 A5
Cleveden Rd KVD/HLHD G12 .....52 A5
Cleveland La CGLW G2 .....2 C5
Cleveland St KVGV G3 .....2 B5
Clifford Gdns GOV/IBX G51 .....88 A4
Clifford La GOV/IBX G51 .....88 B4
Clifford St GOV/IBX G51 .....88 A4
Cliff Rd KVGV G3 .....67 E5
Clifton Pl CTBR ML5 .....97 F3
 KVGV G3 .....66 D5
Clifton Rd GIF/THBK G46 .....127 G4
Clifton St KVGV G3 .....66 D5
Clifton Ter BLTYR/CAMB G72 .....130 D4
Clincarthill Rd RUTH G73 .....110 A4
Clincart Rd GVH/MTFL G42 .....109 G4
Clippens Rd CRG/CRSL/HOU PA6 .....81 F3
Cloan Av DRUM G15 .....33 G5
Cloan Crs BSHPBGS G64 .....38 A4
Clober Farm La MLNGV G62 .....16 C2
Cloberfield MLNGV G62 .....16 D1
Cloberfield Gdns MLNGV G62 .....16 D1
Cloberhill Rd KNTSWD G13 .....50 D2
Clober Rd MLNGV G62 .....16 D2
Clochbar Av MLNGV G62 .....16 D1
Clochbar Gdns MLNGV G62 .....16 D3
Clochoderick Av KLBCH PA10 .....100 C4

Cloch St STPS/GTHM/RID G33 .....92 B1
Clockerhill Pl MTHW ML1 .....138 B3
Cloister Av AIRDRIE ML6 .....98 D5
Clonbeith St
 STPS/GTHM/RID G33 .....71 F4
Closeburn St PPK/MIL G22 .....67 H1
Cloth St BRHD/NEIL G78 .....124 B5
Clouden Rd CUMB G67 .....26 D3
Cloudhowe Ter
 BLTYR/CAMB G72 .....151 F1
Clouston La MRYH/FIRH G20 .....66 D2
Clouston St MRYH/FIRH G20 .....66 C2
Clova Pl UD/BTH/TAN G71 .....134 A1
Clova St GIF/THBK G46 .....126 C3
Cloverbank St
 SPRGB/BLRNK G21 .....68 D5
Clovergate BSHPBGS G64 .....54 B2
Cloverhill Pl
 BAIL/MDB/MHD G69 .....58 B3
Cloverhill Ter EKILN G74 .....166 A3
Cloverhill Vw EKILN G74 .....166 A4
Clunie Pl CTBR ML5 .....117 E1
 WISHAW ML2 .....158 A4
Clunie Rd PLK/PH/NH G53 .....107 E5
Cluny Av BSDN G61 .....51 H1
 CLYDBK G81 .....32 B1
Cluny Dr BSDN G61 .....51 H1
 NMRNS G77 .....143 G5
 PSLYN/LNWD PA3 .....84 D3
Clutha Pl EKILS G75 .....177 F1
Clutha St GOV/IBX G51 .....88 A1
Clyde Av BRHD/NEIL G78 .....142 C1
 BSHPBGS G64 .....19 F5
 HMLTN ML3 .....151 G4
 UD/BTH/TAN G71 .....152 A1
Clydebrae Dr UD/BTH/TAN G71 .....152 C2
Clydebrae St GOV/IBX G51 .....88 A1
Clyde Dr BLSH ML4 .....136 B3
Clydeford Dr CAR/SHTL G32 .....111 H1
 UD/BTH/TAN G71 .....114 C5
Clydeford Rd
 BLTYR/CAMB G72 .....131 G1
 CAR/SHTL G32 .....112 B5
Clydeholm Rd SCOT G14 .....65 G4
Clydeholm Ter CLYDBK G81 .....49 G4
Clydeneuk Dr
 UD/BTH/TAN G71 .....114 C5
Clyde Pl BLTYR/CAMB G72 .....132 A3
 GBLS G5 .....2 C7
 JNSTN PA5 .....101 E5
 MTHW ML1 .....137 F3
Clyde Rd PSLYN/LNWD PA3 .....82 C5
Clydesdale Av HMLTN ML3 .....180 D2
 PSLYN/LNWD PA3 .....62 D5
 WISHAW ML2 .....173 E4
Clydesdale Pl HMLTN ML3 .....180 D2
Clydeside Expressway
 HMLTN ML3 .....169 H1
Clydeside Rd RUTH G73 .....110 C2
Clydesmill Dr CAR/SHTL G32 .....112 B5
Clydesmill Gv CAR/SHTL G32 .....112 B5
Clydesmill Pl CAR/SHTL G32 .....112 B4
Clydesmill Rd CAR/SHTL G32 .....112 B4
Clyde St CGLE G1 .....2 E7
 CTBR ML5 .....97 F2
 RNFRW PA4 .....63 G1
Clyde Ter MTHW ML1 .....155 F5
 UD/BTH/TAN G71 .....152 B1
Clydevale UD/BTH/TAN G71 .....152 C1
Clyde Valley Av MTHW ML1 .....171 H1
Clydeview HMLTN ML3 .....169 H5
Clydeview DMBTN G82 .....12 D5
 UD/BTH/TAN G71 .....152 D1
Clyde View PSLYS PA2 .....105 E2
Clydeview Ter CAR/SHTL G32 .....112 D4
Clynder St GOV/IBX G51 .....88 A3
Clyth Dr GIF/THBK G46 .....127 G5
Coach Cl KSYTH G65 .....9 E2
Coach Pl KSYTH G65 .....8 D3
Coach Rd KSYTH G65 .....8 D3
Coalburn Rd UD/BTH/TAN G71 .....134 C2
Coalhall Av MTHW ML1 .....155 F1
Coalhill St DEN/PKHD G31 .....91 E4
Coatbank St CTBR ML5 .....97 E5
Coatbank Wy CTBR ML5 .....97 E5
Coatbridge Rd AIRDRIE ML6 .....75 G3
 BAIL/MDB/MHD G69 .....93 H3
 BAIL/MDB/MHD G69 .....94 B4
 CTBR ML5 .....95 F3
Coathill St CTBR ML5 .....96 D5
Coats Dr PSLYS PA2 .....103 G1
Coatshill Av BLTYR/CAMB G72 .....151 F1
Coats St CTBR ML5 .....97 E2
Cobblebank MTHW ML1 .....154 A5
Cobbleton Rd MTHW ML1 .....137 E5
Cobington Pl
 STPS/GTHM/RID G33 .....70 C5
Cobinshaw St CAR/SHTL G32 .....92 B5
Coburg St GBLS G5 .....89 G4
Cochno St CLYDBK G81 .....32 D1
Cochno St CLYDBK G81 .....49 F3
Cochranemill Rd JNSTN PA5 .....100 D5
Cochrane Sq PSLYN/LNWD PA3 .....82 A1
Cochrane St BLSH ML4 .....135 G1
 BRHD/NEIL G78 .....124 A5
 CGLE G1 .....3 G5
Cochran St PSLY PA1 .....84 C5
Cockburn Pl CTBR ML5 .....96 C5
Cockels Loan RNFRW PA4 .....63 E5
Cockenzie St CAR/SHTL G32 .....92 B4
Cockmuir St
 SPRGB/BLRNK G21 .....68 D2
Coddington Crs BLSH ML4 .....118 A5
Cogan Pl BRHD/NEIL G78 .....124 A5
Cogan Rd PLKSW/MSWD G43 .....127 F1
Cogan St BRHD/NEIL G78 .....124 A5
 PLKSW/MSWD G43 .....108 B5
Colbert St DMNK/BRGTN G40 .....90 C5
Colbreggan Ct CLYDBK G81 .....32 B2
Colbreggan Gdns CLYDBK G81 .....32 B2
Colchester Dr KVD/HLHD G12 .....51 H5
Coldingham Av SCOT G14 .....49 H5
Coldstream Crs WISHAW ML2 .....157 H4
Coldstream Dr PSLYS PA2 .....103 F3
 RUTH G73 .....130 C1
Coldstream Pl
 SPRGB/BLRNK G21 .....68 A3
Coldstream Rd CLYDBK G81 .....49 G2
Coldstream St
 BLTYR/CAMB G72 .....151 G3
Colebrooke La KVD/HLHD G12 .....66 D3

Colebrooke St
 BLTYR/CAMB G72 .....131 F1
 KVD/HLHD G12 .....66 D3
Colebrooke Ter KVD/HLHD G12 .....66 D3
Coleridge EKILS G75 .....177 H1
Coleridge Av UD/BTH/TAN G71 .....134 C5
Colfin St ESTRH G34 .....72 B5
Colgrain Av MRYH/FIRH G20 .....53 F5
Colgrain St MRYH/FIRH G20 .....67 F1
Colgrain Ter MRYH/FIRH G20 .....53 F5
Colgrave Crs CAR/SHTL G32 .....112 A1
Colinbar Cir BRHD/NEIL G78 .....142 A1
Colinslee Av PLK/PH/NH G53 .....125 G1
Colinslee Crs PLK/PH/NH G53 .....125 G1
Colinslee Dr PLK/PH/NH G53 .....125 G1
Colinslie Rd PLK/PH/NH G53 .....106 D4
Colinton Pl CAR/SHTL G32 .....92 C2
Colintraive Av
 STPS/GTHM/RID G33 .....69 H3
Colintraive Crs
 STPS/GTHM/RID G33 .....69 H3
Collace Av BRWEIR PA11 .....79 G4
Colla Gdns BSHPBGS G64 .....55 G1
Coll Av RNFRW PA4 .....63 G5
Coll Dr CTBR ML5 .....116 B1
College La CGLE G1 .....3 H6
College St CGLE G1 .....3 H6
 DMBTN G82 .....13 E4
Collessie Dr
 STPS/GTHM/RID G33 .....70 D4
Collier St JNSTN PA5 .....101 G3
Colliertree Rd AIRDRIE ML6 .....99 E1
Collina St MRYH/FIRH G20 .....66 C1
Collins St CLYDBK G81 .....32 B2
 COWCAD G4 .....3 K5
Coll Lea HMLTN ML3 .....169 E4
Coll Pl AIRDRIE ML6 .....98 D4
 SPRGB/BLRNK G21 .....68 D4
Coll St SPRGB/BLRNK G21 .....68 D4
 WISHAW ML2 .....158 A4
Collylinn Rd BSDN G61 .....34 B4
Colmonell Av KNTSWD G13 .....50 A4
Colonsay EKILN G74 .....179 F1
Colonsay Av RNFRW PA4 .....63 F5
Colonsay Crs CTBR ML5 .....96 A5
Colonsay Rd
 CARD/HILL/MSPK G52 .....87 A4
 PSLYS PA2 .....104 A5
Colquhoun Av
 CARD/HILL/MSPK G52 .....86 B2
Colquhoun Dr BSDN G61 .....34 A3
Colquhoun St DMBTN G82 .....13 E5
Colson Pl BLSH ML4 .....136 B1
Colston Av SPRGB/BLRNK G21 .....54 C4
Colston Dr BSHPBGS G64 .....54 C4
Colston Gdns AIRDRIE ML6 .....98 A2
 BSHPBGS G64 .....54 B4
Colston Path BSHPBGS G64 .....54 B4
Colston Pl AIRDRIE ML6 .....98 A2
 BSHPBGS G64 .....54 C4
Colston Rd AIRDRIE ML6 .....98 A2
 BSHPBGS G64 .....54 C4
Colt Av CTBR ML5 .....74 B5
Coltmuir Crs BSHPBGS G64 .....54 B3
Coltmuir Dr BSHPBGS G64 .....54 B3
Coltmuir Gdns BSHPBGS G64 .....54 B3
Coltmuir St PPK/MIL G22 .....53 G5
Coltness Av SHOTTS ML7 .....159 G2
Coltness La
 STPS/GTHM/RID G33 .....92 D2
Coltness Rd WISHAW ML2 .....157 F5
Coltness St
 STPS/GTHM/RID G33 .....92 D1
Coltpark Av BSHPBGS G64 .....54 B3
Coltpark La BSHPBGS G64 .....54 B3
Colt Pl CTBR ML5 .....96 D1
Coltsfoot Dr PLK/PH/NH G53 .....125 G4
Coltswood Rd CTBR ML5 .....74 D5
Colt Ter CTBR ML5 .....96 D2
Columba Crs MTHW ML1 .....136 C5
Columba Path
 BLTYR/CAMB G72 .....151 F2
Columba Pl GOV/IBX G51 .....88 A2
Columba St GOV/IBX G51 .....88 A2
Columbia Wy EKILS G75 .....165 G5
Colvend Dr RUTH G73 .....130 A4
Colvend St DMNK/BRGTN G40 .....110 C1
Colville Dr RUTH G73 .....130 C1
Colvilles Pl EKILS G75 .....179 E2
Colvilles Rd EKILS G75 .....178 D3
Colwood Av PLK/PH/NH G53 .....125 F4
Colwood Gdns
 PLK/PH/NH G53 .....125 F4
Colwood Path PLK/PH/NH G53 .....125 F4
Colwyn Ct AIRDRIE ML6 .....76 B5
Coizium Vw AIRDRIE ML6 .....98 D2
Combe Qd BLSH ML4 .....135 F4
Comedie Rd
 STPS/GTHM/RID G33 .....71 E3
Comely Bank HMLTN ML3 .....169 E2
Comelybank La DMBTN G82 .....12 C3
Comelybank Rd DMBTN G82 .....12 C3
Comelypark St DEN/PKHD G31 .....90 C3
Commerce St GBLS G5 .....89 H5
Commercial Rd
 BRHD/NEIL G78 .....124 B4
 GBLS G5 .....89 H5
Common Gn HMLTN ML3 .....170 B1
Commonhead Av AIRDRIE ML6 .....76 A5
Commonhead La AIRDRIE ML6 .....76 A5
Commonhead Rd ESTRH G34 .....94 A1
Commonhead St AIRDRIE ML6 .....76 A5
Commonside St AIRDRIE ML6 .....76 A5
Commore Av BRHD/NEIL G78 .....142 C1
Commore Dr KNTSWD G13 .....50 A4
Community Av BLSH ML4 .....135 H4
Community Pl BLSH ML4 .....135 H3
Community Rd BLSH ML4 .....135 G3
Comrie Crs HMLTN ML3 .....168 D1
Comrie Rd STPS/GTHM/RID G33 .....70 D1
Comrie St CAR/SHTL G32 .....112 C1
Cona St GIF/THBK G46 .....126 B3
Condor Gln BLSH ML4 .....117 H5
Condorrat Ring Rd CUMB G67 .....26 A4
Condorrat Rd CUMB G67 .....43 H4
Congress Rd KVGV G3 .....88 C2
Congress Wy KVGV G3 .....88 D2
Conifer Pl KKNTL G66 .....39 G2
Conisborough Rd ESTRH G34 .....71 G4
Coniston EKILS G75 .....177 G3
Coniston Dr BLSH ML4 .....136 C3

Coniston Dr BLSH ML4 .....136 A4
Conistone Crs
 BAIL/MDB/MHD G69 .....93 G5
Connal St DMNK/BRGTN G40 .....111 E1
Connell Crs MLNGV G62 .....17 G4
Conniston St CAR/SHTL G32 .....91 H2
Connor Rd BRHD/NEIL G78 .....124 A4
Connor St AIRDRIE ML6 .....77 F1
Conon Av BSDN G61 .....34 A5
Conservation Pl WISHAW ML2 .....174 A4
Consett La STPS/GTHM/RID G33 .....92 D1
Consett St STPS/GTHM/RID G33 .....92 D1
Constantine Wy MTHW ML1 .....154 B1
Constarry Rd BALLOCH G68 .....25 E2
 KSYTH G65 .....25 F2
Consul Wy MTHW ML1 .....154 D1
Contin Pl MRYH/FIRH G20 .....66 C1
Cook St GBLS G5 .....89 F4
Coolgardie Gn EKILS G75 .....177 H1
Coolgardie Pl EKILS G75 .....177 H1
Cooperage Ct KNTSWD G13 .....49 G5
Co-operative Ter JNSTN PA5 .....101 H3
Copenhagen Av EKILS G75 .....178 B2
Copland Pl GOV/IBX G51 .....88 A3
Copland Qd GOV/IBX G51 .....88 A4
Copland Rd GOV/IBX G51 .....88 A4
Coplaw St GVH/MTFL G42 .....109 F1
Copperfield La
 UD/BTH/TAN G71 .....115 F5
Coralmount Gdns KKNTL G66 .....40 B1
Corbett Ct CAR/SHTL G32 .....112 A1
Corbett St CAR/SHTL G32 .....112 B1
Corbie Pl MLNGV G62 .....16 B3
Corbie St LNPK/KPK G44 .....109 G5
Corkerhill La
 CARD/HILL/MSPK G52 .....87 F5
Corkerhill Pl
 CARD/HILL/MSPK G52 .....107 E2
Corkerhill Rd
 CARD/HILL/MSPK G52 .....107 E1
Corlaich Av GVH/MTFL G42 .....110 D5
Corlaich Dr RUTH G73 .....110 B5
Cormack Av BSHPBGS G64 .....37 H1
Cormorant Av
 CRG/CRSL/HOU PA6 .....81 E3
Cornaig Rd PLK/PH/NH G53 .....106 C4
Cornalee Gdns
 PLK/PH/NH G53 .....106 C5
Cornalee Pl PLK/PH/NH G53 .....106 C5
Cornalee Rd PLK/PH/NH G53 .....106 C5
Cornelian Ter BLSH ML4 .....135 H3
Cornelia St MTHW ML1 .....154 A1
Cornhill Dr CTBR ML5 .....96 B1
Cornhill St SPRGB/BLRNK G21 .....68 C1
Cornock Crs CLYDBK G81 .....32 A5
Cornock St CLYDBK G81 .....32 A5
Corn St COWCAD G4 .....67 G4
Cornwall Av RUTH G73 .....130 C2
Cornwall St EKILS G75 .....166 B4
 GOV/IBX G51 .....88 C4
Cornwall St South
 PLKSD/SHW G41 .....88 C5
Coronation Pl
 BAIL/MDB/MHD G69 .....58 D4
Coronation Rd MTHW ML1 .....137 E3
Coronation Rd East MTHW ML1 .....155 E1
Coronation Wy BSDN G61 .....51 G1
Corpach Pl ESTRH G34 .....72 C5
Corra Linn HMLTN ML3 .....169 F2
Corran Av NMRNS G77 .....143 H4
Corran St STPS/GTHM/RID G33 .....92 A1
Correen Gdns BSDN G61 .....33 G1
Corrie Brae KSYTH G65 .....8 C2
Corrie Ct HMLTN ML3 .....169 E3
Corrie Dr MTHW ML1 .....157 F5
 PSLY PA1 .....85 H5
Corrie Gdns EKILS G75 .....177 G4
Corrie Gv LNPK/KPK G44 .....128 A3
Corrie Pl KKNTL G66 .....40 B4
Corrie Rd KSYTH G65 .....8 C1
Corrie Vw BALLOCH G68 .....24 D5
Corrour Rd NMRNS G77 .....143 H4
Corsebar Av PSLYS PA2 .....103 H2
Corsebar Crs PSLYS PA2 .....103 H3
Corsebar Dr PSLYS PA2 .....103 H2
Corsebar La PSLYS PA2 .....103 G3
Corsebar Rd PSLYS PA2 .....103 F3
Corse Dr BRHD/NEIL G78 .....124 A3
Corseford Av JNSTN PA5 .....120 D1
Corsehill Pl ESTRH G34 .....94 B1
Corsehill St ESTRH G34 .....94 B1
Corse Rd PLK/PH/NH G53 .....143 F1
Corsewall Av CAR/SHTL G32 .....113 F1
Corsewall St CTBR ML5 .....96 B2
Corsford Dr PLK/PH/NH G53 .....125 H1
Corsock Av HMLTN ML3 .....168 D3
Corsock St DEN/PKHD G31 .....91 G1
Corston St STPS/GTHM/RID G33 .....91 G2
Cortachy Pl BSHPBGS G64 .....55 G2
Coruisk Dr
 CRMNK/CLK/EAG G76 .....145 G2
Corunna St KVGV G3 .....88 D1
Coshneuk Rd
 STPS/GTHM/RID G33 .....70 C1
Cottar St MRYH/FIRH G20 .....52 D4
Cotton Av PSLYN/LNWD PA3 .....82 A4
Cotton St DMNK/BRGTN G40 .....110 D2
 PSLY PA1 .....84 C5
Cotton V MTHW ML1 .....156 B2
Coulin Gdns PPK/MIL G22 .....68 A1
Coulter Av CTBR ML5 .....96 B1
County Av BLTYR/CAMB G72 .....111 G5
County Pl PSLY PA1 .....84 B4
County Sq PSLY PA1 .....84 B4
Couper St COWCAD G4 .....3 H2
Coursington Crs MTHW ML1 .....155 F3
Coursington Gdns MTHW ML1 .....155 F3
Coursington Rd MTHW ML1 .....155 E3
Courthill BSDN G61 .....34 A2
Courthill Av LNPK/KPK G44 .....128 C2
Courthill Crs KSYTH G65 .....8 D2
Coustonholm Rd
 PLKSW/MSWD G43 .....108 C5
Couther Qd AIRDRIE ML6 .....76 C3
Covanburn Av HMLTN ML3 .....170 C4
Coventry Dr DEN/PKHD G31 .....91 E1
Cowal Dr PSLYN/LNWD PA3 .....101 H1
Cowal Rd MRYH/FIRH G20 .....52 B4
Cowal St MRYH/FIRH G20 .....52 B4
Cowan Crs BRHD/NEIL G78 .....124 C5

Cowan La KVD/HLHD G12 .....66 D4
Cowan Rd BALLOCH G68 .....25 F3
Cowan St KVD/HLHD G12 .....66 D4
Cowan Wilson Av
 BLTYR/CAMB G72 .....151 G2
Cowan Wynd
 UD/BTH/TAN G71 .....115 F4
Cowcaddens Rd COWCAD G4 .....2 D2
Cowcaddens St CGLW G2 .....2 E3
Cowdenhill Circ KNTSWD G13 .....51 E3
Cowdenhill Pl KNTSWD G13 .....51 E3
Cowdenhill Rd KNTSWD G13 .....50 D3
Cowden St GOV/IBX G51 .....87 E2
Cowdray Crs RNFRW PA4 .....63 G3
Cowgate KKNTL G66 .....21 E5
Cowglen Rd PLK/PH/NH G53 .....106 D5
Cowlairs Rd SPRGB/BLRNK G21 .....68 A2
Coxdale Av KKNTL G66 .....20 D5
Coxhill St SPRGB/BLRNK G21 .....68 A3
Coxton Pl STPS/GTHM/RID G33 .....71 E5
Coylton Crs HMLTN ML3 .....168 D4
Coylton Rd PLKSW/MSWD G43 .....128 A2
Crabb Qd MTHW ML1 .....154 B1
Cragdale EKILN G74 .....165 H2
Cragan Dr KNTSWD G13 .....50 A5
Crags Av PSLYS PA2 .....104 C3
Crags Crs PSLYS PA2 .....104 C2
Crags Rd PSLYS PA2 .....104 C3
Cragwell Pk
 CRMNK/CLK/EAG G76 .....147 F3
Craigallian Av
 BLTYR/CAMB G72 .....132 A3
 MLNGV G62 .....17 F1
Craiganour La
 PLKSW/MSWD G43 .....127 F1
Craigard Pl RUTH G73 .....130 C4
Craigash Qd MLNGV G62 .....16 C3
Craigash Rd MLNGV G62 .....16 C3
Craigbank Dr PLK/PH/NH G53 .....125 F3
Craigbarnet Av BSHPBGS G64 .....19 E5
Craigbarnet Crs
 STPS/GTHM/RID G33 .....70 C2
Craigbarnet Rd MLNGV G62 .....16 B3
Craigbet Av BRWEIR PA11 .....78 B1
Craigbet Crs BRWEIR PA11 .....78 B1
Craigbet Pl BRWEIR PA11 .....78 B1
Craigbo Av SMSTN G23 .....52 C2
Craigbog Av JNSTN PA5 .....121 E1
Craigbo Rd SMSTN G23 .....52 C2
Craigburn Av
 CRG/CRSL/HOU PA6 .....81 E4
Craigburn Crs
 CRG/CRSL/HOU PA6 .....81 E4
Craigburn Pl
 CRG/CRSL/HOU PA6 .....81 E4
Craigburn St HMLTN ML3 .....170 A5
Craigdhu Av AIRDRIE ML6 .....99 E3
 MLNGV G62 .....16 D4
Craigdhu Rd MLNGV G62 .....16 C4
Craigdonald Pl JNSTN PA5 .....101 G3
Craigellan Rd
 PLKSW/MSWD G43 .....127 G1
Craigelvan Av CUMB G67 .....43 G2
Craigelvan Ct CUMB G67 .....43 G2
Craigelvan Dr CUMB G67 .....43 G2
Craigelvan Gdns CUMB G67 .....43 G2
Craigelvan Gv CUMB G67 .....43 G2
Craigelvan Pl CUMB G67 .....43 G2
Craigelvan Vw CUMB G67 .....43 G2
Craigenbay Rd KKNTL G66 .....40 B3
Craigenbay St SPRGB/BLRNK G21 .....69 E2
Craigendmuir Rd
 STPS/GTHM/RID G33 .....71 F2
Craigendmuir St
 STPS/GTHM/RID G33 .....69 G5
Craigend Ov PSLYS PA2 .....122 D1
Craigend Pl KNTSWD G13 .....51 F5
Craigend Rd CUMB G67 .....26 B3
Craigends Dr KLBCH PA10 .....100 B3
Craigends Rd
 CRG/CRSL/HOU PA6 .....81 E4
Craigend St KNTSWD G13 .....51 F5
Craigend Vw CUMB G67 .....43 G2
Craigenfeoch Av JNSTN PA5 .....101 E5
Craigens Rd AIRDRIE ML6 .....101 H1
Craigfaulds Av PSLYS PA2 .....103 G2
Craigfell Ct HMLTN ML3 .....168 D3
Craigflower Gdns
 PLK/PH/NH G53 .....125 F3
Craigflower Rd
 PLK/PH/NH G53 .....125 F3
Craig Gdns NMRNS G77 .....161 F1
Craighalbert Rd BALLOCH G68 .....25 G1
Craighalbert Wy BALLOCH G68 .....25 G1
Craighall Qd BRHD/NEIL G78 .....141 E4
Craighall Rd COWCAD G4 .....67 G4
Craighaw St
 STPS/GTHM/RID G33 .....69 G3
Craighead Av MLNGV G62 .....16 B3
Craighead Dr MLNGV G62 .....16 B3
Craighead Rd BSHPTN PA7 .....46 A1
 KKNTL G66 .....40 B3
Craighead St AIRDRIE ML6 .....99 F1
Craig Hi EKILS G75 .....177 H1
Craighill Dr
 CRMNK/CLK/EAG G76 .....145 G4
Craighill Gv
 CRMNK/CLK/EAG G76 .....145 G4
Craighirst Dr CLYDBK G81 .....31 H1
Craighirst Rd MLNGV G62 .....16 C3
Craighlaw Av
 CRMNK/CLK/EAG G76 .....163 E5
Craighlaw Dr
 CRMNK/CLK/EAG G76 .....163 E5
Craighouse St
 STPS/GTHM/RID G33 .....70 B5
Craighurst Rd MLNGV G62 .....16 B3
Craigie St
 CRMNK/CLK/EAG G76 .....145 G4
Craigiebar Dr PSLYS PA2 .....103 H4
Craigieburn Gdns
 MRYH/FIRH G20 .....52 A3
Craigieburn Rd CUMB G67 .....26 B4
Craigie Dr NMRNS G77 .....161 H2
Craigiehall Av ERSK PA8 .....47 F4
Craigiehall Crs ERSK PA8 .....47 F4
Craigiehall Pl GOV/IBX G51 .....88 C3
Craigiehall St GOV/IBX G51 .....88 C3
Craigiehall Wy ERSK PA8 .....47 F4
Craigielea Crs MLNGV G62 .....16 C3

Craigielea Dr PSLYN/LNWD PA3 ..83 G3
Craigielea Pk RNFRW PA4 ......63 F5
Craigielea Rd CLYDBK G81 ....31 G1
  RNFRW PA4 ....63 F5
Craigielea St DEN/PKHD G31 ..90 D1
Craigiellyn Av PSLYS PA2 ....122 C1
Craigie Pk KKNTL G66 ....40 B3
Craigie St GVH/MTFL G42 ....109 F2
Craigievar Pl NMRNS G77 ....143 G5
Craigievar St
  STPS/GTHM/RID G33 ......71 F4
Craiglea Pl AIRDRIE ML6 ......98 D1
Craiglea Ter AIRDRIE ML6 ....77 F1
Craiglee EKILS G75 ....178 B4
Craigleith St CAR/SHTL G32 ..91 H5
Craiglinn Park Rd BALLOCH G68 ..25 E4
Craiglockhart St
  STPS/GTHM/RID G33 ......71 E5
Craigmaddie Gdns
  BSHPBGS G64 ....19 G5
Craigmaddie Terrace La
  KVGV G5 ....66 D5
Craigmarloch Av BSHPBGS G64 ..19 F5
Craigmillar Av MLNGV G62 ....17 F5
Craigmillar Rd GVH/MTFL G42 ..109 F5
Craigmochan Av AIRDRIE ML6 ..77 F5
Craigmont Dr MRYH/FIRH G20 ..66 D1
Craigmont St MRYH/FIRH G20 ..52 D5
Craigmore Rd BSDN G61 ....33 G1
Craigmore St DEN/PKHD G31 ..90 D2
Craigmount Av PSLYS PA2 ....122 D1
Craigmuir Crs
  CARD/HILL/MSPK G52 ......86 A3
Craigmuir Gdns
  BLTYR/CAMB G72 ....151 E4
Craigmuir Pl
  CARD/HILL/MSPK G52 ......85 H3
Craigmuir Rd
  CARD/HILL/MSPK G52 .....151 E4
  CARD/HILL/MSPK G52 ......85 H3
Craigneil St
  STPS/GTHM/RID G33 ......71 F4
Craigneith Ct EKILN G74 ....167 H1
Craignestock St
  DMNK/BRGTN G40 ....90 B4
Craigneuk Av AIRDRIE ML6 ....98 D5
Craigneuk St WISHAW ML2 ....155 G5
Craignure Crs AIRDRIE ML6 ....98 D5
Craignure Rd RUTH G73 ......130 A4
Craigpark DEN/PKHD G31 ....90 D2
Craigpark Dr DEN/PKHD G31 ..90 D2
Craigpark St CLYDBK G81 ....32 C1
Craigpark Wy
  UD/BTH/TAN G71 ....115 F5
Craig Pl NMRNS G77 ....143 F5
Craig Rd BRHD/NEIL G78 ....141 E4
  LNPK/KPK G44 ....128 B2
  PSLYN/LNWD PA3 ....81 G4
Craigs Av CLYDBK G81 ....32 B1
Craigsheen Av
  CRMNK/CLK/EAG PA6 .....147 E3
Craigside Ct BALLOCH G68 ....43 G1
Craigside Pl BALLOCH G68 ....43 G1
Craigside Rd BALLOCH G68 ....43 G1
Craigson Pl AIRDRIE ML6 ......99 G5
Craigstone Vw KSYTH G65 ......8 D2
Craig St AIRDRIE ML6 ....98 A2
  CTBR ML5 ....95 E5
Craigton Av BRHD/NEIL G78 ..142 D1
  MLNGV G62 ....16 D5
Craigton Crs NMRNS G77 ....143 G5
Craigton Dr BRHD/NEIL G78 ..142 D1
  GOV/IBX G51 ....87 F3
  NMRNS G77 ....143 H5
Craigton Gdns MLNGV G62 ....16 D2
Craigton Pl BLTYR/CAMB G72 ..151 G1
  GOV/IBX G51 ....87 F3
Craigton Rd GOV/IBX G51 ....87 F3
  MLNGV G62 ....16 C2
Craigvale Crs AIRDRIE ML6 ....99 F2
Craigvicar Gdns CAR/SHTL G32 ..93 E4
Craigview Av JNSTN PA5 ....101 E5
Craigview Rd MTHW ML1 ....154 A1
Craigview Ter JNSTN PA5 ....101 E5
Craigwell Av RUTH G73 ......130 C1
Crail St DEN/PKHD G31 ....91 H5
Crammond Av CTBR ML5 ......95 H5
Cramond Av RNFRW PA4 ......63 H4
Cramond St GBLS G5 ....110 A2
Cramond Ter CAR/SHTL G32 ..92 C4
Cranborne Rd KVD/HLHD G12 ..65 H1
Cranbrooke Dr MRYH/FIRH G20 ..52 C4
Crannog Rd DMBTN G82 ......14 B4
Cranston St KVGV G3 ....89 E2
Cranworth La KVD/HLHD G12 ..66 C3
Cranworth St KVD/HLHD G12 ..66 C3
Crarae Av BSDN G61 ....51 G1
Crarea Pl NMRNS G77 ....143 F5
Crathes Ct LNPK/KPK G44 ....127 H3
Crathie Dr AIRDRIE ML6 ......65 H4
  KVGV G3 ....65 H4
Crathie Pl NMRNS G77 ....143 G4
Crathie Qd WISHAW ML2 ....157 E5
Crawford Av KKNTL G66 ......40 B5
Crawford Crs
  BLTYR/CAMB G72 ....151 G1
  UD/BTH/TAN G71 ....114 D5
Crawford Dr DRUM G15 ......50 B2
  EKILN G74 ....167 E3
Crawford Hl EKILN G74 ......167 E3
Crawford Rd
  CRG/CRSL/HOU PA6 ....81 G2
  MLNGV G62 ....16 D1
Crawfurd Dr PSLYN/LNWD PA3 ..83 G3
Crawfurd Gdns RUTH G73 ....130 A3
Crawfurd Rd RUTH G73 ......130 A3
Crawriggs Av KKNTL G66 ......40 A2
Craw Rd PSLYS PA2 ....104 A2
Creamery Rd WISHAW ML2 ....174 B4
Credon Dr BRHD/NEIL G78 ....126 B5
Crebar St GIF/THBK G46 ....126 B3
Credon Av AIRDRIE ML6 ......98 B4
Credon Gdns RUTH G73 ......130 C2
Cree Av BSHPBGS G64 ....55 G2
Cree Gdns CAR/SHTL G32 .....92 A4
Cree Pl EKILS G75 ....165 G4
Creighton Gv EKILN G74 ....166 B4

Creran Ct HMLTN ML3 ....169 F4
Creran Dr RNFRW PA4 ....63 F2
Crescent Rd SCOT G14 ....64 C1
The Crescent CLYDBK G81 ....31 F5
  CRMNK/CLK/EAG G76 .....146 B5
Cressdale Ct CSMK G45 .....129 G5
Cressdale Dr CSMK G45 .....129 G5
Cresswell Gv NMRNS G77 ....161 G2
Cresswell La KVD/HLHD G12 ..66 C3
Cresswell Pl NMRNS G77 ....161 H3
Cresswell St KVD/HLHD G12 ..66 C3
Cressy St GOV/IBX G51 ....87 F1
Crest Av KNTSWD G13 ....50 C3
Crestlea Av PSLYS PA2 .....104 B4
Crichton St CTBR ML5 ....96 D1
  SPRGB/BLRNK G21 ....68 B2
Crieff Av AIRDRIE ML6 ......119 E3
Criffell Gdns CAR/SHTL G32 ..113 E1
Criffell Rd CAR/SHTL G32 ....93 E1
Crighton Wynd
  UD/BTH/TAN G71 ....135 E2
Crimea St CGLW G2 ....2 A5
Crimond Pl KSYTH G65 ....7 H1
Crinan Crs CTBR ML5 ....74 A5
Crinan Gdns BSHPBGS G64 ....55 F2
Crinan Pl BLSH ML4 ....136 A3
Crinan St DEN/PKHD G31 .....91 E2
Clindledyke Crs WISHAW ML2 ..158 B4
Cripps Av CLYDBK G81 ....49 G2
Croftbank Av
  UD/BTH/TAN G71 ....152 C1
Croftbank Crs
  UD/BTH/TAN G71 ....134 A1
  UD/BTH/TAN G71 ....152 C1
Croftbank Ga
  UD/BTH/TAN G71 ....152 C1
Croftburn Dr LNPK/KPK G44 ..129 E3
Croftcot Av BLSH ML4 ......135 G4
Croftcroighn Rd
  STPS/GTHM/RID G33 ......70 C5
Croftend Av LNPK/KPK G44 ..129 F1
Croftend La LNPK/KPK G44 ..129 F2
Croftfoot Crs CSMK G45 ....129 H5
Croftfoot Dr CSMK G45 .....129 G5
Croftfoot Qd CSMK G45 .....129 F5
Croftfoot Rd CSMK G45 .....129 E5
Croftfoot St CSMK G45 .....129 H4
Croftfoot Ter CSMK G45 ....129 G5
Crofthead St UD/BTH/TAN G71 ..134 A2
Crofthill Av UD/BTH/TAN G71 ..134 A1
Crofthill Rd LNPK/KPK G44 ..129 F2
Crofthouse Dr LNPK/KPK G44 ..129 F3
Croftmont Av LNPK/KPK G44 ..129 F2
Croftmoraig Av
  BAIL/MDB/MHD G69 ....42 B4
Crofton Av LNPK/KPK G44 ..129 E2
Croftpark Av LNPK/KPK G44 ..129 F2
Croftpark Crs
  BLTYR/CAMB G72 ....151 H4
Croftpark Rd CLYDBK G81 ....32 A1
Croftpark St BLSH ML4 .....135 H1
Croft Rd BLTYR/CAMB G72 ....151 E5
  EKILS G75 ....178 B1
Croftside Av LNPK/KPK G44 ..129 F3
Croftspar Ct
  STPS/GTHM/RID G33 ......93 E3
Croftspar Dr CAR/SHTL G32 ..92 D3
Croftspar Ga
  STPS/GTHM/RID G33 ......93 E3
Croftspar Pl CAR/SHTL G32 ..92 D3
Croftwood Av LNPK/KPK G44 ..129 E3
Croftwood Rd HMLTN ML3 ....170 A4
Croft Wynd UD/BTH/TAN G71 ..134 B1
Crogal Crs AIRDRIE ML6 ....119 E2
Cromalt Av EKILS G75 ......177 G4
Cromalt Crs BSDN G61 ....16 A5
Cromarty Av BSHPBGS G64 ....55 G1
  PLKSW/MSWD G43 ....109 E5
Cromarty Crs BSDN G61 ......34 C1
Cromarty Gdns
  CRMNK/CLK/EAG PA6 .....146 B1
Cromarty Pl
  BAIL/MDB/MHD G69 ....58 C2
  EKILN G74 ....167 F2
Cromarty Rd AIRDRIE ML6 ....98 A5
Crombie Gdns
  BAIL/MDB/MHD G69 ....113 G1
Cromdale Rd OLDK G60 ....30 A3
Cromdale St GOV/IBX G51 ....87 F3
Cromdale Wy MTHW ML1 ....137 F5
Cromer St MRYH/FIRH G20 ....67 E1
Cromer Wy PSLY PA1 ....83 H4
Compton La LNPK/KPK G44 ..103 G1
Crompton Av LNPK/KPK G44 ..128 C2
Cromwell La COWCAD G4 ......67 F4
Cromwell St COWCAD G4 ......67 F4
Crona Dr HMLTN ML3 ....168 D1
Cronberry Qd
  CARD/HILL/MSPK G52 ....106 A1
Cronberry Ter
  CARD/HILL/MSPK G52 ....106 A1
Cronin Pl BLSH ML4 ....117 E5
Cronulla Pl KSYTH G65 ......8 B2
Crookedshields Rd EKILN G74 ..149 G3
Crookfur Rd NMRNS G77 ....143 H4
Crookston Av
  CARD/HILL/MSPK G52 .....86 B5
Crookston Ct
  CARD/HILL/MSPK G52 .....86 B5
Crookston Dr
  CARD/HILL/MSPK G52 .....86 A5
Crookston Gv
  CARD/HILL/MSPK G52 .....86 B5
Crookston Pl
  CARD/HILL/MSPK G52 .....86 A5
Crookston Qd
  CARD/HILL/MSPK G52 .....86 A5
Crookston Rd
  CARD/HILL/MSPK G52 ....106 A1
  GOV/IBX G51 ....85 F2
Crookston Ter
  CARD/HILL/MSPK G52 .....86 B5
Crosbie Dr PSLYS PA2 ......102 D5
Crosbie La MRYH/FIRH G20 ...52 B3
Crosbie St MRYH/FIRH G20 ...52 B3
Crosbie Wd PSLYS PA2 ......103 G3
Cross Arthurlie St
  BRHD/NEIL G78 ....124 A4
Crossbank Av GVH/MTFL G42 ..110 B3
Crossbank Dr GVH/MTFL G42 ..110 A3

Crossbank Rd GVH/MTFL G42 ..110 A3
Crossbank Ter GVH/MTFL G42 ..110 A3
Crossburn Av MLNGV G62 ....16 D4
Crossdykes KKNTL G66 ....40 D1
Crossflat Crs PSLY PA1 .....84 D4
Crossford Dr SMSTN G23 ....52 D2
Cross Gates BLSH ML4 ......135 H3
Crosshill Av GVH/MTFL G42 ..109 G3
  KKNTL G66 ....40 A2
Crosshill Dr MTHW ML1 .....139 E4
  RUTH G73 ....130 A1
Crosshill Rd BSHPBGS G64 ....38 C3
  KKNTL G66 ....40 A5
Crosshill St AIRDRIE ML6 ....98 A2
  CTBR ML5 ....95 H5
  MTHW ML1 ....155 E4
Crosshouse Rd EKILS G75 ..177 E3
Crosslea Gdns
  CRG/CRSL/HOU PA6 ....80 C2
Crosslee Crs
  CRG/CRSL/HOU PA6 ....80 D2
Crosslee Pk CRG/CRSL/HOU PA6 ..80 D2
Crosslee Rd BRWEIR PA11 ...80 B4
Crosslees Dr GIF/THBK G46 ..126 C4
Crosslees Pk GIF/THBK G46 ..126 C4
Crosslees Rd GIF/THBK G46 ..126 C5
Crosslee St
  CARD/HILL/MSPK G52 .....87 E4
Crosslet Ct DMBTN G82 ......13 G4
Crosslet Pl DMBTN G82 ......13 G4
Crosslet Rd DMBTN G82 ......13 F4
Crossloan Rd GOV/IBX G51 ..87 G2
Crossloan Ter GOV/IBX G51 ..87 G2
Crossmill Av BRHD/NEIL G78 ..124 C3
Crossmyloof Gdns
  PLKSD/SHW G41 ....108 C3
Crosspoint Dr SMSTN G23 ....52 D2
Cross Stone Pl MTHW ML1 ..154 D4
Cross St CAR/SHTL G32 ......112 D5
Crossstobs Rd PLK/PH/NH G53 ..106 B3
Crossveggate MLNGV G62 ....17 F4
Crossview Av
  BAIL/MDB/MHD G69 ....94 C4
Crossview Pl
  BAIL/MDB/MHD G69 ....94 C4
Crossways CRG/CRSL/HOU PA6 ..81 E3
Crovie Rd PLK/PH/NH G53 ..106 B5
Crow Av MTHW ML1 ....137 G2
Crowflats Rd UD/BTH/TAN G71 ..133 H1
Crowflat Vw UD/BTH/TAN G71 ..115 H5
Crowhill Crs AIRDRIE ML6 ....76 A4
Crowhill Rd BSHPBGS G64 ....54 C3
Crowhill St PPK/MIL G22 .....53 H5
Crow La KNTSWD G13 ....65 G1
Crowlin Crs
  STPS/GTHM/RID G33 ......92 C1
Crown Av CLYDBK G81 ....31 H5
Crown Circ KVD/HLHD G12 ....66 B3
Crown Gdns KVD/HLHD G12 ..66 B3
Crownhall Pl CAR/SHTL G32 ..92 D4
Crownhall Rd CAR/SHTL G32 ..92 D4
Crownpoint Rd
  DMNK/BRGTN G40 ....90 D4
Crown Rd North KVD/HLHD G12 ..66 A3
Crown Rd South KVD/HLHD G12 ..66 B3
Crown St AIRDRIE ML6 ......118 C1
  BAIL/MDB/MHD G69 ....93 G5
  CTBR ML5 ....97 F2
  GBLS G5 ....89 H5
Crown Ter KVD/HLHD G12 ....66 A3
Cruachan Av RNFRW PA4 ....63 G5
Cruachan Crs AIRDRIE ML6 ..118 C2
Cruachan Dr BRHD/NEIL G78 ..142 B1
  NMRNS G77 ....162 A2
Cruachan Rd BSDN G61 ......33 G1
  RUTH G73 ....130 D4
Cruachan St GIF/THBK G46 ..126 C3
Cruachan Wy BRHD/NEIL G78 ..142 B1
Cruden St GOV/IBX G51 ......87 G3
Crum Av GIF/THBK G46 ......126 D4
Crusader Av KNTSWD G13 ....51 E2
Cubie St DMNK/BRGTN G40 ..90 C4
Cuckoo Wy MTHW ML1 ......137 G2
Cuilhill Rd CTBR ML5 ....95 E1
Cuillin Pl AIRDRIE ML6 ....119 G3
The Cuillins
  BAIL/MDB/MHD G69 ....42 B4
  UD/BTH/TAN G71 ....114 D3
Cuillin Wy BRHD/NEIL G78 ..124 B5
Cuilmuir Ter KSYTH G65 ......8 D5
Cuilmuir Vw KSYTH G65 ......8 D5
Culbin Dr KNTSWD G13 ......50 A3
Cullen La EKILS G75 ....178 A1
Cullen Pl UD/BTH/TAN G71 ..115 F4
Cullen Rd EKILS G75 ....178 A1
  MTHW ML1 ....154 B5
Cullen St CAR/SHTL G32 .....92 B5
Cullins Rd RUTH G73 ....130 D4
Cullion Wy MTHW ML1 ......138 C2
Culloch Rd BSDN G61 ....33 E5
Culloden Av BLSH ML4 ......136 C5
Culloden St DEN/PKHD G31 ..91 E1
Culrain Gdns CAR/SHTL G32 ..92 B4
Culrain St CAR/SHTL G32 ....92 B4
Culross Hl EKILN G74 ......166 A4
Culross La CAR/SHTL G32 ....93 E5
Culross St CAR/SHTL G32 ....93 E5
Culross Wy BAIL/MDB/MHD G69 ..42 B5
Culterfell Pl AIRDRIE ML6 ....99 F2
Cults St GOV/IBX G51 ......87 G3
Culvain Av BSDN G61 ....33 G1
Culzean AIRDRIE ML6 ....99 F2
Culzean Av CTBR ML5 ....96 B5
Culzean Crs
  BAIL/MDB/MHD G69 ....93 H5
  NMRNS G77 ....144 D5
Culzean Dr CAR/SHTL G32 ....93 E4
  MTHW ML1 ....137 H4
Culzean Pl EKILN G74 ......166 A2
Cumberland Pl CTBR ML5 ....96 B5
  GBLS G5 ....89 H5
Cumberland St GBLS G5 .....89 H5
Cumbernauld Rd
  BAIL/MDB/MHD G69 ....58 B4

  CUMB G67 ....43 E4
  DEN/PKHD G31 ....91 E2
  STPS/GTHM/RID G33 ......69 G5
Cumbrae EKILN G74 ....167 F4
Cumbrae Ct CLYDBK G81 .....49 H1
Cumbrae Crs CTBR ML5 ......97 H4
Cumbrae Crs North DMBTN G82 ..12 B2
Cumbrae Crs South DMBTN G82 ..12 A2
  KKNTL G66 ....40 A2
Cumbrae Dr MTHW ML1 ......154 B5
Cumbrae Pl AIRDRIE ML6 ....97 H5
Cumbrae Rd PSLYS PA2 ....104 D5
  RNFRW PA4 ....63 G5
Cumbrae St
  STPS/GTHM/RID G33 ......92 B1
Cumlodden Dr MRYH/FIRH G20 ..52 B4
Cumming Dr GVH/MTFL G42 ..109 G4
Cumnock Dr AIRDRIE ML6 ....98 B5
  BRHD/NEIL G78 ....142 B1
  HMLTN ML3 ....168 C4
Cumnock Rd
  STPS/GTHM/RID G33 ......55 H5
Cunard St CLYDBK G81 ......49 E3
Cunningham Rd KLBCH PA10 ..100 C4
Cunningair Dr MTHW ML1 ..171 H1
Cunningham Dr GIF/THBK G46 ..127 H4
Cunninghame Rd EKILN G74 ..166 B4
  RUTH G73 ....111 F4
Cunningham Gdns
  CRG/CRSL/HOU PA6 ....81 C2
Cunningham Rd
  CARD/HILL/MSPK G52 .....86 A1
Cunningham St MTHW ML1 ..154 B4
Cuparhead Av CTBR ML5 ......96 B5
Curfew Rd KNTSWD G13 ......51 E2
Curle St SCOT G14 ....65 F4
Curlew Pl JNSTN PA5 ....120 D2
Curling Crs GVH/MTFL G42 ..109 H5
Curlinghaugh Crs
  WISHAW ML2 ....174 B2
Curlingmire EKILS G75 .....178 B2
Curran Av WISHAW ML2 .....173 F4
Currie Pl MRYH/FIRH G20 ....66 D1
Currie St MRYH/FIRH G20 ....52 D5
Curtis Av LNPK/KPK G44 ....109 H5
Curzon St MRYH/FIRH G20 ....52 D5
Cuthbertson St
  PLKSD/SHW G41 ....109 E1
Cuthbert St UD/BTH/TAN G71 ..115 G5
Cuthelton Dr DEN/PKHD G31 ..91 H5
Cuthelton St DEN/PKHD G31 ..91 G5
Cuthelton Ter DEN/PKHD G31 ..91 G5
Cypress Av BLTYR/CAMB G72 ..151 G4
  UD/BTH/TAN G71 ....115 G4
Cypress Ct EKILS G75 ......177 H3
  HMLTN ML3 ....170 A4
  KKNTL G66 ....39 G2
Cypress Crs EKILS G75 ....177 H3
Cypress Gv CTBR ML5 ....95 F3
Cypress Pl EKILS G75 ......177 H3
Cypress St PPK/MIL G22 ....54 A5
Cypress Wy BLTYR/CAMB G72 ..132 C3
Cyprus Av JNSTN PA5 ......102 A2
Cyril St PSLY PA1 ....84 D5

D

Daer Av RNFRW PA4 ....63 H5
Daffodil Wy MTHW ML1 .....154 D2
Dairsie Gdns BSHPBGS G64 ..55 G2
Dairsie St LNPK/KPK G44 ..128 A3
Daisy St GVH/MTFL G42 ....109 G3
Dalbeattie Braes AIRDRIE ML6 ..119 F3
Dalbeth Rd CAR/SHTL G32 ..112 A2
Dalcharn Pl ESTRH G34 ....93 H1
Dalcraig Crs BLTYR/CAMB G72 ..151 F1
Dalcross St PTCK G11 ......66 B4
Dalcruin Gdns
  BAIL/MDB/MHD G69 ....42 B4
Daldowie Av CAR/SHTL G32 ..112 D2
Daldowie Rd UD/BTH/TAN G71 ..113 H2
Daldowie St CTBR ML5 ......116 A1
Dale Av EKILS G75 ....178 A2
Dale Ct WISHAW ML2 ....173 H3
Dale Dr MTHW ML1 ....137 F5
Daleview Av KVD/HLHD G12 ..52 A5
Daleview Gv
  CRMNK/CLK/EAG G76 .....145 G4
Daleview Rd
  CRMNK/CLK/EAG G76 .....145 G4
Dale Wy RUTH G73 ....129 H3
Dalfoil Ct PSLY PA1 ....85 H4
Dalgarroch Av KNTSWD G13 ..49 H5
Dalgleish Av CLYDBK G81 ....31 E3
Dalgraig Crs BLTYR/CAMB G72 ..133 F5
Dalhousie Gdns BSHPBGS G64 ..54 C1
Dalhousie La KVGV G3 ......2 D1
Dalhousie Rd KLBCH PA10 ..100 C4
Dalhousie St COWCAD G4 ....2 D2
Daliea Dr ESTRH G34 ....72 C5
Dalilea Pl ESTRH G34 ......72 C5
Dalintober St GBLS G5 .....89 E4
Dalkeith Av BSHPBGS G64 ....38 A5
  PLKSD/SHW G41 ....88 A5
Dalkeith Rd BSHPBGS G64 ....38 A4
Dalmacoulter Rd AIRDRIE ML6 ..77 H3
Dalmahoy Crs BRWEIR PA11 ..79 F5
Dalmahoy St CAR/SHTL G32 ..91 H3
Dalmally St MRYH/FIRH G20 ..67 E2
Dalmarnock Rd
  DMNK/BRGTN G40 ....90 C5
Dalmary Dr PSLY PA1 ....85 G3
Dalmellington Ct EKILN G74 ..166 B2
  HMLTN ML3 ....168 C4
Dalmellington Dr EKILN G74 ..166 B2
  PLK/PH/NH G53 ....106 B3
Dalmellington Rd
  PLK/PH/NH G53 ....106 B4
Dalmeny Av GIF/THBK G46 ..127 F4
Dalmeny Dr BRHD/NEIL G78 ..123 H5
Dalmeny Rd HMLTN ML3 ....170 A3
Dalmeny St GBLS G5 ....110 B2
Dalmore Dr AIRDRIE ML6 ....98 B5
Dalnair Pl MLNGV G62 ......16 B3
Dalnair St KVGV G3 ....66 B5
Dalness St CAR/SHTL G32 ..92 B5
Dalnottar Av OLDK G60 ......30 C2
Dalnottar Dr OLDK G60 ......30 B3
Dalnottar Gdns OLDK G60 ....30 B3
Dalnottar Hill Rd OLDK G60 ..30 C3

Dalreoch Av
  BAIL/MDB/MHD G69 ....94 B3
Dalreoch Ct DMBTN G82 .....12 C3
Dalriada Crs MTHW ML1 ....154 C1
Dalriada Dr BSHPBGS G64 ....19 G4
Dalriada St DMNK/BRGTN G40 ..91 F4
Dairy Gdns HMLTN ML3 .....168 C5
Dalrymple Dr CTBR ML5 ......96 C5
  EKILN G74 ....166 B3
  NMRNS G77 ....162 B1
Dalry Pl AIRDRIE ML6 ......119 E4
Dalry Rd UD/BTH/TAN G71 ..115 G5
Dalry St CAR/SHTL G32 ......92 C5
Dalserf Crs GIF/THBK G46 ..126 D5
Dalserf Gdns DEN/PKHD G31 ..91 E4
Dalserf St DMNK/BRGTN G40 ..91 E4
Dalsetter Av DRUM G15 ......50 A1
Dalsetter Pl DRUM G15 ......50 B1
Dalshannon Pl CUMB G67 ....44 A1
Dalshannon Rd CUMB G67 ....44 A1
Dalshannon Vw CUMB G67 ....44 A1
Dalsholm Rd MRYH/FIRH G20 ..52 B3
Dalskeith Av PSLYN/LNWD PA3 ..83 F4
Dalskeith Crs PSLYN/LNWD PA3 ..83 F4
Dalskeith Rd PSLYN/LNWD PA3 ..83 F5
Dalswinton Pth ESTRH G34 ..94 B1
Dalswinton St ESTRH G34 ....94 B1
Dalton Av CLYDBK G81 ....50 A4
Dalton Hl HMLTN ML3 ......168 C3
Dalton St DEN/PKHD G31 ....91 H4
Dalveen Ct BRHD/NEIL G78 ..142 B1
Dalveen Dr UD/BTH/TAN G71 ..114 D4
Dalveen Qd CTBR ML5 ....97 G2
Dalveen St CAR/SHTL G32 ....92 A4
Dalveen Wy RUTH G73 ......130 B4
Dalwhinnie Av
  BLTYR/CAMB G72 ....133 F5
Daly Gdns BLTYR/CAMB G72 ..151 G1
Dalzell Av MTHW ML1 ......172 B1
Dalziel Dr PLKSD/SHW G41 ..108 B1
Dalziel Rd CARD/HILL/MSPK G52 ..86 A1
Dalziel St HMLTN ML3 ......152 C5
  MTHW ML1 ....154 C3
Damshot Crs PLK/PH/NH G53 ..107 E4
Damshot Rd PLK/PH/NH G53 ..107 E5
Danby Rd BAIL/MDB/MHD G69 ..93 G5
Danes Av SCOT G14 ....64 D2
Danes Crs SCOT G14 ....64 C2
Danes Dr SCOT G14 ....64 C2
Danes La North SCOT G14 ...64 D2
Daniel McLaughlin Pl
  KKNTL G66 ....21 G4
Dargarvel Av PLKSD/SHW G41 ..88 A5
Dargavel Av BSHPTN PA7 ....46 A1
Dargavel Rd ERSK PA8 ......46 C2
Darkwood Ct
  PSLYN/LNWD PA3 ....83 G3
Darkwood Dr PSLYN/LNWD PA3 ..83 G3
Darleith St CAR/SHTL G32 ....92 A4
Darley Pl HMLTN ML3 ......169 F5
Darley Rd BALLOCH G68 ......25 F3
Darluith Rd PSLYN/LNWD PA3 ..81 F5
Darnaway Av
  STPS/GTHM/RID G33 ......71 E4
Darnaway Dr
  STPS/GTHM/RID G33 ......71 E4
Darnaway St
  STPS/GTHM/RID G33 ......71 E4
Darngaber Gdns HMLTN ML3 ..181 E5
Darngaber Rd HMLTN ML3 ....181 E5
Darnick St SPRGB/BLRNK G21 ..68 D4
Darnley Crs BSHPBGS G64 ....37 G5
Darnley Gdns PLKSD/SHW G41 ..108 D2
Darnley Pl PLKSD/SHW G41 ..108 D2
Darnley Rd BRHD/NEIL G78 ..124 C4
  PLKSD/SHW G41 ....108 D2
Darnley St PLKSD/SHW G41 ..109 E1
Darragh Gn WISHAW ML2 ....158 B4
Darroch Dr ERSK PA8 ....30 A5
Darroch Wy CUMB G67 ....26 D2
Dartford St PPK/MIL G22 ....67 G3
Darvel Crs PSLY PA1 ....85 G5
Darvel Dr NMRNS G77 ......144 D5
Darvel St PLK/PH/NH G53 ..125 E1
Darwin Pl CLYDBK G81 ......31 E5
Darwin St EKILS G75 ....165 H5
Davaar EKILN G74 ....167 F4
Davaar Dr CTBR ML5 ....96 B5
  MTHW ML1 ....136 B5
  PSLYS PA2 ....104 B5
Davaar Pl NMRNS G77 ......143 H4
Davaar Rd RNFRW PA4 ......63 H5
Davaar St DMNK/BRGTN G40 ..91 E5
Dava St GOV/IBX G51 ....87 H2
Daventry Dr KVD/HLHD G12 ..65 H1
David Gray Dr KKNTL G66 ...22 A4
David Pl BAIL/MDB/MHD G69 ..93 G5
Davidson Crs KSYTH G65 ......23 E2
Davidson Gdns CAR/SHTL G32 ..92 D3
Davidson Qd CLYDBK G81 ....31 G1
Davidson St AIRDRIE ML6 ....98 C1
  CLYDBK G81 ....49 H1
  CTBR ML5 ....97 E5
  DMNK/BRGTN G40 ....90 D4
Davieland Rd GIF/THBK G46 ..144 D1
Davies Qd MTHW ML1 ......136 C5
Davington Dr HMLTN ML3 ....168 B3
Daviot St GOV/IBX G51 ......87 E3
Dawson Av EKILS G75 ......165 G4
Dawson Pl COWCAD G4 ......67 G3
Deaconsbank Av
  GIF/THBK G46 ....144 A1
Deaconsbank Crs
  GIF/THBK G46 ....144 A1
Deacons Rd KSYTH G65 ....8 B2
Dealston Rd BRHD/NEIL G78 ..124 A3
Deanbrae St UD/BTH/TAN G71 ..134 A2
Dean Crs BAIL/MDB/MHD G69 ..58 C2
  HMLTN ML3 ....169 H4
Deanfield Qd
  CARD/HILL/MSPK G52 .....86 A3
Dean Park Av
  UD/BTH/TAN G71 ....134 B5
Dean Park Dr
  BLTYR/CAMB G72 ....132 A3
Dean Park Rd RNFRW PA4 ....63 G4
Deanside Av BLTYR/CAMB G72 ..132 A4
Deanside Rd
  CARD/HILL/MSPK G52 .....86 B1
Deans Av BLTYR/CAMB G72 ..132 A4
Dean St BLTYR/CAMB G72 ....108 C5
  CLYDBK G81 ....49 F1
Deanston Av BRHD/NEIL G78 ..142 A1
Deanston Dr PLKSD/SHW G41 ..108 C4
Deanston Pk CTBR ML5 .....119 F1
Deanstone Wk CTBR ML5 .....117 G2

Deanston Gv CTBR ML5 ....116 B1
Deanston Pk BRHD/NEIL G78 ...141 H1
Dean St BLSH ML4 ....136 A2
  CLYDBK G81 ....49 F2
Deanwood Av GIF/THBK G46 ...128 A4
Deanwood Rd GIF/THBK G46 ...128 A4
Dechmont Av
  BLTYR/CAMB G72 ....132 A4
  MTHW ML1 ....154 B3
Dechmont Gdns
  BLTYR/CAMB G72 ....151 F1
Dechmont Pl
  BLTYR/CAMB G72 ....132 A4
Dechmont Rd
  UD/BTH/TAN G71 ....114 D3
Dechmont St DEN/PKHD G31 ...91 F5
  HMLTN ML3 ....169 H5
Dechmont Vw BLSH ML4 ....135 G4
  UD/BTH/TAN G71 ....115 F5
Dee Av PSLYS PA2 ....103 E2
  RNFRW PA4 ....63 H3
Deedes St AIRDRIE ML6 ....97 G3
Dee Dr PSLYS PA2 ....103 E2
Deep Dl EKILN G74 ....165 H2
Deepdene Rd
  BAIL/MDB/MHD G69 ....59 E3
  BSDN G61 ....51 E1
Dee PI EKILS G75 ....176 D1
  JNSTN PA5 ....120 D1
Deerdykes Ct North
  BALLOCH G68 ....43 F2
Deerdykes Ct South
  BALLOCH G68 ....43 F3
Deerdykes Rd BALLOCH G68 ...43 F2
Deerdykes Vw BALLOCH G68 ...43 E3
Deer Park Pl BLSH ML4 ....180 D1
Deer Park Pl HMLTN ML3 ....181 E1
Dee St CTBR ML5 ....73 H4
  STPS/GTHM/RID G33 ....91 G1
Dee Ter HMLTN ML3 ....169 G5
Delhi Av CLYDBK G81 ....30 D4
Deliburn St MTHW ML1 ....155 E5
The Dell BLSH ML4 ....136 C4
Delny Pl STPS/GTHM/RID G33 ...93 F2
Delvin Rd LNPK/KPK G44 ....128 B1
Dempsey Rd BLSH ML4 ....135 G4
Denbak Av HMLTN ML3 ....169 F5
Denbeck St CAR/SHTL G32 ....92 A4
Denbrae St CAR/SHTL G32 ....92 A4
Denewood Av PSLYS PA2 ....104 A4
Denham St PPK/MIL G22 ....67 G3
Denholm Crs EKILS G75 ....166 B5
Denholm Dr GIF/THBK G46 ....145 F2
  WISHAW ML2 ....157 F4
Denholm Gdns HMLTN ML3 ...181 E5
Denholm Grn EKILS G75 ....166 C5
Denholm Ter HMLTN ML3 ....168 D2
Denmark St PPK/MIL G22 ....67 H2
Denmilne Rd
  BAIL/MDB/MHD G69 ....94 C2
Denmilne St ESTRH G34 ....94 B2
Dennistoun St BLSH ML4 ....135 H2
Dennystoun Forge DMBTN G82 ...12 D3
Dentdale EKILN G74 ....165 H2
Deramore Av GIF/THBK G46 ...144 D3
Derby St KVGV G3 ....88 D1
Derby Terrace La KVGV G3 ....66 C5
Derby Wynd MTHW ML1 ....155 G1
Derrywood Rd KKNTL G66 ....5 H5
Derwent Dr CTBR ML5 ....73 H4
Derwent St PPK/MIL G22 ....67 G2
Derwentwater EKILS G75 ....177 E2
Despard Av CAR/SHTL G32 ....93 E5
Despard Gdns CAR/SHTL G32 ...93 F5
Deveron Av GIF/THBK G46 ....127 G5
Deveron Crs HMLTN ML3 ....168 C1
Deveron Rd BSDN G61 ....50 D1
  EKILN G74 ....167 E4
  MTHW ML1 ....137 G1
Deveron St CTBR ML5 ....73 H4
  STPS/GTHM/RID G33 ....69 G5
Devine Gv WISHAW ML2 ....158 B3
Devlin Ct BLTYR/CAMB G72 ...151 H5
Devlin Gv BLTYR/CAMB G72 ...151 H5
Devol Crs PLK/PH/NH G53 ....106 C4
Devondale Av
  BLTYR/CAMB G72 ....151 F1
Devon Dr BSHPTN PA7 ....29 F5
Devon Gdns BSHPTN PA7 ....37 G5
Devonhill Av HMLTN ML3 ....180 D1
Devon Pl GVH/MTFL G42 ....89 G5
Devonport Pk EKILS G75 ....177 F1
Devonshire Gardens La
  KVD/HLHD G12 ....66 A2
Devonshire Terrace La
  KVD/HLHD G12 ....66 A2
Devon St GBLS G5 ....89 G5
Devonview Pl AIRDRIE ML6 ...98 A3
Devonview St AIRDRIE ML6 ...98 A3
Devon Wk BALLOCH G68 ....24 C5
Devon Wy MTHW ML1 ....154 A4
Dewar Cl UD/BTH/TAN G71 ...115 F3
Dewar Ga DRUM G15 ....33 H5
Dewar Rd STPS/GTHM/RID G33...57 H5
Diamond St BLSH ML4 ....135 H3
Diana Av KNTSWD G13 ....50 C5
Diana Qd MTHW ML1 ....137 F2
Dickens Av CLYDBK G81 ....31 G4
Dicks Pk EKILS G75 ....166 A5
Dick St MRYH/FIRH G20 ....67 E3
Differ Av KSYTH G65 ....23 F5
Dilwara Av SCOT G14 ....65 E4
Dimity St JNSTN PA5 ....101 G4
Dimsdale Crs WISHAW ML2 ...174 B4
Dimsdale Rd WISHAW ML2 ...174 B4
Dinard Dr GIF/THBK G46 ....127 F3
Dinduff St ESTRH G34 ....72 B5
Dinmont Av PSLYS PA2 ....103 E5
Dinmont Crs MTHW ML1 ....136 A5
Dinmont Rd PLKSD/SHW G41 ...108 C3
Dinwiddie St SPRGB/BLRNK G21...69 F4
Dinyra Pl CTBR ML5 ....59 H5
Dipple Pl DRUM G15 ....50 C1
Dirleton Ga PLKSD/SHW G41...34 A5
Divernia Wy BRHD/NEIL G78...142 C2
Dixon Av DMBTN G82 ....12 C5
Dixon Dr DMBTN G82 ....12 C5
Dixon Pl EKILN G74 ....165 G2
Dixon Rd GVH/MTFL G42 ....109 H3
Dixon St CGLE G1 ....2 E7

  CTBR ML5 ....97 E5
  HMLTN ML3 ....170 A2
  PSLY PA1 ....84 C5
Dickens Gv MTHW ML1 ....138 A5
Dobbie's Loan COWCAD G4 ...3 G2
Dobbie's Loan Pl COWCAD G4...2 D3
Dochart Av RNFRW PA4 ....63 H5
Dochart Dr CTBR ML5 ....73 H4
Dochart St STPS/GTHM/RID G33...69 H4
Dock St CLYDBK G81 ....49 G4
Dodhill Pl KNTSWD G13 ....50 C5
Dodside Gdns CAR/SHTL G32...92 D5
Dodside Pl CAR/SHTL G32 ....92 D5
Dodside St CAR/SHTL G32 ....92 D5
Dolan St BAIL/MDB/MHD G69...94 A4
Dollar Pk MTHW ML1 ....172 C2
Dollar Ter MRYH/FIRH G20 ....52 B3
Dolphin Rd PLKSD/SHW G41...108 C2
Domnica Gn EKILS G75 ....165 F4
Donaldfield Rd BRWEIR PA11...79 E4
Donaldson Crs KKNTL G66 ....39 H1
Donaldson Dr RNFRW PA4 ....63 G2
Donaldson Gn
  UD/BTH/TAN G71 ....115 G4
Donaldswood Pk PSLYS PA2...103 H4
Donaldswood Rd PSLYS PA2...103 H4
Donald Ter HMLTN ML3 ....169 H4
Donald Wy UD/BTH/TAN G71...115 F5
Don Av RNFRW PA4 ....63 H4
Don Ct HMLTN ML3 ....169 F5
Don Dr PSLYS PA2 ....103 E3
Donnelly Wy WISHAW ML2 ...172 D1
Donnies Brae BRHD/NEIL G78...141 G1
Don Pl JNSTN PA5 ....120 D1
Don St STPS/GTHM/RID G33...91 G1
Doonfoot Gdns
  PLKSW/MSWD G43 ....127 F1
Doonfoot Rd
  PLKSW/MSWD G43 ....127 F1
Doon HI KKNTL G66 ....21 H5
Doon Rd KKNTL G66 ....21 H4
Doon Side CUMB G67 ....26 D3
Doon St CLYDBK G81 ....32 B5
  MTHW ML1 ....172 B1
Doon Wy KKNTL G66 ....22 A2
Dorain Rd MTHW ML1 ....138 A4
Dora St DMNK/BRGTN G40 ....110 D1
Dorchester Av KVD/HLHD G12...51 H5
Dorchester Ct KVD/HLHD G12...51 H5
Dorchester Pl KVD/HLHD G12...65 H1
Dorian Dr
  CRMNK/CLK/EAG G76 ....145 F2
Dorlin Rd STPS/GTHM/RID G33...71 F1
Dormanside Ct
  PLK/PH/NH G53 ....106 C1
Dormanside Gv
  PLK/PH/NH G53 ....106 C1
Dormanside Rd
  PLK/PH/NH G53 ....106 C1
Dornal Av KNTSWD G13 ....50 A4
Dornford Av CAR/SHTL G32 ...113 E2
Dornford Rd CAR/SHTL G32...113 E2
Dornie Dr CAR/SHTL G32 ....112 C4
  GIF/THBK G46 ....144 C5
Dornoch Av GIF/THBK G46 ...145 H4
Dornoch Ct BLSH ML4 ....135 H2
Dornoch Dr BLTYR/CAMB G72...168 C1
Dornoch Pl BAIL/MDB/MHD G69...58 C2
  EKILN G74 ....166 B5
Dornoch Rd BSDN G61 ....51 E1
  MTHW ML1 ....137 G2
Dornoch St DMNK/BRGTN G40...90 C4
Dornoch Wy AIRDRIE ML6 ....60 B4
  BALLOCH G68 ....10 C5
Dorset St KVGV G3 ....89 E1
Dosk Av KNTSWD G13 ....49 H5
Dosk Pl KNTSWD G13 ....50 A3
Double Hedges Rd
  BRHD/NEIL G78 ....141 G4
Dougalston Av MLNGV G62 ...17 F4
Dougalston Crs MLNGV G62...17 F4
Dougalston Gdns North
  MLNGV G62 ....17 F4
Dougalston Gdns South
  MLNGV G62 ....17 F4
Douglas Av AIRDRIE ML6 ....98 B3
  BLTYR/CAMB G72 ....131 G3
  GIF/THBK G46 ....145 F1
  JNSTN PA5 ....102 A2
  KKNTL G66 ....40 A5
  RUTH G73 ....130 D2
Douglas Crs AIRDRIE ML6 ....98 B3
  ERSK PA8 ....30 A5
  UD/BTH/TAN G71 ....115 G4
Douglasdale EKILN G74 ....166 A3
Douglas Dr BAIL/MDB/MHD G69...93 G4
  BLSH ML4 ....135 H3
  BLTYR/CAMB G72 ....151 E1
  DRUM G15 ....50 A2
  EKILS G75 ....176 D1
  NMRNS G77 ....144 B4
Douglas Gdns BSDN G61 ....34 C4
  GIF/THBK G46 ....145 F1
  UD/BTH/TAN G71 ....134 A2
Douglas Ga BLTYR/CAMB G72...131 F4
Douglas La CGLW G2 ....2 C4
Douglas Muir Dr MLNGV G62...16 A2
Douglas Muir Gdns MLNGV G62...16 A2
Douglas Muir Pl MLNGV G62...16 A2
Douglas Muir Rd CLYDBK G81...32 C1
  MLNGV G62 ....16 B3
Douglas Park Crs BSDN G61...34 D2
Douglas Park La HMLTN ML3...169 H1
Douglas Pl BSDN G61 ....34 B3
  HMLTN ML3 ....180 D2
  KKNTL G66 ....40 A3
Douglas Rd DMBTN G82 ....13 H3
  RNFRW PA4 ....84 D1
Douglas St AIRDRIE ML6 ....98 B3
  BLTYR/CAMB G72 ....151 F4
  HMLTN ML3 ....152 D5
  MLNGV G62 ....17 E4
  MTHW ML1 ....154 D3
  PSLY PA1 ....83 H4
  UD/BTH/TAN G71 ....134 A2
Douglas Ter PLKSD/SHW G41...108 E2
Dougray Pl BRHD/NEIL G78...124 B5
Dougrie Dr CSMK G45 ....129 E4
Dougrie Pl CSMK G45 ....129 F4
Dougrie Rd CSMK G45 ....129 E4

Dougrie St CSMK G45 ....129 E4
Dougrie Ter CSMK G45 ....129 E5
Dougrie Gdns CSMK G45 ....129 E5
Doune Av AIRDRIE ML6 ....119 E3
  BSHPBGS G64 ....38 A4
Doune Crs AIRDRIE ML6 ....119 E3
  NMRNS G77 ....144 C5
Doune Gdns La
  MRYH/FIRH G20 ....66 D3
Doune Park Wy CTBR ML5 ....96 C5
Doune Qd MRYH/FIRH G20...66 D3
Doune Ter CTBR ML5 ....74 A5
Dovecot PLKSW/MSWD G43...108 B4
Dovecote Vw KKNTL G66 ....40 C1
Dovecotwood KSYTH G65 ....8 B1
Doveholm DMBTN G82 ....13 F2
Doveholm Av DMBTN G82 ....13 G3
Dove Pl EKILS G75 ....177 E2
Dover St CTBR ML5 ....74 A4
  KVGV G3 ....89 E1
Dowanfield Rd CUMB G67 ....25 H4
Dowanhill St PTCK G11 ....66 B4
Dowan Rd MLNGV G62 ....17 H5
Dowanside La
  KVD/HLHD G12 ....66 B3
Dowanside Rd KVD/HLHD G12...66 B3
Downcraig Dr CSMK G45 ...128 D5
Downcraig Gv CSMK G45 ....128 C5
Downcraig Rd CSMK G45 ....128 C5
Downcraig Ter CSMK G45 ....128 D5
Downfield Dr HMLTN ML3 ....180 A2
Downfield Gdns
  UD/BTH/TAN G71 ....134 A5
Downfield St CAR/SHTL G32...111 H1
Downhill St KVD/HLHD G12...66 C3
Downiebrae Rd RUTH G73 ....111 E2
Downie Cl UD/BTH/TAN G71...115 F4
Downie St HMLTN ML3 ....170 B2
Dowrie Crs PLK/PH/NH G53...106 C3
Draffen St MTHW ML1 ....155 E3
Drakemire Av CSMK G45 ....128 C4
Drakemire Dr CSMK G45 ....128 C5
Drake St DMNK/BRGTN G40 ...90 B4
Dreghorn St DEN/PKHD G31...91 F2
Drimmin Rd
  STPS/GTHM/RID G33 ....71 G1
Drive Rd GOV/IBX G51 ....87 F1
Drochil St ESTRH G34 ....71 H5
Drove HI BALLOCH G68 ....25 F2
Drumbathie Rd AIRDRIE ML6...98 D1
Drumbeg Dr PLK/PH/NH G53...125 F1
Drumbeg Ter MLNGV G62 ....16 A3
Drumbottie Rd
  SPRGB/BLRNK G21 ....68 D1
Drumbreck Pl KKNTL G66 ....40 B4
Drumby Crs
  CRMNK/CLK/EAG G76 ....145 G1
Drumby Dr
  CRMNK/CLK/EAG G76 ....145 G2
Drumcarn Dr MLNGV G62 ....16 D4
Drumcavel Rd
  BAIL/MDB/MHD G69 ....58 C4
Drumchapel Gdns DRUM G15...50 C1
Drumchapel Pl DRUM G15 ....50 C1
Drumchapel Rd DRUM G15 ...50 C1
Drumclair Pl AIRDRIE ML6 ....99 E2
Drumclog Av MLNGV G62 ....17 E1
Drumclog Gdns
  STPS/GTHM/RID G33 ....56 A5
Drumcross Rd BSHPTN PA7...29 G5
  PLK/PH/NH G53 ....106 D3
Drumduff EKILS G75 ....178 A3
Drumgelloch St AIRDRIE ML6...99 E1
Drumglass Vw KSYTH G65 ....24 D1
Drumhead Pl CAR/SHTL G32...112 A3
Drumhead Rd CAR/SHTL G32...112 A3
Drumhill KKNTL G66 ....22 A2
Drumilaw Rd RUTH G73 ....129 H2
Drumilaw Wy RUTH G73 ....129 H2
Drumlaken Av MRYH/FIRH G20...52 B2
Drumlaken Ct MRYH/FIRH G20...52 B2
Drumlaken St MRYH/FIRH G20...52 B2
Drumlanrig Av ESTRH G34 ....94 C1
Drumlanrig Pl ESTRH G34 ....94 C1
Drumlin Dr MLNGV G62 ....16 D5
Drumloch Gdns EKILS G75 ...178 A4
Drumlochy Rd
  STPS/GTHM/RID G33 ....70 B5
Drum Mains Pk BALLOCH G68...24 A5
Drummond Dr PSLY PA1 ....110 A5
Drummond Dr PSLY PA1 ....85 F5
  WISHAW ML2 ....174 A3
Drummond HI EKILN G74 ....167 E2
Drummond Pl EKILN G74 ....167 E2
Drummore Av CTBR ML5 ....117 F2
Drummore Rd DRUM G15 ....33 F4
Drumnessie Ct BALLOCH G68 * ...25 F3
Drumnessie Rd BALLOCH G68...25 F3
Drumnessie Vw BALLOCH G68...25 F3
Drumore Av AIRDRIE ML6 ....119 E3
Drumover Dr DEN/PKHD G31...91 H5
Drumoyne Av GOV/IBX G51...87 F2
Drumoyne Circ GOV/IBX G51...87 F3
Drumoyne Dr GOV/IBX G51...87 F2
Drumoyne Pl GOV/IBX G51...87 F3
Drumoyne Qd GOV/IBX G51...87 F3
Drumoyne Rd GOV/IBX G51...87 F3
Drumpark St CTBR ML5 ....115 H1
  GIF/THBK G46 ....126 C3
Drumpellier Av
  BAIL/MDB/MHD G69 ....114 A1
  CTBR ML5 ....96 A2
  CUMB G67 ....44 B1
Drumpellier Ct CUMB G67 ....44 B1
Drumpellier Crs CTBR ML5 ....95 H3
Drumpellier Gdns CUMB G67...44 B1
Drumpellier Gv CUMB G67 ....44 B1
Drumpellier Pl
  BAIL/MDB/MHD G69 ....94 A5
  CTBR ML5 ....95 H2
  CUMB G67 ....44 B1
Drumpellier Rd
  BAIL/MDB/MHD G69 ....113 H1
Drumpellier St
  STPS/GTHM/RID G33 ....69 H3
Drumreoch Dr GVH/MTFL G42...110 B3
Drumreoch Pl GVH/MTFL G42...110 B3
Drumry Rd East DRUM G15 ...49 H1
Drumsack Av
  BAIL/MDB/MHD G69 ....58 A3
Drumsargard Rd RUTH G73...130 C2
Drums Av PSLYN/LNWD PA3...83 H3
Drums Crs PSLYN/LNWD PA3...83 H3

Drumshangie Pl AIRDRIE ML6...76 B4
Drumshangie St AIRDRIE ML6...76 B4
Drumshaw Dr CAR/SHTL G32...112 D4
Drums Rd PLK/PH/NH G53 ....106 B1
Drumtrocher St KSYTH G65 ....8 B2
Drury St CGLW G2 ....2 E5
Dryad St GIF/THBK G46 ....126 B2
Dryad St GIF/THBK G46 ....126 B2
Dryburgh Av PSLYS PA2 ....103 F3
  RUTH G73 ....111 E5
Dryburgh Gdns MRYH/FIRH G20...66 D4
Dryburgh HI EKILN G74 ....166 A4
Dryburgh La EKILN G74 ....166 A4
Dryburgh Pl CTBR ML5 ....96 C2
Dryburgh Rd BSDN G61 ....33 H2
  WISHAW ML2 ....173 H1
Dryburgh St HMLTN ML3 ....152 C4
Dryburgh Wk
  BAIL/MDB/MHD G69 ....42 B5
Dryburn Av
  CARD/HILL/MSPK G52 ....86 B4
Dryden St HMLTN ML3 ....152 C4
Drygait HWWD PA9 ....120 B3
Drygate COWCAD G4 ....3 K5
Drygrange Rd
  STPS/GTHM/RID G33 ....70 D4
Drymen Rd BSDN G61 ....34 C5
Drymen St
  CARD/HILL/MSPK G52 ....87 F4
Drynoch Pl PPK/MIL G22 ....53 G4
Drysdale St SCOT G14 ....64 C1
Duart Dr EKILN G74 ....166 A2
  JNSTN PA5 ....102 A3
  NMRNS G77 ....144 D5
Duart St MRYH/FIRH G20 ....52 B3
Dubs Rd BRHD/NEIL G78 ....124 D4
Dubton St ESTRH G34 ....72 A5
Duchall Pl SCOT G14 ....64 C2
Duchess Ct HMLTN ML3 ....170 D3
Duchess Palace RUTH G73 ....111 F4
Duchess Rd RUTH G73 ....111 F3
Duchray Dr PSLY PA1 ....86 A5
Duchray La
  STPS/GTHM/RID G33 ....69 G5
Duchray St
  STPS/GTHM/RID G33 ....69 G5
Dudhope St
  STPS/GTHM/RID G33 ....71 E4
Dudley Dr CTBR ML5 ....73 H4
  KVD/HLHD G12 ....65 H3
Dudley La KVD/HLHD G12 ....65 H3
Duffus Pl CAR/SHTL G32 ....112 D4
Duffus St ESTRH G34 ....71 G5
Duffus Ter CAR/SHTL G32 ....112 D4
Duich Gdns SMSTN G23 ....52 D1
Duisdale Rd CAR/SHTL G32...112 D4
Dukes Ga UD/BTH/TAN G71...133 H5
Dukes Rd BAIL/MDB/MHD G69...95 E4
  RUTH G73 ....130 C2
Duke St COWCAD G4 ....3 J3
  DEN/PKHD G31 ....91 G5
  HMLTN ML3 ....170 B2
  MTHW ML1 ....154 D2
  PSLYS PA2 ....104 B2
  WISHAW ML2 ....158 A4
Dulnain St BLTYR/CAMB G72...132 A2
Dulsie Rd SPRGB/BLRNK G21...55 F5
Dumbarton Rd CLYDBK G81...31 H4
  OLDK G60 ....15 F3
  PTCK G11 ....65 H4
  SCOT G14 ....49 H5
Dumbreck Av PLKSD/SHW G41...107 H1
Dumbreck Ct PLKSD/SHW G41...107 H1
Dumbreck Pl KKNTL G66 ....40 B4
Dumbreck Rd PLKSD/SHW G41...87 H5
Dumbreck Sq PLKSD/SHW G41...107 H1
Dumbuck Crs DMBTN G82 ....13 H5
Dumbuck Gdns DMBTN G82...13 G5
Dumbuck Rd DMBTN G82 ....13 G3
Dumbuie Av DMBTN G82 ....13 G3
Dumfries Crs AIRDRIE ML6 ....98 A4
Dumgoyne Av MLNGV G62 ....16 C4
Dumgoyne Dr BSDN G61 ....34 A1
Dumgoyne Gdns MLNGV G62...16 C5
Dumgoyne Pl
  CRMNK/CLK/EAG G76 ....145 F3
Dumgoyne St MRYH/FIRH G20...52 B3
Dunagoil Rd CSMK G45 ....129 E5
Dunagoil Sq CSMK G45 ....129 E5
Dunagoil St CSMK G45 ....129 F5
Dunalastair Dr
  STPS/GTHM/RID G33 ....70 C1
Dunan Pl STPS/GTHM/RID G33...93 F1
Dunard Rd RUTH G73 ....111 E5
Dunard St MRYH/FIRH G20...66 D3
Dunaskin St PTCK G11 ....66 B5
Dunavon Pl CTBR ML5 ....116 D1
Dunbar Av JNSTN PA5 ....101 G5
  RUTH G73 ....111 F5
Dunbar Dr MTHW ML1 ....154 C1
Dunbar HI EKILN G74 ....165 H1
Dunbar La MTHW ML1 ....137 F5
Dunbar Pl EKILN G74 ....165 H4
Dunbar Rd PSLYS PA2 ....103 F3
Dunbar St HMLTN ML3 ....152 C3
Dunbeath Av NMRNS G77 ....144 C5
Dunbeith Pl MRYH/FIRH G20...66 C2
Dunblane Dr EKILN G74 ....166 C3
Dunblane Pl CTBR ML5 ....117 F2
  EKILN G74 ....166 C4
Dunblane St COWCAD G4 ....2 E2
Dunbrach Rd BALLOCH G68...25 E2
Dunbritton Rd DMBTN G82 ....13 H3
Duncan Av SCOT G14 ....64 D2
Duncan La MTHW ML1 ....154 C1
Duncan La North SCOT G14...64 D2
Duncan La South SCOT G14...64 D2
Duncan McIntosh Rd
  BALLOCH G68 ....10 D3
Duncansby Dr
  BLTYR/CAMB G72 ....168 B2
Duncansby Rd
  STPS/GTHM/RID G33 ....93 E3
Duncan St CLYDBK G81 ....31 H5
Duncarnock Av
  BRHD/NEIL G78 ....141 F3
Duncarnock Crs
  BRHD/NEIL G78 ....141 F3
Dunchattan Pl DEN/PKHD G31...90 C2
Dunchattan St DEN/PKHD G31...90 C2
Dunchurch Rd PSLY PA1 ....85 G4
Dunclutha Dr
  UD/BTH/TAN G71 ....152 B1

Dunclutha St
  DMNK/BRGTN G40 ....111 E2
Duncolm Pl MLNGV G62 ....16 B3
Duncombe Av CLYDBK G81 ...32 A1
Duncombe St MRYH/FIRH G20...52 B3
Duncrub Dr BSHPBGS G64 ...54 B2
Duncruin St MRYH/FIRH G20...52 C4
Duncruin Ter MRYH/FIRH G20...52 C4
Duncryne Av CAR/SHTL G32...93 F5
Duncryne Gdns CAR/SHTL G32...93 F5
Duncryne Pl BSHPBGS G64...54 B3
Duncryne Rd CAR/SHTL G32...93 F5
Dundaff HI BALLOCH G68 ....25 F4
Dundas Av BSHPBGS G64 ....19 F4
Dundashill COWCAD G4 ....67 G4
Dundas La CGLE G1 ....3 F5
Dundas Pl EKILN G74 ....166 B3
Dundas St CGLE G1 ....3 F5
Dundee Dr
  CARD/HILL/MSPK G52 ....106 C1
Dundonald Av JNSTN PA5 ....101 E5
Dundonald Crs NMRNS G77...162 B3
Dundonald Pl BRHD/NEIL G78...180 D1
Dundonald Rd KVD/HLHD G12...66 B2
  PSLYN/LNWD PA3 ....85 E1
Dundrennan Rd
  GVH/MTFL G42 ....109 E5
Dundyvan Av WISHAW ML2...173 H5
Dundyvan Ga CTBR ML5 ....96 C4
Dundyvan La WISHAW ML2...173 H5
Dundyvan Rd CTBR ML5 ....96 C4
Dundyvan St WISHAW ML2...173 H5
Dundyvan Wy CTBR ML5 ....96 C4
Dunearn Pl PSLYS PA2 ....104 D1
Dunearn St COWCAD G4 ....67 E4
Dunedin Ct EKILS G75 ....165 F5
Dunedin Dr EKILS G75 ....165 F5
Dunellan Av
  BAIL/MDB/MHD G69 ....59 F1
Dunellan Dr CLYDBK G81 ....32 A1
Dunellan Gdns
  BAIL/MDB/MHD G69 ....59 F1
Dunellan Pl
  BAIL/MDB/MHD G69 ....59 F1
Dunellan St
  CARD/HILL/MSPK G52 ....87 F4
Dungavel Gdns HMLTN ML3...170 D3
Dungeonhill Rd ESTRH G34...94 C1
Dunglass Av EKILN G74 ....166 C2
  SCOT G14 ....64 D2
Dunglass La SCOT G14 ....64 D2
Dunglass La North SCOT G14...64 D2
Dunglass La South SCOT G14...64 D2
Dunglass Pl MLNGV G62 ....16 C2
  NMRNS G77 ....143 H5
Dunglass Sq BSHPTN PA7 ....46 B1
Dungoil Av BALLOCH G68 ....25 E2
Dungoil Rd KKNTL G66 ....40 B4
Dungoyne St MRYH/FIRH G20...52 B3
Dunira St CAR/SHTL G32 ....112 A1
Dunivaig St
  STPS/GTHM/RID G33 ....93 E1
Dunkeld Av RUTH G73 ....111 E5
Dunkeld Dr BSDN G61 ....35 E4
Dunkeld Pl CTBR ML5 ....96 C3
  HMLTN ML3 ....168 D2
  NMRNS G77 ....162 C1
Dunkeld St DEN/PKHD G31...91 F5
Dunkenny Pl DRUM G15 ....33 E4
Dunkenny Rd DRUM G15 ....33 E4
Dunlin EKILN G74 ....166 A1
Dunlin Crs CRG/CRSL/HOU PA6...80 D2
Dunlop Crs UD/BTH/TAN G71...152 C1
Dunlop Gv UD/BTH/TAN G71...115 F3
Dunlop Pl MLNGV G62 ....16 D2
Dunlop St BLTYR/CAMB G72...132 B1
  CGLE G1 ....3 F7
  PSLYN/LNWD PA3 ....82 B3
  RNFRW PA4 ....63 G2
Dunmore Dr MLNGV G62 ....17 G5
Dunmore St CLYDBK G81 ....49 G2
Dunnachie Dr CTBR ML5 ....95 G5
Dunnet Av AIRDRIE ML6 ....76 A3
Dunnet Dr CRG/CRSL/HOU PA6...80 C2
Dunnichen Gdns BSHPBGS G64...55 G2
Dunnikier Wk BALLOCH G68...24 C4
Dunning St DEN/PKHD G31...91 G5
Dunnottar Ct EKILN G74 ....165 H1
Dunnottar Crs EKILN G74 ....165 H2
Dunnottar St BSHPBGS G64...55 G1
  STPS/GTHM/RID G33 ....70 C4
Dunns Wood Rd CUMB G67...11 F4
Dunolly Dr NMRNS G77 ....144 C5
Dunolly St SPRGB/BLRNK G21...68 D5
Dunottar Av CTBR ML5 ....117 E2
Dunottar Pl CTBR ML5 ....117 E2
Dunottar St DEN/PKHD G31...70 C4
  STPS/GTHM/RID G33 ....70 C4
Dunphail Dr ESTRH G34 ....94 C1
Dunphail Rd ESTRH G34 ....94 C1
Dunragit St DEN/PKHD G31...91 F2
Dunrobin Av JNSTN PA5 ....102 A3
Dunrobin Ct EKILN G74 ....166 A2
Dunrobin Crs EKILN G74 ....166 A1
Dunrobin Dr EKILN G74 ....166 A2
Dunrobin Pl CTBR ML5 ....96 B3
Dunrobin Rd AIRDRIE ML6 ....99 E2
Dunrobin St DEN/PKHD G31...91 F3
Dunrod HI EKILN G74 ....166 C2
Dunrod St CAR/SHTL G32 ....92 C5
Dunscore Brae HMLTN ML3...169 E3
Duns Crs WISHAW ML2 ....157 F4
Dunside Dr PLK/PH/NH G53...125 F1
Dunskaith Pl ESTRH G34 ....94 C1
Dunskaith St ESTRH G34 ....94 C2
Dunsmore Rd BSHPTN PA7...28 D4
Dunsmuir St GOV/IBX G51 ....88 A2
Duns Pth CTBR ML5 ....117 G1
Dunster Gdns BSHPBGS G64...19 E4
Dunswin Av CLYDBK G81 ....31 F5
Dunsyre Pl SMSTN G23 ....52 D2
Dunsyre St STPS/GTHM/RID G33...91 H1
Duntarvie Av ESTRH G34 ....94 B1
Duntarvie Crs ESTRH G34 ....94 B1
Duntarvie Dr ESTRH G34 ....94 A1
Duntarvie Gdns ESTRH G34...94 B1
Duntarvie Pl ESTRH G34 ....94 A1
Duntarvie Qd ESTRH G34 ....94 B1

Duntarvie Rd *ESTRH* G34 ....94 A1
Dunterlie Av *KNTSWD* G13 ....50 B5
Dunterlie Ct *BRHD/NEIL* G78 ....124 B4
Duntiblae Rd *KKNTL* G66 ....40 D1
Duntiglennan Rd *CLYDBK* G81 ....31 H2
Duntocher Rd *BSDN* G61 ....34 B3
CLYDBK G81 ....31 H4
Duntreath Av *DRUM* G15 ....50 A2
KNTSWD G13 ....49 H3
Duntreath Dr *DRUM* G15 ....50 A2
Duntreath Gdns *DRUM* G15 ....50 A1
Duntreath Gv *DRUM* G15 ....50 A2
Duntreath Ter *KSYTH* G65 ....8 B2
Duntroon St *DEN/PKHD* G31 ....91 E1
Dunure Dr *HMLTN* ML3 ....168 C3
NMRNS G77 ....144 D5
RUTH G73 ....129 G2
Dunure Pl *CTBR* ML5 ....116 B1
NMRNS G77 ....162 B1
Dunure St *CTBR* ML5 ....116 B1
MRYH/FIRH G20 ....52 C4
Dunvegan *AIRDRIE* ML6 ....75 H2
Dunvegan Av *CTBR* ML5 ....74 A5
JNSTN PA5 ....102 A3
Dunvegan Dr *BSHPBGS* G64 ....37 H4
NMRNS G77 ....144 D5
Dunvegan Pl *EKILN* G74 ....166 A2
UD/BTH/TAN G71 ....114 C4
Dunvegan Qd *RNFRW* PA4 ....63 E2
Dunwan Av *KNTSWD* G13 ....50 A4
Dunwan Pl *KNTSWD* G13 ....50 A4
Durban Av *CLYDBK* G81 ....31 E4
EKILS G75 ....177 G4
Durham St *PLKSD/SHW* G41 ....88 C4
Durisdeer Dr *HMLTN* ML3 ....168 D4
Durness Av *BSDN* G61 ....35 E3
Duror St *CAR/SHTL* G32 ....92 B3
Durris Gdns *CAR/SHTL* G32 ....113 E1
Durrockstock Crs *PSLYS* PA2 ....103 E5
Durrockstock Rd *PSLYS* PA2 ....103 E5
Durward *EKILN* G74 ....167 H1
Durward Av *PLKSD/SHW* G41 ....108 C3
Durward Ct *PLKSD/SHW* G41 ....108 C3
Durward Crs *PSLYS* PA2 ....103 E3
Duthil St *GOV/IBX* G51 ....87 E3
Dyce Av *AIRDRIE* ML6 ....97 H5
Dyce La *PTCK* G11 ....65 H4
Dyer's La *CGLE* G1 ....90 A3
Dyfrig St *BLTYR/CAMB* G72 ....151 F2
Dykebar Av *KNTSWD* G13 ....50 B5
Dykebar Crs *PSLYS* PA2 ....105 E2
Dykehead Crs *AIRDRIE* ML6 ....76 A4
Dykehead La
STPS/GTHM/RID G33 ....93 E2
Dykehead Rd *AIRDRIE* ML6 ....76 A4
BAIL/MDB/MHD G69 ....95 F4
BALLOCH G68 ....9 G4
KSYTH G65 ....7 E1
Dykehead Sq *HMLTN* ML3 ....169 E2
Dykehead St
STPS/GTHM/RID G33 ....93 E2
Dykemuir Pl *SPRGB/BLRNK* G21 ....69 E2
Dykemuir Qd
SPRGB/BLRNK G21 ....68 D2
Dykemuir St *SPRGB/BLRNK* G21 ....68 D2
Dyke Rd *KNTSWD* G13 ....50 B4
Dyke St *BAIL/MDB/MHD* G69 ....94 B4
CTBR ML5 ....95 G5
Dysart Ct *BALLOCH* G68 ....24 C4
Dysart Wy *AIRDRIE* ML6 ....99 H3

E

Eagle Crs *BSDN* G61 ....33 G2
Eaglesham Ct *GOV/IBX* G51 ....88 D3
Eaglesham Pl *GOV/IBX* G51 ....88 D3
Eaglesham Rd
CRMNK/CLK/EAG G76 ....163 F1
EKILS G75 ....176 A2
NMRNS G77 ....161 G2
Eagle St *COWCAD* G4 ....67 H4
Earlbank Av *SCOT* G14 ....64 D2
Earlbank La North *SCOT* G14 ....64 D2
Earlbank La South *SCOT* G14 ....64 D3
Earl Haig Rd
CARD/HILL/MSPK G52 ....86 A2
Earl La *SCOT* G14 ....64 D3
Earl Pl *BRWEIR* PA11 ....79 G5
SCOT G14 ....64 D2
Earlsburn Rd *KKNTL* G66 ....40 B4
Earlscourt *BAIL/MDB/MHD* G69 ....59 E2
Earlsgate *CRG/CRSL/HOU* PA6 ....80 C2
Earl's Ga *UD/BTH/TAN* G71 ....133 H4
Earl's Hl *BALLOCH* G68 ....25 F3
Earlspark Av
PLKSW/MSWD G43 ....128 A1
Earlston Crs *CTBR* ML5 ....117 G1
Earlston St *WISHAW* ML2 ....157 F4
Earl St *SCOT* G14 ....64 D3
Earlybraes Gdns *CAR/SHTL* G32 ....93 E3
Earn Av *BLSH* ML4 ....135 F1
BSDN G61 ....35 E4
RNFRW PA4 ....63 H4
Earn Crs *WISHAW* ML2 ....174 A4
Earnock Av *MTHW* ML1 ....154 B3
Earnock Gdns *HMLTN* ML3 ....169 F3
Earnock Rd *HMLTN* ML3 ....168 C3
Earnock St *HMLTN* ML3 ....169 F1
STPS/GTHM/RID G33 ....69 G2
Earn Rd *NMRNS* G77 ....144 A3
Earnside St *CAR/SHTL* G32 ....92 C4
Earn St *STPS/GTHM/RID* G33 ....69 H5
Easdale *EKILN* G74 ....179 E1
Easdale Dr *CAR/SHTL* G32 ....92 A5
Easdale Pth *CTBR* ML5 ....97 G5
Easdale Pl *NMRNS* G77 ....143 G5
Easdale Ri *HMLTN* ML3 ....168 D2
East Academy St *WISHAW* ML2 ....174 A3
East Av *AIRDRIE* ML6 ....77 H3
BLTYR/CAMB G72 ....151 H5
MTHW ML1 ....137 F5
RNFRW PA4 ....63 G3
UD/BTH/TAN G71 ....134 D1
Eastbank Dr *CAR/SHTL* G32 ....92 D4
East Barns St *CLYDBK* G81 ....49 G3
East Bath La *CGLE* G1 ....3 F4
East Buchanan St *PSLY* PA1 ....84 C4
Eastburn Crs *SPRGB/BLRNK* G21 ....55 E5
Eastburn Rd *SPRGB/BLRNK* G21 ....69 E1
East Burnside St *KSYTH* G65 ....8 B2
East Campbell St *COWCAD* G4 ....3 K7
Eastcote Av *SCOT* G14 ....65 F2
Eastcroft *RUTH* G73 ....111 E4
Eastcroft Ter
SPRGB/BLRNK G21 ....68 D2
East Dean St *BLSH* ML4 ....136 A2
Eastend Av *MTHW* ML1 ....155 G1
Easterbrae *MTHW* ML1 ....171 G1
Easter Craigs *DEN/PKHD* G31 ....91 E1
Easter Crs *WISHAW* ML2 ....174 D1
Easter Garngaber Rd
KKNTL G66 ....40 B3
Easterhill Pl *CAR/SHTL* G32 ....112 A1
Easterhill St *CAR/SHTL* G32 ....112 B2
Easterhouse Pl *ESTRH* G34 ....94 B1
Easterhouse Qd *ESTRH* G34 ....94 B1
Easterhouse Rd
BAIL/MDB/MHD G69 ....94 A4
Eastermains *KKNTL* G66 ....22 B3
Easter Ms *UD/BTH/TAN* G71 ....133 H2
Easter Queenslie Rd
STPS/GTHM/RID G33 ....93 F1
Easter Rd
CRMNK/CLK/EAG G76 ....146 B5
Easterton Av
CRMNK/CLK/EAG G76 ....146 B5
Easter Wood Crs
UD/BTH/TAN G71 ....116 A3
Eastfield Av *BLTYR/CAMB* G72 ....130 D2
Eastfield Crs *DMBTN* G82 ....13 C5
Eastfield Pl *DMBTN* G82 ....13 C5
Eastfield Rd *BALLOCH* G68 ....25 G1
SPRGB/BLRNK G21 ....68 B2
Eastfield Ter *BLSH* ML4 ....136 C3
Eastgate *BAIL/MDB/MHD* G69 ....73 F1
East Ga *WISHAW* ML2 ....174 C2
East George St *CTBR* ML5 ....97 E1
East Glebe Ter *HMLTN* ML3 ....170 A3
East Greenlees Av
BLTYR/CAMB G72 ....131 H4
East Greenlees Crs
BLTYR/CAMB G72 ....131 G4
East Greenlees Dr
BLTYR/CAMB G72 ....131 H4
East Greenlees Rd
BLTYR/CAMB G72 ....131 F4
East Hallhill Rd
BAIL/MDB/MHD G69 ....93 G3
Easthall Pl *STPS/GTHM/RID* G33 ....93 G2
East Hamilton St *WISHAW* ML2 ....174 A3
East High St *AIRDRIE* ML6 ....98 B1
KKNTL G66 ....21 E4
East Kilbride Rd
BLTYR/CAMB G72 ....131 E5
CRMNK/CLK/EAG G76 ....164 C1
East La *PSLY* PA1 ....85 E4
Eastlea Pl *AIRDRIE* ML6 ....98 C3
East Mains Rd *EKILN* G74 ....166 B3
East Milton Gv *EKILS* G75 ....165 G4
Eastmuir St *CAR/SHTL* G32 ....92 C4
WISHAW ML2 ....174 D2
Easton Pl *CTBR* ML5 ....97 E4
East Rd *KLBCH* PA10 ....100 B2
MTHW ML1 ....137 F3
East Scott Ter *HMLTN* ML3 ....170 A4
Eastside *KKNTL* G66 ....21 F4
East Springfield Ter
BSHPBGS G64 ....55 E3
East Stewart Pl *CTBR* ML5 ....97 F2
East Stewart St *CTBR* ML5 ....97 F3
East Thomson St *CLYDBK* G81 ....32 A5
East Thornlie St *WISHAW* ML2 ....174 A3
Eastvale Pl *KVGV* G3 ....88 B1
East Wellbrae Crs *HMLTN* ML3 ....169 G4
East Wellington St
DEN/PKHD G31 ....91 G4
Eastwood Av *GIF/THBK* G46 ....127 F5
PLKSD/SHW G41 ....108 C4
Eastwood Crs *GIF/THBK* G46 ....126 C3
Eastwood Dr *WISHAW* ML2 ....158 B5
Eastwoodmains Rd
GIF/THBK G46 ....145 F1
Eastwood Rd
BAIL/MDB/MHD G69 ....59 E1
Eastwood Vw
BLTYR/CAMB G72 ....132 B1
Easwald Bank *KLBCH* PA10 ....100 C4
Ebroch Dr *KSYTH* G65 ....8 C2
Ebroch Pk *KSYTH* G65 ....8 C2
Eccles St *PPK/MIL* G22 ....68 B1
Eckford St *CAR/SHTL* G32 ....92 B5
Eday St *PPK/MIL* G22 ....54 A5
Edderton Pl
STPS/GTHM/RID G33 ....93 H2
Edderton Wy
STPS/GTHM/RID G33 ....93 H2
Eddington Dr *NMRNS* G77 ....161 F2
Eddlewood Ct
STPS/GTHM/RID G33 ....93 G2
Eddlewood Pth
STPS/GTHM/RID G33 ....93 G2
Eddlewood Pl
STPS/GTHM/RID G33 ....93 G2
Eddlewood Rd
STPS/GTHM/RID G33 ....93 G2
Eden Dr *EKILS* G75 ....177 E2
Eden Gdns *EKILS* G75 ....177 E1
Eden Gv *EKILS* G75 ....177 E1
Edenhall Ct *NMRNS* G77 ....161 G3
Edenhall Gv *NMRNS* G77 ....161 G3
Eden La *STPS/GTHM/RID* G33 ....69 G5
Eden Pk *UD/BTH/TAN* G71 ....134 A5
Eden Pl *RNFRW* PA4 ....63 H4
Edenside *BALLOCH* G68 ....10 D3
Eden St *STPS/GTHM/RID* G33 ....69 G5
Edenwood St *DEN/PKHD* G31 ....91 H4
Edgam Dr
CARD/HILL/MSPK G52 ....86 D4
Edgefauld Av
SPRGB/BLRNK G21 ....68 C3
Edgefauld Dr
SPRGB/BLRNK G21 ....68 C2
Edgefauld Pl
SPRGB/BLRNK G21 ....68 C1
Edgefauld Rd
SPRGB/BLRNK G21 ....68 D3
Edgehill La *PTCK* G11 ....65 H2
Edgehill Rd *BSDN* G61 ....34 B2
PTCK G11 ....65 G2
Edgemont Pk *HMLTN* ML3 ....169 H5
Edgemont St *PLKSD/SHW* G41 ....108 D4
Edinbeg Av *GVH/MTFL* G42 ....110 B4
Edinbeg Pl *GVH/MTFL* G42 ....110 B4
Edinburgh Rd *CAR/SHTL* G32 ....92 B2
MTHW ML1 ....119 F5
STPS/GTHM/RID G33 ....91 H2
Edington Gdns
BAIL/MDB/MHD G69 ....42 A5
Edington St *COWCAD* G4 ....67 G4
Edison St *CARD/HILL/MSPK* G52 ....85 H1
Edmiston Dr *GOV/IBX* G51 ....87 H3
PSLYN/LNWD PA3 ....81 G5
Edmonstone Dr *KSYTH* G65 ....8 B3
Edmonton Ter *EKILS* G75 ....165 H5
Edmund Kean *EKILN* G74 ....149 H5
Edrom Ct *CAR/SHTL* G32 ....92 A4
Edrom St *CAR/SHTL* G32 ....92 A5
Edward Av *RNFRW* PA4 ....63 G2
Edward St *BAIL/MDB/MHD* G69 ....95 E4
CLYDBK G81 ....49 G4
HMLTN ML3 ....170 A3
KSYTH G65 ....8 B1
MTHW ML1 ....155 E5
Edwin St *GOV/IBX* G51 ....88 C4
Edzell Ct *SCOT* G14 ....65 E4
Edzell Dr *JNSTN* PA5 ....102 C2
NMRNS G77 ....161 H1
Edzell Gdns *BSHPBGS* G64 ....55 F3
WISHAW ML2 ....173 H3
Edzell Pl *SCOT* G14 ....65 E3
Edzell St *CTBR* ML5 ....96 A5
SCOT G14 ....65 E4
Egidia Av *GIF/THBK* G46 ....127 E5
Egilsay Crs *PPK/MIL* G22 ....53 H3
Egilsay Pl *PPK/MIL* G22 ....53 H3
Egilsay St *PPK/MIL* G22 ....53 H3
Egilsay Ter *PPK/MIL* G22 ....53 H3
Eglinton Ct *GBLS* G5 ....89 G4
Eglinton Dr *GIF/THBK* G46 ....127 F5
Eglinton St *CTBR* ML5 ....97 E1
GBLS G5 ....89 G5
Egmont Pk *EKILS* G75 ....177 F1
Eider *KVD/HLHD* G12 ....51 H4
Eider Av *EKILS* G75 ....177 F4
Eider Gv *EKILS* G75 ....177 F3
Eider Pl *EKILS* G75 ....177 F4
Eighth St *UD/BTH/TAN* G71 ....114 D3
Eildon Crs *AIRDRIE* ML6 ....119 G3
Eildon Dr *BRHD/NEIL* G78 ....142 B1
Eildon Rd *KKNTL* G66 ....21 H5
Eileen Gdns *BSHPBGS* G64 ....55 E1
Elcho St *DMNK/BRGTN* G40 ....90 C3
Elderbank *BSDN* G61 ....34 B5
Elder Crs *BLTYR/CAMB* G72 ....132 B3
Elder Gv *UD/BTH/TAN* G71 ....115 G5
Elder Grove Av *GOV/IBX* G51 ....87 E2
Elder Grove Pl *GOV/IBX* G51 ....87 E2
Elderpark Gdns *GOV/IBX* G51 ....87 G2
Elderpark Gv *GOV/IBX* G51 ....87 G2
Elderpark St *GOV/IBX* G51 ....87 G2
Elderslie St *KVGV* G3 ....89 E1
Elder St *GOV/IBX* G51 ....87 G2
Eldin Pl *BRWEIR* PA11 ....79 H5
JNSTN PA5 ....102 A2
Eldon Gdns *BSHPBGS* G64 ....54 B2
Eldon St *KVGV* G3 ....66 D4
Elgin Av *EKILN* G74 ....166 C2
Elgin Gdns
CRMNK/CLK/EAG G76 ....146 A2
Elgin Pl *AIRDRIE* ML6 ....97 H4
CTBR ML5 ....117 E1
EKILN G74 ....166 C2
KSYTH G65 ....8 B1
Elgin Rd *BSDN* G61 ....34 C1
Elgin Ter *HMLTN* ML3 ....168 D1
Elgin Wy *BLSH* ML4 ....135 H1
Elibank St *STPS/GTHM/RID* G33 ....70 B5
Elie Rd *HMLTN* ML3 ....168 C2
Elie St *PTCK* G11 ....66 B4
Eliot Crs *HMLTN* ML3 ....170 A4
Eliot Ter *HMLTN* ML3 ....170 A3
Elizabeth Av *KKNTL* G66 ....5 F4
Elizabeth Crs *GIF/THBK* G46 ....126 D4
Elizabeth Qd *MTHW* ML1 ....137 E2
Elizabeth St *GOV/IBX* G51 ....88 B4
Elizabeth Wynd *HMLTN* ML3 ....180 D1
Ella Gdns *BLSH* ML4 ....136 B3
Ellangowan Rd *MLNGV* G62 ....17 E3
PLKSD/SHW G41 ....108 B4
Ellergreen Rd *BSDN* G61 ....34 B4
Ellerslie St *JNSTN* PA5 ....101 H3
Ellesmere St *PPK/MIL* G22 ....67 F3
Elliot Av *GIF/THBK* G46 ....127 F5
PSLYS PA2 ....102 D5
Elliot Ct *MTHW* ML1 ....154 C1
Elliot Crs *EKILN* G74 ....167 E3
Elliot Dr *GIF/THBK* G46 ....127 F4
Elliot Pl *KVGV* G3 ....88 D2
Elliot St *KVGV* G3 ....88 D2
Ellisland *EKILN* G74 ....167 G2
KKNTL G66 ....22 B3
Ellisland Av *CLYDBK* G81 ....32 B5
Ellisland Crs *CSMK* G45 ....129 G2
Ellisland Dr *BLTYR/CAMB* G72 ....151 E4
KKNTL G66 ....22 A3
Ellisland Rd
CRMNK/CLK/EAG G76 ....145 H5
CUMB G67 ....26 D3
PLKSW/MSWD G43 ....127 G1
Ellismuir Farm Rd
BAIL/MDB/MHD G69 ....94 C5
Ellismuir Pl
BAIL/MDB/MHD G69 ....94 B5
Ellismuir Rd
BAIL/MDB/MHD G69 ....94 B5
Ellismuir St *CTBR* ML5 ....116 A1
Ellismuir Wy *UD/BTH/TAN* G71 ....115 F3
Ellis St *CTBR* ML5 ....96 D3
Elliston Av *PLK/PH/NH* G53 ....125 H2
Elliston Crs *PLK/PH/NH* G53 ....125 H2
Elliston Dr *PLK/PH/NH* G53 ....125 H2
Elliston Pl *HWWD* PA9 ....120 A4
Elliston Rd *HWWD* PA9 ....120 A4
Ellis Wy *MTHW* ML1 ....155 E5
Ellon Dr *PSLYN/LNWD* PA3 ....101 H1
Ellon Gv *PSLYN/LNWD* PA3 ....84 C2
Ellon Wy *PSLYN/LNWD* PA3 ....84 D2
Elirig *EKILS* G75 ....178 A3
Elm Av *KKNTL* G66 ....39 H2
RNFRW PA4 ....63 F2
Elm Bank *BSHPBGS* G64 ....55 E2
KKNTL G66 ....21 F5
Elmbank Av *UD/BTH/TAN* G71 ....115 G5
Elmbank Crs *CGLW* G2 ....2 B3
HMLTN ML3 ....169 F1
Elmbank St *BLSH* ML4 ....135 H2
CGLW G2 ....2 B4
Elmbank Street La *KVGV* G3 ....2 B4
Elm Ct *HMLTN* ML3 ....181 F4
Elm Crs *UD/BTH/TAN* G71 ....116 A5
Elm Dr *AIRDRIE* ML6 ....119 F1
BLTYR/CAMB G72 ....131 H1
CUMB G67 ....27 H1
JNSTN PA5 ....121 G1
Elmfoot St *GBLS* G5 ....110 A2
Elm Gdns *BSDN* G61 ....34 B2
Elmhurst *MTHW* ML1 ....171 G1
Elmira Rd *BAIL/MDB/MHD* G69 ....58 B4
Elmore Av *LNPK/KPK* G44 ....128 D3
Elm Pl *EKILS* G75 ....177 H2
Elm Qd *AIRDRIE* ML6 ....99 E3
Elm Rd *BRWEIR* PA11 ....79 H3
CLYDBK G81 ....31 H3
DMBTN G82 ....13 E3
MTHW ML1 ....137 F5
MTHW ML1 ....137 G2
PSLYS PA2 ....104 D3
RUTH G73 ....130 A3
Elmslie Ct *BAIL/MDB/MHD* G69 ....94 B5
Elm St *BLTYR/CAMB* G72 ....151 H3
CRMNK/CLK/EAG G76 ....146 A4
CTBR ML5 ....97 F4
KKNTL G66 ....4 C2
MTHW ML1 ....154 C3
SCOT G14 ....65 E3
Elmvale Rw *SPRGB/BLRNK* G21 ....68 B2
Elmvale St *PPK/MIL* G22 ....68 B1
Elm View Ct *BLSH* ML4 ....136 C3
Elm Wk *BSDN* G61 ....34 B2
Elm Wy *BLTYR/CAMB* G72 ....132 B3
Elmwood *WISHAW* ML2 ....173 F4
Elmwood Av *NMRNS* G77 ....144 C4
PTCK G11 ....65 G2
Elmwood Ct *UD/BTH/TAN* G71 ....134 B5
Elmwood La *PTCK* G11 ....65 G2
Elphinstone Crs *EKILS* G75 ....178 C1
Elphinstone Pl *GOV/IBX* G51 ....88 B2
Elphinstone Rd *GIF/THBK* G46 ....144 D3
Elphin St *SMSTN* G23 ....52 C2
Elrig Rd *LNPK/KPK* G44 ....128 A2
Elspeth Gdns *BSHPBGS* G64 ....55 F1
Eltham St *PPK/MIL* G22 ....67 G3
Elvan Pl *EKILS* G75 ....176 D1
Elvan St *CAR/SHTL* G32 ....92 A4
MTHW ML1 ....154 C4
Embo Dr *KNTSWD* G13 ....50 C5
Emerald Ter *BLSH* ML4 ....135 H3
Emerson Rd *BSHPBGS* G64 ....54 D3
Emerson Rd West
BSHPBGS G64 ....54 D2
Emerson St *MRYH/FIRH* G20 ....53 F5
Emily Dr *MTHW* ML1 ....171 H1
Emma Jay Rd *BLSH* ML4 ....136 A2
Empire Wy *MTHW* ML1 ....154 B1
Endfield Av *KVD/HLHD* G12 ....52 A5
Endrick Bank *BSHPBGS* G64 ....37 H4
Endrick Dr *BSDN* G61 ....34 C4
PSLY PA1 ....85 E3
Endrick St *SPRGB/BLRNK* G21 ....68 A3
English Rw *AIRDRIE* ML6 ....118 D2
English St *WISHAW* ML2 ....173 E2
Ennerdale *EKILS* G75 ....177 E2
Ennisfree Rd *BLTYR/CAMB* G72 ....151 G2
Ensay St *PPK/MIL* G22 ....54 A4
Enterkin St *CAR/SHTL* G32 ....92 A5
Eriboll Pl *PPK/MIL* G22 ....53 G4
Eriboll St *PPK/MIL* G22 ....53 G4
Ericht Rd *PLKSW/MSWD* G43 ....127 F2
Eriska Av *SCOT* G14 ....64 B1
Eriskay Av *HMLTN* ML3 ....169 E3
NMRNS G77 ....143 G5
Eriskay Crs *NMRNS* G77 ....143 G5
Eriskay Dr *OLDK* G60 ....30 D2
Ermelo Gdns *EKILS* G75 ....177 G4
Erradale St *PPK/MIL* G22 ....53 F4
Errogie St *ESTRH* G34 ....94 A1
Erskine Av *PLKSD/SHW* G41 ....88 A5
Erskine Br *ERSK* PA8 ....30 B3
Erskine Crs *AIRDRIE* ML6 ....98 A4
Erskinefauld Rd
PSLYN/LNWD PA3 ....82 A3
Erskine Ferry Rd *OLDK* G60 ....30 B3
Erskine Rd *GIF/THBK* G46 ....145 E4
Erskine Sq
CARD/HILL/MSPK G52 ....86 A2
Ervie St *ESTRH* G34 ....94 B2
Esdaile Ct *MTHW* ML1 ....137 F4
Esk Av *RNFRW* PA4 ....63 H4
Eskbank St *CAR/SHTL* G32 ....92 B3
Esk Dl *EKILN* G74 ....165 H2
Eskdale Dr *RUTH* G73 ....111 G5
Eskdale Rd *BSDN* G61 ....51 E1
Eskdale St *GVH/MTFL* G42 ....109 G3
Esk Dr *PSLYS* PA2 ....102 D3
Esk St *SCOT* G14 ....64 A1
Esmond St *KVGV* G3 ....66 B5
Espedair St *PSLYS* PA2 ....104 B1
Espieside Crs *CTBR* ML5 ....96 B1
Essenside Av *DRUM* G15 ....50 D1
Essex Dr *SCOT* G14 ....65 F2
Essex La *SCOT* G14 ....65 F3
Esslemont Av *SCOT* G14 ....64 C2
Estate Qd *CAR/SHTL* G32 ....112 D4
Estate Rd *CAR/SHTL* G32 ....112 D4
Etive Av *BSDN* G61 ....35 E4
HMLTN ML3 ....169 F4
Etive Ct *CLYDBK* G81 ....32 B3
CUMB G67 ....44 A2
Etive Crs *BSHPBGS* G64 ....55 E2
CUMB G67 ....44 A2
WISHAW ML2 ....174 A5
Etive Dr *AIRDRIE* ML6 ....98 D4
BSHPTN PA7 ....46 B1
CUMB G67 ....44 A2
GIF/THBK G46 ....145 G1
Etive Pl *CUMB* G67 ....44 B2
Etive St *CAR/SHTL* G32 ....92 B4
WISHAW ML2 ....174 A4
Etna St *WISHAW* ML2 ....172 D1
Eton La *KVD/HLHD* G12 ....66 D4
Ettrick Av *BLSH* ML4 ....116 D5
RNFRW PA4 ....64 A4
Ettrick Crs *RUTH* G73 ....111 F5
Ettrick Dr *BSDN* G61 ....33 H1
BSHPTN PA7 ....46 B1
Ettrick Hl *EKILN* G74 ....166 D2
Ettrick Pl *PLKSD/SHW* G41 ....108 C5
Ettrick St *WISHAW* ML2 ....156 D5
Ettrick Ter *JNSTN* PA5 ....120 D1
Evan Crs *GIF/THBK* G46 ....127 G5
Evan Dr *GIF/THBK* G46 ....145 G1
Evanton Dr *GIF/THBK* G46 ....126 B4
Evanton Pl *GIF/THBK* G46 ....126 B4
Everard Ct *SPRGB/BLRNK* G21 ....54 B4
Everard Dr *SPRGB/BLRNK* G21 ....54 B5
Everard Pl *SPRGB/BLRNK* G21 ....54 B4
Everard Qd *SPRGB/BLRNK* G21 ....54 B4
Eversley St *CAR/SHTL* G32 ....112 B1
Everton Rd *PLK/PH/NH* G53 ....106 D2
Ewart Crs *HMLTN* ML3 ....169 F3
Ewart Ter *HMLTN* ML3 ....169 F3
Ewing Ct *HMLTN* ML3 ....180 C1
Ewing Pl *DEN/PKHD* G31 ....91 F4
Ewing St *KLBCH* PA10 ....100 B3
RUTH G73 ....110 D5
Ewing Wk *MLNGV* G62 ....17 G4
Excelsior St *WISHAW* ML2 ....173 E2
Exeter Dr *PTCK* G11 ....65 H4
Exeter St *CTBR* ML5 ....96 D4
Eynort St *PPK/MIL* G22 ....53 F4
Eyrepoint Ct
STPS/GTHM/RID G33 ....92 B1

F

Factory Rd *MTHW* ML1 ....154 D5
Fagan Ct *BLTYR/CAMB* G72 ....151 H1
Faifley Rd *CLYDBK* G81 ....32 B1
Fairbairn Crs *GIF/THBK* G46 ....126 D5
Fairburn St *CAR/SHTL* G32 ....92 A5
Fairfax Av *LNPK/KPK* G44 ....128 D2
Fairfield Ct
CRMNK/CLK/EAG G76 ....145 H5
Fairfield Dr
CRMNK/CLK/EAG G76 ....145 H5
RNFRW PA4 ....63 G5
Fairfield Gdns *GOV/IBX* G51 ....87 G1
Fairfield Pl *EKILN* G74 ....165 G3
GOV/IBX G51 ....87 G1
HMLTN ML3 ....170 B4
UD/BTH/TAN G71 ....134 C5
Fairfield St *GOV/IBX* G51 ....87 G1
Fairford Dr *CUMB* G67 ....44 C2
Fairhaven Av *AIRDRIE* ML6 ....99 F3
Fairhaven Rd *SMSTN* G23 ....52 C3
Fairhill Av *HMLTN* ML3 ....169 H4
PLK/PH/NH G53 ....106 D5
Fairhill Crs *HMLTN* ML3 ....169 H4
Fairhill Pl *HMLTN* ML3 ....180 B1
Fairholm Av *HMLTN* ML3 ....171 G4
Fairholm St *CAR/SHTL* G32 ....92 A5
Fairley St *GOV/IBX* G51 ....88 A3
Fairlie *EKILN* G74 ....166 A3
Fairlie Park Dr *PTCK* G11 ....65 H4
Fair Oaks *CRMNK/CLK/EAG* G76 ....147 F2
Fairway *BSDN* G61 ....33 G3
Fairway Av *PSLYS* PA2 ....104 A5
The Fairways
UD/BTH/TAN G71 ....134 B5
Fairways Vw *CLYDBK* G81 ....32 C2
Fairweather Pl *NMRNS* G77 ....161 F1
Fairyknowe Gdns
UD/BTH/TAN G71 ....134 C5
Faith Av *BRWEIR* PA11 ....78 B1
Falconbridge Rd *EKILN* G74 ....167 F1
Falcon Crs *PSLYN/LNWD* PA3 ....83 G4
Falconer Ter *HMLTN* ML3 ....169 H4
Falcon Rd *JNSTN* PA5 ....121 E2
Falcon Ter *MRYH/FIRH* G20 ....52 B3
Falcon Terrace La
MRYH/FIRH G20 ....52 B3
Falfield St *GBLS* G5 ....89 F5
Falkland Av *NMRNS* G77 ....144 D4
Falkland Crs *BSHPBGS* G64 ....55 G3
Falkland Dr *EKILN* G74 ....165 H4
Falkland La *KVD/HLHD* G12 ....66 A3
Falkland Pk *EKILN* G74 ....166 A4
Falkland Pl *CTBR* ML5 ....117 E1
EKILN G74 ....166 A4
Falkland St *KVD/HLHD* G12 ....66 A3
Falloch Pl *WISHAW* ML2 ....158 A4
Falloch Rd *BSDN* G61 ....50 D1
GVH/MTFL G42 ....109 F5
MLNGV G62 ....16 C2
Fallside Av *UD/BTH/TAN* G71 ....134 D1
Fallside Rd *UD/BTH/TAN* G71 ....134 B5
UD/BTH/TAN G71 ....134 C2
Falside Av *PSLYS* PA2 ....104 B3
Falside Rd *CAR/SHTL* G32 ....112 B2
PSLYS PA2 ....104 A3
Falstaff *EKILN* G74 ....149 H5
Faraday Av *WISHAW* ML2 ....174 B1
Fara St *SMSTN* G23 ....53 E3
Farie St *RUTH* G73 ....110 C4
Farm Ct *UD/BTH/TAN* G71 ....134 C3
Farm Crs *MTHW* ML1 ....138 C3
Farme Castle Ct *RUTH* G73 ....111 F3
Farmeloan Rd *RUTH* G73 ....111 E4
Farmgate Sq *BLSH* ML4 ....135 G3
Farmington Av *CAR/SHTL* G32 ....93 E4
Farmington Gdns
CAR/SHTL G32 ....93 E4
Farmington Gv *CAR/SHTL* G32 ....93 E4
Farm La *BLSH* ML4 ....135 G4
Farm Pk *KKNTL* G66 ....40 A4
Farm Rd *BLTYR/CAMB* G72 ....151 G1
CLYDBK G81 ....31 E5
CLYDBK G81 ....31 H1
HMLTN ML3 ....169 E1
PLKSD/SHW G41 ....88 A4
Farm St *MTHW* ML1 ....154 C3
Farm Ter *HMLTN* ML3 ....169 E1
Farndale *EKILN* G74 ....165 H2
Farne Dr *LNPK/KPK* G44 ....128 C3
Farnell St *COWCAD* G4 ....67 G4
Farrier Ct *JNSTN* PA5 ....101 G3
Faskally Av *BSHPBGS* G64 ....37 F5
Faskin Crs *PLK/PH/NH* G53 ....106 A5
Faskine Av *AIRDRIE* ML6 ....98 A4
Faskine Crs *AIRDRIE* ML6 ....98 A3
Faskin Pl *PLK/PH/NH* G53 ....106 A5
Faskin Rd *PLK/PH/NH* G53 ....106 A5
Fasque Pl *DRUM* G15 ....32 D4
Fauldhouse St *GBLS* G5 ....110 A1
Faulds *BAIL/MDB/MHD* G69 ....94 B4
Faulds Gdns
BAIL/MDB/MHD G69 ....94 B4
Fauldshead Rd *RNFRW* PA4 ....63 F3
Fauldspark Crs
BAIL/MDB/MHD G69 ....94 B3
Faulds St *CTBR* ML5 ....116 B1
Fauldswood Crs *PSLYS* PA2 ....103 G3
Fauldswood Dr *PSLYS* PA2 ....103 G2
Faulkner Gv *MTHW* ML1 ....156 C2
Fearnach Pl *MRYH/FIRH* G20 ....52 A4
Fearnmore Rd *MRYH/FIRH* G20 ....52 C4
The Fells *KKNTL* G66 ....4 C2
Fellsview Av *KKNTL* G66 ....21 H4
Felton Pl *KNTSWD* G13 ....50 A4
Fendoch St *CAR/SHTL* G32 ....92 B5
Fenella St *CAR/SHTL* G32 ....92 C4
Fennsbank Av *RUTH* G73 ....130 C4
Fenwick Dr *BRHD/NEIL* G78 ....142 C1

HMLTN ML3 ....181 E1
Fenwick Pl GIF/THBK G46 ....145 E1
Fenwick Rd GIF/THBK G46 ......145 E1
Ferclay St CLYDBK G81 ....32 C1
Fereneze Av BRHD/NEIL G78 ...124 A4
  CRMNK/CLK/EAG G76 ....145 F4
  RNFRW PA4 ....84 D1
Fereneze Crs HMLTN ML3 ....169 E2
  KNTSWD G13 ....50 A4
Fereneze Dr PSLYS PA2 ....103 H5
Fereneze Rd BRHD/NEIL G78 ...124 A4
Fereneze Rd BRHD/NEIL G78 ...124 A4
Fergus Av PSLYN/LNWD PA3 ......83 F4
Fergus Dr MRYH/FIRH G20 ....66 D2
  PSLYN/LNWD PA3 ....83 F4
Fergus Gdns HMLTN ML3 ....170 C3
Fergus La MRYH/FIRH G20 ....67 E2
Ferguslie PSLY PA1 ....85 G5
Ferguslie Park Av
  PSLYN/LNWD PA3 ....83 F5
Ferguslie Park Crs
  PSLYN/LNWD PA3 ....85 G5
Ferguslie Wk PSLY PA1 ....85 G5
Ferguson Av MLNGV G62 ....17 E4
  RNFRW PA4 ....63 G3
Ferguson Dr MTHW ML1 ....171 H2
Ferguson St PSLYN PA5 ....101 F3
  RNFRW PA4 ....63 G3
Ferguson Wy AIRDRIE ML6 ....76 B4
Fergusson Pl EKILN G74 ....150 A5
Fergusson Rd CUMB G67 ....26 B5
Ferguston Rd BSDN G61 ....34 C4
Fernan St CAR/SHTL G32 ....92 A4
Fern Av BSHPBGS G64 ....55 E5
  ERSK PA8 ....47 G4
  KNTSWD G13 ....65 G1
Fernbae Av G61 ....34 B5
Fernbank Av BLYTR/CAMB G72 .131 H5
Fernbank St PPK/MIL G22 ....68 B1
Fernbrae Av RUTH G73 ....130 A4
Fernbrae Wy RUTH G73 ....130 A4
Ferncroft Dr LNPK/KPK G44 .....129 E2
Ferndale Ct SMSTN G23 ....52 C3
Ferndale Dr SMSTN G23 ....52 C3
Ferndale Gdns SMSTN G23 ....52 C3
Ferndale Pl SMSTN G23 ....52 C3
Fern Dr BRHD/NEIL G78 ....124 A3
Ferness Ov SPRGB/BLRNK G21 ...55 H4
Ferness Pl SPRGB/BLRNK G21 ...55 H4
Ferness Rd SPRGB/BLRNK G21 ...55 H4
Ferness Gv BAIL/MDB/MHD G69 .59 F5
Ferngrove Av KVD/HLHD G12 .....52 A5
Fernhill Gra UD/BTH/TAN G71 ...129 H5
Fernhill Rd RUTH G73 ....129 H3
Fernie Gdns MRYH/FIRH G20 .....52 D4
Fern La KNTL G66 ....4 A1
  KNTSWD G13 ....65 G1
Fernlea BSDN G61 ....34 B5
Fernleigh Rd
  PLKSW/MSWD G43 ....127 G2
Fernslea Av BLTYR/CAMB G72 ..131 H5
Fern St MTHW ML1 ....172 B1
Ferryden St SCOT G14 ....65 F4
Ferry Rd BSHPTN PA7 ....28 D5
  KVGV G3 ....66 B5
  RNFRW PA4 ....63 G2
  UD/BTH/TAN G71 ....133 H1
Fersit St PLKSW/MSWD G43 .....127 F1
Fetlar Dr LNPK/KPK G44 ....128 D2
Fetlar Rd BRWEIR PA11 ....79 F3
Fettercairn Av DRUM G15 ....32 D4
Fettes St STPS/GTHM/RID G33 ...92 A1
Fiddoch Ct WISHAW ML2 ....158 A4
Fidra St STPS/GTHM/RID G33 .....92 A1
Fielden Pl DMNK/BRGTN G40 .....90 D4
Fielden St DMNK/BRGTN G40 .....90 D4
Field Gv CRMNK/CLK/EAG G76 ..146 A5
Fieldhead Dr
  PLKSW/MSWD G43 ....126 D2
Fieldhead Sq
  PLKSW/MSWD G43 ....126 D2
Field St HMLTN ML3 ....170 A4
  CARD/HILL/MSPK G52 ....86 C5
Fife Crs UD/BTH/TAN G71 ....152 B1
Fife Dr MTHW ML1 ....136 C5
Fife Wy BSHPBGS G64 ....55 G3
Fifth Av AIRDRIE ML6 ....98 B4
  KVD/HLHD G12 ....65 G1
  RNFRW PA4 ....63 G1
  STPS/GTHM/RID G33 ....70 C1
Fifth Rd BLTYR/CAMB G72 ....151 H5
Fifty Pitches Pl GOV/IBX G51 .....86 D2
Fifty Pitches Rd GOV/IBX G51 ....86 D2
Finart Dr PSLYS PA2 ....105 E3
Finch Dr KNTSWD G13 ....50 A5
Finch Pl JNSTN PA5 ....121 E2
Finch Wy BLSH ML4 ....116 C4
Findhorn Av ERSK PA8 ....47 G4
  RNFRW PA4 ....63 H5
Findhorn Pl EKILS G75 ....164 C5
Findhorn St
  STPS/GTHM/RID G33 ....91 G1
Finlay Dr KSYTH G65 ....8 B2
  MTHW ML1 ....155 E5
Findochty St
  STPS/GTHM/RID G33 ....71 F5
Fingal La MRYH/FIRH G20 ....52 B4
Fingal St MRYH/FIRH G20 ....52 C4
Fingalton Rd NMRNS G77 ....142 C5
Fingask St CAR/SHTL G32 ....92 D5
Finglas Av PSLYS PA2 ....105 E3
Finglen Pl PLK/PH/NH G53 ......125 E5
Fingleton Av BRHD/NEIL G78 ...142 C1
Finhaven St CAR/SHTL G32 .....111 H1
Finlarig St ESTRH G34 ....94 B2
Finlas St PPK/MIL G22 ....68 A2
Finlay Dr DEN/PKHD G31 ....91 E3
  PSLYN/LNWD PA3 ....101 G1
Finlay Ri MLNGV G62 ....17 G5
Finlayson Dr AIRDRIE ML6 ....99 F2
Finlayson Qd AIRDRIE ML6 ....99 F2
Finlaystone St CTBR ML5 ....96 C2
Finnart Sq DMNK/BRGTN G40 ..110 C1
Finnart St DMNK/BRGTN G40 ...110 C1
Finnieston Sq KVGV G3 ....88 B2
Finnieston St KVGV G3 ....88 B2
Finnie Wynd MTHW ML1 ....172 C1
Finsbay St GOV/IBX G51 ....87 E3
Fintaig La WISHAW ML2 ....174 B3
Fintrie Ter HMLTN ML3 ....168 D1
Fintry Av PSLYS PA2 ....104 B4
Fintry Crs BRHD/NEIL G78 ....142 C1
  BSHPBGS G64 ....55 F2
Fintry Dr LNPK/KPK G44 ....109 H5

Fintry Gdns BSDN G61 ....16 A5
Fintry Pl EKILS G75 ....177 G4
Firbank Av BSHPBGS G64 ....19 F5
Firbank Qd AIRDRIE ML6 ....119 F1
Firbank Ter BRHD/NEIL G78 ....142 D1
Fir Ct BLTYR/CAMB G72 ....132 B3
Firdon Crs DRUM G15 ....50 B2
Fir Dr EKILS G75 ....177 G4
Fir Gv MTHW ML1 ....137 F5
  UD/BTH/TAN G71 ....115 H5
Firhill Av AIRDRIE ML6 ....98 A5
Firhill Rd MRYH/FIRH G20 ....67 F2
Firhill St MRYH/FIRH G20 ....67 F2
Firpark Rd BSHPBGS G64 ....55 E5
Firpark St DEN/PKHD G31 ....90 C1
Fir Park St MTHW ML1 ....172 A1
Firpark Ter DEN/PKHD G31 ....90 C2
Fir Pl BAIL/MDB/MHD G69 ......113 H1
  CAR/SHTL G32 ....92 A5
  JNSTN PA5 ....101 H5
First Av BSDN G61 ....34 D5
  DMBTN G82 ....13 H5
  KKNTL G66 ....57 E2
  LNPK/KPK G44 ....128 A5
  RNFRW PA4 ....63 G1
  STPS/GTHM/RID G33 ....70 C1
  UD/BTH/TAN G71 ....114 D4
First Gdns PLKSD/SHW G41 ....87 H5
First Rd BLTYR/CAMB G72 ....151 H5
First Ter CLYDBK G81 ....31 H5
Firthview Ter DMBTN G82 ....12 B4
Firtree Pl WISHAW ML2 ....158 C4
Firtree Rd WISHAW ML2 ....158 C4
Fir Vw AIRDRIE ML6 ....118 C2
Firwood Crs NMRNS G77 ....161 H1
Firwood Dr LNPK/KPK G44 ......128 D1
Firwood Rd NMRNS G77 ....144 B5
Fischer Gdns PSLYN/LNWD PA3 ..83 E5
Fisher Av KSYTH G65 ....8 B2
  PSLYN/LNWD PA3 ....83 E5
Fisher Crs CLYDBK G81 ....32 A3
Fisher Dr PSLYN/LNWD PA3 ......83 E5
Fisher Pl PSLYN/LNWD PA3 ......83 E5
Fishescoates Av RUTH G73 ......130 C2
Fishescoates Gdns RUTH G73 ...130 B2
Fitzalan Dr PSLYN/LNWD PA3 ....84 D3
Fitzalan Rd PSLYN/LNWD PA3 ....62 D5
Fitzroy La KVGV G3 ....88 D1
Flakefield EKILN G74 ....165 G5
Flanders St CLYDBK G81 ....32 B2
Flaxfield Gv MTHW ML1 ....136 C5
Flaxmill Av WISHAW ML2 ....173 E1
Flax Rd UD/BTH/TAN G71 ....134 B2
Fleet Av RNFRW PA4 ....63 H5
Fleet St CAR/SHTL G32 ....92 C5
Fleming Av
  BAIL/MDB/MHD G69 ....58 B4
  CLYDBK G81 ....49 G3
Fleming Ct HMLTN ML3 ....168 D1
  MTHW ML1 ....172 B1
Fleming Pl EKILS G75 ....166 A5
Fleming Rd BLSH ML4 ....116 A4
  BSHPTN PA7 ....29 E5
  CRG/CRSL/HOU PA6 ....80 D1
  CUMB G67 ....26 B3
Fleming St DEN/PKHD G31 ....91 E3
  PSLYN/LNWD PA3 ....84 B2
Flemington St
  SPRGB/BLRNK G21 ....68 C3
Fleming Wy HMLTN ML3 ....168 C1
Flenders Av
  CRMNK/CLK/EAG G76 ....145 F4
Flenders Rd
  CRMNK/CLK/EAG G76 ....145 F4
Fleurs Av PLKSD/SHW G41 ....108 A1
Fleurs Rd PLKSD/SHW G41 ....88 A5
Flinders Pl EKILS G75 ....165 G5
Floyd St CTBR ML5 ....96 C2
Floorsburn Crs JNSTN PA5 ....101 F4
Floors Rd
  CRMNK/CLK/EAG G76 ....162 D4
Floors St JNSTN PA5 ....101 G4
Flora Gdns BSHPBGS G64 ....55 F2
Florence Dr GIF/THBK G46 ......127 F5
Florence Gdns RUTH G73 ....130 B3
Florence St GBLS G5 ....89 H4
Florida Av GVH/MTFL G42 ....109 G4
Florida Crs GVH/MTFL G42 ......109 G4
Florida Dr GVH/MTFL G42 ....109 F4
Florida Gdns
  BAIL/MDB/MHD G69 ....93 H4
Florida Sq GVH/MTFL G42 ....109 G4
Florida St GVH/MTFL G42 ....109 G4
Florish Rd ERSK PA8 ....48 A3
Flowerdale Pl PLK/PH/NH G53 ..125 G4
Flowerhill St AIRDRIE ML6 ....98 C1
Flures Av ERSK PA8 ....48 B3
Flures Crs ERSK PA8 ....48 B3
Flures Dr ERSK PA8 ....48 B3
Flures Pl ERSK PA8 ....48 B3
Fochabers Dr
  CARD/HILL/MSPK G52 ....86 D3
Foinaven Dr GIF/THBK G46 .....126 C2
Foinaven Gdns GIF/THBK G46 ...126 C1
Foinaven Wy GIF/THBK G46 .....126 D1
Foinavon Rd HMLTN ML3 ....181 D5
Footfield Rd BLSH ML4 ....135 G4
Forbes Dr DMNK/BRGTN G40 ....90 C3
  MTHW ML1 ....136 A5
Forbes Pl PSLY PA1 ....84 B5
Forbes St DMNK/BRGTN G40 .....90 C3
Fordneuk St DMNK/BRGTN G40 ..90 D4
Fordoun St ESTRH G34 ....94 C1
Ford Rd KVD/HLHD G12 ....66 C2
  NMRNS G77 ....161 G2
Fordyce St PTCK G11 ....66 A4
Fore Rw HMLTN ML3 ....170 B1
Forest Av BLSH ML4 ....136 A4
  HMLTN ML3 ....180 D2
Forest Dr UD/BTH/TAN G71 .....134 B4
Forest Gdns KKNTL G66 ....39 F4
Forest Ga UD/BTH/TAN G71 .....115 G3
Foresthall Crs
  SPRGB/BLRNK G21 ....68 D3
Foresthall Gdns
  SPRGB/BLRNK G21 ....68 D3
Forest La HMLTN ML3 ....180 D2
Forest Pk WISHAW ML2 ....157 G5
Forest Pl KKNTL G66 ....39 F4
  PSLYS PA2 ....104 B2
Fore St SCOT G14 ....64 D3
Forest Rd CUMB G67 ....11 H4
  CUMB G67 ....27 E4

Forest Vw CUMB G67 ....27 E2
Forfar Av CARD/HILL/MSPK G52 ..86 C5
Forfar Crs BSHPBGS G64 ....55 F5
Forgan Gdns BSHPBGS G64 ....55 G3
Forge Dr CTBR ML5 ....96 C2
Forge Pl SPRGB/BLRNK G21 ......69 E4
Forge Rd AIRDRIE ML6 ....118 C1
Forge Rw AIRDRIE ML6 ....118 D1
Forge St SPRGB/BLRNK G21 ......69 E4
Forgewood Pth AIRDRIE ML6 .....99 G3
Forgewood Rd MTHW ML1 ....136 D5
Forglen St ESTRH G34 ....72 C5
Formby Dr SMSTN G23 ....52 C3
Forres Av GIF/THBK G46 ....127 G4
Forres Crs BLSH ML4 ....116 C5
Forres Ga GIF/THBK G46 ....127 G5
Forres Qd WISHAW ML2 ....157 G5
Forres St BLTYR/CAMB G72 ....151 H5
  SMSTN G23 ....52 D2
Forrester Ct BSHPBGS G64 ....68 D1
Forrestfield Crs NMRNS G77 ....144 A5
Forrestfield Gdns NMRNS G77 ...144 A5
Forrestfield St
  SPRGB/BLRNK G21 ....68 D5
Forsa St HMLTN ML3 ....169 G4
Forsyth St AIRDRIE ML6 ....98 C1
Forteviot Av
  BAIL/MDB/MHD G69 ....94 B4
Forteviot Pl
  BAIL/MDB/MHD G69 ....94 B4
Forth Av PSLYS PA2 ....103 G4
Forth Ct EKILS G75 ....176 D1
Forth Crs EKILS G75 ....164 D5
Forth Gv EKILS G75 ....176 D1
Forth Pl JNSTN PA5 ....120 D2
Forth Rd BSDN G61 ....51 E1
  BSHPBGS G64 ....55 E1
Forth St CLYDBK G81 ....49 F5
  PLKSD/SHW G41 ....109 E1
Forth Ter HMLTN ML3 ....169 G5
Forties Ct GIF/THBK G46 ....126 C2
Forties Crs GIF/THBK G46 ....126 C2
Forties Gdns GIF/THBK G46 .....126 C2
Forties Rd CRG/CRSL/HOU PA6 ..80 D3
Forties Wy GIF/THBK G46 ....126 C2
Fortieth Av EKILS G75 ....178 C3
Fortingall Av KVD/HLHD G12 .....52 B5
Fortingall Pl KVD/HLHD G12 .....52 B5
Fortingall Rd
  BLTYR/CAMB G72 ....152 A5
Fortrose St PTCK G11 ....66 A4
Fort St MTHW ML1 ....154 B2
Forum Pl MTHW ML1 ....154 D2
Fossil Gv KKNTL G66 ....22 A4
Foswell Dr DRUM G15 ....33 E3
Foswell Pl DRUM G15 ....33 E3
Fotheringay La
  PLKSD/SHW G41 ....108 C2
Fotheringay Rd
  PLKSD/SHW G41 ....108 C2
Foulis La KNTSWD G13 ....51 G5
Foulis St KNTSWD G13 ....51 G5
Foulsykes Rd WISHAW ML2 ....174 D1
Foundry La BRHD/NEIL G78 .....124 A4
Foundry Rd MTHW ML1 ....139 F5
Fountain Av RNFRW PA4 ....61 G2
Fountain Crs RNFRW PA4 ....61 G2
Fountainwell Av
  SPRGB/BLRNK G21 ....68 A4
Fountainwell Dr
  SPRGB/BLRNK G21 ....68 A4
Fountainwell Pl
  SPRGB/BLRNK G21 ....68 A4
Fountainwell Rd
  SPRGB/BLRNK G21 ....68 A4
Fountainwell Sq
  SPRGB/BLRNK G21 ....68 B4
Fourth Av DMBTN G82 ....13 H5
  KKNTL G66 ....57 E2
  RNFRW PA4 ....63 G1
  STPS/GTHM/RID G33 ....70 C1
Fourth Gdns PLKSD/SHW G41 ....87 H5
Fourth St UD/BTH/TAN G71 ....115 E3
Four Windings
  CRG/CRSL/HOU PA6 ....80 C1
Fowler Pl EKILS G75 ....177 H3
Fowlis Dr NMRNS G77 ....143 H4
Foxbar Crs PSLYS PA2 ....103 G5
Foxbar Dr KNTSWD G13 ....50 D5
  PSLYS PA2 ....102 D5
Foxbar Rd PSLYS PA2 ....102 D5
Foxes Gv KKNTL G66 ....40 D5
Foxglove Pl PLK/PH/NH G53 ....125 G4
Fox Gv MTHW ML1 ....154 A3
Foxhills Pl SMSTN G23 ....52 D2
Foxley St CAR/SHTL G32 ....112 D5
Foyers Ter SPRGB/BLRNK G21 ...68 D2
Francis St GBLS G5 ....89 F5
Frankfield Rd
  STPS/GTHM/RID G33 ....71 F1
Frankfield St
  STPS/GTHM/RID G33 ....69 G4
Frankfort St PLKSD/SHW G41 ...108 D3
Franklin Pl EKILS G75 ....165 G4
Franklin St DMNK/BRGTN G40 ..110 C1
Fraser Av DMBTN G82 ....28 D4
  DMBTN G82 ....12 B3
  JNSTN PA5 ....101 H4
  NMRNS G77 ....144 A4
  RUTH G73 ....111 F5
Fraser Ct HMLTN ML3 ....169 G5
Fraser Gdns KKNTL G66 ....20 D5
Fraser St BLTYR/CAMB G72 .....130 D1
  MTHW ML1 ....139 E5
Frazer St DMNK/BRGTN G40 .....91 E4
Frederick St CTBR ML5 ....96 B1
Freeland Ct PLK/PH/NH G53 ....125 H1
Freeland Crs PLK/PH/NH G53 ...125 G1
Freeland Dr BRWEIR PA11 ....79 G2
  ERSK PA8 ....47 G4
  PLK/PH/NH G53 ....125 G1
Freeland Rd ERSK PA8 ....47 G4
Freelands Crs OLDK G60 ....30 A3
Freelands Rd OLDK G60 ....30 A4
Freesia Ct MTHW ML1 ....154 D5
French St CLYDBK G81 ....31 F5
  DMNK/BRGTN G40 ....110 D1
  RNFRW PA4 ....63 E3
  WISHAW ML2 ....174 A2
Freuchie St ESTRH G34 ....94 A2

Frew St AIRDRIE ML6 ....98 B1
Friar Av BSHPBGS G64 ....38 A4
Friarscourt Av KNTSWD G13 .....51 E3
Friarscourt Rd
  BAIL/MDB/MHD G69 ....58 A2
Friars Ct KKNTL G66 ....21 G5
Friars Cft KKNTL G66 ....51 E3
Friars Wy AIRDRIE ML6 ....98 D5
Friarton Rd PLKSW/MSWD G43 .128 A1
Frood St MTHW ML1 ....154 B1
Fruin Av NMRNS G77 ....144 B5
Fruin Pl SPRGB/BLRNK G21 ......68 C3
Fruin Ri HMLTN ML3 ....168 D3
Fruin Rd DRUM G15 ....32 D1
Fruin St SPRGB/BLRNK G21 ......68 C3
Fulbar Av RNFRW PA4 ....63 F2
Fulbar Ct RNFRW PA4 ....63 F2
Fulbar Crs PSLYS PA2 ....103 E2
Fulbar Gdns PSLYS PA2 ....103 E2
Fulbar La RNFRW PA4 ....63 G2
Fulbar Rd GOV/IBX G51 ....86 D2
  PSLYS PA2 ....103 E2
Fulbar St RNFRW PA4 ....63 G2
Fullarton Av CAR/SHTL G32 .....112 B2
Fullarton La CAR/SHTL G32 ......112 B2
Fullarton Pl CAR/SHTL G32 ......112 A2
Fullarton Rd BALLOCH G68 ....116 A1
  CAR/SHTL G32 ....112 B3
Fullers Gt CLYDBK G81 ....32 B1
Fullerton St PSLYN/LNWD PA3 ..69 E4
Fullerton Ter PSLYN/LNWD PA3 .84 D2
Fulmar Pk EKILN G74 ....166 A2
Fulmar Pl JNSTN PA5 ....120 D2
Fulton Crs KLBCH PA10 ....32 E1
Fulton Dr CRG/CRSL/HOU PA6 ...81 F3
Fulton Gdns
  CRG/CRSL/HOU PA6 ....81 F2
Fulton Rd MLNGV G62 ....17 F4
Fulton St KNTSWD G13 ....50 A4
Fulwood Av KNTSWD G13 ....50 A4
  PSLYN/LNWD PA3 ....82 A3
Fulwood Pl KNTSWD G13 ....50 A4
The Furlongs HMLTN ML3 ....170 A1
Furnace Rd HMLTN ML3 ....181 F5
Fyneart St WISHAW ML2 ....174 D1
Fyne Av BLSH ML4 ....116 A5
Fyne Ct HMLTN ML3 ....169 F4
Fynloch Pl CLYDBK G81 ....31 F1
Fyvie Av PLKSW/MSWD G43 ....126 D2
Fyvie Crs AIRDRIE ML6 ....99 F3

G

Gadie Av RNFRW PA4 ....63 H4
Gadie St STPS/GTHM/RID G33 ...91 G1
Gadloch Av KKNTL G66 ....57 E1
Gadloch Gdns KKNTL G66 ....39 E5
Gadloch St PPK/MIL G22 ....54 A5
Gadloch Vw KKNTL G66 ....39 E5
Gadsburn Ct SPRGB/BLRNK G21 .55 F5
Gadshill St SPRGB/BLRNK G21 ...68 C5
Gailes Pk UD/BTH/TAN G71 .....134 A5
Gailes Rd BALLOCH G68 ....9 H5
Gailes St DMNK/BRGTN G40 .....91 E5
Gain & Shankburn Rd
  CRG/CRSL/HOU PA6 ....80 C1
Gainburn Crs CUMB G67 ....43 G2
Gainburn Ct CUMB G67 ....43 G2
Gainburn Gdns CUMB G67 ....43 G3
Gainburn Pl CUMB G67 ....43 G2
Gainburn Vw CUMB G67 ....43 H2
Gainside Rd CTBR ML5 ....59 H5
Gairbraid Av MRYH/FIRH G20 ...52 C5
Gairbraid Ct MRYH/FIRH G20 ....52 C5
Gairbraid Pl MRYH/FIRH G20 ....52 D5
Gairbraid Ter
  BAIL/MDB/MHD G69 ....95 F4
Gair Crs WISHAW ML2 ....174 A4
Gala Av RNFRW PA4 ....63 H5
Gala Crs WISHAW ML2 ....156 D5
Gala St STPS/GTHM/RID G33 .....69 H4
Galbraith Dr GOV/IBX G51 ....16 D5
  MLNGV G62 ....16 D5
Galdenoch St
  STPS/GTHM/RID G33 ....70 C4
Gallacher Av PSLYS PA2 ....103 F3
Gallan Av SMSTN G23 ....52 D2
Galloway Av HMLTN ML3 ....180 B2
Galloway Dr RUTH G73 ....130 A4
Galloway Rd AIRDRIE ML6 ....98 A4
  EKILN G74 ....166 A3
Galloway St SPRGB/BLRNK G21 ..54 D5
Gallowflat St RUTH G73 ....111 E6
Gallowgate CGLE G1 ....3 J7
  DEN/PKHD G31 ....91 E4
  DMNK/BRGTN G40 ....90 C4
Gallowhill Av KKNTL G66 ....39 H2
Gallowhill Rd
  CRMNK/CLK/EAG G76 ....147 F2
  KKNTL G66 ....39 H2
  PSLYN/LNWD PA3 ....84 C3
Galston Av NMRNS G77 ....144 D5
Galston Ct HMLTN ML3 ....181 E1
Galston St PLK/PH/NH G53 .....125 E2
Galt Pl EKILS G75 ....178 A1
Gamrie Dr PLK/PH/NH G53 ......125 E1
Gamrie Gdns PLK/PH/NH G53 ...106 B4
Gamrie Rd PLK/PH/NH G53 ......106 B4
Gannochy Dr BSHPBGS G64 ......55 F1
Gantock Crs
  STPS/GTHM/RID G33 ....92 C2
Gardenhall EKILS G75 ....164 C5
Gardenhall Ct EKILS G75 ....164 C5
Gardenside BLSH ML4 ....136 B4
Gardenside Av CAR/SHTL G32 ..112 B4
  UD/BTH/TAN G71 ....133 H1
Gardenside Crs CAR/SHTL G32 ..112 B4
Gardenside Gv CAR/SHTL G32 ..112 B4
Gardenside Rd HMLTN ML3 .....170 A3
Gardenside St
  UD/BTH/TAN G71 ....133 H1
Garden Square Wk AIRDRIE ML6 .97 G1
Gardner Gv UD/BTH/TAN G71 ...115 F4
Gardner St PTCK G11 ....66 A4
Gardyne St ESTRH G34 ....72 A5
Gareloch Av AIRDRIE ML6 ....76 A4
  PSLYS PA2 ....103 E2
Garfield Av BLSH ML4 ....136 B2
Garfield St DEN/PKHD G31 ....90 D3
Garforth Rd
  BAIL/MDB/MHD G69 ....93 G5

Gargrave Av
  BAIL/MDB/MHD G69 ....93 G5
Garion Dr KNTSWD G13 ....64 C1
Garlieston Rd
  STPS/GTHM/RID G33 ....93 G3
Garmouth Ct GOV/IBX G51 ....87 H1
Garmouth Gdns GOV/IBX G51 ....87 G1
Garmouth St GOV/IBX G51 ....87 G1
Garnethill St KVGV G3 ....2 C2
Garnet St KVGV G3 ....2 B2
Garngaber Av KKNTL G66 ....40 A3
Garngaber Ct KKNTL G66 ....40 B3
Garnhall Farm Rd BALLOCH G68 .7 H2
Garnie Av ERSK PA8 ....48 A3
Garnieland Rd ERSK PA8 ....48 A3
Garnie La ERSK PA8 ....48 A3
Garnie Ov ERSK PA8 ....48 A3
Garnie Pl ERSK PA8 ....48 A2
Garnkirk La
  STPS/GTHM/RID G33 ....71 E1
Garnock St SPRGB/BLRNK G21 ...68 C4
Garrell Av KSYTH G65 ....8 B1
Garrell Rd KSYTH G65 ....8 A2
Garrell Wy CUMB G67 ....26 A5
  KSYTH G65 ....8 A2
Garrick Av NMRNS G77 ....161 G3
Garrioch Crs MRYH/FIRH G20 ...66 C1
Garrioch Dr MRYH/FIRH G20 ....66 C1
Garrioch Ga MRYH/FIRH G20 ....66 C1
Garriochmill Rd
  MRYH/FIRH G20 ....66 C2
Garrioch Qd MRYH/FIRH G20 ....66 C1
Garrioch Rd MRYH/FIRH G20 ....66 C2
Garrowhill Dr
  BAIL/MDB/MHD G69 ....93 G4
Garry Av BSDN G61 ....51 H1
Garry Dr PSLYS PA2 ....103 F2
Garry St LNPK/KPK G44 ....109 F5
Garscadden Rd DRUM G15 ......50 A1
Garscadden Rd South
  DRUM G15 ....50 A3
Garscube Rd COWCAD G4 ....2 D2
Garshake Av DMBTN G82 ....13 H2
Garshake Rd DMBTN G82 ....13 H3
Gartartan Rd PSLY PA1 ....86 A4
Gartcarron Hl BALLOCH G68 .....25 G2
Gartcloss Rd CTBR ML5 ....73 H4
Gartconnell Dr BSDN G61 ....34 B2
Gartconnell Gdns BSDN G61 .....34 B2
Gartconnell Rd BSDN G61 ....34 B2
Gartconner Av KKNTL G66 ....22 B5
Gartcosh Rd
  BAIL/MDB/MHD G69 ....95 E3
Gartcosh Wk BLSH ML4 ....135 H3
Gartcraig Rd
  STPS/GTHM/RID G33 ....70 A5
Gartferry Av
  BAIL/MDB/MHD G69 ....58 D1
Gartferry Rd
  BAIL/MDB/MHD G69 ....58 D1
Gartferry St SPRGB/BLRNK G21 .68 D2
Gartgill Rd CTBR ML5 ....74 B4
Garthamlock Rd
  STPS/GTHM/RID G33 ....71 F5
Garthland Dr DEN/PKHD G31 ....90 D2
Garthland La PSLY PA1 ....84 C4
Garth St CGLE G1 ....3 G5
Gartlea Av AIRDRIE ML6 ....98 B2
Gartleahill AIRDRIE ML6 ....98 B3
Gartlea Rd AIRDRIE ML6 ....98 B2
Gartliston Ter
  BAIL/MDB/MHD G69 ....95 F4
Gartloch Rd
  BAIL/MDB/MHD G69 ....71 G4
  STPS/GTHM/RID G33 ....70 A5
Gartly St LNPK/KPK G44 ....128 A3
Gartmore Gdns
  UD/BTH/TAN G71 ....114 D4
Gartmore La PSLY PA1 ....85 F5
Gartmore Ter
  BLTYR/CAMB G72 ....130 D4
Gartness Dr AIRDRIE ML6 ....119 H1
Gartness Rd AIRDRIE ML6 ....119 H1
Gartocher Dr CAR/SHTL G32 ....92 D4
Gartocher Rd CAR/SHTL G32 ....92 D4
Gartocher Ter CAR/SHTL G32 ...92 D4
Gartons Rd SPRGB/BLRNK G21 ..55 F5
Gartsherrie Av BLSH ML4 ....116 D1
Gartsherrie Rd CTBR ML5 ....96 B1
Gartshore Crs KSYTH G65 ....23 F3
Gartshore Gdns BALLOCH G68 ...24 C4
Gartshore Rd BALLOCH G68 ......42 D2
Garturk St GVH/MTFL G42 ....109 G2
Garvald Ct DMNK/BRGTN G40 ..111 E1
Garvald St DMNK/BRGTN G40 ..111 E1
Garvel Crs STPS/GTHM/RID G33 .93 F3
Garvel Pl MLNGV G62 ....16 B3
Garvel Rd MLNGV G62 ....16 B3
  STPS/GTHM/RID G33 ....93 F3
Garvin Lea BLSH ML4 ....116 D4
Garvock Dr PLKSW/MSWD G43 .127 E2
Garwhitter Dr MLNGV G62 ....17 F3
Gascoyne EKILS G75 ....177 H2
Gask Pl KNTSWD G13 ....50 A3
Gask St JNSTN PA5 ....101 H5
Gatehouse St CAR/SHTL G32 ...92 C4
Gateshead Pl KLBCH PA10 ......100 B3
Gateside Av BLTYR/CAMB G72 ..152 A5
  KSYTH G65 ....8 B2
Gateside Crs AIRDRIE ML6 ....98 B1
  BRHD/NEIL G78 ....141 H1
Gateside Pl KLBCH PA10 ....100 B3
  WISHAW ML2 ....173 F1
Gateside Rd BRHD/NEIL G78 ....141 F1
Gateside St DEN/PKHD G31 ....91 E3
  HMLTN ML3 ....170 B3
The Gateway EKILN G74 ....166 D1
Gauldry Av
  CARD/HILL/MSPK G52 ....106 D1
Gauze St PSLY PA1 ....84 C4
Gavell Rd KSYTH G65 ....23 F2
Gavinburn Gdns OLDK G60 ....30 A1
Gavinburn Pl OLDK G60 ....30 B1
Gavinburn St OLDK G60 ....30 B1
Gavins Rd CLYDBK G81 ....32 A2
Gavin St MTHW ML1 ....154 D5
Gavinton St LNPK/KPK G44 .....128 A2
Gean Ct CUMB G67 ....11 G5
Geary St SMSTN G23 ....52 B2
Geddes Hl EKILN G74 ....167 G1

Geddes Rd SPRGB/BLRNK G21....55 F4
Geils Av DMBTN G82 ...13 H5
Geils Qd DMBTN G82 ...13 H5
Gelston St CAR/SHTL G32....92 C5
Gemmel Pl NMRNS G77 ...161 E1
Gentle Rw CLYDBK G81 ...31 G2
George Av CLYDBK G81....32 B5
George Crs CLYDBK G81....32 B5
George Gray St RUTH G73....111 F4
George La PSLY PA1 ....84 B5
George Mann Ter RUTH G73...129 H5
George Pl PSLY PA1....84 B5
George Reith Av KVD/HLHD G12..65 G1
George Sq CGLE G1 ....3 F5
George St AIRDRIE ML6....97 F2
AIRDRIE....119 E1
BAIL/MDB/MHD G69....94 A5
BRHD/NEIL G78 ...124 A4
CGLE G1 ...3 H5
HMLTN ML3 ...152 B5
HWWD PA9....120 A4
JNSTN PA5....137 F5
MTHW ML1 ...171 H1
PSLY PA1....83 H5
George V Br KVGV G3 ...2 D7
Gerard Pl BLSH ML4....117 E5
Germiston Crs EKILS G75 ...177 E4
Germiston Crs EKILS G75 ...177 F4
Gertrude Pl BRHD/NEIL G78...123 H5
Ghillies La MTHW ML1 ...154 B1
Gibbon Crs EKILN G74 ...167 F2
Gibb St AIRDRIE ML6....119 E1
MTHW ML1....157 E1
Gibson Av DMBTN G82 ...13 G5
Gibson Crs JNSTN PA5....101 F4
Gibson Qd MTHW ML1 ...154 B1
Gibson Rd RNFRW PA4 ...85 E1
Gibson St DMBTN G82....13 F3
DMNK/BRGTN G40 ...90 B3
KVD/HLHD G12 ....66 D4
Giffnock Park Av
GIF/THBK G46 ...127 F3
Gifford Dr
CARD/HILL/MSPK G52...86 B4
Gifford Wynd JNSTN PA5...103 E2
Gigha Qd WISHAW ML2 ...173 F4
Gilbertfield Pl
STPS/GTHM/RID G33 ...70 C4
Gilbertfield Rd
BLTYR/CAMB G72 ...132 C3
Gilbertfield St
STPS/GTHM/RID G33 ...70 C4
Gilbert St KVGV G3 ...88 B1
Gilchrist St CTBR ML5 ...97 E1
Gilchrist Wy WISHAW ML2...174 B4
Gilderdale EKILN G74 ...149 H5
Gilhill St MRYH/FIRH G20....52 C4
Gillies Crs EKILN G74 ...150 A5
Gillies La BAIL/MDB/MHD G69 ..94 B5
Gilmerton St CAR/SHTL G32...92 B5
Gilmour Av CLYDBK G81 ...32 A3
EKILN G74 ...164 A1
Gilmour Crs RUTH G73 ...110 C4
Gilmour Dr HMLTN ML3 ...169 E3
Gilmour Pl BLSH ML4....135 F2
CTBR ML5 ...96 B1
Gilmour St CLYDBK G81 ...32 B4
PSLY PA1....84 B4
Gilmourton Crs NMRNS G77...161 G1
Gimmerscroft Crs AIRDRIE ML6..99 G3
Girthon St CAR/SHTL G32...92 D5
Girvan Crs AIRDRIE ML6....119 E3
Girvan St STPS/GTHM/RID G33..69 G5
Gladney Av KNTSWD G13 ...49 H3
Gladsmuir Rd
CARD/HILL/MSPK G52...86 B3
Gladstone Av BRHD/NEIL G78..124 A5
JNSTN PA5....121 E2
Gladstone Ct HMLTN ML3...152 C5
Gladstone St BLSH ML4 ...136 A2
CLYDBK G81 ...48 C1
COWCAD G4....67 F4
Glaive Rd KNTSWD G13 ...51 E2
Glamis Av JNSTN PA5 ...102 A3
NMRNS G77....144 C5
Glamis Ct MTHW ML1 ...137 H4
Glamis Gdns EKILN G74....166 C2
Glamis Rd DEN/PKHD G31...91 H5
Glanderston Av
BRHD/NEIL G78 ...124 D5
Glanderston Ct KNTSWD G13....50 B4
Glanderston Dr KNTSWD G13..50 B4
Glanderston Ga NMRNS G77...143 G4
Glanderston Rd NMRNS G77...142 B5
Glasgow & Edinburgh Rd
BAIL/MDB/MHD G69....69 H4
BLSH ML4....117 H3
MTHW ML1 ...119 F4
Glasgow Br CGLE G1 ....2 E7
KKNTL G66....39 E1
Glasgow Rd BLTYR/CAMB G72...149 E2
BRHD/NEIL G78 ...124 A4
CLYDBK G81 ...32 B2
CRMNK/CLK/EAG G76...163 E3
CTBR ML5 ...95 G3
CUMB G67 ...26 D1
CUMB G67....44 B1
DMBTN G82 ...12 D4
HMLTN ML3 ...152 B5
KKNTL G66....20 C5
KSYTH G65 ...7 F3
MLNGV G62 ...17 F5
RNFRW PA4 ...63 H4
RUTH G73....110 C2
UD/BTH/TAN G71 ...114 B4
WISHAW ML2 ...173 E1
Glasgow St KVD/HLHD G12...66 D3
Glassel Rd ESTRH G34 ...72 C5
Glasserton Pl
PLKSW/MSWD G43...128 A2
Glasserton Rd
PLKSW/MSWD G43...128 A2
Glassford St CGLE G1 ....3 G6
Glaudhall Av
BAIL/MDB/MHD G69....58 D4
Glazert Meadow KKNTL G66....4 C1
Glazert Park Dr KKNTL G66....4 C1
Glazert Pl KKNTL G66....5 F5
Glebe Av CRMNK/CLK/EAG G76..147 E5
CTBR ML5 ...116 A1
UD/BTH/TAN G71 ...134 C5
Glebe Ct COWCAD G4 ....3 J5
Glebe Crs AIRDRIE ML6....99 E1

HMLTN ML3 ...169 H3
Glebe Gdns CRG/CRSL/HOU PA6..80 C1
Glebe Hollow
UD/BTH/TAN G71 ...134 C5
Glebe La NMRNS G77 ...161 G1
Glebe Pk DMBTN G82 ...13 G2
Glebe Pl BLTYR/CAMB G72...131 G2
RUTH G73 ...110 C4
Glebe Rd NMRNS G77 ...161 G1
Glebe St BLSH ML4 ...116 A1
COWCAD G4....3 J2
EKILN G74....166 C3
HMLTN ML3....170 A3
RNFRW PA4....63 G3
The Glebe UD/BTH/TAN G71..134 B5
Glebe Wynd UD/BTH/TAN G71...134 C5
Gleddoch Rd
CARD/HILL/MSPK G52...85 H3
Gledstane Rd BSHPTN PA7...46 A1
Glenacre Crs UD/BTH/TAN G71..114 D4
Glenacre Dr AIRDRIE ML6....99 E3
Glenacre Qd CSMK G45....129 E4
Glenacre St CSMK G45....129 E4
Glenacre Ter CSMK G45....129 E4
Glen Affric EKILN G74 ...167 E4
Glen Affric Av PLK/PH/NH G53..125 H5
Glen Affric Dr AIRDRIE ML6....119 E3
Glen Affric Wy AIRDRIE ML6...119 E3
Glenafton Vw HMLTN ML3...169 E5
Glen Alby Pl PLK/PH/NH G53...125 H5
Glenallan Ter MTHW ML1...136 C5
Glen Almond EKILN G74...167 F5
Glenalmond St CAR/SHTL G32..92 B5
Glenalva Ct KSYTH G65 ....8 B1
Glenapp Av PSLY PA2 ...105 F3
Glenapp Rd PSLY PA2 ...105 E3
Glenapp St PLKSD/SHW G41...109 E1
Glenarklet Dr PSLY PA2 ...104 D5
Glen Arroch EKILN G74 ...167 E4
Glenartney CRG/CRSL/HOU PA6..80 D1
Glenartney Rd
BAIL/MDB/MHD G69...58 B2
Glenashdale Wy PSLY PA2...104 D5
Glen Av BAIL/MDB/MHD G69...59 E1
BRHD/NEIL G78 ...141 F3
CAR/SHTL G32 ....92 C2
Glenavon Ct HMLTN ML3...169 C4
Glen Avon Dr AIRDRIE ML6...119 E3
Glenavon Rd MRYH/FIRH G20..52 C4
Glenbank Av KKNTL G66 ....40 A4
Glenbank Dr GIF/THBK G46...126 C5
Glenbank Rd KKNTL G66 ...40 A4
Glenbarr St SPRGB/BLRNK G21...68 C5
Glen Bervie EKILN G74 ...167 E5
Glenbervie Pl NMRNS G77...143 F5
SMSTN G23....52 C2
Glenboig Rd CTBR ML5....59 H5
Glen Brae BRWEIR PA11 ...79 G3
Glenbrittle Dr PSLY PA2....104 D5
Glenbrittle Wy PSLY PA2...104 D5
Glenbuck Av
STPS/GTHM/RID G33...56 A5
Glenbuck Dr
STPS/GTHM/RID G33...56 A5
Glenburn Av
BAIL/MDB/MHD G69....59 E1
BLTYR/CAMB G72....130 C2
MTHW ML1 ...137 H5
Glenburn Crs KKNTL G66....21 H5
PSLY PA2....104 A5
UD/BTH/TAN G71 ...115 G4
Glenburn Gdns BSHPBGS G64...54 C1
CTBR ML5....59 H5
Glenburnie Pl
STPS/GTHM/RID G33 ...93 H2
Glenburn La MRYH/FIRH G20...52 D4
Glenburn Rd BSDN G61 ....34 A3
EKILN G74....165 F2
GIF/THBK G46 ...145 E1
HMLTN ML3 ...169 G2
PSLY PA2....103 G4
Glenburn St MRYH/FIRH G20...52 D4
Glenburn Ter MTHW ML1...155 C1
Glenburn Wy EKILN G74 ...165 E2
Glencairn Av WISHAW ML2...173 E1
Glencairn Ct RUTH G73 ...110 C4
Glencairn Dr
BAIL/MDB/MHD G69...58 D1
PLKSD/SHW G41 ...108 D2
RUTH G73 ...110 C4
Glencairn Gdns
BLTYR/CAMB G72 ...132 A2
PLKSD/SHW G41 ...108 D2
Glencairn La PLKSD/SHW G41...108 D2
Glencairn Rd CUMB G67....27 E3
DMBTN G82....12 B4
PSLYN/LNWD PA3 ...84 D2
Glencairn St MRYH/FIRH G20..154 D5
Glencaple Crs BLSH ML4 ...116 A3
Glen Cally EKILN G74 ...167 E5
Glencally Av PSLY PA2 ...105 E3
Glen Cannich EKILN G74 ...167 E4
Glen Carron EKILN G74....167 E4
Glencart Gv KLBCH PA10....100 D5
Glencleland Rd WISHAW ML2..173 E1
Glenclora Dr PSLY PA2 ...104 D5
Glen Clova EKILN G74 ...167 E4
Glen Clova Dr BALLOCH G68...25 G1
Glencloy St MRYH/FIRH G20...52 B4
Glen Clunie Dr PLK/PH/NH G53..125 H5
Glen Clunie Pl PLK/PH/NH G53..125 H5
Glencoats Crs PSLYN/LNWD PA3..83 F5
Glencoats Dr PSLYN/LNWD PA3...83 F5
Glencoe Pl HMLTN ML3 ...137 F2
KNTSWD G13 ....51 F4
Glencoe Rd RUTH G75 ...130 C4
Glencoe St KNTSWD G13 ....51 G4
Glen Cona Dr PLK/PH/NH G53..125 H2
Glencorse Rd PSLY PA2 ...104 A2
Glencorse St
STPS/GTHM/RID G33...91 H2
Glencraig St AIRDRIE ML6...97 H2
Glen Creran Crs
BRHD/NEIL G78 ...140 D4
Glen Crs KNTSWD G13 ...49 H4
Glen Cs BRHD/NEIL G78...171 C4
Glencroft Rd LNPK/KPK G44..114 A2
Glencryan Rd CUMB G67 ...26 D4
Glendale Av AIRDRIE ML6....99 E3
Glendale Crs BSHPBGS G64...55 F5
Glendale Dr BSHPBGS G64...55 F5
Glendale Gv CTBR ML5 ...116 B1

Glendale Pl BSHPBGS G64 ....55 F4
Glendale St DEN/PKHD G31...91 E3
Glendaruel Av BSDN G61 ...35 E4
Glendaruel Rd
CRMNK/CLK/EAG C76...130 D5
Glendarvel Gdns PPK/MIL G22...68 A2
Glendee Gdns RNFRW PA4...63 G4
Glendee Rd RNFRW PA4 ...63 G4
Glen Dene Wy PLK/PH/NH G53..125 H5
Glendentan Rd BRWEIR PA11..79 F4
Glen Derry EKILN G74 ...167 E5
Glen Dessary EKILN G74....167 E5
Gleneveron Wy MTHW ML1...137 F5
Glen Devon EKILN G74....167 G4
Glendevon Pl CLYDBK G81...31 G5
HMLTN ML3....169 E5
Glendevon Sq
STPS/GTHM/RID G33....70 C4
Glen Dewar Pl PLK/PH/NH G53..125 H5
Glendinning Rd KNTSWD G13...51 F2
Glen Dochart Dr BALLOCH G68..25 G1
Glendoick Pl NMRNS G77....143 F5
Glen Doll EKILN G74 ...167 F4
Glen Doll Rd BRHD/NEIL G78..140 C4
Glendorch Av WISHAW ML2...157 F3
Glendore St SCOT G14....65 F4
Glen Douglas Dr BALLOCH G68..25 F1
Glendoune Rd
CRMNK/CLK/EAG G76...145 H4
Glen Dr MTHW ML1 ...137 G2
Glenduffhill Rd
BAIL/MDB/MHD G69...93 G4
Glen Dye EKILN G74 ...167 G4
Gleneagles Av BALLOCH G68...10 C5
Gleneagles Dr NMRNS G77...162 C1
Gleneagles Gdns BSHPBGS G64..37 G5
Gleneagles La North SCOT G14..64 D2
Gleneagles La South SCOT G14..64 D3
Gleneagles Pk
UD/BTH/TAN G71 ...134 A5
Glenelg Crs KKNTL G66 ...21 H5
Glenelg Qd ESTRH G34 ...72 C5
Gleneim Pl BLSH ML4 ...117 G1
Glen Esk EKILN G74 ...167 F5
Glen Esk Dr PLK/PH/NH G53..125 H5
Glen Esk Dr PLK/PH/NH G53..125 H5
Glenesk Pl PLK/PH/NH G53...125 H5
Glen Etive Pl
CRMNK/CLK/EAG G76...130 D5
Glen Falloch EKILN G74 ...167 E5
Glen Falloch Crs
BRHD/NEIL G78 ...140 D5
Glen Falloch Wy BALLOCH G68..25 G1
Glen Fairy EKILN G74 ...167 E4
Glenfarg Ct HMLTN ML3 ...169 C5
Glenfarg Crs BSDN G61 ...35 E4
Glenfarg Rd RUTH G73 ...130 A3
Glenfarg St MRYH/FIRH G20...66 D1
Glenfield Av PSLY PA2 ...123 E1
Glenfield Crs PSLY PA2 ...123 F1
Glenfield Gdns PSLY PA2 ...123 E1
Glenfield Gv PSLY PA2 ...123 E1
Glenfield Rd EKILS G75 ...177 H3
PSLY PA2....123 E1
Glen Finlet Rd BRHD/NEIL G78..140 C5
Glenfinnan Dr BSDN G61....34 D4
MRYH/FIRH G20 ...52 C4
Glenfinnan Gv BLSH ML4...136 C3
Glenfinnan Pl MRYH/FIRH G20..52 C4
Glenfinnan Rd MRYH/FIRH G20..66 C1
Glen Fruin Pl AIRDRIE ML6...119 E3
Glenfruin Rd BLTYR/CAMB G72..151 F3
Glen Fyne Rd BALLOCH G68...25 F1
Glen Gairn EKILN G74 ...167 G4
Glen Gairn Crs BRHD/NEIL G78..140 D4
Glen Gdns JNSTN PA5 ...102 B1
Glen Garrell Pl KSYTH G65....7 H1
Glengarriff Rd BLSH ML4 ...117 E4
Glen Garry EKILN G74 ...167 E5
Glengarry Dr
CARD/HILL/MSPK G52...86 D4
Glengavel Gdns WISHAW ML2..157 F3
Glengowan Rd BRWEIR PA11..79 F3
Glen Gv EKILS G75 ...178 A1
Glengyre St ESTRH G34 ...72 B5
Glenhead Crs CLYDBK G81...31 H1
Glenhead Rd CLYDBK G81 ...31 H3
KKNTL G66....39 H4
Glenhead St PPK/MIL G22...54 A4
Glenholme Av PSLY PA2 ...103 G3
Glen Isla EKILN G74 ...167 G4
Gleniffer Av KNTSWD G13 ...50 B5
Gleniffer Crs JNSTN PA5 ...102 B3
Gleniffer Rd PSLY PA2 ...103 E5
RNFRW PA4....62 D5
Gleniffer Vw BRHD/NEIL G78..141 E1
Glenisla Av BAIL/MDB/MHD G69..59 E1
Glenisla St DEN/PKHD G31...91 G5
Glenkirk Dr DRUM G15....50 C1
Glen Kyle Dr PLK/PH/NH G53..125 H3
Glen Lednock Dr BALLOCH G68..25 F1
Glen Lee EKILN G74....167 F4
Glenlee St HMLTN ML3 ...152 A5
Glen Lethnot EKILN G74 ...167 F4
Glen Livet Pl PLK/PH/NH G53..125 H3
Glenlivet Rd BRHD/NEIL G78..140 D5
Glen Lochay Gdns BALLOCH G68..25 F1
Glenlora Dr PLK/PH/NH G53...106 C5
Glenlora Ter PLK/PH/NH G53...106 C5
Glen Loy Pl PLK/PH/NH G53...125 H3
Glen Luce Dr CAR/SHTL G32...113 E1
Glenluce Gdns
BAIL/MDB/MHD G69...42 B5
Glenluce Ter EKILN G74 ...165 H5
Glenluggie Rd KKNTL G66...40 D1
Glenlui Av RUTH G73 ...130 A1
Glen Luss Gdns BALLOCH G68..25 G1
Glen Luss Pl CTBR ML5 ...97 G4
PLK/PH/NH G53 ...125 H3
Glen Lyon EKILN G74 ...167 F4
Glen Lyon Ct BALLOCH G68...25 F1
Glenlyon Ct HMLTN ML3 ...170 B4
Glenlyon Pl RUTH G73 ...130 B4
Glen Lyon Rd BRHD/NEIL G78..140 D4

Glen Mallie EKILN G74 ...167 E4
Glenmalloch Pl JNSTN PA5...102 B1
Glenmanor Av
BAIL/MDB/MHD G69...41 H5
Glen Mark EKILN G74 ...167 F5
Glen Mark Rd BRHD/NEIL G78..140 D4
Glenmavis Rd AIRDRIE ML6...75 H5
Glenmavis St COWCAD G4....2 D2
Glen More EKILN G74....166 D4
Glenmore Av BLSH ML4 ...136 A4
GVH/MTFL G42 ...110 D4
Glenmore Rd MTHW ML1...137 H5
Glen Moriston EKILN G74...167 E4
Glen Moriston Rd BALLOCH G68..25 F1
PLK/PH/NH G53 ...126 A4
Glenmoss Av ERSK PA8 ....47 E2
Glen Moy EKILN G74 ...167 G4
Glenmuir Dr PLK/PH/NH G53...125 H3
Glen Muir Rd BRHD/NEIL G78..140 D4
Glen Nevis EKILN G74....167 G4
Glen Nevis Pl RUTH G73....130 B5
Glen Noble MTHW ML1 ...156 D2
Glenochil Rd AIRDRIE ML6...119 G3
Glen Ogilvie EKILN G74....167 F5
Glen Ogle St CAR/SHTL G32...92 D5
Glenorchard Rd BSHPBGS G64...18 B2
Glen Orchy Dr BALLOCH G68...25 F1
Glen Orchy Dr PLK/PH/NH G53..125 H3
PLK/PH/NH G53....126 A4
Glen Orchy Pl AIRDRIE ML6...119 E3
BALLOCH G68....25 F1
Glenorrin Wy BRHD/NEIL G78..140 D4
Glenpark AIRDRIE ML6 ...98 C3
Glenpark Av GIF/THBK G46...126 C5
Glenpark Gdns
BLTYR/CAMB G72 ...111 G5
Glenpark Rd DEN/PKHD G31...91 E3
Glenpark St WISHAW ML2...173 H1
Glenpark Ter BLTYR/CAMB G72..111 H5
Glenpath DMBTN G82 ...13 H4
Glenpatrick Rd JNSTN PA5...102 B5
Glen Pl CRMNK/CLK/EAG G76..145 H3
Glen Prosen EKILN G74 ...167 F4
Glen Quoich EKILN G74 ...167 G2
Glenraith Rd
STPS/GTHM/RID G33...70 B1
Glen Rannoch Dr AIRDRIE ML6..119 C3
Glen Rinnes Dr BRHD/NEIL G78..141 E5
Glen Rd AIRDRIE ML6 ...98 D5
BSHPTN PA7....28 D4
CAR/SHTL G32 ....92 C2
EKILN G74 ...166 D4
MTHW ML1 ...119 E5
OLDK G60 ...30 C2
WISHAW ML2 ...173 H1
Glen Rosa Gdns BALLOCH G68..25 F1
Glen Roy Dr BRHD/NEIL G78..140 D4
Glen Sannox Dr BALLOCH G68..25 H1
Glen Sannox Gv BALLOCH G68..25 H1
Glen Sannox Loan BALLOCH G68..25 H1
Glen Sannox Vw BALLOCH G68..25 H1
Glen Sannox Wy BALLOCH G68..25 H1
Glen Sax Dr RNFRW PA4 ...63 H5
Glen Shee EKILN G74 ...167 F5
Glen Shee Av BRHD/NEIL G78..140 D4
Glen Shee Crs AIRDRIE ML6...119 E3
Glenshee Gdns DEN/PKHD G31..91 G5
Glenshee St DEN/PKHD G31...91 G5
Glenshiel Av PSLY PA2....104 D5
Glenshira Av PSLY PA2 ...104 D5
Glen Shirva Rd KSYTH G65....23 C1
Glenside Av PLK/PH/NH G53...106 C3
Glenside Dr RUTH G73 ...130 C1
Glenside Rd DMBTN G82....13 H2
Glenspean St
PLKSW/MSWD G43...127 G1
Glen St BLTYR/CAMB G72...132 A3
BRHD/NEIL G78 ...124 A4
MTHW ML1....138 A3
MTHW ML1 ...154 D1
PSLYN/LNWD PA3 ...84 A4
Glentanar Dr
BAIL/MDB/MHD G69...59 F1
Glentanar Pl PPK/MIL G22...53 G4
Glentanar Rd PPK/MIL G22...53 G4
Glen Tanner EKILN G74 ...167 G3
Glen Tarbert Dr
BRHD/NEIL G78 ...140 D4
Glentarbert Rd RUTH G73...130 C4
Glen Tennet EKILN G74 ...167 F5
Glentore Qd AIRDRIE ML6....76 B4
Glentrool Gdns
BAIL/MDB/MHD G69...42 B5
PPK/MIL G22 ...68 A2
Glen Turret EKILN G74 ...167 G3
Glentyan Av KLBCH PA10....100 B2
Glentyan Dr PLK/PH/NH G53..106 B5
Glentyan Pl PLK/PH/NH G53...106 B5
Glen Urquhart EKILN G74...167 E4
Glenview AIRDRIE ML6 ...99 E3
Glen Vw CUMB G67 ...180 D2
Glenview
BAIL/MDB/MHD G69...42 A5
Glenview Crs
BAIL/MDB/MHD G69...42 A5
Glenview Pl BLTYR/CAMB G72..151 G1
Glenville Av GIF/THBK G46...127 E4
Glenville Ga
CRMNK/CLK/EAG G76...146 B5
Glenville Ter
CRMNK/CLK/EAG G76...146 B5
Glenward Av KNTL G66 ...4 C1
Glenwell St AIRDRIE ML6....99 G1
Glenwood Av AIRDRIE ML6...98 D5
Glenwood Ct KKNTL G66 ...39 F3
Glenwood Dr GIF/THBK G46...126 C5
Glenwood Gdns KKNTL G66...39 F3
Glenwood Pth CSMK G45...129 F4
Glenwood Pl CSMK G45 ...129 F4
KKNTL G66....39 F3
Glenwood Rd KKNTL G66...39 F3
Glorat Av KVD/HLHD G12...52 A3
Gloucester Av
CRMNK/CLK/EAG G76...145 H3
RUTH G73....130 C1
Gloucester St GBLS G5....89 F4
Gockston Rd PSLYN/LNWD PA3..84 A3
Goddard Pl WISHAW ML2....158 C5
Gogar Pl STPS/GTHM/RID G33..69 H5
Gogar St STPS/GTHM/RID G33..69 H5
Goil Av UD/BTH/TAN G71 ...135 C1
Goldberry Av SCOT G14....64 C1
Goldenacre Pl AIRDRIE ML6...77 G3

Goldenlee Vw
CRG/CRSL/HOU PA6...80 B3
Goldie Rd UD/BTH/TAN G71...134 B5
Golf Av BLSH ML4 ...135 H4
Golf Course Rd BRWEIR PA11..79 E5
BSHPBGS G64 ...18 B5
Golf Dr DRUM G15 ...50 A2
PSLY PA1....85 F5
Golfhill Dr DEN/PKHD G31...90 D1
Golfhill Qd AIRDRIE ML6 ...76 B4
Golfhill Rd WISHAW ML2...173 H3
Golf Pl BLSH ML4 ...136 A4
Golf Rd BSHPTN PA7 ....28 D3
CRMNK/CLK/EAG C76...145 G2
RUTH G73....130 A3
Golfview BSDN G61 ...33 C5
Golf Vw CLYDBK G81 ...31 G4
Golfview Pl CTBR ML5 ...95 H3
Golspie Av AIRDRIE ML6....99 H4
Golspie St GOV/IBX G51 ...87 H1
Goosedubbs CGLE G1 ...89 H3
Gooseholm Crs DMBTN G82...13 F2
Gooseholm Rd DMBTN G82...13 F2
Gopher Av UD/BTH/TAN G71..115 G4
Gorbals St GBLS G5 ...89 H4
Gordon Av BAIL/MDB/MHD G69..93 G4
BSHPTN PA7....28 D4
CARD/HILL/MSPK G52...85 H2
LNPK/KPK G44 ...127 H5
Gordon Crs NMRNS G77 ...144 B4
Gordon Dr EKILN G74 ...166 C4
LNPK/KPK G44 ...127 H4
Gordon La CGLE G1 ....2 E5
Gordon Pl BLSH ML4....135 G4
Gordon Rd HMLTN ML3 ...153 G5
LNPK/KPK G44 ...127 H5
Gordon St CGLE G1 ....2 E5
PSLY PA1....84 B5
Gore St BLTYR/CAMB G72...131 H2
HMLTN ML3....169 E2
Gorebridge St CAR/SHTL G32..91 H2
Gorget Av KNTSWD G13 ...50 D2
Gorget Pl KNTSWD G13 ...50 D2
Gorget Qd DRUM G15 ...50 C2
Gorse Crs BRWEIR PA11 ...79 H4
Gorsehall St MTHW ML1 ...139 E5
Gorse Pl UD/BTH/TAN G71...115 H4
Gorsewood BSHPBGS G64...54 B2
Gorstan Pl MRYH/FIRH G20...66 B1
Gorstan St SMSTN G23 ...52 C3
Gosford La SCOT G14 ...64 B2
Goudie St PSLYN/LNWD PA3...84 A2
Gough St STPS/GTHM/RID G33..91 G1
Gourlay St SPRGB/BLRNK G21..68 B2
Gourock St PLKSD/SHW G41...89 G5
Govanhill St GVH/MTFL G42...109 H2
Govan Rd GOV/IBX G51 ...65 G5
Gowanbank Gdns JNSTN PA5..101 F4
Gowanbank Gdns JNSTN PA5..101 F4
Gowanlea Av DRUM G15....50 B2
Gowanlea Dr GIF/THBK G46...127 G3
Gowanlea Ter
UD/BTH/TAN G71 ...115 G5
Gower St PLKSD/SHW G41....88 B4
Gowkhall Av MTHW ML1 ...138 C4
Goyle Av DRUM G15....33 H5
Grace Av BAIL/MDB/MHD G69..95 G2
Grace St KVGV G3....2 B5
Graeme Ct MTHW ML1 ...136 C5
Graffham Av GIF/THBK G46...127 G4
Grafton Pl CGLE G1 ....3 G4
Graham Av BLTYR/CAMB G72..132 A3
CLYDBK G81 ...32 A5
EKILN G74 ...166 B3
HMLTN ML3 ...169 H5
Graham Rd DMBTN G82 ...12 B6
Grahamsdyke Rd KKNTL G66..21 C4
Grahamshill Av AIRDRIE ML6...99 E1
Grahamshill St AIRDRIE ML6...98 D1
Graham Sq DEN/PKHD G31...90 C4
Grahamston Crs PSLY PA2...105 C4
Grahamston Pk
BRHD/NEIL G78 ...124 A2
Grahamston Pl PSLY PA2...105 G4
Grahamston Rd PSLY PA2...124 B1
Graham St AIRDRIE ML6....98 B2
BRHD/NEIL G78 ...124 A4
HMLTN ML3 ...170 B2
JNSTN PA5....101 F4
MTHW ML1 ...137 F2
WISHAW ML2 ...174 A3
Graham Ter BSHPBGS G64...55 E4
Grainger Rd BSHPBGS G64...55 G2
Grampian Av PSLY PA2 ...104 A4
Grampian Ct BSDN G61 ...16 C5
CAR/SHTL G32 ....112 C5
Grampian Dr EKILS G75 ...177 C4
Grampian Pl CAR/SHTL G32...92 C5
Grampian Rd WISHAW ML2...173 G1
Grampian St CAR/SHTL G32...92 C5
Grampian Wy BALLOCH G68...25 C1
BRHD/NEIL G78 ...142 B1
BSDN G61....33 G1
Granby La KVD/HLHD G12...66 D3
Grandtully Dr KVD/HLHD G12...52 B5
Grange Av MLNGV G62 ...17 F3
WISHAW ML2 ...157 F4
Grangeneuk Gdns
BALLOCH G68 ...25 G4
Grange Rd BSDN G61 ...34 C3
GVH/MTFL G42 ...109 F4
Grange St HMLTN ML3 ...172 B1
Grannoch Pl CTBR ML5 ...117 G2
Gran St CLYDBK G81 ...49 H5
Grant Ct HMLTN ML3 ...180 C1
Granthall Av MTHW ML1 ...137 G1
Grantlea Gv CAR/SHTL G32...93 E5
Grantlea Ter CAR/SHTL G32...93 E5
Grantley Gdns
PLKSD/SHW G41 ...108 C4
Grantley St PLKSD/SHW G41...108 C4
Grantoften Pth EKILS G75...178 A3
Granton St GBLS G5 ...110 B2
Grantown Av AIRDRIE ML6 ...98 B3
Grantown Gdns AIRDRIE ML6..76 A1
Grants Av PSLY PA2 ...103 H4
Grants Crs PSLY PA2 ...104 A4
Grants Pl PSLY PA2 ...103 H5
Grant St CGLE G1....2 A1
Grants Wy PSLY PA2 ...103 H4
Granville St CLYDBK G81...32 A5
KVGV G3 ....2 A3
Grasmere EKILS G75 ...177 E3

Grasmere Ct *HMLTN* ML3 ......180 D2
Grathellen Ct *MTHW* ML1 ......155 F2
Gray Dr *BSDN* G61 ......34 C5
Grayshill Rd *BALLOCH* G68 ......43 E1
Gray's Rd *UD/BTH/TAN* G71 ......134 C2
Grayston Mnr
  BAIL/MDB/MHD G69 ......58 C2
Gray St *KKNTL* G66 ......41 E1
  KVGV G3 ......2 A5
  MTHW ML1 ......157 E1
Great Dovehill *COWCAD* G4 ......3 J7
Great George La *KVD/HLHD* G12 ......66 C4
Great George St *KVD/HLHD* G12 ......66 C4
Great Hamilton St *PSLYS* PA2 ......104 B2
Great Kelvin La *KVD/HLHD* G12 ......66 B3
Great Western Rd *CLYDBK* G81 ......32 B4
  KNTSWD G13 ......50 D5
  OLDK G60 ......15 E5
Great Western Ter
  KVD/HLHD G12 ......66 B2
Great Western Terrace La
  KVD/HLHD G12 ......66 B2
Greenacres *MTHW* ML1 ......154 B5
Greenacres Ct *PLK/PH/NH* G53 ......125 H3
Greenacres Dr *PLK/PH/NH* G53 ......125 H3
Greenacres Wy
  PLK/PH/NH G53 ......125 H3
Greenan Av *LNPK/KPK* G44 ......108 D5
Greenbank Dr *PSLYS* PA2 ......104 A5
Green Bank Rd *BALLOCH* G68 ......43 E4
Greenbank Rd *WISHAW* ML2 ......174 B2
Green Dl *WISHAW* ML2 ......157 G5
Greendyke St *CCLE* G1 ......90 A3
Greenend Av *JNSTN* PA5 ......101 E5
Greenend Pl *CAR/SHTL* G32 ......92 D2
Greenend Vw *BLSH* ML4 ......135 G3
Greenfarm Rd *NMRNS* G77 ......145 G5
Green Farm Rd
  PSLYN/LNWD PA3 ......82 A3
Greenfaulds Crs *CUMB* G67 ......26 C5
Greenfaulds Rd *CUMB* G67 ......44 C1
Greenfaulds Crs *WISHAW* ML2 ......174 C1
Greenfield Dr *WISHAW* ML2 ......174 C1
Greenfield Qd *MTHW* ML1 ......138 C3
Greenfield Rd *CAR/SHTL* G32 ......92 D5
  CRMNK/CLK/EAG G76 ......145 H4
  HMLTN ML5 ......152 B4
Greenfield St *GOV/IBX* G51 ......87 G1
  WISHAW ML2 ......174 C1
Greengairs Av *GOV/IBX* G51 ......87 E2
Green Gdns *MTHW* ML1 ......139 F5
Greenhall Pl *BLTYR/CAMB* G72 ......151 E4
Greenhead Rd *BSDN* G61 ......34 C4
  DMBTN G82 ......13 H5
  RNFRW PA4 ......64 C1
  WISHAW ML2 ......174 C2
Greenhead St
  DMNK/BRGTN G40 ......90 B5
Greenhill *BSHPBGS* G64 ......55 F5
Greenhill Av
  BAIL/MDB/MHD G69 ......58 D4
  GIF/THBK G46 ......145 F1
Greenhill Crs *JNSTN* PA5 ......102 C2
  PSLYN/LNWD PA3 ......82 A4
Greenhill Dr *PSLYN/LNWD* PA3 ......82 B4
Greenhill Rd *MTHW* ML1 ......139 H2
  PSLYN/LNWD PA3 ......82 A4
  RUTH G73 ......110 D5
Greenhills Crs *EKILS* G75 ......177 G3
Greenhills Rd *EKILS* G75 ......176 D1
Greenhills St *RUTH* G73 ......110 D5
Greenholm Av
  CRMNK/CLK/EAG G76 ......145 H3
  UD/BTH/TAN G71 ......114 D5
Greenknowe Rd
  PLKSW/MSWD G43 ......127 E1
Greenlaw Av *PSLY* PA1 ......84 D4
Greenlaw Dr *PSLY* PA1 ......84 D4
Greenlaw Rd *NMRNS* G77 ......143 H5
  SCOT G14 ......49 G5
Greenlea Rd
  BLTYR/CAMB G72 ......131 E4
Greenlea St *KNTSWD* G13 ......51 F5
Greenlees Gdns
  BLTYR/CAMB G72 ......131 E4
Greenlees Gv *CTBR* ML5 ......97 G4
Greenlees Pk
  BLTYR/CAMB G72 ......131 E4
Greenlees Rd
  BLTYR/CAMB G72 ......131 E3
Greenloan Av *GOV/IBX* G51 ......87 E2
Greenmoss Pl *BLSH* ML4 ......136 A1
Greenmount *PPK/MIL* G22 ......53 F4
Greenock Av *LNPK/KPK* G44 ......128 C2
Greenock Rd *BSHPTN* PA7 ......46 A1
  PSLYN/LNWD PA3 ......83 H1
  RNFRW PA4 ......63 E5
Green Pl *AIRDRIE* ML6 ......118 C2
Greenrig *UD/BTH/TAN* G71 ......134 A1
Greenrigg Rd *CUMB* G67 ......26 D4
Greenrigg St *UD/BTH/TAN* G71 ......134 A1
Greenrig St
  STPS/GTHM/RID G33 ......69 G3
Green Rd *PSLYS* PA2 ......103 F1
Greens Av *KKNTL* G66 ......39 H1
Greens Crs *KKNTL* G66 ......39 H1
Greenshields Rd
  BAIL/MDB/MHD G69 ......94 A4
Greenside Crs
  STPS/GTHM/RID G33 ......69 H3
Greenside Rd *CLYDBK* G81 ......32 A1
  MTHW ML1 ......118 D5
  MTHW ML1 ......174 B3
Greenside St *CTBR* ML5 ......96 C2
  MTHW ML1 ......138 C3
  STPS/GTHM/RID G33 ......69 H3
Green St *CLYDBK* G81 ......31 H5
Green St *CLYDBK* G81 ......31 H5
  DMNK/BRGTN G40 ......90 B4
  UD/BTH/TAN G71 ......134 D1
The Green *DMNK/BRGTN* G40 ......90 B5
Greentree Dr
  BAIL/MDB/MHD G69 ......113 G1
Greenview St
  PLKSW/MSWD G43 ......108 B4
Greenways Ct *PSLYS* PA2 ......103 F2
Greenways Ct *PSLYS* PA2 ......103 F2
Greenwood Av
  BLTYR/CAMB G72 ......132 A1
Greenwood Crs *CTBR* ML5 ......97 F4
Greenwood Dr *BSDN* G61 ......35 E4
  JNSTN PA5 ......121 E3

Greenwood Qd *CLYDBK* G81 ......49 G2
Greenwood Rd
  CRMNK/CLK/EAG G76 ......145 G3
Greer Qd *CLYDBK* G81 ......32 A4
Grenada Pl *EKILS* G75 ......165 F4
Grenadier Gdns *MTHW* ML1 ......171 G2
Grenville Dr *BLTYR/CAMB* G72 ......131 E3
Gresham St *DMNK/BRGTN* G40 ......91 E5
Greta Meek La *KKNTL* G66 ......5 E1
Gretna St *DMNK/BRGTN* G40 ......91 E5
Greyfriars Rd
  UD/BTH/TAN G71 ......114 B4
Greyfriars St *CAR/SHTL* G32 ......92 A2
Greystone Av *KNTSWD* G13 ......130 B1
Greywood St *KNTSWD* G13 ......51 F4
Grierson La
  STPS/GTHM/RID G33 ......91 G1
Grierson St
  STPS/GTHM/RID G33 ......91 G1
Grieve Cft *UD/BTH/TAN* G71 ......152 B1
Grieve Rd *CUMB* G67 ......26 C2
Griffen Av *PSLYN/LNWD* PA3 ......82 D4
Griffin Pl *BLSH* ML4 ......116 D4
Griqua Ter *UD/BTH/TAN* G71 ......134 C5
Grogarry Rd *DRUM* G15 ......33 F4
Grosvenor Crescent La
  KVD/HLHD G12 ......66 C3
Grosvenor La *KVD/HLHD* G12 ......66 C3
Grosvenor Ter *KVD/HLHD* G12 ......66 C3
Groveburn Av *GIF/THBK* G46 ......126 D3
Grove Pk *KKNTL* G66 ......40 A4
Grovepark Ct *MRYH/FIRH* G20 ......67 F4
Grove Park Gdns
  MRYH/FIRH G20 ......67 F4
Grovepark St *MRYH/FIRH* G20 ......67 F4
The Groves *BSHPBGS* G64 ......55 F4
The Grove *BRHD/NEIL* G78 ......140 D4
  BRWEIR PA11 ......79 H5
  BSHPTN PA7 ......28 D5
  GIF/THBK G46 ......145 E2
  KLBCH PA10 ......100 B3
Grudie St *ESTRH* G34 ......93 H1
Gryfebank Av
  CRG/CRSL/HOU PA6 ......81 F2
Gryfebank Cl
  CRG/CRSL/HOU PA6 ......81 F2
Gryfebank Crs
  CRG/CRSL/HOU PA6 ......81 F2
Gryfebank Wy
  CRG/CRSL/HOU PA6 ......81 F2
Gryfe Rd *BRWEIR* PA11 ......79 G4
Gryfewood Crs
  CRG/CRSL/HOU PA6 ......81 F2
Gryfewood Wy
  CRG/CRSL/HOU PA6 ......81 F2
Gryffe Av *BRWEIR* PA11 ......79 G2
Gryffe Crs *PSLYS* PA2 ......103 E3
Gryffe Gv *BRWEIR* PA11 ......79 G4
Gryffe St *LNPK/KPK* G44 ......128 B1
Guildford St
  STPS/GTHM/RID G33 ......70 D5
Gullane Av *BALLOCH* G68 ......10 D5
Gullane St *PTCK* G11 ......65 H5
Gunn Ms *WISHAW* ML2 ......173 G5
Gunn Qd *BLSH* ML4 ......135 F4
Guthrie Dr *UD/BTH/TAN* G71 ......115 F3
Guthrie Pl *BSHPBGS* G64 ......19 E5
  EKILN G74 ......166 C5
Guthrie St *HMLTN* ML3 ......170 A1
  MRYH/FIRH G20 ......52 C5
Gyle St *WISHAW* ML2 ......174 D2

H

Haberlea Av *PLK/PH/NH* G53 ......125 H4
Haberlea Gdns
  PLK/PH/NH G53 ......125 H5
Haddington Wy *CTBR* ML5 ......116 B1
Haddow Gv *UD/BTH/TAN* G71 ......115 F4
Haddow St *HMLTN* ML3 ......170 B2
Hadrian Ter *MTHW* ML1 ......154 B2
Hagart Rd *CRG/CRSL/HOU* PA6 ......81 E1
Hagen Dr *MTHW* ML1 ......156 D1
Hagg Crs *JNSTN* PA5 ......101 F3
Hagg Pl *JNSTN* PA5 ......101 F3
Hagg Rd *JNSTN* PA5 ......101 F4
Haggs La *PLKSD/SHW* G41 ......108 B2
Haggs Rd *PLKSD/SHW* G41 ......108 B3
Haggswood Av
  PLKSD/SHW G41 ......108 B2
Haghill Rd *DEN/PKHD* G31 ......91 F3
Hagmill Crs *CTBR* ML5 ......117 F2
Hagmill Rd *CTBR* ML5 ......117 E2
Haig Dr *BAIL/MDB/MHD* G69 ......93 G5
Haig St *SPRGB/BLRNK* G21 ......68 C2
Hailes Av *CAR/SHTL* G32 ......93 E4
Haining Rd *RNFRW* PA4 ......63 G3
The Haining *RNFRW* PA4 ......63 F4
Hairmyres Dr *EKILS* G75 ......164 D5
Hairmyres La *EKILS* G75 ......164 D4
Hairmyres Pk *EKILS* G75 ......165 E5
Hairmyres St *CVH/MTFL* G42 ......109 H3
Hairst St *RNFRW* PA4 ......63 G2
Halbeath Av *DRUM* G15 ......33 E5
Halbert St *PLKSD/SHW* G41 ......108 D3
Haldane La *SCOT* G14 ......65 E3
Haldane Pl *EKILS* G75 ......178 C1
Haldane St *SCOT* G14 ......65 E3
Halfmerk North *EKILN* G74 ......166 D5
Halfmerk South *EKILN* G74 ......166 D5
Halgreen Av *DRUM* G15 ......32 D5
Haldon Av *CUMB* G67 ......45 E1
Halkirk Ga *BLTYR/CAMB* G72 ......168 B1
Hallbrae St *STPS/GTHM/RID* G33 ......69 H4
Hallcraig St *AIRDRIE* ML6 ......98 B1
Halley Dr *KNTSWD* G13 ......49 H5
Halley Pl *KNTSWD* G13 ......49 H5
Halley St *KNTSWD* G13 ......49 H4
Hallforest St
  STPS/GTHM/RID G33 ......70 C4
Hallhill Crs *STPS/GTHM/RID* G33 ......93 F3
Hallhill Rd *CAR/SHTL* G32 ......92 D3
Halliburton Crs *ESTRH* G34 ......93 G3
Halliburton Ter *ESTRH* G34 ......93 H2
Hallidale Crs *RNFRW* PA4 ......64 A4
Hallinan Gdns *WISHAW* ML2 ......173 G4
Hall Pl *STPS/GTHM/RID* G33 ......71 G1

Hallrule Dr
  CARD/HILL/MSPK G52 ......86 D4
Hallside Av *BLTYR/CAMB* G72 ......132 B2
Hallside Bvd *BLTYR/CAMB* G72 ......132 B3
Hallside Crs *BLTYR/CAMB* G72 ......132 B2
Hallside Dr *BLTYR/CAMB* G72 ......132 B2
Hallside Pl *GBLS* G5 ......89 H5
Hallside Rd *BLTYR/CAMB* G72 ......132 C3
Hallside St *HWWD* PA9 ......120 D5
Hall St *CLYDBK* G81 ......49 E2
  HMLTN ML3 ......170 B3
  MTHW ML1 ......157 G2
Hallydown Dr *KNTSWD* G13 ......64 D1
Halpin Cl *UD/BTH/TAN* G71 ......135 E2
Halton Gdns
  BAIL/MDB/MHD G69 ......93 G5
Hamersley Pl *EKILS* G75 ......177 E1
Hamilcomb Rd *BLSH* ML4 ......135 H4
Hamill Dr *KSYTH* G65 ......8 D2
Hamilton Av *PLKSD/SHW* G41 ......108 A1
Hamilton Crs *BLTYR/CAMB* G72 ......131 H5
  BSDN G61 ......34 C1
  BSHPTN PA7 ......28 C5
  CTBR ML5 ......96 D5
Hamilton Dr *AIRDRIE* ML6 ......76 C5
  BLTYR/CAMB G72 ......131 F2
  BLTYR/CAMB G72 ......151 E5
  BSDN G61 ......34 A5
  GIF/THBK G46 ......127 G5
  KVD/HLHD G12 ......66 D3
  MTHW ML1 ......172 A1
  UD/BTH/TAN G71 ......152 C1
Hamilton Park Av
  KVD/HLHD G12 ......66 D3
Hamilton Pk North
  HMLTN ML3 ......153 E4
Hamilton Pk South
  HMLTN ML3 ......153 E4
Hamilton Pl *EKILS* G75 ......178 B1
  HMLTN ML3 ......170 B5
  MTHW ML1 ......137 H5
Hamilton Rd *BLSH* ML4 ......135 H2
  BLTYR/CAMB G72 ......131 C2
  BLTYR/CAMB G72 ......150 D5
  CAR/SHTL G32 ......112 D2
  EKILN G74 ......167 E1
  MTHW ML1 ......154 A4
  RUTH G73 ......111 E5
  UD/BTH/TAN G71 ......113 G2
  UD/BTH/TAN G71 ......152 C1
Hamilton St *CLYDBK* G81 ......49 G4
  CVH/MTFL G42 ......109 H3
  PSLYN/LNWD PA3 ......84 B4
Hamilton Ter *CLYDBK* G81 ......49 G4
Hamlet *EKILN* G74 ......149 H5
Hampden Dr *GVH/MTFL* G42 ......109 G4
Hampden La *GVH/MTFL* G42 ......109 G4
Hampden Ter *GVH/MTFL* G42 ......109 G4
Hangingshaw Pl
  GVH/MTFL G42 ......109 H4
Hanover Cl *GVH/MTFL* G42 ......109 G1
Hanover Ct *CCLE* G1 ......3 G4
Hanover St *CCLE* G1 ......3 G5
Hanson St *DEN/PKHD* G31 ......90 C1
Hapland Av *PLK/PH/NH* G53 ......106 D3
Hapland Rd *PLK/PH/NH* G53 ......106 D3
Harbour La *PSLY* PA1 ......84 B4
Harbour Rd *PSLYN/LNWD* PA3 ......84 B2
Harburn Pl *SCOT* G14 ......50 A5
Harbury Pl *SCOT* G14 ......49 H4
Harcourt Dr *DEN/PKHD* G31 ......91 E1
Hardgate Dr *GOV/IBX* G51 ......86 D2
Hardgate Gdns *GOV/IBX* G51 ......86 D2
Hardgate Pl *GOV/IBX* G51 ......86 D2
Hardgate Rd *GOV/IBX* G51 ......86 D2
Hardie Av *RUTH* G73 ......111 F4
Hardie St *BLTYR/CAMB* G72 ......151 G3
  HMLTN ML3 ......169 G3
  MTHW ML1 ......154 D2
Hardmuir Gdns *KKNTL* G66 ......21 G4
Hardridge Av
  CARD/HILL/MSPK G52 ......107 F2
Hardridge Pl
  CARD/HILL/MSPK G52 ......107 F2
Hardridge Rd
  CARD/HILL/MSPK G52 ......107 F2
Harefield Dr *SCOT* G14 ......64 C1
Hareleeshill Rd *LRKH* ML9 ......176 A5
Harelaw Av *BRHD/NEIL* G78 ......141 F4
  LNPK/KPK G44 ......127 H5
Harelaw Crs *PSLYS* PA2 ......103 H5
Hareshaw Rd *MTHW* ML1 ......139 G2
Harestanes Gdns *KKNTL* G66 ......21 H4
Harestone Crs *WISHAW* ML2 ......174 B3
Harestone Rd *WISHAW* ML2 ......174 B3
Harhill St *GOV/IBX* G51 ......87 F1
Harkins Av *BLTYR/CAMB* G72 ......151 E3
Harkness Av *KKNTL* G66 ......5 F5
Harland St *SCOT* G14 ......65 E3
Harley St *GOV/IBX* G51 ......88 B3
Harmetray St *PPK/MIL* G22 ......54 A4
Harmony Pl *GOV/IBX* G51 ......87 H2
Harmony Rw *GOV/IBX* G51 ......87 H2
Harmony Sq *GOV/IBX* G51 ......87 H2
Harmsworth St *PTCK* G11 ......65 F3
Harper Crs *WISHAW* ML2 ......158 A5
Harport St *GIF/THBK* G46 ......126 B3
Harriet Pl *PLKSW/MSWD* G43 ......127 E1
Harriet St *RUTH* G73 ......111 E5
Harrington Rd *EKILN* G74 ......166 B4
Harris Cl *NMRNS* G77 ......143 G5
Harris Crs *OLDK* G60 ......30 C3
Harris Dr *OLDK* G60 ......30 C3
Harris Gdns *OLDK* G60 ......30 C3
Harrison Dr *GOV/IBX* G51 ......88 A3
Harris Rd *OLDK* G60 ......30 C3
  SMSTN G23 ......52 C2
Harrow Ct *DRUM* G15 ......33 E5
Harrow Pl *DRUM* G15 ......33 E5
Hartfield Ct *DMBTN* G82 ......13 H4
Hartfield Ter *PSLYS* PA2 ......104 C2
Hartlaw Crs
  CARD/HILL/MSPK G52 ......86 B3
Hartree Av *KNTSWD* G13 ......49 H4
Hartstone Rd *PLK/PH/NH* G53 ......106 C5
Hart St *CLYDBK* G81 ......31 H2
  DEN/PKHD G31 ......91 H4
  PSLYN/LNWD PA3 ......82 A4
Heathcliffe Av
  BLTYR/CAMB G72 ......151 F1

Hartwood Rd *SHOTTS* ML7 ......159 G1
Harvest Dr *MTHW* ML1 ......171 H1
Harvey St *COWCAD* G4 ......67 H4
Harvey Wy *BLSH* ML4 ......117 F5
Harvie Av *NMRNS* G77 ......144 A4
Harvie St *GOV/IBX* G51 ......88 C3
Harwood Gdns
  BAIL/MDB/MHD G69 ......42 B5
Harwood St *CAR/SHTL* G32 ......92 A2
Hastie St *KVGV* G3 ......66 C5
Hastings *EKILS* G75 ......177 F1
Hatfield Dr *KVD/HLHD* G12 ......65 G1
Hathaway Dr *GIF/THBK* G46 ......127 E5
Hathaway La *MRYH/FIRH* G20 ......66 D1
Hathaway St *MRYH/FIRH* G20 ......66 D1
Hathersage Av
  BAIL/MDB/MHD G69 ......94 A4
Hathersage Dr
  BAIL/MDB/MHD G69 ......94 A4
Hathersage Gdns
  BAIL/MDB/MHD G69 ......94 A4
Hatton Gdns
  CARD/HILL/MSPK G52 ......86 B5
Hatton Crs *BLTYR/CAMB* G72 ......131 H5
  BSDN G61 ......34 C3
  BSHPTN PA7 ......28 C5
  CTBR ML5 ......96 D5
Haughburn Pl *PLK/PH/NH* G53 ......106 C5
Haughburn Rd
  PLK/PH/NH G53 ......106 C5
Haughburn Ter
  PLK/PH/NH G53 ......106 D5
Haugh Pl *HMLTN* ML3 ......170 B4
Haugh Rd *KVGV* G3 ......88 C1
  KSYTH G65 ......8 A2
Haughton Av *KSYTH* G65 ......8 C1
Haughview Rd *MTHW* ML1 ......154 A4
Havelock La *PTCK* G11 ......66 B4
Havelock Pk *EKILS* G75 ......177 E2
Havelock St *PTCK* G11 ......66 B4
Haven Pk *EKILS* G75 ......177 E2
Havoc Rd *DMBTN* G82 ......12 A4
Hawbank Rd *EKILN* G74 ......165 F2
Hawick Av *PSLYS* PA2 ......103 G3
Hawick St *KNTSWD* G13 ......49 H4
  WISHAW ML2 ......157 F5
Hawkhead Av *PSLYS* PA2 *......105 E3
Hawkhead Rd *PSLY* PA1 ......105 F2
Hawkwood *EKILS* G75 ......178 A3
Hawkwood Rd *AIRDRIE* ML6 ......119 F2
Hawthorn Av *BSDN* G61 ......34 D1
  BSHPBGS G64 ......55 E3
  DMBTN G82 ......12 A3
  ERSK PA8 ......48 A3
  JNSTN PA5 ......101 H5
  KKNTL G66 ......39 H1
  WISHAW ML2 ......158 D4
Hawthornden Gdns *SMSTN* G23 ......52 D2
Hawthorn Dr *AIRDRIE* ML6 ......99 E2
  BRHD/NEIL G78 ......142 C2
  CTBR ML5 ......97 G4
  MTHW ML1 ......174 B1
Hawthorn Gdns *BLSH* ML4 ......136 A3
  BLTYR/CAMB G72 ......132 B3
  CRMNK/CLK/EAG G76 ......145 G4
Hawthornhill Rd *DMBTN* G82 ......12 C4
Hawthorn Qd *PPK/MIL* G22 ......67 H1
Hawthorn Rd
  CRMNK/CLK/EAG G76 ......145 H4
  ERSK PA8 ......48 A3
  CLYDBK G81 ......31 H4
  PPK/MIL G22 ......53 H5
  SPRGB/BLRNK G21 ......68 B5
Hawthorn Ter *EKILS* G75 ......177 G2
  UD/BTH/TAN G71 ......115 G5
Hawthorn Wk *CTBR* ML5 ......130 C2
Hawthorn Wy *ERSK* PA8 ......48 A3
Hay Av *BSHPTN* PA7 ......29 E5
Hayburn Crs *PTCK* G11 ......65 H5
Hayburn La *KVD/HLHD* G12 ......66 A5
Hayburn St *PTCK* G11 ......65 H5
Hay Dr *JNSTN* PA5 ......102 A1
Hayfield St *GBLS* G5 ......90 A5
Hayhill *EKILN* G74 ......176 A1
Hayle Gdns *BAIL/MDB/MHD* G69 ......42 A5
Haymarket St *CAR/SHTL* G32 ......92 A2
Haystack Pl *KKNTL* G66 ......40 A4
Hayston Crs *MRYH/FIRH* G20 ......67 C1
Hayston Rd *BALLOCH* G68 ......25 H3
Hayston St *MRYH/FIRH* G20 ......67 C1
Hazel Av *BSDN* G61 ......35 E1
  JNSTN PA5 ......101 H5
  KKNTL G66 ......40 A3
  LNPK/KPK G44 ......128 A3
Hazel Bank *KKNTL* G66 ......5 E1
Hazelbank Wk *AIRDRIE* ML6 ......97 H2
Hazeldean Crs *WISHAW* ML2 ......157 F5
Hazel Dene *BSHPBGS* G64 ......54 D2
Hazelden Gdns *LNPK/KPK* G44 ......127 H4
Hazelden Rd *NMRNS* G77 ......161 E1
Hazelfield Gv *AIRDRIE* ML6 ......119 F3
Hazel Gdns *MTHW* ML1 ......171 H1
Hazel Gv *KKNTL* G66 ......40 A3
  OLDK G60 ......30 C3
Hazel Pl *BLTYR/CAMB* G72 ......151 F5
  EKILS G75 ......177 G2
Hazel Rd *CUMB* G67 ......27 E2
Hazel Ter *UD/BTH/TAN* G71 ......115 G5
Hazel Wd *WISHAW* ML2 ......157 G5
Hazelwood Av *NMRNS* G77 ......161 H1
  PSLYS PA2 ......102 D5
Hazelwood Dr
  BLTYR/CAMB G72 ......151 F2
Hazelwood Gdns *RUTH* G73 ......130 B3
Hazelwood La *BRWEIR* PA11 ......79 G4
Hazelwood Rd
  PLKSD/SHW G41 ......88 B5
Hazlitt Gdns *MRYH/FIRH* G20 ......53 F5
Hazlitt Pl *MRYH/FIRH* G20 ......53 F5
Hazlitt St *MRYH/FIRH* G20 ......53 F5
Heath Av *BSHPBGS* G64 ......55 E3
  KKNTL G66 ......40 A5
Heathcliffe Av
  BLTYR/CAMB G72 ......151 F1

Heathcot Av *DRUM* G15 ......49 H1
Heathcot Pl *DRUM* G15 ......49 G1
Heather Av *BRHD/NEIL* G78 ......123 H2
  BSDN G61 ......16 B5
  CLYDBK G81 ......31 H1
  MTHW ML1 ......137 F2
Heatherbank Wk *CTBR* ML5 ......97 G1
Heatherbrae *BSHPBGS* G64 ......54 B2
Heathergardens *KKNTL* G66 ......5 H4
Heather Pl *JNSTN* PA5 ......101 H5
Heather Vw *KKNTL* G66 ......4 C1
Heathery Knowe *EKILS* G75 ......178 B1
Heatheryknowe Rd
  BAIL/MDB/MHD G69 ......94 D1
Heathery Lea Av *CTBR* ML5 ......117 G1
Heathery Rd *WISHAW* ML2 ......173 G2
Heathfield Av
  BAIL/MDB/MHD G69 ......59 F1
Heathfield Dr *MLNGV* G62 ......17 F1
Heathfield St
  STPS/GTHM/RID G33 ......92 D1
Heathside Rd *GIF/THBK* G46 ......126 D4
Heathwood Dr *GIF/THBK* G46 ......126 D4
Hecla Av *DRUM* G15 ......33 E5
Hecla Pl *DRUM* G15 ......33 E5
Hecla Sq *DRUM* G15 ......33 E5
Hector Rd *PLKSD/SHW* G41 ......108 C4
Helensburgh Dr *KNTSWD* G13 ......51 F5
Helenslee Crs *DMBTN* G82 ......12 B4
Helenslee Pl *DMBTN* G82 ......12 C4
Helenslee Rd *DMBTN* G82 ......12 B4
Helenslee Crs *DMBTN* G82 ......12 C4
Helenslee St *GOV/IBX* G51 ......87 G4
Helenvale Ct *DEN/PKHD* G31 ......91 G4
Helenvale St *DEN/PKHD* G31 ......91 F5
Helmsdale Av
  BLTYR/CAMB G72 ......133 F4
Helmsdale Ct *BLTYR/CAMB* G72 ......168 C1
Helmsdale Dr *PSLYS* PA2 ......103 E2
Hemlock St *KNTSWD* G13 ......51 F1
Henderland Dr *BSDN* G61 ......51 F1
Henderland Rd *BSDN* G61 ......51 F3
Henderson Av
  BLTYR/CAMB G72 ......132 A1
Henderson St *AIRDRIE* ML6 ......98 C1
  CTBR ML5 ......96 C3
  KNTSWD G13 ......67 E3
  MRYH/FIRH G20 ......67 F3
  PSLY PA1 ......84 A4
Henrietta St *SCOT* G14 ......64 D2
Henry St *BRHD/NEIL* G78 ......124 A4
Hepburn Rd
  CARD/HILL/MSPK G52 ......86 B2
Hepburn Gv *MTHW* ML1 ......171 G1
Herald Av *KNTSWD* G13 ......51 E3
Herald Gv *MTHW* ML1 ......171 G1
Herbertson Gv
  BLTYR/CAMB G72 ......151 E1
Herbertson St
  BLTYR/CAMB G72 ......151 E1
Herbert St *MRYH/FIRH* G20 ......67 E3
Heriot Av *PSLYS* PA2 ......103 E4
Heriot Crs *BSHPBGS* G64 ......37 H5
Heriot Rd *KKNTL* G66 ......39 H5
Heritage Ct *NMRNS* G77 ......144 A5
Heritage Wy *CTBR* ML5 ......96 C1
Herma St *SMSTN* G23 ......52 D3
Hermes Wy *BLSH* ML4 ......137 E2
Hermiston Av *CAR/SHTL* G32 ......92 C3
Hermiston Pl *CAR/SHTL* G32 ......92 C3
Hermiston Rd *CAR/SHTL* G32 ......92 C3
Hermitage Av *KNTSWD* G13 ......50 D4
Hermitage Crs *CTBR* ML5 ......117 E1
Herndon Ct *NMRNS* G77 ......144 D4
Heron Ct *CLYDBK* G81 ......32 A3
Heron Pl *JNSTN* PA5 ......121 F2
Herries Rd *PLKSD/SHW* G41 ......108 B3
Herriet St *PLKSD/SHW* G41 ......109 E1
Herriot St *CTBR* ML5 ......96 B2
Herschell St *KNTSWD* G13 ......51 G5
Hertford Av *KVD/HLHD* G12 ......52 A5
Hewett Crs *CRG/CRSL/HOU* PA6 ......80 D2
Hexham Gdns *PLKSD/SHW* G41 ......108 C3
Hickman St *GVH/MTFL* G42 ......109 H2
Hickman Ter *GVH/MTFL* G42 ......109 H2
Hickory Crs *UD/BTH/TAN* G71 ......115 G3
Hickory St *PPK/MIL* G22 ......68 B1
High Barholm *KLBCH* PA10 ......100 C3
High Barrwood Rd *KSYTH* G65 ......8 D2
High Beeches
  CRMNK/CLK/EAG G76 ......147 E3
High Blantyre Rd
  BLTYR/CAMB G72 ......152 A5
Highburgh Dr *RUTH* G73 ......130 A2
Highburgh Rd *KVD/HLHD* G12 ......66 B4
High Burnside Av *CTBR* ML5 ......116 B1
High Calside *PSLYS* PA2 ......104 A2
High Common Rd *EKILN* G74 ......167 F5
High Craighall Rd *COWCAD* G4 ......67 G5
Highcroft Av *LNPK/KPK* G44 ......129 E2
Highcross Av *CTBR* ML5 ......116 A1
Highermess Wy *CTBR* ML5 ......116 A1
Highfield Av *PSLYS* PA2 ......103 H5
Highfield Crs *MTHW* ML1 ......172 A1
  PSLYS PA2 ......103 H5
Highfield Dr
  CRMNK/CLK/EAG G76 ......145 G3
  KVD/HLHD G12 ......66 A1
  RUTH G73 ......130 A3
Highfield Pl *EKILN* G74 ......166 C2
Highfield Rd *KKNTL* G66 ......21 G4
High Flender Rd
  CRMNK/CLK/EAG G76 ......145 G5
High Kirk Vw *JNSTN* PA5 ......101 G4
Highland Av
  BLTYR/CAMB G72 ......151 F2
Highland La *GOV/IBX* G51 ......88 B2
Highland Pk *KSYTH* G65 ......8 A1
High Mains Av *DMBTN* G82 ......13 G2
Highland Pl *KSYTH* G65 ......8 A1
High Parks Crs *HMLTN* ML3 ......180 D2
High Patrick St *HMLTN* ML3 ......170 B3
High Rd *MTHW* ML1 ......154 C3
  PSLYS PA2 ......103 H2
Highstonehall Rd *HMLTN* ML3 ......168 D5
High St *AIRDRIE* ML6 ......98 A1
  BRHD/NEIL G78 ......141 E3
  COWCAD G4 ......3 J6
  DMBTN G82 ......12 C4
  JNSTN PA5 ......101 G4
  MTHW ML1 ......138 B3

PSLY PA1 .....84 A5
RNFRW PA4 .....63 G3
High Whitehills Rd EKILS G75 .....178 B3
Hilary Dr BAIL/MDB/MHD G69 .....93 G4
Hillary Av RUTH G73 .....130 C1
Hill Av NMRNS G77 .....161 F1
Hill Crs CRMNK/CLK/EAG G76 .....146 A4
Hillcrest BAIL/MDB/MHD G69 .....58 C3
CRMNK/CLK/EAG G76 .....147 E2
Hilbert Crs CLYDBK G81 .....112 C4
CLYDBK G81 .....31 H1
CTBR ML5 .....97 F3
CUMB G67 .....26 A5
LNPK/KPK G44 .....122 C5
PSLYS PA2 .....122 C1
WISHAW ML2 .....173 F2
Hillcrest Dr NMRNS G77 .....144 D5
Hillcrest Rd BALL G61 .....34 C4
CAR/SHTL G32 .....112 D4
KSYTH G65 .....7 F2
UD/BTH/TAN G71 .....115 F5
Hillcrest St MLNGV G62 .....17 F3
Hillcroft Ter BSHPBGS G64 .....54 C3
Hillcroft Ter BSHPBGS G64 .....55 E4
CRMNK/CLK/EAG G76 .....145 F4
Hillend Rd CRMNK/CLK/EAG G76 .....145 G4
PPK/MIL G22 .....53 F4
RUTH G73 .....130 A3
Hillfoot CRG/CRSL/HOU PA6 .....81 E3
Hillfoot Av DMBTN G82 .....13 H2
RUTH G73 .....110 D5
WISHAW ML2 .....157 G3
Hillfoot Crs WISHAW ML2 .....157 G3
Hillfoot Dr BSDN G61 .....96 A3
CTBR ML5 .....96 A3
HWWD PA9 .....120 A4
WISHAW ML2 .....157 G3
Hillfoot Gdns UD/BTH/TAN G71 .....114 D4
WISHAW ML2 .....157 G5
Hillfoot Rd AIRDRIE ML6 .....98 C3
Hillfoot St DEN/PKHD G31 .....90 D2
Hillhead Av BAIL/MDB/MHD G69 .....59 E1
MTHW ML1 .....137 F5
RUTH G73 .....130 A3
Hillhead Crs HMLTN ML3 .....168 D2
MTHW ML1 .....137 F5
Hillhead Dr AIRDRIE ML6 .....98 B3
MTHW ML1 .....155 F1
Hillhead Pl RUTH G73 .....130 A3
Hillhead Rd KKNTL G66 .....21 H4
SPRGB/BLRNK G21 .....55 G4
Hillhead St KVD/HLHD G12 .....66 C4
MLNGV G62 .....17 E3
Hillhead Ter HMLTN ML3 .....168 D2
Hillhouse Crs HMLTN ML3 .....168 D3
Hillhouse Rd BLTYR/CAMB G72 .....151 F5
HMLTN ML3 .....168 D2
Hillhouse St SPRGB/BLRNK G21 .....68 D2
Hillhouse Ter HMLTN ML3 * 169 E2
Hillington Gdns
CARD/HILL/MSPK G52 .....86 D5
Hillington Park Circ
CARD/HILL/MSPK G52 .....86 D4
Hillington Qd
CARD/HILL/MSPK G52 .....86 D4
Hillington Rd
CARD/HILL/MSPK G52 .....64 A5
Hillington Rd South
CARD/HILL/MSPK G52 .....86 D3
Hillkirk Pl SPRCB/BLRNK G21 .....68 C2
Hillkirk St SPRCB/BLRNK G21 .....68 C2
Hillneuk Av BSDN G61 .....34 C3
Hillneuk Dr BSDN G61 .....34 D3
Hillpark Av PSLYS PA2 .....104 A2
Hillpark Dr PLKSW/MSWD G43 .....127 F1
Hill Pl BLSH ML4 .....135 H3
MTHW ML1 .....137 H5
Hillrigg Av AIRDRIE ML6 .....98 D1
Hill Rd CUMB G67 .....26 A3
MTHW ML1 .....120 A4
Hillsborough Rd
BAIL/MDB/MHD G69 .....93 G5
KSYTH G65 .....8 D5
Hillside Av BSDN G61 .....34 C3
CRMNK/CLK/EAG G76 .....145 G5
Hillside Ct GIF/THBK G46 .....126 C4
Hillside Crs BRHD/NEIL G78 .....141 E5
CTBR ML5 .....96 C5
HMLTN ML3 .....169 H5
MTHW ML1 .....138 A3
Hillside Dr BRHD/NEIL G78 .....123 H4
BSDN G61 .....34 D3
Hillside Gardens La
KVD/HLHD G12 .....66 A3
Hillside Gv BRHD/NEIL G78 .....123 H5
Hillside La HMLTN ML3 .....169 H5
Hillside Pk CLYDBK G81 .....32 A2
Hillside Pl MTHW ML1 .....138 A3
Hillside Qd PLKSW/MSWD G43 .....127 E2
Hillside Rd BRHD/NEIL G78 .....141 E5
PLKSW/MSWD G43 .....127 E2
PSLYS PA2 .....104 D2
Hillside Ter HMLTN ML3 .....169 H5
KKNTL G66 .....5 F5
Hill St AIRDRIE ML6 .....119 E2
DMBTN G82 .....12 C4
HMLTN ML3 .....169 E2
KVGV G3 .....2 C3
WISHAW ML2 .....173 H5
Hillswick Crs PPK/MIL G22 .....53 G3
Hill Ter MTHW ML1 .....137 H5
Hilltop Av BLSH ML4 .....116 D5
Hilltop Rd BAIL/MDB/MHD G69 .....59 E1
Hill Vw DMBTN G82 .....14 C4
EKILS G75 .....166 B5
Hillview Av KKNTL G66 .....4 C3
KSYTH G65 .....8 B3
Hillview Crs BLSH ML4 .....116 C4
UD/BTH/TAN G71 .....114 C6
Hillview Dr BLTYR/CAMB G72 .....133 G5
CRMNK/CLK/EAG G76 .....145 G5
Hillview Pl
CRMNK/CLK/EAG G76 .....145 H3
NMRNS G77 .....161 G5
Hillview Rd BRWEIR PA11 .....79 H4
JNSTN PA5 .....101 H5
Hillview St CAR/SHTL G32 .....92 A4
Hiltonbank St HMLTN ML3 .....169 G1

Hilton Gdns KNTSWD G13 .....51 G4
Hilton Pk BSHPBGS G64 .....37 G5
Hilton Rd BSHPBGS G64 .....37 G5
MLNGV G62 .....16 C5
Hilton Ter BLTYR/CAMB G72 .....130 D4
BSHPBGS G64 .....37 G5
KNTSWD G13 .....51 F4
Hinshaw St MRYH/FIRH G20 .....67 E3
Hinshelwood Dr GOV/IBX G51 .....87 H4
Hinshelwood Pl GOV/IBX G51 .....88 A4
Hobart Crs CLYDBK G81 .....31 E3
Hobart Qd WISHAW ML2 .....174 D2
Hobart Rd EKILS G75 .....177 H1
Hobart St PPK/MIL G22 .....67 G2
Hobden St SPRGB/BLRNK G21 .....68 D3
Hoddam Av CSMK G45 .....129 H4
Hoddam Ter CSMK G45 .....129 H4
Hogan Wy MTHW ML1 .....156 B2
Hogarth Av CAR/SHTL G32 .....91 G2
Hogarth Gdns CAR/SHTL G32 .....91 G2
Hogganfield St
STPS/GTHM/RID G33 .....69 G4
Hogg Av JNSTN PA5 .....101 F5
Hogg Rd AIRDRIE ML6 .....99 E5
Hogg St AIRDRIE ML6 .....98 B2
Holeburn La
PLKSW/MSWD G43 .....127 F1
Holeburn Rd
PLKSW/MSWD G43 .....127 F1
Holehills Pl AIRDRIE ML6 .....76 C4
Holehills Pl AIRDRIE ML6 .....76 C4
Holehouse Brae
BRHD/NEIL G78 .....140 D3
Holehouse Dr KNTSWD G13 .....50 B5
Holehouse Ter BRHD/NEIL G78 .....140 D3
Hollandhush Cr HMLTN ML3 .....169 H5
Hollandhurst Rd CTBR ML5 .....74 D3
Holland St CCLW G2 .....2 B4
Hollinwell Rd SMSTN G23 .....52 C3
Hollowglen Rd CAR/SHTL G32 .....92 C3
Hollows Av PSLYS PA2 .....103 E5
Hollows Crs PSLYS PA2 .....103 E5
Hollybank Pl BLTYR/CAMB G72 .....131 G3
Hollybank St SPRGB/BLRNK G21 .....68 D5
Hollybrook St GVH/MTFL G42 .....109 G3
Hollybush Av PSLYS PA2 .....122 C1
Hollybush Rd
CARD/HILL/MSPK G52 .....86 A4
Holly Dr DMBTN G82 .....12 A3
SPRGB/BLRNK G21 .....68 D3
Holly Gv BLSH ML4 .....137 E2
Holly St AIRDRIE ML6 .....98 D2
CLYDBK G81 .....31 H4
Holm Av PSLYS PA2 .....104 C2
UD/BTH/TAN G71 .....114 D5
Holmbank Av PLKSD/SHW G41 .....108 C5
Holmbrae Av UD/BTH/TAN G71 .....115 E5
Holmbrae Rd
UD/BTH/TAN G71 .....115 E5
Holmbyre Rd CSMK G45 .....146 C1
Holmbyre Ter CSMK G45 .....128 D5
Holmes Av RNFRW PA4 .....63 F5
Holmes Qd BLSH ML4 .....136 A4
Holmfauld Dr GOV/IBX G51 .....87 F1
Holmfauldhead Dr GOV/IBX G51 .....65 F5
Holmfauld Rd GOV/IBX G51 .....65 F5
Holm Gdns BLSH ML4 .....136 B3
Holmhead Crs LNPK/KPK G44 .....128 B1
Holmhead Pl LNPK/KPK G44 .....128 B1
Holmhead Rd LNPK/KPK G44 .....128 B2
Holmhill Av BLTYR/CAMB G72 .....131 F3
Holmhills Dr BLTYR/CAMB G72 .....131 E4
Holmhills Gdns
BLTYR/CAMB G72 .....131 E3
Holmhills Gv BLTYR/CAMB G72 .....131 E3
Holmhills Pl BLTYR/CAMB G72 .....131 E3
Holmhills Rd BLTYR/CAMB G72 .....131 E4
Holmhills Ter
BLTYR/CAMB G72 .....131 E3
Holm La EKILN G74 .....166 D3
Holmlea Rd GVH/MTFL G42 .....109 F5
Holm Pl PLYN/LNWD PA3 .....82 A2
Holms Crs ERSK PA8 .....47 E1
Holms Pl BAIL/MDB/MHD G69 .....58 D4
Holm St CCLW G2 .....2 C6
MTHW ML1 .....137 F4
Holmswood Av
UD/BTH/TAN G71 .....115 E5
Holmwood Gdns
UD/BTH/TAN G71 .....134 A1
Holyknowe Crs KKNTL G66 .....4 C2
Holyknowe Rd KKNTL G66 .....4 C3
Holyrood Crs MRYH/FIRH G20 .....67 E4
Holyrood Qd MRYH/FIRH G20 .....67 E4
Holyrood St HMLTN ML3 .....152 D5
Holytown Rd BLSH ML4 .....136 D2
Holywell St DEN/PKHD G31 .....91 E4
Homer Pl BLSH ML4 .....136 D2
Homeston Av
UD/BTH/TAN G71 .....134 B4
Honeybog Rd
CARD/HILL/MSPK G52 .....85 H3
Honeywell Crs AIRDRIE ML6 .....119 F3
Hood St CLYDBK G81 .....49 G1
Hope Av BRWEIR PA11 .....78 B1
Hopefield Av KVD/HLHD G12 .....66 B1
Hopehill Gdns MRYH/FIRH G20 .....67 F3
Hopehill Rd MRYH/FIRH G20 .....67 E3
Hopeman ERSK PA8 .....30 B5
Hopeman Av GIF/THBK G46 .....126 B3
Hopeman Dr GIF/THBK G46 .....126 B3
Hopeman Rd GIF/THBK G46 .....126 B3
Hopeman St GIF/THBK G46 .....126 B3
Hope St BLSH ML4 .....136 B2
CGLW G2 .....2 D6
HMLTN ML3 .....170 B2
MTHW ML1 .....154 D3
WISHAW ML2 .....175 F1
Hopetoun Pl SMSTN G23 .....52 D1
Hopetoun Ter
SPRGB/BLRNK G21 .....68 D3
Horatius St MTHW ML1 .....154 A1
Hornal Rd UD/BTH/TAN G71 .....134 B3
Hornbeam Dr CLYDBK G81 .....31 G4
Hornbeam Rd CUMB G67 .....44 B1
UD/BTH/TAN G71 .....115 G4
Horne St PPK/MIL G22 .....68 B1
Hornock Rd CTBR ML5 .....74 C5
Hornshill Dr MTHW ML1 .....139 E5
Hornshill Farm Rd
STPS/GTHM/RID G33 .....57 F4
Hornshill St SPRGB/BLRNK G21 .....68 D2
Horsbrugh Av KSYTH G65 .....8 B1

Horsburgh St
STPS/GTHM/RID G33 .....71 E4
Horse Shoe Rd BSDN G61 .....34 B4
Horsewood Rd BRWEIR PA11 .....79 F4
Horslethill Rd KVD/HLHD G12 .....66 B2
Horslet St CTBR ML5 .....95 H5
Hospital Rd WISHAW ML2 .....174 B4
Hospital St CTBR ML5 .....96 D5
GBLS G5 .....89 G5
Hotspur St MRYH/FIRH G20 .....66 D2
Houldsworth Crs SHOTTS ML7 .....159 H2
Houldsworth La KVGV G3 .....88 D1
Househillmuir Crs
PLK/PH/NH G53 .....125 H1
Househillmuir Pl
PLK/PH/NH G53 .....125 H1
Househillmuir Rd
PLK/PH/NH G53 .....125 F2
Househillwood Crs
PLK/PH/NH G53 .....106 C5
Househillwood Rd
PLK/PH/NH G53 .....125 G1
Housel Av KNTSWD G13 .....50 C5
Houstonfield Qd
CRG/CRSL/HOU PA6 .....80 B1
Houston Pl GBLS G5 .....89 E3
JNSTN PA5 .....102 B2
Houston Rd BRWEIR PA11 .....79 F3
CRG/CRSL/HOU PA6 .....60 B3
CRG/CRSL/HOU PA6 .....80 D2
RNFRW PA4 .....61 F2
Houston Sq JNSTN PA5 .....101 G3
Houston St HMLTN ML3 .....170 A4
PLKSD/SHW G41 .....89 E4
RNFRW PA4 .....63 G2
WISHAW ML2 .....174 C3
Howard Av EKILN G74 .....166 A3
Howard St JNSTN PA5 .....101 G5
Howard St CGLE G1 .....2 E7
PSLY PA1 .....84 D4
Howat's Rd DMBTN G82 .....13 H4
Howat St GOV/IBX G51 .....87 H1
Howden Dr PSLYN/LNWD PA3 .....101 H1
Howden Pl MTHW ML1 .....137 G2
Howe Gdns UD/BTH/TAN G71 .....115 F5
Howe Rd KSYTH G65 .....8 B3
Howes St CTBR ML5 .....97 E5
Howe St PSLY PA1 .....83 E5
Howford Rd
CARD/HILL/MSPK G52 .....86 C5
Howgate Av DRUM G15 .....33 E5
Howgate Rd HMLTN ML3 .....169 H5
Howieshill Av
BLTYR/CAMB G72 .....131 G2
Howieshill Rd
BLTYR/CAMB G72 .....131 G3
Howletnest Rd AIRDRIE ML6 .....98 D3
Howlet Pl HMLTN ML3 .....170 B4
Howson Lea MTHW ML1 .....172 C1
Howson Vw MTHW ML1 .....154 A3
Howth Dr KNTSWD G13 .....51 G3
Howth Ter KNTSWD G13 .....51 G3
Hoylake Pk UD/BTH/TAN G71 .....134 A5
Hoylake Pl SMSTN G23 .....52 D2
Hozier Crs UD/BTH/TAN G71 .....115 E4
Hozier St CTBR ML5 .....96 D5
Hudson Ter EKILS G75 .....165 G5
Hudson Wy EKILS G75 .....165 H5
Hughenden Dr KVD/HLHD G12 .....66 A2
Hughenden Gdns
KVD/HLHD G12 .....65 H2
Hughenden La KVD/HLHD G12 .....66 A2
Hughenden Rd KVD/HLHD G12 .....66 A2
Hugh Murray Gv
BLTYR/CAMB G72 .....131 H2
Hugo St MRYH/FIRH G20 .....67 E2
Hulks Rd AIRDRIE ML6 .....45 G5
Humbie Ct NMRNS G77 .....161 H5
Humbie Ga NMRNS G77 .....161 H5
Humbie Lawns NMRNS G77 .....161 H5
Humbie Rd NMRNS G77 .....161 G5
Hume Dr UD/BTH/TAN G71 .....134 B4
UD/BTH/TAN G71 .....115 H5
Hume Pl EKILS G75 .....166 A5
Hume Rd CUMB G67 .....26 C2
Hume St CLYDBK G81 .....49 E2
Hunter Dr NMRNS G77 .....161 E2
Hunterfield Dr
BLTYR/CAMB G72 .....130 D2
Hunterhill Av PSLYS PA2 .....104 C1
Hunterhill Rd PSLYS PA2 .....104 C1
Hunter Pl KLBCH PA10 .....100 B3
MLNGV G62 .....16 C4
Hunter Rd HMLTN ML3 .....152 C4
MLNGV G62 .....16 D1
RUTH G73 .....111 F3
Hunter's Av DMBTN G82 .....13 H4
Huntersfield Rd JNSTN PA5 .....100 D5
Hunters Hill Ct
SPRGB/BLRNK G21 .....54 C3
Huntershill Rd BSHPBGS G64 .....54 C3
Huntershill St
SPRGB/BLRNK G21 .....54 B5
Huntershill Wy BSHPBGS G64 .....54 C4
Hunter St AIRDRIE ML6 .....76 A5
BLSH ML4 .....135 H2
COWCAD G4 .....90 B3
PSLY PA1 .....84 B4
Hunthill La BLTYR/CAMB G72 .....151 E4
Hunthill Pl
CRMNK/CLK/EAG G76 .....146 A5
Hunthill Rd BLTYR/CAMB G72 .....151 E4
Huntingdon Rd
SPRGB/BLRNK G21 .....68 B4
Huntingdon Sq
SPRGB/BLRNK G21 .....68 B4
Hunting Lodge Gdns
HMLTN ML3 .....170 D3
Huntingtower Rd
BAIL/MDB/MHD G69 .....93 G5
Huntley Gdns KVD/HLHD G12 .....66 A3
Huntly Av BLSH ML4 .....135 H1
GIF/THBK G46 .....127 G4
Huntly Ct BSHPBGS G64 .....54 B3
Huntly Dr BLTYR/CAMB G72 .....151 F3
BSDN G61 .....34 B1
GIF/THBK G46 .....126 D5
Huntly Gdns KVD/HLHD G12 .....66 A3
Huntly Pth BLTYR/CAMB G72 .....151 F3
Huntly Qd WISHAW ML2 .....157 E5
Huntly Rd CARD/HILL/MSPK G52 .....86 A1
KVD/HLHD G12 .....66 A3
Huntly Ter PSLYS PA2 .....104 D3
Hurlet Rd PSLYS PA2 .....105 F4

Hurlford Av KNTSWD G13 .....50 A4
Hurly Hawkin BSHPBGS G64 .....55 G3
Hutcheson Rd GIF/THBK G46 .....126 D5
Hutcheson St CGLE G1 .....3 G5
Hutchinson Pl
BLTYR/CAMB G72 .....132 B4
Hutchison Dr BSDN G61 .....51 H1
Hutchison Pl CTBR ML5 .....96 C5
Hutchison St HMLTN ML3 .....170 A5
Hutchison KVD/HLHD G12 .....51 H5
Hutton Dr EKILN G74 .....166 C1
GOV/IBX G51 .....87 F4
Huxley St MRYH/FIRH G20 .....53 E5
Huxley St MRYH/FIRH G20 .....53 E5
Hydepark St KVGV G3 .....2 A6
Hyndal Av PLK/PH/NH G53 .....106 D3
Hyndland Av PTCK G11 .....66 A4
Hyndland Rd KVD/HLHD G12 .....66 A3
Hyndland St PTCK G11 .....66 B4
Hyndlee Dr
CARD/HILL/MSPK G52 .....86 D5
Hyndshaw Rd WISHAW ML2 .....175 H5
Hyslop Pl CLYDBK G81 .....31 H5
Hyslop St AIRDRIE ML6 .....97 H1

I

Iain Dr BSDN G61 .....33 H2
Iain Rd BSDN G61 .....33 H2
Ian Smith Ct CLYDBK G81 .....49 G3
Ibroxholm Ov GOV/IBX G51 .....88 A5
Ibroxholm Pl GOV/IBX G51 .....88 A4
Ibrox Ter GOV/IBX G51 .....88 B3
Ibrox Ter GOV/IBX G51 .....88 A3
Ida Qd BLSH ML4 .....135 G2
Iddesleigh Av MLNGV G62 .....17 E3
Ilay Av BSDN G61 .....51 H1
Ilay Ct BSDN G61 .....51 H1
Ilay Rd BSDN G61 .....51 H1
Imlach Pl MTHW ML1 .....154 C5
Imperial Dr AIRDRIE ML6 .....98 A4
Inchbrae Rd
CARD/HILL/MSPK G52 .....86 D5
Inchcolm Pl EKILN G74 .....165 H3
Inchfad Crs DRUM G15 .....32 D5
Inchfad Dr DRUM G15 .....32 D5
Inchfad Pl DRUM G15 .....32 D5
Inch Carve EKILN G74 .....167 G4
Inchholm La PTCK G11 .....65 F4
Inchinnan Dr RNFRW PA4 .....61 H2
Inchinnan Rd BLSH ML4 .....116 C5
PSLYN/LNWD PA3 .....84 A2
RNFRW PA4 .....62 D2
Inch Keith EKILN G74 .....167 G4
Inchkeith Pl CAR/SHTL G32 .....92 C2
Inchlaggan Pl DRUM G15 .....32 D4
Inchlee St SCOT G14 .....65 H3
Inch Marnock EKILN G74 .....167 F5
Inch Murrin EKILN G74 .....167 G4
Inchmurrin Av KKNTL G66 .....22 B5
Inchmurrin Dr
CRMNK/CLK/EAG G76 .....130 C5
Inchmurrin Gdns
CRMNK/CLK/EAG G76 .....130 C5
Inchmurrin Pl
CRMNK/CLK/EAG G76 .....130 C5
Inchnock Av
BAIL/MDB/MHD G69 .....59 F5
Inchoch St STPS/GTHM/RID G33 .....71 F4
Incholm Gdns
BAIL/MDB/MHD G69 .....42 B5
Inchrory Pl DRUM G15 .....32 D4
Inchwood Ct BALLOCH G68 .....43 H1
Inchwood Pl BALLOCH G68 .....43 G1
Inchwood Rd BALLOCH G68 .....43 G1
Incle St PSLY PA1 .....84 C4
India Dr RNFRW PA4 .....61 H1
India St CGLW G2 .....2 B3
Industry St KNTL G66 .....40 A1
Inga St MRYH/FIRH G20 .....52 D4
Ingerbreck Av RUTH G73 .....130 C2
Ingleby Dr DEN/PKHD G31 .....90 D2
Inglefield Ct AIRDRIE ML6 .....98 A2
Inglefield St GVH/MTFL G42 .....109 G2
Ingleneuk Av
STPS/GTHM/RID G33 .....70 C1
Inglestone Av GIF/THBK G46 .....126 D5
Inglewood Crs EKILS G75 .....165 F5
Inglewood Pl KLBCH PA10 .....178 B1
Inglis St DEN/PKHD G31 .....91 E3
MTHW ML1 .....173 E3
Ingliston Dr BSHPTN PA7 .....28 C5
Ingram St CGLE G1 .....3 F5
Inishail Rd STPS/GTHM/RID G33 .....71 F1
Inkerman Rd
CARD/HILL/MSPK G52 .....86 A4
Innellan Gdns MRYH/FIRH G20 .....52 A4
Innellan Pl MRYH/FIRH G20 .....52 A4
Innermanse Qd MTHW ML1 .....138 C2
Innerwick Dr
CARD/HILL/MSPK G52 .....86 C4
Innes Ct EKILN G74 .....166 B1
International Av
BLTYR/CAMB G72 .....168 C1
Inveraray Dr BSHPBGS G64 .....38 A4
Inveraray Gdns MTHW ML1 .....137 H5
Inverarish ERSK PA8 .....47 H4
Inverary Dr BSHPBGS G64 .....38 A3
Invercanny Dr DRUM G15 .....33 F4
Invercanny Pl DRUM G15 .....33 F4
Invercargill EKILS G75 .....177 F1
Invercloy Pl KNTL G66 .....22 B5
Inverclyde Gdns RUTH G73 .....130 D4
Inveresk Pl CTBR ML5 .....96 D1
Inveresk Qd CAR/SHTL G32 .....92 B3
Inveresk St CAR/SHTL G32 .....92 B3
Inverewe Av GIF/THBK G46 .....126 A5
Inverewe Dr GIF/THBK G46 .....126 A5
Inverewe Gdns GIF/THBK G46 .....126 A5
Inverewe Pl GIF/THBK G46 .....126 A4
Inverewe Wy NMRNS G77 .....143 H5
Invergarry Av GIF/THBK G46 .....144 A5
Invergarry Ct GIF/THBK G46 .....144 B5
Invergarry Dr GIF/THBK G46 .....126 A5
Invergarry Gdns
GIF/THBK G46 .....144 A5
Invergarry Gv GIF/THBK G46 .....126 A5
Invergarry Pl GIF/THBK G46 .....126 A5

Invergarry Quad
GIF/THBK G46 .....126 B5
Invergarry Vw GIF/THBK G46 .....126 B5
Inverglas Av RNFRW PA4 .....64 A5
Invergordon Av
PLKSW/MSWD G43 .....109 G5
Invergordon Dr AIRDRIE ML6 .....98 B2
Invergyle Dr
CARD/HILL/MSPK G52 .....86 D4
Inverkar Dr PSLYS PA2 .....103 F2
Inverlair Av PLKSW/MSWD G43 .....128 A1
Inverleith St CAR/SHTL G32 .....91 H2
Inverlochy St
STPS/GTHM/RID G33 .....71 E5
Inverness St GOV/IBX G51 .....87 E3
Inveroran Dr BSDN G61 .....35 E4
Inver Rd STPS/GTHM/RID G33 .....93 F2
Invershiel Rd SMSTN G23 .....52 C2
Invershin Dr MRYH/FIRH G20 .....66 C1
Inverurie St SPRGB/BLRNK G21 .....68 A3
Invervale Av AIRDRIE ML6 .....99 G3
Inzievar Ter CAR/SHTL G32 .....112 C3
Iona Av EKILN G74 .....166 D1
Iona Crs OLDK G60 .....30 D3
Iona Gdns OLDK G60 .....30 D3
Iona Pl CTBR ML5 .....74 A5
Iona Rd RNFRW PA4 .....63 F5
RUTH G73 .....130 D4
WISHAW ML2 .....158 A4
Iona St GOV/IBX G51 .....88 A2
MTHW ML1 .....154 C1
Iona Wk CTBR ML5 .....96 B5
Iona Wy KKNTL G66 .....22 A5
Iris Av CSMK G45 .....129 H4
Irongray St DEN/PKHD G31 .....91 F2
Irvine Crs CTBR ML5 .....97 F2
Irvine Dr PSLYN/LNWD PA3 .....81 G4
Irvine Gdns KKNTL G66 .....5 F5
Irvine Pl KSYTH G65 .....7 H1
Irvine St AIRDRIE ML6 .....76 A2
DMNK/BRGTN G40 .....111 E1
Irvine Ter HMLTN ML3 .....170 A5
Irving Av CLYDBK G81 .....32 A3
Irving Ct CLYDBK G81 .....32 A2
Irving Qd CLYDBK G81 .....32 A2
Isabella Gdns HMLTN ML3 .....171 E4
Isla Av WISHAW ML2 .....158 A4
Island Rd CUMB G67 .....25 H5
Islay Av RUTH G73 .....130 D4
Islay Crs OLDK G60 .....30 D3
Islay Crs OLDK G60 .....30 D3
Islay Dr NMRNS G77 .....143 G5
OLDK G60 .....30 D3
Islay Od WISHAW ML2 .....173 F4
Islay Rd KKNTL G66 .....22 A5
Islay Wy CTBR ML5 .....96 A5
Ivanhoe EKILN G74 .....167 H2
Ivanhoe Crs WISHAW ML2 .....174 B2
Ivanhoe Rd CUMB G67 .....26 A5
KNTSWD G13 .....51 E5
PSLYS PA2 .....102 D3
Ivybank Av BLTYR/CAMB G72 .....131 H3
Ivy Gv CTBR ML5 .....97 E3
Ivy Pl BLTYR/CAMB G72 .....151 F2
MTHW ML1 .....137 F4
Ivy Rd UD/BTH/TAN G71 .....115 H4
Ivy Ter MTHW ML1 .....137 F2
Ivy Wy AIRDRIE ML6 .....119 F1

J

Jackson Dr STPS/GTHM/RID G33 .....71 H1
Jackson St CTBR ML5 .....97 E2
Jack's Rd UD/BTH/TAN G71 .....134 B3
Jack St HMLTN ML3 .....170 B5
MTHW ML1 .....172 C1
Jackton Rd EKILS G75 .....176 C3
Jacobite Pl BLSH ML4 .....136 C3
Jagger Gdns
BAIL/MDB/MHD G69 .....93 G5
Jamaica Dr EKILS G75 .....165 G4
Jamaica St CGLE G1 .....2 E7
James Dempsey Ct CTBR ML5 .....96 C3
James Dempsey Gdns
CTBR ML5 * 96 C3
James Dunlop Gdns
BSHPBGS G64 .....55 E4
James Gray St
PLKSD/SHW G41 .....108 D3
James Hamilton Dr BLSH ML4 .....136 A2
James Healy Dr HMLTN ML3 .....180 C1
James Leeson Ct KKNTL G66 .....5 F4
James Morrison St CGLE G1 .....3 G6
James Nisbet St
SPRGB/BLRNK G21 .....90 C1
James St BLSH ML4 .....90 B5
DMNK/BRGTN G40 .....110 B1
MTHW ML1 .....154 C3
James Vw MTHW ML1 .....137 E4
James Watt Av EKILS G75 .....166 C5
James Watt Pl EKILN G74 .....165 G2
James Watt Rd MLNGV G62 .....16 D2
James Watt St CGLW G2 .....2 C6
Jamieson Ct CLYDBK G81 .....49 G2
GVH/MTFL G42 .....109 G2
Jamieson Dr EKILN G74 .....166 D3
Jamieson St GVH/MTFL G42 .....109 G2
Janebank Av BLTYR/CAMB G72 .....131 H3
Janefield Av JNSTN PA5 .....101 F4
Janefield Pl BLTYR/CAMB G72 .....151 F4
KKNTL G66 .....4 B1
Janefield St DEN/PKHD G31 .....91 E4
Jane Rae Gdns CLYDBK G81 .....49 G3
Jane's Brae CUMB G67 .....26 B5
Janesmith St WISHAW ML2 .....172 D1
Janetta St CLYDBK G81 .....31 H5
Jardine St MRYH/FIRH G20 .....67 E3
Jardine Ter BAIL/MDB/MHD G69 .....73 E1
Jarvie Crs KSYTH G65 .....8 B3
Jarvie Wy PSLYS PA2 .....102 D4
Jasmine Pl CUMB G67 .....44 A4
Java St MTHW ML1 .....154 B1
Jean Armour Dr CLYDBK G81 .....32 B5
Jeanette Av HMLTN ML3 .....180 D1
Jean Maclean Pl BSHPBGS G64 .....38 A1

Jedburgh Av RUTH G73 111 E5
Jedburgh Dr PSLYS PA2 103 F3
Jedburgh Gdns MRYH/FIRH G20 67 E3
Jedburgh Pl CTBR ML5 116 C1
EKILN G74 166 C3
Jedburgh St BLTYR/CAMB G72 151 G3
WISHAW ML2 157 F5
Jedworth Av DRUM G15 33 G5
Jedworth Rd DRUM G15 33 H5
Jeffrey Pl KSYTH G65 8 A1
Jellicoe St CLYDBK G81 31 F5
Jennys Well Ct PSLYS PA2 105 E2
Jennys Well Rd PSLYS PA2 105 E2
Jervis Ter EKILS G75 177 G1
Jerviston Ct MTHW ML1 155 F1
Jerviston Rd MTHW ML1 155 F1
STPS/GTHM/RID G33 70 D4
Jerviston St MTHW ML1 155 E2
Jerviswood MTHW ML1 155 F1
Jessie St GVH/MTFL G42 110 A3
Joanna Ter BLTYR/CAMB G72 151 G2
John Bowman Gdns BLSH ML4 136 A1
John Brannan Wy
UD/BTH/TAN G71 135 E1
John Brown Pl
BAIL/MDB/MHD G69 58 B3
John Burnside Dr CLYDBK G81 32 B1
John Hendry Rd
UD/BTH/TAN G71 134 B3
John Knox St CLYDBK G81 49 G4
COWCAD G4 90 B2
John Lang St JNSTN PA5 101 H3
John Marshall Dr PPK/MIL G22 54 B3
John Murray Ct MTHW ML1 171 H2
Johnsburn Dr PLK/PH/NH G53 125 G1
Johnsburn Rd PLK/PH/NH G53 125 G1
Johnshaven St
PLKSW/MSWD G43 108 B5
John Smith Ct AIRDRIE ML6 98 A1
John Smith Gdns CTBR ML5 97 F3
John Smith Ga BRHD/NEIL G78 124 B3
Johnson Dr BLTYR/CAMB G72 131 F2
Johnston Av KSYTH G65 8 B3
Johnstone Av
CARD/HILL/MSPK G52 86 C2
CLYDBK G81 49 G3
Johnstone Dr RUTH G73 110 D5
Johnstone Rd HMLTN ML3 170 B3
Johnstone St BLSH ML4 136 B2
Johnstone Ter KSYTH G65 23 F2
Johnston Rd
BAIL/MDB/MHD G69 59 F5
Johnston St AIRDRIE ML6 98 C1
PSLY PA1 84 B5
John St BLSH ML4 135 H2
BLTYR/CAMB G72 151 H3
BRHD/NEIL G78 124 A4
CGLE G1 3 G6
HMLTN ML3 170 B2
KKNTL G66 21 F4
WISHAW ML2 172 D1
John Wilson Dr KSYTH G65 7 H1
Jones Wynd MTHW ML1 156 B1
Joppa St STPS/GTHM/RID G33 91 H1
Jordanhill Crs KNTSWD G13 65 E1
Jordanhill Dr KNTSWD G13 65 E1
Jordanhill La KNTSWD G13 65 F1
Jordan St SCOT G14 65 E4
Jordanvale Av SCOT G14 65 E4
Jowitt Av CLYDBK G81 49 G2
Jubilee Ct CARD/HILL/MSPK G52 86 A2
Jubilee Gdns BSDN G61 34 B4
Jubilee Ter JNSTN PA5 101 E5
Julian Av KVD/HLHD G12 66 B2
Julian La KVD/HLHD G12 66 B2
Juniper Av EKILS G75 178 A2
Juniper Ct KKNTL G66 39 G3
Juniper Dr KKNTL G66 20 D1
Juniper Gv HMLTN ML3 170 C3
Juniper Pl CAR/SHTL G32 93 G5
JNSTN PA5 121 H1
UD/BTH/TAN G71 116 A4
Juniper Rd UD/BTH/TAN G71 116 A4
Juniper Ter CAR/SHTL G32 93 F5
Juno St MTHW ML1 154 C1
Jupiter St MTHW ML1 154 C1
Jura EKILN G74 179 E1
Jura Av RNFRW PA4 63 G5
Jura Dr BLTYR/CAMB G72 133 F4
NMRNS G77 143 G4
OLDK G60 30 D3
Jura Gdns HMLTN ML3 169 F3
Jura Qd WISHAW ML2 173 F4
Jura Rd OLDK G60 30 D3
PSLYS PA2 104 A5
Jura St CARD/HILL/MSPK G52 87 G4
Jura Wynd CTBR ML5 59 H5

K

Kaim Dr PLK/PH/NH G53 125 H1
Katewell Av DRUM G15 32 D4
Katewell Pl DRUM G15 32 D4
Katherine St AIRDRIE ML6 99 F1
Katrine Av BSHPBGS G64 55 E2
UD/BTH/TAN G71 135 E1
Katrine Crs AIRDRIE ML6 76 A5
Katrine Dr NMRNS G77 162 C1
PSLYS PA2 103 E2
Katrine Pl BLTYR/CAMB G72 131 F1
CTBR ML5 74 A5
Kay Gdns MTHW ML1 154 A4
Kaystone Rd DRUM G15 50 B2
Kay St SPRGB/BLRNK G21 68 C2
Keal Av DRUM G15 50 C3
Keal Crs DRUM G15 50 B3
Keal Dr DRUM G15 50 B3
Keal Pl DRUM G15 50 B3
Kearn Av DRUM G15 50 C2
Kearn Pl DRUM G15 50 C2
Keats Pk UD/BTH/TAN G71 134 C4
Keil Crs DMBTN G82 12 C4
Keir Crs WISHAW ML2 174 A1
Keir Dr BSHPBGS G64 54 C1
Keir Hardie Av MTHW ML1 137 G2
Keir Hardie Dr BLSH ML4 135 G3
KSYTH G65 8 B2
Keir St PLKSD/SHW G41 109 E1
Keir's Wk BLTYR/CAMB G72 131 F1
Keith Av GIF/THBK G46 127 F4
Keith Ct PTCK G11 66 B4
Keith Qd WISHAW ML2 157 E5
Keith St BLSH ML4 135 H1
HMLTN ML3 170 C1
PTCK G11 66 B4
Kelbourne Crs BLSH ML4 135 G2
Kelbourne St MRYH/FIRH G20 66 D2
Kelburne Dr PSLY PA1 85 E4
Kelburne Gdns
BAIL/MDB/MHD G69 113 H1
PSLY PA1 84 D4
Kelburne Ov PSLY PA1 84 D4
Kelburn St BRHD/NEIL G78 141 H1
Kelhead Av
CARD/HILL/MSPK G52 86 A5
Kelhead Dr
CARD/HILL/MSPK G52 86 A4
Kelhead Pth
CARD/HILL/MSPK G52 86 A4
Kelhead Pl PSLY PA1 86 A4
Kellas St GOV/IBX G51 87 H2
Kellie Gv EKILN G74 166 A2
Kells Pl DRUM G15 32 D4
Kelso Av BRWEIR PA11 79 F4
PSLYS PA2 103 F3
RUTH G73 111 E5
Kelso Crs WISHAW ML2 157 E4
Kelso Dr EKILN G74 166 D2
Kelso Gdns BAIL/MDB/MHD G69 42 A5
Kelso Pl SCOT G14 49 H5
Kelso Qd CTBR ML5 96 C1
Kelso St KNTSWD G13 50 A4
SCOT G14 49 H5
Kelton St CAR/SHTL G32 92 C5
Kelvin Av CARD/HILL/MSPK G52 86 B1
Kelvin Ct KKNTL G66 21 E4
Kelvin Crs BSDN G61 51 G1
Kelvindale Gdns
MRYH/FIRH G20 52 B5
Kelvindale Pl MRYH/FIRH G20 52 C5
Kelvindale Rd KVD/HLHD G12 66 B1
Kelvin Dr AIRDRIE ML6 76 C5
BAIL/MDB/MHD G69 58 D1
BRHD/NEIL G78 142 C1
BSHPBGS G64 54 D1
EKILS G75 178 C1
KKNTL G66 20 C5
MRYH/FIRH G20 66 C2
Kelvin Gdns HMLTN ML3 168 D1
KSYTH G65 8 B3
Kelvingrove St KVGV G3 88 D1
Kelvinhaugh Ga KVGV G3 88 C1
Kelvinhaugh Pl KVGV G3 88 C1
Kelvinhaugh St KVGV G3 88 C1
Kelvin Pk South EKILS G75 178 D4
Kelvin Pl EKILS G75 178 D1
Kelvin Rd BLSH ML4 117 E5
CUMB G67 26 C5
EKILS G75 178 D1
MLNGV G62 16 C2
UD/BTH/TAN G71 114 D5
Kelvin Rd North CUMB G67 26 C5
Kelvinside Av MRYH/FIRH G20 66 D2
Kelvinside Dr MRYH/FIRH G20 67 E2
Kelvinside Gdns MRYH/FIRH G20 66 D2
Kelvinside Gdns East
MRYH/FIRH G20 67 E2
Kelvinside Gardens La
MRYH/FIRH G20 66 D3
Kelvinside Ter South
KVD/HLHD G12 66 D3
Kelvinside Ter West
MRYH/FIRH G20 66 D3
Kelvin St CTBR ML5 97 F4
Kelvinvale KKNTL G66 21 F4
Kelvin Vw BSHPBGS G64 19 G5
KSYTH G65 23 F3
Kelvin Wy KKNTL G66 20 C5
KSYTH G65 8 A1
KVGV G3 66 C5
Kemp Av PSLYN/LNWD PA3 62 D5
Kempsthorn Crs
PLK/PH/NH G53 106 B3
Kempsthorn Pl
PLK/PH/NH G53 106 C3
Kempsthorn Rd
PLK/PH/NH G53 106 B3
Kemp St HMLTN ML3 170 A2
SPRGB/BLRNK G21 68 B2
Kenbank Crs BRWEIR PA11 79 G3
Kenbank Rd BRWEIR PA11 79 G3
Kendal Av GIF/THBK G46 127 F4
KVD/HLHD G12 51 H5
Kendal Dr KVD/HLHD G12 51 H5
Kendal Rd EKILS G75 177 E2
Kendoon Av DRUM G15 32 D5
Kenilburn Av AIRDRIE ML6 76 C4
Kenilburn Crs AIRDRIE ML6 76 C4
Kenilworth EKILN G74 167 G1
Kenilworth Av
PLKSD/SHW G41 108 C4
PSLYS PA2 103 E4
WISHAW ML2 174 A2
Kenilworth Crs BLSH ML4 135 H1
BSDN G61 33 H2
HMLTN ML3 169 E1
Kenilworth Dr AIRDRIE ML6 98 D1
Kenilworth Rd KKNTL G66 21 G5
Kenllworth Ct CUMB G67 26 A5
Kenmar Gdns
UD/BTH/TAN G71 114 D4
Kenmar Rd HMLTN ML3 152 C5
Kenmar Ter HMLTN ML3 152 C5
Kenmore Gdns BSDN G61 35 E3
Kenmore Rd CUMB G67 26 D3
Kenmore St CAR/SHTL G32 92 B4
Kenmore Wy CTBR ML5 97 F5
Kenmuiraid Pl BLSH ML4 135 G4
Kenmuir Av CAR/SHTL G32 113 F1
Kenmuirhill Rd CAR/SHTL G32 113 E2
Kenmuir Rd CAR/SHTL G32 113 E4
Kenmuir St CTBR ML5 95 G5
Kenmure Av BSHPBGS G64 54 B2
Kenmure Crs BSHPBGS G64 54 C2
Kenmure Dr BSHPBGS G64 54 C2
Kenmure Gdns BSHPBGS G64 54 B2
Kenmure La BSHPBGS G64 54 C2
Kenmure Rd GIF/THBK G46 145 E4
Kenmure St PLKSD/SHW G41 109 E1
Kenmure Wy RUTH G73 130 A4
Kennedar Dr GOV/IBX G51 87 F1
Kennedy Dr AIRDRIE ML6 97 H2
Kennedy St COWCAD G4 3 J2
WISHAW ML2 174 B2
Kennelburn Rd AIRDRIE ML6 119 E3
Kenneth Rd MTHW ML1 154 B5
Kennihill AIRDRIE ML6 76 B5
Kennihill Qd AIRDRIE ML6 76 B5
Kennishead Av GIF/THBK G46 126 B2
Kennishead Pl GIF/THBK G46 126 B2
Kennishead Rd GIF/THBK G46 126 C3
PLK/PH/NH G53 125 H2
Kennisholm Av GIF/THBK G46 126 B2
Kennoway Dr PTCK G11 65 G4
Kennyhill Sq DEN/PKHD G31 91 E1
Kensington Dr GIF/THBK G46 145 G1
Kensington Ga KVD/HLHD G12 66 B2
Kensington Gate La
KVD/HLHD G12 66 B2
Kensington Rd KVD/HLHD G12 66 B2
Kentallen Rd
STPS/GTHM/RID G33 93 E3
Kent Dr RUTH G73 130 C2
Kentigern Ter BSHPBGS G64 54 D3
Kentmere Cl EKILS G75 177 F2
Kentmere Dr EKILS G75 177 F2
Kentmere Pl EKILS G75 177 E2
Kent Pl EKILS G75 177 E2
Kent Rd KVGV G3 88 D1
Kent St DMNK/BRGTN G40 90 B3
Keppel Dr LNPK/KPK G44 110 B5
Keppochhill Dr
SPRGB/BLRNK G21 68 A3
Keppochhill Rd PPK/MIL G22 67 H3
SPRGB/BLRNK G21 68 B3
Keppoch St SPRGB/BLRNK G21 68 A3
Kerfield Pl DRUM G15 32 D4
Kerr Crs HMLTN ML3 169 H4
Kerr Dr DMNK/BRGTN G40 90 C4
MTHW ML1 154 B4
Kerrera Pl STPS/GTHM/RID G33 93 E3
Kerrera Rd STPS/GTHM/RID G33 93 E3
Kerr Gdns UD/BTH/TAN G71 115 F4
Ker Rd MLNGV G62 16 C2
Kerr Pl DMNK/BRGTN G40 90 C4
Kerr St BLTYR/CAMB G72 151 H2
BRHD/NEIL G78 123 H5
DMNK/BRGTN G40 90 C4
KKNTL G66 21 E5
PSLYN/LNWD PA3 84 A4
Kerrycroy Av GVH/MTFL G42 110 A4
Kerrycroy Pl GVH/MTFL G42 110 A4
Kerrycroy St GVH/MTFL G42 110 A4
Kerrydale St DMNK/BRGTN G40 91 E5
Kerrylamont Av
GVH/MTFL G42 110 B5
Kerry Pl DRUM G15 32 D5
Kersland Dr MLNGV G62 17 F3
Kersland La KVD/HLHD G12 66 C3
MLNGV G62 17 F3
Kersland St KVD/HLHD G12 66 C3
Kessington Dr BSDN G61 34 D4
Kessington Rd BSDN G61 35 E5
Kessington Sq BSDN G61 35 E5
Kessock Dr PPK/MIL G22 67 G3
Kessock Pl PPK/MIL G22 67 G3
Kestrel Ct CLYDBK G81 31 H3
Kestrel Pl JNSTN PA5 121 E2
Kestrel Rd KNTSWD G13 50 D5
Kestrel Vw BLSH ML4 116 B3
Keswick Dr HMLTN ML3 180 C2
Keswick Rd EKILS G75 177 E2
Kethers La MTHW ML1 154 A4
Kethers St MTHW ML1 154 B3
Kew Gdns UD/BTH/TAN G71 115 G5
Kew La KVD/HLHD G12 66 C3
Kew Ter KVD/HLHD G12 66 C2
Keystone Av MLNGV G62 17 E5
Keystone Qd MLNGV G62 16 D5
Keystone Rd MLNGV G62 17 E5
Kibbleston Rd KLBCH PA10 100 B5
Kidston Ter GBLS G5 89 H5
Kierhill Rd BALLOCH G68 25 F3
Kilallan Av BRWEIR PA11 79 G2
Kilbarchan Rd JNSTN PA5 80 A5
JNSTN PA5 101 E5
KLBCH PA10 100 D4
Kilbeg Ter GIF/THBK G46 126 A4
Kilberry St SPRGB/BLRNK G21 68 D5
Kilbirnie Pl GBLS G5 89 F5
Kilbirnie St GBLS G5 89 F5
Kilbowie Pl AIRDRIE ML6 99 E4
Kilbowie Rd CLYDBK G81 49 E2
CUMB G67 26 C5
Kilbreck Gdns BSDN G61 16 A5
Kilbrennan Dr MTHW ML1 153 H3
Kilbrennan Rd
PSLYN/LNWD PA3 82 A3
Kilbride St GBLS G5 110 A2
Kilbride Vw UD/BTH/TAN G71 115 F5
Kilburn Gv BLTYR/CAMB G72 151 G1
Kilburn Pl KNTSWD G13 50 C5
Kilchattan Dr LNPK/KPK G44 109 H5
Kilchoan Rd
STPS/GTHM/RID G33 70 D4
Kilcloy Av DRUM G15 33 F4
Kildale Wy RUTH G73 110 C4
Kildary Av LNPK/KPK G44 128 B2
Kildary Rd LNPK/KPK G44 128 B2
Kildermorie Rd ESTRH G34 93 G1
Kildonan Ct WISHAW ML2 158 A3
Kildonan Dr PTCK G11 65 H4
Kildonan Pl MTHW ML1 154 B3
Kildonan St CTBR ML5 97 E2
Kildrostan St PLKSD/SHW G41 109 E2
Kildrummy Pl EKILN G74 166 A2
Kildrum Rd CUMB G67 27 E3
Kilearn Rd PSLYN/LNWD PA3 85 E2
Kilearn Wy PSLYN/LNWD PA3 85 E2
Kilfinan St PPK/MIL G22 53 G4
Kilgarth St CTBR ML5 95 G5
Kilgraston Rd BRWEIR PA11 79 G5
Kilkerran Ct NMRNS G77 161 E1
Kilkerran Dr
STPS/GTHM/RID G33 56 A5
Kilkerran Pk NMRNS G77 161 E1
Kilkerran Wy NMRNS G77 161 E1
Killearn Dr PSLY PA1 86 A5
Killearn St PPK/MIL G22 67 H2
Killermont Av BSDN G61 52 A1
Killermont Mdw
UD/BTH/TAN G71 133 H5
Killermont Rd BSDN G61 34 C5
Killermont St CGLE G1 3 F3
Killermont Vw MRYH/FIRH G20 51 H1
Killiegrew Rd PLKSD/SHW G41 108 C2
Killin Dr PSLYN/LNWD PA3 101 G1
Killin St CAR/SHTL G32 112 C1
Killoch Av PSLYN/LNWD PA3 83 F4
Killoch Dr BRHD/NEIL G78 142 C1
KNTSWD G13 50 B4
Killoch La PSLYN/LNWD PA3 83 F4
Killoch Rd PSLYN/LNWD PA3 83 F4
Killoch Wy PSLYN/LNWD PA3 83 F4
Kilmacolm Rd BRWEIR PA11 79 E1
Kilmailing Rd LNPK/KPK G44 128 C2
Kilmair Pl MRYH/FIRH G20 66 C1
Kilmaluag Ter GIF/THBK G46 126 A4
Kilmany Dr CAR/SHTL G32 92 A4
Kilmany Gdns CAR/SHTL G32 92 A4
Kilmardinny Av BSDN G61 34 C2
Kilmardinny Crs BSDN G61 34 D2
Kilmardinny Dr BSDN G61 34 C2
Kilmardinny Ga BSDN G61 34 C3
Kilmardinny Gv BSDN G61 34 C2
Kilmari Gdns DRUM G15 32 D4
Kilmarnock Rd
PLKSW/MSWD G43 127 G1
Kilmartin Pl GIF/THBK G46 126 B3
UD/BTH/TAN G71 115 F3
Kilmaurs Dr GIF/THBK G46 127 H4
Kilmaurs St GOV/IBX G51 87 G3
Kilmeny Crs WISHAW ML2 157 F5
Kilmichael Av WISHAW ML2 158 B4
Kilmore Crs DRUM G15 32 D4
Kilmorie Dr RUTH G73 110 B5
Kilmory Av UD/BTH/TAN G71 115 F5
Kilmory Ct EKILS G75 177 G4
Kilmory Dr NMRNS G77 144 B4
Kilmuir Crs GIF/THBK G46 126 A3
Kilmuir Dr GIF/THBK G46 126 B3
Kilmuir Rd GIF/THBK G46 126 A4
UD/BTH/TAN G71 115 E3
Kilmun St MRYH/FIRH G20 52 C4
Kilnburn Rd MTHW ML1 154 B3
Kilnside Rd PSLY PA1 84 C4
Kilnwell Qd MTHW ML1 154 C3
Kiloran Gv NMRNS G77 160 D1
Kiloran Pl NMRNS G77 160 D1
Kiloran St GIF/THBK G46 126 C3
Kilpatrick Av PSLYS PA2 103 G2
Kilpatrick Crs PSLYS PA2 104 A3
Kilpatrick Dr BSDN G61 16 A5
EKILS G75 177 G5
ERSK PA8 47 G1
RNFRW PA4 85 E1
STPS/GTHM/RID G33 71 F1
Kilpatrick Gdns
CRMNK/CLK/EAG G76 145 G3
Kilpatrick Vw DMBTN G82 13 G3
Kilpatrick Wy
UD/BTH/TAN G71 115 F4
Kilsyth Gdns EKILS G75 177 F5
Kilsyth Rd KKNTL G66 21 F4
KSYTH G65 7 E3
Kiltarie Crs AIRDRIE ML6 99 G3
Kiltearn Rd
STPS/GTHM/RID G33 93 G2
Kilvaxter Dr GIF/THBK G46 126 B4
Kilwinning Crs AIRDRIE ML6 77 F5
HMLTN ML3 168 D4
Kimberley Gdns EKILS G75 165 H5
Kimberley St CLYDBK G81 31 E3
WISHAW ML2 172 D2
Kinalty Rd PLKSW/MSWD G43 128 B2
Kinarvie Crs PLK/PH/NH G53 106 A5
Kinarvie Pl PLK/PH/NH G53 106 A5
Kinarvie Rd PLK/PH/NH G53 106 A5
Kinarvie Ter PLK/PH/NH G53 106 A5
Kinbuck St PPK/MIL G22 68 A2
Kincaid Fld KKNTL G66 5 G5
Kincaid Gdns BLTYR/CAMB G72 131 F1
Kincaid Wy KKNTL G66 5 F5
Kincardine Dr BSHPBGS G64 55 E3
Kincardine Pl BSHPBGS G64 55 F4
EKILN G74 167 F2
Kincardine Sq
STPS/GTHM/RID G33 71 E5
Kincath Av RUTH G73 130 B4
Kinclaven Av DRUM G15 33 F5
Kinclaven Gdns DRUM G15 33 G5
Kinclaven Pl DRUM G15 33 G5
Kincraig St GOV/IBX G51 87 E3
Kinellan Rd BSDN G61 51 G2
Kinellar Dr SCOT G14 50 B5
Kinfauns Dr DRUM G15 33 E5
NMRNS G77 144 C5
Kingarth La GVH/MTFL G42 109 F2
Kingarth St HMLTN ML3 170 A5
PLKSD/SHW G41 109 F2
King Edward La KNTSWD G13 65 G1
King Edward Rd KNTSWD G13 65 G1
Kingfisher Dr KNTSWD G13 50 A4
King George Ct RNFRW PA4 63 H5
King George Gdns RNFRW PA4 63 H4
King George Park Av
RNFRW PA4 63 H5
King George Pl RNFRW PA4 63 H5
King George Wy RNFRW PA4 63 H5
Kinghorn Dr LNPK/KPK G44 128 D1
Kinglas Rd BSDN G61 50 D1
King Pl BAIL/MDB/MHD G69 95 F4
Kingsacre Rd LNPK/KPK G44 109 H5
RUTH G73 110 B5
Kingsbarns Dr LNPK/KPK G44 109 G5
Kingsborough Gdns
KVD/HLHD G12 66 A2
Kingsborough Ga
KVD/HLHD G12 66 A3
Kingsborough La
KVD/HLHD G12 66 A3
Kingsborough La East
KVD/HLHD G12 66 A3
Kingsbrae Av LNPK/KPK G44 109 H5
Kingsbridge Crs LNPK/KPK G44 129 E1
Kingsbridge Dr LNPK/KPK G44 128 D1
Kingsburgh Dr PSLY PA1 85 E4
Kingsburn Dr RUTH G73 129 H1
Kingsburn Gv RUTH G73 129 H1
Kingscliffe Av LNPK/KPK G44 109 H5
Kingscourt Av LNPK/KPK G44 110 A5
Kings Crs BLTYR/CAMB G72 131 G2
JNSTN PA5 102 B1
Kingsdale Av LNPK/KPK G44 109 H5
King's Dr BALLOCH G68 10 B4
DMNK/BRGTN G40 90 B5
MTHW ML1 137 E4
NMRNS G77 162 A2
Kingsdyke Av LNPK/KPK G44 110 A5
Kingsford Av LNPK/KPK G44 127 H3
Kingsford Ct NMRNS G77 143 G4
King's Gdns NMRNS G77 162 B2
Kingsheath Av RUTH G73 129 F1
Kingshill Av BALLOCH G68 24 C4
Kingshill Dr LNPK/KPK G44 128 D1
Kingshill Rd SHOTTS ML7 159 H2
Kingshouse Av LNPK/KPK G44 109 H5
Kingshurst Av LNPK/KPK G44 128 D1
King's Inch Rd RNFRW PA4 64 A2
Kingsknowe Dr RUTH G73 129 F1
Kingsland Dr
CARD/HILL/MSPK G52 86 C3
Kingslea Rd CRG/CRSL/HOU PA6 80 C1
Kingsley Av GVH/MTFL G42 109 G3
Kingsley Ct UD/BTH/TAN G71 115 F5
Kingslynn Dr LNPK/KPK G44 129 E1
Kings Pk BSHPBGS G64 19 G4
King's Park Av LNPK/KPK G44 128 D1
RUTH G73 129 F1
King's Park Rd GVH/MTFL G42 109 G5
King's Pl PPK/MIL G22 53 G5
King's Rd JNSTN PA5 102 A2
Kingston Av AIRDRIE ML6 98 D2
BRHD/NEIL G78 141 E4
UD/BTH/TAN G71 115 F4
Kingston Br GOV/IBX G51 2 B7
Kingston Flats KSYTH G65 8 B1
Kingston Gv BSHPTN PA7 29 E5
Kingston Pl CLYDBK G81 30 D4
Kingston Rd BRHD/NEIL G78 140 D5
BSHPTN PA7 29 F4
KSYTH G65 8 B1
Kingston St GBLS G5 89 F3
King St CGLE G1 89 H3
CLYDBK G81 49 G3
CTBR ML5 96 B3
HMLTN ML3 169 E1
KSYTH G65 8 B2
PSLY PA1 83 H4
RUTH G73 110 D4
WISHAW ML2 158 A5
WISHAW ML2 174 A3
King Street La RUTH G73 110 D4
King's Vw BALLOCH G68 10 B4
King's Wy DMBTN G82 12 B2
Kingsway EKILN G74 149 F5
KKNTL G66 22 B3
KSYTH G65 8 B1
SCOT G14 64 C1
Kingsway Ct SCOT G14 64 C1
Kingswood Dr LNPK/KPK G44 128 D1
Kingswood Rd BSHPTN PA7 28 C4
Kingussie Dr LNPK/KPK G44 128 D1
Kiniver Dr DRUM G15 50 B2
Kinkell Gdns KKNTL G66 22 B4
Kinloch Av BLTYR/CAMB G72 131 G3
PSLYN/LNWD PA3 101 H1
Kinloch Dr MTHW ML1 136 C5
Kinloch Rd NMRNS G77 143 H4
RNFRW PA4 63 E5
Kinloch St DMNK/BRGTN G40 91 F5
Kinloss Pl EKILN G74 166 C3
Kinmount Av LNPK/KPK G44 109 G5
Kinnaird Av NMRNS G77 144 D5
Kinnaird Crs BSDN G61 35 E3
Kinnaird Dr PSLYN/LNWD PA3 82 A2
Kinnaird Pl BSHPBGS G64 55 E3
Kinnear Rd DMNK/BRGTN G40 111 E1
Kinneil Pl HMLTN ML3 169 E3
Kinnell Av
CARD/HILL/MSPK G52 106 D1
Kinnell Crs
CARD/HILL/MSPK G52 106 D1
Kinnell Pl
CARD/HILL/MSPK G52 107 E1
Kinning St GBLS G5 89 E4
Kinnoul La KVD/HLHD G12 66 B3
Kinnoull Pl BLTYR/CAMB G72 151 G3
Kinpurnie Rd PSLY PA1 85 G4
Kinross Av
CARD/HILL/MSPK G52 86 C5
Kinross Pk EKILN G74 167 G2
Kinsail Dr CARD/HILL/MSPK G52 86 A3
Kinstone Av SCOT G14 64 B1
Kintessack Pl BSHPBGS G64 55 G1
Kintillo Dr KNTSWD G13 50 C5
Kintore Pk HMLTN ML3 180 B1
Kintore Rd PLKSW/MSWD G43 128 A1
Kintra St GOV/IBX G51 88 A3
Kintyre Av PSLYN/LNWD PA3 101 H2
Kintyre Crs AIRDRIE ML6 77 G3
CTBR ML5 96 B5
NMRNS G77 143 H4
Kintyre Dr CTBR ML5 96 B5
Kintyre Gdns KKNTL G66 22 B3
Kintyre Rd BLTYR/CAMB G72 151 F2
Kintyre St SPRGB/BLRNK G21 68 D5
Kipland Wk CTBR ML5 97 G4
Kippen Dr
CRMNK/CLK/EAG G76 146 C5
Kippen St AIRDRIE ML6 97 G3
PPK/MIL G22 54 A5
Kippford Pl AIRDRIE ML6 119 G3
Kippford St CAR/SHTL G32 92 D5
Kipps Av AIRDRIE ML6 97 H1
Kirkaig Av RNFRW PA4 64 A4
Kirkandrews Pl AIRDRIE ML6 119 G3
Kirkbean Av RUTH G73 129 H3
Kirkbriggs Gdns RUTH G73 130 A2
Kirkburn Av BLTYR/CAMB G72 131 F3
Kirkcaldy Rd PLKSD/SHW G41 108 C2
Kirkconnel Av BALLOCH G68 24 C4
KNTSWD G13 50 A5
Kirkconnel Dr RUTH G73 129 G2
Kirk Crs OLDK G60 30 B1
Kirkcudbright Pl EKILN G74 167 G1
Kirkdale Dr
CARD/HILL/MSPK G52 87 F5
Kirkdene Av NMRNS G77 145 E5
Kirkdene Bank NMRNS G77 145 E5
Kirkdene Crs NMRNS G77 145 E5
Kirkdene Gv NMRNS G77 145 E5
Kirkdene Pl NMRNS G77 145 E5
Kirkfield Bank Wy HMLTN ML3 169 F2
Kirkfield Rd UD/BTH/TAN G71 134 B4
Kirkford Rd
BAIL/MDB/MHD G69 58 D1
Kirkgate WISHAW ML2 175 E1
Kirkhall Rd MTHW ML1 138 A3
Kirkhill Av BLTYR/CAMB G72 131 F4
Kirkhill Crs BRHD/NEIL G78 141 F2
Kirkhill Dr MRYH/FIRH G20 66 C1
Kirkhill Gdns BLTYR/CAMB G72 131 F4
Kirkhill Ga NMRNS G77 162 C1
Kirkhill Gv BLTYR/CAMB G72 131 F4
Kirkhill Pl MRYH/FIRH G20 66 C1
WISHAW ML2 172 D3
Kirkhill Rd BAIL/MDB/MHD G69 73 E1
NMRNS G77 145 E5
UD/BTH/TAN G71 114 D4
WISHAW ML2 172 D4
Kirkhill St WISHAW ML2 173 E4
Kirkhill Ter BLTYR/CAMB G72 131 F4
Kirkhope Dr DRUM G15 50 C1
Kirkinner Rd CAR/SHTL G32 113 E1
Kirkintilloch Rd BSHPBGS G64 54 C4
KKNTL G66 20 C3
KKNTL G66 22 B5
KKNTL G66 40 A1

Kirkland Gv JNSTN PA5 ... 101 G3
Kirklandneuk Rd RNFRW PA4 ... 62 D2
Kirklands Crs KSYTH G65 ... 8 B3
　UD/BTH/TAN G71 ... 134 B4
Kirklands Dr NMRNS G77 ... 161 G3
Kirklands Pl NMRNS G77 ... 161 G3
Kirklands Rd NMRNS G77 ... 161 G3
Kirkland St MRYH/FIRH G20 ... 67 E3
　MLNGV G62 ... 154 C5
Kirk La BSDN G61 ... 34 B5
　PLKSW/MSWD G43 ... 108 D5
Kirklea Gdns PSLYN/LNWD PA3 ... 83 F4
Kirklee Dr NMRNS G77 ... 144 D5
Kirklee Circ KVD/HLHD G12 ... 66 B2
Kirklee Gdns KVD/HLHD G12 ... 66 B2
Kirklee Gardens La
　KVD/HLHD G12 ... 66 B2
Kirklee Pl KVD/HLHD G12 ... 66 B2
Kirklee Qd KVD/HLHD G12 ... 66 B2
Kirklee Quadrant La
　KVD/HLHD G12 ... 66 C2
Kirklee Rd BLSH ML4 ... 136 C5
　KVD/HLHD G12 ... 66 B2
　MTHW ML1 ... 154 D1
Kirklee Ter KVD/HLHD G12 ... 66 C2
Kirklee Terrace La
　KVD/HLHD G12 ... 66 C2
Kirklee Terrace Rd
　KVD/HLHD G12 ... 66 B2
Kirkliston St CAR/SHTL G32 ... 92 A3
Kirkmichael Gdns PTCK G11 ... 65 H5
Kirkmuir Dr RUTH G73 ... 130 A4
Kirkness St AIRDRIE ML6 ... 98 B1
Kirknethan WISHAW ML2 ... 173 D4
Kirknewton St CAR/SHTL G32 ... 92 D4
Kirkoswald EKILN G74 ... 167 G2
Kirkoswald Dr CLYDBK G81 ... 32 C5
Kirkoswald Rd MTHW ML1 ... 138 B5
　PLKSW/MSWD G43 ... 127 G1
Kirkpatrick St
　DMNK/BRGTN G40 ... 90 D4
Kirk Pl BSDN G61 ... 34 B3
　CUMB G67 ... 27 F3
Kirkriggs Av RUTH G73 ... 130 A2
Kirk Rd BSDN G61 ... 34 B3
　CRMNK/CLK/EAG G76 ... 147 E3
　MTHW ML1 ... 119 E5
　WISHAW ML2 ... 157 H5
Kirkshaws Av CTBR ML5 ... 116 B1
Kirkshaws Pl CTBR ML5 ... 116 B1
Kirkshaws Rd CTBR ML5 ... 116 B1
Kirkstall Gdns BSHPBGS G64 ... 38 A4
Kirkstone Cl EKILS G75 ... 177 E2
Kirk St CTBR ML5 ... 96 C5
　MLNGV G62 ... 17 E4
　MTHW ML1 ... 154 D3
Kirkstyle Crs AIRDRIE ML6 ... 76 A4
Kirkstyle La BRHD/NEIL G78 ... 141 E5
Kirkstyle Pl AIRDRIE ML6 ... 75 G2
Kirksyde Av KKNTL G66 ... 40 A1
Kirkton ERSK PA8 ... 30 B5
Kirkton Av BRHD/NEIL G78 ... 124 A5
　KNTSWD G13 ... 50 B5
Kirkton Crs CTBR ML5 ... 97 G5
　KNTSWD G13 ... 50 B5
Kirktonfield Dr
　BRHD/NEIL G78 ... 141 G3
Kirktonfield Pl BRHD/NEIL G78 ... 141 F3
Kirktonfield Rd
　BRHD/NEIL G78 ... 141 F3
Kirkton Ga EKILN G74 ... 166 B3
Kirktonholme Crs EKILN G74 ... 165 G3
Kirktonholme Rd EKILN G74 ... 166 C4
Kirkton Pk EKILN G74 ... 166 C4
Kirkton Pl CTBR ML5 ... 97 G5
　EKILN G74 ... 166 D3
Kirkton Rd BLTYR/CAMB G72 ... 151 H4
　DMBTN G82 ... 12 C5
Kirktonside BRHD/NEIL G78 ... 142 A1
Kirkvale Ct NMRNS G77 ... 145 E5
Kirkvale Crs NMRNS G77 ... 145 E5
Kirkvale Dr NMRNS G77 ... 145 E5
Kirkview CUMB G67 ... 43 H2
Kirkview Crs NMRNS G77 ... 161 H1
Kirkview Gdns
　UD/BTH/TAN G71 ... 114 D4
Kirkville Pl DRUM G15 ... 50 C2
Kirkwall CUMB G67 ... 10 D5
Kirkwall Av BLTYR/CAMB G72 ... 133 F5
Kirkwell Rd LNPK/KPK G44 ... 128 C2
Kirkwood Av CLYDBK G81 ... 49 H3
　STPS/GTHM/RID G33 ... 71 G1
Kirkwood Pl CTBR ML5 ... 96 B5
　GOV/IBX G51 ...
Kirkwood St CTBR ML5 ... 96 B5
　RUTH G73 ... 110 D4
Kirn St MRYH/FIRH G20 ... 52 B3
Kirriemuir EKILN G74 ... 150 A5
Kirriemuir Av
　CARD/HILL/MSPK G52 ... 106 D1
Kirriemuir Gdns BSHPBGS G64 ... 55 F1
Kirriemuir Pl
　CARD/HILL/MSPK G52 ... 86 D5
Kirriemuir Rd BSHPBGS G64 ... 55 F1
Kirtle Dr RNFRW PA4 ... 63 H4
Kirtle Pl EKILS G75 ... 176 D1
Kishorn Pl STPS/GTHM/RID G33 ... 70 D5
Kitchener St WISHAW ML2 ... 173 H2
Kittoch Pl EKILN G74 ... 166 C5
Kittochside Rd
　CRMNK/CLK/EAG G76 ... 147 F5
Kittoch St EKILN G74 ... 166 C4
Klondike Ct MTHW ML1 ... 137 G4
Knapdale St PPK/MIL G22 ... 53 G4
Knightsbridge St KNTSWD G13 ... 51 E5
Knightscliffe Av KNTSWD G13 ... 51 E3
Knightswood Ct UD/BTH/TAN G71 ... 132 H3
Knightswood Rd KNTSWD G13 ... 51 E3
Knightswood Ter
　BLTYR/CAMB G72 ... 151 H1
Knivysbridge Pl BLSH ML4 ... 135 H3
Knockburnie Rd
　UD/BTH/TAN G71 ... 134 B3
Knockhall St
　STPS/GTHM/RID G33 ... 71 E4
Knockhill Dr LNPK/KPK G44 ... 109 G5
Knockhill Rd RNFRW PA4 ... 63 E5
Knockside Av PSLYS PA2 ... 104 A5
Knolipark Dr
　CRMNK/CLK/EAG G76 ... 145 G3
Knowe Crs MTHW ML1 ... 138 A3

Knowehead Dr
　UD/BTH/TAN G71 ... 133 H1
Knowehead Gdns
　PLKSD/SHW G41 ... 109 E1
　UD/BTH/TAN G71 ... 133 H1
Knowehead Rd WISHAW ML2 ... 174 B3
Knowehead Ter
　PLKSD/SHW G41 ... 108 D1
Knowenoble St MTHW ML1 ... 139 E5
Knowe Rd BAIL/MDB/MHD G69 ... 58 D5
　PSLYN/LNWD PA3 ... 85 E2
Knowes Av NMRNS G77 ... 144 B5
Knowes Rd NMRNS G77 ... 144 B5
Knowetop Av MTHW ML1 ... 155 G3
Knowetop Crs DMBTN G82 ... 12 B2
Knox Av BRWEIR PA11 ... 79 F4
Knoxland Sq DMBTN G82 ... 13 E4
Knox Pl NMRNS G77 ... 161 E1
Knox St AIRDRIE ML6 ... 98 C1
　PSLY PA1 ... 83 G5
Kronborg Wy EKILS G75 ... 177 G4
Kyleakin Dr BLTYR/CAMB G72 ... 133 F5
Kyleakin Rd GIF/THBK G46 ... 126 A4
Kyleakin Ter GIF/THBK G46 ... 126 A4
Kyle Dr GIF/THBK G46 ... 127 H4
Kyle Gv MTHW ML1 ... 137 F4
Kylemore Crs MTHW ML1 ... 136 C5
Kylepark Av UD/BTH/TAN G71 ... 133 G1
Kylepark Crs UD/BTH/TAN G71 ... 114 C5
Kylepark Dr UD/BTH/TAN G71 ... 114 C5
Kyle Qd MTHW ML2 ... 173 F4
Kylerhea Rd GIF/THBK G46 ... 126 A4
Kyle Rd CUMB G67 ... 26 D3
Kyle Sq CSMK G45 ... 129 G2
Kyle St COWCAD G4 ... 3 H2
　MTHW ML1 ... 154 A3
Kyle Ter DMBTN G82 ... 12 A5

L

La Belle Allee KVGV G3 ... 66 D5
La Belle Pl KVGV G3 ... 66 D5
Laberge Gdns MTHW ML1 ... 137 G4
Laburnum Av
　BLTYR/CAMB G72 ... 132 B4
　EKILS G75 ... 177 H2
Laburnum Ct EKILS G75 ... 177 H2
Laburnum Crs WISHAW ML2 ... 157 F3
Laburnum Dr KKNTL G66 ... 39 G3
Laburnum Gv CTBR ML5 ... 97 E4
Laburnum Lea HMLTN ML3 ... 170 B4
Laburnum Pl JNSTN PA5 ... 121 H1
Laburnum Rd CUMB G67 ... 27 F3
　PLKSD/SHW G41 ... 88 B5
Lacy St PSLY PA1 ... 84 D4
Ladder Ct EKILS G75 ... 177 G4
Ladeside Cl NMRNS G77 ... 143 H4
Ladeside Dr JNSTN PA5 ... 101 E4
　KSYTH G65 ... 8 C1
Lade Ter CARD/HILL/MSPK G52 ... 86 B5
Ladhope Pl KNTSWD G13 ... 49 H3
Ladyacres RNFRW PA4 ... 48 A5
Ladyacres Wy RNFRW PA4 ... 48 A5
Lady Ann Crs AIRDRIE ML6 ... 98 D3
Ladybank BALLOCH G68 ... 10 B4
Ladybank Gdns EKILN G74 ... 166 D3
Ladybank Pl EKILN G74 ... 166 D3
Ladyburn St PSLY PA1 ... 84 D5
Ladyhill Dr BAIL/MDB/MHD G69 ... 93 H5
Lady Isle Crs UD/BTH/TAN G71 ... 133 H1
Lady Jane Ga
　UD/BTH/TAN G71 ... 133 H3
Ladykirk Crs
　CARD/HILL/MSPK G52 ... 86 C3
　PSLYS PA2 ... 104 C1
Ladykirk Dr
　CARD/HILL/MSPK G52 ... 86 C3
Ladykirk Wy EKILN G74 ... 166 C1
Lady La PSLY PA1 ... 84 A5
Ladyloan Av DRUM G15 ... 49 H5
Ladyloan Ct DRUM G15 ... 32 D4
Ladyloan Gdns DRUM G15 ... 32 D4
Ladymuir Cir ERSK PA8 ... 47 G2
Ladymuir Crs PLK/PH/NH G53 ... 106 D2
Ladysmith EKILS G75 ... 177 H3
Ladysmith Av KLBCH PA10 ... 100 C4
Ladysmith St WISHAW ML2 ... 172 D2
Lady Watson Gdns
　HMLTN ML3 ... 169 F2
Ladywell St MTHW ML1 ... 154 A4
Ladywell St COWCAD G4 ... 3 J5
Lady Wilson St AIRDRIE ML6 ... 98 C2
Ladywood MLNGV G62 ... 17 F3
Laggan Av AIRDRIE ML6 ... 75 H5
Laggan Rd AIRDRIE ML6 ... 76 A5
　NMRNS G77 ... 144 A3
　PLKSW/MSWD G43 ... 127 H2
Laggan Ter RNFRW PA4 ... 63 E2
Laidlaw Gdns
　UD/BTH/TAN G71 ... 115 E3
Laidlaw St GBLS G5 ... 89 F4
Laidon Rd AIRDRIE ML6 ... 76 A5
Laigncartside St JNSTN PA5 ... 101 H4
Laighlands Rd
　UD/BTH/TAN G71 ... 134 C5
Laighmuir St
　UD/BTH/TAN G71 ... 134 A4
Laighpark Av BSHPTN PA7 ... 29 E5
Laighpark Vw
　PSLYN/LNWD PA3 ... 84 B2
Laigh Rd NMRNS G77 ... 145 G5
Laighstonehall Rd HMLTN ML3 ... 169 G3
Laightoun Ct CUMB G67 ... 43 H2
Laightoun Dr CUMB G67 ... 43 H2
Laightoun Gdns CUMB G67 ... 43 H2
Lainshaw Dr CSMK G45 ... 128 C1
Laird Gv UD/BTH/TAN G71 ... 115 F4
Laird Pl DMNK/BRGTN G40 ... 90 C5
Lairds Ga UD/BTH/TAN G71 ... 133 G3
Lairds Hill CUMB G67 ... 26 A3
Laird's Hill Ct KSYTH G65 ... 7 G2
Laird's Hill Pl KSYTH G65 ... 7 G2

Laird St CTBR ML5 ... 97 E2
Lairg Dr BLTYR/CAMB G72 ... 133 F5
Lairhills Rd EKILS G75 ... 178 A3
Lairhill Rd EKILS G75 ... 178 B1
Lamberton Dr
　CARD/HILL/MSPK G52 ... 86 C3
Lambhill Qd PLKSD/SHW G41 ... 88 C4
Lambhill St PLKSD/SHW G41 ... 88 C4
Lamb St HMLTN ML3 ... 170 B2
　PPK/MIL G22 ... 53 G5
Lamerton Rd CUMB G67 ... 27 E3
Lamington Rd
　CARD/HILL/MSPK G52 ... 86 C5
Lamlash Crs
　STPS/GTHM/RID G33 ... 92 C1
Lamlash Pl EKILS G75 ... 177 G2
　MTHW ML1 ... 154 B3
　STPS/GTHM/RID G33 ... 92 C1
Lammermoor EKILN G74 ... 167 H1
Lammermoor Av
　CARD/HILL/MSPK G52 ... 106 D1
Lammermoor Crs KKNTL G66 ... 21 H5
Lammermoor Dr CUMB G67 ... 26 D4
Lammermoor Gdns KKNTL G66 ... 21 H5
Lammermoor Rd KKNTL G66 ... 40 C1
Lammermoor Ter
　WISHAW ML2 ... 174 A2
Lammermuir Ct PSLYS PA2 ... 104 B4
Lammermuir Dr PSLYS PA2 ... 104 A4
Lammermuir Gdns BSDN G61 ... 33 H1
Lammermuir Wy AIRDRIE ML6 ... 119 G3
Lamont Av BSHPTN PA7 ... 29 F5
Lamont Rd SPRGB/BLRNK G21 ... 55 E5
Lanark Av AIRDRIE ML6 ... 98 A3
Lancaster Av AIRDRIE ML6 ... 119 F4
Lancaster Crs KVD/HLHD G12 ... 66 B2
Lancaster Crescent La
　KVD/HLHD G12 ... 66 B2
Lancaster Rd BSHPBGS G64 ... 38 A4
Lancefield Quay KVGV G3 ... 88 D2
Lancefield St KVGV G3 ... 2 A5
Landemer Dr RUTH G73 ... 129 G3
Landressy Pl DMNK/BRGTN G40 ... 90 C5
Landressy St DMNK/BRGTN G40 ... 90 C5
Landsdowne Gdns HMLTN ML3 ... 170 C2
The Lane HMLTN ML3 ... 169 G4
Langa St MRYH/FIRH G20 ... 52 D4
Lang Av BSHPTN PA7 ... 29 F5
　RNFRW PA4 ... 63 G5
Langbar Crs
　STPS/GTHM/RID G33 ... 93 G2
Langbyres Rd MTHW ML1 ... 157 G1
Langcraigs Ct PSLYS PA2 ... 103 H4
Langcraigs Dr PSLYS PA2 ... 103 H5
Langcroft Dr BLTYR/CAMB G72 ... 131 H5
Langcroft Pl GOV/IBX G51 ... 86 D2
Langcroft Rd GOV/IBX G51 ... 87 E2
Langcroft Ter GOV/IBX G51 ... 87 E2
Langdale EKILN G74 ... 165 H2
Langdale Av
　STPS/GTHM/RID G33 ... 69 H3
Langdales Av BALLOCH G68 ... 25 G5
Langdale St
　STPS/GTHM/RID G33 ... 69 H3
Langfaulds Crs CLYDBK G81 ... 32 D2
Langford Dr PLK/PH/NH G53 ... 125 F4
Langford Pl PLK/PH/NH G53 ... 125 G4
Langhaul Rd PLK/PH/NH G53 ... 106 A3
Langhill Dr BALLOCH G68 ... 25 H2
Langholm EKILN G74 ... 167 H1
Langholm Ct
　BAIL/MDB/MHD G69 ... 59 H1
Langholm Dr PSLYN/LNWD PA3 ... 82 A4
Langlands Av EKILS G75 ... 178 C4
　GOV/IBX G51 ... 87 E2
Langlands Ct GOV/IBX G51 ... 87 F2
　GOV/IBX G51 ... 87 E2
Langlands Dr
　GOV/IBX G51 ... 87 E2
　EKILS G75 ... 178 C4
Langlands Pl EKILS G75 ... 178 C4
Langlands Rd GOV/IBX G51 ... 87 E2
Langlands Ter DMBTN G82 ... 13 F2
Langlea Av BLTYR/CAMB G72 ... 130 C3
Langlea Ct BLTYR/CAMB G72 ... 130 D3
Langlea Dr BLTYR/CAMB G72 ... 130 D2
Langlea Gdns
　BLTYR/CAMB G72 ... 130 D2
Langlea Gv BLTYR/CAMB G72 ... 130 D3
Langlees Av NMRNS G77 ... 145 E5
Langley Av KNTSWD G13 ... 50 C4
Langlook Rd PLK/PH/NH G53 ... 106 A3
Langmuir Rd
　BAIL/MDB/MHD G69 ... 95 F4
　KKNTL G66 ... 21 H4
Langmuir Wy CTBR ML5 ... 95 F4
Langness Rd
　STPS/GTHM/RID G33 ... 92 C1
Langoreth Av HMLTN ML3 ... 169 E3
Langrig Rd NMRNS G77 ... 161 F2
　SPRGB/BLRNK G21 ... 68 C3
Langshot St GOV/IBX G51 ... 88 C4
Langside Av UD/BTH/TAN G71 ... 108 D3
　PLKSD/SHW G41 ... 134 D1
Langside Ct UD/BTH/TAN G71 ... 134 B4
Langside Dr KLBCH PA10 ... 100 B4
　PLKSW/MSWD G43 ... 127 H2
Langside Gdns GVH/MTFL G42 ... 109 F3
Langside La GVH/MTFL G42 ... 109 F2
Langside Pl PLKSD/SHW G41 ... 109 E4
Langside Rd GVH/MTFL G42 ... 109 F2
　UD/BTH/TAN G71 ... 134 C5
Langside St CLYDBK G81 ... 32 D2
Langstile Pl
　CARD/HILL/MSPK G52 ... 86 A4
Langstile Rd
　CARD/HILL/MSPK G52 ... 86 A4
Lang St PSLY PA1 ... 84 D5
Langton Crs BRHD/NEIL G78 ... 142 C1
　PLK/PH/NH G53 ... 106 D4
Langton Gdns
　BAIL/MDB/MHD G69 ... 93 G5
Langton Pl NMRNS G77 ... 143 H5
Langton Rd PLK/PH/NH G53 ... 106 D4
Langtree Av GIF/THBK G46 ... 144 B1
Lanrig Pl BAIL/MDB/MHD G69 ... 58 A3
Lanrig Rd BAIL/MDB/MHD G69 ... 58 B3
Lansbury Gdns
　PSLYN/LNWD PA3 ... 84 A2

Lansdowne Crs COWCAD G4 ... 67 E4
Lansdowne Crescent La
　COWCAD G4 ... 67 E4
Lansdowne Dr BALLOCH G68 ... 26 B1
Lantana Gv MTHW ML1 ... 156 C4
Lanton Dr CARD/HILL/MSPK G52 ... 86 C4
Lanton Rd PLKSW/MSWD G43 ... 127 H2
Lappin St CLYDBK G81 ... 49 G3
Larbert St COWCAD G4 ... 3 F3
Larch Av BSHPBGS G64 ... 56 C1
　KKNTL G66 ... 39 H5
Larch Ct BLTYR/CAMB G72 ... 132 B4
　CUMB G67 ... 27 G1
　EKILS G75 ... 177 G3
Larch Crs KKNTL G66 ... 39 H5
Larchfield Av NMRNS G77 ... 161 H1
　SCOT G14 ... 64 D2
Larchfield Crs WISHAW ML2 ... 157 F4
Larchfield Dr RUTH G73 ... 130 A3
Larchfield Gdns WISHAW ML2 ... 157 G3
Larchfield Pl SCOT G14 ... 64 C2
Larchfield Rd BSDN G61 ... 51 G1
　BAIL/MDB/MHD G69 ...
Larch Gv CUMB G67 ... 27 G1
　HMLTN ML3 ... 170 B3
　KKNTL G66 ... 5 F5
Larchgrove Av CAR/SHTL G32 ... 92 D3
Larchgrove Pl CAR/SHTL G32 ... 92 D2
Larchgrove Rd CAR/SHTL G32 ... 92 D2
Larch Pl EKILS G75 ... 177 G3
　JNSTN PA5 ... 121 G1
　UD/BTH/TAN G71 ... 116 A4
Larch Rd CUMB G67 ... 27 G1
　PLKSD/SHW G41 ... 88 A5
Larchwood Dr
　... 142 C1
Largie Rd LNPK/KPK G44 ... 128 A2
Largo Pl GOV/IBX G51 ... 87 F1
Larkfield Ct BLTYR/CAMB G72 ... 151 F4
Larkfield Dr BLTYR/CAMB G72 ... 151 G4
Larkfield Rd KKNTL G66 ... 40 B3
Larkfield St GVH/MTFL G42 ... 109 G1
Larkin Gdns PSLYN/LNWD PA3 ... 83 H3
Larkin Wy BLSH ML4 ... 116 C5
Larkspur Dr EKILN G74 ... 165 H1
Lasswade St SCOT G14 ... 49 H5
Latherton Dr MRYH/FIRH G20 ... 66 C1
Latimer Gdns
　CARD/HILL/MSPK G52 ... 86 B5
Latta St DMBTN G82 ... 13 F3
Lauchope Rd MTHW ML1 ... 119 H5
Lauchope St AIRDRIE ML6 ... 119 H4
Lauderdale Dr NMRNS G77 ... 161 F2
Lauderdale Gdns PTCK G11 ... 65 H3
Lauderdale La PSLYN/LNWD PA3 ... 82 A4
Lauder Dr PSLYN/LNWD PA3 ... 82 A4
　RUTH G73 ... 111 G5
Lauder Gdns BLTYR/CAMB G72 ... 133 H3
　CTBR ML5 ... 117 G1
Lauder St GBLS G5 ... 89 G5
Laughland Dr MTHW ML1 ... 138 A4
Laundry La
　STPS/GTHM/RID G33 ... 70 D1
Lauranne Pl BLSH ML4 ... 135 G3
Laurel Av CLYDBK G81 ... 31 E4
　KKNTL G66 ... 40 A1
Laurelbank CTBR ML5 ... 96 B5
Laurel Bank HMLTN ML3 ... 170 A5
Laurelbank Rd
　BAIL/MDB/MHD G69 ... 58 A5
　CAR/SHTL G32 ... 112 D4
Laurel Ct EKILS G75 ... 178 A3
Laurel Dr EKILS G75 ... 178 A3
　WISHAW ML2 ... 157 F4
Laurel Gdns AIRDRIE ML6 ... 119 F2
　UD/BTH/TAN G71 ... 115 E4
Laurel La BLTYR/CAMB G72 ... 132 B4
Laurel Park Gdns KNTSWD G13 ... 64 D1
Laurel Pl EKILS G75 ... 178 A3
　PTCK G11 ... 65 H4
The Laurels MTHW ML1 ... 157 F2
　NMRNS G77 ... 144 A5
Laurel St PTCK G11 ... 65 H4
Laurel Wy BRHD/NEIL G78 ... 124 A4
Laurel Wynd BLTYR/CAMB G72 ... 132 C3
Laurence Ct DRUM G15 ... 32 D5
Laurence Dr BSDN G61 ... 34 A2
　DRUM G15 ... 32 D5
Lauren Av AIRDRIE ML6 ... 98 D3
Lauren Wy PSLYS PA2 ... 103 E3
Laurieston Crs AIRDRIE ML6 ... 119 G3
Laurieston Rd GBLS G5 ... 89 G5
Laurieston Wy RUTH G73 ... 129 H3
Lauriston Gv NMRNS G77 ... 143 G5
Lavelle Dr CTBR ML5 ... 97 F2
Lavender Dr EKILS G75 ... 178 A3
Laverock Av HMLTN ML3 ... 170 D3
Laverockhall St
　SPRGB/BLRNK G21 ... 68 C3
Laverock Rd AIRDRIE ML6 ... 99 F2
Laverock Ter
　BAIL/MDB/MHD G69 ... 59 G1
Law Dr MTHW ML1 ... 137 H3
Lawers Dr BSDN G61 ... 33 G1
Lawers Rd PLKSW/MSWD G43 ... 127 F2
　RNFRW PA4 ... 63 E5
Lawfield Av NMRNS G77 ... 145 G5
Lawhill Av CSMK G45 ... 129 E5
Lawhope Mill Rd AIRDRIE ML6 ... 99 H2
Lawmarnock Crs BRWEIR PA11 ... 79 F4
Lawmarnock Rd BRWEIR PA11 ... 79 F5
Lawmoor Av GBLS G5 ... 89 H5
Lawmoor Pl GBLS G5 ... 109 H1
Lawmoor Rd GBLS G5 ... 89 H5
Lawmoor St GBLS G5 ... 89 H5
Lawmuir Crs CLYDBK G81 ... 32 D1
Lawmuir Pl BLSH ML4 ... 135 H3
Lawmuir Rd BLSH ML4 ... 135 H3
Lawn Pk MLNGV G62 ... 17 G4
Lawn St PSLY PA1 ... 84 C4
Lawrence Av GIF/THBK G46 ... 145 E1
Lawrence St PTCK G11 ... 66 B4
Lawrie St PTCK G11 ... 66 A4
　WISHAW ML2 ... 158 B5
Lawson Av MTHW ML1 ... 171 H2
Law St DMNK/BRGTN G40 ... 90 D4
Laxford Av LNPK/KPK G44 ... 128 B3

Laxford Pl CTBR ML5 ... 97 G4
Laxford Rd ERSK PA8 ... 46 D2
Laxton Dr KKNTL G66 ... 40 B4
Lea Av BRHD/NEIL G78 ... 141 E5
Leabank Av PSLYS PA2 ... 104 B4
Leadburn Rd SPRGB/BLRNK G21 ... 69 F2
Leadburn St
　STPS/GTHM/RID G33 ... 91 G1
Leader St STPS/GTHM/RID G33 ... 69 G5
Leaend Rd AIRDRIE ML6 ... 75 H5
Leander Crs BLSH ML4 ... 136 D2
　RNFRW PA4 ... 63 H4
Learmonth Pl MLNGV G62 ... 17 F2
Leathem Pl WISHAW ML2 ... 172 D4
Leathen Pl ERSK PA8 ... 46 D2
Leckethill Av BALLOCH G68 ... 43 G1
Leckethill Ct BALLOCH G68 ... 43 G1
Leckethill Pl BALLOCH G68 ... 43 G1
Leckethill Vw BALLOCH G68 ... 43 G1
Leckie Dr HMLTN ML3 ... 169 G2
Ledaig St DEN/PKHD G31 ... 91 F2
Ledard Rd GVH/MTFL G42 ... 109 E5
Ledcameroch Crs BSDN G61 ... 34 A4
Ledcameroch Pk BSDN G61 ... 34 A4
Ledcameroch Rd BSDN G61 ... 34 A4
Ledgate KKNTL G66 ... 21 F4
Ledgowan Pl MRYH/FIRH G20 ... 52 C5
Ledi Dr BSDN G61 ... 33 E5
Ledi Rd PLKSW/MSWD G43 ... 127 F2
Ledmore Dr DRUM G15 ... 33 E4
Lednock Rd
　CARD/HILL/MSPK G52 ... 86 B4
　STPS/GTHM/RID G33 ... 70 D1
Lee Av STPS/GTHM/RID G33 ... 69 H5
Leebank Dr LNPK/KPK G44 ... 146 A1
Leeburn Av CRG/CRSL/HOU PA6 ... 80 D2
Leeburn Gdns CRG/CRSL/HOU PA6 ... 80 D2
Leefield Dr LNPK/KPK G44 ... 128 A5
Leehill Rd SPRGB/BLRNK G21 ... 54 C4
Lee Pl BLSH ML4 ... 136 C3
Leesburn Pl EKILN G74 ... 166 C1
Lee's Ct CTBR ML5 ... 96 C4
Leesland UD/BTH/TAN G71 ... 115 F4
Leeward Cir EKILS G75 ... 165 H5
Leewood Dr LNPK/KPK G44 ... 128 B5
Le Froy Gdns EKILS G75 ... 165 H5
Le Froy La EKILS G75 ... 165 H5
Legbrannock Av MTHW ML1 ... 138 A1
Legbrannock Crs MTHW ML1 ... 138 A3
Legbrannock Rd MTHW ML1 ... 138 B1
Leglen Wood Crs
　STPS/GTHM/RID G33 ... 55 G5
Leglen Wood Dr
　STPS/GTHM/RID G33 ... 55 G5
Leglen Wood Rd
　STPS/GTHM/RID G33 ... 55 G5
Leicester Av KVD/HLHD G12 ... 66 A1
Leighton St MRYH/FIRH G20 ... 52 D5
　WISHAW ML2 ... 174 A3
Leitchland Rd PSLYS PA2 ... 102 C4
Leithland Av PLK/PH/NH G53 ... 106 C3
Leithland Rd PLK/PH/NH G53 ... 106 C3
Leith St STPS/GTHM/RID G33 ... 91 G1
Leman Dr CRG/CRSL/HOU PA6 ... 81 E3
Leman Gv CRG/CRSL/HOU PA6 ... 81 E3
Lembert Dr
　CRMNK/CLK/EAG G76 ... 145 G2
Lendale La BSHPBGS G64 ... 37 H5
Lendalfoot Gdns HMLTN ML3 ... 168 C2
Lendel Pl GOV/IBX G51 ... 88 C4
Lenihall Dr CSMK G45 ... 129 F5
Lenihall Ter CSMK G45 ... 129 F5
Lennox Av BSHPTN PA7 ...
　CTBR ML5 ... 96 B2
　MLNGV G62 ... 17 E4
　SCOT G14 ... 64 D3
Lennox Crs BSHPBGS G64 ... 54 C2
Lennox Dr BSDN G61 ... 34 C2
　CLYDBK G81 ... 32 C1
　NMRNS G77 ... 161 H3
Lennox Gdns SCOT G14 ... 65 E2
Lennox La East SCOT G14 ... 65 E3
Lennox La West SCOT G14 ... 65 E3
Lennox Rd CUMB G67 ... 26 B5
　DMBTN G82 ... 13 G2
　KKNTL G66 ... 4 A1
Lennox St DMBTN G82 ... 13 F5
　MRYH/FIRH G20 ... 52 B4
　WISHAW ML2 ... 174 D1
Lennox Ter PSLYN/LNWD PA3 ... 84 C1
Lentran St ESTRH G34 ... 94 C2
Lenzie Pl SPRGB/BLRNK G21 ... 54 D5
Lenzie Rd KKNTL G66 ... 40 A1
　STPS/GTHM/RID G33 ... 57 E4
Lenziemill Rd CUMB G67 ... 26 D5
Lenzie St SPRGB/BLRNK G21 ... 54 B5
Lenzie Ter SPRGB/BLRNK G21 ... 54 B5
Lenzie Wy SPRGB/BLRNK G21 ... 54 B5
Lesley Qd BLSH ML4 ... 135 G5
Leslie Av BSHPTN PA7 ... 29 E3
　NMRNS G77 ... 144 B3
Leslie Rd PLKSD/SHW G41 ... 108 D2
Leslie St MTHW ML1 ... 155 E3
　PLKSD/SHW G41 ... 109 E1
Lesmuir Dr SCOT G14 ... 64 B1
Lesmuir Pl SCOT G14 ... 64 A1
Letham Ct PLKSW/MSWD G43 ... 127 H2
Letham Dr BSHPBGS G64 ... 55 F3
　PLKSW/MSWD G43 ... 127 H2
Letham Gra BALLOCH G68 ... 26 B1
Lethamhill Pl
　STPS/GTHM/RID G33 ... 69 H5
Lethamhill Rd
　STPS/GTHM/RID G33 ... 69 H5
Letham Ov BSHPBGS G64 ... 55 G3
Lethbridge Pl EKILS G75 ... 165 H5
Letherby Dr LNPK/KPK G44 ... 109 G5
Letheron Dr WISHAW ML2 ... 157 E5
Lethington Av
　PLKSD/SHW G41 ... 108 D3
Lethington Pl PLKSD/SHW G41 ... 109 E3
Lethington Rd NMRNS G77 ... 161 E4
Letterfearn Rd SMSTN G23 ... 52 C1
Letterickhills Crs
　BLTYR/CAMB G72 ... 132 B4
Lettoch St GOV/IBX G51 ... 87 H2
Leven Av BSHPBGS G64 ... 55 E1
Leven Ct BRHD/NEIL G78 ... 124 A2
　DMBTN G82 ... 13 G3
Leven Dr BSDN G61 ... 34 B4
　HMLTN ML3 ... 169 G5
Leven Qd AIRDRIE ML6 ... 76 A4

Leven Rd CTBR ML5.....73 H5
Leven St DMBTN G82.....13 E1
MTHW ML1.....154 D1
PLKSD/SHW G41.....109 E1
Leven Ter MTHW ML1.....137 H5
Leven Wy EKILS G75.....177 E2
Levern Bridge Ct
PLK/PH/NH G53.....106 A5
Levern Bridge Gv
PLK/PH/NH G53.....106 A5
Levern Bridge Pl
PLK/PH/NH G53.....125 E1
Levern Bridge Wy
PLK/PH/NH G53.....125 E1
Levern Crs BRHD/NEIL G78.....142 A1
Leverndale Ct PLK/PH/NH G53.....106 A3
Leverndale Rd PLK/PH/NH G53.....106 A3
Levern Gdns BSHPBGS G64.....124 A4
Levernside Av PLK/PH/NH G53.....123 H5
PLK/PH/NH G53.....106 D4
Levernside Crs
PLK/PH/NH G53.....106 C3
Levernside Rd PLK/PH/NH G53.....106 C3
Lewis Av RNFRW PA4.....63 G5
WISHAW ML2.....157 H5
Lewis Ct KLBCH PA10.....100 C4
OLDK G60.....30 D3
Lewis Dr OLDK G60.....30 C3
OLDK G60.....30 D3
Lewis Gdns BSDN.....33 G2
OLDK G60.....30 D5
Lewis Gv OLDK G60.....30 D5
Lewis Pl AIRDRIE ML6.....99 E3
NMRNS G77.....143 G4
OLDK G60.....30 D5
Lewiston Dr SMSTN G23.....52 C1
Lewiston Pl SMSTN G23.....52 C2
Lewiston Rd SMSTN G23.....52 C2
Lexwell Av JNSTN PA5.....102 C1
Leyden Gdns MRYH/FIRH G20.....66 D1
Leyden St MRYH/FIRH G20.....66 D1
Leys Pk HMLTN ML3.....169 F1
The Leys BSHPBGS G64.....54 D2
Libberton Wy HMLTN ML3.....169 F2
Liberton St
STPS/GTHM/RID G33.....91 H1
Liberty Av BAIL/MDB/MHD G69.....95 E4
Liberty Rd BLSH ML4.....135 H4
Libo Av PLK/PH/NH G53.....107 E3
Libo Pl ERSK PA8.....46 D1
Library Gdns BLTYR/CAMB G72.....131 E1
Library La GIF/THBK G46.....126 C4
Library Rd WISHAW ML2.....174 A2
Lickprivick Rd EKILS G75.....177 G1
Liddell Gv EKILS G75.....178 A1
Liddells Ct BSHPBGS G64.....54 C4
Liddell St CAR/SHTL G32.....112 D5
Liddel Rd CUMB G67.....26 A4
Liddesdale Pl PPK/MIL G22.....54 B4
Liddesdale Rd PPK/MIL G22.....54 B4
Liddesdale Sq PPK/MIL G22.....54 B4
Liddesdale Ter PPK/MIL G22.....54 B4
Liddoch Wy RUTH G73.....110 C4
Liff Gdns BSHPBGS G64.....55 G3
Liff Pl ESTRH G34.....94 A1
Lightburn Pl CAR/SHTL G32.....92 C2
Lightburn Rd
BLTYR/CAMB G72.....132 A3
DEN/PKHD G31.....91 G3
Lilac Av CLYDBK G81.....31 F4
CUMB G67.....11 G5
Lilac Ct CUMB G67.....11 G5
Lilac Crs UD/BTH/TAN G71.....115 G3
Lilac Gdns BSHPBGS G64.....55 E3
Lilac Hl CUMB G67.....11 H5
HMLTN ML3.....170 C3
Lilac Pl CUMB G67.....11 H5
Lilac Wynd BLTYR/CAMB G72.....132 C3
Lillyburn Pl DRUM G15.....32 D4
Lilybank Av AIRDRIE ML6.....76 C4
BAIL/MDB/MHD G69.....58 A4
BLTYR/CAMB G72.....131 G3
Lilybank Gdns KVD/HLHD G12.....66 C4
Lilybank Gardens La
KVD/HLHD G12.....66 C4
Lilybank St HMLTN ML3.....169 H1
Lilybank Ter HMLTN ML3.....169 H1
Lilybank Terrace La
KVD/HLHD G12.....66 C4
Lily St DMNK/BRGTN G40.....110 D1
Limecraigs Av PSLYS PA2.....103 H5
Limecraigs Crs PSLYS PA2.....103 H5
Limecraigs Rd PSLYS PA2.....103 H5
Lime Crs AIRDRIE ML6.....99 F1
CUMB G67.....27 G2
Lime Gv BLTYR/CAMB G72.....151 F1
KNTL G66.....40 A3
Limegrove St BLSH ML4.....116 D5
Limekilns Rd CUMB G67.....45 E2
Limekilns St CLYDBK G81.....32 C2
Lime La MTHW ML1.....154 D1
Lime Rd DMBTN G82.....13 E3
Limeside Av RUTH G73.....111 F5
Limeside Gdns RUTH G73.....111 F5
Lime St SCOT G14.....65 E3
Limetree Av UD/BTH/TAN G71.....115 G4
Limetree Ct HMLTN ML3.....152 B5
Limetree Crs NMRNS G77.....161 G1
Limetree Dr CLYDBK G81.....32 A3
Limetree Qd UD/BTH/TAN G71.....115 H4
Limetree Wk KNTL G66.....20 D1
Limeview Av PSLYS PA2.....103 G5
Limeview Crs PSLYS PA2.....103 G5
Limeview Wy PSLYS PA2.....103 G5
Linacre Dr CAR/SHTL G32.....92 D4
Linacre Gdns CAR/SHTL G32.....93 E4
Linburn Pl
CARD/HILL/MSPK G52.....86 B3
Linburn Rd
CARD/HILL/MSPK G52.....86 A2
ERSK PA8.....46 D2
Lincan Av KNTSWD G13.....50 D4
UD/BTH/TAN G71.....115 F3
Lincuan Av GIF/THBK G46.....145 F2
Lindams UD/BTH/TAN G71.....134 A2
Linden Av WISHAW ML2.....157 H4
Linden Dr CLYDBK G81.....31 H2
Linden Lea HMLTN ML3.....169 G1
KNTL G66.....5 F5
Lindores Av RUTH G73.....111 G5
Lindores Dr EKILN G74.....165 G4
Lindores St EKILN G74.....165 G4
Lindrick Dr SMSTN G23.....52 C1

Lindsaybeg Ct
BAIL/MDB/MHD G69.....58 B3
Lindsaybeg Rd
BAIL/MDB/MHD G69.....58 B3
KKNTL G66.....40 B3
Lindsay Dr KVD/HLHD G12.....52 A5
Lindsayfield Av EKILS G75.....177 H4
Lindsayfield Rd EKILS G75.....177 G4
Lindsay Gv EKILN G74.....166 C3
Lindsay Pl EKILN G74.....166 D4
KVD/HLHD G12.....52 A5
Lindsay Rd EKILN G74.....166 C4
Lindsay Ter KKNTL G66.....4 C2
Lindum Crs MTHW ML1.....154 B2
Lindum St MTHW ML1.....154 A2
Linfern Rd KVD/HLHD G12.....66 B5
Linghope Pl WISHAW ML2.....173 G5
Lingley Av AIRDRIE ML6.....98 B3
Linhead Dr PLK/PH/NH G53.....125 H1
Linhope Pl EKILS G75.....176 D1
Links Rd CAR/SHTL G32.....113 E1
The Links BALLOCH G68.....10 D4
Linksview Rd MTHW ML1.....155 C1
Linkwood Av DRUM G15.....33 E5
Linkwood Crs DRUM G15.....33 F5
Linkwood Dr DRUM G15.....33 E5
Linkwood Gdns DRUM G15.....33 F5
Linkwood Pl DRUM G15.....33 E5
Linlithgow Gdns CAR/SHTL G32.....93 E4
Linn Crs PSLYS PA2.....103 H5
Linn Dr LNPK/KPK G44.....128 A4
Linnet Av JNSTN PA5.....120 D2
Linnet Pl KNTSWD G13.....50 A4
Linnet Rd BLSH ML4.....116 C4
Linnet Wy BLSH ML4.....116 C4
Linn Gdns BALLOCH G68.....24 D5
Linn Gln KKNTL G66.....4 D2
Linnhead Dr PLK/PH/NH G53.....125 H1
Linnhead Pl SCOT G14.....64 C2
Linnhe Av BSHPBGS G64.....55 E2
HMLTN ML3.....169 F4
LNPK/KPK G44.....128 B3
Linnhe Dr BRHD/NEIL G78.....124 A2
ERSK PA8.....46 D2
Linnpark Av LNPK/KPK G44.....128 A5
Linn Park Gdns JNSTN PA5.....101 H4
Linnvale Wy BALLOCH G68.....9 G4
Linn Valley Vw CSMK G45.....129 E4
Linnwell Crs PSLYS PA2.....103 H5
Linside Av PSLY PA1.....84 D5
Linthaugh Rd PLK/PH/NH G53.....106 C1
Linthaugh Ter PLK/PH/NH G53.....107 E3
Linthouse Buildings
GOV/IBX G51.....87 F1
Linthouse Rd GOV/IBX G51.....87 F1
Lintie Rd MTHW ML1.....137 H3
Lintlaw BLTYR/CAMB G72.....151 F2
Lintlaw Dr
CARD/HILL/MSPK G52.....86 C3
Lintmill Ter BRHD/NEIL G78.....140 D4
Linton St STPS/GTHM/RID G33.....91 H1
Lintwhite Crs BRWEIR PA11.....79 H4
Linwood Av
CRMNK/CLK/EAG G76.....146 A3
EKILN G74.....166 C3
Linwood Rd PSLYN/LNWD PA3.....82 C4
Linwood Ter HMLTN ML3.....169 G1
Lion Bank KKNTL G66.....21 E4
Lismore EKILN G74.....167 F5
Lismore Av MTHW ML1.....154 A2
RNFRW PA4.....63 G5
Lismore Dr CTBR ML5.....96 B5
PSLYN/LNWD PA3.....82 A3
Lismore Gdns KLBCH PA10.....100 D4
Lismore Hl HMLTN ML3.....168 C2
Lismore Pl NMRNS G77.....143 G5
Lismore Rd KVD/HLHD G12.....66 A1
Lister Gdns
CRMNK/CLK/EAG G76.....146 B5
Lister Pl CARD/HILL/MSPK G52.....86 B2
Lister Rd CARD/HILL/MSPK G52.....86 B2
Lister St COWCAD G4.....3 J2
Lithgow Crs PSLYS PA2.....104 D2
Lithgow Dr MTHW ML1.....155 E4
Lithgow Pl EKILN G74.....165 E1
Little Dovehill COWCAD G4.....3 J7
Littlehill St SPRGB/BLRNK G21.....68 D3
Littleholm Pl CLYDBK G81.....31 F4
Little John Gdns WISHAW ML2.....175 E4
Littlemill Av BALLOCH G68.....25 E4
Littlemill Dr PLK/PH/NH G53.....106 C1
Littlemill Gdns PLK/PH/NH G53.....106 B4
Littlemill La OLDK G60.....15 F5
Littlemill Wy MTHW ML1.....155 C1
Littlesdale Av PSLYS PA2.....102 C5
Littleton Gdns ERSK PA8.....47 F2
Little St KVGV G3.....2 A5
Littleton St MRYH/FIRH G20.....52 C2
Livingston Dr AIRDRIE ML6.....77 H1
Livingstone Av
CARD/HILL/MSPK G52.....86 B1
Livingstone Bvd
BLTYR/CAMB G72.....151 F3
Livingstone Crs
BLTYR/CAMB G72.....151 F1
EKILS G75.....178 A1
Livingstone Dr EKILS G75.....178 A1
Livingstone Pl AIRDRIE ML6.....98 C3
Livingstone St CLYDBK G81.....49 G2
HMLTN ML3.....152 C5
Lloyd Av CAR/SHTL G32.....112 B2
Lloyd Dr MTHW ML1.....155 F1
Lloyds St CTBR ML5.....96 D4
Lloyd St DEN/PKHD G31.....90 D1
MTHW ML1.....155 F1
RUTH G73.....111 E3
Loanbank Pl GOV/IBX G51.....87 H2
Loanbank Qd GOV/IBX G51.....87 H2
Loancroft Av
BAIL/MDB/MHD G69.....94 B5
Loancroft Gdns
UD/BTH/TAN G71.....133 H2
Loancroft Ga
UD/BTH/TAN G71.....133 H2
Loancroft Pl
BAIL/MDB/MHD G69.....114 A1
Loanfoot Av BRHD/NEIL G78.....140 B4
KNTSWD G13.....50 B4
Loanfoot Rd BLTYR/CAMB G72.....151 G3
Loanhead Av MTHW ML1.....138 A4
PSLYN/LNWD PA3.....84 A3
RNFRW PA4.....63 G3
Loanhead Crs MTHW ML1.....138 A4

Loanhead Rd MTHW ML1.....137 H4
PSLYN/LNWD PA3.....81 H5
Loanhead St CAR/SHTL G32.....92 A2
CTBR ML5.....116 B1
The Loaning DMBTN G82.....13 E4
Loaninghead Dr DMBTN G82.....13 E2
MTHW ML1.....154 B3
The Loan MLNGV G62.....16 A1
Lobnitz Av RNFRW PA4.....63 G3
Lochaber Dr RUTH G73.....130 C3
Lochaber Pl EKILN G74.....166 A2
Lochaber Rd BSDN G61.....52 A1
Loch Achray St CAR/SHTL G32.....92 D5
Lochaline Av RUTH G73.....110 D5
Lochaline Dr LNPK/KPK G44.....128 B3
Lochalsh Crs KKNTL G66.....5 C2
Lochalsh Dr PSLYS PA2.....103 G1
Lochalsh Pl BLTYR/CAMB G72.....133 G5
Lochar Crs PLK/PH/NH G53.....107 E2
Lochar Pl EKILS G75.....176 D1
Lochay St CAR/SHTL G32.....92 D5
Lochbrae Dr RUTH G73.....130 C3
Lochbridge Rd ESTRH G34.....93 H2
Lochbroom Dr NMRNS G77.....144 C4
PSLYS PA2.....103 F2
Loch Brora Crs CTBR ML5.....116 B1
Lochburn Crs MRYH/FIRH G20.....52 D4
Lochburn Pas MRYH/FIRH G20.....52 D4
Lochburn Rd MRYH/FIRH G20.....52 D4
Lochdochart Rd ESTRH G34.....94 C1
Lochearn Crs AIRDRIE ML6.....76 A4
PSLYS PA2.....103 F2
Lochend Av
BAIL/MDB/MHD G69.....58 D5
Lochend Crs BSDN G61.....34 A5
Lochend Dr BSDN G61.....34 A5
BSDN G61.....34 B5
ESTRH G34.....72 A5
Lochend St MTHW ML1.....155 C4
Locher Av CRG/CRSL/HOU PA6.....81 F2
Locher Crs CRG/CRSL/HOU PA6.....81 F3
Locher Gait CRG/CRSL/HOU PA6.....81 F3
Locher Gdns
CRG/CRSL/HOU PA6.....81 F3
Locher Pl CTBR ML5.....117 G1
Locher Rd KLBCH PA10.....100 A1
Locher Wk CTBR ML5.....117 F1
Lochfauld Rd SMSTN G23.....53 E4
Lochfield Crs PSLYS PA2.....104 C3
Lochfield Dr PSLYS PA2.....104 D3
Lochfield Gdns ESTRH G34.....72 C5
Lochfield Rd PSLYS PA2.....104 C3
Lochgarry Wy CTBR ML5.....117 F1
Lochgilp St MRYH/FIRH G20.....52 B4
Loch Goil EKILN G74.....166 D4
Lochgoin Av DRUM G15.....32 D4
Lochgreen Pl CTBR ML5.....73 H4
HMLTN ML3.....169 G5
Lochgreen St
STPS/GTHM/RID G33.....69 G3
Lochiel La PSLYN/LNWD PA3.....82 A4
Lochiel Dr KKNTL G66.....5 C1
Lochiel Rd GIF/THBK G46.....126 C5
Lochinch Pl NMRNS G77.....143 F5
Lochinver Crs PSLYS PA2.....103 F2
Lochinver Dr LNPK/KPK G44.....128 B2
Lochinver Gv
BLTYR/CAMB G72.....131 G2
Loch Laidon St CAR/SHTL G32.....93 E5
Loch Laxford EKILN G74.....167 E5
Lochlea Av CLYDBK G81.....32 B4
Lochlea Lea KKNTL G66.....21 H3
Loch Lea KKNTL G66.....21 H3
Lochlea Rd CRMNK/CLK/EAG G76.....145 G2
CUMB G67.....26 D2
PLKSW/MSWD G43.....127 G1
RUTH G73.....129 H4
Lochleven La GVH/MTFL G42.....109 F5
Lochleven Rd GVH/MTFL G42.....109 F5
Lochlibo Av KNTSWD G13.....49 H5
Lochlibo Crs BRHD/NEIL G78.....141 H1
Lochlibo Rd BRHD/NEIL G78.....141 H1
Loch Long EKILN G74.....166 D5
Loch Loyal EKILN G74.....167 E5
Lochmaben Rd
CARD/HILL/MSPK G52.....86 A5
Lochmaddy Av LNPK/KPK G44.....128 B3
Loch Maree EKILN G74.....167 E4
Loch Meadie EKILN G74.....167 E5
Loch Naver EKILN G74.....167 E5
Lochore Av PSLYN/LNWD PA3.....84 B1
Loch Pk WISHAW ML2.....173 H4
Loch Pl BRWEIR PA11.....79 G3
Lochranza Dr EKILS G75.....177 G4
Lochranza La EKILS G75.....177 H4
Loch Rd AIRDRIE ML6.....
BRWEIR PA11.....79 G3
KKNTL G66.....40 B1
MLNGV G62.....17 F3
STPS/GTHM/RID G33.....71 E1
Loch Shin EKILN G74.....167 E5
Lochside BAIL/MDB/MHD G69.....58 D5
BSDN G61.....51 H1
Lochside St PLKSD/SHW G41.....108 D3
Loch St AIRDRIE ML6.....98 C2
Loch Striven EKILN G74.....166 D4
Loch Torridon EKILN G74.....167 E5
Lochview Crs
STPS/GTHM/RID G33.....70 A3
Lochview Dr
STPS/GTHM/RID G33.....70 A3
Lochview Gdns
STPS/GTHM/RID G33.....70 A3
Lochview Pl
STPS/GTHM/RID G33.....70 A3
Lochview Rd BSDN G61.....34 B5
CTBR ML5.....73 H5
Loch Voil St CAR/SHTL G32.....93 E5
Lochwood Loan
BAIL/MDB/MHD G69.....42 B5

Lochwood St
STPS/GTHM/RID G33.....69 H4
Lochy Av RNFRW PA4.....64 A5
Lochy Pl ERSK PA8.....46 D1
Lochy St WISHAW ML2.....173 H4
Locke Gv MTHW ML1.....156 C1
Lockerbie Av
PLKSW/MSWD G43.....128 A1
Locket Yett Vw BLSH ML4.....135 F2
Lockhart Av BLTYR/CAMB G72.....132 C1
Lockhart Ct NMRNS G77.....161 G5
Lockhart Dr BLTYR/CAMB G72.....132 A1
NMRNS G77.....161 G5
Lockhart Pl UD/BTH/TAN G71.....134 A2
WISHAW ML2.....174 D1
Lockhart St HMLTN ML3.....180 C2
SPRGB/BLRNK G21.....69 E4
Lockhart Ter EKILN G74.....167 E5
Locksley Av CUMB G67.....44 D3
KVD/HLHD G12.....66 A2
Locksley Crs CUMB G67.....44 D3
Locksley Pl CUMB G67.....44 D3
Locksley Rd CUMB G67.....44 D3
PSLYS PA2.....103 E5
Locks St CTBR ML5.....97 G3
Logan Av NMRNS G77.....143 H4
Logandale Av WISHAW ML2.....158 A4
Logan Dr BALLOCH G68.....25 H2
PSLYN/LNWD PA3.....83 H5
Logan Gdns MTHW ML1.....155 F1
Loganlea Dr MTHW ML1.....155 F1
Logans Rd MTHW ML1.....154 A2
Logan St BLTYR/CAMB G72.....151 H3
GBLS G5.....110 A2
Loganswell Dr GIF/THBK G46.....126 B5
Loganswell Gdns
GIF/THBK G46.....126 B5
Loganswell Pl GIF/THBK G46.....126 B5
Loganswell Rd GIF/THBK G46.....126 B5
Logie Pk EKILN G74.....166 D2
Logie Sq EKILN G74.....166 D2
Lomax St STPS/GTHM/RID G33.....91 G1
Lomond Av RNFRW PA4.....63 E5
Lomond Ct BRHD/NEIL G78.....124 B5
CUMB G67.....44 B1
Lomond Crs BRWEIR PA11.....79 G4
CUMB G67.....44 A1
PSLYS PA2.....104 A3
Lomond Dr AIRDRIE ML6.....75 H5
BRHD/NEIL G78.....123 H5
BSHPBGS G64.....37 G5
CUMB G67.....44 A1
DMBTN G82.....13 G1
NMRNS G77.....161 G1
UD/BTH/TAN G71.....134 C4
WISHAW ML2.....173 H4
Lomond Gdns JNSTN PA5.....102 B2
Lomond Gv CUMB G67.....44 B1
Lomond Pl CTBR ML5.....74 B5
ERSK PA8.....46 D2
STPS/GTHM/RID G33.....71 E2
Lomond Rd BSDN G61.....51 G1
CTBR ML5.....74 A1
KKNTL G66.....40 A3
UD/BTH/TAN G71.....115 E3
Lomondside Av
CRMNK/CLK/EAG G76.....145 F2
Lomond St PPK/MIL G22.....67 G1
Lomond Vw BLTYR/CAMB G72.....149 F1
CUMB G67.....44 B1
HMLTN ML3.....169 E5
London Dr CAR/SHTL G32.....112 C1
London La DEN/PKHD G31.....111 G1
London Rd CGLE G1.....90 A3
DEN/PKHD G31.....111 G1
Lonend PSLY PA1.....104 C1
Longay Pl PPK/MIL G22.....53 H3
Longay St PPK/MIL G22.....53 H3
Long Crags Vw DMBTN G82.....13 H3
Longden St CLYDBK G81.....49 G3
Long Dr EKILS G75.....178 D1
Longford St
STPS/GTHM/RID G33.....91 G1
Longlee BAIL/MDB/MHD G69.....94 A5
Longmeadow JNSTN PA5.....100 D5
Longmorn Pl MTHW ML1.....155 G1
Long Rw BAIL/MDB/MHD G69.....94 B3
Longstone Rd
STPS/GTHM/RID G33.....92 C1
Longwill Ter CUMB G67.....26 D1
Lonmay Rd
STPS/GTHM/RID G33.....92 D1
Lonsdale Av GIF/THBK G46.....127 F4
Loom Wk KLBCH PA10.....100 B3
Lora Dr CARD/HILL/MSPK G52.....87 F5
Loretto Pl STPS/GTHM/RID G33.....92 A1
Loretto St STPS/GTHM/RID G33.....92 A1
Lorimer Crs EKILS G75.....178 A1
Lorn Av BAIL/MDB/MHD G69.....58 C3
Lorne Crs BSHPBGS G64.....38 C4
Lorne Dr MTHW ML1.....136 C5
PSLYN/LNWD PA3.....101 H1
Lorne Pl CTBR ML5.....97 G4
Lorne Rd CARD/HILL/MSPK G52.....86 A1
Lorne St BLTYR/CAMB G72.....131 E4
GOV/IBX G51.....89 E4
HMLTN ML3.....169 H1
Lorne Ter BLTYR/CAMB G72.....131 E4
Lorraine Gdns KVD/HLHD G12.....66 B2
Lorraine Gardens La
KVD/HLHD G12.....66 B2
Lorraine Rd KVD/HLHD G12.....66 B2
Loskin Dr PPK/MIL G22.....53 G4
Lossie Crs RNFRW PA4.....64 A4
Lossie St STPS/GTHM/RID G33.....69 G5
Lothian Crs PSLYS PA2.....104 A3
Lothian Dr
CRMNK/CLK/EAG G76.....145 G2
Lothian Gdns MRYH/FIRH G20.....66 D3
Lothian St
CARD/HILL/MSPK G52.....85 H1
Lothian Wy EKILN G74.....166 D2
Louden Hill Dr
STPS/GTHM/RID G33 *.....55 H5
Louden Hill Pl
STPS/GTHM/RID G33.....55 H5
Louden Hill Rd
STPS/GTHM/RID G33.....
Louden St AIRDRIE ML6.....98 D3
Loudon Gdns JNSTN PA5.....101 H3
Loudon Rd STPS/GTHM/RID G33.....70 C3
Loudonhill Av HMLTN ML3.....170 B4
Loudon Rd STPS/GTHM/RID G33.....56 C5
Loudon St WISHAW ML2.....157 H3
Louise Gdns BLSH ML4.....135 H2
Louisville Av WISHAW ML2.....157 G5
Lounsdale Av PSLYS PA2.....103 G1

Lounsdale Av PSLYS PA2.....103 F2
Lounsdale Crs PSLYS PA2.....103 F2
Lounsdale Dr PSLYS PA2.....103 G2
Lounsdale Pl SCOT G14.....64 C2
Lounsdale Rd PSLYS PA2.....103 F2
Lourdes Av
CARD/HILL/MSPK G52.....87 E5
Lovat Av BSDN G61.....34 B1
Lovat Dr KKNTL G66.....20 C5
Lovat Pl CARD/HILL/MSPK G52.....85 G3
RUTH G73.....130 C3
Love Av BRWEIR PA11.....78 B1
Love St PSLYN/LNWD PA3.....84 B3
Low Barholm KLBCH PA10.....100 C4
Low Broadlie Rd
BRHD/NEIL G78.....141 E2
Low Craigends KSYTH G65.....8 C2
Low Crs CLYDBK G81.....49 H2
Lower Auchingramont Rd
HMLTN ML3.....170 B1
Lower Bourtree Dr RUTH G73.....130 B3
Lower Mill Rd
CRMNK/CLK/EAG G76.....146 A4
Low Flender Rd
CRMNK/CLK/EAG G76.....145 G5
Lowndes St BRHD/NEIL G78.....142 A5
Low Parksail ERSK PA8.....47 E3
Low Patrick St HMLTN ML3.....170 C2
Low Rd PSLYS PA2.....104 B2
Lowther Av BSDN G61.....33 H1
Lowther Ter KVD/HLHD G12.....66 B2
Low Waters Rd HMLTN ML3.....170 B4
Loyal Av ERSK PA8.....47 E2
Loyal Gdns BSDN G61.....33 G1
Loyal Pl ERSK PA8.....47 E2
Loyne Dr RNFRW PA4.....64 A4
Luath St GOV/IBX G51.....88 A1
Lubas Av GVH/MTFL G42.....110 A5
Lubas Pl GVH/MTFL G42.....110 A5
Lubnaig Dr ERSK PA8.....46 C1
Lubnaig Gdns BSDN G61.....33 H1
Lubnaig Pl AIRDRIE ML6.....75 H4
Lubnaig Rd PLKSW/MSWD G43.....127 H2
Luckiesfauld BRHD/NEIL G78.....141 E3
Luckingsford Av RNFRW PA4.....47 H4
Luckingsford Dr RNFRW PA4.....47 H4
Luckingsford Rd RNFRW PA4.....47 H4
Lucy Brae UD/BTH/TAN G71.....114 D4
Luffness Gdns CAR/SHTL G32.....112 C1
Lugar Dr CARD/HILL/MSPK G52.....87 F5
Lugar Pl LNPK/KPK G44.....129 E1
Lugar St CTBR ML5.....97 E1
Luggiebank Pl
BAIL/MDB/MHD G69.....95 E5
Luggiebank Rd KKNTL G66.....21 F5
Luggie Vw CUMB G67.....43 H1
Luing Rd CARD/HILL/MSPK G52.....87 F2
Luma Gdns GOV/IBX G51.....86 D2
Lumloch St SPRGB/BLRNK G21.....68 D2
Lumsden La KVGV G3.....66 A5
Lumsden St KVGV G3.....88 A1
Lunan Dr BSHPBGS G64.....55 G3
Lunan Pl GOV/IBX G51.....87 F2
Luncarty Pl CAR/SHTL G32.....112 B1
Luncarty St CAR/SHTL G32.....112 B1
Lunderston Dr
PLK/PH/NH G53.....106 B5
Lundie Gdns BSHPBGS G64.....55 G3
Lundie St CAR/SHTL G32.....111 H1
Luss Brae HMLTN ML3.....168 D5
Lusset Gln OLDK G60.....30 C2
Lusset Rd OLDK G60.....30 C2
Lusshill Ter UD/BTH/TAN G71.....114 A2
Lye Brae CUMB G67.....27 E2
Lyell Gv EKILN G74.....166 B2
Lyell Pl EKILN G74.....166 B2
Lyle Crs BSHPTN PA7.....28 C2
Lyle Pl PSLYS PA2.....104 C2
Lyle Rd AIRDRIE ML6.....99 G2
Lylesland Ct PSLYS PA2.....104 B2
Lyle Sq MLNGV G62.....16 C3
Lyman Dr WISHAW ML2.....157 F3
Lymburn St KVGV G3.....66 C5
Lymekilns Rd EKILN G74.....166 A3
Lyndale Pl MRYH/FIRH G20.....52 C3
Lyndale Rd MRYH/FIRH G20.....52 C3
Lyndhurst Gdns MRYH/FIRH G20.....67 E3
Lyndhurst Gardens La
MRYH/FIRH G20.....67 E3
Lynebank Gv NMRNS G77.....161 G3
Lynebank Pl NMRNS G77.....161 G3
Lyne Cft BSHPBGS G64.....37 H4
Lyne Crs KVGV G3.....
Lynedoch Crs KVGV G3.....67 E5
Lynedoch Crescent La KVGV G3.....
Lynedoch Pl KVGV G3.....67 E5
Lynedoch St KVGV G3.....67 E5
Lynedoch Ter KVGV G3.....
Lyne St WISHAW ML2.....156 D5
Lynnburn Av BLSH ML4.....135 H2
Lynn Dr MLNGV G62.....17 F3
Lynne Dr SMSTN G23.....52 D2
Lynnhurst UD/BTH/TAN G71.....115 E5
Lynnwood Br AIRDRIE ML6.....
Lynton Av GIF/THBK G46.....144 D1
Lyoncross Av BRHD/NEIL G78.....124 C4
Lyoncross Crs BRHD/NEIL G78.....124 C4
Lyoncross Rd PLK/PH/NH G53.....106 C2
Lyon Rd ERSK PA8.....46 D2
PSLYN/LNWD PA3.....82 A5
Lysa Vale Pl BLSH ML4.....135 F2
Lytham Dr SMSTN G23.....52 D2
Lytham Mdw
UD/BTH/TAN G71.....133 H5
Lyttelton EKILS G75.....177 G1

M

Mabel St MTHW ML1.....154 D5
Macadam Gdns BLSH ML4.....135 H1
Macadam Pl EKILS G75.....196 B5
Macarthur Av AIRDRIE ML6.....
Macarthur Ct EKILN G74.....165 H2
Macarthur Crs EKILN G74.....165 H1
Macarthur Dr EKILN G74.....165 H2
Macarthur Wynd
BLTYR/CAMB G72.....131 H2
Macbeth EKILN G74.....149 G5
Macbeth Pl DEN/PKHD G31.....91 F5

Macbeth St *DEN/PKHD* G31 .....91 G5
Maccallum Dr
  BLTYR/CAMB G72 ....131 H2
Maccrimmon Pk *EKILN* G74 ....165 G1
Macdairmid Dr *HMLTN* ML3 .....180 B1
Macdonald Av *EKILN* G74 ......165 F1
Macdonald Crs *KSYTH* G65 ......23 G2
Macdonald Gv *BLSH* ML4 ....135 G5
Macdonald St *MTHW* ML1 ....137 H3
  RUTH G73 ....110 D4
Macdougal Dr
  BLTYR/CAMB G72 ....131 H2
Macdougall St
  PLKSW/MSWD G43 ....108 B5
Macdougall Rd *BLSH* ML4 ......135 G5
Macdowall St *JNSTN* PA5 ......101 G3
Macduff Pl *DEN/PKHD* G31 ......91 G5
Macduff St *DEN/PKHD* G31 ......91 G5
Macedonian Gv *MTHW* ML1 ......137 H3
Mace Rd *KNTSWD* G13 ....50 D2
Macfarlane Crs
  BLTYR/CAMB G72 ....131 H2
Macfarlane Rd *BSDN* G61 ....34 C5
Macfie Pl *EKILN* G74 ....165 G1
Machrie Dr *CSMK* G45 ....129 G3
  NMRNS G77 ....144 B4
Machrie Grn *EKILN* G74 ....165 G1
Machrie Rd *CSMK* G45 ....129 G3
Machrie St *CSMK* G45 ....129 G3
Macintosh Pl *EKILS* G75 ......177 H1
Macintyre St *KVGV* G3 ....2 A5
Macivor Crs *EKILN* G74 ....165 F1
Mackean St *PSLYN/LNWD* PA3 ...83 H3
Mackeith St *DMNK/BRGTN* G40 ..90 C5
Mackenzie Ct *EKILN* G74 ......165 F1
Mackenzie Gdns *EKILN* G74 ....165 F1
Mackenzie Ter *BLSH* ML4 ......116 D5
Mackie's Mill Rd *JNSTN* PA5 ..102 C4
Mackinlay St *GBLS* G5 ....89 G5
Mack St *AIRDRIE* ML6 ....98 B1
Maclay Pk *KLBCH* PA10 ....100 B4
Maclean Ct *EKILN* G74 ....165 G1
Maclean Gv *EKILN* G74 ....165 G1
Maclean Pl *EKILN* G74 ....165 G1
Maclean St *GOV/IBX* G51 ....89 F3
  CLYDBK G81 ....49 H5
  GOV/IBX G51 ....88 C3
Maclehose Rd *CUMB* G67 ....27 E2
Maclellan Rd *BRHD/NEIL* G78 ..141 F4
Maclellan St *PLKSD/SHW* G41 ...88 C4
Macleod Pl *EKILN* G74 ....167 E3
Macleod St *COWCAD* G4 ....3 K5
Macleod Wy *BLTYR/CAMB* G72 ..131 H2
Macmillan Gdns
  UD/BTH/TAN G71 ....115 F4
Macneill Dr *EKILN* G74 ....165 F1
Macneill Gdns *EKILN* G74 .....165 F1
Macneish Wy *EKILN* G74 ....165 F1
Macnicol Ct *EKILN* G74 ....165 F1
Macnicol Pk *EKILN* G74 ....165 F1
Macnicol Pl *EKILN* G74 ....165 F1
Macpherson Pk *EKILN* G74 .....165 G1
Macphie Rd *DMBTN* G82 ....13 H5
Macrae Gdns *EKILN* G74 ....165 G2
Macrimmon Pl *EKILS* G75 ......166 B5
Mactaggart Rd *CUMB* G67 ....26 A5
Madison Av *LNPK/KPK* G44 .....128 C2
Madras Pl *BRHD/NEIL* G78 .....141 F3
Madras St *DMNK/BRGTN* G40 ...110 C1
Mafeking St *GOV/IBX* G51 ....88 C3
  WISHAW ML2 ....173 F1
Magna St *MTHW* ML1 ....154 A2
Magnolia Dr *BLTYR/CAMB* G72 .132 C4
Magnolia Pl *UD/BTH/TAN* G71 .115 H4
Magnolia St *WISHAW* ML2 ......157 E5
Magnus Crs *LNPK/KPK* G44 ....128 C3
Magnus Rd *CRC/CRSL/HOU* PA6 ..80 D3
Mahon Ct *BAIL/MDB/MHD* G69 ...58 C5
Maidens *EKILN* G74 ....166 A2
Maidens Av *NMRNS* G77 ....144 D5
Maitland Pl *PLK/PH/NH* G53 ..106 D5
Maitland Rd
  AIRDRIE ML6 ....118 D2
  BAIL/MDB/MHD G69 ....58 C2
  BAIL/MDB/MHD G69 ....94 B5
  BLSH ML4 ....135 H4
  BLTYR/CAMB G72 ....131 E1
  BLTYR/CAMB G72 ....151 F4
  BRHD/NEIL G78 ....124 B5
  BRWEIR PA11 ....79 G3
  BSDN G61 ....34 C1
  BSHPBGCS G64 ....19 F5
  CRMNK/CLK/EAG G76 ....146 A4
  CTBR ML5 ....96 D3
  CUMB G67 ....10 D5
  DMNK/BRGTN G40 ....90 B5
  EKILN G74 ....166 C3
  GIF/THBK G46 ....126 C4
  PLK/PH/NH G53 ....120 A4
  KKNTL G66 ....4 B2
  KSYTH G65 ....8 C4
  KSYTH G65 ....23 F1
  MLNGV G62 ....17 E4
  MTHW ML1 ....157 F1
  RUTH G73 ....111 F3
  UD/BTH/TAN G71 ....133 H1
  UD/BTH/TAN G71 ....134 B5
  WISHAW ML2 ....173 H2
Mains Wd *ERSK* PA8 ....48 A3
Mair St *GOV/IBX* G51 ....88 D3

Maitland Dr *BSHPBGCS* G64 .....19 F4
Maitland Pl *RNFRW* PA4 ....63 E4
Maitland St *COWCAD* G4 ....2 E1
Malborough La North *PTCK* G11 .65 G5
Malborough La South *PTCK* G11 .65 G5
Malcolm Gdns *EKILN* G74 ......165 H5
Malcolm St *MTHW* ML1 ....154 B4
Mallaig Pl *GOV/IBX* G51 ....87 E2
Mallaig Rd *GOV/IBX* G51 ....87 E2
Mallard Crs *EKILS* G75 ....177 F3
Mallard Pl *EKILS* G75 ....177 F3
Mallard Rd *CLYDBK* G81 ....32 A3
Mallard Ter *EKILS* G75 ....178 B3
Mallard Wy *BLSH* ML4 ....116 C3
Malleable Gdns *MTHW* ML1 .....136 B5
Malletsheugh Rd *NMRNS* G77 ..161 E2
Malloch Crs *JNSTN* PA5 ....102 A2
Malloch Pl *EKILN* G74 ....167 E3
Malloch St *MRYH/FIRH* G20 ......66 D1
Mallot's Vw *NMRNS* G77 ....161 E2
Malov Ct *EKILS* G75 ....178 B3
Maltbarns St *MRYH/FIRH* G20 ...67 F3
Mamberg Dr *GOV/IBX* G51 ....87 F1
Mamore Pl *PLKSW/MSWD* G43 ...127 F1
Mamore St *PLKSW/MSWD* G43 ...127 F1
Manchester Dr *KVD/HLHD* G12 ...51 H5
Manitoba Crs *EKILS* G74 ......165 G4
Mannering *EKILN* G74 ....167 G1
Mannering Ct *PLKSD/SHW* G41 .108 B4
Mannering Rd
  PLKSD/SHW G41 ....108 B4
  PSLYS PA2 ....102 D4
Mannoch Pl *CTBR* ML5 ....97 H4
Mannofield *BSDN* G61 ....34 A4
Manor Dr *AIRDRIE* ML6 ....97 H1
Manor Ga *NMRNS* G77 ....162 A2
Manor Rd *BAIL/MDB/MHD* G69 ...75 E1
  BRHD/NEIL G78 ....141 E5
  BSDN G61 ....34 A4
  CAR/SHTL G32 ....93 E5
  CRMNK/CLK/EAG G76 ....147 E5
  KSYTH G65 ....8 C5
  PTCK G11 ....171 H3
  OLDK G60 ....30 D2
  WISHAW ML2 ....175 E1
Manse St *CTBR* ML5 ....96 A5
Manse Brae *LNPK/KPK* G44 .....128 C1
Manse Ct *BRHD/NEIL* G78 ......124 C4
  KSYTH G65 ....8 B1
Mansefield Av
  BLTYR/CAMB G72 ....151 E1
Mansefield Crs *OLDK* G60 ....30 B2
Mansel St *SPRGB/BLRNK* G21 ...68 C1
Manse Pl *AIRDRIE* ML6 ....99 E2
Manse Rd *BAIL/MDB/MHD* G69 ...94 D3
  BRHD/NEIL G78 ....141 E5
  BSDN G61 ....34 A4
  CAR/SHTL G32 ....93 E5
  CRMNK/CLK/EAG G76 ....147 E5
  KSYTH G65 ....8 C5
Mansewood Dr *DMBTN* G82 ....13 G2
Mansewood Rd *GIF/THBK* G46 ..127 E3
Mansfield Crs
  CRMNK/CLK/EAG G76 ....145 G4
Mansfield Rd *BLSH* ML4 ....135 G3
  CARD/HILL/MSPK G52 ....86 A2
  GOV/IBX G51 ....88 B3
Mansfield St *PTCK* G11 ....66 A4
Mansion Ct *BLTYR/CAMB* G72 ..131 F1
Mansionhouse Av
  CAR/SHTL G32 ....112 D4
Mansionhouse Dr
  CAR/SHTL G32 ....92 D3
Mansionhouse Gdns
  PLKSD/SHW G41 ....108 D5
Mansionhouse Gv
  CAR/SHTL G32 ....113 F1
Mansionhouse Rd
  CAR/SHTL G32 ....93 F5
  PLKSD/SHW G41 ....108 D5
  PSLY PA1 ....84 D4
Mansion St *BLTYR/CAMB* G72 ..131 F1
  PPK/MIL G22 ....67 H1
Manson Pl *EKILS* G75 ....178 D3
Maple Av *KKNTL* G66 ....5 F5
Maple Bank *HMLTN* ML3 ....170 C3
Maple Ct *CUMB* G67 ....27 E1
Maple Crs *BLTYR/CAMB* G72 ..132 C4
Maple Dr *BRHD/NEIL* G78 ......142 C2
  CLYDBK G81 ....121 C1
  JNSTN PA5 ....102 A4
  KKNTL G66 ....39 F5
Maple Pl *EKILS* G75 ....177 G2
  UD/BTH/TAN G71 ....116 A4
Maple Qd *AIRDRIE* ML6 ....11 H5
Maple Rd *CUMB* G67 ....137 G2
  MTHW ML1 ....137 G2
  PLKSD/SHW G41 ....88 A5
Maple Ter *EKILS* G75 ....177 G2
Maplewood *WISHAW* ML2 ....173 E4
Mar Av *BSHPTN* PA7 ....46 B1
Marchbank Gdns *PSLY* PA1 ......85 G5
Marchfield Av
  PSLYN/LNWD PA3 ....84 A1
Marchglen Pl *GOV/IBX* G51 .....87 E2
Marchmont Gdns *BSHPBGCS* G64 ..37 G5
Marchmont Ter *KVD/HLHD* G12 ...66 C4
March St *PLKSD/SHW* G41 .....109 E2
Mardale *EKILN* G74 ....166 A2
Mar Dr *BSDN* G61 ....34 C1
Maree Dr *CARD/HILL/MSPK* G52 .87 H4
  CUMB G67 ....26 C4
Maree Gdns *BSHPBGCS* G64 ......55 E2
Maree Rd *PSLYS* PA2 ....103 G3
Marfield St *CAR/SHTL* G32 ......91 H3
Margaret Dr *AIRDRIE* ML6 ......118 C2
Margaret Pl *BLSH* ML4 ....135 G3
Margaret Rd *HMLTN* ML3 ....152 C4
Margaret St *CTBR* ML5 ....96 C2
Marguerite Av *KKNTL* G66 ......39 H2
Marguerite Gdns
  UD/BTH/TAN G71 ....135 F3
  UD/BTH/TAN G71 ....134 B5
  WISHAW ML2 ....173 H2
Marian Dr *MTHW* ML1 ....154 D2
Marigold Av *MTHW* ML1 ....155 F4
Marina Ct *BLSH* ML4 ....135 F4
Marine Crs *GOV/IBX* G51 ....88 D3

Marine Gdns *GOV/IBX* G51 ....89 E3
Mariner Ct *BLSH* ML4 ....48 D1
Marion St *BLSH* ML4 ....136 C2
Mariscat Rd *PLKSD/SHW* G41 ..108 D2
Marius Crs *MTHW* ML1 ....154 B1
Marjory Dr *PSLYN/LNWD* PA3 ...84 D2
Marjory Rd *RNFRW* PA4 ....62 D5
Markdow Av *PLK/PH/NH* G53 ..106 B5
Markethill Rd *EKILN* G74 .....148 C4
Market Rd *KKNTL* G66 ....40 D1
  UD/BTH/TAN G71 ....115 H5
Market St *AIRDRIE* ML6 ....98 B2
  UD/BTH/TAN G71 ....115 H5
Marlach Pl *PLK/PH/NH* G53 ...106 B4
Marlborough Av *PTCK* G11 ......65 G3
Marlborough Pk *EKILS* G75 ....177 F1
Marldon La *PTCK* G11 ....65 G3
Marley Wy *KKNTL* G66 ....5 E4
Marlfield Gdns *BLSH* ML4 .....116 D5
Marlow St *PLKSD/SHW* G41 ......88 D5
Marlow Ter *PLKSD/SHW* G41 .....88 D5
Marmion Crs *HMLTN* ML3 ....66 F1
Marmion Dr *KKNTL* G66 ....21 H5
Marmion Pl *CUMB* G67 ....44 D1
Marmion Rd *CUMB* G67 ....44 D1
  PSLYS PA2 ....102 D4
Marne St *DEN/PKHD* G31 ....91 E2
Marnock Ter *PSLYS* PA2 ....104 C2
Marquis Av *HMLTN* ML3 ....152 C4
Marrswood Av *HMLTN* ML3 .....169 F1
Marrwood Av *KKNTL* G66 ....41 E2
Marshall La *WISHAW* ML2 ......173 G2
Marshall's La *PSLY* PA1 ....84 B5
Marshall St *CTBR* ML5 ....96 A5
  WISHAW ML2 ....173 G3
Martha St *CCLE* G1 ....3 G4
Martin Ct *HMLTN* ML3 ....169 H2
Martin Crs *BAIL/MDB/MHD* G69 .94 B4
Martin Pl *MTHW* ML1 ....137 H4
Martinside *EKILS* G75 ....178 C3
Martin St *CTBR* ML5 ....97 G2
  DMNK/BRGTN G40 ....110 C1
Mart St *CCLE* G1 ....3 G7
Martyn St *AIRDRIE* ML6 ....97 H2
Martyrs Pl *BSHPBGCS* G64 ......54 D3
Marwick St *DEN/PKHD* G31 ......91 E2
Mary Dr *BLSH* ML4 ....135 G4
Mary Gln *WISHAW* ML2 ....157 G4
Maryhill Rd *BSDN* G61 ....51 H1
  COWCAD G4 ....2 B1
  MRYH/FIRH G20 ....67 G3
Maryknowe Rd *MTHW* ML1 ......155 H1
Maryland Dr
  CARD/HILL/MSPK G52 ....87 H4
Maryland Gdns
  CARD/HILL/MSPK G52 ....87 H4
Maryland Rd *DMBTN* G82 ....13 H1
Mary Rae Rd *BLSH* ML4 ....135 F4
Maryston St
  STPS/GTHM/RID G33 ....69 G4
Mary St *HMLTN* ML3 ....170 A3
  JNSTN PA5 ....101 H3
  PSLYS PA2 ....104 B2
Maryville Av *GIF/THBK* G46 ...127 E5
Maryville Gdns *GIF/THBK* G46 .127 F5
Maryville Vw *UD/BTH/TAN* G71 .114 C3
Marywood Sq *PLKSD/SHW* G41 ..109 E2
Mary Young Pl
  CRMNK/CLK/EAG G76 ....146 A4
Masonfield Av *BALLOCH* G68 ....25 H3
Mason La *MTHW* ML1 ....154 D4
Masterton St *COWCAD* G4 ....67 H3
Masterton Wy
  UD/BTH/TAN G71 ....115 G3
Matherton Av *NMRNS* G77 .....145 E5
Mathieson Crs
  STPS/GTHM/RID G33 ....71 G1
Mathieson Rd *RUTH* G73 ....111 F3
Matilda Rd *PLKSD/SHW* G41 ...108 D1
Mauchline *EKILN* G74 ....166 A2
Mauchline Av *KKNTL* G66 ....22 A3
Mauchline St *HMLTN* ML3 .....168 C3
  GBLS G5 ....89 F5
Maukinfauld Ct *CAR/SHTL* G32 .111 E1
Mauldslie St *BLSH* ML4 ....135 H3
  CTBR ML5 ....96 D4
  DMNK/BRGTN G40 ....110 D1
Maule Dr *PTCK* G11 ....65 H4
Mavis Bank *BSHPBGCS* G64 ......54 A5
Mavisbank Gdns *BLSH* ML4 ....135 H1
  GOV/IBX G51 ....88 D3
Mavisbank Rd *AIRDRIE* ML6 .....97 H1
Mavisbank St *AIRDRIE* ML6 .....97 H1
Mavisbank Ter *JNSTN* PA5 ....101 G4
  PSLY PA1 ....104 C1
Mavor Av *EKILN* G74 ....149 F5
Maxton Av *BRHD/NEIL* G78 ....124 A4
Maxton Crs *WISHAW* ML2 ......157 F4
Maxton Gv *BRHD/NEIL* G78 ....123 H5
Maxton Ter *BLTYR/CAMB* G72 ..131 E4
Maxwell Av
  BAIL/MDB/MHD G69 ....93 H5
  BSDN G61 ....51 F1
  PLKSD/SHW G41 ....88 D5
Maxwell Dr
  BAIL/MDB/MHD G69 ....93 G4
  EKILN G74 ....166 C3
  ERSK PA8 ....30 A5
  PLKSD/SHW G41 ....88 C5
Maxwell Gdns *PLKSD/SHW* G41 ..88 C5
Maxwell Gv *PLKSD/SHW* G41 ....88 C5
Maxwell Oaks *PLKSD/SHW* G41 ..88 D5
Maxwell Pl *BRWEIR* PA11 ......79 E3
  PLKSD/SHW G41 ....109 F1
  UD/BTH/TAN G71 ....134 B1
Maxwell Rd *BSHPTN* PA7 ....46 A1
  PLKSD/SHW G41 ....89 E5
Maxwell St *BAIL/MDB/MHD* G69 .94 A5
  CCLE G1 ....3 F6
  CLYDBK G81 ....31 G4
  PSLYN/LNWD PA3 ....84 A3
Maxwellton Av *EKILN* G74 ....166 D3
Maxwellton Pl *EKILN* G74 ....167 E2
Maxwellton Rd *EKILN* G74 ....166 C3
  PSLY PA1 ....83 G5
Maxwellton St *PSLYS* PA2 .....103 H1
Maxwelton Rd
  STPS/GTHM/RID G33 ....69 G4

Maybank La *GVH/MTFL* G42 ....109 F3
Maybank St *GVH/MTFL* G42 ....109 F3
Mayberry Crs *CAR/SHTL* G32 ....92 D4
Mayberry Gdns *CAR/SHTL* G32 ..93 E4
Mayberry Gv *CAR/SHTL* G32 ....93 E4
Mayberry Pl *BLTYR/CAMB* G72 .151 G2
Maybole Crs *NMRNS* G77 ......162 B1
Maybole Gdns *HMLTN* ML3 .....168 D4
Maybole Gv *NMRNS* G77 ....162 B1
Maybole Pl *CTBR* ML5 ....117 G1
Maybole St *PLK/PH/NH* G53 ...106 A5
Mayfield Av
  CRMNK/CLK/EAG G76 ....145 H3
Mayfield Ct *HWWD* PA9 ....120 A4
Mayfield Crs *HWWD* PA9 ....120 A3
Mayfield Dr *HWWD* PA9 ....120 A3
Mayfield Pl *CTBR* ML5 ....116 D1
Mayfield Rd *HMLTN* ML3 ......169 E1
Mayfield St *MRYH/FIRH* G20 ....67 E2
May Rd *PSLYS* PA2 ....103 H5
May St *HMLTN* ML3 ....153 E5
May Ter *GIF/THBK* G46 ....127 F4
  GVH/MTFL G42 ....109 G4
McAllister Av *AIRDRIE* ML6 ....99 E1
McAlpine St *KVGV* G3 ....2 C6
  WISHAW ML2 ....174 A3
McArdle Av *MTHW* ML1 ....155 H1
McArthur Pk *KKNTL* G66 ....39 H1
McArthur St
  PLKSW/MSWD G43 ....108 B5
McAslin Ct *COWCAD* G4 ....3 J5
McAslin St *COWCAD* G4 ....3 J4
McCallum Av *RUTH* G73 ....111 E5
McCallum Gdns *BLSH* ML4 .....116 A4
McCallum Gv *EKILN* G74 ......165 G1
McCallum Pl *EKILN* G74 ......165 G1
McCarrison Rd *WISHAW* ML2 ...158 B4
McCash Pl *KKNTL* G66 ....39 H1
McClue Av *RNFRW* PA4 ....63 E2
McClue Rd *RNFRW* PA4 ....63 E1
McCormack Gdns *MTHW* ML1 ..138 B3
McCracken Av *RNFRW* PA4 .....63 E4
McCracken Dr
  UD/BTH/TAN G71 ....115 H4
McCreery St *CLYDBK* G81 ......49 G3
McCulloch Av
  UD/BTH/TAN G71 ....134 D1
McCulloch St *PLKSD/SHW* G41 ..89 E5
McDonald Av *JNSTN* PA5 ......101 F5
McDonald Crs *CLYDBK* G81 .....49 G3
McDonald Pl *BRHD/NEIL* G78 ..141 F3
  MTHW ML1 ....137 G2
McEwan Gdns *EKILN* G74 ......165 F1
McFarlane St *COWCAD* G4 ....3 K7
  PSLYN/LNWD PA3 ....83 H2
McGhee St *CLYDBK* G81 ....32 A1
McGowan Pl *HMLTN* ML3 ......152 B5
McGown St *PSLYN/LNWD* PA3 ...84 A3
McGregor Av *AIRDRIE* ML6 ......99 E1
  RNFRW PA4 ....63 E4
McGregor Dr *DMBTN* G82 ....13 G3
McGregor Rd *CUMB* G67 ....26 A4
McGregor St *CLYDBK* G81 ......49 G3
  GOV/IBX G51 ....87 E3
McGregor Rd *MLNGV* G62 ....90 C3
McIntosh Ct *DEN/PKHD* G31 ....90 C2
McIntosh St *DEN/PKHD* G31 ....90 C2
McIntosh Qd *BLSH* ML4 ....135 G5
McIntyre Pl *PSLYS* PA2 ......104 A2
McIntyre Ter *BLTYR/CAMB* G72 131 F1
McIver St *BLTYR/CAMB* G72 ...132 A1
McKay Crs *JNSTN* PA5 ....101 H4
McKay Gv *BLSH* ML4 ....135 G2
McKay Pl *EKILN* G74 ....165 F1
  NMRNS G77 ....161 F1
McKechnie St *GOV/IBX* G51 .....87 H1
McKenna Dr *AIRDRIE* ML6 ......97 H1
McKenzie Av *CLYDBK* G81 ......32 A4
McKenzie St *PSLYN/LNWD* PA3 .83 H4
McKeown Gdns *BLSH* ML4 .....136 C2
McKerrell St *PSLY* PA1 ....84 D4
McLaren Av *RNFRW* PA4 ....63 F4
McLaren Ct *GIF/THBK* G46 ....145 E1
McLaren Crs *MRYH/FIRH* G20 ...52 D4
McLaren Dr *BLSH* ML4 ....136 C3
McLaren Gdns *MRYH/FIRH* G20 .52 D4
McLaurin Crs *JNSTN* PA5 .....101 E5
McLean Dr *BLSH* ML4 ....135 G5
McLean Pl *PSLYN/LNWD* PA3 ...84 A2
McLees La *MTHW* ML1 ....154 B3
McLennan St *GVH/MTFL* G42 ..109 G4
McLeod Rd *DMBTN* G82 ....13 H3
McMahon Dr *WISHAW* ML2 .....158 B4
McMahon Gv *BLSH* ML4 ....136 A1
McMillan Rd *WISHAW* ML2 .....157 E4
McNair St *CAR/SHTL* G32 ....92 C4
McNeil Av *CLYDBK* G81 ....49 H2
McNeil Dr *MTHW* ML1 ....138 C1
McNeil Gdns *GBLS* G5 ....90 A5
McNeil St *GBLS* G5 ....90 A5
McPhail Av *MTHW* ML1 ....138 C2
McPhail St *DMNK/BRGTN* G40 ..90 B5
McPherson Crs *AIRDRIE* ML6 ..119 E3
McPherson Dr
  UD/BTH/TAN G71 ....134 C4
McPherson St *BLSH* ML4 ......135 H4
McShannon Gv *BLSH* ML4 .....136 A3
Meadow Av *BLTYR/CAMB* G72 ..151 G4
  ERSK PA8 ....47 E2
Meadowbank La *UD/BTH/TAN* G71 133 H1
Meadowbank St *DMBTN* G82 .....13 E4
Meadowburn *BSHPBGCS* G64 .....37 H4
Meadowburn Av *NMRNS* G77 ....40 B3
  NMRNS G77 ....162 A1
Meadowburn Rd *WISHAW* ML2 .174 B2
Meadow Ct *EKILS* G75 ....177 F4
Meadowfield Pl *WISHAW* ML2 .158 B4
Meadowhead Av
  BAIL/MDB/MHD G69 ....59 E1
Meadowhead Rd *AIRDRIE* ML6 ..77 G3
  WISHAW ML2 ....173 E1
Meadowhill *NMRNS* G77 ....144 B5
Meadow La *RNFRW* PA4 ....63 G1
Meadowpark St *DEN/PKHD* G31 ..91 E2
Meadow Ri *NMRNS* G77 ....143 H5
Meadow Rd *DMBTN* G82 ....13 E4
  MTHW ML1 ....155 H1
  PTCK G11 ....65 H4
Meadows Dr *ERSK* PA8 ....47 H2

Meadowside *HMLTN* ML3 ....180 D2
Meadowside Av *JNSTN* PA5 ....102 C2
Meadowside Gdns *AIRDRIE* ML6 .99 E2
Meadowside Pl *AIRDRIE* ML6 ...99 E2
Meadowside Rd *KSYTH* G65 .....23 G1
Meadowside St *PTCK* G11 ......65 H5
  RNFRW PA4 ....63 G1
The Meadows
  CRC/CRSL/HOU PA6 ....81 E3
Meadow St *CTBR* ML5 ....97 E5
Meadow Vw *AIRDRIE* ML6 ....77 H5
  CUMB G67 ....27 E1
Meadow Wk *CTBR* ML5 ....97 E4
Meadow Wy *NMRNS* G77 ....144 A5
Meadowwell St *CAR/SHTL* G32 ..92 D4
Meadside Av *KLBCH* PA10 ......100 B2
Meadside Rd *KLBCH* PA10 ......100 B2
Mealkirk St *CLYDBK* G81 ....32 B1
Mearns Ct *HMLTN* ML3 ....181 E1
Mearnscroft Gdns *NMRNS* G77 .162 A2
Mearnscroft Rd *NMRNS* G77 ...161 G4
Mearnskirk Rd *NMRNS* G77 ...161 G4
Mearns Rd *MTHW* ML1 ....154 B2
  NMRNS G77 ....161 F5
Medlar Rd *CUMB* G67 ....27 F1
Medroc Gdns *CUMB* G67 ....43 G5
Medwin Gdns *EKILS* G75 ......176 D1
Medwin St *BLTYR/CAMB* G72 ..132 A2
Meek Pl *BLTYR/CAMB* G72 .....131 G2
Meetinghouse La *PSLY* PA1 ....84 B4
Megan St *DMNK/BRGTN* G40 ....90 C5
Meikle Av *RNFRW* PA4 ....63 F4
Meikle Bin Brae *KKNTL* G66 .....4 C3
Meikle Crs *HMLTN* ML3 ....180 C1
Meikle Earnock Rd
  HMLTN ML3 ....180 C1
Meiklehill Av *KKNTL* G66 ......21 G4
Meiklehill Rd *KKNTL* G66 ......21 G4
Meiklerig Crs *PLK/PH/NH* G53 106 D2
Meiklerigs Dr *PSLYS* PA2 .....103 F3
Meikle Rd *PLK/PH/NH* G53 ....106 D4
Meiklewood Rd *GOV/IBX* G51 ...87 E3
Melbourne Av *CLYDBK* G81 .....31 E3
Melbourne Ct *GIF/THBK* G46 ..127 G4
Melbourne Gn *EKILS* G75 .....165 H5
Melbourne St
  DMNK/BRGTN G40 ....90 C3
Meldon Pl *GOV/IBX* G51 ....87 E2
Meldrum Gdns
  PLKSD/SHW G41 ....108 C2
Meldrum Mains *AIRDRIE* ML6 ...75 H2
Meldrum St *CLYDBK* G81 ....49 H3
Melford Av *GIF/THBK* G46 ....127 G5
  KKNTL G66 ....20 D5
Melford Rd *BLSH* ML4 ....135 F1
Melford Av *CLYDBK* G81 ....31 G4
Melfort Av *PLKSD/SHW* G41 ....88 A5
Melfort Rd *HMLTN* ML3 ....168 D2
Mellerstain Dr *SCOT* G14 ......49 H5
Melness Pl *GOV/IBX* G51 ....86 D2
Melrose Av *AIRDRIE* ML6 .....119 E2
  BAIL/MDB/MHD G69 ....95 E4
  MTHW ML1 ....137 G2
  PSLYN/LNWD PA3 ....101 H1
  PSLYS PA2 ....103 F4
  RUTH G73 ....111 E5
Melrose Crs *WISHAW* ML2 .....173 F2
Melrose Gdns *MRYH/FIRH* G20 ..67 E3
  BLTYR/CAMB G72 ....151 F1
  CTBR ML5 ....96 C2
Melrose Rd *CUMB* G67 ....44 D1
Melrose St *COWCAD* G4 ....2 B1
  HMLTN ML3 ....152 C5
Melrose Ter *MRYH/FIRH* G20 ...67 E3
  HMLTN ML3 ....152 C4
Melvaig Pl *MRYH/FIRH* G20 ....66 C1
Melvick Pl *GOV/IBX* G51 ....87 E2
Melville Ct *CGLE* G1 ....3 G7
Melville Dr *MTHW* ML1 ....154 D4
Melville Gdns *BSHPBGCS* G64 ..54 D1
Melville Pk *EKILN* G74 ....167 E2
Melville St *PLKSD/SHW* G41 ..109 E1
Memel St *PPK/MIL* G22 ....68 B1
Memus Av
  CARD/HILL/MSPK G52 ....86 D5
Mendip La *EKILS* G75 ....177 F3
Mennock Ct *HMLTN* ML3 ....168 D3
Mennock Dr *BSHPBGCS* G64 .....37 H4
Mennock St *MTHW* ML1 ....139 F5
Menock Rd *LNPK/KPK* G44 ....128 C1
Menteith Av *BSHPBGCS* G64 ....55 E2
Menteith Ct *MTHW* ML1 ....155 E3
Menteith Dr *RUTH* G73 ....130 C5
Menteith Gdns *BSDN* G61 ......16 A5
Menteith Pl *RUTH* G73 ....130 C5
Menteith Rd *MTHW* ML1 ....154 D1
Menzies Dr *SPRGB/BLRNK* G21 ..68 D1
Menzies Pl *SPRGB/BLRNK* G21 ..68 D1
Menzies Rd *SPRGB/BLRNK* G21 ..68 D1
Merchant La *KLBCH* PA10 .....100 B2
Merchiston Av
  PSLYN/LNWD PA3 ....101 G1
Merchiston Dr *JNSTN* PA5 ....101 E1
Merchiston St *CAR/SHTL* G32 ..91 H2
Merkins Av *DMBTN* G82 ....13 G1
Merkland Dr *KKNTL* G66 ....22 A4
Merkland Pl *KKNTL* G66 ....21 H4
Merkland Rd *CTBR* ML5 ....96 A4
Merkland St *PTCK* G11 ....66 A4
Merkland Wy *EKILS* G75 ......177 H4
Merlewood Av
  BAIL/MDB/MHD G69 ....34 C3
Merlin Av *BLSH* ML4 ....116 A4
Merlinford Av *RNFRW* PA4 .....63 H3
Merlinford Crs *RNFRW* PA4 ....63 H3
Merlinford Dr *RNFRW* PA4 .....63 H3
Merlinford Wy *RNFRW* PA4 .....63 H3
Merlin Wy *PSLYN/LNWD* PA3 ...85 E3
Merrick Ct *KLBCH* PA10 ....100 A3
Merrick Gdns *BSDN* G61 ....33 H1
  GOV/IBX G51 ....88 A4
Merrick Wy *RUTH* G73 ....130 A4
Merry St *MTHW* ML1 ....154 D3
Merrycrest Av *GIF/THBK* G46 .127 G3
Merrycroft Av *GIF/THBK* G46 .127 G3
Merryflats *KSYTH* G65 ....23 E1
Merryland Pl *GOV/IBX* G51 .....88 B2
Merryland St *GOV/IBX* G51 .....88 A2
Merrylee Crs
  PLKSW/MSWD G43 ....127 F2

Merrylee Pk GIF/THBK G46......127 F2
Merrylee Park Av
  GIF/THBK G46......127 G3
Merrylee Rd
  PLKSW/MSWD G43......127 H2
Merrylees Rd
  BLTYR/CAMB G72......151 F5
Merrystone St CTBR ML5......96 C2
Merrick Av MTHW ML1......154 D3
Merryton Av DRUM G15......33 G5
Merryton Pl DRUM G15......33 G5
Merryton Rd MTHW ML1......172 C3
Merryvale Av
  PLKSW/MSWD G43......127 G3
Merryvale Pl
  PLKSW/MSWD G43......127 F2
Merton Dr
  CARD/HILL/MSPK G52......86 B4
Meryon Gdns CAR/SHTL G32......113 G2
Meryon Rd CAR/SHTL G32......113 F1
Methil St SCOT G14......64 D3
Methlan Pk DMBTN G82......12 C5
Methlan Park Gdns DMBTN G82......12 C5
Methlick Av AIRDRIE ML6......117 F5
Methuen Rd PSLYN/LNWD PA3......84 C1
Methven Av BSDN G61......35 E3
Methven Pl EKILN G74......165 H5
Methven St CLYDBK G81......144 D4
  DEN/PKHD G31......111 G1
Metropole La CGLE G1......89 H5
Mews La PSLYN/LNWD PA3......84 C1
Mey Ct NMRNS G77......160 D1
Mey Pl NMRNS G77......160 D1
Michael McParland Dr
  BSHPBGS G64......19 F5
Michael Ter AIRDRIE ML6......119 E3
Micklehouse Ov
  BAIL/MDB/MHD G69......94 A3
Micklehouse Pl
  BAIL/MDB/MHD G69......94 A3
Micklehouse Rd
  BAIL/MDB/MHD G69......94 A3
Micklehouse Wynd
  BAIL/MDB/MHD G69......94 A3
Midas Pl BLSH ML4......136 D2
Mid Barrwood Rd KSYTH G65......8 D3
Mid Barwood Rd KSYTH G65......9 E2
Mid Carbarns WISHAW ML2......173 E4
Midcroft Av LNPK/KPK G44......128 C3
Middlefield EKILS G75......178 B3
Middlemuir Rd KKNTL G66......40 A2
Middlerigg Rd BALLOCH G68......25 H3
Middlesex Gdns
  PLKSD/SHW G41......88 D4
Middlesex St PLKSD/SHW G41......88 D4
Middleton Crs
  PSLYN/LNWD PA3......83 G3
Middleton Dr MLNGV G62......17 E3
Middleton Rd PSLYN/LNWD PA3......82 B2
Middleton St GOV/IBX G51......88 C3
Middle Ward St CLYDBK G81......32 C1
Midfaulds Av RNFRW PA4......63 H4
Midland St CGLE G1......3 G6
Midlem Dr
  CARD/HILL/MSPK G52......86 D4
Midlem Ov
  CARD/HILL/MSPK G52......86 D4
Midlock St GOV/IBX G51......88 B4
Midlothian Dr PLKSD/SHW G41......108 C5
Mid Pk EKILS G75......166 B5
Mid Rd CUMB G67......45 E2
Midton St SPRGB/BLRNK G21......68 C3
Mid-Wharf St COWCAD G4......67 F1
Migvie Pl MRYH/FIRH G20......66 B1
Milford EKILS G75......177 G1
Milford St STPS/GTHM/RID G33......92 B1
Milands Av BLTYR/CAMB G72......151 F1
Millarbank St
  SPRGB/BLRNK G21......68 B2
Millar Gv HMLTN ML3......169 G2
Millars Pl KKNTL G66......40 A5
Millarston Dr PSLY PA1......83 F5
Millarston Dr PSLY PA1......83 F5
Millar St PSLY PA1......84 B4
Millbank Av BLSH ML4......136 A4
Millbank Rd WISHAW ML2......175 G3
Millbeg Crs STPS/GTHM/RID G33......93 G4
Millbeg Pl STPS/GTHM/RID G33......93 G4
Mill Brae BRWEIR PA11......79 G3
Millbrae Av BAIL/MDB/MHD G69......58 C3
Millbrae Crs CVH/MTFL G42......108 D5
  KNTSWD......49 C4
Millbrae Gdns PLKSD/SHW G41......109 E5
Millbrae Rd CVH/MTFL G42......108 D5
Millbrix Av SCOT G14......64 B3
Millbrook EKILN G74......165 F4
Millburn Av KNTSWD G13......49 H5
  RNFRW PA4......63 H3
  RUTH G73......129 H1
Millburn Ct EKILS G75......176 D1
Millburn Crs DMBTN G82......13 G4
Millburn Dr RNFRW PA4......63 H3
Millburn Gdns EKILS G75......176 D1
Millburn Rd BSDN G61......13 G4
  RNFRW PA4......63 G3
Millburn St KKNTL G66......6 B2
  MTHW ML1......154 D3
  SPRGB/BLRNK G21......68 D5
Millburn Wy EKILS G75......176 D1
  RNFRW PA4......63 H3
Mill Ct HMLTN ML3......169 H3
  RUTH G73......110 D4
Mill Crs BSHPBGS G64......19 G4
  DMNK/BRGTN G40......110 C1
Millcroft Rd CUMB G67......44 D4
  CUMB G67......110 C2
Milldam Rd CLYDBK G81......32 B1
Millennium Gdns ESTRH G34......94 B2
Miller Ct DMBTN G82......13 G3
Millerfield Pl
  DMNK/BRGTN G40......111 E1
Miller Field Pl HMLTN ML3......170 C2
Millerfield Rd
  DMNK/BRGTN G40......111 E1
Millersneuk Av KKNTL G66......40 A4
Millersneuk Crs
  STPS/GTHM/RID G33......70 B1
Millersneuk Dr KKNTL G66......40 A4
Millersneuk Rd KKNTL G66......40 A4
Miller's Pl AIRDRIE ML6......98 C2
Millerston St DMNK/BRGTN G40......90 D5
Miller St BAIL/MDB/MHD G69......94 A5

CGLE G1......3 F6
CLYDBK G81......49 E2
CTBR ML5......97 E4
DMBTN G82......13 H3
HMLTN ML3......170 C2
JNSTN PA5......102 A1
WISHAW ML2......173 H2
Millfield Av ERSK PA8......47 F2
  MTHW ML1......155 E2
Millfield Crs ERSK PA8......47 F2
Millfield Dr ERSK PA8......47 F2
Millfield Gdns ERSK PA8......47 F2
Millfield Hl ERSK PA8......47 F2
Millfield Mdw ERSK PA8......47 F2
Millfield Pl ERSK PA8......47 F2
Millfield Vw ERSK PA8......47 F2
Millfield Wk RNFRW PA4......47 F3
Millfield Wynd ERSK PA8......47 F2
Milford Dr PSLYN/LNWD PA3......82 A4
Millgate Av UD/BTH/TAN G71......115 E4
Millgate Ct UD/BTH/TAN G71......115 E5
Millgate Rd HMLTN ML3......169 H4
Mill Gv HMLTN ML3......169 H3
Millheugh Pl BLTYR/CAMB G72......151 F4
Millhall Rd LNPK/KPK G44......115 G5
Millhouse Crs MRYH/FIRH G20......52 A4
Millhouse Dr MRYH/FIRH G20......52 A4
Millichen Rd SMSTN G23......35 H5
Milliken Dr KLBCH PA10......100 D4
Milliken Park Rd KLBCH PA10......100 D5
Mill Loan AIRDRIE ML6......98 B1
Mill of Gryffe Rd BRWEIR PA11......79 G3
Mill Pl PSLYN/LNWD PA3......82 A4
Millport Av LNPK/KPK G44......109 H5
Mill Rig EKILS G75......178 A3
Mill Ri KKNTL G66......40 A5
Mill Rd AIRDRIE ML6......98 B5
  BLTYR/CAMB G72......131 H1
  HMLTN ML3......169 H4
  KNTSWD G13......49 G4
  KSYTH G65......7 E3
  MTHW ML1......155 G2
  SHOTTS ML7......159 G2
  UD/BTH/TAN G71......152 B1
Millroad Dr DMNK/BRGTN G40......90 B3
Millroad St DMNK/BRGTN G40......90 B3
Millstream Ct PSLY PA1......84 C5
Mill St DMNK/BRGTN G40......110 C1
  PSLY PA1......84 C5
  RUTH G73......129 H1
Millview BRHD/NEIL G78......124 C4
Millview Pl PLK/PH/NH G53......125 G5
Millview Rd BRHD/NEIL G78......140 D3
Millview Ter BRHD/NEIL G78......125 G5
Mill Wy KKNTL G66......40 B5
Millwood St PLKSD/SHW G41......108 D4
Milnbank St DEN/PKHD G31......90 D1
Milncroft Pl
  STPS/GTHM/RID G33......70 B5
Milncroft Rd
  STPS/GTHM/RID G33......70 B5
Milner La KNTSWD G13......65 F1
Milner Rd KNTSWD G13......65 F1
Milngavie Rd BSDN G61......34 C5
Milnpark Gdns PLKSD/SHW G41......88 C4
Milnpark St PLKSD/SHW G41......88 C4
Milnwood Dr MTHW ML1......136 D5
Milovaig Av SMSTN G23......52 C1
Milovaig St SMSTN G23......52 C1
Milrig Rd RUTH G73......110 C5
Milroy Gdns BLSH ML4......116 A4
Milton Av BLTYR/CAMB G72......130 D2
Milton Brae DMBTN G82......14 A2
Milton Ct DMBTN G82......14 C3
Milton Douglas Rd CLYDBK G81......31 H2
Milton Dr BSHPBGS G64......54 B4
Milton Gdns UD/BTH/TAN G71......114 D4
Milton La DMBTN G82......14 C4
Milton Mains Rd CLYDBK G81......31 H3
Milton Pl EKILN G74......165 F3
  KKNTL G66......21 E5
Milton St AIRDRIE ML6......98 B1
  COWCAD G4......67 F4
  HMLTN ML3......152 B5
  MTHW ML1......154 D2
Milton Ter HMLTN ML3......152 B5
Milverton Av BSDN G61......33 H2
Milverton Rd GIF/THBK G46......144 D1
Mimosa Rd BRWEIR PA11......79 G3
Minard Rd PLKSD/SHW G41......108 D3
Minard Wy UD/BTH/TAN G71......115 F5
Mincher Crs MTHW ML1......171 H1
Minch Wy AIRDRIE ML6......99 E4
Minella Gdns BLSH ML4......116 D4
Minerva St KVGV G3......88 C1
Minerva Wy KVGV G3......88 C1
Mingarry La MRYH/FIRH G20......66 D2
Mingarry St MRYH/FIRH G20......66 D2
Mingulay Crs PPK/MIL G22......54 A3
Mingulay Pl PPK/MIL G22......54 B3
Mingulay St PPK/MIL G22......54 A3
Ministers Pk EKILN G74......165 E1
Minmoir Rd PLK/PH/NH G53......106 A5
Minstrel Rd KNTSWD G13......51 E2
Minto Av RUTH G73......130 C3
Minto Crs CARD/HILL/MSPK G52......87 H4
Minto Pk WISHAW ML2......157 F4
Minto St CARD/HILL/MSPK G52......87 H4
Mireton St PPK/MIL G22......53 H4
Mirren Dr CLYDBK G81......31 G1
Mirrlees Dr KVD/HLHD G12......66 B2
Mirrlees La KVD/HLHD G12......66 B2
Mitchell Av BLTYR/CAMB G72......132 B3
  RNFRW PA4......63 E4
Mitchell Ct EKILN G74......165 H5
Mitchell Dr MLNGV G62......17 G4
  RUTH G73......130 B1
Mitchell Hill Rd CSMK G45......129 G5
Mitchell La CGLE G1......3 G5
Mitchell St AIRDRIE ML6......98 A1
  CGLE G1......3 G5
  CTBR ML5......95 H4
Mitchison Rd CUMB G67......26 C2
Mitre Ct PTCK G11......65 G2
Mitre La SCOT G14......65 F2
Mitre La West SCOT G14......65 E2
Mitre Rd PTCK G11......65 G2
Mochrum Rd
  PLKSW/MSWD G43......127 H1
Moffat Ct EKILS G75......176 D1
Moffathill AIRDRIE ML6......99 F5

Moffat Pl BLTYR/CAMB G72......151 G1
  CTBR ML5......97 G5
  EKILS G75......176 D1
Moffat Rd AIRDRIE ML6......99 G2
Moffat St GBLS G5......90 A5
Moffat Vw AIRDRIE ML6......77 H4
Mogarth Av PSLYS PA2......103 E4
Moidart Av RNFRW PA4......63 E2
Moidart Crs
  CARD/HILL/MSPK G52......87 F4
Moidart Gdns KKNTL G66......22 B4
Moidart Pl
  CARD/HILL/MSPK G52......87 F4
  NMRNS G77......144 B4
Moidart Rd
  CARD/HILL/MSPK G52......87 F4
Moir St CGLE G1......90 A3
Molendinar Ter
  BRHD/NEIL G78......140 D4
Mollinsburn Rd CUMB G67......43 F5
Mollinsburn St
  SPRGB/BLRNK G21......68 B3
Mollins Ct BALLOCH G68......43 E5
Mollins Rd BALLOCH G68......23 H4
Monach Rd
  STPS/GTHM/RID G33......92 D1
Monar Dr PPK/MIL G22......67 G3
Monar St PPK/MIL G22......67 G3
Monart Pl MRYH/FIRH G20......67 E3
Moncrieff Av KKNTL G66......40 A3
Moncrieffe Rd AIRDRIE ML6......99 E5
Moncrieff St PSLY PA1......84 B4
Moncur St DMNK/BRGTN G40......90 B3
Moness Dr
  CARD/HILL/MSPK G52......87 F5
Money Gv MTHW ML1......172 C1
Monieburgh Crs KSYTH G65......8 C1
Monieburgh Rd KSYTH G65......8 C1
Monifieth Av
  CARD/HILL/MSPK G52......87 E5
Monikie Gdns BSHPBGS G64......55 G2
Monkcastle Dr
  BLTYR/CAMB G72......131 F1
Monkland Av KKNTL G66......40 A2
Monkland St AIRDRIE ML6......98 C1
Monkland Vw AIRDRIE ML6......118 C2
  UD/BTH/TAN G71......115 F4
Monkland View Crs
  BAIL/MDB/MHD G69......95 E4
Monksbridge Av KNTSWD G13......50 D2
Monkscourt Av AIRDRIE ML6......97 H1
Monkscroft Av PTCK G11......65 H1
Monkscroft Ct PTCK G11......65 H3
Monks Rd AIRDRIE ML6......98 D5
Monkton Dr DRUM G15......50 B2
Monkton Gdns NMRNS G77......162 B1
Monmouth Av KVD/HLHD G12......65 H1
Monreith Av BSDN G61......51 E1
Monreith Rd
  PLKSW/MSWD G43......127 H1
Monreith Rd East
  LNPK/KPK G44......128 B2
Monroe Pl UD/BTH/TAN G71......115 E3
Monroe Pl UD/BTH/TAN G71......115 E3
Montague La KVD/HLHD G12......66 A2
Montague St KVD/HLHD G12......66 D4
Montalto Av MTHW ML1......155 F1
Montclair Pl PSLYN/LNWD PA3......81 H5
Monteith Dr
  CRMNK/CLK/EAG G76......146 B2
Monteith Gdns
  CRMNK/CLK/EAG G76......146 A2
Monteith Pl DMNK/BRGTN G40......90 A3
  UD/BTH/TAN G71......134 C5
Monteith Rw CGLE G1......90 A3
Montford Av LNPK/KPK G44......110 A5
Montfort Av
  PSLYN/LNWD PA3......96 C1
Montgomery Av CTBR ML5......96 B5
  PSLYN/LNWD PA3......84 D1
Montgomery Crs WISHAW ML2......173 H4
Montgomery Dr GIF/THBK G46......166 C3
Montgomery Rd
  PSLYN/LNWD PA3......84 D1
Montgomery St
  BLTYR/CAMB G72......132 A2
  DMNK/BRGTN G40......90 D4
  EKILN G74......166 C3
Montgomery Ter KKNTL G66......5 F5
Montraive St RUTH G73......111 F3
Montrave St
  CARD/HILL/MSPK G52......87 E5
Montreal Pk EKILS G75......165 H4
Montrose Av CAR/SHTL G32......112 C3
  CARD/HILL/MSPK G52......86 A1
Montrose Crs HMLTN ML3......170 A1
Montrose Gdns
  BLTYR/CAMB G72......133 F5
  KSYTH G65......17 G2
  MLNGV G62......17 G2
Montrose Pl PSLYN/LNWD PA3......81 H5
Montrose Rd PSLYS PA2......103 E4
Montrose St CGLE G1......3 J4
  CLYDBK G81......49 F2
Montrose Ter BRWEIR PA11......79 H4
  BSHPBGS G64......55 F2
Monymusk Gdns BSHPBGS G64......55 G1
Monymusk Pl CLYDBK G81......31 F1
Moodiesburn St
  STPS/GTHM/RID G33......69 G4
Moorburn Pl PSLYN/LNWD PA3......81 G5
Moorburn Av GIF/THBK G46......127 E5
Moorcroft Dr AIRDRIE ML6......119 E4
Moorcroft Rd NMRNS G77......161 F2
Moore Dr BSDN G61......34 C5
Moore Gdns HMLTN ML3......181 E1
Moore St DMNK/BRGTN G40......90 D5
  MTHW ML1......137 H4
Moorfield Crs AIRDRIE ML6......99 E3
Moorfield Rd
  BLTYR/CAMB G72......151 F4
Moorfoot Av GIF/THBK G46......126 D5
  PSLYS PA2......104 A3
Moorfoot Gdns EKILS G75......177 G5
Moorfoot St CAR/SHTL G32......92 A3
Moorfoot Wy BSDN G61......33 H1
Moorhill Crs NMRNS G77......161 F2
Moorhill Rd NMRNS G77......161 F2
Moorhouse Av KNTSWD G13......50 A5
  PSLYS PA2......103 G2
Moorhouse St BRHD/NEIL G78......124 B5
The Moorings PSLYS PA1......103 H1

Moorland Dr AIRDRIE ML6......99 F4
Moorpark Av AIRDRIE ML6......99 F2
  BAIL/MDB/MHD G69......58 B4
  CARD/HILL/MSPK G52......86 A3
Moorpark Dr
  CARD/HILL/MSPK G52......86 B3
Moorpark Sq RNFRW PA4......63 E4
Morar Rd MLNGV G62......17 F3
  CARD/HILL/MSPK G52......87 F5
Moraine Av DRUM G15......50 B2
Moraine Circ DRUM G15......50 B2
Moraine Dr
  CRMNK/CLK/EAG G76......145 F2
  DRUM G15......50 B2
Moraine Pl DRUM G15......50 C2
Morar Av CLYDBK G81......32 A4
Morar Crs AIRDRIE ML6......75 H5
  BSHPBGS G64......54 C1
  BSHPTN PA7......29 H3
  CLYDBK G81......32 A4
Morar Dr BSDN G61......35 E5
  CLYDBK G81......32 A4
  CTBR ML5......116 C2
  CUMB G67......25 G5
  PSLYS PA2......103 E2
  RUTH G73......130 B3
Morar Pl CLYDBK G81......32 A4
  NMRNS G77......144 B3
Morar Rd CARD/HILL/MSPK G52......87 F4
  CLYDBK G81......32 A4
Morar St WISHAW ML2......173 H4
Morar Ter RUTH G73......130 C3
  UD/BTH/TAN G71......115 G5
Moravia Av UD/BTH/TAN G71......134 B4
Moray Av AIRDRIE ML6......98 B4
Moray Dr BSHPBGS G64......19 E5
  CRMNK/CLK/EAG G76......146 A3
Moray Gdns BALLOCH G68......10 B5
  CRMNK/CLK/EAG G76......146 A3
  UD/BTH/TAN G71......115 E4
Moray Ga UD/BTH/TAN G71......134 A4
Moray Pl BAIL/MDB/MHD G69......58 C3
  BLTYR/CAMB G72......151 F4
  BSHPBGS G64......55 F2
  KKNTL G66......22 A4
  PLKSD/SHW G41......108 D2
  PSLYN/LNWD PA3......81 H5
Moray Qd BLSH ML4......135 H2
Mordaunt St
  DMNK/BRGTN G40......110 D1
Moredun Crs CAR/SHTL G32......92 D2
Moredun Dr PSLYS PA2......103 G3
Moredun Rd PSLYS PA2......103 G3
Moredun St CAR/SHTL G32......92 D2
Morefield Rd GOV/IBX G51......87 E2
Morgan Ms GVH/MTFL G42......109 G1
Morgan St HMLTN ML3......170 A3
Morina Gdns PLK/PH/NH G53......125 H5
Morion Rd KNTSWD G13......51 E3
Moriston Ct WISHAW ML2......158 A4
Morland EKILN G74......150 A5
Morley St GVH/MTFL G42......109 F5
Morna La SCOT G14......65 F4
Morningside Rd WISHAW ML2......175 F1
Morningside St
  STPS/GTHM/RID G33......91 G1
Morris Crs BLTYR/CAMB G72......151 G5
  MTHW ML1......156 B1
Morrishall Rd EKILN G74......166 D5
Morrison Dr KKNTL G66......4 C5
Morrison Qd CLYDBK G81......49 H2
Morrison St CLYDBK G81......31 G2
  GBLS G5......89 H2
Morris St HMLTN ML3......170 A4
Morriston Crs RNFRW PA4......64 A5
Morriston Park Dr
  BLTYR/CAMB G72......112 B5
Morriston St BLTYR/CAMB G72......131 F1
Morton Gdns PLKSD/SHW G41......108 B3
Morton St MTHW ML1......154 D2
Morven Av BLTYR/CAMB G72......151 F1
  BSHPBGS G64......55 F2
  PSLYS PA2......104 A4
Morven Dr
  CRMNK/CLK/EAG G76......145 G2
  PSLYN/LNWD PA3......101 H1
Morven Gait ERSK PA8......48 B3
Morven Gdns
  UD/BTH/TAN G71......115 E4
Morven Rd GOV/IBX G51......131 E4
  BSDN G61......34 B2
Morven St CAR/SHTL G32......93 E4
  CTBR ML5......96 D1
Mosesfield St
  SPRGB/BLRNK G21......68 C1
Mosque Av GBLS G5......89 H4
Mossacre Rd WISHAW ML2......174 D1
Moss Av PSLYN/LNWD PA3......82 A3
Mossbank BLTYR/CAMB G72......151 F5
  EKILS G75......165 G5
Mossbank Av
  STPS/GTHM/RID G33......70 A2
Mossbank Dr
  STPS/GTHM/RID G33......70 A2
Mossbank Rd BLSH ML4......135 F1
  WISHAW ML2......174 D1
Mossburn St WISHAW ML2......174 C4
Mosscastle Rd
  STPS/GTHM/RID G33......70 D4
Mossdale EKILN G74......165 H2
Mossdale Gdns HMLTN ML3......168 D3
Moss Dr BRHD/NEIL G78......123 H2
  ERSK PA8......47 G4
Mossend La
  STPS/GTHM/RID G33......93 E1
Mossend St
  STPS/GTHM/RID G33......93 E2
Mossgiel EKILS G75......177 G1
Mossgiel Av RUTH G73......129 H2
Mossgiel Crs
  CRMNK/CLK/EAG G76......146 A3
Mossgiel Dr CLYDBK G81......32 B5
Mossgiel Gdns KKNTL G66......21 H4
  UD/BTH/TAN G71......114 D4
Mossgiel Pl RUTH G73......129 H2
Mossgiel Rd BALLOCH G68......26 D2
  PLKSW/MSWD G43......127 G1
Mossgiel Ter BLTYR/CAMB G72......133 F5

Mosshall Gv MTHW ML1......138 C3
Mosshall Rd MTHW ML1......119 E5
Mosshall St MTHW ML1......138 C4
Moss Heights Av
  CARD/HILL/MSPK G52......87 E4
Mosshill Rd BLSH ML4......117 E5
Moss Knowe CUMB G67......26 D5
Mossland Dr WISHAW ML2......174 A4
Mossland Rd
  CARD/HILL/MSPK G52......85 G1
Mossland Rd
  PSLYN/LNWD PA3......84 A2
Mosslingal EKILS G75......178 B3
Mossmulloch EKILS G75......178 A3
Mossneuk Crs WISHAW ML2......174 D1
Mossneuk Dr EKILS G75......177 E1
  PSLYS PA2......103 H4
  WISHAW ML2......174 D1
Mossneuk Pk WISHAW ML2......174 B1
Mossneuk Rd EKILS G75......165 F5
Mossneuk St CTBR ML5......116 C1
Mosspark Av
  CARD/HILL/MSPK G52......107 G1
  MLNGV G62......17 E2
Mosspark Bvd
  CARD/HILL/MSPK G52......107 E1
Mosspark Dr
  CARD/HILL/MSPK G52......106 D1
Mosspark Ov
  CARD/HILL/MSPK G52......107 F1
Mosspark Rd CTBR ML5......96 A1
  MLNGV G62......17 E2
Mosspark Sq
  CARD/HILL/MSPK G52......107 F1
Moss Rd AIRDRIE ML6......76 D5
  BAIL/MDB/MHD G69......58 B4
  BRWEIR PA11......79 H4
  CRG/CRSL/HOU PA6......60 A3
  CUMB G67......27 G1
  EKILS G75......177 H4
  GOV/IBX G51......87 E1
  KKNTL G66......39 G2
  PSLYN/LNWD PA3......41 E1
  WISHAW ML2......173 G3
Moss Side Av AIRDRIE ML6......97 H1
Moss-Side Rd PLKSD/SHW G41......108 D3
Moss St PSLY PA1......84 B4
Mossvale La PSLYN/LNWD PA3......84 A3
Mossvale Rd
  STPS/GTHM/RID G33......70 D4
Mossvale Sq
  STPS/GTHM/RID G33......70 C4
Mossvale St PSLYN/LNWD PA3......84 A3
Mossvale Ter
  BAIL/MDB/MHD G69......42 B5
Mossview Crs AIRDRIE ML6......98 D4
Mossview La
  CARD/HILL/MSPK G52......86 D4
Mossview Qd
  CARD/HILL/MSPK G52......87 E4
Mossview Rd
  STPS/GTHM/RID G33......71 F1
Mosswell Rd MLNGV G62......17 E2
Mosswood Dr BALLOCH G68......43 G1
Mossywood Pl BALLOCH G68......43 G1
Mossywood Rd BALLOCH G68......43 G1
Mote Hl HMLTN ML3......153 F5
Motehill Rd PSLYN/LNWD PA3......85 E2
Motherwell Rd BLSH ML4......135 H3
  HMLTN ML3......170 C2
  MTHW ML1......138 D1
  MTHW ML1......155 H1
Motherwell St AIRDRIE ML6......76 D5
Moulin Circ
  CARD/HILL/MSPK G52......86 B5
Moulin Pl
  CARD/HILL/MSPK G52......106 B1
Mountainblue St
  DMNK/BRGTN G40......90 D4
Mountblow Rd
  CLYDBK G81......31 E2
Mount Cameron Dr North
  EKILN G74......166 D5
Mount Cameron Dr South
  EKILN G74......166 D5
Mount Harriet Av
  STPS/GTHM/RID G33......57 F5
Mount Harriet Dr
  STPS/GTHM/RID G33......57 F5
Mount Lockhart
  UD/BTH/TAN G71......114 A2
Mount Pleasant Crs KKNTL G66......5 F5
Mount Pleasant Dr OLDK G60......30 C1
Mount St MRYH/FIRH G20......67 E3
Mount Stuart St
  PLKSD/SHW G41......108 D4
Mount Vernon Av
  CAR/SHTL G32......113 F1
  CTBR ML5......96 B2
Mournian Wy HMLTN ML3......170 A4
  HMLTN ML3......167 F1
Mowbray Av
  BAIL/MDB/MHD G69......59 E1
Moyne Rd PLK/PH/NH G53......106 B2
Muckcroft Rd
  BAIL/MDB/MHD G69......41 E4
Mugdock Rd MLNGV G62......17 E3
Muirbank Av RUTH G73......129 H2
Muirbank Gdns RUTH G73......129 H2
Muirbrae Rd RUTH G73......130 A3
Muirbrae Wy RUTH G73......130 A3
Muirburn Av
  LNPK/KPK G44......127 H4
Muircroft Dr MTHW ML1......139 F1
Muirdrum Av
  CARD/HILL/MSPK G52......86 D4
Muirdykes Rd CTBR ML5......74 D1
  CTBR ML5......96 B1
Muirdykes Av
  CARD/HILL/MSPK G52......86 A4
Muirdykes Crs
  PSLYN/LNWD PA3......83 G3
Muirdykes Rd
  PSLYN/LNWD PA3......83 G3
Muiredge Ct
  UD/BTH/TAN G71......134 A1

Muiredge Ter
BAIL/MDB/MHD G69....94 A5
Muirend Av LNPK/KPK G44...128 A2
Muirend Rd LNPK/KPK G44...127 H3
Muirfield Ct LNPK/KPK G44...128 A3
Muirfield Crs SMSTN G23...52 D2
Muirfield Mdw
UD/BTH/TAN G71...133 H5
Muirfield Rd BALLOCH G68...10 D5
Muirhead Dr MTHW ML1...138 C3
PSLYN/LNWD PA5...101 H1
Muirhead Gdns
BAIL/MDB/MHD G69...94 B5
Muirhead Ga UD/BTH/TAN G71..115 F4
Muirhead Gv
BAIL/MDB/MHD G69...94 B5
Muirhead Rd
BAIL/MDB/MHD G69...114 A1
Muirhead Wy BSHPBGS G64...55 G2
Muirhill Av LNPK/KPK G44...127 H3
Muirhill Ct HMLTN ML3...170 A1
Muirhill Crs KNTSWD G13...50 A4
Muirhouse Av MTHW ML1...172 D5
WISHAW ML2...158 C4
Muirhouse Dr MTHW ML1...172 D5
Muirhouse La EKILS G75...166 B5
Muirhouse Pk BSDN G61...16 B5
Muirhouse Rd MTHW ML1...172 C3
Muirkirk Dr HMLTN ML3...168 C3
KNTSWD G13...51 G4
Muirlees Crs MLNGV G62...16 C3
Muirmadkin Rd BLSH ML4...136 A2
Muirmaillen Av MTHW ML1...157 F1
Muirpark Av RNFRW PA4...63 F4
Muirpark Dr BSHPBGS G64...54 D5
Muirpark Ter BSHPBGS G64...54 D5
Muir Rd DMBTN G82...13 H1
Muirshiel Crs PLK/PH/NH G53..125 H1
Muirside Av CAR/SHTL G32...115 F1
KNTSL G66...22 A5
Muirside Pl BAIL/MDB/MHD G69.94 A5
Muirside Rd
BAIL/MDB/MHD G69...94 A5
Muirside St BAIL/MDB/MHD G69..94 A5
Muirskeith Crs
PLKSW/MSWD G43...128 A1
Muirskeith Pl
PLKSW/MSWD G43...128 A1
Muirskeith Rd
PLKSW/MSWD G43...128 A1
Muir St BLTYR/CAMB G72...151 F4
BSHPBGS G64...54 C3
CTBR ML5...96 B2
HMLTN ML3...170 B1
MTHW ML1...154 C2
RNFRW PA4...63 G2
Muir Ter PSLYN/LNWD PA3...84 D2
Muirton Dr BSHPBGS G64...37 G5
Muiryfauld Dr CAR/SHTL G32...91 H5
Mulben Crs PLK/PH/NH G53...106 A5
Mulben Pl PLK/PH/NH G53...106 A5
Mulben Ter PLK/PH/NH G53...106 A5
Mulberry Crs AIRDRIE ML6...119 F1
Mulberry Dr EKILS G75...177 H3
Mulberry Rd
PLKSW/MSWD G43...127 G2
UD/BTH/TAN G71...115 H3
Mulberry Wy EKILS G75...177 G5
Mulberry Wynd
BLTYR/CAMB G72...132 C4
Mull EKILN G74...179 F1
Mullardoch St SMSTN G23...52 C2
Mull Av PSLYS PA2...104 B5
RNFRW PA4...63 F5
Mull Ct HMLTN ML3...169 E4
Mullen Ct STPS/GTHM/RID G33..71 G1
Mull Qd WISHAW ML2...157 H5
Mull St SPRGB/BLRNK G21...69 E4
Mulvey Crs AIRDRIE ML6...97 H3
Mungo Pk EKILS G75...166 A5
Mungo Pl UD/BTH/TAN G71...115 F3
Munlochy Rd GOV/IBX G51...87 E2
Munro Ct CTBR ML5...31 G2
Munro Dr KKNTL G66...5 F5
Munro La KNTSWD G13...65 E1
Munro La East KNTSWD G13...65 F1
Munro Pl EKILN G74...150 A4
KNTSWD G13...51 F4
Munro Rd KNTSWD G13...65 E1
Murano St MRYH/FIRH G20...67 E2
Murchison EKILS G75...165 G5
Murchison Rd
CRG/CRSL/HOU PA6...80 D2
Murdoch Dr MLNGV G62...17 H5
Murdoch Dr MTHW ML1...137 E4
Murdoch Rd EKILS G75...166 D5
Murdoch Sq BLSH ML4...117 F5
Murdostoun Gdns
WISHAW ML2...157 H5
Murdostoun Ter MTHW ML1...157 H1
Murdostoun Vw WISHAW ML2..158 A4
Muriel La BRHD/NEIL G78...124 B4
Muriel St BRHD/NEIL G78...124 B4
Murray Av KSYTH G65...8 B2
Murray Crs WISHAW ML2...158 B3
Murrayfield BSDN G61...51 F2
Murrayfield St CAR/SHTL G32...91 H2
Murrayhill EKILS G75...165 H5
Murray Pl BLSH ML4...116 B5
BRHD/NEIL G78...124 C3
Murray Rd UD/BTH/TAN G71...134 B4
The Murray Rd EKILS G75...165 H5
The Murray Sq EKILS G75...178 B1
Murray St PSLYN/LNWD PA3...83 H5
RNFRW PA4...63 F3
Murray Ter MTHW ML1...154 A3
Murrin Av BSHPBGS G64...55 G2
Murroch Av DMBTN G82...13 G1
Murroes Rd GOV/IBX G51...87 E2
Musgrove Pl EKILS G75...165 H5
Muslin St DMNK/BRGTN G40...90 C5
Muttonhole Rd HMLTN ML3...168 A5
Myers Ct UD/BTH/TAN G71...134 B2
Myreside Pl CAR/SHTL G32...91 G3
Myreside St CAR/SHTL G32...91 G3
Myres Rd PLK/PH/NH G53...107 E1
Myrie Gdns BSHPBGS G64...55 E1
Myrtle Av KNTSL G66...39 H5
Myrtle Dr MTHW ML1...137 G2

WISHAW ML2...173 E1
Myrtle Hill La GVH/MTFL G42..109 H4
Myrtle Pk GVH/MTFL G42...109 G3
Myrtle Rd CLYDBK G81...31 E4
Myrtle Rd UD/BTH/TAN G71...115 C4
Myrtle Sq BSHPBGS G64...54 D3
Myrtle St BLTYR/CAMB G72...151 C1
Myrtle View Rd GVH/MTFL G42..109 H4
Myrtle Wk BLTYR/CAMB G72...131 E1
Myvot Av CUMB G67...44 A2
Myvot Rd CUMB G67...43 H4
CUMB G67...44 A2

N

Naburn Ga GBLS G5...89 H5
Nagle Gdns MTHW ML1...156 C2
Nairn Av BLSH ML4...135 G2
Nairn Ct PLYDBK G81...31 C5
EKILN G74...167 F2
Nairn Qd WISHAW ML2...157 E5
Nairnside Rd SPRGB/BLRNK G21..55 F4
Nairn St BLTYR/CAMB G72...151 F4
CLYDBK G81...31 C4
KVGV G3...66 C5
Nairn Wy BALLOCH G68...10 C3
Naismith St CAR/SHTL G32...112 D4
Naismith Wk BLSH ML4...117 F5
Nansen St MRYH/FIRH G20...67 F5
Napier Ct GALLOCH G68...11 F2
OLDK G60...30 D3
Napier Crs DMBTN G82...12 C4
Napier Dr GOV/IBX G51...88 A1
Napier Gdns PSLYN/LNWD PA3...84 A1
Napier Hl EKILS G75...166 B5
Napier Pk BALLOCH G68...11 E2
Napier Pl BALLOCH G68...11 E2
GOV/IBX G51...88 A1
OLDK G60...30 D3
Napier Rd BALLOCH G68...11 E2
CARD/HILL/MSPK G52...64 A5
GOV/IBX G51...88 A1
Napiershall La COWCAD G4...67 E4
Napiershall Pl MRYH/FIRH G20..67 E4
Napiershall St COWCAD G4...67 E4
Napier Sq BLSH ML4...117 F5
Napier St CLYDBK G81...49 F4
GOV/IBX G51...88 A1
JNSTN PA5...101 F5
PSLYN/LNWD PA3...82 B3
Napier Ter GOV/IBX G51...88 A1
Napier Wy BALLOCH G68...11 E2
Naproch Pl NMRNS G77...145 E5
Naseby Av PTCK G11...65 G3
Naseby La PTCK G11...65 G3
Nasmyth Av EKILS G75...178 D1
Nasmyth Pl EKILS G75...178 C1
Nasmyth Rd
CARD/HILL/MSPK G52...86 B2
Nasmyth Rd North
CARD/HILL/MSPK G52...86 B2
Nasmyth Rd South
CARD/HILL/MSPK G52...86 B2
Nassau Pl EKILS G75...165 F4
National Bank La CGLE G1...2 E5
Navar Pl PSLYS PA2...104 D2
Naver St STPS/GTHM/RID G33...69 H5
Naylor La AIRDRIE ML6...98 C1
Naysmyth Bank EKILS G75...178 D1
Neidpath Av CTBR ML5...116 D1
Neidpath Pl CTBR ML5...116 D1
Neidpath Rd East NMRNS G77..144 D3
Neidpath Rd West NMRNS G77..144 D3
Neilsland Dr HMLTN ML3...180 C1
MTHW ML1...154 A4
Neilsland Ov PLK/PH/NH G53...106 A4
Neilsland Rd HMLTN ML3...169 G4
Neilsland Sq PLK/PH/NH G53...106 A3
HMLTN ML3...169 G4
Neilsland St HMLTN ML3...169 H4
Neilson Ct HMLTN ML3...170 C2
Neilston Av PLK/PH/NH G53...125 H3
Neilston Pl KSYTH G65...8 B1
Neilston Rd BRHD/NEIL G78...141 F3
PSLYS PA2...104 B2
Neil St RNFRW PA4...63 G1
Neilvaig Dr RUTH G73...130 B4
Neistpoint Dr
STPS/GTHM/RID G33...92 B1
Nelson Av CTBR ML5...96 B5
Nelson Crs MTHW ML1...172 C1
Nelson Mandela Pl CCLW G2...3 F4
Nelson Pl BAIL/MDB/MHD G69...94 A5
Nelson St BAIL/MDB/MHD G69...94 A5
GBLS G5...89 F3
Nelson Ter EKILN G74...166 D5
Neptune St GOV/IBX G51...88 A2
Neptune Wy BLSH ML4...136 D2
Nerston Rd EKILN G74...148 C4
Ness Av JNSTN PA5...120 D1
Ness Dr BLTYR/CAMB G72...151 H1
EKILN G74...167 E4
Ness Gdns BSHPBGS G64...54 D1
Ness Rd RNFRW PA4...63 E2
Ness St STPS/GTHM/RID G33...69 H5
WISHAW ML2...173 G4
Ness Ter HMLTN ML3...169 H4
Nethan Av WISHAW ML2...172 D3
Nethan Ga HMLTN ML3...169 H3
Nethan Pl HMLTN ML3...180 C2
Nethan St MTHW ML1...154 C1
Nether Auldhouse Rd
PLKSW/MSWD G43...127 F1
Netherbog Rd DMBTN G82...13 G3
Netherburn Av
CRG/CRSL/HOU PA6...81 F4
LNPK/KPK G44...128 A5
Netherburn Gdns
CRG/CRSL/HOU PA6...81 F4
Netherby Dr PLKSD/SHW G41...88 C5
Nethercairn Pl NMRNS G77...145 G4
Nethercairn Rd GIF/THBK G46..127 F3
Nethercliffe Av LNPK/KPK G44..128 A5
Nethercommon Harbour
PSLYN/LNWD PA3...84 B3
Nethercroft Rd
BAIL/MDB/MHD G69...58 D1
Nethercraigs Dr PSLYS PA2...103 G4
Nethercraigs Rd PSLYS PA2...103 G5

JNSTN PA5...102 D1
Netherdale Crs WISHAW ML2..172 D3
Netherdale Dr PSLY PA1...106 A1
Netherdale Rd WISHAW ML2...173 F5
Netherfield St DEN/PKHD G31...91 F3
Nethergreen Crs RNFRW PA4...63 F3
Nethergreen Wynd RNFRW PA4..63 F3
Netherhall Av WISHAW ML2...173 F3
Netherhall Rd LNPK/KPK G44..146 A1
Netherhill Crs
PSLYN/LNWD PA3...84 D5
Netherhill Rd
BAIL/MDB/MHD G69...59 E2
PSLYN/LNWD PA3...85 E2
KKNTL G66...116 C1
Netherhouse Av CTBR ML5...116 D1
KKNTL G66...40 B4
Netherhouse Pl
BAIL/MDB/MHD G69...94 D1
Netherhouse Rd
BAIL/MDB/MHD G69...94 D2
Netherlee Pl LNPK/KPK G44...128 B3
Netherlee Rd LNPK/KPK G44...128 B3
Nethermains Rd MLNGV G62...17 E5
Netherpark Av LNPK/KPK G44..146 A1
Netherplace Crs NMRNS G77...160 C1
PLK/PH/NH G53...106 A3
Netherplace Rd NMRNS G77...160 A1
PLK/PH/NH G53...106 C4
Netherton Av KVD/HLHD G12...65 H1
Netherton Ct NMRNS G77...144 C4
Netherton Dr BRHD/NEIL G78..124 C5
Netherton Rd EKILS G75...177 E4
KNTSWD G13...51 E4
NMRNS G77...144 C4
WISHAW ML2...172 D3
Netherton St KNTSWD G13...51 G4
WISHAW ML2...158 A3
Netherview Rd LNPK/KPK G44..146 A1
Netherway LNPK/KPK G44...146 A1
Netherwood Av BALLOCH G68...25 E5
Netherwood Ct BALLOCH G68...25 E5
Netherwood Gv BALLOCH G68...25 E5
Netherwood Rd BALLOCH G68...24 D5
MTHW ML1...138 A2
Netherwood Wy BALLOCH G68...25 E5
Neuk Av BAIL/MDB/MHD G69...58 B4
CRG/CRSL/HOU PA6...80 D2
Neuk Crs CRG/CRSL/HOU PA6...80 D1
The Neuk WISHAW ML2...173 F2
Neville EKILN G74...149 H5
Nevis Av HMLTN ML3...169 F4
Nevis Dr BSHPBGS G64...19 F4
Nevis Rd BSDN G61...33 C1
PLKSW/MSWD G43...127 E2
RNFRW PA4...63 E5
Nevis Wy PSLYN/LNWD PA3...62 B5
Newark Dr PLKSD/SHW G41...108 D1
PSLYS PA2...103 H4
Newark Ga SHOTTS ML7...159 G2
Newark Pl WISHAW ML2...157 G4
Newarthill Rd MTHW ML1...137 H5
New Ashtree St WISHAW ML2...173 F2
Newbank Ct DEN/PKHD G31...91 H5
Newbank Gdns DEN/PKHD G31..91 G5
Newbank Rd DEN/PKHD G31...91 H5
Newbattle Av AIRDRIE ML6...118 C2
Newbattle Ct CAR/SHTL G32...112 C2
Newbattle Gdns CAR/SHTL G32.112 C2
Newbattle Pl CAR/SHTL G32...112 C2
Newbattle Rd CAR/SHTL G32...112 B5
Newbold Av SPRGB/BLRNK G21..54 B4
Newburgh St
PLKSW/MSWD G43...108 C5
Newcastleton Dr SMSTN G23...52 D2
New City Rd COWCAD G4...2 D1
Newcraigs Drive
CRMNK/CLK/EAG G76...147 E3
Newcroft Dr LNPK/KPK G44...129 E2
Newdyke Rd KKNTL G66...21 G5
New Edinburgh Rd
UD/BTH/TAN G71...114 D5
Newfield Crs HMLTN ML3...169 F1
Newfield Pl GIF/THBK G46...126 C5
RUTH G73...110 B5
Newfield Sq PLK/PH/NH G53...125 F1
Newford Gv
CRMNK/CLK/EAG G76...145 H5
Newhall St DMNK/BRGTN G40..110 B1
Newhaven Rd
STPS/GTHM/RID G33...92 C1
Newhaven St CAR/SHTL G32...92 B2
Newhills Rd
STPS/GTHM/RID G33...93 F2
Newhousemill Rd EKILN G74..179 F1
Newhut Rd MTHW ML1...154 C2
New Inchinnan Rd
PSLYN/LNWD PA3...84 B2
New Kirk Rd BSDN G61...34 B5
New Lairdsland Rd KKNTL G66..21 F5
Newlands Dr HMLTN ML3...170 A5
Newlandsfield Rd
PLKSW/MSWD G43...108 C5
Newlands Gdns JNSTN PA5...102 B3
Newlandsmuir Rd EKILS G75...177 E2
Newlands Pl EKILN G74...166 B4
Newlands Rd EKILS G75...176 D4
PLKSW/MSWD G43...127 H1
UD/BTH/TAN G71...115 E4
Newlands St CTBR ML5...96 D5
New Luce Dr CAR/SHTL G32...113 E1
Newmains Av RNFRW PA4...61 F1
Newmains Rd RNFRW PA4...63 F5
Newmill Rd SPRGB/BLRNK G21..55 E5
New Park St HMLTN ML3...152 D5
New Plymouth EKILS G75...177 F1
New Rd BLTYR/CAMB G72...112 B5
Newrose Av BLSH ML4...117 E5
Newshot Dr ERSK PA8...47 H2
New St BLTYR/CAMB G72...151 F4
CLYDBK G81...31 H1
KLBCH PA10...100 B3
PSLY PA1...84 B5
Newton Av BLTYR/CAMB G72...132 A1
BRHD/NEIL G78...142 C2

Newton Brae
BLTYR/CAMB G72...132 C2
Newton Brai WISHAW ML1...172 D3
Newton Dr JNSTN PA5...161 G2
Newton Dr UD/BTH/TAN G71...115 F1
WISHAW ML2...158 B5
Newton Farm Rd
BLTYR/CAMB G72...113 G5
Newtongrange Av
CAR/SHTL G32...112 C2
Newtongrange Gdns
CAR/SHTL G32...112 C2
Newton Gv NMRNS G77...161 G2
Newtonlea Av NMRNS G77...161 H1
Newton Pl NMRNS G77...161 H2
KVGV G3...2 B5
Newton Rd KKNTL G66...40 B4
Newton St CGLW G2...2 B3
Newton St KSYTH G65...8 A1
Newton St PSLY PA1...83 H5
Newton Terrace La KVGV G3...89 E1
Newton St KSYTH G65...8 A1
Newtyle Dr PLK/PH/NH G53...106 A3
Newtyle Pl BSHPBGS G64...55 G2
Newtyle Rd PSLY PA1...85 F5
New View Dr BLSH ML4...135 H4
New View Pl BLSH ML4...135 H4
New Wynd CGLE G1...3 G7
Nicholas St CGLE G1...3 J5
Nicholson St GBLS G5...89 G4
Nicklaus Wy MTHW ML1...119 F5
Nicolson Ct
STPS/GTHM/RID G33...71 E1
Nicol St AIRDRIE ML6...76 D5
Niddrie Rd GVH/MTFL G42...109 E3
Niddrie Sq GVH/MTFL G42...109 E3
Niddry St PSLYN/LNWD PA3...84 B4
Nigel Gdns PLKSD/SHW G41...108 C3
Nigel St MTHW ML1...154 C3
Nigg Pl ESTRH G34...93 H1
Nightingale Pl JNSTN PA5...121 E2
Nimmo Dr GOV/IBX G51...87 F2
Nimmo Pl WISHAW ML2...174 B2
Ninian Av CRG/CRSL/HOU PA6...96 A1
Ninian Rd AIRDRIE ML6...98 C3
Nisbet Rd DEN/PKHD G31...91 G4
Nisbet St DEN/PKHD G31...91 C4
Nisbett Av AIRDRIE ML6...119 F2
Nisbett St AIRDRIE ML6...119 F2
Nissen Pl PLK/PH/NH G53...106 A3
Nith Av PSLYS PA2...103 E3
Nith Dr RNFRW PA4...63 H5
Nith Pl JNSTN PA5...120 D1
Nithsdale EKILN G74...167 G2
Nithsdale Crs BSDN G61...33 H2
Nithsdale Dr PLKSD/SHW G41..109 E2
Nithsdale Pl PLKSD/SHW G41..109 E1
Nithsdale Rd PLKSD/SHW G41..107 G2
Nithsdale St PLKSD/SHW G41..109 E2
Nith St STPS/GTHM/RID G33...69 G4
Nitshill Rd GIF/THBK G46...125 G5
PLK/PH/NH G53...125 F2
Niven St MRYH/FIRH G20...52 B5
Noble Rd BLSH ML4...135 H2
Nobles Pl BLSH ML4...135 G3
Nobles Vw BLSH ML4...135 G3
Noldrum Av CAR/SHTL G32...112 D4
Noldrum Gdns CAR/SHTL G32..112 D4
Norbreck Dr GIF/THBK G46...127 F3
Norby Rd PTCK G11...65 G3
Nordic Gv BLTYR/CAMB G72...151 H1
Norfield Dr LNPK/KPK G44...109 G5
Norfolk Ct GBLS G5...89 G4
Norfolk Crs BSHPBGS G64...53 H4
Norfolk St GBLS G5...89 G4
Norham St PLKSD/SHW G41...108 D3
Norman St DMNK/BRGTN G40..110 C1
Norse La North SCOT G14...64 D2
Norse La South SCOT G14...64 D2
Norse Pl SCOT G14...64 D2
Norse Rd SCOT G14...64 D2
Northall Qd MTHW ML1...155 F1
Northampton Dr
KVD/HLHD G12...52 A5
North & South Rd MTHW ML1..157 H1
North Av BLTYR/CAMB G72...131 G2
CLYDBK G81...49 E1
MTHW ML1...137 F5
Northbank Av
BLTYR/CAMB G72...132 A3
North Bank Pl CLYDBK G81...49 G2
North Bank St CLYDBK G81...49 G2
Northbank St KKNTL G66...21 G5
North Berwick Av BALLOCH G68..10 B5
North Berwick Av EKILS G75...177 F2
North Biggar Rd AIRDRIE ML6...98 D2
North Birbiston Rd KKNTL G66..21 F1
North Bridge St AIRDRIE ML6...98 B1
North British Rd
UD/BTH/TAN G71...134 A1
Northburn Av AIRDRIE ML6...76 C5
Northburn Pl AIRDRIE ML6...76 D4
Northburn Rd AIRDRIE ML6...118 B1
Northburn St AIRDRIE ML6...98 D1
North Bute St CTBR ML5...97 F5
North Caldeen Rd CTBR ML5...97 F4
North Calder Dr AIRDRIE ML6...99 E3
North Calder Pl
UD/BTH/TAN G71...114 A2
North Calder Rd
UD/BTH/TAN G71...115 H3
North Campbell Av MLNGV G62..16 D4
North Claremont La
MLNGV G62...17 E3
North Claremont St KVGV G3...66 C5
North Corsebar Rd PSLYS PA2..103 H2
North Ct CGLE G1...3 G5
North Court La CGLE G1...3 G5
Northcroft Rd
BAIL/MDB/MHD G69...58 D1
North Croft St
PSLY PA1...84 B5
North Dean Park Av
UD/BTH/TAN G71...134 B4
North Douglas St CLYDBK G81...49 F3

North Dr PSLYN/LNWD PA3...82 A3
North Dryburgh Rd
WISHAW ML2...156 D5
North Dumgoyne Av
MLNGV G62...16 D3
North Elgin Pl CLYDBK G81...49 F4
North Elgin St CLYDBK G81...49 G3
North Erskine Pk BSDN G61...34 A5
Northfield EKILS G75...177 E1
Northfield Rd KSYTH G65...7 H1
Northfield St MTHW ML1...154 D2
North Frederick St CGLE G1...3 G5
North Gardner St PTCK G11...66 A4
Northgate Qd
SPRGB/BLRNK G21...55 F5
Northgate Rd
SPRGB/BLRNK G21...55 F4
North Gower St GOV/IBX G51...88 B4
North Grange Rd BSDN G61...34 B2
North Hanover St CGLE G1...3 G4
Northinch St SCOT G14...65 E4
North Iverton Park Rd
JNSTN PA5...101 H3
North Kilmeny Crs
WISHAW ML2...157 F4
Northland Av SCOT G14...64 D1
Northland Dr SCOT G14...64 D2
Northland Gdns SCOT C14...64 D1
Northland La SCOT C14...64 D2
North La PSLYN/LNWD PA3...82 B3
North Lodge Av MTHW ML1...171 H1
North Lodge Rd RNFRW PA4...63 F2
Northmuir Dr WISHAW ML2...174 B2
Northmuir Rd DRUM G15...33 G4
North Orchard St MTHW ML1..154 C3
North Park Av BRHD/NEIL G78..124 A4
North Portland St COWCAD G4...3 H5
North Rd BALLOCH G68...25 E5
BLSH ML4...116 D3
JNSTN PA5...101 F4
North St CGLW G2...2 A4
MTHW ML1...155 E2
PSLYN/LNWD PA3...84 B3
Northumberland St
MRYH/FIRH G20...66 D2
North Vw BSDN G61...51 E1
North Vw Rd BRWEIR PA11...80 A4
North Wallace St COWCAD G4...3 H2
Northway BLTYR/CAMB G72...151 F1
North Woodside Rd
COWCAD G4...67 E4
North Wy BLTYR/CAMB G72...151 F1
Norwich Dr KVD/HLHD G12...66 A1
Norwood Av KKNTL G66...20 D4
Norwood Dr GIF/THBK G46...144 D1
Norwood Pk BSDN G61...34 C5
Norwood Ter
UD/BTH/TAN G71...115 F5
Nottingham Av KVD/HLHD G12..52 A5
Nottingham La KVD/HLHD G12..52 A5
Novar Dr KVD/HLHD G12...65 H2
Novar Gdns BSHPBGS G64...54 B2
Novar St HMLTN ML3...170 A3
Nuneaton St
DMNK/BRGTN G40...110 D1
Nurseries Rd
BAIL/MDB/MHD G69...93 G3
Nursery Av BSHPTN PA7...29 H4
Nursery La PLKSD/SHW G41...109 E2
Nursery Pl BLTYR/CAMB G72...151 G4
Nursery St PLKSD/SHW G41...109 F1
Nutberry Ct GVH/MTFL G42...109 G3

O

Oak Av BSDN G61...34 C1
EKILS G75...177 G2
Oakbank Av WISHAW ML2...173 F4
Oakbank Dr BRHD/NEIL G78..142 D2
Oakbank St AIRDRIE ML6...99 E2
Oakburn Av MLNGV G62...16 D4
Oakburn Pl MLNGV G62...16 D4
Oak Crs BAIL/MDB/MHD G69...93 H5
Oakdene Av BLSH ML4...116 C5
UD/BTH/TAN G71...115 G5
Oakdene Crs MTHW ML1...137 H3
Oak Dr BLTYR/CAMB G72...131 H3
KKNTL G66...39 H4
Oak Fern Dr EKILN G74...166 A1
Oak Fern Gv EKILN G74...166 A1
Oakfield Av KVD/HLHD G12...66 D4
Oakfield Dr MTHW ML1...154 D4
Oakfield La KVD/HLHD G12...66 D4
Oakfield Rd MTHW ML1...154 D5
Oak Gv AIRDRIE ML6...119 E3
Oakhall Av CAR/SHTL G32...113 G1
Oak Lea HMLTN ML3...170 C3
Oaklea Gdns BLTYR/CAMB G72..151 F2
Oakley Dr LNPK/KPK G44...128 A4
Oakley Ter DEN/PKHD G31...90 D2
Oak Pk BSHPBGS G64...54 D2
MTHW ML1...171 G1
Oak Rd CLYDBK G81...31 G2
EKILS G75...177 G2
UD/BTH/TAN G71...115 H5
Oakridge Rd
BAIL/MDB/MHD G69...95 G3
Oak Rd CLYDBK G81...31 G5
CUMB G67...27 F1
PSLYS PA2...104 D2
Oakshaw Brae PSLY PA1...84 A4
Oakshaw St East PSLY PA1...84 A4
Oakshaw St West PSLY PA1...84 A4
The Oaks JNSTN PA5...101 E4
Oak St CGLW G2...2 C5
Oaktree Gdns CSMK G45...129 G3
Oakwood Av PSLYS PA2...103 G3
Oakwood Crs ESTRH G34...72 D5
Oakwood Dr BLSH ML4...135 G4
Oakwood Dr CTBR ML5...95 G4
NMRNS G77...161 H1
Oak Wynd BLTYR/CAMB G72...132 C3
Oatfield St SPRGB/BLRNK G21...69 E2
Oban Ct MRYH/FIRH G20...66 D2
Oban Dr MRYH/FIRH G20...66 D3
Oban La MRYH/FIRH G20...66 D3
Oban Wy MTHW ML1...137 G5
Oban Dr MRYH/FIRH G20...66 D3
Obiston Gdns CAR/SHTL G32...92 B4
Observatory Rd KVD/HLHD G12..66 C3

Ocean Fld CLYDBK G81 ....31 G2
Ochil Ct EKILS G75 ....177 C4
Ochil Dr BRHD/NEIL G78 ...142 A1
  PSLYS PA2 ...104 A4
Ochil Pl CAR/SHTL G32 ...92 B5
Ochil Rd BSDN G61 ...33 G1
  BSHPBGS G64 ...55 F2
  RNFRW PA4 ...63 E5
Ochil St CAR/SHTL G32 ...92 B5
  WISHAW ML2 ...173 G1
Ochiltree Av KNTSWD G13 ...51 G4
Ochiltree Dr HMLTN ML3 ...168 D4
Ochil Vw UD/BTH/TAN G71 ...115 F4
Odense St EKILS G75 ...178 B2
Ogilvie Pl DEN/PKHD G31 ...91 G5
Ogilvie St DEN/PKHD G31 ...91 G5
Old Aisle Rd KKNTL G66 ...40 C1
Old Avon Rd HMLTN ML3 ...170 D5
Old Balmore Rd BSHPBGS G64 ...37 F1
Old Bore Rd AIRDRIE ML6 ...99 E1
Old Bridge of Weir Rd
  UD/BTH/TAN G71 ...152 C1
Old Castle Gdns LNPK/KPK G44 ...128 C1
Old Castle Rd LNPK/KPK G44 ...128 B1
Old Church Gdns
  BAIL/MDB/MHD G69 ...95 F4
Old Coach Rd EKILN G74 ...166 C2
Old Dalmarnock Rd
  DMNK/BRGTN G40 ...90 C5
Old Dalnottar Rd OLDK G60 ...30 C3
Old Dullatur Rd BALLOCH G68 ...9 H4
Old Dumbarton Rd KVGV G3 ...66 C5
Old Edinburgh Rd
  UD/BTH/TAN G71 ...114 D3
Old Gartloch Rd
  BAIL/MDB/MHD G69 ...73 E2
Old Glasgow Rd CUMB G67 ...26 C1
  UD/BTH/TAN G71 ...114 C4
Old Govan Rd RNFRW PA4 ...64 A3
Old Greenock Rd BSHPTN PA7 ...46 B2
  ERSK PA8 ...47 E5
Oldhall Rd PSLY PA1 ...85 G4
Old Humbie Rd NMRNS G77 ...161 H3
Old Manse Gdns CTBR ML5 ...96 D2
Old Manse Rd CAR/SHTL G32 ...93 E5
  WISHAW ML2 ...173 F5
Old Mill Rd BLTYR/CAMB G72 ...132 A2
  CLYDBK G81 ...31 H2
  EKILN G74 ...166 C4
  PSLY PA1 ...105 G1
  SHOTTS ML7 ...159 H1
  UD/BTH/TAN G71 ...152 B1
Old Mill Vw KSYTH G65 ...24 D2
Old Monkland Rd CTBR ML5 ...116 A1
Old Playfield Rd
  CRMNK/CLK/EAG G76 ...147 E2
Old Quarry Rd BALLOCH G68 ...43 E3
Old Renfrew Rd RNFRW PA4 ...64 B4
Old Rd JNSTN PA5 ...102 B1
Old Rutherglen Rd GBLS G5 ...89 H4
Old Shettleston Rd
  CAR/SHTL G32 ...92 B4
Old Sneddon St PSLY PA1 ...84 B4
Old Stable Rw CTBR ML5 ...97 E3
Old St CLYDBK G81 ...31 G2
Old Union St AIRDRIE ML6 ...98 C2
Old Wood Rd
  BAIL/MDB/MHD G69 ...113 H1
Old Wynd CGLE G1 ...3 G7
Olifard Av UD/BTH/TAN G71 ...134 C4
Oliphant Crs
  CRMNK/CLK/EAG G76 ...145 H5
  PSLYS PA2 ...102 D4
Olive Bank UD/BTH/TAN G71 ...115 H3
Olive St STPS/GTHM/RID G33 ...69 G2
Ollach ERSK PA8 ...47 H4
Olympia EKILN G74 ...166 C5
Olympia St EKILN G74 ...166 C5
Olympia St DMNK/BRGTN G40 ...90 C4
Omoa Rd MTHW ML1 ...156 D1
O'Neill Av BSHPBGS G64 ...55 E3
Onslow EKILS G75 ...177 H1
Onslow Dr DEN/PKHD G31 ...90 D2
Onslow Sq DEN/PKHD G31 ...90 D2
Ontario Pk EKILS G75 ...165 G4
Ontario Pl EKILS G75 ...165 G4
Onyx St BLSH ML4 ...135 H5
Oran Gdns MRYH/FIRH G20 ...66 D1
Oran Pl MRYH/FIRH G20 ...66 D2
Oran St MRYH/FIRH G20 ...66 D2
Orbiston Dr BLSH ML4 ...136 A4
  CLYDBK G81 ...32 C1
Orbiston Pl CLYDBK G81 ...32 C1
Orbiston Rd BLSH ML4 ...135 G3
Orbiston Sq BLSH ML4 ...135 E5
Orbiston St MTHW ML1 ...155 E5
Orcades Dr LNPK/KPK G44 ...128 C5
Orchard Av UD/BTH/TAN G71 ...152 C1
Orchard Brae HMLTN ML3 ...170 A2
Orchard Ct CAR/SHTL G32 ...112 C5
  GIF/THBK G46 ...126 D4
Orchard Dr BLTYR/CAMB G72 ...151 F2
  GIF/THBK G46 ...127 E4
  RUTH G73 ...110 C4
Orchard Fld KKNTL G66 ...40 A4
Orchard Gn EKILN G74 ...167 E1
Orchard Gv CTBR ML5 ...97 E5
  GIF/THBK G46 ...127 E5
Orchard Park Av
  GIF/THBK G46 ...126 D5
Orchard Pl BLSH ML4 ...135 G4
  HMLTN ML3 ...170 A2
  KKNTL G66 ...40 C1
Orchard St
  BAIL/MDB/MHD G69 ...113 G1
  HMLTN ML3 ...170 B2
  MTHW ML1 ...154 C3
  PSLY PA1 ...84 B5
Orchardton Rd BALLOCH G68 ...43 G2
Orchid Pl KKNTL G66 ...A A2
Orchy Av CRMNK/CLK/EAG G76 ...146 A2
Orchy Ct CLYDBK G81 ...32 B3
Orchy Crs AIRDRIE ML6 ...98 C4
  BSDN G61 ...51 E2
  PSLYS PA2 ...103 E4
Orchy Dr CRMNK/CLK/EAG G76 ...146 A1
Orchy Gdns
  CRMNK/CLK/EAG G76 ...146 A1
Orchy St LNPK/KPK G44 ...128 B1
Orefield Pl EKILN G74 ...166 B2

Oregon Pl GBLS G5 ...89 H5
Orion Pl BLSH ML4 ...136 D2
Orion Wy BLTYR/CAMB G72 ...131 F5
Orkney Pl GOV/IBX G51 ...88 A2
Orkney Qd WISHAW ML2 ...174 C1
Orkney St GOV/IBX G51 ...88 A2
Orlando EKILN G74 ...149 H5
Orleans Av SCOT G14 ...65 F3
Orleans La SCOT G14 ...65 F3
Ormiston Av SCOT G14 ...65 F3
Ormiston Dr HMLTN ML3 ...169 H5
Ormiston La SCOT G14 ...64 D2
Ormiston La North SCOT G14 ...64 D2
Ormiston La South SCOT G14 ...64 D2
Ormonde Av LNPK/KPK G44 ...128 A4
Ormonde Crs LNPK/KPK G44 ...128 A4
Ormonde Dr LNPK/KPK G44 ...128 A4
Ornsay St PPK/MIL G22 ...54 A2
Oronsay Crs BSDN G61 ...35 E5
  OLDK G60 ...30 D2
Oronsay Gdns OLDK G60 ...30 D2
Oronsay Pl OLDK G60 ...30 D2
  WISHAW ML2 ...174 A4
Orr Sq PSLY PA1 ...84 B4
Orr St DMNK/BRGTN G40 ...90 C4
  PSLY PA1 ...84 A4
  PSLYS PA2 ...104 B1
Orr Ter BRHD/NEIL G78 ...140 D4
Orton Pl GOV/IBX G51 ...87 H3
Osborne Crs EKILN G74 ...164 A2
Osborne St CGLE G1 ...3 F7
  CLYDBK G81 ...31 H5
Osprey Dr UD/BTH/TAN G71 ...115 F5
Ossian Av PSLY PA1 ...86 A4
Ossian Rd PLKSW/MSWD G43 ...127 H1
Oswald St CGLE G1 ...2 C6
Oswald Wk MLNGV G62 ...17 G5
Otago La KVD/HLHD G12 ...66 D4
Otago St EKILS G75 ...165 F4
Otago St KVD/HLHD G12 ...66 D4
Othello EKILN G74 ...149 G5
Ottawa Crs CLYDBK G81 ...31 E5
Otterburn Dr GIF/THBK G46 ...127 F5
Ottershick Pl
  STPS/GTHM/RID G33 ...70 D4
The Oval CRMNK/CLK/EAG G76 ...146 A1
  CTBR ML5 ...59 H5
Overbrae Gdns DRUM G15 ...33 E3
Overbrae Pl DRUM G15 ...33 E3
Overburn Av DMBTN G82 ...13 E3
Overburn Crs DMBTN G82 ...13 E2
Overdale Av GVH/MTFL G42 ...109 F4
Overdale Gdns GVH/MTFL G42 ...109 F4
Overdale St GVH/MTFL G42 ...109 F4
Overjohnstone Dr
  WISHAW ML2 ...172 D1
Overlea Av RUTH G73 ...130 C1
Overlee Rd
  CRMNK/CLK/EAG G76 ...147 E3
Overnewton Pl KVGV G3 ...88 C1
Overnewton Sq KVGV G3 ...66 C5
Overnewton St KVGV G3 ...66 C5
Overton Crs JNSTN PA5 ...102 A2
Overton St BLTYR/CAMB G72 ...132 A3
Overtoun Av DMBTN G82 ...13 E5
Overtoun Dr CLYDBK G81 ...31 G4
  RUTH G73 ...110 D5
Overtoun Rd CLYDBK G81 ...31 G4
Overtown Av PLK/PH/NH G53 ...125 F1
Overtown Rd WISHAW ML2 ...174 D5
Overtown St DEN/PKHD G31 ...90 D4
Overwood Dr DMBTN G82 ...13 H4
  LNPK/KPK G44 ...128 D1
Owen Av EKILS G75 ...178 A1
Owendale Av BLSH ML4 ...117 E5
Owen Pk EKILS G75 ...177 H1
O'wood Av MTHW ML1 ...137 G1
Oxford Dr PSLYN/LNWD PA3 ...82 A3
Oxford La GBLS G5 ...89 G4
  RNFRW PA4 ...63 F3
Oxford Rd RNFRW PA4 ...63 F3
Oxford St CTBR ML5 ...96 B2
  GBLS G5 ...89 G3
  KKNTL G66 ...40 B1
Oxgang Pl KKNTL G66 ...40 B1
Oxhill Pl DMBTN G82 ...12 C4
Oxhill Rd DMBTN G82 ...12 C4
Oxton Dr CARD/HILL/MSPK G52 ...86 C4

P

Paddock St CTBR ML5 ...97 G5
The Paddock
  CRMNK/CLK/EAG G76 ...146 B5
  HMLTN ML3 ...152 D4
Paidmyre Crs NMRNS G77 ...161 G2
Paidmyre Gdns NMRNS G77 ...161 G2
Paidmyre Rd NMRNS G77 ...161 G2
Paisley Rd BRHD/NEIL G78 ...124 A3
  GBLS G5 ...89 F3
  GOV/IBX G51 ...88 A2
  RNFRW PA4 ...63 E5
Paisley Rd West
  CARD/HILL/MSPK G52 ...86 B5
  GOV/IBX G51 ...88 A3
Palacecraig St CTBR ML5 ...116 D1
Palace Grounds Rd
  HMLTN ML3 ...170 C1
Paladin Av KNTSWD G13 ...50 C3
Palladium Pl SCOT G14 ...65 E3
Palmer Av KNTSWD G13 ...51 E2
Palmerston EKILS G75 ...177 F1
Palmerston Pl JNSTN PA5 ...120 D2
  KVGV G3 ...88 C1
Palm Pl UD/BTH/TAN G71 ...115 F3
Pandora Wy UD/BTH/TAN G71 ...115 F5
Pandrup Pl EKILN G74 ...166 C3
Panmure Pl MRYH/FIRH G20 ...67 F1
Panmure St MRYH/FIRH G20 ...67 F1
Pannure Rd BRHD/NEIL G78 ...142 A1
  BSHPBGS G64 ...55 E1
  DMBTN G82 ...13 G2
  JNSTN PA5 ...101 G5
  KKNTL G66 ...21 E5
  KSYTH G65 ...23 E1
  KVGV G3 ...66 C4
  MLNGV G62 ...17 E4

MTHW ML1 ...137 F2
  PSLYS PA2 ...103 H3
Park Bank ERSK PA8 ...47 G2
Park Brae ERSK PA8 ...47 H3
Parkbrae Dr MRYH/FIRH G20 ...53 F5
Parkbrae Gdns MRYH/FIRH G20 ...53 F5
Parkbrae La MRYH/FIRH G20 ...53 F5
Parkburn Av KKNTL G66 ...39 H2
Park Burn Ct HMLTN ML3 ...152 B4
Parkburn Rd KSYTH G65 ...8 B3
Park Circ KVGV G3 ...66 D5
Park Circus La KVGV G3 ...66 D5
Park Crs BLTYR/CAMB G72 ...151 E5
  BSDN G61 ...33 H5
  BSHPBGS G64 ...19 G5
  DMBTN G82 ...13 E3
  RNFRW PA4 ...47 H4
Park Dr BLSH ML4 ...135 H5
  EKILN G74 ...164 B2
  ERSK PA8 ...47 H3
  HMLTN ML3 ...171 F4
  RUTH G73 ...110 D5
Parker Pl KSYTH G65 ...8 B2
Parkfield EKILS G75 ...178 B3
Parkfoot St KSYTH G65 ...8 B1
Park Gdns KLBCH PA10 ...100 C2
  KVGV G3 ...66 D5
Park Gate EKILS G75 ...66 D5
Park Gdns KVGV G3 ...66 D5
Park Gate Pl BLSH ML4 ...135 G2
Park Gld ERSK PA8 ...47 H3
Park Gn ERSK PA8 ...47 H3
Park Gv ERSK PA8 ...47 H3
Parkgrove Av GIF/THBK G46 ...127 G4
Parkgrove Ter KVGV G3 ...66 D5
Parkgrove Terrace La KVGV G3 ...66 D5
Parkhall Rd CLYDBK G81 ...31 G3
Parkhall St EKILN G74 ...166 B3
Parkhall Ter CLYDBK G81 ...31 G3
Parkhead St AIRDRIE ML6 ...98 B1
  MTHW ML1 ...154 D3
Park Hill ERSK PA8 ...47 G2
Parkhill Dr RUTH G73 ...110 D5
Parkhill Rd PLKSW/MSWD G43 ...108 B4
Parkholm La GBLS G5 ...89 E3
Parkhouse Rd PLK/PH/NH G53 ...125 E3
Parkinch ERSK PA8 ...47 H4
Parklands Rd LNPK/KPK G44 ...128 A4
Parklands Vw PLK/PH/NH G53 ...106 B4
Park La BLTYR/CAMB G72 ...151 G2
  DMNK/BRGTN G40 ...90 C4
  KSYTH G65 ...8 B2
Park Moor ERSK PA8 ...47 G3
Parkneuk Rd
  PLKSW/MSWD G43 ...127 F3
Park Pl BLSH ML4 ...135 F4
  EKILN G74 ...164 B2
Park Quadrant KVGV G3 ...66 D5
Park Rd AIRDRIE ML6 ...118 C2
  BAIL/MDB/MHD G69 ...58 B3
  BLSH ML4 ...135 H5
  BRWEIR PA11 ...79 F4
  BSHPBGS G64 ...54 D1
  CAR/SHTL G32 ...112 D4
  CLYDBK G81 ...31 G5
  GIF/THBK G46 ...127 E5
  HMLTN ML3 ...170 A2
  JNSTN PA5 ...101 G5
  KVGV G3 ...66 D4
  KVGV G3 ...66 D5
  MTHW ML1 ...137 G4
  PSLYS PA2 ...104 A2
  RNFRW PA4 ...48 A4
Parksail ERSK PA8 ...47 H4
Parkside Gdns MRYH/FIRH G20 ...53 F5
Parkside Pl MRYH/FIRH G20 ...53 F5
Parkside Rd MTHW ML1 ...154 A4
Park St AIRDRIE ML6 ...98 B2
  CTBR ML5 ...96 D2
  DMBTN G82 ...13 F4
  KKNTL G66 ...41 E1
  MTHW ML1 ...139 E4
  MTHW ML1 ...154 D3
Park St South KVGV G3 ...66 D5
Park Terrace East La KVGV G3 ...66 D5
Park Terrace La KVGV G3 ...66 D5
Park Top ERSK PA8 ...47 H2
Parkvale Av ERSK PA8 ...48 A3
Parkvale Crs ERSK PA8 ...48 A3
Parkvale Dr ERSK PA8 ...48 A3
Parkvale Gdns ERSK PA8 ...48 A3
Parkvale Wy ERSK PA8 ...48 A3
Park Vw KLBCH PA10 ...100 B2
  PSLYS PA2 ...104 A2
Parkview Av KKNTL G66 ...40 A1
Parkview Ct KKNTL G66 ...40 A1
Parkview Crs WISHAW ML2 ...175 F1
Parkview Dr CTBR ML5 ...96 B2
  STPS/GTHM/RID G33 ...57 F3
Parkville Dr BLTYR/CAMB G72 ...151 H4
Parkville Rd BLSH ML4 ...117 F5
Park Wy CUMB G67 ...26 D1
Parkway ERSK PA8 ...47 G2
Parkway Ct CTBR ML5 ...96 B3
Parkway Pl CTBR ML5 ...96 B4
Park Winding ERSK PA8 ...47 H3
Park Wd ERSK PA8 ...47 H2
Parliament Rd KKNTL G66 ...40 A1
Parnell St AIRDRIE ML6 ...98 A4
Parnie St CGLE G1 ...3 G6
Parry Ter EKILS G75 ...165 G4
Parsonage Rw COWCAD G4 ...3 J6
Parsonage Sq COWCAD G4 ...3 H6
Partick Bridge St KVGV G3 ...66 B5
Partickhill Av PTCK G11 ...66 A4
Partickhill Rd PTCK G11 ...66 A4
Paterson Pl BSDN G61 ...16 A5
Paterson's Laun BSHPBGS G64 ...37 G3
Paterson St GBLS G5 ...89 F4
  MTHW ML1 ...154 D3
Paterson Ter EKILS G75 ...178 A1
Pather St WISHAW ML2 ...174 A3

Pathhead Gdns
  STPS/GTHM/RID G33 ...56 A5
Pathhead Rd
  CRMNK/CLK/EAG G76 ...147 E3
Patna Ct HMLTN ML3 ...168 D4
Patna St DMNK/BRGTN G40 ...91 E5
Paton St DEN/PKHD G31 ...91 E2
Patrick St PSLYS PA2 ...104 C1
Patterton Dr BRHD/NEIL G78 ...142 C1
Pattison St CLYDBK G81 ...31 F5
Paxton Ct EKILN G74 ...166 C1
Paxton Crs EKILN G74 ...166 C1
Payne St COWCAD G4 ...3 F1
Peacock Av PSLYS PA2 ...103 E2
Peacock Dr HMLTN ML3 ...169 H1
  PSLYS PA2 ...103 E2
Pearce La GOV/IBX G51 ...87 H1
Pearce St GOV/IBX G51 ...87 H1
Pearl St BLSH ML4 ...136 A4
Pearson Dr RNFRW PA4 ...63 G4
Pearson Pl PSLYN/LNWD PA3 ...82 A4
Peathill Av BAIL/MDB/MHD G69 ...58 A3
Peathill St SPRGB/BLRNK G21 ...67 H3
Peat Rd BRWEIR PA11 ...79 H4
  PLK/PH/NH G53 ...125 G1
Pedmyre La
  CRMNK/CLK/EAG G76 ...147 E5
Peebles Dr RUTH G73 ...111 G5
Peebles Pth CTBR ML5 ...117 F2
Peel Av MTHW ML1 ...171 H1
Peel Glen Gdns DRUM G15 ...33 F3
Peel Glen Rd DRUM G15 ...33 F2
Peel La PTCK G11 ...65 H4
Peel Park Pl EKILN G74 ...165 E3
Peel Pl CTBR ML5 ...117 H1
  UD/BTH/TAN G71 ...134 B4
Peel Rd EKILN G74 ...164 B1
Peel St PTCK G11 ...66 A4
Pegasus Av PSLYN/LNWD PA3 ...82 C4
Pegasus Rd BLSH ML4 ...136 D3
Pembroke EKILN G74 ...167 F1
Pembroke St KVGV G3 ...88 D1
Pencaitland Dr CAR/SHTL G32 ...112 B1
Pencaitland Gv CAR/SHTL G32 ...112 B2
Pencaitland Pl SMSTN G23 ...52 D2
Pendale Ri CSMK G45 ...129 E4
Pendeen Crs
  STPS/GTHM/RID G33 ...93 F4
Pendeen Pl
  STPS/GTHM/RID G33 ...93 G3
Pendeen Rd
  STPS/GTHM/RID G33 ...93 F4
Pendicle Crs BSDN G61 ...34 A5
Pendicle Rd BSDN G61 ...34 A5
Pendle Ct BAIL/MDB/MHD G69 ...59 F1
Penfold Crs EKILS G75 ...166 A5
Penilee Rd PSLYN/LNWD PA3 ...85 C1
Penilee Ter
  CARD/HILL/MSPK G52 ...85 H2
Peninver Dr GOV/IBX G51 ...87 E1
Penman Av RUTH G73 ...110 C4
Pennan Pl SCOT G14 ...64 B1
Penneld Rd
  CARD/HILL/MSPK G52 ...86 A4
Pennine Gv AIRDRIE ML6 ...119 G3
Pennycroft Av DMBTN G82 ...13 H2
Pennyroyal Ct EKILN G74 ...166 C4
Penrioch Dr EKILS G75 ...177 H4
Penrith Av GIF/THBK G46 ...127 F5
Penrith Dr KVD/HLHD G12 ...51 H5
Penrith Pl EKILS G75 ...177 H4
Penryn Gdns CAR/SHTL G32 ...113 E1
Penston Rd
  STPS/GTHM/RID G33 ...93 E1
Pentland Av PSLYN/LNWD PA3 ...81 H4
Pentland Crs PSLYS PA2 ...104 A4
Pentland Dr BRHD/NEIL G78 ...142 A1
  BSHPBGS G64 ...55 G1
  RNFRW PA4 ...63 E5
Pentland Pl BSDN G61 ...33 G1
Pentland Rd
  BAIL/MDB/MHD G69 ...58 C2
  PLKSW/MSWD G43 ...127 F2
  WISHAW ML2 ...157 F4
Pentland Wy HMLTN ML3 ...180 B1
Penzance Wy
  BAIL/MDB/MHD G69 ...58 D1
Peockland Gdns JNSTN PA5 ...101 H3
Peockland Pl JNSTN PA5 ...101 H3
Peploe Dr EKILN G74 ...150 A5
Percy Dr GIF/THBK G46 ...145 F1
Percy Rd RNFRW PA4 ...62 D1
Percy St GOV/IBX G51 ...88 A4
Perran Gdns
  BAIL/MDB/MHD G69 ...58 D1
Perray Av DMBTN G82 ...12 A2
Perth Av AIRDRIE ML6 ...98 B4
Perth Crs CLYDBK G81 ...31 E3
Peter D Stirling Rd KKNTL G66 ...21 F4
Petersburn Pl AIRDRIE ML6 ...99 E3
Petersburn Rd AIRDRIE ML6 ...99 E3
Petershill Dr SPRGB/BLRNK G21 ...68 D3
Petershill Pl SPRGB/BLRNK G21 ...68 D2
Petershill Rd SPRGB/BLRNK G21 ...68 D3
Peterson Dr KNTSWD G13 ...49 H5
Peterson Gdns KNTSWD G13 ...49 H5
Petition Pl UD/BTH/TAN G71 ...134 B2
Pettigrew St CAR/SHTL G32 ...92 B4
Peveril Av PLKSD/SHW G41 ...108 C3
  RUTH G73 ...130 B2
Pharonhill St DEN/PKHD G31 ...91 H4
Philip Murry Rd
  UD/BTH/TAN G71 ...133 E1
Philipshill Ga EKILN G74 ...164 D2
Philipshill Rd EKILN G74 ...164 D2
Phoenix Crs BLSH ML4 ...116 C5
Phoenix Pl JNSTN PA5 ...102 C1
Phoenix Rd COWCAD G4 ...2 D1
Piccadilly St KVGV G3 ...2 A6
Pickerstonhill MTHW ML1 ...138 D3
Picketlaw Dr
  CRMNK/CLK/EAG G76 ...147 E5
Picketlaw Farm Rd
  CRMNK/CLK/EAG G76 ...146 D5
Piershill St CAR/SHTL G32 ...92 B2
Pikeman Av KNTSWD G13 ...50 D5
Pikeman Rd KNTSWD G13 ...50 D5
Pillans Ct HMLTN ML3 ...152 B4
Pilmuir Av LNPK/KPK G44 ...128 A3
Pilrig St CAR/SHTL G32 ...91 H2
Pilton Rd DRUM G15 ...33 F3
Pine Av BLTYR/CAMB G72 ...132 C4
Pine Cl CUMB G67 ...27 G1

Pine Ct CUMB G67 ...27 G1
  EKILS G75 ...177 G1
Pine Crs CUMB G67 ...27 G1
  EKILS G75 ...177 G3
  JNSTN PA5 ...101 H5
Pine Gv AIRDRIE ML6 ...118 C2
  CUMB G67 ...27 G1
  UD/BTH/TAN G71 ...115 G4
  CTBR ML5 ...95 F3
Pine Lawn WISHAW ML2 ...157 G5
Pine Pk HMLTN ML3 ...170 B4
Pine Pl CUMB G67 ...27 G1
  GBLS G5 ...89 H5
Pine Qd AIRDRIE ML6 ...119 E3
Pine Rd CLYDBK G81 ...31 E4
  CUMB G67 ...27 G1
  DMBTN G82 ...13 E3
Pine St AIRDRIE ML6 ...4 C2
  KKNTL G66 ...40 C2
  PSLYS PA2 ...104 D2
Pinewood Av KKNTL G66 ...39 F3
Pinewood Ct DMBTN G82 ...13 G2
  KKNTL G66 ...39 F3
Pinewood Pl KKNTL G66 ...39 F3
Pinkerton Av RUTH G73 ...110 A4
Pinkerton La RNFRW PA4 ...63 G5
Pinkston Dr SPRGB/BLRNK G21 ...68 B4
Pinkston Rd SPRGB/BLRNK G21 ...68 A4
Pinmore Pl PLK/PH/NH G53 ...125 E2
Pinmore St PLK/PH/NH G53 ...125 E2
Pinwherry Dr
  STPS/GTHM/RID G33 ...56 A5
Pinwherry Pl UD/BTH/TAN G71 ...134 B4
Piper Av CRG/CRSL/HOU PA6 ...80 D5
Piper Rd AIRDRIE ML6 ...98 B3
  CRG/CRSL/HOU PA6 ...80 D5
Pirnie Pl KSYTH G65 ...8 B2
Pirnmill Av EKILS G75 ...177 G4
  MTHW ML1 ...154 A3
Pitcairn Crs EKILS G75 ...165 F5
Pitcairn Gv EKILS G75 ...165 F5
Pitcairn Pl EKILS G75 ...165 E5
Pitcairn St DEN/PKHD G31 ...91 H5
Pitcairn Ter HMLTN ML3 ...169 F1
Pitcaple Dr PLKSW/MSWD G43 ...127 F1
Pitlochry Dr
  CARD/HILL/MSPK G52 ...86 D5
Pitmedden Rd BSHPBGS G64 ...55 G1
Pitmilly Rd DRUM G15 ...33 H4
Pitreavie Ct HMLTN ML3 ...169 G5
Pitreavie Pl
  STPS/GTHM/RID G33 ...70 D4
Pitt St CGLW G2 ...2 C5
Pladda Rd RNFRW PA4 ...63 G5
Pladda St MTHW ML1 ...154 A2
Plaintrees Ct PSLYS PA2 ...104 B3
Plane Pl UD/BTH/TAN G71 ...115 G3
Planetree Pl JNSTN PA5 ...101 H5
Planetree Rd CLYDBK G81 ...31 H4
Plantation Av MTHW ML1 ...138 C5
Plantation Park Gdns
  GOV/IBX G51 ...88 C4
Plantation Sq GOV/IBX G51 ...88 D3
Plant St DEN/PKHD G31 ...91 F3
Platthorn Dr EKILN G74 ...166 C3
Platthorn Rd EKILN G74 ...166 C3
Playfair St DMNK/BRGTN G40 ...110 D1
Plaza EKILN G74 ...166 B5
Pleaknowe Crs
  BAIL/MDB/MHD G69 ...58 D1
Pleamuir Pl BALLOCH G68 ...25 G4
Plean St SCOT G14 ...64 B1
Pleasance La
  PLKSW/MSWD G43 ...108 B4
Plover Dr EKILS G75 ...177 G3
Plover Pl JNSTN PA5 ...120 D2
Pochard Wy BLSH ML4 ...116 C4
Poet's Vw KKNTL G66 ...40 C1
Poindfauld Ter DMBTN G82 ...13 F3
Pointhouse Rd KVGV G3 ...88 B1
Polden Av EKILS G75 ...177 F5
Polden Ct EKILS G75 ...177 F5
Pollock Av HMLTN ML3 ...169 E5
Pollock Rd BSDN G61 ...34 D5
  NMRNS G77 ...161 F1
Pollock St BLSH ML4 ...136 B2
  MTHW ML1 ...154 D3
Pollok Dr BSHPBGS G64 ...54 B1
Pollok La EKILN G74 ...167 E2
Pollok Pl EKILN G74 ...167 E2
Pollokshaws Rd
  PLKSW/MSWD G43 ...108 A5
Pollokshields Sq
  PLKSD/SHW G41 ...108 D2
Polmadie Av GBLS G5 ...110 A2
Polmadie Rd GBLS G5 ...109 H2
  GVH/MTFL G42 ...109 H2
Polmadie St GVH/MTFL G42 ...109 H3
Polnoon Av KNTSWD G13 ...50 B5
Polquhap Ct PLK/PH/NH G53 ...106 D4
Polquhap Gdns
  PLK/PH/NH G53 ...106 D4
Polquhap Pl PLK/PH/NH G53 ...106 D4
Polquhap Rd PLK/PH/NH G53 ...106 D4
Polson Dr JNSTN PA5 ...101 F4
Polsons Crs PSLYS PA2 ...104 A2
Polwarth La KVD/HLHD G12 ...66 A4
Polwarth St KVD/HLHD G12 ...66 A4
Pomona Pl HMLTN ML3 ...169 E3
Poplar Av BSHPTN PA7 ...46 A1
  JNSTN PA5 ...101 H5
  NMRNS G77 ...161 H2
Poplar Crs BSHPTN PA7 ...46 A1
Poplar Dr CLYDBK G81 ...31 G3
  KKNTL G66 ...39 F3
Poplar Gdns EKILS G75 ...177 H3
Poplar Pl BLTYR/CAMB G72 ...151 F1
  MTHW ML1 ...137 G3
  UD/BTH/TAN G71 ...116 A4
Poplar Rd DMBTN G82 ...13 E2
The Poplars BSDN G61 ...16 D5
Poplar St AIRDRIE ML6 ...98 D2
Poplar Wy BLTYR/CAMB G72 ...132 A3
  MTHW ML1 ...138 A5
Poplin St DMNK/BRGTN G40 ...110 D1
Porchester St
  STPS/GTHM/RID G33 ...71 E4
Portal Rd KNTSWD G13 ...50 D3
Port Dundas Pl COWCAD G4 ...3 F3
Port Dundas Rd COWCAD G4 ...3 F1
Porterfield Rd RNFRW PA4 ...62 D3
Porter St GOV/IBX G51 ...88 A4
Porters Well UD/BTH/TAN G71 ...133 H2

Portessie ERSK PA8......................47 F1
Portland Pk HMLTN ML5 ....170 B3
Portland Pl HMLTN ML5 ....170 B3
Portland Rd BALLOCH G68 ....10 B5
 PSLYS PA2....................................105 E1
Portland St HMLTN ML3 ....170 B5
Portland St CTBR ML5 ....97 E1
Portman St PLKSD/SHW G41 ....88 D4
Portmarnock Dr SMSTN G23 ....52 D3
Portpatrick Rd OLDK G60 ....30 A1
Portreath Rd
 BAIL/MDB/MHD G69....................44 A3
Portree Av CTBR ML5......................96 B5
Portree Pl HMLTN ML5 ....52 D4
Portsoy Av KNTSWD G13 ....50 A3
Portsoy Pl KNTSWD G13 ....50 A3
Port St KVGV G3 ....89 E2
Portugal St CBLS G5 ....C5
Portwell HMLTN ML3 ....170 B1
Possil Rd COWCAD G4 ....67 G4
Postgate HMLTN ML5......................170 B1
Potassels Rd
 BAIL/MDB/MHD G69......................58 B4
Potrail Pl HMLTN ML5 ....169 F2
Potter Cl CAR/SHTL G32 ....111 H1
Potter Gv CAR/SHTL G32 ....111 H1
Potterhill Av PSLYS PA2 ....104 B3
Potterhill Rd PLK/PH/NH G53 ......106 B2
Potter Pl CAR/SHTL G32 ....111 H1
Potter St CAR/SHTL G32 ....111 H1
Potts Wy HMLTN ML1......................154 B1
Powbrone EKILS G75 ....178 B3
Powburn Crs UD/BTH/TAN G71 ....114 C5
Powfoot St DEN/PKHD G31 ....91 G4
Powrie St STPS/GTHM/RID G33 ....69 H4
Prentice La UD/BTH/TAN G71 ......115 F4
Prentice Rd HMLTN ML3................154 A5
Prestonfield MLNGV G62 ....16 C5
Preston Pl GVH/MTFL G42 ....109 G2
Prestwick Ct BALLOCH G68 ....26 B1
Prestwick Pl NMRNS G77 ....162 B1
Prestwick St PLK/PH/NH G53 ......125 H1
Pretoria Ct KVGV G3 ....177 C4
Priesthill St BLTYR/CAMB G72 ....151 F4
Priesthill Crs PLK/PH/NH G53 ....125 H1
Priesthill Gdns PLK/PH/NH G53 ..125 H1
Priesthill Rd PLK/PH/NH G53 ......125 G1
Preston Rd BRWEIR PA11 ....79 C4
Primrose Av BLSH ML4 ....116 D5
Primrose Crs HMLTN ML1 ....154 D5
Primrose Pl CUMB G67 ....44 C4
 UD/BTH/TAN G71 ....115 H4
Primrose St SCOT G14 ....64 D3
Primrose Wy KNTTL G66....................4 C4
Prince Albert Rd KVD/HLHD G12 ..66 A5
Prince Edward St
 GVH/MTFL G42 ....109 F2
Prince of Wales Gdns
 MRYH/FIRH G20 ....52 B5
Prince Pl WISHAW ML2 ....158 B4
Prince's Gdns KVD/HLHD G12 ......66 A3
Prince's Pl KVD/HLHD G12 ....66 B5
Princes Ga RUTH G73 ....110 D4
 UD/BTH/TAN G71 ....133 H5
Princes Ms EKILN G74 ....166 C4
Princes Pk BSHPTN PA7 ....29 H4
Prince's Pl KVD/HLHD G12 ....66 B5
Princess Crs PSLY PA1 ....85 E3
Princes Dr
 BAIL/MDB/MHD G69........................95 F4
Princes Sq BRHD/NEIL G78 ....124 B4
 EKILN G74 ....166 B4
Princess Rd MTHW ML1..................137 H4
Princes St MTHW ML1 ....154 D2
 RUTH G73......................................110 D4
Princes' Ter KVD/HLHD G12 ....66 B3
Princes Terrace La
 KVD/HLHD G12 ....66 B3
Printers Lea KKNTL G66......................4 A2
Priorwood Ga NMRNS G77............160 D1
Priorwood Pl KNTSWD G13 ....51 E5
Priorwood Rd NMRNS G77............160 D1
Priorwood Wy NMRNS G77 ....160 D1
Priory Av PSLYN/LNWD PA3 ....84 D2
Priory Dr UD/BTH/TAN G71 ....114 C5
Priory Pl BALLOCH G68 ....26 A1
 KNTSWD G13 ....51 E4
Priory Rd KNTSWD G13 ....51 E4
Priory St BLTYR/CAMB G72 ....151 G5
Priory Ter WISHAW ML2 ....158 A5
Procession Rd PSLYS PA2 ....123 E1
Prosen St CAR/SHTL G32 ....111 H1
Prospect Av BLTYR/CAMB G72 ....151 E1
 UD/BTH/TAN G71 ....115 E5
Prospect St E BLTYR/CAMB G72 ..151 G5
Prospecthill Circ
 GVH/MTFL G42 ....110 B3
Prospecthill Crs
 GVH/MTFL G42 ....110 B3
Prospecthill Dr GVH/MTFL G42 ..109 H4
Prospecthill Pl RUTH G73 ....110 B4
Prospecthill Rd GVH/MTFL G42 ..109 G4
Prospecthill Sq GVH/MTFL G42 ..110 A4
Prospect Rd BALLOCH G68 ....9 G4
 PLKSD/SHW G41 ....108 C4
Provand Hall Crs
 BAIL/MDB/MHD G69......................114 A1
Provanmill St SPRGB/BLRNK G21..68 C5
Provanmill Rd
 STPS/GTHM/RID G33......................69 H4
Provan Rd DEN/PKHD G31 ....69 H4
Provost Driver Ct RNFRW PA4 ......63 G5
Purdie EKILN G74 ....150 A5
Purdie St HMLTN ML3....................152 B5
Purdon St PTCK G11 ....66 A4

Quadrant Rd
 PLKSW/MSWD G43 ....127 H2
The Quadrant
 CRMNK/CLK/EAG G76..................146 A2
Quantock Gv EKILS G75 ....177 F4
Quarreiton Gv JNSTN PA5 ....101 G5
Quarreiton Rd JNSTN PA5 ....101 F4
Quarrybank KLBCH PA10 ....100 D4
Quarrybrae Av
 CRMNK/CLK/EAG G76....................145 G3
Quarrybrae Gdns
 UD/BTH/TAN G71 ....134 D1

Quarrybrae St DEN/PKHD G31 ....91 H4
Quarry Dr KKNTL G66 ....21 H5
Quarry Knowe DMBTN G82 ....12 C2
Quarryknowe RUTH G73 ....110 C5
Quarryknowe Gdns
 DEN/PKHD G31 ....91 H4
Quarry knowe Pl BLSH ML4............135 C4
Quarryknowe St CLYDBK G81 ....32 D1
 DEN/PKHD G31 ....91 H4
Quarry La KKNTL G66..........................4 B1
Quarry Pk EKILS G75 ....166 B5
Quarry Pl BLTYR/CAMB G72 ....130 D1
 DMBTN G82....................................12 C3
Quarry Rd AIRDRIE ML6 ....76 A5
 BRHD/NEIL G78 ....123 H4
 EKILS G75......................................178 A3
 PSLYS PA2 ....104 C3
Quarryside St AIRDRIE ML6 ....77 H1
Quarry St CTBR ML5 ....97 C3
 HMLTN ML3 ....170 B2
 JNSTN PA5 ....101 C3
 MTHW ML1 ....137 H5
 WISHAW ML2..................................173 H2
Quarrywood Av
 SPRGB/BLRNK G21 ....69 F2
Quarrywood Rd
 SPRGB/BLRNK G21 ....69 C2
Quay Pend DMBTN G82 ....12 D4
Quay Rd RUTH G73 ....110 D4
Quay Rd North RUTH G73 ....110 D3
Quay St DMBTN G82 ....13 E4
Quebec Dr EKILS G75 ....165 H4
Quebec Wynd BLTYR/CAMB G72 ..132 C4
Queen Elizabeth Av
 CARD/HILL/MSPK G52....................85 H2
Queen Elizabeth Ct
 CLYDBK G81 ....31 H5
Queen Elizabeth Gdns
 CLYDBK G81 ....31 H5
Queen Margaret Dr
 KVD/HLHD G12 ....66 C3
Queen Margaret Rd
 MRYH/FIRH G20..............................66 D2
Queen Mary Av CLYDBK G81 ....49 F1
 GVH/MTFL G42..............................109 G3
Queen Mary St
 DMNK/BRGTN G40 ....90 D5
Queen's Av BLTYR/CAMB G72 ......151 H5
Queensbank Av
 BAIL/MDB/MHD G69........................58 D4
Queensberry Av BSDN G61 ....34 B3
 CRMNK/CLK/EAG G76....................145 H3
Queensborough Gdns
 KVD/HLHD G12 ....65 H2
Queensby Av
 BAIL/MDB/MHD G69........................94 A4
Queensby Pl
 BAIL/MDB/MHD G69........................94 A3
Queensby Rd
 BAIL/MDB/MHD G69........................94 A3
Queen's St KNTSWD G13 ....50 C2
Queen's Crs AIRDRIE ML6 ....119 E1
 BAIL/MDB/MHD G69........................95 E4
 BLSH ML4 ....135 C3
 COWCAD G4 ....67 E4
 MTHW ML1 ....137 E4
Queens Dr BALLOCH G68 ....10 B4
 BSHPTN PA7 ....29 F4
 GVH/MTFL G42..............................109 F3
 HMLTN ML3 ....180 D2
Queen's Drive La
 GVH/MTFL G42..............................109 F3
Queensferry St GBLS G5 ....110 B2
Queen's Gdns KVD/HLHD G12 ......66 B3
Queen's Ga
 CRMNK/CLK/EAG G76....................145 H2
Queenside Crs ERSK PA8................47 E2
Queensland Dr
 CARD/HILL/MSPK G52....................86 D3
Queensland Gdns
 CARD/HILL/MSPK G52....................86 D3
Queensland La East
 CARD/HILL/MSPK G52....................86 D4
Queensland La West
 CARD/HILL/MSPK G52....................86 D3
Queenslie St
 STPS/GTHM/RID G33......................69 G4
Queen's Park Av
 GVH/MTFL G42..............................109 G3
Queen's Rd PLKSD/SHW G41 ......109 E2
Queen Sq PLKSD/SHW G41 ....109 E2
Queen St AIRDRIE ML6 ....98 B2
 MTHW ML1 ....139 E5
Queen St CGLE G1................................3 F6
 HMLTN ML3 ....152 B5
 KKNTL G66......................................21 E5
 PSLY PA1..83 H5
 RNFRW PA4 ....63 G3
 RUTH G73......................................110 D4
 WISHAW ML2 ....158 A4
Queens Wy BSHPBGS G64 ....19 F5
Queensway EKILS G75 ....165 H4
 EKILS G75......................................166 C5
Queen Victoria Ga
 KNTSWD G13 ....64 D1
Queen Victoria St SCOT G14 ....64 D2
Quendale Dr CAR/SHTL G32 ....112 A1
Quentin St PLKSD/SHW G41 ....108 D2
Quinton Gdns
 BAIL/MDB/MHD G69........................93 H4

Raasay Crs AIRDRIE ML6 ....99 F3
Raasay Dr PSLYS PA2 ....104 F3
Raasay Gdns NMRNS G77 ....143 G5
Raasay Pl PPK/MIL G22 ....53 H3
Racecourse Vw HMLTN ML3 ....153 F5
Rachan St ESTRH G34 ....72 C5
Radnor St CLYDBK G81 ....31 H5
Raeberry St MRYH/FIRH G20 ....67 E3
Raebog Crs AIRDRIE ML6 ....76 A4
Raebog Rd AIRDRIE ML6 ....75 H2
Raeburn Av EKILN G74 ....167 E3
 PSLY PA1 ....84 D5
Raeburn Crs HMLTN ML3 ....168 D1
Raeburn Pl EKILN G74 ....167 E1
Raeside Av NMRNS G77 ....161 G2

Raeswood Dr PLK/PH/NH G53 ......106 A4
Raeswood Rd PLK/PH/NH G53 ....106 A4
Raewell Crs BLSH ML4 ....135 G4
Rafford St GOV/IBX G51 ....87 H2
Raglan St COWCAD G4 ....67 H4
Railway Rd AIRDRIE ML6 ....97 G2
Raith Av CSMK G45 ....129 E3
Raithburn Av CSMK G45 ....128 D3
Raithburn Rd CSMK G45 ....128 D4
Raith Dr BALLOCH G68 ....24 B4
 BLSH ML4 ....136 A3
Ralston Av
 CARD/HILL/MSPK G52....................86 A5
 PSLY PA1 ....106 A1
Ralston Ct
 CARD/HILL/MSPK G52....................86 A5
Ralston Dr
 CARD/HILL/MSPK G52....................86 A5
Ralston Pl
 CARD/HILL/MSPK G52....................86 A5
Ralston Rd
 BRHD/NEIL G78 ....124 B5
 BSDN G61 ....34 B3
Ralston St AIRDRIE ML6 ....97 H2
 PSLY PA1 ....84 D5
Rampart Av KNTSWD G13 ....50 B3
Ramsay Av JNSTN PA5 ....101 F5
Ramsay Ct NMRNS G77 ....161 H2
Ramsay Crs KLBCH PA10 ....100 C4
Ramsay Hl EKILN G74 ....166 D2
Ramsay Pl CTBR ML5 ....95 H4
 JNSTN PA5 ....101 F5
Ramsay St CLYDBK G81 ....31 G5
Ram St CAR/SHTL G32 ....92 A4
Ranald Gdns RUTH G73 ....130 C4
Randolph Av
 CRMNK/CLK/EAG G76....................146 A1
Randolph Dr
 CRMNK/CLK/EAG G76....................146 A1
Randolph Gdns
 CRMNK/CLK/EAG G76....................146 A1
Randolph La PTCK G11 ....65 G5
Randolph Rd PTCK G11 ....65 G5
Ranfurly Dr BALLOCH G68 ....26 A1
Ranfurly Pl BRWEIR PA11 ....79 G4
Ranfurly Rd BRWEIR PA11 ....79 H5
 CARD/HILL/MSPK G52....................86 A4
Range Av MTHW ML1......................172 D2
Range Pl HMLTN ML3 ....170 B4
Rangerhouse Rd EKILS G75 ....178 C3
Range Rd MTHW ML1 ....172 C1
Range St MTHW ML1 ....172 C1
Rankin Dr NMRNS G77 ....143 H4
Rankine Av EKILS G75 ....178 D1
Rankine Pl JNSTN PA5 ....101 G3
Rankine St JNSTN PA5 ....101 G3
Rankin Rd WISHAW ML2 ....174 D1
Rannoch Av BSHPBGS G64 ....55 E2
 CTBR ML5 ....74 A5
 HMLTN ML3 ....169 H3
 NMRNS G77....................................144 A5
Rannoch Ct CUMB G67 ....44 A2
Rannoch Dr BSDN G61 ....51 H1
 CUMB G67 ....44 A2
 KKNTL G66 ....22 A4
 RNFRW PA4 ....63 F2
Rannoch Gn EKILN G74 ....166 D2
Rannoch Pl PSLYS PA2 ....104 D1
Rannoch Rd AIRDRIE ML6 ....76 A5
 JNSTN PA5 ....101 G5
 UD/BTH/TAN G71 ....114 D3
Rannoch St LNPK/KPK G44 ....128 B1
Raploch Av SCOT G14 ....64 C2
Raploch Crs CLYDBK G81 ....32 C1
Raploch La SCOT G14 ....64 C2
Raploch Rd LRKH ML9....................175 H1
Rashielee Av ERSK PA8 ....47 E1
Rashielee Rd ERSK PA8 ....47 E1
Rashiewood ERSK PA8 ....47 F1
Rathlin St GOV/IBX G51 ....87 H1
Rathlin Ter DMBTN G82 ....12 B2
Ratho Dr BALLOCH G68 ....10 A5
 SPRGB/BLRNK G21 ....68 B2
Ratho Pk HMLTN ML3 ....180 B1
Rattray St CAR/SHTL G32 ....111 H1
Ravel Rw DEN/PKHD G31 ....91 G4
Ravelston Rd BSDN G61 ....51 F1
Ravelston St CAR/SHTL G32 ....91 G5
Ravel Wynd UD/BTH/TAN G71 ......115 H4
Ravenscliffe Dr GIF/THBK G46 ....127 E4
Ravenscourt EKILN G74 ....164 B2
Ravenscraig Av PSLYS PA2 ....103 H2
Ravenscraig Dr BLSH ML4 ....136 A2
Ravenscraig Dr
 PLK/PH/NH G53 ....125 G1
Ravenscraig Ter
 PLK/PH/NH G53 ....125 H2
Ravenshall Rd
 PLKSD/SHW G41 ....108 B4
Ravenshill Dr MTHW ML1 ....157 F1
Ravenstone Dr GIF/THBK G46 ......127 F2
Ravenswood Av PSLYS PA2 ....102 D5
Ravenswood Dr
 PLKSD/SHW G41 ....108 C3
Ravenswood Rd
 BAIL/MDB/MHD G69........................94 B5
Rawyards Av AIRDRIE ML6 ....76 C4
Raymond Pl EKILS G75 ....165 H4
Rayne Pl DRUM G15 ....33 G5
Ream Av AIRDRIE ML6 ....99 G3
Reay Av EKILN G74 ....165 G5
Reay Gdns EKILN G74 ....165 G5
Redan St DMNK/BRGTN G40 ....90 C4
Redburn Av GIF/THBK G46 ....145 E2
Redburn Ct CUMB G67 ....11 H4
Redburn Pl CUMB G67 ....11 H4
Redburn Rd CUMB G67....................11 H4
Redcastle Sq
 STPS/GTHM/RID G33......................71 E3
Redclift Dr EKILS G75 ....165 G5
Rederech Crs HMLTN ML3 ....169 E3
Redford St
 STPS/GTHM/RID G33......................91 G1
Redgrave EKILN G74 ....166 C4
Redgrave EKILN G74 ....149 H5
Redhill Rd BALLOCH G68 ....25 H2
Redhills Vw KKNTL G66......................4 C5
Redhurst Crs PSLYS PA2 ....103 G5
Redhurst La PSLYS PA2 ....103 G5
Redhurst Wy PSLYS PA2 ....103 G5
Redlands La KVD/HLHD G12 ....66 B2
Redlands Rd KVD/HLHD G12 ....66 B2
Redlands Ter KVD/HLHD G12 ....66 B2

Redlands Terrace La
 KVD/HLHD G12 ....66 B2
Redlawood Pl
 BLTYR/CAMB G72 ....132 D1
Redlawood Rd
 BLTYR/CAMB G72 ....132 D1
Redmoss Rd CLYDBK G81 ....31 G2
 KKNTL G66..5 F5
Redmoss St MRYH/FIRH G20 ....67 F2
Rednock St PPK/MIL G22 ....67 H2
Redpath Dr
 CARD/HILL/MSPK G52....................86 C3
Red Rd SPRGB/BLRNK G21 ....69 E2
Red Road Ct SPRGB/BLRNK G21 ..69 E3
Redwing Gdns WISHAW ML2 ....173 H4
Redwood Ct EKILN G74..................164 D4
Redwood Crs BLTYR/CAMB G72 ..132 C3
 BSHPTN PA7 ....29 F5
 EKILN G74......................................164 D3
Redwood Dr
 BLTYR/CAMB G72 ....132 C3
Redwood Gv CTBR ML5 ....96 C5
Redwood Pl EKILN G74 ....164 D3
 UD/BTH/TAN G71 ....115 H4
 MTHW ML1 ....137 G2
Redwood Wy
 BLTYR/CAMB G72 ....132 C4
Reelick Av KNTSWD G13 ....49 H3
Reelick Qd KNTSWD G13 ....49 H3
Reema Rd BLSH ML4 ....136 B1
Reen Pl UD/BTH/TAN G71 ....134 C3
Regency Wy HMLTN ML3 ....170 D3
 MTHW ML1 ....137 E3
Regent Dr RUTH G73 ....110 D4
Regent Moray St KVGV G3 ....66 C5
Regent Park Sq
 PLKSD/SHW G41 ....109 E2
Regent Pl CLYDBK G81 ....31 F4
Regent Sq KKNTL G66 ....39 H4
Regent St CLYDBK G81 ....31 F4
 KKNTL G66 ....21 E5
 PSLY PA1..84 D4
Register Av BLSH ML4 ....135 H4
Register Rd KSYTH G65......................8 C2
Regwood St PLKSD/SHW G41 ......108 C4
Reid Av BSDN G61 ....34 D5
 PSLYN/LNWD PA3 ....82 A4
Reid Gv MTHW ML1........................172 C1
Reid Pl DMNK/BRGTN G40 ....90 C5
Reid St AIRDRIE ML6 ....98 C1
 DMNK/BRGTN G40 ....110 C1
 HMLTN ML3 ....152 B5
 RUTH G73......................................111 E4
Reidvale St DEN/PKHD G31 ....90 D3
Reith Dr EKILS G75........................178 A1
Remus Pl BLSH ML4........................136 D2
Renfield La CCLW G2 ....2 E5
Renfield St CCLW G2 ....2 E4
 RNFRW PA4 ....63 G2
Renfrew Ct CCLW G2 ....3 F3
Renfrew Rd PSLYN/LNWD PA3 ......84 A3
 RNFRW PA4 ....64 B5
Renfrew St COWCAD G4 ....95 H5
 RNFRW PA4 ....2 D3
Rennie Pl EKILN G74 ....165 F2
Rennie Rd KSYTH G65........................7 H1
Renshaw Dr
 CARD/HILL/MSPK G52....................86 C3
Renshaw Rd BSHPTN PA7 ....29 F5
 JNSTN PA5....................................102 B5
Renton Rd DMBTN G82 ....12 C1
Renton St COWCAD G4 ....67 H5
Resipol Rd STPS/GTHM/RID G33 ..71 F1
Reston Dr CARD/HILL/MSPK G52 ..86 B3
Reuther Av RUTH G73 ....111 E5
Revoch Dr KNTSWD G13 ....50 B4
Reynolds Av EKILS G75 ....178 D1
Reynolds Dr
 STPS/GTHM/RID G33......................71 G1
Reynolds Pth WISHAW ML2 ....174 C4
Rhannan Rd LNPK/KPK G44 ....128 B2
Rhannan Ter LNPK/KPK G44 ....128 B2
Rhindhouse Pl
 BAIL/MDB/MHD G69........................94 C4
Rhindhouse Rd
 BAIL/MDB/MHD G69........................94 C4
Rhindmuir Av
 BAIL/MDB/MHD G69........................94 B4
Rhindmuir Ct
 BAIL/MDB/MHD G69........................94 B3
Rhindmuir Crs
 BAIL/MDB/MHD G69........................94 B3
Rhindmuir Dr
 BAIL/MDB/MHD G69........................94 B3
Rhindmuir Gdns
 BAIL/MDB/MHD G69........................94 B3
Rhindmuir Pth
 BAIL/MDB/MHD G69........................94 B3
Rhindmuir Pl
 BAIL/MDB/MHD G69........................94 B3
Rhindmuir Rd
 BAIL/MDB/MHD G69........................94 B3
Rhindmuir Vw
 BAIL/MDB/MHD G69........................94 B3
Rhindmuir Wynd
 BAIL/MDB/MHD G69........................94 B3
Rhindsdale Crs
 BAIL/MDB/MHD G69........................93 H4
Rhinds St CTBR ML5 ....95 G5
Rhymer St SPRGB/BLRNK G21 ......68 C5
Rhymie Rd CAR/SHTL G32 ....113 E1
Rhynie Dr GOV/IBX G51 ....88 A4
Riach Gdns MTHW ML1 ....154 B1
Ribblesdale EKILN G74 ....165 H2
Riccarton EKILS G75 ....177 G1
Riccarton St GVH/MTFL G42 ....109 H2
Riccartsbar Av PSLYS G77 ....103 H1
Rice Wy MTHW ML1 ....172 D2
Richmond Av
 CRMNK/CLK/EAG G76....................145 H3
Richmond Ct RUTH G73 ....111 G5
Richmond Dr
 BLTYR/CAMB G72 ....130 D2
 PSLYN/LNWD PA3 ....84 D2
 RUTH G73......................................111 G5
Richmond Gdns
 BAIL/MDB/MHD G69........................58 A2
Richmond Gv RUTH G73 ....111 F5
Richmond Pl RUTH G73 ....111 G5
Richmond Rd RUTH G73 ....111 G5
Richmond St CGLE G1 ....3 H5
 CLYDBK G81 ....49 F2
Riddell St CLYDBK G81 ....32 B5

 CTBR ML5..97 F2
Riddon Av KNTSWD G13 ....49 H3
Riddon Pl KNTSWD G13 ....49 H3
Riddrie Crs STPS/GTHM/RID G33 ..91 H1
Ridrie Knowes
 STPS/GTHM/RID G33 ....91 H1
Riddrievale Ct
 STPS/GTHM/RID G33......................69 H5
Rigby St CAR/SHTL G32 ....91 G3
Rigghead Av CUMB G67 ....10 C5
Rigside Rd
 STPS/GTHM/RID G33......................70 D4
The Riggs MLNGV G62 ....17 E2
Riglaw Pl KNTSWD G13 ....50 B4
Rimsdale St DMNK/BRGTN G40 ....90 D4
Ringford St SPRGB/BLRNK G21 ....68 B2
Ripon Dr KVD/HLHD G12 ....51 H5
Risk St CLYDBK G81 ....31 G4
 DMBTN G82....................................12 D4
Ritchie Crs JNSTN PA5 ....102 B1
Ritchie Pk JNSTN PA5 ....82 A5
Ritchie St NMRNS G77 ....161 F1
Ritchie St GBLS G5 ....89 F5
Riverbank Dr BLSH ML4 ....136 C4
Riverbank St
 PLKSW/MSWD G43 ....108 B5
Riverbank St
 PLKSW/MSWD G43 ....108 B5
River Ct CRMNK/CLK/EAG G76 ....146 A5
Riverdale La SCOT G14 ....64 B1
Riverford Rd
 PLKSW/MSWD G43 ....108 B5
 RUTH G73......................................111 F5
River Rd CAR/SHTL G32 ....112 C5
Riversdale La SCOT G14 ....64 B1
Riverside CRC/CRSL/HOU PA6 ......81 F2
 MLNGV G62....................................16 C4
Riverside Ct LNPK/KPK G44 ....128 A5
Riverside Gdns
 CRMNK/CLK/EAG G76....................146 A5
Riverside La DMBTN G82 ....12 D4
Riverside Pl BLTYR/CAMB G72 ....132 D1
Riverside Rd
 CRMNK/CLK/EAG G76....................163 F5
 PLKSW/MSWD G43 ....108 D5
Riverside Ter
 CRMNK/CLK/EAG G76....................146 A5
Riverside Wk MTHW ML1 ....155 E2
Riverton Dr EKILS G75 ....165 G5
Riverview Dr GBLS G5 ....2 D7
Riverview Gdns KVGV G3 ....2 C7
Riverview Pl GBLS G5 ....2 D7
Roadside CUMB G67 ....10 C1
Roaden Av PSLYS PA2 ....103 E5
Roaden Rd PSLYS PA2 ....103 E5
Robert Burns Av CLYDBK G81 ......32 B5
 HMLTN ML1 ....138 B3
Robert Burns Od BLSH ML4 ....135 G2
Robert Dr GOV/IBX G51 ....87 H2
Robert Gilson Gdns CTBR ML5 ......97 E4
Robertland Sq SPRGB/BLRNK G40 ..108 B2
Robertson Av PLKSD/SHW G41 ..108 A1
Robertson St AIRDRIE ML6 ....119 E1
Robertson Av RNFRW PA4 ....63 E3
Robertson Cl RNFRW PA4 ....135 H3
Robertson Crs BRHD/NEIL G78 ....141 G5
Robertson Dr BLSH ML4 ....135 H3
 EKILN G74......................................167 F1
 RNFRW PA4 ....63 E3
Robertson La CCLW G2 ....2 D6
Robertson St AIRDRIE ML6 ....98 B2
 BRHD/NEIL G78 ....124 A4
 HMLTN ML3 ....152 A5
 KVGV G3 ....2 D7
Roberts Od BLSH ML4 ....136 A4
Roberts St WISHAW ML2 ....173 H2
Robert St GOV/IBX G51 ....87 H2
Robert Templeton Dr
 BLTYR/CAMB G72 ....131 G2
Robert Wynd WISHAW ML2 ....158 B4
Robin Pl WISHAW ML2 ....174 A2
Robroyston Av
 STPS/GTHM/RID G33......................69 H3
Robroyston Rd
 STPS/GTHM/RID G33......................69 G3
Robslee Crs GIF/THBK G46 ....126 D4
Robslee Dr GIF/THBK G46 ....127 E4
Robslee Rd GIF/THBK G46 ....126 D4
Robson Gv GVH/MTFL G42 ....109 G2
Rochsoles Crs AIRDRIE ML6 ....76 B4
Rochsoles Dr AIRDRIE ML6 ....76 B4
Rochsolloch Rd AIRDRIE ML6 ....97 G3
Rockall Dr LNPK/KPK G44 ....128 C3
Rockbank Pl DMNK/BRGTN G40 ..90 D4
Rockbank St DMNK/BRGTN G40 ..90 D4
Rockburn Crs BLSH ML4 ....116 C5
Rockburn Dr
 CRMNK/CLK/EAG G76....................145 F2
Rockcliffe Pth AIRDRIE ML6 ....119 G3
Rockcliffe St
 DMNK/BRGTN G40 ....110 C1
Rock Dr KLBCH PA10......................100 C4
Rockfield Pl SPRGB/BLRNK G21 ....69 F1
Rockfield Rd SPRGB/BLRNK G21 ..69 F1
Rockhampton Av EKILS G75 ....177 E3
Rockmount Av
 BRHD/NEIL G78 ....142 C1
 GIF/THBK G46 ....126 D4
Rock St COWCAD G4 ....67 G3
Rockwell Av PSLYS PA2 ....103 H4
Roddinghead Rd NMRNS G77 ......144 D4
Rodger Av NMRNS G77 ....161 G2
Rodger Dr RUTH G73 ....129 H1
Rodger Pl RUTH G73 ....129 H1
Rodil Av LNPK/KPK G44 ....128 D3
Rodney St COWCAD G4 ....67 G4
Roebank Dr BRHD/NEIL G78 ....142 B1
Roebank St DEN/PKHD G31 ....91 E1
Roffey Park Rd PSLY PA1 ....85 H4
Rogart St DMNK/BRGTN G40 ....90 C4
Rogerfield Rd
 BAIL/MDB/MHD G69........................94 B2
Roland Crs NMRNS G77 ....162 A2
Roman Av BSDN G61 ....34 C3
 DRUM G15..50 B2
Roman Ct BSDN G61 ....34 B3
Roman Crs OLDK G60 ....30 A3
Roman Dr BSDN G61 ....34 B3
 BLSH ML4 ....136 A3
Roman Gdns BSDN G61 ....34 B3
Roman Hill Rd CLYDBK G81 ....31 H1
Roman Pl BLSH ML4 ....135 H3
Roman Rd BSDN G61 ....34 A3
 CLYDBK G81 ....31 H1
 KKNTL G66 ....21 G4
 MTHW ML1 ....154 D3

Roman Wy UD/BTH/TAN G71 134 D1
Romney Av LNPK/KPK G44 128 D2
Romulus Ct MTHW ML1 154 B1
Ronaldsay Dr BSHPBGS G64 55 G1
Ronaldsay Pl CUMB G67 25 H5
Ronaldsay St PPK/MIL G22 53 H4
Rona St SPRGB/BLRNK G21 69 E4
Rona Ter BLTYR/CAMB G72 131 E4
Ronay St PPK/MIL G22 54 A4
WISHAW ML2 157 H5
Rooksdell Av PSLYS PA2 103 H3
Ropework La CGLE G1 89 H3
Rosa Burn Av EKILS G75 177 G4
Rosebank Av
BLTYR/CAMB G72 151 H1
KKNTL G66 21 G4
Rosebank Dr BLTYR/CAMB G72 131 H3
UD/BTH/TAN G71 115 H5
Rosebank Gdns
UD/BTH/TAN G71 114 A2
Rosebank Pl BALLOCH G68 9 G4
HMLTN ML3 169 F2
Rosebank Rd BLSH ML4 117 E4
Rosebank St AIRDRIE ML6 99 F1
Rosebank Ter
BAIL/MDB/MHD G69 95 F5
Roseberry La AIRDRIE ML6 119 E1
Roseberry Pl HMLTN ML3 169 F1
Roseberry Rd AIRDRIE ML6 99 E5
Roseberry St GBLS G5 110 B2
Roseburn Ct CUMB G67 11 H5
Rose Crs HMLTN ML3 169 E1
Rose Dl BSHPBGS G64 55 E3
Rosedale EKILN G74 165 H2
Rosedale Av PSLYS PA2 102 C5
Rosedale Dr
BAIL/MDB/MHD G69 93 H5
Rosedale Gdns MRYH/FIRH G20 52 B3
Rosedene Ter BLSH ML4 135 H1
Rosefield Gdns
UD/BTH/TAN G71 114 D5
Rosegreen Crs BLSH ML4 116 D4
Rosehall Av CTBR ML5 97 E5
Rosehall Rd BLSH ML4 135 G1
Rosehall Ter WISHAW ML2 173 F4
Rosehill Dr CUMB G67 43 H1
Rosehill Rd BSHPBGS G64 19 G5
Rose Knowe Rd
GVH/MTFL G42 110 A4
Roselea Dr MLNGV G62 17 F2
Roselea Gdns KNTSWD G13 51 G4
Roselea Pl BLTYR/CAMB G72 151 F1
Roselea Rd UD/BTH/TAN G71 114 D4
Rosemary Crs EKILN G74 166 A1
Rosemary Pl EKILN G74 166 A1
Rosemount BALLOCH G68 10 B5
Rosemount Av NMRNS G77 161 G3
Rose Mount Ct AIRDRIE ML6 98 D1
Rosemount Ct NMRNS G77 161 G4
Rosemount La BRWEIR PA11 79 E5
Rosemount Mdw
UD/BTH/TAN G71 133 H5
Rosemount St
SPRGB/BLRNK G21 90 D1
Rosendale Wy
BLTYR/CAMB G72 151 H3
Roseness Pl
STPS/GTHM/RID G33 92 B1
Rosenheath Ga EKILN G74 165 H3
Rosepark Av UD/BTH/TAN G71 134 D1
Rose St CUMB G67 44 A2
KKNTL G66 21 F5
KVGV G3 2 D3
MTHW ML1 155 F5
Rosevale Crs BLSH ML4 136 B3
HMLTN ML3 169 G3
Rosevale Rd BSDN G61 34 B4
Rosevale St PTCK G11 65 H4
Rosewood Av BLSH ML4 117 E5
PSLYS PA2 103 G3
Rosewood Pth BLSH ML4 135 F2
Rosewood St KNTSWD G13 51 F4
Roslea Dr DEN/PKHD G31 90 D2
Roslyn Dr BAIL/MDB/MHD G69 95 E4
Rosneath St GOV/IBX G51 87 H1
Ross Av KKNTL G66 21 H5
RNFRW PA4 62 D5
Ross Crs MTHW ML1 154 B5
Ross Dr AIRDRIE ML6 97 H5
MTHW ML1 154 B5
UD/BTH/TAN G71 115 H3
Rossendale Ct
PLKSD/SHW G41 108 B4
Rossendale Rd
PLKSD/SHW G41 108 B4
Ross Gdns MTHW ML1 154 B5
Rosshall Av PSLY PA1 85 F5
Ross Hall Pl RNFRW PA4 63 G3
Rosshill Av
CARD/HILL/MSPK G52 86 A4
Rosshill Rd
CARD/HILL/MSPK G52 86 A4
Rossie Crs BSHPBGS G64 55 F3
Rossie Gv NMRNS G77 143 G5
Rossland Crs BSHPTN PA7 28 D5
Rosslea Dr GIF/THBK G46 127 F5
Rosslyn Av EKILN G74 166 C2
RUTH G73 111 F5
Rosslyn Ct HMLTN ML3 169 F1
Rosslyn Rd BSDN G61 33 G2
Rosslyn Ter KVD/HLHD G12 66 B2
Ross Pl RUTH G73 130 C3
Ross St CGLE G1 90 A3
CTBR ML5 96 D2
PSLY PA1 104 D1
Ross Ter HMLTN ML3 171 F4
Rostan Rd PLKSW/MSWD G43 127 F2
Rosyth Rd GBLS G5 110 B2
Rosyth St GBLS G5 110 B2
Rotherwick Dr PSLY PA1 85 H5
Rotherwood Av KNTSWD G13 50 D2
PSLYS PA2 103 E4
Rotherwood La KNTSWD G13 50 D1
Rotherwood Pl KNTSWD G13 51 E3
Rothesay Crs CTBR ML5 117 E1
Rothesay Pl CTBR ML5 97 E5
Rothesay St EKILS G75 166 C5
Rothes Dr SMSTN G23 52 C3
Rothes Pl MRYH/FIRH G20 52 B2
Rottenrow COWCAD G4 3 H4
Rottenrow East COWCAD G4 3 J5
Roughcraig St AIRDRIE ML6 76 B4
Roughrigg Rd AIRDRIE ML6 99 H3
Roukenburn St GIF/THBK G46 126 B3
Rouken Glen Rd
GIF/THBK G46 126 C5
The Roundel WISHAW ML2 174 B2
Roundhill Dr JNSTN PA5 102 D1
Roundknowe Rd
UD/BTH/TAN G71 114 B3
Round Riding Rd DMBTN G82 13 F3
Rowallan Gdns PTCK G11 65 G3
Rowallan La
CRMNK/CLK/EAG G76 145 H3
PTCK G11 65 G3
Rowallan La East PTCK G11 65 H3
Rowallan Rd GIF/THBK G46 126 C5
Rowallan Ter
STPS/GTHM/RID G33 70 C2
Rowan Av KKNTL G66 5 F5
RNFRW PA4 63 F2
Rowanbank Pl CTBR ML5 97 G1
Rowan Crs AIRDRIE ML6 119 F1
KKNTL G66 39 H3
Rowandale Av
BAIL/MDB/MHD G69 93 H5
Rowand Av GIF/THBK G46 127 F5
Rowanden Av BLSH ML4 135 H1
Rowan Dr BSDN G61 34 C1
CLYDBK G81 31 G4
Rowan Gdns PLKSD/SHW G41 88 A5
Rowan Ga PSLYS PA2 104 C2
Rowan Gv HMLTN ML3 181 F5
Rowanlea Av PSLYS PA2 102 C5
Rowanlea Dr GIF/THBK G46 127 G3
Rowanpark Dr BRHD/NEIL G78 123 H2
Rowan Pl BLTYR/CAMB G72 131 H1
BLTYR/CAMB G72 151 G2
CTBR ML5 96 B5
Rowan Ri HMLTN ML3 170 B3
Rowan Rd CUMB G67 27 F2
PLKSD/SHW G41 88 A5
PSLYN/LNWD PA3 81 G4
Rowans Gdns
UD/BTH/TAN G71 134 C3
The Rowans BSHPBGS G64 54 C1
Rowan St PSLYS PA2 104 C2
WISHAW ML2 157 E5
Rowantree Av MTHW ML1 119 E5
RUTH G73 130 A3
UD/BTH/TAN G71 115 H5
Rowantree Pl JNSTN PA5 * 101 G5
KKNTL G66 4 C3
Rowantree Rd JNSTN PA5 101 G5
Rowantree Ter KKNTL G66 4 C4
MTHW ML1 137 G2
Rowanwood Crs CTBR ML5 96 A4
Rowena Av KNTSWD G13 51 E2
Roxburgh Dr BSDN G61 34 B1
CTBR ML5 97 G5
Roxburgh Pk EKILN G74 166 C4
Roxburgh Rd PSLYS PA2 102 C5
Roxburgh St KVD/HLHD G12 66 C3
Royal Crs KVGV G3 88 D1
Royal Dr HMLTN ML3 170 D3
Royal Exchange Ct CGLE G1 3 F5
Royal Exchange Sq CGLE G1 3 F5
Royal Gdns UD/BTH/TAN G71 133 H5
Royal Inch Ter RNFRW PA4 63 G1
Royal Ter KVGV G3 66 D5
WISHAW ML2 157 F3
Royal Terrace La KVGV G3 66 D5
Royellen Av HMLTN ML3 169 E3
Roystonhill SPRGB/BLRNK G21 68 C5
Royston Rd SPRGB/BLRNK G21 68 C5
STPS/GTHM/RID G33 69 H3
Royston Sq SPRGB/BLRNK G21 68 B5
Roy St SPRGB/BLRNK G21 68 A3
Rozelle Av DRUM G15 33 G5
NMRNS G77 161 E1
Rozelle Dr NMRNS G77 161 E1
Rozelle Pl NMRNS G77 161 E1
Rubislaw Dr BSDN G61 34 B5
Ruby St DMNK/BRGTN G40 90 D5
Ruchazie Pl
STPS/GTHM/RID G33 92 A1
Ruchazie Rd
STPS/GTHM/RID G33 92 A1
Ruchill Pl MRYH/FIRH G20 67 E1
Ruchill St MRYH/FIRH G20 66 D1
Ruel St LNPK/KPK G44 109 F5
Rufflees Av BRHD/NEIL G78 124 C4
Rugby Av KNTSWD G13 50 C3
Rullion Pl STPS/GTHM/RID G33 92 A1
Rumford St DMNK/BRGTN G40 110 C1
Runciman Pl EKILN G74 167 E1
Rupert St COWCAD G4 67 E4
Rushyhill St SPRGB/BLRNK G21 68 D2
Ruskin La KVD/HLHD G12 66 D3
Ruskin Pl KSYTH G65 8 B2
Ruskin Ter KVD/HLHD G12 66 D3
Russell Colt St CTBR ML5 96 D1
Russell Dr BSDN G61 34 C2
Russell Gdns UD/BTH/TAN G71 115 F4
Russell La WISHAW ML2 173 H2
Russell Pl
CRMNK/CLK/EAG G76 146 B5
EKILS G75 177 H1
PSLYN/LNWD PA3 81 G5
Russell Rd CLYDBK G81 31 F1
Russell St AIRDRIE ML6 119 F2
BLSH ML4 136 C2
HMLTN ML3 152 A5
JNSTN PA5 101 H3
PSLYN/LNWD PA3 84 A2
WISHAW ML2 173 H3
Rutherford Ct CLYDBK G81 48 D1
Rutherford La EKILS G75 178 C1
Rutherford Sq EKILS G75 166 B5
Rutherglen Rd GBLS G5 110 B1
Ruthven Av GIF/THBK G46 145 G1
Ruthven La KVD/HLHD G12 66 B3
Ruthven Pl BSHPBGS G64 55 F3
Ruthven St KVD/HLHD G12 66 B3
Rutland Crs GOV/IBX G51 88 D3
Rutland Pl GOV/IBX G51 88 D3
Ryan Rd BSHPBGS G64 55 E2
Ryan Wy RUTH G73 130 B4
Ryat Dr NMRNS G77 143 H4
Ryat Gn NMRNS G77 143 H5
Ryatt Linn ERSK PA8 47 E2
Rydal Gv EKILS G75 177 E2
Rydal Pl EKILS G75 177 E2
Ryden Mains Rd AIRDRIE ML6 75 G2
Ryde Rd WISHAW ML2 174 B2
Rye Crs SPRGB/BLRNK G21 69 E1
Ryecroft Dr
BAIL/MDB/MHD G69 94 A4
Ryedale Pl DRUM G15 33 F4
Ryefield Av CTBR ML5 96 A2
JNSTN PA5 101 E5
Ryefield Pl JNSTN PA5 101 E5
Ryefield Rd SPRGB/BLRNK G21 69 E1
Ryehill Pl SPRGB/BLRNK G21 69 F1
Ryehill Rd SPRGB/BLRNK G21 69 F1
Ryemount Rd
SPRGB/BLRNK G21 69 F1
Rye Rd SPRGB/BLRNK G21 69 E1
Ryeside Rd SPRGB/BLRNK G21 69 E2
Ryewraes Rd PSLYN/LNWD PA3 82 A4
Rylands Dr CAR/SHTL G32 93 E5
Rylands Gdns CAR/SHTL G32 93 F5
Rylees Crs
CARD/HILL/MSPK G52 85 H2
Rylees Rd
CARD/HILL/MSPK G52 85 H3
Rysland Av NMRNS G77 144 B5
Rysland Crs NMRNS G77 144 B5
Ryvra Rd KNTSWD G13 51 E5

S

Sachelcourt Av BSHPTN PA7 46 A1
Sackville Av KNTSWD G13 65 G1
Sackville La KNTSWD G13 65 G1
Saddell Rd DRUM G15 33 G4
Saffron Crs WISHAW ML2 173 E4
Saffronhall Crs HMLTN ML3 170 A1
Saffronhall La HMLTN ML3 170 A1
St Abb's Dr PSLYS PA2 103 F3
St Aidan's Pth WISHAW ML2 * 157 F4
St Andrews Av
UD/BTH/TAN G71 152 B1
St Andrew's Brae DMBTN G82 13 G2
St Andrews Ct EKILS G75 177 H2
St Andrew's Crs DMBTN G82 13 G2
PLKSD/SHW G41 88 D5
PSLYN/LNWD PA3 61 H5
St Andrews Dr BALLOCH G68 10 D4
BRWEIR PA11 79 E5
BSDN G61 34 A1
HMLTN ML3 168 C1
PLKSD/SHW G41 108 B2
PSLYN/LNWD PA3 62 B5
St Andrew's Dr West
PSLYN/LNWD PA3 83 H1
St Andrew's Gdns AIRDRIE ML6 98 C1
St Andrew's La CGLE G1 3 H7
St Andrews Pl KSYTH G65 8 A1
St Andrew's Rd
PLKSD/SHW G41 89 E5
RNFRW PA4 63 F3
St Andrew's Sq CGLE G1 90 A3
St Andrew's St CGLE G1 3 H7
MTHW ML1 137 F2
St Andrew's Wy WISHAW ML2 157 F4
St Annes Av ERSK PA8 48 A3
St Annes Wynd ERSK PA8 47 H3
St Ann's Dr GIF/THBK G46 127 F5
St Barchan's Rd KLBCH PA10 100 C4
St Blane's Dr RUTH G73 129 F1
St Boswell's Crs PSLYS PA2 103 F3
St Boswells Dr CTBR ML5 97 G5
St Bride's Av UD/BTH/TAN G71 115 H5
St Bride's Rd
PLKSW/MSWD G43 127 G1
St Brides Wy UD/BTH/TAN G71 134 B3
St Bryde St EKILN G74 166 C3
St Catherine's Rd
GIF/THBK G46 127 F5
St Clair Av GIF/THBK G46 127 F4
St Clair St MRYH/FIRH G20 67 E4
St Columba Dr KKNTL G66 40 B1
St Cyrus Gdns BSHPBGS G64 55 F2
St Cyrus Rd BSHPBGS G64 55 F2
St Davids Dr AIRDRIE ML6 98 D5
St Denis Wy CTBR ML5 96 C1
St Edmunds Gv MLNGV G62 17 E2
St Enoch Av UD/BTH/TAN G71 115 H4
St Enoch Pl CGLE G1 2 E7
St Fillans Dr
CRG/CRSL/HOU PA6 80 B1
St Fillans Rd
STPS/GTHM/RID G33 70 D1
St Flanan Rd KKNTL G66 22 D3
St George's Rd COWCAD G4 67 F4
KVGV G3 2 B2
St Germains BSDN G61 34 B4
St Giles Pk HMLTN ML3 169 G3
St Giles Wy HMLTN ML3 169 G2
St Helena Crs CLYDBK G81 32 B2
St Ives Rd BAIL/MDB/MHD G69 42 A5
St James Av PSLYN/LNWD PA3 83 G2
St James Ct CTBR ML5 116 B1
St James Rd COWCAD G4 3 K4
St James' St PSLYN/LNWD PA3 84 B4
St James Wy CTBR ML5 116 B1
St John's Ct PLKSD/SHW G41 88 D5
St John's Qd PLKSD/SHW G41 88 D5
St John's Rd PLKSD/SHW G41 108 D1
St John St CTBR ML5 96 D2
St Joseph's Ct
SPRGB/BLRNK G21 68 C5
St Joseph's Vw
SPRGB/BLRNK G21 68 C5
St Kenneth Dr GOV/IBX G51 87 E1
St Kilda Dr SCOT G14 65 F2
St Kilda Wy WISHAW ML2 157 H5
St Lawrence Pk EKILS G75 165 H4
St Leonard's Dr GIF/THBK G46 127 F4
St Leonards Rd EKILN G74 167 F3
St Leonards Wk CTBR ML5 117 F1
St Lukes Pl GBLS G5 89 H4
St Lukes Ter GBLS G5 89 H4
St Machan's Wy KKNTL G66 4 B1
St Machars Rd BRWEIR PA11 79 H4
St Margaret's Ct
PSLYN/LNWD PA3 84 C3
St Margaret's Dr WISHAW ML2 173 F4
St Margaret's Pl CGLE G1 89 H3
St Mark Gdns CAR/SHTL G32 92 A4
St Mark's Ct WISHAW ML2 157 F4
St Mark St CAR/SHTL G32 91 H4
St Marnock St
DMNK/BRGTN G40 90 D4
St Martins Ga CTBR ML5 96 D5
St Mary's Crs BRHD/NEIL G78 124 B5
St Marys Gdns BRHD/NEIL G78 124 B5
St Mary's La CGLW G2 2 E5
St Mary's Rd BLSH ML4 135 F2
BSHPBGS G64 54 B1
St Mary's Wy DMBTN G82 13 E4
St Michael Rd WISHAW ML2 172 C4
St Mirren's Rd KSYTH G65 8 C2
St Mirren St PSLY PA1 84 B5
St Monance St
SPRGB/BLRNK G21 68 C1
St Mungo Av COWCAD G4 3 G3
St Mungo Ct BRWEIR PA11 79 H3
St Mungo Pl COWCAD G4 3 J3
HMLTN ML3 168 C1
St Mungos Crs MTHW ML1 137 G5
St Mungo's Rd CUMB G67 26 B4
St Mungo St BSHPBGS G64 54 C3
St Ninian's Crs PSLYS PA2 104 C2
St Ninian's Pl HMLTN ML3 168 D2
St Ninian's Rd HMLTN ML3 168 D2
PSLYS PA2 104 C2
St Ninian Ter GBLS G5 89 H4
St Peter's La CGLW G2 2 C5
St Peter's St COWCAD G4 67 F4
St Ronan's Dr HMLTN ML3 169 H5
PLKSD/SHW G41 108 C3
RUTH G73 130 B2
St Stephens Av RUTH G73 130 B4
St Stephen's Crs RUTH G73 130 C4
St Vigeans Av NMRNS G77 161 E1
St Vigeans Pl NMRNS G77 161 F2
St Vincent Crs KVGV G3 88 C1
St Vincent Crescent La KVGV G3 88 C1
St Vincent La CGLW G2 2 C4
St Vincent Pl CGLE G1 3 F5
EKILS G75 165 F5
MTHW ML1 154 D3
St Vincent St CGLW G2 2 C4
KVGV G3 89 E1
St Vincent Ter KVGV G3 2 A4
St Winifred's Wy WISHAW ML2 173 H1
Salamanca St DEN/PKHD G31 91 G4
Salasaig Ct STPS/GTHM/RID G33 92 B2
Salen St CARD/HILL/MSPK G52 87 G4
Saline St AIRDRIE ML6 97 G3
Salisbury EKILN G74 167 G1
Salisbury Crs MTHW ML1 154 A1
Salisbury Pl CLYDBK G81 31 E3
Salisbury St GBLS G5 89 G5
Salkeld St GBLS G5 89 F5
Salmona St PPK/MIL G22 67 G2
Saltaire Av UD/BTH/TAN G71 134 B2
Salterland Rd BRHD/NEIL G78 124 D2
Saltmarket CGLE G1 89 H4
Saltmarket Pl CGLE G1 89 H3
Saltoun La KVD/HLHD G12 66 C3
Saltoun St KVD/HLHD G12 66 C3
Salvia St BLTYR/CAMB G72 130 D1
Sandaig Rd
STPS/GTHM/RID G33 93 F4
Sandalwood Av EKILN G74 166 A1
Sandalwood Ct EKILN G74 166 A1
Sanda St MRYH/FIRH G20 66 D2
Sandbank Av MRYH/FIRH G20 52 C4
Sandbank Crs MRYH/FIRH G20 52 C5
Sandbank Dr MRYH/FIRH G20 52 C4
Sandbank St MRYH/FIRH G20 52 C5
Sandbank Ter MRYH/FIRH G20 52 C4
Sandend Rd PLK/PH/NH G53 106 B5
Sanderling Pl JNSTN PA5 121 E3
Sanderling Rd
PSLYN/LNWD PA3 84 A1
Sanderson Av
UD/BTH/TAN G71 135 E1
Sandfield Av MLNGV G62 17 E2
Sandfield St MRYH/FIRH G20 66 D1
Sandgate Av CAR/SHTL G32 113 E1
Sandhaven Pl PLK/PH/NH G53 106 B5
Sandhaven Rd
PLK/PH/NH G53 106 B5
Sandhead Crs AIRDRIE ML6 119 F3
Sandholes Rd JNSTN PA5 100 D1
Sandholes St PSLY PA1 83 H5
Sandholm Pl SCOT G14 64 A1
Sandholm Ter SCOT G14 64 A1
Sandiefield Rd GBLS G5 89 H5
Sandielands Av ERSK PA8 48 A4
Sandilands Crs MTHW ML1 154 A5
Sandilands St CAR/SHTL G32 92 C4
Sandmill St SPRGB/BLRNK G21 68 D5
Sandpiper Dr EKILS G75 177 F3
Sandpiper Pl EKILS G75 177 F3
Sandpiper Wy BLSH ML4 116 B4
Sandra Rd BSHPBGS G64 55 F1
Sandringham Av NMRNS G77 144 D4
Sandringham Dr JNSTN PA5 102 A3
Sandringham La KVD/HLHD G12 66 C3
Sandwood Rd
CARD/HILL/MSPK G52 86 B3
Sandyfaulds Sq GBLS G5 89 H5
Sandyfaulds St GBLS G5 90 A5
Sandyford Av MTHW ML1 119 E4
Sandyford Pl MTHW ML1 119 E5
Sandyford Place La KVGV G3 88 D1
Sandyford Rd MTHW ML1 119 E5
PSLYN/LNWD PA3 84 C1
Sandyford St KVGV G3 88 B1
Sandyhills Crs CAR/SHTL G32 112 C1
Sandyhills Dr CAR/SHTL G32 112 C1
Sandyhills Gv CAR/SHTL G32 112 D2
Sandyhills Pl CAR/SHTL G32 112 C1
Sandyhills Rd CAR/SHTL G32 112 D1
Sandyknowes Rd CUMB G67 26 B5
Sandy Rd PTCK G11 65 H5
RNFRW PA4 63 F5
Sannox Dr MTHW ML1 154 A3
Sannox Gdns DEN/PKHD G31 91 E1
Sannox Pl EKILS G75 177 G4
Sanquhar Dr PLK/PH/NH G53 106 B4
Sanquhar Gdns
BLTYR/CAMB G72 133 E5
PLK/PH/NH G53 106 B4
Sanquhar Pl PLK/PH/NH G53 106 B4
Sanquhar Rd PLK/PH/NH G53 106 B4
Sapphire Rd BLSH ML4 135 H4
Saracen Head Rd COWCAD G4 3 K7
Saracen St PPK/MIL G22 67 H2
Sarazen Ct MTHW ML1 156 B2
Sardinia La KVD/HLHD G12 66 C3
Saskatoon Pl EKILS G75 165 G4
Saturn Av PSLYN/LNWD PA3 82 D5
Saucel Hill Ter PSLYS PA2 104 B1
Saucel St PSLY PA1 84 C5
Sauchiehall La CGLW G2 2 B3
Sauchiehall St KVGV G3 2 B3
Saughs Av STPS/GTHM/RID G33 56 A5
Saughs Dr STPS/GTHM/RID G33 56 A5
Saughs Ga STPS/GTHM/RID G33 56 A5
Saughs Pl STPS/GTHM/RID G33 56 A5
Saughs Rd STPS/GTHM/RID G33 56 B5
Saughton St CAR/SHTL G32 91 H2
Savoy St DMNK/BRGTN G40 90 C5
Sawmillfield St COWCAD G4 67 G4
Saxon Rd KNTSWD G13 51 E4
Scadlock Rd PSLYN/LNWD PA3 83 G3
Scalpay EKILN G74 167 F4
Scalpay Pl PPK/MIL G22 54 A4
Scalpay St PPK/MIL G22 53 H4
Scapa St SMSTN G23 52 D3
Scaraway Dr PPK/MIL G22 54 A3
Scaraway Pl PPK/MIL G22 54 A3
Scaraway St PPK/MIL G22 53 H3
Scaraway Ter PPK/MIL G22 54 A3
Scarba Dr PLKSW/MSWD G43 127 E1
Scarba Qd WISHAW ML2 173 F4
Scarffe Av PSLYN/LNWD PA3 101 G1
Scarhill Av AIRDRIE ML6 98 A4
Scarhill La AIRDRIE ML6 98 B4
Scarhill St CTBR ML5 116 C1
MTHW ML1 139 E5
Scarrel Dr CSMK G45 129 H3
Scarrel Rd CSMK G45 129 H3
Scarrel Ter CSMK G45 129 H3
Scavaig Crs DRUM G15 32 D4
Schaw Dr BSDN G61 34 B2
CLYDBK G81 32 C2
Schaw Rd PSLYN/LNWD PA3 84 D3
Scholar's Ga EKILS G75 178 A2
School Av BLTYR/CAMB G72 131 G2
Schoolhouse La
BLTYR/CAMB G72 151 F4
School La BLTYR/CAMB G72 132 B3
DMBTN G82 12 C3
KKNTL G66 4 B2
School Qd AIRDRIE ML6 76 A4
School Rd BSHPBGS G64 19 G4
NMRNS G77 161 G1
PSLY PA1 85 H4
STPS/GTHM/RID G33 57 F5
WISHAW ML2 175 G2
School St AIRDRIE ML6 119 E2
CTBR ML5 96 D5
HMLTN ML3 170 A4
School Wynd PSLY PA1 84 B4
Scioncroft Av RUTH G73 111 F5
Scone Pl EKILN G74 166 A2
NMRNS G77 162 C1
Scone St PPK/MIL G22 67 H3
Sconser St SMSTN G23 52 D2
Scorton Gdns CAR/SHTL G32 93 G5
Scotia Gdns HMLTN ML3 180 C1
Scotia St MTHW ML1 154 B3
Scotland St GBLS G5 89 E4
Scotland St West GOV/IBX G51 88 C4
Scotsblair Av KKNTL G66 39 H1
Scotsburn Rd
SPRGB/BLRNK G21 69 F2
Scotstoun St SCOT G14 64 D3
Scott Av JNSTN PA5 121 F1
KKNTL G66 5 G4
OLDK G60 15 G5
Scott Crs CUMB G67 44 C1
Scott Dr BSDN G61 33 H2
CUMB G67 44 C1
Scott Gv HMLTN ML3 170 A3
Scott Hl EKILN G74 166 D2
Scott Pl BLSH ML4 117 E5
Scott Rd CARD/HILL/MSPK G52 86 A1
Scott's Pl AIRDRIE ML6 98 C1
Scott's Rd PSLYS PA2 105 F1
Scott St BAIL/MDB/MHD G69 94 A5
CLYDBK G81 31 F4
HMLTN ML3 170 A4
KVGV G3 2 C2
MTHW ML1 154 D3
Seafar Rd CUMB G67 26 B3
Seafield Av BSDN G61 34 C1
Seafield Crs BALLOCH G68 24 C4
Seafield Dr RUTH G73 130 C4
Seaforth Crs BRHD/NEIL G78 124 A2
Seaforth Pl BLSH ML4 135 G5
Seaforth Rd
CARD/HILL/MSPK G52 86 B2
CLYDBK G81 49 E2
Seaforth Rd North
CARD/HILL/MSPK G52 86 B2
Seaforth Rd South
CARD/HILL/MSPK G52 86 B2
Seagrove St CAR/SHTL G32 91 G3
Seamill Gdns EKILN G74 166 A3
Seamill St PLK/PH/NH G53 125 E2
Seamore St MRYH/FIRH G20 67 E4
Seath Av AIRDRIE ML6 97 H1
Seath Rd RUTH G73 110 D3
Seath St GVH/MTFL G42 109 H2
Seaton Ter HMLTN ML3 169 F1
Seaward La PLKSD/SHW G41 88 D3
Seaward Pl PLKSD/SHW G41 89 E4
Seaward St GOV/IBX G51 89 E3
PLKSD/SHW G41 88 D5
Second Av BSDN G61 34 D5
CLYDBK G81 31 H5
DMBTN G82 13 H5
KKNTL G66 56 D2
LNPK/KPK G44 128 C1
RNFRW PA4 63 F5
STPS/GTHM/RID G33 70 C1
UD/BTH/TAN G71 114 D3
Second Gdns PLKSD/SHW G41 87 H5
Second Rd BLTYR/CAMB G72 151 H5
Second St UD/BTH/TAN G71 115 E4
Seedhill PSLY PA1 84 C5
Seedhill Rd PSLY PA1 84 C5
Seggielea La KNTSWD G13 51 E5
Seggielea Rd KNTSWD G13 51 E5
Seil Dr LNPK/KPK G44 128 C3
Selborne Pl KNTSWD G13 65 F1
Selborne Place La KNTSWD G13 65 F1
Selborne Rd KNTSWD G13 65 F1
Selby Gdns CAR/SHTL G32 93 E4
Selby Pl CTBR ML5 74 A4
Selby St CTBR ML5 74 A4
Selkirk Av CARD/HILL/MSPK G52 86 D5
PSLYS PA2 103 F4
Selkirk Dr RUTH G73 111 F5
Selkirk Pl EKILN G74 167 G2
HMLTN ML3 170 B3
Selkirk St BLTYR/CAMB G72 151 G3
HMLTN ML3 170 B3
WISHAW ML2 157 F5
Selkirk Wy CTBR ML5 117 H1
Sella Rd BSHPBGS G64 55 G1
Selvieland Rd
CARD/HILL/MSPK G52 85 H4
Semphill Gdns EKILN G74 167 E3
Sempie St HMLTN ML3 169 E1
Sempill Av ERSK PA8 47 E1
Semple Av BSHPTN PA7 29 E5
Semple Pl PSLYN/LNWD PA3 82 A2
Semple Vw HWWD PA9 120 A4
Senate Pl MTHW ML1 154 B1
Senga Crs BLSH ML4 116 D5

Seres Rd CRMNK/CLK/EAG G76 .....145 G2
Sergeant Law Rd PSLYS PA2 ......122 A2
Service St KKNTL G66 ....4 A1
Seton Ter DEN/PKHD G31 ....90 C2
Settle Gdns
  BAIL/MDB/MHD G69 ....93 G5
Seven Sisters KKNTL G66 ....40 B3
Seventh Av UD/BTH/TAN G71 ...115 E4
Seventh Rd BLTYR/CAMB G72 ...151 H5
Severn Rd EKILS G75 ....176 D1
Seymour Gn EKILS G75 ....165 G5
Seyton Av GIF/THBK G46 ....145 F1
Seyton La KLBCH PA10 ....2 A4
Shaftesbury St CLYDBK G81 ....48 C1
  KVCV G3 ....2 A4
Shafton Pl KNTSWD G13 ....51 F3
Shafton Rd KNTSWD G13 ....51 F3
Shakespeare Av CLYDBK G81 ......31 F4
Shakespeare St
  MRYH/FIRH G20 ....66 D1
Shamrock St COWCAD C4 ....2 D1
  KKNTL G66 ....21 F5
Shandon Brae BLSH ML4 ....116 D5
Shandon Ter HMLTN ML3 ....169 E3
Shand St WISHAW ML2 ....174 B3
Shandwick St ESTRH G34 ....93 H1
Shanks Av BRHD/NEIL G78 ....124 D4
Shanks Crs JNSTN PA5 ....101 F4
Shanks Pl BRHD/NEIL 76 B5
  MRYH/FIRH G20 ....66 D1
Shanks Wy BRHD/NEIL G78 ......124 B2
Shannon St MRYH/FIRH G20 ......67 E1
Shapinsay St PPK/MIL G22 ....54 A3
Sharp Av CTBR ML5 ....95 H5
Sharp St MTHW ML1 ....154 A3
Shaw Av BSHPTN PA7 ....29 F5
Shawbridge St
  PLKSW/MSWD G43 ....108 B5
Shawburn St HMLTN ML3 ....169 F1
Shaw Ct ERSK PA8 ....30 A3
Shawfield Dr GBLS G5 ....110 B2
Shawfield Rd GBLS G5 ....110 C1
Shawhead Av CTBR ML5 ....97 E5
Shawhill Ct PLKSD/SHW G41 .....108 C4
Shawhill Crs NMRNS G77 ....161 H2
Shawhill Rd PLKSW/MSWD G43..108 C4
Shawholm Crs
  PLKSW/MSWD G43 ....108 A5
Shawmoss Rd PLKSD/SHW G41..108 B5
Shawpark St MRYH/FIRH G20 .....67 E1
Shaw Pl PSLYN/LNWD PA3 ....82 A4
Shaw Rd MLNGV G62 ....17 E5
  NMRNS G77 ....161 H1
Shawstonfoot Rd MTHW ML1 ...158 D1
Shaw St GOV/IBX G51 ....87 H1
Shawwood Crs NMRNS G77 ......161 H2
Shearer Dr HMLTN ML3 ....180 C1
Sheddens Pl CAR/SHTL G32 ....92 A4
Sheepburn Rd
  UD/BTH/TAN G71 ....114 C5
Sheila St STPS/GTHM/RID G33 .....69 H2
Sheldaig Hl HMLTN ML3 ....170 B1
Sheldaig Rd PPK/MIL G22 ....53 H5
Sheldrake Pl JNSTN PA5 ....121 E5
Shelley Dr CLYDBK G81 ....31 H4
  UD/BTH/TAN G71 ....134 C1
Shelley Rd KVD/HLHD G12 ....65 G1
Shells Rd KKNTL G66 ....21 F5
Sherbrooke Av
  PLKSD/SHW G41 ....108 B1
Sherbrooke Dr PLKSD/SHW G41..88 B5
Sherbrooke Gdns
  PLKSD/SHW G41 ....108 B1
Sherbrooke Pl EKILS G75 ....178 D2
Sherburn Gdns CAR/SHTL G32 ....111 F5
Sherdale Av AIRDRIE ML6 ....119 E2
Sheriff Park Av RUTH G73 ....110 D5
Sherry Av MTHW ML1 ....137 F2
Sherry Dr HMLTN ML3 ....169 F4
Sherwood Av PSLY PA1 ....84 D3
  UD/BTH/TAN G71 ....134 D2
Sherwood Dr GIF/THBK G46 .....126 D4
Sherwood Pl DRUM 33 G5
Shetland Dr LNPK/KPK G44 ......128 D3
Shettleston Rd DEN/PKHD G31...91 H4
Shiel Av EKILN G74 ....166 C2
Shielbridge Gdns SMSTN G23 .....52 D2
Shiel Ct BRHD/NEIL G78 ....124 A2
Shieldaig Dr RUTH G73 ....130 A3
Shieldburn Rd GOV/IBX G51 ....86 B2
Shieldhall Gdns GOV/IBX G51 .....86 D2
Shieldhall Rd GOV/IBX G51 ....86 C2
Shieldmuir St WISHAW ML2 ....172 D1
Shields Ct MTHW ML1 ....172 C2
Shields Dr MTHW ML1 ....172 C2
Shields Rd MTHW ML1 ....172 C2
  PLKSD/SHW G41 ....88 D5
Shiel Pl CTBR ML5 ....97 G4
  EKILN G74 ....166 C2
Shiel Rd BSHPBGS G64 ....55 E2
Shiel Ter WISHAW ML2 ....158 A4
Shillay St PPK/MIL G22 ....54 B3
Shillingworth Pl BRWEIR PA11 ....79 G5
Shilton Dr PLK/PH/NH G53 ....125 H2
Shilton La BSHPTN PA7 ....28 A5
Shinwell Av CLYDBK G81 ....49 G2
Shira Ter EKILN G74 ....167 E4
Shirley Qd MTHW ML1 ....171 G2
Shirrel Av BLSH ML4 ....116 C5
Shirrel Rd MTHW ML1 ....137 E4
Shirva Lea KSYTH G65 ....23 F1
Shiskine Dr MRYH/FIRH G20 ....52 B3
Shiskine Pl MRYH/FIRH G20 ....52 B3
Shiskine St MRYH/FIRH G20 ....52 B3
Shore Crs DMNK/BRGTN G40 .....110 C2
Shortridge St MRYH/FIRH G20 ....66 D1
Shortroods Av
  PSLYN/LNWD PA3 ....84 A2
Shortroods Crs
  PSLYN/LNWD PA3 ....84 A2
Shortroods Rd
  PSLYN/LNWD PA3 ....84 A2
Shotts St STPS/GTHM/RID G33 ....93 E1
Shuna Gdns MRYH/FIRH G20 .....66 D1
  NMRNS G77
Shuna Pl MRYH/FIRH G20 ....66 D1
  NMRNS G77 ....143 G4
Shuna St MRYH/FIRH G20 ....52 D5
Shuttle St CCLE G1 ....3 J5
  KLBCH PA10 ....100 B2
  KSYTH G65 ....8 B2
Sidaird Rd SPRGB/BLRNK G21 .....84 B5
Sidlaw Av BRHD/NEIL G78 ....142 B1
  HMLTN ML3 ....169 E3
Sidlaw Dr WISHAW ML2 ....173 G2

Sidlaw Rd BSDN G61 ....33 G2
Sidlaw Wy AIRDRIE ML6 ....119 G3
Sielga Pl ESTRH G34 ....93 H1
Siemens Pl SPRGB/BLRNK G21 ....69 E4
Siemens St SPRGB/BLRNK G21 ....68 D4
Sievewright St RUTH G73 ....111 F5
Sikeside Pl CTBR ML5 ....97 G4
Sikeside St CTBR ML5 ....97 G4
Silkin Av CLYDBK G81 ....49 G2
Silk St PSLY PA1 ....84 C4
Silvan Pl CRMNK/CLK/EAG G76 .146 B5
Silver Birch Dr GOV/IBX G51 ....87 E2
Silver Birch Gdns GOV/IBX G51 ....87 E2
Silverburn Crs MTHW ML1 ....138 A4
Silverburn St
  STPS/GTHM/RID G33 ....91 H1
Silverdale EKILN G74 ....165 H2
Silverdale St DEN/PKHD G31 ....91 F5
Silverdale Ter AIRDRIE ML6 ....77 G3
Silver Firs MTHW ML1 ....137 G4
Silverfir St GBLS G5 ....110 A1
Silvergrove St
  DMNK/BRGTN G40 ....90 B5
Silverton Av DMBTN G82 ....13 G5
Silvertonhill Av HMLTN ML3 ......170 B5
Silverwells Crs UD/BTH/TAN G71 114 D1
Silverwells UD/BTH/TAN G71 .....134 D1
Silverwells Crs
  UD/BTH/TAN G71 ....152 B1
Simons Crs RNFRW PA4 ....63 G1
Simpson Ct CLYDBK G81 ....48 D1
  UD/BTH/TAN G71 ....134 A1
Simpson Dr EKILS G75 ....178 A1
Simpson Pl EKILS G75 ....178 A1
Simpson St MRYH/FIRH G20 ....67 E5
Simpson Wy BLSH ML4 ....117 F5
Sinclair Av BSDN G61 ....34 B2
Sinclair Dr CTBR ML5 ....96 A2
  GVH/MTFL G42 ....109 E5
Sinclair Gdns BSHPBGS G64 ....55 E3
Sinclair Gv BLSH ML4 ....116 B5
Sinclair Pk EKILS G75 ....166 C5
Sinclair Pl EKILS G75 ....166 C5
Sinclair St CLYDBK G81 ....49 G5
  MLNGV G62 ....17 E3
Singer Rd CLYDBK G81 ....31 G5
  EKILS G75 ....178 C2
Singer St CLYDBK G81 ....32 A5
Sir Michael Pl PSLY PA1 ....84 A5
Sixth Av RNFRW PA4 ....63 F5
Sixth St UD/BTH/TAN G71 ....114 D5
Skaethorn Rd MRYH/FIRH G20 ...52 A4
Skaterigg La KNTSWD G13 ....65 F1
Skelbo Pl ESTRH G34 ....72 C5
Skene Rd GOV/IBX G51 ....87 H3
Skerne Gv EKILS G75 ....177 E2
Skerray Qd PPK/MIL G22 ....53 H3
Skerray St PPK/MIL G22 ....53 H3
Skerryvore Pl
  STPS/GTHM/RID G33 ....92 C1
Skerryvore Rd
  STPS/GTHM/RID G33 ....92 C1
Skipness Dr GOV/IBX G51 ....87 E1
Skirsa Ct SMSTN G23 ....53 F3
Skirsa Pl SMSTN G23 ....53 E4
Skirsa Sq SMSTN G23 ....53 E3
Skirsa St SMSTN G23 ....53 E3
Skirving St PLKSD/SHW G41 ......108 D4
Skovlunde Wy EKILS G75 ....178 B2
Skye EKILN G74 ....167 F4
Skye Av RNFRW PA4 ....63 F5
Skye Ct CUMB G67 ....25 H5
Skye Crs OLDK G60 ....30 D3
  PA4
Skye Dr CUMB G67 ....25 H5
Skye Gdns BSDN G61 ....33 G2
Skye Pl CUMB G67 ....25 H5
Skye Qd WISHAW ML2 ....157 H5
Skye Rd CUMB G67 ....25 H5
  RUTH G73 ....130 C4
Skye Wynd HMLTN ML3 ....169 E4
Slakiewood Av
  BAIL/MDB/MHD G69 ....58 D4
Slatefield KKNTL G66 ....4 B2
Slatefield St DEN/PKHD G31 ....90 D3
Sleaford Av MTHW ML1 ....171 G1
Slenavon Av RUTH G73 ....130 C4
Slessor Dr EKILS G75 ....178 B1
Sloy St PPK/MIL G22 ....68 A2
  WISHAW ML2 ....173 H3
Small Crs BLTYR/CAMB G72 ......151 G3
Smeaton Av BSHPBGS G64 ....19 F5
Smeaton Dr BSHPBGS G64 ....37 H4
Smeaton Gv MRYH/FIRH G20 .....53 G5
Smeaton St MRYH/FIRH G20 ......53 G5
Smith Crs CLYDBK G81 ....32 A3
Smithhills St PSLY PA1 ....84 B4
Smith Qd CTBR ML5 ....97 F2
Smith's La PSLYN/LNWD PA3 ....84 B3
Smithstone Crs KSYTH G65 ....24 C3
Smithstone Rd BALLOCH G68 ......24 D3
Smithview WISHAW ML2 ....174 D5
Smithycroft HMLTN ML3 ....170 D5
Smithycroft Rd
  STPS/GTHM/RID G33 ....69 H5
Smithyends CUMB G67 ....10 D5
Smollett Rd DMBTN G82 ....13 G3
Snaefell Av RUTH G73 ....130 B3
Snaefell Crs RUTH G73 ....130 B2
Sneddon Av WISHAW ML2 ....174 B4
Sneddon St HMLTN ML3 ....152 A4
Sneddon Ter HMLTN ML3 ....152 A4
Snowdon St GBLS G5 ....90 A5
Snuff Mill Rd LNPK/KPK G44 ......128 C2
Society St DEN/PKHD G31 ....91 E4
Sollas Pl KNTSWD G13 ....49 H4
Solway Ct HMLTN ML3 ....169 G5
Solway Pl BAIL/MDB/MHD G69 ...58 D2
Solway Rd BSHPBGS G64 ....55 F2
Solway St DMNK/BRGTN G40 ....110 C2
Somerford Rd BSDN G61 ....51 G2
Somerled Av PSLYN/LNWD PA3 ...62 C5
Somerset Av HMLTN ML3 ....169 G2
Somerset Pl KVGV G3 ....67 E5
Somerset Place La
  KVGV G3 ....67 E5
Somerville Dr EKILS G75 ....178 C1
  GVH/MTFL G42 ....109 G4
Somerville La EKILS G75 ....178 C1
Sorby St DEN/PKHD G31 ....91 G4
Sorley St PTCK G11 ....65 H4
Sorn St DMNK/BRGTN G40 ....111 E1
Souterhouse Pth CTBR ML5 ....96 C4
Souterhouse Rd CTBR ML5 ....96 C4

Southampton Dr
  KVD/HLHD G12 ....52 A5
Southampton La
  KVD/HLHD G12 ....52 A5
South Annandale St
  GVH/MTFL G42 ....109 G2
South Av BLTYR/CAMB G72 ....151 H5
  CLYDBK G81 ....48 D1
  PSLYS PA2 ....104 C4
  RNFRW PA4 ....63 G3
Southbank Dr KKNTL G66 ....39 G1
Southbank St CLYDBK G81 ....49 F4
South Bank St CLYDBK G81 ....49 F4
Southbank St DEN/PKHD G31 ......91 G4
Southbar Av KNTSWD G13 ....50 B4
Southbar Rd ERSK PA8 ....4 A3
South Biggar Rd AIRDRIE ML6 .....98 C2
South Brae KKNTL G66 ....4 A5
Southbrae Av BRWEIR PA11 ....79 E4
Southbrae Dr KNTSWD G13 ....65 E2
South Burn Rd AIRDRIE ML6 ....97 G2
South Caldeen Rd CTBR ML5 ....97 E4
South Campbell St PSLYS PA2 ....104 B1
South Carbrain Rd CUMB G67 ......26 C5
South Chester St CAR/SHTL G32 ..92 B4
South Circular Rd CTBR ML5 ....96 D2
South Claremont La
  MLNGV G62 ....17 E4
South Commonhead Av
  AIRDRIE ML6 ....76 A5
Southcroft Rd RUTH G73 ....110 B3
Southcroft St GOV/IBX G51 ....88 A2
South Crosshill Rd
  BSHPBGS G64 ....54 D2
South Dean Park Av
  UD/BTH/TAN G71 ....134 B5
Southdeen Av DRUM G15 ....33 G5
Southdeen Rd DRUM G15 ....33 G5
South Douglas St CLYDBK G81 .....49 F5
South Dr PSLYN/LNWD PA3 ....82 A3
South Dumbreck Rd KSYTH G65 ....7 H2
South Elgin Pl CLYDBK G81 ....49 F4
South Elgin St CLYDBK G81 ....49 F4
Southend Pl BLSH ML4 ....135 G3
Southend Rd CLYDBK G81 ....32 A3
Southern Av RUTH G73 ....130 A2
Southernness Dr BALLOCH G68 ....10 C5
South Erskine Pk BSDN G61 ....34 A3
Southesk Av BSHPBGS G64 ....37 G5
South Exchange Ct CCLE G1 ....3 H6
Southfield Av PSLYS PA2 ....104 B4
Southfield Crs CTBR ML5 ....97 F4
  PLK/PH/NH G53 ....106 D4
Southfield Rd BALLOCH G68 ....25 G4
South Frederick St CCLE G1 ....3 G6
Southgate EKILN G74 ....166 B5
South Glassford St MLNGV G62 ....17 E4
Southhill Av RUTH G73 ....130 B2
Southinch Av SCOT G14 ....49 H5
Southinch La SCOT G14 ....49 H5
Southlea Av GIF/THBK G46 ....126 C4
Southloch Gdns
  SPRGB/BLRNK G21 ....68 C3
Southloch St SPRGB/BLRNK G21 ..68 C3
South Mains Rd MLNGV G62 ....16 D4
South Medros St CTBR ML5 ....97 F4
South Mound
  CRG/CRSL/HOU PA6 ....80 B1
South Muirhead Rd CUMB G67 ....26 C3
Southmuir Pl MRYH/FIRH G20 .....66 C1
South Nimmo St AIRDRIE ML6 .....98 C2
South Park Av BRHD/NEIL G78 ...124 B4
Southpark Av KVD/HLHD G12 ......66 D4
South Park Dr PSLYS PA2 ....104 B2
South Park Gv HMLTN ML3 ....170 A2
Southpark La KVD/HLHD G12 ......66 D4
South Pl BLSH ML4 ....135 G3
South Portland St GBLS G5 ....89 G4
South Rd CRMNK/CLK/EAG G76 .146 B5
South Robertson Pl
  AIRDRIE ML6 ....97 H2
South Scott St
  BAIL/MDB/MHD G69 ....94 A5
Southside Crs GBLS G5 ....89 G5
South St CRG/CRSL/HOU PA6 ......61 G2
  RNFRW PA4 ....64 B3
  SCOT G14 ....65 E4
South Vesalius St
  CAR/SHTL G32 ....92 B4
South Vw BLSH ML4 ....135 F3
  BLTYR/CAMB G72 ....151 F1
  CLYDBK G81 ....31 G5
Southview BSDN G61 ....33 H3
Southview Av
  CRMNK/CLK/EAG G76 ....145 H5
Southview Ct BSHPBGS G64 ....54 C4
Southview Crs BRWEIR PA11 ....79 G2
Southview Pl
  BAIL/MDB/MHD G69 ....58 D5
Southview Ter
  SPRGB/BLRNK G21 ....54 C4
South William St JNSTN PA5 ......101 G4
Southwold Rd PSLY PA1 ....85 H4
Southwood Dr LNPK/KPK G44 ....128 D2
South Woodside Rd
  COWCAD C4 ....67 E4
  MRYH/FIRH G20 ....67 E4
South Vw STPS/GTHM/RID G33 ....92 C1
Spairdrum Rd CUMB G67 ....47 E1
Spalehall Dr MTHW ML1 ....138 C4
Spateston Rd HWWD PA9 ....120 B5
Spean Av EKILN G74 ....167 E4
Spean St LNPK/KPK G44 ....108 D5
Speirsfield Gdns PSLYS PA2 ....104 B1
Speirshall Ct SCOT G14 ....49 H4
Speirshall Ter SCOT G14 ....49 H4
Speirs Pl PSLYN/LNWD PA3 ....82 C2
Speirs Rd BSDN G61 ....51 H1
Spencer Dr PSLYS PA2 ....102 C5
Spencer Field Gdns
  HMLTN ML3 ....170 C2
Spencer St CLYDBK G81 ....31 H5
  KNTSWD G13 ....51 F4
Spence St MRYH/FIRH G20 ....52 B3
Spey Av PSLYS PA2 ....102 D3
Spey Ct AIRDRIE ML6 ....98 A3
Spey Dr CTBR ML5 ....96 B5
Spey Gdns HMLTN ML3 ....169 G5

Spey Gv EKILS G75 ....177 E1
Spey Pl JNSTN PA5 ....120 D1
Spey Rd BSDN G61 ....51 F1
Spey St STPS/GTHM/RID G33 ......92 A1
Spey Ter EKILS G75 ....177 E1
Spiersbridge Av GIF/THBK G46 ...126 C4
Spiersbridge La GIF/THBK G46 ....126 C4
Spiersbridge Rd GIF/THBK G46 ...126 C5
Spiersbridge Ter GIF/THBK G46 ...126 B4
Spiers Gv GIF/THBK G46 ....126 C4
Spiers Rd CRG/CRSL/HOU PA6 ....80 C1
  JNSTN PA5 ....102 A3
Spindlehowe Rd
  UD/BTH/TAN G71 ....115 F5
Spindleside Rd MTHW ML1 ....157 G1
Spinners Dr CLYDBK G81 ....32 A1
Spinners La CLYDBK G81 ....32 A1
Spittal Rd CSMK C45 ....129 H2
Spoolers Rd PSLY PA1 ....103 G1
Spoutmouth CCLE G1 ....3 J7
Springbank Crs HMLTN ML3 ....155 F1
  MTHW ML1 ....155 F1
Springbank Rd
  PSLYN/LNWD PA3 ....84 A3
Springbank St MRYH/FIRH G20 ...67 E2
Springbank Ter AIRDRIE ML6 ....77 G3
  PSLYN/LNWD PA3 ....84 A2
Springboig Av CAR/SHTL G32 ......92 D3
Springboig Rd CAR/SHTL G32 ......92 D2
Springburn Pl EKILN G74 ....165 F1
Springburn Rd
  PSLY/LNWD PA3 ....84 A3
Springburn Wy
  SPRGB/BLRNK G21 ....68 C2
Springcroft Av
  BAIL/MDB/MHD G69 ....94 A3
Springcroft Crs
  BAIL/MDB/MHD G69 ....94 A3
Springcroft Dr
  BAIL/MDB/MHD G69 ....93 H3
Springcroft Gdns
  BAIL/MDB/MHD G69 ....94 B3
Springcroft Rd
  BAIL/MDB/MHD G69 ....94 A3
Springcroft Wynd
  BAIL/MDB/MHD G69 ....94 A3
Springfield Av BSHPBGS G64 ....54 D3
  PSLY PA1 ....85 E5
  UD/BTH/TAN G71 ....134 A1
Springfield Ct CGLE G1 ....3 F6
Springfield Crs
  BLTYR/CAMB G72 ....151 F3
  BSHPBGS G64 ....54 D3
Springfield Dr BRHD/NEIL G78 ...142 D1
Springfield Gv BRHD/NEIL G78 ...142 C2
Springfield Pk JNSTN PA5 ....101 H4
Springfield Park Rd RUTH G73 ....130 B1
Springfield Quay GOV/IBX G51 ....88 D2
Springfield Rd AIRDRIE ML6 ....141 G3
  BRHD/NEIL G78 ....141 G3
  BSHPBGS G64 ....54 D3
  CUMB G67 ....26 C1
  DEN/PKHD G31 ....91 E5
  DMNK/BRGTN G40 ....111 E1
Springfield Sq BSHPBGS G64 ....54 D3
Springfield Woods JNSTN PA5 ....101 H4
Springhead Rd SHOTTS ML7 ......159 F2
Springhill Av AIRDRIE ML6 ....98 C1
Springhill Dr South
  BAIL/MDB/MHD G69 ....93 H3
Springhill Farm Gv
  BAIL/MDB/MHD G69 ....93 H3
Springhill Farm Pl
  BAIL/MDB/MHD G69 ....93 H3
Springhill Farm Rd
  BAIL/MDB/MHD G69 ....93 H3
Springhill Farm Wy
  BAIL/MDB/MHD G69 ....93 H3
Springhill Gdns
  PLKSD/SHW G41 ....108 D3
Springhill Pkwy
  BAIL/MDB/MHD G69 ....94 A2
Springhill Pl CTBR ML5 ....95 H5
Springhill Rd
  BAIL/MDB/MHD G69 ....93 G4
  BRHD/NEIL G78 ....141 E5
  CRMNK/CLK/EAG G76 ....146 B5
Springholm Dr AIRDRIE ML6 ....76 A4
Springkell Av PLKSD/SHW G41 ...108 A2
Springkell Dr PLKSD/SHW G41 ...108 A2
Springkell Gdns
  PLKSD/SHW G41 ....108 B2
Springkell Ga PLKSD/SHW G41 ..108 C2
Springside Gdns DRUM G15 ....33 F3
Springside Pl DRUM G15 ....33 F3
Springvale Dr PSLYS PA2 ....103 G2
Springvale Ter
  SPRGB/BLRNK G21 ....68 B2
Springwells Av AIRDRIE ML6 ....98 D1
Springwells Crs AIRDRIE ML6 ....98 D1
Spruce Av BLTYR/CAMB G72 ......132 C3
  HMLTN ML3 ....170 B4
  JNSTN PA5 ....101 H5
Spruce Ct HMLTN ML3 ....170 B4
Spruce Dr BLTYR/CAMB G72 ......132 C3
  KKNTL G66 ....39 H3
Spruce Rd CUMB G67 ....27 F1
  UD/BTH/TAN G71 ....115 H5
Spruce St PPK/MIL G22 ....68 A1
Spruce Wy BLTYR/CAMB G72 .....132 C3
Squire St SCOT G14 ....65 F3
Stable Gv PSLY PA1 ....83 G5
Stable Rd MLNGV G62 ....16 D2
Staffa EKILN G74 ....167 F5
Staffa Av RNFRW PA4 ....63 F5
Staffa Dr AIRDRIE ML6 ....99 G2
  PSLYS PA2 ....104 B5
Staffa Rd BLTYR/CAMB G72 ....131 G4
Staffa St DEN/PKHD G31 ....91 F1
Staffin Dr SMSTN G23 ....52 C2
Staffin St SMSTN G23 ....52 D2
Stafford St BLSH ML4 ....135 G3
  COWCAD C4 ....3 H2
Stag Ct UD/BTH/TAN G71 ....116 B5
Stag St GOV/IBX G51 ....88 A2
Staig Wynd MTHW ML1 ....172 B1
Stalker St WISHAW ML2 ....172 D1

Stamford St DEN/PKHD G31 ....91 E4
Stamperland Av
  CRMNK/CLK/EAG G76 ....146 A2
Stamperland Dr
  CRMNK/CLK/EAG G76 ....146 A3
Stamperland Gdns
  CRMNK/CLK/EAG G76 ....146 A3
Stamperland Hl
  CRMNK/CLK/EAG G76 ....145 H2
Stanalane St GIF/THBK G46 ....126 B4
Standburn Rd
  SPRGB/BLRNK G21 ....55 G5
St Andrew's Av BSHPBGS G64 ......54 B3
Staneacre Pk HMLTN ML3 ....170 C2
Stanecraigs Pl WISHAW ML2 ......158 A4
Stanefield Dr MTHW ML1 ....138 B3
Stanely Av PSLYS PA2 ....103 G3
Stanely Crs PSLYS PA2 ....103 G4
Stanely Dr PSLYS PA2 ....103 H3
Stanely Rd PSLYS PA2 ....103 H5
Stanford St CLYDBK G81 ....49 F1
Stanhope Dr RUTH G73 ....130 C2
Stanhope Pl WISHAW ML2 ....173 H5
Stanistone Rd BLTYR/CAMB G72 ..168 C1
Stanley Dr BLSH ML4 ....135 H1
  BSHPBGS G64 ....55 E1
Stanley La JNSTN PA5 ....100 D1
Stanley Pl BLTYR/CAMB G72 ......151 G1
Stanley St HMLTN ML3 ....169 E1
  PLKSD/SHW G41 ....88 D4
Stanley Street La
  PLKSD/SHW G41 ....88 D4
Stanmore Rd GVH/MTFL G42 .....109 G4
Stanrigg St AIRDRIE ML6 ....77 H4
Stark Av CLYDBK G81 ....31 F2
Starling Wy UD/BTH/TAN G71 ....116 B4
Startpoint St
  STPS/GTHM/RID G33 ....92 B1
Station Av HWWD PA9 ....120 A4
Station Brae BRHD/NEIL G78 ......140 D2
Station Crs RNFRW PA4 ....64 B1
Station Pk BAIL/MDB/MHD G69 ...94 B5
Station Rd AIRDRIE ML6 ....99 F1
  BAIL/MDB/MHD G69 ....94 B5
  BLTYR/CAMB G72 ....151 F2
  BRHD/NEIL G78 ....141 E3
  BSDN G61 ....33 H5
  BSHPTN PA7 ....29 E4
  CRMNK/CLK/EAG G76 ....146 B5
  DMBTN G82 ....13 E4
  GIF/THBK G46 ....127 F4
  KKNTL G66 ....21 F5
  KLBCH PA10 ....100 B4
  KSYTH G65 ....8 B1
  MRYH/FIRH G20 ....36 B1
  MTHW ML1 ....137 G4
  MTHW ML1 ....157 E1
  OLDK G60 ....30 C3
  PSLY PA1 ....84 C5
  RNFRW PA4 ....63 G2
  STPS/GTHM/RID G33 ....70 B1
  UD/BTH/TAN G71 ....133 H1
  WISHAW ML2 ....173 H5
Station Wynd KLBCH PA10 ....100 C4
Staybrae Dr PLK/PH/NH G53 ......106 A3
Staybrae Gv PLK/PH/NH G53 ......106 A3
The Steading WISHAW ML2 ....157 E5
Steel St CCLE G1 ....3 J7
  WISHAW ML2 ....174 A3
Stenhouse Av
  BAIL/MDB/MHD G69 ....58 B4
Stenton Crs WISHAW ML2 ....173 E4
Stenton Pl WISHAW ML2 ....173 E4
Stenton St CAR/SHTL G32 ....91 H2
Stenzel Pl STPS/GTHM/RID G33 ...71 G1
Stepford Pl
  STPS/GTHM/RID G33 ....93 G2
Stepford Rd
  STPS/GTHM/RID G33 ....93 G2
Stephen Crs
  BAIL/MDB/MHD G69 ....93 G4
Stephenson Pl EKILS G75 ....166 A5
Stephenson St
  CARD/HILL/MSPK G52 ....85 H1
Stepps Rd KKNTL G66 ....70 D5
  STPS/GTHM/RID G33 ....70 C5
Stevenson Pl BLSH ML4 ....117 E5
Stevenson St CLYDBK G81 ....31 G4
  DMNK/BRGTN G40 ....90 B5
  PSLYS PA2 ....104 B1
Stevenston Ct MTHW ML1 ....137 F3
Stevenston St MTHW ML1 ....137 F3
Stewart Av BLTYR/CAMB G72 .....151 H4
  HMLTN ML3 ....180 A1
  NMRNS G77 ....144 B4
  RNFRW PA4 ....62 D5
Stewart Ct BRHD/NEIL G78 ....124 B3
Stewart Crs BRHD/NEIL G78 ....124 B3
  WISHAW ML2 ....158 B4
Stewart Dr CLYDBK G81 ....32 A2
  CRMNK/CLK/EAG G76 ....146 A1
  CTBR ML5 ....95 C5
Stewartfield Crs EKILN G74 ....165 H2
Stewartfield Dr EKILN G74 ....166 A1
Stewartfield Rd EKILN G74 ....165 H2
Stewarton Dr
  BLTYR/CAMB G72 ....130 D2
Stewarton St WISHAW ML2 ....174 B3
Stewart Qd MTHW ML1 ....137 G1
Stewart Rd PSLYS PA2 ....104 C4
Stewarts La WISHAW ML2 ....174 B2
Stewart St BLSH ML4 ....136 B2
  BRHD/NEIL G78 ....124 C3
  COWCAD C4 ....2 E1
  CTBR ML5 ....96 B1
  HMLTN ML3 ....152 B5
  MLNGV G62 ....16 D3
  WISHAW ML2 ....173 G2
Stewartville St PTCK G11 ....66 A4
Stirling Av BSDN G61 ....51 F1
  EKILN G74 ....166 D2
Stirling Dr BSDN G61 ....33 H2
  BSHPBGS G64 ....54 B1
  HMLTN ML3 ....169 E5
  JNSTN PA5 ....101 E4
  PSLYN/LNWD PA3 ....83 H4
  RUTH G73 ....130 A2

Stirlingfauld Pl GBLS G5 ....89 G5
Stirling Gdns BSHPBGS G64 ....37 F5
Stirling Rd KKNTL G66 ....12 C4
Stirling Rd AIRDRIE ML6 ....76 C2
  BAIL/MDB/MHD G69 ....99 E5
  COWCAD G4 ....3 J4
  CUMB G67 ....45 F2
  DMBTN G82 ....13 C3
  KSYTH G65 ....8 D1
Stirling St AIRDRIE ML6 ....98 A2
  CUMB G67 ....45 F2
  CUMB G67 ....26 D1
  MTHW ML1 ....172 C1
Stirrat St MRYH/FIRH G20 ....52 B5
  PSLYN/LNWD PA3 ....83 G2
Stobcross Rd KVGV G3 ....88 B1
Stobcross St CTBR ML5 ....96 D5
Stobcross Wynd KVGV G3 ....88 B1
Stobhill Rd SPRGB/BLRNK G21 ....54 C2
Stobo EKILN G74 ....167 F1
Stobo St EKILN G74 ....167 F1
Stobo St WISHAW ML2 ....157 F5
Stobs Dr BRHD/NEIL G78 ....124 A5
Stock Av PSLYS PA2 ....104 B2
Stockholm Crs PSLYS PA2 ....104 B1
Stockiemuir Av BSDN G61 ....34 B1
Stockiemuir Rd BSDN G61 ....34 A1
Stock Rd MTHW ML1 ....158 A1
Stock St PSLYS PA2 ....104 B2
Stockwell Pl CGLE G1 ....3 F7
Stockwell St CGLE G1 ....89 G1
Stoneyburns Ct HMLTN ML3 ....169 F2
Stonecraig Rd WISHAW ML2 ......174 B3
Stonedyke Gv DRUM G15 ....50 C1
Stonedyke Av KVD/HLHD G12 .....52 A5
Stonefall Av CTBR ML5 ....104 C3
Stonefield Crs
  BLTYR/CAMB G72 ....151 F4
  CRMNK/CLK/EAG G76 ....145 F2
  PSLYS PA2 ....104 C3
Stonefield Dr PSLYS PA2 ....104 C3
Stonefield Pk PSLYS PA2 ....104 B3
Stonefield Park Gdns
  BLTYR/CAMB G72 ....151 F4
Stonefield Rd
  BLTYR/CAMB G72 ....151 F4
Stonehall Av AIRDRIE ML6 ....76 B5
Stonehall Av HMLTN ML3 ....169 G3
Stonehaven Crs AIRDRIE ML6 ....97 H4
Stonelaw Dr RUTH G73 ....111 E5
Stonelaw Rd RUTH G73 ....111 E5
Stoneside Dr
  PLKSW/MSWD G43 ....127 E1
Stoneside Sq
  PLKSW/MSWD G43 ....126 D1
Stoney Brae PSLYN/LNWD PA3 .....84 B2
  PSLYS PA2 ....104 B3
Stoneyetts Rd
  BAIL/MDB/MHD G69 ....59 E1
Stoneymeadow Rd
  BLTYR/CAMB G72 ....150 C5
  EKILN G74 ....149 G5
Stonyflatt Av DMBTN G82 ....13 G2
Stonyflatt Rd DMBTN G82 ....13 G2
Stonyhurst St PPK/MIL G22 ....67 H2
Stonylee Rd CUMB G67 ....26 C4
Stonyvale St PSLY PA2 ....84 B5
Stormyland Wy
  BRHD/NEIL G78 ....124 B5
Stornoway Crs WISHAW ML2 ......174 D1
Stornoway St PPK/MIL G22 ....54 A1
Stow Brae PSLY PA1 ....104 B1
Stow St PSLY PA1 ....84 B5
Strachan St BLSH ML4 ....135 H3
Strachur St PPK/MIL G22 ....53 G4
Strain Crs AIRDRIE ML6 ....98 C3
Straiton Dr HMLTN ML3 ....168 D5
Straiton St STPS/GTHM/RID G33 ..91 H2
Stranka Av PSLYS PA2 ....103 H1
Stranraer Dr DRUM G15 ....50 C1
Stratford EKILN G74 ....150 A5
Stratford St MRYH/FIRH G20 ....52 D5
Strathallan Crs AIRDRIE ML6 ....76 B3
Strathallan Ga EKILS G75 ....165 E4
Strathallan Pl RUTH G73 ....130 C4
Strathaven Rd EKILS G75 ....166 D5
  HMLTN ML3 ....180 D5
Strathavon Crs AIRDRIE ML6 ....76 B3
Strathblane Crs AIRDRIE ML6 ....76 B3
Strathblane Dr EKILS G75 ....166 C4
Strathblane Gdns KNTSWD G13 ....51 G3
Strathblane Rd MLNGV G62 ....17 E3
Strathbran St DEN/PKHD G31 ....91 G5
Strathcairn Crs AIRDRIE ML6 ....76 B3
Strathcarron Crs PSLYS PA2 ....105 E4
Strathcarron Dr PSLYS PA2 ....105 E3
Strathcarron Pl
  MRYH/FIRH G20 ....66 C1
  PSLYS PA2 ....105 E4
Strathcarron Rd PSLYS PA2 ....105 E4
Strathcarron Wy PSLYS PA2 ....105 E3
Strathclyde Dr RUTH G73 ....110 D5
Strathclyde Rd DMBTN G82 ....13 F2
Strathclyde St
  DMNK/BRGTN G40 ....110 D2
Strathclyde Vw
  UD/BTH/TAN G71 ....152 C1
Strathclyde Wy EKILS G75 ....51 C4
Strathcona Gdns
  MRYH/FIRH G20 ....51 H4
Strathcona La EKILS G75 ....178 B1
Strathcona Pl EKILS G75 ....178 B1
  RUTH G73 ....130 C4
Strathcona St KNTSWD G13 ....51 G5
Strathconon Gdns EKILS G75 ......164 D4
Strathdearn Gv EKILS G75 ....164 D5
Strathdee Av CLYDBK G81 ....32 A5
Strathdee Rd LNPK/KPK G44 ......127 H5
Strathdon Av LNPK/KPK G44 ......127 H5
  PSLYS PA2 ....104 B2
Strathdon Dr LNPK/KPK G44 ......128 A5
Strathdon Pl EKILS G75 ....164 D5
Strathearn Gv KKNTL G66 ....22 D1
Strathearn Rd
  CRMNK/CLK/EAG G76 ....145 H4
Strathendrick Dr
  PLKSW/MSWD G43 ....127 H1
Strathfillan Rd EKILN G74 ....166 C2
Strathgoil Crs AIRDRIE ML6 ....76 B3
Strathgryffe Crs BRWEIR PA11 .....79 E5
Strathisla Wy MTHW ML1 ....137 G5

Strathkelvin Av
  SPRGB/BLRNK G21 ....54 C4
Strathkelvin La EKILS G75 ....164 D5
Strathmiglo Ct EKILS G75 ....164 D5
Strathmore Av
  BLTYR/CAMB G72 ....151 F1
  PSLY PA1 ....85 G5
Strathmore Crs AIRDRIE ML6 * 76 B4
Strathmore Gdns RUTH G73 ....130 C3
Strathmore Pl CTBR ML5 * 97 G4
Strathmore Rd HMLTN ML3 ....170 B2
  PPK/MIL G22 ....53 H4
Strathmore Wk CTBR ML5 ....97 G4
Strathmungo Crs AIRDRIE ML6 .....76 A4
Strathnairn Av EKILS G75 ....164 D5
Strathnairn Ct EKILS G75 ....164 D5
Strathnairn Dr EKILS G75 ....164 D5
Strathnairn Wy EKILS G75 ....164 D5
Strathnaver Crs AIRDRIE ML6 ....76 B3
Strathnaver Gdns EKILS G75 ....164 D5
Strathord Pl
  BAIL/MDB/MHD G69 ....42 B4
Strathord St CAR/SHTL G32 ....112 B1
Strathpeffer Crs AIRDRIE ML6 ....76 B4
Strathrannoch Wy EKILS G75 .....164 D5
Strathspey Av EKILS G75 ....164 D5
Strathspey Crs AIRDRIE ML6 ....76 B3
Strathtay Av EKILS G75 ....164 D5
  LNPK/KPK G44 ....127 H5
Strathummel Crs AIRDRIE ML6 .....76 B3
Strathview Gv LNPK/KPK G44 .....127 H5
Strathview Pk LNPK/KPK G44 .....127 H5
Strathview Rd BLSH ML4 ....135 F5
Strathvithie Gv EKILS G75 ....166 A1
Strathyre Gdns AIRDRIE ML6 ....76 B3
  BSDN G61 ....34 E3
  EKILS G75 ....164 D5
Strathyre St PLKSD/SHW G41 ......108 D4
Stratton Dr GIF/THBK G46 ....127 E5
Strauss Av CLYDBK G81 ....49 H2
Stravaig Pth PSLYS PA2 ....103 F5
Stravaig Wk PSLYS PA2 ....103 F5
Stravanan Ct CSMK G45 ....129 F5
Stravanan Rd CSMK G45 ....129 E5
Stravanan St CSMK G45 ....129 F5
Stravanan Ter CSMK G45 ....129 F5
Strawberry Field Rd
  CRG/CRSL/HOU PA6 ....80 C2
Strawhill Rd
  CRMNK/CLK/EAG G76 ....145 H3
Streamfield Gdns
  STPS/GTHM/RID G33 ....55 H4
Streamfield Ga
  STPS/GTHM/RID G33 ....55 G4
Streamfield Lea
  STPS/GTHM/RID G33 ....55 G4
Streamfield Pl
  STPS/GTHM/RID G33 ....55 H4
Strenabey Av RUTH G73 ....130 C3
Striven Crs WISHAW ML2 ....173 H4
Striven Gdns MRYH/FIRH G20 ......67 E3
Striven Ter HMLTN ML3 ....169 F4
Stroma St SPRGB/BLRNK G21 ......69 E4
Stromness St GBLS G5 ....89 F5
Strone Gdns KSYTH G65 ....7 H2
Stronend St PPK/MIL G22 ....53 G4
Strone Rd STPS/GTHM/RID G33 ...92 C2
Stronsay St SPRGB/BLRNK G21 ....69 E4
Stronvar Dr SCOT G14 ....64 C2
Stroud Rd EKILS G75 ....177 H3
Struthers Crs EKILN G74 ....167 E1
Stuart Av OLDK G60 ....30 C3
  RUTH G73 ....130 A4
Stuart Dr BSHPBGS G64 ....54 B3
Stuarton Pk EKILN G74 ....166 B3
Stuart Qd WISHAW ML2 ....173 E4
Stuart Rd BSHPTN PA7 ....29 F4
  CRMNK/CLK/EAG G76 ....145 H4
  DMBTN G82 ....13 H1
Stuart St EKILN G74 ....166 C3
  OLDK G60 ....30 C3
Succoth St KNTSWD G13 ....51 G4
Sudbury Crs EKILS G75 ....164 D4
Sugworth Av
  BAIL/MDB/MHD G69 ....94 A4
Sumburgh St
  STPS/GTHM/RID G33 ....92 A2
Summerfield Pl *
  DMNK/BRGTN G40 ....111 E2
Summerfield St
  CUMB G67 ....44 B5
Summerhill Gdns DRUM G15 ....33 G4
Summerhill Pl DRUM G15 ....33 G4
Summerhill Rd
  CRMNK/CLK/EAG G76 ....146 A3
  DRUM G15 ....33 G4
Summerlea Rd GIF/THBK G46 ......126 C3
Summerlee Rd WISHAW ML2 ......172 D1
Summerlee St CTBR ML5 ....96 D4
  STPS/GTHM/RID G33 ....92 D1
Summer St DMNK/BRGTN G40 .....90 C4
Summertown Rd GOV/IBX G51 ......88 A2
Sunart Av RNFRW PA4 ....63 E2
Sunart Gdns BSHPBGS G64 ....55 F2
Sunart Rd BSHPBGS G64 ....55 F2
  CARD/HILL/MSPK G52 ....87 F4
Sunart St WISHAW ML2 ....173 H4
Sunbury Av
  CRMNK/CLK/EAG G76 ....145 F3
Sundale Av
  CRMNK/CLK/EAG G76 ....145 G4
Sunderland Av DMBTN G82 ....12 B3
Sunflower Gdns MTHW ML1 ....154 C5
Sunningdale Av NMRNS G77 ....144 C5
Sunningdale Dr BRWEIR PA11 ......79 E5
Sunningdale Rd SMSTN G23 ....52 C3
Sunningdale Wynd
  UD/BTH/TAN G71 ....133 H4
Sunnybank Dr
  CRMNK/CLK/EAG G76 ....145 G4
Sunnybank Gv
  CRMNK/CLK/EAG G76 ....145 G4
Sunnyhill KSYTH G65 ....23 F2

Sunnylaw Dr PSLYS PA2 ....103 G2
Sunnylaw St PPK/MIL G22 ....67 G2
Sunnyside Av MTHW ML1 ....137 G5
  UD/BTH/TAN G71 ....134 A2
Sunnyside Crs MTHW ML1 ....137 F2
Sunnyside Dr
  BAIL/MDB/MHD G69 ....95 A4
  CRMNK/CLK/EAG G76 ....145 G2
  DRUM G15 ....50 B2
Sunnyside Ov PSLYS PA2 ....103 H3
Sunnyside Rd CTBR ML5 ....78 A4
  DRUM G15 ....50 B2
  HMLTN ML3 ....181 G4
  MTHW ML1 ....157 E2
  PSLYS PA2 ....104 A3
Sunnyside Ter MTHW ML1 ....137 F2
Surrey La GBLS G5 ....89 G5
Surrey St GBLS G5 ....89 G5
Sussex St PLKSD/SHW G41 ....88 D4
Sutcliffe Ct KNTSWD G13 ....51 F4
Sutcliffe Rd KNTSWD G13 ....51 F3
Sutherland Av BSDN G61 ....34 B1
  PLKSD/SHW G41 ....108 B1
Sutherland Crs HMLTN ML3 ....169 H1
Sutherland Dr AIRDRIE ML6 ....98 A4
  GIF/THBK G46 ....145 G1
Sutherland La KVGV G3 * 66 B4
Sutherland Rd BLSH ML4 ....135 G5
  CLYDBK G81 ....49 E1
Sutherland St
  BLTYR/CAMB G72 ....151 F5
  PSLY PA1 ....84 A4
Sutherland Wy EKILN G74 ....167 F2
Sutherness Dr
  STPS/GTHM/RID G33 ....92 B2
Swaledale EKILN G74 ....165 H2
Swallow Gdns KNTSWD G13 ....50 A4
Swallow Rd CLYDBK G81 ....32 C1
  WISHAW ML2 ....174 A2
Swan Pl JNSTN PA5 ....120 D2
Swan St
  DMNK/BRGTN G40 ....110 D2
  CLYDBK G81 ....31 G5
  COWCAD G4 ....3 G1
Swan La LNPK/KPK G44 * 128 B5
Sween Dr RNFRW PA4 ....169 F4
Sweethope Gdns
  UD/BTH/TAN G71 ....134 C5
Sweethope Pl
  UD/BTH/TAN G71 ....134 B3
Swift Bank HMLTN ML3 ....168 D4
Swift Cl WISHAW ML2 ....174 A2
Swift Crs KNTSWD G13 ....50 B3
Swift Pl EKILS G75 ....176 D2
  JNSTN PA5 ....121 E2
Swindon St CLYDBK G81 ....31 F5
Swinstie Rd MTHW ML1 ....157 F2
Swinstie Vw MTHW ML1 ....157 F1
Swinton Av
  BAIL/MDB/MHD G69 ....94 C4
Swinton Crs
  BAIL/MDB/MHD G69 ....94 B4
  CTBR ML5 ....95 C5
Swinton Dr
  CARD/HILL/MSPK G52 ....86 C4
Swinton Pth
  BAIL/MDB/MHD G69 ....94 C4
Swinton Pl
  CARD/HILL/MSPK G52 ....86 C4
Swinton Rd
  BAIL/MDB/MHD G69 ....94 B4
Swinton Vw
  BAIL/MDB/MHD G69 ....94 B4
Swisscot Av HMLTN ML3 ....169 G5
Swisscot Wk HMLTN ML3 ....169 G5
Switchback Rd BSDN G61 ....51 C2
Sword St DEN/PKHD G31 ....90 C3
Sword St AIRDRIE ML6 ....98 A2
Sycamore Av JNSTN PA5 ....101 H5
  KKNTL G66 ....40 A3
  UD/BTH/TAN G71 ....115 H5
Sycamore Crs EKILS G75 ....178 A2
  EKILS G75 ....178 A2
Sycamore Dr AIRDRIE ML6 ....98 A4
  CLYDBK G81 ....31 G4
  HMLTN ML3 ....170 C5
Sycamore Gv
  BLTYR/CAMB G72 ....151 F2
Sycamore Pl EKILS G75 ....178 A2
  MTHW ML1 ....137 G4
Sycamore Wy
  BLTYR/CAMB G72 ....132 C5
  KKNTL G66 ....40 A3
Sydenham Rd KVD/HLHD G12 ......66 A4
Sydney Dr EKILS G75 ....177 G3
Sydney Pl EKILS G75 ....177 G5
Sydney St CLYDBK G81 ....31 E4
  DEN/PKHD G31 ....90 B5
Sykehead Av BLSH ML4 ....136 A2
Sykeside Rd AIRDRIE ML6 ....97 H5
Symington Dr CLYDBK G81 ....49 E2
Syriam Pl SPRGB/BLRNK G21 ....68 C1
Syriam St SPRGB/BLRNK G21 ......68 C1

T

Tabard Pl KNTSWD G13 ....50 D3
Tabard Rd KNTSWD G13 ....50 D3
Tabernacle La
  BLTYR/CAMB G72 ....131 F2
Tabernacle St
  BLTYR/CAMB G72 ....131 F2
Taggart Rd KSYTH G65 ....24 D2
Taig Rd KKNTL G66 ....21 H5
Tait Av BRHD/NEIL G78 ....124 C5
Talbot EKILN G74 ....167 F1
Talbot Ct KNTSWD G13 ....64 C1
Talbot Dr KNTSWD G13 ....64 C1
Talbot Pl KNTSWD G13 ....64 C1
Talbot Ter KNTSWD G13 ....64 C1
  UD/BTH/TAN G71 ....114 D4
Talisman Av DMBTN G82 ....12 B3
Talisman Crs MTHW ML1 ....136 C5
Talisman Rd KNTSWD G13 ....50 D5
  PSLYS PA2 ....102 D5

Tallant Rd DRUM G15 ....33 G5
Tallant Ter DRUM G15 ....33 H5
Talla Rd CARD/HILL/MSPK G52 ....86 C4
Tamarack Crs
  UD/BTH/TAN G71 ....115 H3
Tamar Dr EKILS G75 ....177 E2
Tambowie Crs MLNGV G62 ....16 D3
Tambowie Crs MLNGV G62 ....16 D3
Tambowie St KNTSWD G13 ....51 F4
Tamshill St MRYH/FIRH G20 ....53 E5
Tanar Av RNFRW PA4 ....64 A5
Tandlehill Rd KLBCH PA10 ....100 A4
Tanera Av LNPK/KPK G44 ....128 D2
Tanfield Pl CAR/SHTL G32 ....92 D2
Tanfield St CAR/SHTL G32 ....92 D2
Tankerland Rd
  PLKSW/MSWD G43 ....128 B1
Tannadice Av
  CARD/HILL/MSPK G52 ....106 D1
Tanna Dr
  CARD/HILL/MSPK G52 ....107 G1
Tannahill Crs JNSTN PA5 ....101 G5
Tannahill Dr EKILN G74 ....167 F2
Tannahill Rd
  PLKSW/MSWD PA3 ....127 H1
  PLKSW/MSWD PA3 ....83 G3
Tannahill Ter PSLYN/LNWD PA3 ...83 G4
Tannoch Dr CUMB G67 ....45 E1
  MLNGV G62 ....17 F2
Tannoch Pl CUMB G67 ....45 E1
Tannochside Dr
  UD/BTH/TAN G71 ....115 F3
Tannock St PPK/MIL G22 ....73 H5
  PSLYS PA2 ....103 F5
Tantallon Pk EKILN G74 ....166 A3
Tantallon Rd
  BAIL/MDB/MHD G69 ....113 H1
  PLKSD/SHW G41 ....108 D5
Tanzieknowe Av
  BLTYR/CAMB G72 ....131 G3
Tanzieknowe Dr
  BLTYR/CAMB G72 ....131 G4
Tanzieknowe Pl
  BLTYR/CAMB G72 ....131 G4
Tanzieknowe Rd
  BLTYR/CAMB G72 ....131 G4
Taransay St GOV/IBX G51 ....87 G1
Tarbert Av BLTYR/CAMB G72 ......133 F5
  WISHAW ML2 ....157 G4
Tarbert Ct HMLTN ML3 ....169 F4
Tarbert Wy CTBR ML5 ....96 B5
Tarbolton EKILN G74 ....167 G2
Tarbolton Crs AIRDRIE ML6 ....32 B5
Tarbolton Dr CLYDBK G81 ....32 B5
Tarbolton Rd CUMB G67 ....26 D3
  PLKSW/MSWD G43 ....127 G1
Tarbrax Wy HMLTN ML3 ....169 F2
Tarfside Av
  CARD/HILL/MSPK G52 ....87 E5
Tarfside Gdns
  CARD/HILL/MSPK G52 ....87 E5
Tarfside Ov
  CARD/HILL/MSPK G52 ....87 E5
Target Rd AIRDRIE ML6 ....98 C3
Tarland St GOV/IBX G51 ....87 G3
Tarn Gv STPS/GTHM/RID G33 ....55 E2
Tarquin Pl MTHW ML1 ....154 B2
Tarras Dr RNFRW PA4 ....63 H5
Tasman Dr EKILS G75 ....177 G1
Tasmania Qd WISHAW ML2 ....174 B3
Tassie St PLKSD/SHW G41 ....108 C4
Tattershall Rd
  STPS/GTHM/RID G33 ....70 D4
Tavistock Dr
  PLKSW/MSWD G43 ....127 G2
Tay Av PSLYS PA2 ....103 E3
  RNFRW PA4 ....64 A3
Tay Ct EKILS G75 ....164 D5
Tay Crs BSHPBGS G64 ....55 E2
  STPS/GTHM/RID G33 ....69 H5
Taylor Av KLBCH PA10 ....100 A4
Taylor Pl COWCAD G4 ....3 J4
Taylor St CLYDBK G81 ....49 F1
  COWCAD G4 ....3 J5
Taymouth St CAR/SHTL G32 ....112 C1
Taynish Dr LNPK/KPK G44 ....128 C3
Tay Pl DMBTN G82 ....13 G1
  JNSTN PA5 ....120 D1
Tay Rd BSDN G61 ....51 F1
  BSHPBGS G64 ....55 E2
Tayside AIRDRIE ML6 ....76 A5
Teak Pl UD/BTH/TAN G71 ....116 A3
Teal Ct BLSH ML4 ....116 B4
Teal Crs EKILS G75 ....176 D2
Teal Dr KNTSWD G13 ....50 B4
Tealing Av
  CARD/HILL/MSPK G52 ....86 D5
Tealing Crs
  CARD/HILL/MSPK G52 ....86 D5
Teasel Av PLK/PH/NH G53 ....125 G4
Teawell Rd NMRNS G77 ....144 A5
Technology Av
  BLTYR/CAMB G72 ....151 F5
Teesdale EKILN G74 ....165 H2
Teign Gv EKILS G75 ....177 E2
Teith Av RNFRW PA4 ....63 H4
Teith Dr BSDN G61 ....33 H5
Teith St STPS/GTHM/RID G33 ....69 H5
Telephone La KVD/HLHD G12 ....66 A4
Telford Pl CUMB G67 ....45 E1
Telford Rd CUMB G67 ....45 E1
  EKILS G75 ....166 B5
Telford St BLSH ML4 ....135 H1
Temple Pl EKILS G75 ....177 E1
Templar Av KNTSWD G13 ....51 E2
Temple Gdns KNTSWD G13 ....51 G4
Temple Locks Ct KNTSWD G13 .....51 F4
Temple Locks Pl KNTSWD G13 .....51 F4
Temple Rd MRYH/FIRH G20 ....51 H4
Templeton St
  DMNK/BRGTN G40 ....90 B4
Tennant Av EKILN G74 ....165 H4
Tennant St RNFRW PA4 ....63 H2
Tennent St CTBR ML5 ....97 E4
Tennyson Dr
  BLTYR/CAMB G72 ....151 F2
Tenters Wy PSLY PA1 ....103 G1

Tern Pl JNSTN PA5 ....121 E2
Terregles Av PLKSD/SHW G41 ....108 B2
Terregles Crs PLKSD/SHW G41 ...108 B2
Terregles Dr PLKSD/SHW G41 ....108 B2
Teviot Av BSHPBGS G64 ....37 H5
  PSLYS PA2 ....102 D4
Teviot Crs BSDN G61 ....51 E1
Teviot Dr BSHPTN PA7 ....46 B1
Teviot St CTBR ML5 ....96 B1
  KVGV G3 ....88 B1
Teviot Ter JNSTN PA5 ....120 D1
Tewkesbury Rd EKILN G74 ....150 A5
Thane Ga KNTSWD G13 * 51 F5
Thanes Ga SPRGB/BLRNK G21 .....68 C5
Thankerton Av MTHW ML1 ....137 E2
Tharsis St SPRGB/BLRNK G21 ......68 C5
The Loaning KKNTL G66 ....21 G5
Third Av DMBTN G82 ....13 H5
  KKNTL G66 ....57 E2
Third Gdns PLKSD/SHW G41 ....87 H5
Thirdpart Crs KNTSWD G13 ....49 H4
Third Rd BLTYR/CAMB G72 ....151 H5
Third St UD/BTH/TAN G71 ....115 E4
Thirlmere EKILS G75 ....176 D2
Thistle Bank KKNTL G66 ....40 A3
Thistledown Gv CTBR ML5 ....116 B1
Thistledown Gv CTBR ML5 ....97 F3
Thistle Gdns MTHW ML1 ....137 G4
Thistle Pl EKILN G74 ....166 A2
Thistle Rd MTHW ML1 ....137 G5
Thistle St AIRDRIE ML6 ....76 C5
  GBLS G5 ....89 H4
  KKNTL G66 ....66 C1
  MTHW ML1 ....157 F1
  PSLYS PA2 ....103 H2
Thistle Ter GBLS G5 ....89 G5
Thomas Muir Av BSHPBGS G64 ....55 E3
Thomas St PSLY PA1 ....83 G5
Thompson Av KKNTL G66 ....21 G5
Thompson Pl CLYDBK G81 ....32 B2
Thompson St DEN/PKHD G31 ....90 D3
Thomson Av KNTSWD G13 ....173 G4
  WISHAW ML2 ....173 G4
Thomson Dr AIRDRIE ML6 ....98 A3
  BSDN G61 ....51 H1
Thomson Gv BLTYR/CAMB G72 ...132 A1
Thomson St JNSTN PA5 ....101 F4
  RNFRW PA4 ....63 F4
Thorn Av KNTSWD G74 ....164 B2
Thornbank St KVGV G3 ....88 B1
Thorn Brae JNSTN PA5 ....101 H3
Thornbridge Av
  BAIL/MDB/MHD G69 ....94 A4
  KVD/HLHD G12 ....66 B1
Thornbridge Gdns
  BAIL/MDB/MHD G69 ....93 H4
Thornbridge Rd
  BAIL/MDB/MHD G69 ....93 H4
Thorncliffe Gdns
  PLKSD/SHW G41 ....108 D2
Thorncroft Dr LNPK/KPK G44 .....129 E3
Thorndean Av BLSH ML4 ....136 A3
Thorndean Crs BLSH ML4 ....136 A3
Thorndene JNSTN PA5 ....101 H3
Thorndene Av MTHW ML1 ....137 H5
Thornden La SCOT G14 ....64 B2
Thorn Dr BSDN G61 ....34 A3
  RUTH G73 ....130 B3
Thorndyke EKILN G74 ....149 H4
Thornhill JNSTN PA5 ....101 H4
Thornhill Av BLTYR/CAMB G72 ...151 G2
  JNSTN PA5 ....102 A2
Thornhill Dr JNSTN PA5 ....101 H4
Thornhill Gdns JNSTN PA5 ....101 H3
  NMRNS G77 ....161 G5
Thornhill La HMLTN ML3 ....168 C1
Thornhill Wy CTBR ML5 ....117 G1
Thorniecroft Dr CUMB G67 ....44 B2
Thorniecroft Pl CUMB G67 ....44 B2
Thorniewood Gdns
  UD/BTH/TAN G71 ....134 B1
Thorniewood Rd
  UD/BTH/TAN G71 ....115 G4
Thornkip Pl CTBR ML5 ....97 G4
Thornlea Dr GIF/THBK G46 ....127 G3
Thornley Av KNTSWD G13 ....50 C5
Thornliebank Rd
  GIF/THBK G46 ....126 D3
Thornlie Gill WISHAW ML2 ....174 B3
Thornly Park Av PSLYS PA2 ....104 B3
Thornly Park Dr PSLYS PA2 ....104 B3
Thornly Park Gdns PSLYS PA2 .....104 B3
Thornly Park Rd PSLYS PA2 ....104 B3
Thorn Rd BLSH ML4 ....135 A2
  BSDN G61 ....34 A2
Thornside Rd JNSTN PA5 ....101 H3
Thornton La MRYH/FIRH G20 ......52 D4
Thornton Pl HMLTN ML3 ....180 D2
Thornton Rd EKILN G74 ....164 B2
Thornton St CTBR ML5 ....74 A4
  MRYH/FIRH G20 ....52 D4
Thorntree Av HMLTN ML3 ....152 A5
Thorntree Wy
  UD/BTH/TAN G71 ....134 C4
Thornwood Av KKNTL G66 ....39 F3
  PTCK G11 ....65 H4
Thornwood Crs PTCK G11 ....65 G3
Thornwood Dr BRWEIR PA11 ....79 F4
  PSLYS PA2 ....103 G2
  PTCK G11 ....65 G3
Thornwood Gdns PTCK G11 ....65 H4
Thornwood Pl PTCK G11 ....65 H3
Thornwood Qd PTCK G11 ....65 G3
Thornwood Rd PTCK G11 ....65 G4
Thornwood Ter PTCK G11 ....65 G4
Thornyburn Dr
  BAIL/MDB/MHD G69 ....94 B5
Thornyburn Pl
  BAIL/MDB/MHD G69 ....94 B5
Thrashbush Av WISHAW ML2 ......174 C1
Thrashbush Crs WISHAW ML2 .....174 C1
Thrashbush Rd WISHAW ML2 .....174 C1
Threave Pl NMRNS G77 ....143 H5
Threestonehill Av
  CAR/SHTL G32 ....92 C3
Threshold EKILN G74 ....150 C5
Threshold Pk EKILN G74 ....166 D5
Thriplee Rd BRWEIR PA11 ....79 F3
Thrums EKILN G74 ....150 C5
Thrums Av BSHPBGS G64 ....55 F2
Thrums Gdns BSHPBGS G64 ....55 F2
Thrushbush Qd AIRDRIE ML6 ....76 B3
Thrushbush Rd AIRDRIE ML6 ....76 B4

Thrushcraig Crs *PSLYS* PA2 ......104 E3
Thrush Pl *JNSTN* PA5 ....121 E2
Thurso St *PTCK* G11 ....66 B5
Thurston Rd
  CARD/HILL/MSPK G52 ....86 B4
Thyme Sq *MTHW* ML1 ....154 D2
Tibbermore Rd *PTCK* G11 ....65 H5
Tiber Av *MTHW* ML1 ....154 E1
Tillanburn Rd *MTHW* ML1 ....138 C4
Tillet Ov *PSLYN/LNWD* PA3 ....84 A2
Tillet St *MRYH/FIRH* G20 ....67 E3
Till St *WISHAW* ML2 ....157 E4
Tillycairn Dr
  STPS/GTHM/RID G33 ....71 E4
Tillycairn Rd
  STPS/GTHM/RID G33 ....71 E4
Tillycairn St
  STPS/GTHM/RID G33 ....71 E4
Tilt Rd *WISHAW* ML2 ....158 A4
Tilt St *STPS/GTHM/RID* G33 ......69 H4
Timmons Gv *BLSH* ML4 ....136 C2
Timmons Ter *AIRDRIE* ML6 ....119 E3
Tinker's La *MTHW* ML1 ....154 B4
Tintagel Gdns
  BAIL/MDB/MHD G69 ....42 A5
Tintock Rd *KKNTL* G66 ....22 B3
Tinto Crs *WISHAW* ML2 ....174 B3
Tinto Dr *BRHD/NEIL* G78 ....142 B2
Tinto Rd *AIRDRIE* ML6 ....98 C3
  BSDN G61 ....33 G2
  CTBR ML5 ....95 G3
  PLKSW/MSWD G43 ....127 F2
Tinto St *WISHAW* ML2 ....174 B3
Tinto Vw *HMLTN* ML3 ....170 B5
Tinto Wy *EKILS* G75 ....177 G3
Tinwald Pth
  CARD/HILL/MSPK G52 ....86 B4
Tiree *EKILN* G74 ....179 F1
Tiree Av *RNFRW* PA4 ....85 F1
Tiree Ct *CUMB* G67 ....25 H5
Tiree Crs *WISHAW* ML2 ....158 A5
Tiree Dr *CUMB* G67 ....25 H5
Tiree Gdns *AIRDRIE* ML6 ....76 A1
  BSDN G61 ....33 G2
  OLDK G60 ....30 D2
Tiree Gra *HMLTN* ML3 ....169 E4
Tiree Pl *CTBR* ML5 * 96 B5
  NMRNS G77 ....145 G5
  OLDK G60 ....30 D5
Tiree Rd *CUMB* G67 ....25 H5
Tiree St *SPRGB/BLRNK* G21 ......69 F4
Tirry Av *RNFRW* PA4 ....64 A4
Titwood Rd *NMRNS* G77 ....161 H4
  PLKSD/SHW G41 ....108 B2
Tiverton Av *CAR/SHTL* G32 ......113 E1
Tivoli Ct *EKILS* G75 ....178 B2
Tobago Pl *DMNK/BRGTN* G40 ....90 C4
  EKILS G75 ....165 F4
Tobago St *DMNK/BRGTN* G40 ....90 B4
Tobermory Rd *RUTH* G73 ....130 C4
Todburn Dr *PSLY* PA2 ....104 C5
Todd St *DEN/PKHD* G31 ....91 F2
Todhills North *EKILS* G75 ....166 C5
Todhills South *EKILS* G75 ......166 C5
Todholm Crs *PSLY* PA2 ....105 E2
Todholm Rd *PSLY* PA2 ....105 E2
Todholm Ter *PSLY* PA2 ....105 E2
Tofthill Av *BSHPBGS* G64 ....54 C1
Tofthill Gdns *BSHPBGS* G64 .....54 B1
Tollbrae Av *AIRDRIE* ML6 ....98 C2
Tollcross Park Gdns
  CAR/SHTL G32 ....111 H1
Tollcross Park Gv
  CAR/SHTL G32 ....112 A1
Tollcross Park Vw
  CAR/SHTL G32 ....111 H1
Tollcross Rd *CAR/SHTL* G32 .....112 C1
  DEN/PKHD G31 ....91 G4
Tollhouse Gdns *BLSH* ML4 ......136 B4
Toll La *GOV/IBX* G51 ....88 C3
Tollpark Crs *WISHAW* ML2 ....158 B5
Tollpark Pl *BALLOCH* G68 ....11 G2
Tollpark Rd *BALLOCH* G68 ....11 G2
Toll St *MTHW* ML1 ....155 E5
Toll Wynd *HMLTN* ML3 ....180 C1
Tolsta St *SMSTN* G23 ....52 D2
Toman Brae *BALLOCH* G68 ....43 G1
Tomtain Ct *BALLOCH* G68 ....43 G1
Tontine La *CGLE* G1 ....3 H7
Tontine Pl *RUTH* G73 ....130 D3
Topaz Ter *BLSH* ML4 ....135 H4
Toppersfield *KLBCH* PA10 ....100 D4
Torbeg Gdns *EKILS* G75 ....177 E2
Torbracken *HWWD* PA9 ....120 B3
Torbreck St
  CARD/HILL/MSPK G52 ....87 G4
Torbrex Rd *CUMB* G67 ....26 C4
Torburn Av *GIF/THBK* G46 ......127 E3
Tordene Pth *BALLOCH* G68 ....25 H2
Torgyle St *SMSTN* G23 ....52 B3
Tormeadow Rd *NMRNS* G77 ....144 A5
Tormore St *GOV/IBX* G51 ....87 E3
Tormusk Dr *CSMK* G45 ....129 H5
Tormusk Gdns *CSMK* G45 ....129 H5
Tormusk Gv *CSMK* G45 ....129 H5
Tormusk Rd *CSMK* G45 ....129 H4
Torness St *PTCK* G11 ....66 B4
Torogay Pl *PPK/MIL* G22 ....54 B3
Torogay St *PPK/MIL* G22 ....53 H4
Torogay Ter *PPK/MIL* G22 ....53 H3
Torphin Crs *CAR/SHTL* G32 ......92 B2
Torphin Wk *CAR/SHTL* G32 ......92 B2
Torrance Av *AIRDRIE* ML6 ....99 E3
Torrance Rd *BSHPBGS* G64 ....38 B1
  EKILN G74 ....166 B3
Torrance St *SPRGB/BLRNK* G21 ..68 C2
Torran Dr *RNFRW* PA4 ....64 B4
Torran Rd
  STPS/GTHM/RID G33 ....93 G2
Torranyard Ter *HMLTN* ML3 ......168 D4
Torr Av *BRWEIR* PA11 ....79 E3
Torriden Pl *CTBR* ML5 ....96 A4
Torriden St *CTBR* ML5 ....96 A4
Torridon Av *MTHW* ML1 ....154 A1
  PLKSD/SHW G41 ....108 A1
Torridon Gdns *NMRNS* G77 .....162 C1
Torrington Av *GIF/THBK* G46 ....126 C1
Torrington Crs *CAR/SHTL* G32 ..113 E1
Torrin Rd *SMSTN* G23 ....52 B3
Torrisdale Pl *CTBR* ML5 ....96 B2
Torrisdale St *CTBR* ML5 ....96 B2
  GVH/MTFL G42 ....109 E2
Torr La *BRWEIR* PA11 ....79 E4
Torr Pl *PPK/MIL* G22 ....68 A2

Torryburn Rd
  SPRGB/BLRNK G21 ....69 G2
Torwood Brae *HMLTN* ML3 ......169 E3
Toryglen Rd *RUTH* G73 ....110 B4
Toryglen St *GBLS* G5 ....110 B2
Tourmaline Ter *BLSH* ML4 ....136 A4
Toward Ct *BLTYR/CAMB* G72 ...151 H1
Toward Rd
  STPS/GTHM/RID G33 ....92 D2
Tower Av *BRHD/NEIL* G78 ....124 C5
Tower Crs *RNFRW* PA4 ....63 E4
Tower Dr *RNFRW* PA4 ....63 E4
Towerhill Rd *KNTSWD* G13 ....51 E2
Tower Pl *JNSTN* PA5 ....101 G5
  MLNCV G62 ....17 F5
Tower Rd *BSHPBGS* G64 ....18 A2
  CUMB G67 ....45 F2
  JNSTN PA5 ....101 G5
Towerside Crs *PLK/PH/NH* G53 ..106 B2
Towerside Rd *PLK/PH/NH* G53 ..106 B2
Towers Rd *AIRDRIE* ML6 ....99 G2
Tower St *PLKSD/SHW* G41 ....108 B1
Tower Ter *PSLY* PA1 ....84 A5
Towie Pl *UD/BTH/TAN* G71 .....134 A1
Townend Rd *DMBTN* G82 ....13 F3
Townhead Av *BLSH* ML4 ....117 H5
Townhead Dr *MTHW* ML1 ....138 C4
Townhead Pl
  UD/BTH/TAN G71 ....115 F4
Townhead Rd *CTBR* ML5 ....73 F5
  NMRNS G77 ....161 F1
Townhead St *HMLTN* ML3 ......170 C2
  KSYTH G65 ....8 A2
Townhill Rd *HMLTN* ML3 ....168 D2
Townhill Ter *HMLTN* ML3 ....168 D2
Townmill Rd *DEN/PKHD* G31 ....90 D2
Townsend St *COWCAD* G4 ....3 F1
Tradeston St *GBLS* G5 ....89 F4
Trafalgar St *CLYDBK* G81 ....31 G5
  DMNK/BRGTN G40 ....110 C1
Trainard Av *CAR/SHTL* G32 .....111 H1
Tranent Pl *MTHW* ML1 ....139 F5
  STPS/GTHM/RID G33 ....91 H1
Traquair Av *PSLY* PA2 ....157 F5
Traquair Dr
  CARD/HILL/MSPK G52 ....86 C5
Treeburn Av *GIF/THBK* G46 ......127 E4
Treemain Rd *GIF/THBK* G46 ....144 D2
Trees Park Av *BRHD/NEIL* G78 ..124 A3
Trefoil Av *PLKSD/SHW* G41 .....108 C4
Trent Pl *EKILS* G75 ....176 D2
Trent St *CTBR* ML5 ....74 A4
Tresta Rd *SMSTN* G23 ....53 E3
Trinidad Gn *EKILS* G75 ....165 F4
Trinity Av
  CARD/HILL/MSPK G52 ....86 D5
Trinity Dr *BLTYR/CAMB* G72 ....131 H4
Trinley Rd *KNTSWD* G13 ....51 E2
Triton Pl *BLSH* ML4 ....137 E2
Trondra Pth *ESTRH* G34 ....93 G1
Trondra Pl *ESTRH* G34 ....93 G1
Trongate *CGLE* G1 ....3 H6
Troon Av *EKILS* G75 ....177 F2
Troon Ct *EKILS* G75 ....177 G2
Troon Dr *BRWEIR* PA11 ....79 F4
Troon Gdns *BALLOCH* G68 ....10 B4
Troon Pl *NMRNS* G77 ....162 B1
Troon St *DMNK/BRGTN* G40 ...111 E1
Trossachs Av *MTHW* ML1 ....137 F2
Trossachs Rd *RUTH* G73 ....130 C5
Trossachs St *MRYH/FIRH* G20 ...67 F3
Troubridge Av *KLBCH* PA10 .....100 C5
Troubridge Crs *KLBCH* PA10 ....100 C5
Truce Rd *KNTSWD* G13 ....50 C3
Truro Av *BAIL/MDB/MHD* G69 ...42 A5
Tryst Rd *CUMB* G67 ....26 B4
Tudor La *CARD/SHTL* G32 .... 65 E5
Tudor Rd *SCOT* G14 ....65 F5
Tudor St *BAIL/MDB/MHD* G69 ..113 G1
Tulley Wynd *MTHW* ML1 ....136 C5
Tullallan Pl *EKILN* G74 ....166 D5
Tullis St *DMNK/BRGTN* G40 ......90 B5
Tulloch-ard Pl *RUTH* G73 ....130 C4
Tulloch Gdns *MTHW* ML1 ....172 C1
Tulloch St *LNPK/KPK* G44 ......128 B1
Tullymet Rd *HMLTN* ML3 ....170 A5
Tummel Dr *AIRDRIE* ML6 ....99 H4
Tummel Gn *EKILN* G74 ....166 B2
Tummel St
  STPS/GTHM/RID G33 ....69 H5
Tunnel St *CUMB* G67 ....45 G2
Tunnel St *KVGV* G3 ....88 D2
Tuphall Rd *HMLTN* ML3 ....170 A3
Turnberry Av *KVD/HLHD* G12 ...66 A3
Turnberry Crs *CTBR* ML5 ....95 H4
Turnberry Dr *BRWEIR* PA11 ......79 F5
  HMLTN ML3 ....168 C4
  NMRNS G77 ....143 H4
  RUTH G73 ....129 G3
Turnberry Gdns *AIRDRIE* ML6 ...119 F3
  BALLOCH G68 ....10 C5
Turnberry Pl *EKILS* G75 ....177 G2
  RUTH G73 ....129 G3
Turnberry Rd *PTCK* G11 ....65 H5
Turnberry Wynd *UD/BTH/TAN* G71 ..133 H4
Turner Rd *PSLYN/LNWD* PA3 ....84 C1
Turners Av *PSLY* PA1 ....83 G5
Turner St *CTBR* ML5 ....96 C3
Turnhill Av *ERSK* PA8 ....47 F4
Turnhill Crs *ERSK* PA8 ....47 F4
Turnhill Dr *ERSK* PA8 ....47 G4
Turnhill Gdns *ERSK* PA8 ....47 F4
Turnlaw *EKILS* G75 ....178 A3
Turnlaw Rd *BLTYR/CAMB* G72 ..151 F5
Turnlaw St *GBLS* G5 ....90 A5
Turnyland Mdw *ERSK* PA8 ....47 G4
Turnyland Ter *BLSH* ML4 ....47 G4
Turquoise Ter *BLSH* ML4 ....136 A4
Turret Crs *KNTSWD* G13 ....50 D3
Turret Rd *KNTSWD* G13 ....50 D3
Turriff St *GBLS* G5 ....89 G5
Tweed Av *PSLY* PA2 ....103 G2
Tweed Ct *AIRDRIE* ML6 ....98 D4
Tweed Crs *RNFRW* PA4 ....63 H4
  STPS/GTHM/RID G33 ....69 G5
  WISHAW ML2 ....157 F5
Tweed Dr *BSDN* G61 ....34 A4
Tweedmuir Pl *CTBR* ML5 ....117 F1
Tweed Pl *JNSTN* PA5 ....120 D1
Tweedsmuir *BSHPBGS* G64 ....55 F1
Tweedsmuir Crs *BSDN* G61 ....34 B1
Tweedsmuir Rd *HMLTN* ML3 ....169 H5
Tweedsmuir Rd

Tweed St *CTBR* ML5 ....116 D1
  EKILS G75 ....176 D1
Tweedvale Av *SCOT* G14 ....49 H5
Tweedvale Pl *SCOT* G14 ....49 H5
Twinlaw St *ESTRH* G34 ....72 C5
Tylney Rd *PSLY* PA1 ....85 G4
Tyndrum Rd *BSDN* G61 ....35 E3
Tyndrum St *COWCAD* G4 ....3 F1
Tynecastle Crs *CAR/SHTL* G32 ...92 C2
Tynecastle Pl *CAR/SHTL* G32 .....92 C2
Tynecastle St *CAR/SHTL* G32 .....92 C2
Tyne Pl *EKILS* G75 ....176 D2
Tynron Ct *HMLTN* ML3 ....168 C4
Tynwald Av *RUTH* G73 ....130 B3

U

Udston Rd *HMLTN* ML3 ....168 D1
Udston Ter *HMLTN* ML3 ....152 A5
Uig Pl *STPS/GTHM/RID* G33 ......93 F3
Uist Crs *STPS/GTHM/RID* G33 ....71 F2
Uist Dr *KKNTL* G66 ....22 A5
Uist Pl *AIRDRIE* ML6 ....99 E3
Uist St *GOV/IBX* G51 ....87 G2
Uist Wy *WISHAW* ML2 ....157 H5
Ullswater *EKILS* G75 ....177 E3
Ulundi Rd *JNSTN* PA5 ....101 F4
Ulva St *CARD/HILL/MSPK* G52 ...87 E4
Ulverston Ter *HMLTN* ML3 ....180 D2
Underwood Dr *WISHAW* ML2 ....158 A3
Underwood La *PSLY* PA1 ....84 A4
Underwood Rd *PSLY* PA1 ....83 H4
  RUTH G73 ....130 B1
Underwood St
  PLKSD/SHW G41 ....108 D4
Union Pl *CGLE* G1 ....2 E5
Union St *CGLE* G1 ....2 E5
  HMLTN ML3 ....170 A1
  KKNTL G66 ....21 E5
  MTHW ML1 ....137 F3
  PSLY PA1 ....83 H5
Unitas Rd *BLSH* ML4 ....136 B2
Unity Pl *COWCAD* G4 ....67 F4
University Av *KVD/HLHD* G12 ....66 C4
University Gdns *KVD/HLHD* G12 ..66 C4
University Pl *KVD/HLHD* G12 .....66 C4
Unsted Pl *PSLY* PA1 ....84 D5
Unthank Rd *BLSH* ML4 ....136 B2
Uphall Pl *STPS/GTHM/RID* G33 ..91 H2
Upland La *SCOT* G14 ....64 D2
Upland Rd *SCOT* G14 ....64 D2
U P La *PSLY* PA1 ....8 B2
Upper Bourtree Ct *RUTH* G73 ...130 B3
Upper Bourtree Dr *RUTH* G73 ...130 A3
Upper Glenburn Rd *BSDN* G61 ...34 A3
Upper Mill St *AIRDRIE* ML6 ....98 B1
U P Rd *KSYTH* G65 ....8 C2
Urquhart Crs *RNFRW* PA4 ....63 F4
Urquhart Dr *EKILN* G74 ....166 D2
Urrdale Rd *PLKSD/SHW* G41 ......88 A4
Usmore Pl *STPS/GTHM/RID* G33 ..93 F3

V

Vaila St *SMSTN* G23 ....53 E4
Valerio Ct *BLTYR/CAMB* G72 ....151 G2
Valetta Pl *CLYDBK* G81 ....31 E5
Valeview Ter *DMBTN* G82 ....13 F1
  GVH/MTFL G42 ....109 F4
Vallantine Crs
  UD/BTH/TAN G71 ....115 F4
Valley Ct *PPK/MIL* G22 ....54 A5
Valley Ct *HMLTN* ML3 ....169 H3
Valleyfield *EKILS* G75 ....166 A4
Valleyfield St
  SPRGB/BLRNK G21 ....68 C2
Valley Vw *BLTYR/CAMB* G72 ....131 H1
  MTHW ML1 ....172 C2
Vancouver Dr *EKILS* G75 ....165 F4
Vancouver La *SCOT* G14 ....64 D2
Vancouver Pl *CLYDBK* G81 ....31 E5
Vancouver Rd *SCOT* G14 ....64 D3
Vanguard St *CLYDBK* G81 ....49 G1
Vardar Av
  CRMNK/CLK/EAG G76 .....145 G2
Vardon Lea *MTHW* ML1 ....156 B1
Varna La *SCOT* G14 ....65 F3
Varna Rd *SCOT* G14 ....65 F3
Varnsdorf Wy *AIRDRIE* ML6 ......99 E3
Vassart Pl *MRYH/FIRH* G20 ....67 E1
Veir Ter *DMBTN* G82 ....13 E3
Veitches Ct *CLYDBK* G81 ....31 H2
Veitch Pl *KKNTL* G66 ....4 B2
Vennacher Rd *RNFRW* PA4 ....62 D2
Vennard Gdns
  PLKSD/SHW G41 ....109 E2
Vermont Av *RUTH* G73 ....110 D5
Vermont St *PLKSD/SHW* G41 .....88 C4
Vernon Bank *EKILN* G74 ....166 B2
Vernon Dr *PSLYN/LNWD* PA3 ....81 H5
Verona Av *SCOT* G14 ....64 D2
Verona Gdns *SCOT* G14 ....64 D2
Vesalius St *CAR/SHTL* G32 ....92 B4
Viaduct Rd
  CRMNK/CLK/EAG G76 .....146 A4
Vicarfield St *GOV/IBX* G51 ....88 A2
Vicarland Rd
  BLTYR/CAMB G72 ....131 F2
Vicars Wk *BLTYR/CAMB* G72 ...131 G3
Vickers St *MTHW* ML1 ....154 A1
Victor St *AIRDRIE* ML6 ....99 E3
Victoria Br *GBLS* G5 ....89 H3
Victoria Circ *KVD/HLHD* G12 .....66 B3
Victoria Crs *AIRDRIE* ML6 ....99 H3
  BRHD/NEIL G78 ....124 B4
  KSYTH G65 ....7 H2
  WISHAW ML2 ....173 E4
Victoria Crescent La
  KVD/HLHD G12 ....66 B3
Victoria Crescent Pl
  KVD/HLHD G12 ....66 B3

Victoria Crescent Rd
  KVD/HLHD G12 ....66 B3
Victoria Dr *BRHD/NEIL* G78 .....124 A3
Victoria Dr East *RNFRW* PA4 .....63 F4
Victoria Dr West *RNFRW* PA4 ....63 E5
Victoria Gdns *BRHD/NEIL* G78 ..124 A3
Victoria La *NMRNS* G77 ....161 G5
Victoria Pk *KSYTH* G65 ....7 H2
Victoria Park Cnr *SCOT* G14 ......65 F3
Victoria Park Dr North
  SCOT G14 ....65 F3
Victoria Park Dr South
  SCOT G14 ....65 E3
Victoria Park Gdns North
  PTCK G11 ....65 G3
Victoria Park Gdns South
  PTCK G11 ....65 G3
Victoria Park La South
  SCOT G14 ....65 G3
Victoria Pl *AIRDRIE* ML6 ....98 A3
  BLSH ML4 ....135 G5
  BRHD/NEIL G78 ....124 A3
  KSYTH G65 ....8 A2
  MLNCV G62 ....17 G5
Victoria Qd *MTHW* ML1 ....137 E2
Victoria Rd *BALLOCH* G68 ....9 H4
  BRHD/NEIL G78 ....124 A3
  CVH/MTFL G42 ....109 F1
  JNSTN PA5 ....99 F1
  KKNTL G66 ....20 D4
  PSLYS PA2 ....103 H2
  RUTH G73 ....111 E5
  STPS/GTHM/RID G33 ....57 E4
Victoria St *BLTYR/CAMB* G72 ...151 G4
  DMBTN G82 ....13 F5
  HMLTN ML3 ....152 C4
  KKNTL G66 ....20 D4
  RUTH G73 ....110 D5
  WISHAW ML2 ....175 F1
Victor St *AIRDRIE* ML6 ....77 H4
Victory Dr *KLBCH* PA10 ....100 B2
Viewbank *AIRDRIE* ML6 ....118 D4
Viewbank St *CTBR* ML5 ....74 C1
Viewfield *AIRDRIE* ML6 ....97 H2
Viewfield Av
  BAIL/MDB/MHD G69 ....93 G4
  BLTYR/CAMB G72 ....151 F4
  BSHPBGS G64 ....54 B3
  KKNTL G66 ....4 B1
  KKNTL G66 ....39 H5
Viewfield Dr
  BAIL/MDB/MHD G69 ....93 G4
  BSHPBGS G64 ....54 B3
Viewfield La *KVD/HLHD* G12 .....66 D4
Viewfield Rd *BLSH* ML4 ....135 G4
  BSHPBGS G64 ....54 B3
  CTBR ML5 ....95 H5
Viewglen Ct *CSMK* G45 ....147 E1
Viewmount Dr *MRYH/FIRH* G20 ..52 C4
Viewpark Av *DEN/PKHD* G31 .....91 E1
Viewpark Dr *RUTH* G73 ....130 A1
Viewpark Gdns *RNFRW* PA4 ......63 E4
Viewpark Pl *MTHW* ML1 ....154 B4
Viewpark Rd *MTHW* ML1 ....154 B4
Viewpoint Pl
  SPRGB/BLRNK G21 ....54 C5
Viking Crs *CRG/CRSL/HOU* PA6 ..81 E5
Viking Rd *AIRDRIE* ML6 ....98 C4
Viking Ter *EKILS* G75 ....178 B2
Viking Wy *GIF/THBK* G46 ....126 C2
Villafield Av *BSHPBGS* G64 ....37 H5
Villafield Dr *BSHPBGS* G64 ....37 H5
Village Gdns *BLTYR/CAMB* G72 ..151 H1
Vine St *PTCK* G11 ....66 A4
Vinicombe La *KVD/HLHD* G12 ....66 C3
Vinicombe St *KVD/HLHD* G12 ....66 C3
Vintner St *COWCAD* G4 ....67 H4
Viola Pl *BSHPBGS* G64 ....19 G5
Violet Pl *MTHW* ML1 ....137 G1
Violet St *PSLY* PA1 ....84 D5
Virginia Ct *CGLE* G1 ....3 G5
Virginia Gdns *MLNCV* G62 ....17 G5
Virginia Pl *CGLE* G1 ....3 G5
Virginia St *CGLE* G1 ....3 G5
Viscount Av *RNFRW* PA4 ....63 F5
Viscount Ga *UD/BTH/TAN* G71 ..133 G2
Vivian Av *MLNCV* G62 ....16 D4
Voil Dr *LNPK/KPK* G44 ....128 B3
Vorlich Ct *BRHD/NEIL* G78 ......142 B1
Vorlich Gdns *BSDN* G61 ....16 A4
Vryburg Crs *EKILS* G75 ....177 F4
Vulcan St *MTHW* ML1 ....154 D1
  SPRGB/BLRNK G21 ....68 B2

W

Waddell Av *AIRDRIE* ML6 ....75 G2
Waddell St *AIRDRIE* ML6 ....76 B5
  GBLS G5 ....90 A5
Waid Av *NMRNS* G77 ....143 H4
Waldemar Rd *KNTSWD* G13 ....50 D4
Waldo St *KNTSWD* G13 ....51 G4
Walkerburn Dr *WISHAW* ML2 ...157 H4
Walkerburn Rd
  CARD/HILL/MSPK G52 ....86 C5
Walker Ct *PTCK* G11 ....66 A5
Walker Dr *JNSTN* PA5 ....102 A2
Walker Pth *UD/BTH/TAN* G71 ...115 F4
Walker St *PSLY* PA1 ....84 A5
  PTCK G11 ....66 A5
Walkinshaw Crs
  PSLYN/LNWD PA3 ....83 G3
Walkinshaw Rd
  PSLYN/LNWD PA3 ....61 G3
Walkinshaw St
  DMNK/BRGTN G40 ....90 D5
  JNSTN PA5 ....101 G3
Wallace Av *BSHPTN* PA7 ....29 G2
Wallace Ga *BSHPBGS* G64 ....55 F1
Wallace Pl *BLTYR/CAMB* G72 ...152 H1
  HMLTN ML3 ....170 D1
Wallace Rd *MTHW* ML1 ....137 G5
  RNFRW PA4 ....62 D5
Wallace St *AIRDRIE* ML6 ....77 H4
  CLYDBK G81 ....49 E3
  CTBR ML5 ....96 D4
  DMBTN G82 ....13 E3

  GBLS G5 ....89 F4
Wallace St *MTHW* ML1 ....154 C3
  PSLYN/LNWD PA3 ....83 G3
  RUTH G73 ....110 D5
Wallacewell Crs
  SPRGB/BLRNK G21 ....69 E1
Wallacewell Pl
  SPRGB/BLRNK G21 ....69 E1
Wallacewell Qd
  SPRGB/BLRNK G21 ....69 F1
Wallacewell Rd
  SPRGB/BLRNK G21 ....55 F5
Wallbrae Rd *CUMB* G67 ....26 B5
Wallneuk *PSLY* PA1 ....84 C4
Wallneuk Rd *PSLYN/LNWD* PA3 ..84 C4
Walls St *CGLE* G1 ....3 H5
Walmer Crs *GOV/IBX* G51 ....88 B4
Walnut Crs *JNSTN* PA5 ....102 A4
  PPK/MIL G22 ....68 A1
Walnut Dr *KKNTL* G66 ....68 A1
Walnut Ga *BLTYR/CAMB* G72 ...132 E3
Walnut Pl *UD/BTH/TAN* G71 ....115 H5
Walnut Rd *PPK/MIL* G22 ....67 H1
Walpole Pl *JNSTN* PA5 ....120 D2
Walter St *DEN/PKHD* G31 ....91 E2
  WISHAW ML2 ....174 C2
Walton Av *NMRNS* G77 ....143 H4
Walton St *BRHD/NEIL* G78 ......124 B4
  PLKSD/SHW G41 ....108 D4
Wamba Av *KNTSWD* G13 ....51 F3
Wamphray Pl *EKILS* G75 ....176 C1
Wandilla Av *CLYDBK* G81 ....49 G1
Wanlock St *GOV/IBX* G51 ....87 H1
Wardend Rd *KNTSWD* G13 ....51 E4
Warden Rd *KNTSWD* G13 ....51 E4
Wardhill Rd *SPRGB/BLRNK* G21 ..69 F1
Wardhouse Rd *PSLYS* PA2 ......103 H5
Wardie Pl *STPS/GTHM/RID* G33 ..93 G2
Wardie Rd *BAIL/MDB/MHD* G69 ..93 H2
Wardlaw Av *RUTH* G73 ....111 G5
Wardlaw Crs *EKILS* G75 ....178 C2
Wardlaw Dr *RUTH* G73 ....111 E4
Wardlaw Rd *BSDN* G61 ....51 G2
Wardpark Ct *CUMB* G67 ....11 F4
Wardpark Pl *CUMB* G67 ....11 F4
Wardpark Rd *CUMB* G67 ....11 F4
Wardrop Pl *EKILN* G74 ....166 C2
Wardrop St *GOV/IBX* G51 ....87 H1
  PSLY PA1 ....84 B5
Wards Crs *CTBR* ML5 ....96 B4
Ware Rd *STPS/GTHM/RID* G33 ...93 G2
Warlock Dr *BRWEIR* PA11 ....79 G2
Warlock Rd *BRWEIR* PA11 ....79 F2
Warnock Crs *BLSH* ML4 ....136 A3
Warnock Rd *NMRNS* G77 ....143 H5
Warnock St *COWCAD* G4 ....90 B1
Warren St *GVH/MTFL* G42 ....109 G3
Warriston Crs
  STPS/GTHM/RID G33 ....91 H1
Warriston Pl *CAR/SHTL* G32 ......92 C2
Warriston St
  STPS/GTHM/RID G33 ....91 G1
Warroch St *KVGV* G3 ....2 A4
Warwick *EKILN* G74 ....167 F1
Warwick Gv *BLTYR/CAMB* G72 ..151 H5
Washington St *KVGV* G3 ....2 A6
Watchmeal Crs *CLYDBK* G81 ......32 B1
Waterbank Rd
  CRMNK/CLK/EAG G76 .....147 E4
Waterfoot Av *PLK/PH/NH* G53 ..106 D4
Waterfoot Rd *NMRNS* G77 ......162 A2
Waterfoot Rw
  CRMNK/CLK/EAG G76 .....163 F2
Waterford Ter *PLK/PH/NH* G53 ..106 D4
Waterford Rd *GIF/THBK* G46 ....127 E4
Waterhaughs Gdns
  STPS/GTHM/RID G33 ....55 G4
Waterhaughs Gv
  SPRGB/BLRNK G21 ....55 G4
Waterloo Cl *KKNTL* G66 ....21 F4
Waterloo La *CGLE* G1 ....2 C5
Waterloo St *CGLE* G1 ....2 C5
Watermill Av *KKNTL* G66 ....40 A4
Water Rd *BRHD/NEIL* G78 ....124 B4
Waterside Av *NMRNS* G77 ......162 A2
Waterside Rd *KKNTL* G66 ....87 H1
Watersaugh Dr *MTHW* ML1 .....139 E5
Waterside Av *NMRNS* G77 ......161 F1
Waterside Rd *NMRNS* G77 ......161 F1
Waterside Rd
  CRMNK/CLK/EAG G76 .....147 E3
  HMLTN ML3 ....170 B4
Waterside St *GBLS* G5 ....90 A5
  KKNTL G66 ....40 B1
Watling St *MTHW* ML1 ....154 B1
  UD/BTH/TAN G71 ....114 D4
Watson Av *PSLYN/LNWD* PA3 ....82 A4
  RUTH G73 ....110 C5
Watson Crs *KSYTH* G65 ....8 C2
Watson Pl *BLTYR/CAMB* G72 ....151 F5
  CGLE G1 ....3 J7
Watson St *MTHW* ML1 ....154 D5
  UD/BTH/TAN G71 ....134 C1
Watsonville Pk *MTHW* ML1 ......154 D4
Watt Av *STPS/GTHM/RID* G33 ....71 G1
Watt Ct *BLSH* ML4 ....117 E5
Watt La *BRWEIR* PA11 ....79 E4
Watt Low Av *RUTH* G73 ....129 H1
Watt Pl *MLNCV* G62 ....16 D2
  CARD/HILL/MSPK G52 ....86 D5
Watt St *AIRDRIE* ML6 ....98 B2
  GBLS G5 ....89 E4
Waukglen Av *PLK/PH/NH* G53 ..125 G5
Waukglen Crs *PLK/PH/NH* G53 ..125 H4
Waukglen Dr *PLK/PH/NH* G53 ..125 G4
Waukglen Gdns
  PLK/PH/NH G53 ....125 G5
Waukglen Pth
  PLK/PH/NH G53 ....125 G4
Waukglen Pl *PLK/PH/NH* G53 ..125 G4
Waukglen Rd *PLK/PH/NH* G53 ..125 G4
Waulking Mill Rd *CLYDBK* G81 ..32 B1
Waulkmill Av *BRHD/NEIL* G78 ..124 C3
Waulkmill St *GIF/THBK* G46 ....126 B3
Waulkmill Wy *BRHD/NEIL* G78 ..124 C3
Waverley *EKILN* G74 ....167 G1
Waverley Crs
  UD/BTH/TAN G71 ....134 B5

Waverley Crs *CUMB* G67 ....44 C1
   HMLTN ML3 ....169 E1
Waverley Ct *WISHAW* ML2 ....21 C5
Waverley Dr *AIRDRIE* ML6 ....76 C5
   RUTH G73 ....111 F5
   WISHAW ML2 ....174 B1
Waverley Gdns *JNSTN* PA5 ....102 C2
   PLKSD/SHW G41 ....108 D3
Waverley Pk *KKNTL* G66 ....21 C5
Waverley Rd *PLSYS* PA2 ....103 H4
Waverley St *CTBR* ML5 ....75 E5
   HMLTN ML3 ....169 E1
   PLKSD/SHW G41 ....108 D3
Waverley Ter *BLTYR/CAMB* G72 ....151 F5
   DMBTN G82 ....12 A3
Weardale La *STPS/GTHM/RID* G33 ....92 D1
Weardale St *STPS/GTHM/RID* G33 ....92 D1
Weaver Av *NMRNS* G77 ....144 A4
Weaver La *KLBCH* PA10 ....100 B2
Weaver Pl *EKILS* G75 ....176 D1
Weavers Av *PLSY* PA1 ....103 C1
Weavers Rd *COWCAD* G4 3
Weaver Ter *PLSYS* PA2 ....104 C2
Webster Gdns *WISHAW* ML2 ....157 G5
Webster St *DMNK/BRGTN* G40 ....110 D1
   KNTSWD G13 ....49 H5
Wedderlea Dr *CARD/HILL/MSPK* G52 ....86 C4
Weensmoor Rd *PLK/PH/NH* G53 ....125 F2
Weeple Dr *PSLYN/LNWD* PA3 ....81 H5
Weighhouse Cl *PLSY* PA1 ....84 B5
Weir Av *BRHD/NEIL* G78 ....124 B5
Weir St *CTBR* ML5 ....96 D2
   PLSY PA1 ....84 B4
Weirwood Av *BAIL/MDB/MHD* G69 ....93 G5
Weirwood Gdns *BAIL/MDB/MHD* G69 ....93 G4
Welbeck Rd *PLK/PH/NH* G53 ....125 G2
Weldon Pl *KSYTH* G65 ....24 D2
Welfare Av *BLTYR/CAMB* G72 ....132 B3
Welland Pl *EKILS* G75 ....176 D1
Wellbank Pl *UD/BTH/TAN* G71 ....134 A2
Wellbrae Rd *HMLTN* ML3 ....169 G4
Wellcroft Pl *GBLS* G5 ....89 G5
Wellcroft Rd *HMLTN* ML3 ....168 D2
Wellcroft Ter *HMLTN* ML3 ....168 D2
Wellesley Crs *BALLOCH* G68 ....24 B4
   EKILS G75 ....177 F1
Wellesley Dr *GIF/THBK* G46 ....127 E4
   BALLOCH G68 ....24 B4
Wellfield Av *GIF/THBK* G46 ....127 E4
Wellfield St *SPRGB/BLRNK* G21 ....68 C2
Well Gn *PLKSW/MSWD* G43 ....108 B4
Wellhall Rd *HMLTN* ML3 ....169 C1
Wellhouse Crs *STPS/GTHM/RID* G33 ....93 F2
Wellhouse Gdns *STPS/GTHM/RID* G33 ....93 G2
Wellhouse Rd *STPS/GTHM/RID* G33 ....93 G1
Wellington *EKILS* G75 ....177 G1
Wellington Pl *CLYDBK* G81 ....31 E5
   CTBR ML5 ....95 H4
   WISHAW ML2 ....173 H3
Wellington Rd *BSHPBGS* G64 ....38 A4
Wellington St *AIRDRIE* ML6 ....76 B5
   CGLW G2 ....2 D5
   PSLYN/LNWD PA3 ....83 H4
   WISHAW ML2 ....155 H5
Wellknowe Av *EKILN* G74 ....164 B2
Wellknowe Pl *EKILN* G74 ....164 B2
Wellknowe Rd *EKILN* G74 ....164 A2
Well La *KKNTL* G66 4
Wellmeadow Av *NMRNS* G77 ....144 A5
Wellmeadow Gn *NMRNS* G77 ....144 A5
Wellmeadow Rd *PLKSW/MSWD* G43 ....126 D1
Wellmeadow St *PLSY* PA1 ....84 A5
Wellmeadow Wy *NMRNS* G77 ....144 A5
Wellpark Rd *MTHW* ML1 ....154 B4
Wellpark St *COWCAD* G4 ....90 D2
Wellpark Ter *BRHD/NEIL* G78 ....141 E4
Well Rd *KLBCH* PA10 ....100 B3
Wellshot Dr *BLTYR/CAMB* G72 ....131 E2
Wellshot Rd *CAR/SHTL* G32 ....112 A1
Wellside Av *AIRDRIE* ML6 ....76 B5
Wellside Dr *BLTYR/CAMB* G72 ....131 H3
Wellside La *AIRDRIE* ML6 ....76 B5
Wellside Qd *AIRDRIE* ML6 ....76 B5
Wellsquarry Rd *EKILN* G74 ....165 H1
Wellside Ct *EKILS* G75 ....31 C5
Well St *PSLY* PA1 ....83 H4
Wellview Dr *MTHW* ML1 ....154 C3
Wellwynd *AIRDRIE* ML6 ....76 A4
Welsh Dr *BLTYR/CAMB* G72 ....151 G4
Welsh Rw *AIRDRIE* ML6 ....118 D1
Wemyss Av *NMRNS* G77 ....143 H5
Wemyss Dr *BALLOCH* G68 ....24 C4
Wemyss Gdns *BAIL/MDB/MHD* G69 ....113 H1
Wenlock Rd *PLSYS* PA2 ....104 C2
Wensleydale *EKILN* G74 ....165 H2
Wentworth Dr *SMSTN* G23 ....52 D2
Wesley St *AIRDRIE* ML6 ....98 A2
West Academy St *WISHAW* ML2 ....173 F2
Westacres Rd *NMRNS* G77 ....161 E1
West Av *AIRDRIE* ML6 ....77 H3
   BLTYR/CAMB G72 ....151 F5
   MTHW ML1 ....137 F5
   RNFRW PA4 ....63 G2
   STPS/GTHM/RID G33 ....71 E1
   UD/BTH/TAN G71 ....134 C1
West Balgrochan Rd *BSHPBGS* G64 ....19 F4
Westbank La *KVD/HLHD* G12 ....66 D4
Westbank Qd *KVD/HLHD* G12 ....66 D4
Westbourne Crs *BSDN* G61 ....33 H3
Westbourne Dr *BSDN* G61 ....33 H3
Westbourne Gardens La *KVD/HLHD* G12 ....66 B2
Westbourne Gdns South *KVD/HLHD* G12 ....66 B2
Westbourne Gdns West *KVD/HLHD* G12 ....66 B2
Westbourne Rd *KVD/HLHD* G12 ....66 A2

Westbourne Terrace La North *KVD/HLHD* G12 ....66 A2
Westbourne Terrace La South *KVD/HLHD* G12 ....66 A2
West Brae *PSLY* PA1 ....84 A5
West Brae Dr *KNTSWD* G13 ....65 F2
Westbrae Rd *NMRNS* G77 ....144 C2
West Bridgend *DMBTN* G82 ....12 D4
Westburn Av *BLTYR/CAMB* G72 ....132 A1
   PSLYN/LNWD PA3 ....83 F4
Westburn Crs *CLYDBK* G81 ....32 A1
   RUTH G73 ....110 C5
Westburn Farm Rd *BLTYR/CAMB* G72 ....131 G1
Westburn Rd *BLTYR/CAMB* G72 ....131 G1
West Burnside St *KSYTH* G65 ....8 B2
West Campbell St *CGLW* G2 ....2 D4
   PSLY PA1 ....83 G5
West Canal St *CTBR* ML5 ....96 C3
Westcastle Ct *CSMK* G45 ....129 E4
Westcastle Crs *CSMK* G45 ....129 E4
Westcastle Gdns *CSMK* G45 ....129 E4
Westcastle Gv *CSMK* G45 ....129 E4
West Chapelton Av *BSDN* G61 ....34 C4
West Chapelton Crs *BSDN* G61 ....34 C4
West Chapelton Dr *BSDN* G61 ....34 C4
Westcliff *DMBTN* G82 ....12 A3
Westclyffe St *PLKSD/SHW* G41 ....108 D3
West Coats Rd *BLTYR/CAMB* G72 ....131 G3
West Dr *AIRDRIE* ML6 ....99 F3
West End Rd *MTHW* ML1 ....135 G3
Westend Park St *COWCAD* G4 ....67 E4
   KVGV G3 ....2 A1
West End Pl *BLSH* ML4 ....135 G3
Westerburn St *CAR/SHTL* G32 ....92 A3
Wester Carriagehill *PLSYS* PA2 ....104 B2
Wester Cleddens Rd *BSHPBGS* G64 ....54 D1
Wester Common Dr *PPK/MIL* G22 ....67 F2
Wester Common Rd *PPK/MIL* G22 ....67 F2
Westercraigs *DEN/PKHD* G31 ....90 C2
Westerdale *EKILN* G74 ....165 H2
Westerfield Rd *CRMNK/CLK/EAG* G76 ....164 C1
Westergill Av *AIRDRIE* ML6 ....99 F5
Westergreens Av *KKNTL* G66 ....39 H2
Westerhill Rd *BSHPBGS* G64 ....38 A4
Westerhouse Rd *ESTRH* G34 ....93 H1
Westerkirk Dr *SMSTN* G23 ....52 D2
Westerlands *KVD/HLHD* G12 ....51 G5
Westerlands Dr *NMRNS* G77 ....161 E1
Westerlands Gv *NMRNS* G77 ....161 E1
Westermains Av *KKNTL* G66 ....39 G1
Wester Mavisbank Av *AIRDRIE* ML6 ....97 H1
Wester Moffat Av *AIRDRIE* ML6 ....99 F1
Wester Moffat Crs *AIRDRIE* ML6 ....99 F1
Wester Myvot St *CUMB* G67 ....43 H4
Westerpark Av *HMLTN* ML3 ....168 D2
Western Av *RUTH* G73 ....110 C4
Western Isles Rd *OLDK* G60 ....30 D3
Western Rd *CAR/SHTL* G32 ....111 G1
Westerton Av *CRMNK/CLK/EAG* G76 ....146 B5
   KNTSWD G13 ....51 G3
Westerton La *CRMNK/CLK/EAG* G76 ....146 B5
Westerton Rd *BALLOCH* G68 ....44 C1
Westfield *DMBTN* G82 ....12 B3
Westfield Av *RUTH* G73 ....110 C5
Westfield Crs *BSDN* G61 ....51 F1
Westfield Dr *BALLOCH* G68 ....43 E1
   BSDN G61 ....51 F1
   CARD/HILL/MSPK G52 ....86 B4
Westfield Pl *BALLOCH* G68 ....43 E2
Westfield Rd *BALLOCH* G68 ....43 E2
   GIF/THBK G46 ....126 D5
   KSYTH G65 ....7 H1
   MTHW ML1 ....118 D5
Westfields *BSHPBGS* G64 ....37 F5
Westgarth Pl *EKILN* G74 ....165 F1
West Ga *WISHAW* ML2 ....174 C2
West George La *CGLW* G2 ....2 C4
West George St *CGLE* G1 ....3 F5
   CTBR ML5 ....96 A4
West Glebe Ter *HMLTN* ML3 ....169 H3
West Graham St *COWCAD* G4 ....2 D2
West Greenhill Pl *KVGV* G3 ....88 D1
West Hamilton St *MTHW* ML1 ....154 D4
West High St *KKNTL* G66 ....21 E4
Westhouse Av *RUTH* G73 ....110 B5
Westhouse Gdns *RUTH* G73 ....110 B5
West Kirk St *AIRDRIE* ML6 ....98 A2
Westland Dr *SCOT* G14 ....65 E3
Westlands Gdns *PLSYS* PA2 ....104 A2
West La *PSLY* PA1 ....83 G5
Westlea Pl *AIRDRIE* ML6 ....98 B3
West Lodge Rd *RNFRW* PA4 ....63 F2
West Mains Rd *EKILN* G74 ....165 G3
Westmoreland St *GVH/MTFL* G42 ....109 F2
Westmuir Pl *RUTH* G73 ....110 B4
Westmuir St *DEN/PKHD* G31 ....91 G4
West Nile St *CGLE* G1 ....3 E4
Westpark Dr *PSLYN/LNWD* PA3 ....158 B5
West Pl *WISHAW* ML2 ....165 E4
West Prince's La *COWCAD* G4 ....67 E4
West Prince's St *COWCAD* G4 ....67 E4
Westray Av *NMRNS* G77 ....143 H5
Westray Circ *PPK/MIL* G22 ....53 H5
Westray Dr *NMRNS* G77 ....143 H5
Westray Pl *PPK/MIL* G22 ....53 H5
   BSHPBGS G64 ....55 G1
Westray Sq *PPK/MIL* G22 ....53 H5
West Regent La *CGLW* G2 ....2 D4
West Regent St *CGLW* G2 ....2 D4
   KLBCH PA10 ....100 B2
West Scott Ter *HMLTN* ML3 ....169 H4
West Stewart St *HMLTN* ML3 ....169 H3
West St *CLYDBK* G81 ....49 H1
   GBLS G5 ....89 F4
   PSLY PA1 ....84 A5
West Thomson St *CLYDBK* G81 ....31 H5
West Thornlie St *WISHAW* ML2 ....173 H3

West Wellbrae Crs *HMLTN* ML3 ....169 G5
West Whitby St *DEN/PKHD* G31 ....91 F5
Westwood Crs *HMLTN* ML3 ....169 H5
Westwood Dr *MTHW* ML1 ....157 H1
Westwood Gdns *PSLYN/LNWD* PA3 ....83 G4
Westwood Hl *EKILS* G75 ....177 G1
Westwood Qd *CLYDBK* G81 ....49 G1
Westwood Rd *EKILS* G75 ....165 G4
   WISHAW ML2 ....158 B4
Weymouth Dr *KVD/HLHD* G12 ....51 H5
Whamflet Av *BAIL/MDB/MHD* G69 ....94 B2
Wheatfield Rd *BSDN* G61 ....34 A5
Wheatholm St *AIRDRIE* ML6 ....76 C5
Wheatland Av *BLTYR/CAMB* G72 ....151 F2
Wheatlandhead Ct *BLTYR/CAMB* G72 ....151 F2
Wheatland Dr *KLBCH* PA10 ....100 B2
Wheatlands Dr *KLBCH* PA10 ....100 B2
Wheatlands Farm Rd *KLBCH* PA10 ....100 B2
Wheatley Ct *CAR/SHTL* G32 ....92 B4
Wheatley Crs *KSYTH* G65 ....8 B3
Wheatley Dr *CAR/SHTL* G32 ....92 B4
Wheatley Loan *BSHPBGS* G64 ....55 F1
Wheatley Pl *CAR/SHTL* G32 ....92 B4
Whifflet St *CTBR* ML5 ....116 D1
Whin Av *BRHD/NEIL* G78 ....123 H5
Whinfell Dr *EKILS* G75 ....177 E2
Whinfell Gdns *EKILS* G75 ....177 E2
Whinfield Rd *PLK/PH/NH* G53 ....125 F5
Whinhall Av *AIRDRIE* ML6 ....75 H5
Whinhall Rd *AIRDRIE* ML6 ....75 H5
Whinhill Rd *PLK/PH/NH* G53 ....106 D1
   PSLYS PA2 ....105 E2
Whin Loan *KSYTH* G65 ....6 C2
Whinney Gv *WISHAW* ML2 ....174 D1
Whinpark Av *BLSH* ML4 ....135 G3
Whins Rd *PLKSD/SHW* G41 ....108 B3
Whirlie Ct *CRG/CRSL/HOU* PA6 ....80 C3
Whirlie Dr *CRG/CRSL/HOU* PA6 ....80 C3
Whirlow Gdns *BAIL/MDB/MHD* G69 ....93 H4
Whirlow Rd *BAIL/MDB/MHD* G69 ....93 H4
Whistleberry Crs *HMLTN* ML3 ....152 B3
Whistleberry Dr *HMLTN* ML3 ....152 C3
Whistleberry Rd *HMLTN* ML3 ....152 C4
Whistlefield Ct *BSDN* G61 ....34 B3
Whitacres Rd *PLK/PH/NH* G53 ....125 F3
Whitburn St *CAR/SHTL* G32 ....92 A2
Whiteadder Pl *EKILS* G75 ....176 C1
White Cart Rd *PSLYN/LNWD* PA3 ....84 B3
Whitecraigs Pl *SMSTN* G23 ....52 D5
Whitecrook St *CLYDBK* G81 ....49 G3
Whitefield Av *BLTYR/CAMB* G72 ....131 F3
Whitefield Rd *GOV/IBX* G51 ....88 B3
Whiteford Av *DMBTN* G82 ....13 H3
Whiteford Ct *HMLTN* ML3 ....180 C2
Whiteford Pl *DMBTN* G82 ....13 H3
Whiteford Rd *PSLYS* PA2 ....104 D2
   STPS/GTHM/RID G33 ....71 G1
Whitehall St *KVGV* G3 ....2 A6
Whitehaugh Av *PSLY* PA1 ....85 E4
Whitehaugh Crs *PLK/PH/NH* G53 ....125 F5
Whitehaugh Dr *PSLY* PA1 ....85 E4
Whitehaugh Rd *PLK/PH/NH* G53 ....125 F5
Whitehill Av *AIRDRIE* ML6 ....118 A1
   BALLOCH G68 ....25 H3
   KKNTL G66 ....21 G4
   STPS/GTHM/RID G33 ....70 C3
Whitehill Crs *CLYDBK* G81 ....32 C1
   KKNTL G66 ....21 G4
Whitehill Farm Rd *STPS/GTHM/RID* G33 ....57 E5
Whitehill Gdns *DEN/PKHD* G31 ....90 D2
Whitehill Gv *NMRNS* G77 ....162 A3
Whitehill Rd *BSDN* G61 ....34 A4
   HMLTN ML3 ....152 C5
Whitehills Dr *EKILS* G75 ....178 B1
Whitehills Pl *EKILS* G75 ....178 B2
Whitehills Ter *EKILS* G75 ....178 B2
Whitehill St *DEN/PKHD* G31 ....90 D2
Whitehurst *BSDN* G61 ....33 H2
Whitelaw Av *CTBR* ML5 ....74 C1
Whitelaw Crs *BLSH* ML4 ....136 C3
Whitelaw St *MRYH/FIRH* G20 ....52 B4
Whitelaw Ter *KSYTH* G65 ....8 B2
Whitelee *EKILS* G75 ....177 G3
Whitelee Crs *NMRNS* G77 ....143 H4
Whitelee Ga *NMRNS* G77 ....143 H4
Whitelees Rd *CUMB* G67 ....11 H4
Whitemoss Av *UD/BTH/TAN* G71 ....134 C4
   EKILN G74 ....166 C4
Whitemoss Rd *EKILN* G74 ....166 C4
Whitepond Av *BLSH* ML4 ....135 G2
Whites Bridge Av *PSLY* PA1 ....83 E5
White St *CLYDBK* G81 ....49 G4
Whitevale St *DEN/PKHD* G31 ....90 D2
Whitlop Rd *PLK/PH/NH* G53 ....125 G2
Whithorn Crs *BAIL/MDB/MHD* G69 ....42 B5
Whitlawburn Av *BLTYR/CAMB* G72 ....130 D3
Whitlawburn Rd *BLTYR/CAMB* G72 ....130 D3
Whitlawburn Ter *BLTYR/CAMB* G72 ....130 D3
Whitriggs Rd *PLK/PH/NH* G53 ....125 F3
Whitslade St *ESTRH* G34 ....71 H5
Whitsun Dt *EKILN* G74 ....149 E3
Whittagreen Av *MTHW* ML1 ....138 A4
Whittagreen Crs *MTHW* ML1 ....138 A4
Whittingehame Dr *KVD/HLHD* G12 ....65 G1

Whittingehame La *KNTSWD* G13 ....65 G1
Whittington St *CTBR* ML5 ....97 E4
Whittlemuir Av *LNPK/KPK* G44 ....128 A3
Whitton Dr *GIF/THBK* G46 ....127 G3
Whitton St *MRYH/FIRH* G20 ....52 B3
Whitworth Dr *CLYDBK* G81 ....49 E1
Whitworth St *MRYH/FIRH* G20 ....53 F5
Whyte Av *BLTYR/CAMB* G72 ....130 D1
Wick Av *AIRDRIE* ML6 ....97 G5
Wickham Av *NMRNS* G77 ....144 A4
Wigton Av *NMRNS* G77 ....143 H3
Wigtoun Pl *CUMB* G67 ....26 B3
Wilkie Rd *UD/BTH/TAN* G71 ....134 B2
Wilkie St *HMLTN* ML3 ....180 D1
William Dr *HMLTN* ML3 ....180 D1
William Mann Dr *NMRNS* G77 ....161 E1
Williamsburgh Ter *PSLY* PA1 ....84 D4
Williamson Av *DMBTN* G82 ....13 F3
Williamson St *CLYDBK* G81 ....32 A4
   DMNK/BRGTN G40 ....111 E1
William St *CLYDBK* G81 ....31 H2
   HMLTN ML3 ....169 G6
   JNSTN PA5 ....101 C4
   KSYTH G65 ....8 B2
   KVGV G3 2
   MTHW ML1 ....155 E4
Williamwood Dr *LNPK/KPK* G44 ....127 H5
Williamwood Pk *LNPK/KPK* G44 ....128 A5
Williamwood Pk West *LNPK/KPK* G44 ....128 A5
Willock Pl *MRYH/FIRH* G20 ....52 D4
Willoughby Dr *KNTSWD* G13 ....51 G5
Willoughby La *KNTSWD* G13 ....51 G5
Willow Av *BSHPBGS* G64 ....54 D3
   JNSTN PA5 ....102 B2
   KKNTL G66 ....39 H5
   MTHW ML1 ....156 D3
Willowbank Crs *KVGV* G3 ....67 E4
Willowbank Gdns *KKNTL* G66 ....21 F5
Willowbank St *KVGV* G3 ....67 E4
Willow Crs *CTBR* ML5 ....117 G2
   HMLTN ML3 ....170 C3
Willow Dr *AIRDRIE* ML6 ....76 A5
Willowdale Crs *BAIL/MDB/MHD* G69 ....93 H5
Willowdale Gdns *BAIL/MDB/MHD* G69 ....93 H5
Willowford Rd *PLK/PH/NH* G53 ....125 E3
Willow Gv *MTHW* ML1 ....137 G4
Willow La *CAR/SHTL* G32 ....112 C2
Willow Pl *JNSTN* PA5 ....101 H4
   UD/BTH/TAN G71 ....116 A4
Willow St *KNTSWD* G13 ....51 G4
The Willows *CRMNK/CLK/EAG* G76 ....147 F2
Willow St *KNTSWD* G13 ....51 G4
Willow Wy *HMLTN* ML3 ....170 B4
Wilmot Rd *KNTSWD* G13 ....51 E5
Wilsgait St *MTHW* ML1 ....139 F5
Wilson Av *PSLYN/LNWD* PA3 ....81 H5
Wilson Pl *EKILN* G74 ....166 C3
   NMRNS G77 ....161 F1
Wilson St *AIRDRIE* ML6 ....98 A1
   CGLE G1 ....3 G5
   CTBR ML5 ....97 F2
   HMLTN ML3 ....152 B5
   MTHW ML1 ....155 E3
   RNFRW PA4 ....63 G2
Wiltonburn Rd *PLK/PH/NH* G53 ....125 F5
Wilton Crescent La *MRYH/FIRH* G20 ....67 E3
Wilton Dr *MRYH/FIRH* G20 ....67 E3
Wilton St *CTBR* ML5 ....74 A1
   MRYH/FIRH G20 ....66 D3
Wilverton Rd *KNTSWD* G13 ....51 G3
Winburne Crs *HMLTN* ML3 ....169 G1
Winchester Dr *KVD/HLHD* G12 ....52 A5
Windemere Gdns *HMLTN* ML3 ....180 C5
Windermere St *BLSH* ML4 ....135 G3
Windermere Ter *EKILS* G75 ....177 E3
Windhill Crs *PLKSW/MSWD* G43 ....127 E2
Windhill Pl *PLKSW/MSWD* G43 ....127 E2
Windlaw Ct *CSMK* G45 ....128 A3
Windlaw Park Gdns *GIF/THBK* G46 ....128 A3
Windmill Ct *MTHW* ML1 ....155 F3
Windmillhill St *MTHW* ML1 ....155 H5
Windmill Rd *HMLTN* ML3 ....170 A1
Windrow Ter *WISHAW* ML2 ....157 H3
Windsor Av *NMRNS* G77 ....144 A5
Windsor Crs *CLYDBK* G81 ....102 A3
   JNSTN PA5 ....102 A3
   PSLY PA1 ....83 H3
Windsor Dr *AIRDRIE* ML6 ....119 E2
Windsor Gdns *HMLTN* ML3 ....152 B5
Windsor Rd *MTHW* ML1 ....137 G2
   RNFRW PA4 ....63 E5
Windsor St *CTBR* ML5 ....74 A1
   MRYH/FIRH G20 ....67 F4
Windsor Ter *MRYH/FIRH* G20 ....67 F4
Windward Rd *EKILS* G75 ....165 H4
Windyedge Crs *KNTSWD* G13 ....64 D1
Windyedge Pl *KNTSWD* G13 ....64 D1
Windyedge Rd *MTHW* ML1 ....139 F1
Windyhill Pk *CRMNK/CLK/EAG* G76 ....147 G2
Windyridge *BLTYR/CAMB* G72 ....151 E4
Windy Yetts *BLTYR/CAMB* G72 ....111 H5
Winfield Av *BLTYR/CAMB* G72 ....132 B3
Wingate Crs *EKILN* G74 ....167 E1
Wingate Dr *EKILN* G74 ....167 E1
Wingate Pk *EKILN* G74 ....167 E1
Wingate St *WISHAW* ML2 ....173 F2
Wingfield Gdns *BLTYR/CAMB* G72 ....152 C1
Winifred St *STPS/GTHM/RID* G33 ....69 G2
Winning Ct *BLTYR/CAMB* G72 ....151 H1

Winning Rw *DEN/PKHD* G31 ....91 G4
Winnipeg Dr *EKILS* G75 ....165 G5
Winston Crs *KKNTL* G66 ....4 A1
Wintergreen Ct *EKILN* G74 ....166 A1
Wintergreen Dr *EKILN* G74 ....166 A1
Winton Av *GIF/THBK* G46 ....127 F5
Winton Crs *BLTYR/CAMB* G72 ....151 G3
Winton Dr *KVD/HLHD* G12 ....66 B1
Winton Gdns *UD/BTH/TAN* G71 ....115 E5
Winton La *KVD/HLHD* G12 ....66 B1
Winton Pk *EKILS* G75 ....165 G4
Wishart Av *CLYDBK* G81 ....32 B1
Wishart St *DEN/PKHD* G31 ....90 B1
Wishaw High Rd *MTHW* ML1 ....157 F2
Wishawhill St *WISHAW* ML2 ....173 H1
Wishaw Low Rd *MTHW* ML1 ....157 E1
Wishaw Rd *WISHAW* ML2 ....175 E5
Wisner Ct *GIF/THBK* G46 ....126 B3
Woddrop St *DMNK/BRGTN* G40 ....111 E2
Wolcott Dr *BLTYR/CAMB* G72 ....151 H1
Wolfe Av *NMRNS* G77 ....143 H5
Wolseley St *GBLS* G5 ....110 A1
Wood Aven Dr *EKILN* G74 ....166 A1
Woodbank Crs *CRMNK/CLK/EAG* G76 ....145 H4
   JNSTN PA5 ....101 G4
Woodburn Av *AIRDRIE* ML6 ....119 E2
   BLTYR/CAMB G72 ....151 H2
   CRMNK/CLK/EAG G76 ....146 A4
Woodburn Pl *CRG/CRSL/HOU* PA6 ....81 F4
Woodburn Rd *MTHW* ML1 ....119 E5
   PLKSW/MSWD G43 ....127 G2
Woodburn St *MTHW* ML1 ....154 D2
Woodburn Wy *BALLOCH* G68 ....25 G5
   MLNGV G62 ....17 E4
Wood Crs *MTHW* ML1 ....155 E3
Woodcroft Av *PTCK* G11 ....65 G2
Woodcroft Ter *MTHW* ML1 1
Woodend Ct *CAR/SHTL* G32 ....113 E2
Woodend Dr *AIRDRIE* ML6 ....76 D5
   PSLY PA1 ....85 F5
Woodend Gdns *CAR/SHTL* G32 ....113 E2
Woodend La *KNTSWD* G13 ....65 E1
Woodend Pl *EKILS* G75 ....113 E2
Woodend Rd *CAR/SHTL* G32 ....113 E2
   RUTH G73 ....130 A3
Wood Farm Rd *GIF/THBK* G46 ....144 C1
Woodfield *UD/BTH/TAN* G71 ....134 B1
Woodfield Av *BSHPBGS* G64 ....55 E3
Woodfoot Pl *PLK/PH/NH* G53 ....125 F3
Woodfoot Qd *PLK/PH/NH* G53 ....125 F3
Woodfoot Rd *HMLTN* ML3 ....169 F3
   PLK/PH/NH G53 ....125 F3
Woodford Pl *PSLYN/LNWD* PA3 ....81 G5
Woodford St *PLKSW/MSWD* G43 ....108 C5
Woodgreen Av *LNPK/KPK* G44 ....128 C1
Wood Gv *UD/BTH/TAN* G71 ....115 H5
Woodhall Av *AIRDRIE* ML6 ....118 C2
   CTBR ML5 ....118 B4
Woodhall Mill Rd *AIRDRIE* ML6 ....118 D3
Woodhall Pl *CTBR* ML5 ....118 C2
Woodhall Rd *AIRDRIE* ML6 ....118 C2
   WISHAW ML2 172
Woodhall Cottage Rd *MTHW* ML1 ....137 E2
Woodhall St *AIRDRIE* ML6 ....118 D3
   CTBR ML5 ....118 C2
   HMLTN ML3 ....137 E2
Woodhead Av *BALLOCH* G68 ....58 A5
   BALLOCH G68 ....40 A1
   KKNTL G66 ....40 A1
   UD/BTH/TAN G71 ....152 C2
Woodhead Crs *HMLTN* ML3 ....169 F5
   UD/BTH/TAN G71 ....115 E4
Woodhead Gdns *UD/BTH/TAN* G71 ....152 C2
Woodhead Gv *BALLOCH* G68 ....43 G1
Woodhead Rd *BAIL/MDB/MHD* G69 ....58 A5
   BALLOCH G68 ....58 A5
   PLK/PH/NH G53 ....125 E2
Woodhead Ter *BAIL/MDB/MHD* G69 ....58 A4
Woodhead Vw *BALLOCH* G68 ....58 A5
Woodhill Rd *BSHPBGS* G64 ....55 E3
   SPRGB/BLRNK G21 ....68 D1
Woodholm Av *LNPK/KPK* G44 ....128 C1
Woodhouse St *KNTSWD* G13 ....51 F4
Woodilee Rd *KKNTL* G66 ....40 B2
   MTHW ML1 ....138 B3
Woodland Av *AIRDRIE* ML6 ....99 F3
   KKNTL G66 ....20 D5
   PSLYS PA2 ....104 B3
Woodland Crs *BLTYR/CAMB* G72 ....131 G3
Woodland Gdns *CRMNK/CLK/EAG* G76 ....147 E3
   HMLTN ML3 ....169 H5
Woodlands Av *BAIL/MDB/MHD* G69 ....58 D4
   UD/BTH/TAN G71 ....134 B4
Woodlands Crs *GIF/THBK* G46 ....126 C5
   JNSTN PA5 ....101 E5
   UD/BTH/TAN G71 ....134 B4
Woodlands Dr *CTBR* ML5 ....96 A2
   KVGV G3 ....67 E4
   MTHW ML1 ....137 E2
Woodlands Gdns *UD/BTH/TAN* G71 ....134 A4
Woodlands Ga *GIF/THBK* G46 ....126 C5
   KVGV G3 ....67 E4
Woodlands Gv *MLNGV* G62 ....17 E3
Woodlands Pl *CTBR* ML5 ....96 A2
Woodlands Rd *CRMNK/CLK/EAG* G76 ....162 D5
   GIF/THBK G46 ....126 C5
   KVGV G3 ....67 E4
   MTHW ML1 ....137 E2
Woodlands St *MLNGV* G62 ....17 E3
   MTHW ML1 ....172 A2
The Woodlands *BLSH* ML4 ....136 C4
Woodlands Ter *CRMNK/CLK/EAG* G76 ....126 C5
   KVGV G3 ....67 E4
   UD/BTH/TAN G71 ....119 E5
Woodland Wy *CUMB* G67 ....26 D2
Woodlea Dr *GIF/THBK* G46 ....127 G3
   HMLTN ML3 ....170 A5
Woodlea Pl *AIRDRIE* ML6 ....76 A5
Woodlinn Av *LNPK/KPK* G44 ....128 C2

Woodmill Dr *BSHPBGS* G64 ....19 G4
Woodmill Gdns *CUMB* G67 ....43 G2
Woodneuk Rd
  BAIL/MDB/MHD G69 ....73 E1
  PLK/PH/NH G53 ....125 G5
Woodneuk St *AIRDRIE* ML6 ....119 E3
Woodneuk Ter
  BAIL/MDB/MHD G69 ....73 E1
Wood Qd *CLYDBK* G81 ....49 H5
Woodrow *MTHW* ML1 ....118 C4
Woodrow Av *MTHW* ML1 ....137 G5
Woodrow Circ *PLKSD/SHW* G41 ....88 C5
Woodrow Pl *PLKSD/SHW* G41 ....88 C5
Woodrow Rd *PLKSD/SHW* G41 ....88 C5
Woodside *BLSH* ML4 ....117 H4
  CRG/CRSL/HOU PA6 ....81 E2
Woodside Av *BRWEIR* PA11 ....19 G3
  GIF/THBK G46 ....126 D4
  HMLTN ML3 ....170 B3
  KKNTL G66 ....40 A3
  KSYTH G65 ....8 D2
  RUTH G73 ....111 F5
Woodside Crs *BRHD/NEIL* G78 .....124 C5
  KVGV G3 ....2 A3
  PSLY PA1 ....83 H5
  WISHAW ML2 ....158 C4
Woodside Dr *AIRDRIE* ML6 ....118 B2
  CRMNK/CLK/EAG G76 ....163 E3
Woodside Gdns
  CRMNK/CLK/EAG G76 ....145 G3
  CRMNK/CLK/EAG G76 ....147 E3
  CTBR ML5 ....96 A5
Woodside La *JNSTN* PA5 ....80 D5
Woodside Pl *KVGV* G3 ....67 E5
  UD/BTH/TAN G71 ....115 H4

Woodside Place La *KVGV* G3 ....67 E5
Woodside Rd
  CRMNK/CLK/EAG G76 ....147 E3
  JNSTN PA5 ....81 E5
Woodside St *AIRDRIE* ML6 ....119 E2
  CTBR ML5 ....116 A1
  MTHW ML1 ....137 H4
  MTHW ML1 ....172 C1
Woodside Ter *KVGV* G3 ....67 E5
Woodside Terrace La *KVGV* G3 ......67 E5
Woodside Wk *MTHW* ML3 ....170 B5
Woodside Gv *RUTH* G73 ....111 F5
Woodstock Av *KKNTL* G66 ....21 H5
  PLKSD/SHW G41 ....108 C4
  PSLY PA2 ....102 D4
Woodstock Dr *WISHAW* ML2 ....174 B1
Woodstock St *AIRDRIE* ML6 ....76 C5
  CTBR ML5 ....96 B2
  DEN/PKHD G31 ....91 E1
  MTHW ML1 ....155 E1
  PSLY PA5 ....105 E1
Woodvale Av *AIRDRIE* ML6 ....98 D5
  BSDN G61 ....52 A1
  GIF/THBK G46 ....145 G2
Woodvale Dr *PSLYN/LNWD* PA3 .....83 F4
Wooddvale Dr *UD/BTH/TAN* G71 ....116 A4
Woodview Dr *AIRDRIE* ML6 ....98 D4
  BLSH ML4 ....117 F5
Woodview Ter *HMLTN* ML3 ....169 G1
Woodville St *GOV/IBX* G51 ....88 A3
Woodville St *GOV/IBX* G51 ....88 A3
Woodyard Rd *DMBTN* G82 ....12 D4
Woodyett Pk
  CRMNK/CLK/EAG G76 ....146 A5

Woodyett Rd
  CRMNK/CLK/EAG G76 ....146 A5
Wordsworth Wy
  UD/BTH/TAN G71 ....134 C4
Worsley Crs *NMRNS* G77 ....143 H4
Wraes Av *BRHD/NEIL* G78 ....124 C3
Wraes Vw *BRHD/NEIL* G78 ....141 G1
Wraisland Crs *BSHPTN* PA7 ....28 C4
Wrangholm Crs *MTHW* ML1 ....137 G4
Wrangholm Dr *MTHW* ML1 ....137 F4
Wren Ct *BLSH* ML4 ....116 B4
Wren Pl *JNSTN* PA5 ....121 F2
Wright Av *BRHD/NEIL* G78 ....123 H5
Wrightlands Crs *ERSK* PA8 ....48 B3
Wright St *RNFRW* PA4 ....62 C5
Wye Crs *CTBR* ML5 ....74 A5
Wykeham Pl *KNTSWD* G13 ....50 D5
Wykeham Rd *KNTSWD* G13 ....50 D5
Wylie Av *NMRNS* G77 ....150 A5
Wylie Av *NMRNS* G77 ....144 A5
Wylie St *HMLTN* ML3 ....170 A3
Wynd Beatson
  UD/BTH/TAN G71 ....115 F3
Wyndford Dr *MRYH/FIRH* G20 ....66 C1
Wyndford Pl *MRYH/FIRH* G20 ....66 C1
Wyndford Rd *MRYH/FIRH* G20 ....66 C1
Wyndford Ter
  UD/BTH/TAN G71 ....115 G5
Wyndham Ct *KVD/HLHD* G12 ....66 C2
Wyndham St *KVD/HLHD* G12 ....66 C2
Wyndham St *KVD/HLHD* G12 ....66 C2
Wynyard Gn *EKILS* G75 ....165 G5
Wyper Pl *DMNK/BRGTN* G40 ....90 D3
Wyvil Av *KNTSWD* G13 ....51 F2
Wyvis Av *BSDN* G61 ....33 H1

KNTSWD G13 ....49 H3
Wyvis Ct *NMRNS* G77 ....161 F3
Wyvis Pl *KNTSWD* G13 ....50 A3
  NMRNS G77 ....161 F3
Wyvis Qd *KNTSWD* G13 ....50 A3

Y

Yair Dr *CARD/HILL/MSPK* G52 ....86 B3
Yarrow Crs *BSHPTN* PA7 ....46 B1
  WISHAW ML2 ....174 A1
Yarrow Gdns *MRYH/FIRH* G20 ....67 E3
Yarrow Gardens La
  MRYH/FIRH G20 ....67 E3
Yarrow Pk *EKILN* G74 ....166 D4
Yarrow Rd *BSHPBGS* G64 ....37 H4
Yate St *DEN/PKHD* G31 ....91 E4
Yetholm Gdns *EKILN* G74 ....166 C1
Yetholm St *SCOT* G14 ....49 H5
Yetholm Ter *HMLTN* ML3 ....168 D2
Yett Rd *MTHW* ML1 ....138 A4
Yetts Crs *KKNTL* G66 ....21 F1
Yew Dr *SPRGB/BLRNK* G21 ....68 D3
Yew Pl *JNSTN* PA5 ....101 G5
Yokerburn Pl *KNTSWD* G13 ....49 H4
Yokerburn Ter *CLYDBK* G81 ....49 G4
Yoker Ferry Rd *SCOT* G14 ....49 H5
Yoker Mill Gdns *KNTSWD* G13 ....49 H4
Yoker Mill Rd *KNTSWD* G13 ....49 H4

York Dr *RUTH* G73 ....130 C2
Yorkhill Pde *KVGV* G3 ....66 B5
Yorkhill St *KVGV* G3 ....88 C1
York Rd *AIRDRIE* ML6 ....119 E4
York St *CCLW* G2 ....2 C6
  CLYDBK G81 ....49 G1
  WISHAW ML2 ....174 A3
Young Pl *EKILS* G75 ....178 D3
  UD/BTH/TAN G71 ....115 F4
  WISHAW ML2 ....158 C5
Young St *CLYDBK* G81 ....32 A4
  WISHAW ML2 ....174 A3
Young Ter *SPRGB/BLRNK* G21 ....68 D2
Young Wynd *BLSH* ML4 ....116 D4
Yukon Ter *EKILS* G75 ....165 G5

Z

Zambesi Dr *BLTYR/CAMB* G72 ....151 F1
Zena Crs *STPS/GTHM/RID* G33 ....69 F2
Zena St *STPS/GTHM/RID* G33 ....69 G2
Zetland Rd
  CARD/HILL/MSPK G52 ....86 A1

Index - featured places

Abbey Cemetery
  JNSTN PA5 ....102 B2
Abbey Mill Business Centre
  PSLY PA1 ....84 C5
Abercorn Industrial Estate
  PSLYN/LNWD PA3 ....84 B2
Abercorn School
  COWCAD G4 ....67 G4
Abronhill Health Centre
  CUMB G67 ....27 G1
Abronhill High School
  CUMB G67 ....27 G1
Abronhill Primary School
  CUMB G67 ....27 F2
Agricultural Museum
  CRMNK/CLK/EAG G76 ....147 G5
Airdrie Academy
  AIRDRIE ML6 ....76 A5
Airdrie Golf Club
  AIRDRIE ML6 ....76 A4
Airdrie Health Centre
  AIRDRIE ML6 ....97 H2
Airdrie United FC
  (Excelsior Stadium)
  AIRDRIE ML6 ....98 D3
Air Link Industrial Estate
  AIRDRIE ML6 ....84 B1
Aitkenbar Primary School
  DMBTN G82 ....13 F3
Aitkenhead Primary School
  UD/BTH/TAN G71 ....115 E3
Aiton Primary School
  BLTYR/CAMB G72 ....131 F1
Albert Primary School
  HMLTN ML3 ....98 C1
  SPRGB/BLRNK G21 ....68 C1
Albion Rovers FC (Cliftonhill)
  CTBR ML5 ....97 F3
Alexander Hospital
  CTBR ML5 ....96 B1
Alexandra Golf Club
  DEN/PKHD G31 ....91 E1
Alexandra Parade
  Primary School
  DEN/PKHD G31 ....90 D2
Alexandra Primary School
  AIRDRIE ML6 ....98 B2
Alison Lea Medical Centre
  EKILN G74 ....167 E2
Allandar Sports Centre
  BSDN G61 ....35 E1
Allanshaw Industrial Estate
  HMLTN ML3 ....169 H1
All Saints Secondary School
  SPRGB/BLRNK G21 ....69 F1
The Anderson Doe
  Podiatry Clinic
  SCOT G14 ....93 G3
Anderson Primary School
  KVGV G3 ....89 E1
Anderston Medical Centre
  KVGV G3 ....88 D1
Annette Street
  Primary School
  GVH/MTFL G42 ....109 F2
Annfield Medical Centre
  DEN/PKHD G31 ....90 D2
Anniesland College
  KVD/HLHD G12 ....65 H1
Anniesland College of Further
  Education
  PTCK G11 ....65 G4
Anniesland Industrial Estate
  KNTSWD G13 ....51 F3
The Antonine Sports Centre
  CLYDBK G81 ....31 H2
Antonine Wall
  Bearsden Bath-House
  BSDN G61 ....34 C4
Aquatec Leisure Centre
  MTHW ML1 ....154 D3
Arcadia Business Centre
  CLYDBK G81 ....48 D2
Arches Theatre
  CGLE G1 ....2 D7
Arden Primary School
  GIF/THBK G46 ....126 A3
Ardoch Medical Centre
  BLTYR/CAMB G72 ....131 E1
Argo Sports Centre
  DRUM G15 ....32 D5

Argyle Indoor Market
  CGLE G1 ....3 F6
Arkleston Primary School
  RNFRW PA4 ....63 G5
Ashcraig School
  STPS/GTHM/RID G33 ....70 C3
Ashfield Medical Practice
  MLNGV G62 ....17 E4
Atholl Preparatory School
  MLNGV G62 ....17 E4
Auchenback Primary School
  BRHD/NEIL G78 ....142 C1
Auchenlodment
  Primary School
  JNSTN PA5 ....101 H1
Auchinairn Primary School
  BSHPBGS G64 ....55 E3
Auchinloch Primary School
  KKNTL G66 ....57 E1
Auchinraith Primary School
  BLTYR/CAMB G72 ....151 G3
Auldhouse Retail Park
  PLKSW/MSWD G43 ....127 F1
Auld Kirk Museum
  KKNTL G66 ....21 E4
Baillieston FC
  BAIL/MDB/MHD G69 ....94 B5
Baillieston Health Centre
  BAIL/MDB/MHD G69 ....94 A5
Baird Memorial
  Primary School
  CUMB G67 ....26 B5
Baljaffray Primary School
  BSDN G61 ....16 A5
Baljaffray Shopping Centre
  BSDN G61 ....16 A5
Ballerup High School
  EKILS G75 ....177 G3
Balmalloch Primary School
  KSYTH G65 ....8 A1
Balmore Golf Club
  BSHPBGS G64 ....18 B5
Balmuildy Primary School
  BSHPBGS G64 ....37 F5
Balornock Primary School
  SPRGB/BLRNK G21 ....69 E2
Bankhead Primary School
  KNTSWD G13 ....50 B5
  RUTH G73 ....110 C5
Bannerman High School
  BAIL/MDB/MHD G69 ....93 H5
Bargarran Primary School
  ERSK PA8 ....30 A5
Bargeddie Primary School
  CTBR ML5 ....95 F3
Barlanark Primary School
  STPS/GTHM/RID G33 ....93 F3
Barmulloch Primary School
  SPRGB/BLRNK G21 ....69 F2
Barncluith Business Centre
  HMLTN ML3 ....170 C2
Barras Market
  DMNK/BRGTN G40 ....90 B3
Barratt Trading Estate
  COWCAD G4 ....67 G4
Barrhead Bowling Club
  BRHD/NEIL G78 ....124 B4
Barrhead High School
  BRHD/NEIL G78 ....124 C4
Barrhead Sports Centre
  BRHD/NEIL G78 ....124 B4
Barrowfield Primary School
  DMNK/BRGTN G40 ....91 E5
Barsail Primary School
  ERSK PA8 ....47 H3
Battlefield Primary School
  GVH/MTFL G42 ....109 E5
Beardmore Hotel
  CLYDBK G81 ....31 E5
Bearsden Academy
  BSDN G61 ....34 B2
Bearsden Golf Club
  BSDN G61 ....33 H1
Bearsden Primary School
  BSDN G61 ....34 B3
Beckford Primary School
  HMLTN ML3 ....152 D5
Beckford Street
  Business Centre
  HMLTN ML3 ....152 D5
Bellahouston Academy
  PLKSD/SHW G41 ....88 B4

Bellahouston Leisure Centre
  CARD/HILL/MSPK G52 ....87 G5
Bellahouston Primary School
  GOV/IBX G51 ....88 B3
Bell College of Technology
  HMLTN ML3 ....153 E5
The Bell Leisure Centre
  DMBTN G82 ....12 D4
Bellshill Academy
  BLSH ML4 ....136 A2
Bellshill Golf Club
  BLSH ML4 ....136 A4
Bellshill Industrial Estate
  BLSH ML4 ....135 G1
Belmont House School
  NMRNS G77 ....144 C4
Belvidere Primary School
  BLSH ML4 ....135 H3
Benburb FC
  GOV/IBX G51 ....87 F3
Bent Cemetery
  HMLTN ML3 ....169 H2
Berryhill Primary School
  WISHAW ML2 ....173 F2
Birkenshaw Industrial Estate
  UD/BTH/TAN G71 ....114 D3
Bishopbriggs Golf Club
  BSHPBGS G64 ....54 C1
Bishopbriggs High School
  BSHPBGS G64 ....54 D2
Bishopbriggs Sports Centre
  BSHPBGS G64 ....37 F4
Bishopknow Primary School
  ESTRH G34 ....72 B5
Bishopton Health Centre
  BSHPTN PA7 ....46 A1
Bishopton Primary School
  BSHPTN PA7 ....28 D5
Blackfriars Primary School
  GBLS G5 ....89 H5
Blacklaw Primary School
  EKILN G74 ....167 E4
Blackwoods Medical Centre
  BAIL/MDB/MHD G69 ....42 A5
Blairbeth Golf Club
  CSMK G45 ....129 H4
Blairdardie Primary School
  DRUM G15 ....50 C2
Blairtummock Primary School
  ESTRH G34 ....94 A1
Blantyre Cemetery
  BLTYR/CAMB G72 ....151 F4
Blantyre High School
  BLTYR/CAMB G72 ....151 G3
Blantyre Victoria FC
  BLTYR/CAMB G72 ....152 A3
Blawarthill Hospital
  KNTSWD G13 ....50 B5
Blythswood Estate
  RNFRW PA4 ....63 E2
Bobbys Leisure Centre
  CUMB G67 ....26 B3
Boclair Academy
  BSDN G61 ....35 F4
Bonnyholm Primary School
  PLK/PH/NH G53 ....106 B1
Bothwell Bridge Hotel
  UD/BTH/TAN G71 ....134 B5
Bothwell Castle
  UD/BTH/TAN G71 ....133 G4
Bothwell Castle Golf Club
  UD/BTH/TAN G71 ....134 A5
Bothwell Cemetery
  UD/BTH/TAN G71 ....135 E2
Bothwell Medical Centre
  UD/BTH/TAN G71 ....134 B5
Bothwell Park High School
  MTHW ML1 ....172 B1
Bothwell Park
  Industrial Estate
  UD/BTH/TAN G71 ....134 A2
Bothwell Primary School
  UD/BTH/TAN G71 ....134 B5
Bowling Alley
  BAIL/MDB/MHD G69 ....115 H1
  CLYDBK G81 ....49 F2
  EKILS G75 ....178 D2
  KKNTL G66 ....21 E3
  KVGV G3 ....89 E2
  PSLYN/LNWD PA3 ....84 C3
Braehead Arena
  RNFRW PA4 ....64 B2

Braehead Business Park
  RNFRW PA4 ....64 A3
Braehead Primary School
  DMBTN G82 ....13 F3
Braehead Retail Park
  RNFRW PA4 ....64 C4
Braehead Shopping Centre
  RNFRW PA4 ....64 B3
Braeside Primary School
  CSMK G45 ....129 G3
Braidbar Primary School
  GIF/THBK G46 ....127 G4
Braidcraft Medical Centre
  PLK/PH/NH G53 ....106 D3
Braidfield High School
  CLYDBK G81 ....49 F1
Braidhurst Business Centre
  MTHW ML1 ....154 B5
Braidhurst High School
  MTHW ML1 ....154 C1
Braidhurst Industrial Estate
  MTHW ML1 ....154 C2
Brannock High School
  MTHW ML1 ....137 H4
Bredisland Primary School
  PSLYS PA2 ....103 F3
Bridge of Weir Hospital
  BRWEIR PA11 ....78 C1
Bridge of Weir Primary School
  BRWEIR PA11 ....79 G2
Bridgeton Business Centre
  DMNK/BRGTN G40 ....90 C4
Bridgeton Health Centre
  DMNK/BRGTN G40 ....90 C4
The Bridgewater
  Shopping Centre
  ERSK PA8 ....47 H1
Broomhill Industrial Estate
  KKNTL G66 ....21 G3
Broomhill Primary School
  PTCK G11 ....65 G2
Broomlee School
  PTCK G11 ....65 G4
Bruce Medical Centre
  BLSH ML4 ....136 A2
Buchanan Business Park
  STPS/GTHM/RID G33 ....57 G5
Buchanan Bus Station
  COWCAD G4 ....3 G4
Buchanan Galleries &
  Shopping Centre
  CGLE G1 ....3 F4
Burgh Primary School
  RUTH G73 ....110 D4
Burmah Doctors Surgery
  PTCK G11 ....66 A4
Burnbank Medical Centre
  HMLTN ML3 ....152 B5
Burnbrae Primary School
  PLK/PH/NH G53 ....126 A2
Burnhead Primary School
  UD/BTH/TAN G71 ....116 A4
Burnhill Sports Centre
  RUTH G73 ....110 C4
Burnside Primary School
  RUTH G73 ....130 A2
Burrell Collection
  PLKSD/SHW G41 ....88 D5
Busby Primary School
  CRMNK/CLK/EAG G76 ....146 A4
Bushes Primary School
  PSLYS PA2 ....104 A4
Byres Road Market
  PTCK G11 ....66 B4
Cadder Primary School
  SMSTN G23 ....53 E4
Cadzow Health Centre
  HMLTN ML3 ....170 A1
Cadzow Industrial Estate
  HMLTN ML3 ....170 A5
Cairnbrook Industrial Estate
  ESTRH G34 ....94 A1
Cairnhill Industrial Estate
  AIRDRIE ML6 ....98 B3
Cairnhill Trading Estate
  AIRDRIE ML6 ....98 B3

Cairns Primary School
  BLTYR/CAMB G72 ....131 H3
Calderbank Primary School
  AIRDRIE ML6 ....118 C1
Calderbraes Golf Club
  UD/BTH/TAN G71 ....114 B3
Caldercuilt Primary School
  SMSTN G23 ....52 D2
Calder Glen Country Park
  EKILN G74 ....179 F2
Caldervale High School
  MTHW ML1 ....155 E3
Caldervale High School
  AIRDRIE ML6 ....99 G2
Calderwood Lodge
  Jewish Primary School
  PLKSW/MSWD G43 ....127 H2
Calderwood Primary School
  RUTH G73 ....130 B1
Caledonian University
  CGLW G2 ....2 E1
Caledonia Primary School
  BAIL/MDB/MHD G69 ....114 A1
Callander Street Clinic
  MRYH/FIRH G20 ....67 F3
Cambuslang Avory Club
  BLTYR/CAMB G72 ....131 F3
Cambuslang College
  BLTYR/CAMB G72 ....131 G2
Cambuslang College
  EKILN G74 ....166 C3
Cambuslang Golf Club
  BLTYR/CAMB G72 ....112 C5
Cambuslang Rangers FC
  BLTYR/CAMB G72 ....131 E1
Cambuslang
  Recreation Centre
  BLTYR/CAMB G72 ....132 A2
Cambuslang RFC
  BLTYR/CAMB G72 ....130 C2
Cambusnethan
  Primary School
  WISHAW ML2 ....174 C1
Campsie Recreation Centre
  KKNTL G66 ....4 B2
Campsie View School
  KKNTL G66 ....39 F3
Canberra Primary School
  EKILS G75 ....165 G5
Cannlesburn Hospital
  BSDN G61 ....51 F1
Carbrain Primary School
  CUMB G67 ....26 D3
Cardinal Newman
  High School
  BLSH ML4 ....135 F2
Cardonald Clinic
  CARD/HILL/MSPK G52 ....86 D4
Cardonald College
  CARD/HILL/MSPK G52 ....107 E1
Cardonald Primary School
  CARD/HILL/MSPK G52 ....86 C5
Carlin Industrial Estate
  MTHW ML1 ....137 G4
Carleith Primary School
  CLYDBK G81 ....31 F2
Carlibar Primary School
  BRHD/NEIL G78 ....124 B4
Carmichael Hall
  GIF/THBK G46 ....127 E5
Carmunnock Cemetery
  CRMNK/CLK/EAG G76 ....146 C1
Carmunnock Primary School
  CRMNK/CLK/EAG G76 ....147 E3
Carmyle Medical Centre
  CAR/SHTL G32 ....112 C4
Carmyle Primary School
  CAR/SHTL G32 ....112 D3
Carnbooth Residential School
  CRMNK/CLK/EAG G76 ....146 C3
Carnbroe Primary School
  CTBR ML5 ....97 G5
Carntyne Primary School
  STPS/GTHM/RID G33 ....91 G1
Carnwadric Primary School
  GIF/THBK G46 ....126 C3
Caroleside Medical Centre
  CRMNK/CLK/EAG G76 ....145 H3
Caroleside Primary School
  CRMNK/CLK/EAG G76 ....145 G4
Carsemeadow School
  BRWEIR PA11 ....78 A1

Cartvale School
GOV/IBX G51 .....88 A2
Castlebank Industrial Estate
PTCK G11 .....65 H5
Castlecary House Hotel
BALLOCH G68 .....11 H1
Castlehead Primary School
EKILS G75 .....177 G3
Castlehead High School
PSLYS PA2 .....104 A1
Castlehill Primary School
BSDN G61 .....33 G2
WISHAW ML2 .....175 H5
Castlemilk Health Centre
CSMK G45 .....129 F4
Castlemilk High School
CSMK G45 .....129 F5
Castlemilk Pool
CSMK G45 .....129 F4
Castlemilk Sports Centre
CSMK G45 .....129 F4
Castleton Primary School
CUMB G67 .....128 D4
Cathcart Castle Golf Club
CRMNK/CLK/EAG G76 .....145 F3
Cathedral Primary School
MTHW ML1 .....154 D3
Cathkin Braes Country Park
.....147 G1
Cathkin Braes Golf Club
CRMNK/CLK/EAG G76 .....148 A1
Cathkin High School
RUTH G73 .....130 D3
Cathkin Primary School
RUTH G73 .....130 C4
Cawder Golf Club
BSHPBGS G64 .....37 G2
Celtic FC (Celtic Park)
DEN/PKHD G31 .....91 E4
Central College of Commerce
.....3 H4
Central Health Centre
CUMB G67 .....26 B4
Chapelgreen Primary School
KSYTH G65 .....7 E3
Chapelhall Industrial Estate
AIRDRIE ML6 .....99 F5
AIRDRIE ML6 .....119 E1
Chapelhall Primary School
AIRDRIE ML6 .....119 E2
Chapelside Primary School
AIRDRIE ML6 .....76 B5
Chapel Street
Industrial Estate
MRYH/FIRH G20 .....52 D5
Charing Cross Clinic
KVGV G3 .....2 A2
The Charleston Surgery
PSLYS PA2 .....104 B1
Chatelherault Country Park
HMLTN ML3 .....181 H1
Chatelherault Primary School
HMLTN ML3 .....170 B4
Chatelherault Visitor Centre
HMLTN ML3 .....170 D5
Child Health Clinic
PLKSW/MSWD G43 .....108 B4
Chirnsyde Primary School
PPK/MIL G22 .....54 A5
Christ the King
Primary School
MTHW ML1 .....137 G1
Chryston High School
BAIL/MDB/MHD G69 .....58 B3
Chryston Primary School
BAIL/MDB/MHD G69 .....58 B3
Chryston Valley
Business Centre
BAIL/MDB/MHD G69 .....58 B3
City Chambers
CGLE G1 .....3 G5
City Halls
CGLE G1 .....3 H6
Claremont High School
EKILN G74 .....167 F5
Clarkston Primary School
AIRDRIE ML6 .....99 E1
Cleland Athletics Track
MTHW ML1 .....156 B2
Cleland Hospital
MTHW ML1 .....157 F1
Cleland Primary School
MTHW ML1 .....157 E1
Cleveden Secondary School
KVD/HLHD G12 .....66 A1
MRYH/FIRH G20 .....66 D2
Clippens Special School
PSLYN/LNWD PA3 .....82 B3
Clober Golf Club
MLNGV G62 .....16 D2
Clober Primary School
MLNGV G62 .....16 C3
Clyde Auditorium
KVGV G3 .....88 C2
Clydebank Business Centre
CLYDBK G81 .....49 F3
Clydebank College
CLYDBK G81 .....32 A5
DMBTN G82 .....12 C3
Clydebank Crematorium
OLDK G60 .....31 E2
Clydebank & District
Golf Course
CLYDBK G81 .....32 B2
Clydebank Health Centre
CLYDBK G81 .....32 A4
Clydebank High School
CLYDBK G81 .....31 H4
Clydebank Town Hall
.....48 D2
Clydebuilt
RNFRW PA4 .....64 B3
Clyde FC (Broadwood Stadium)
BALLOCH G68 .....24 D4
Clyde Industrial Estate
RUTH G73 .....111 G4
Clydemuir Primary School
CLYDBK G81 .....31 E4
Clydesdale Cricket Club
PLKSD/SHW G41 .....108 C2
Clyde Tunnel
GOV/IBX G51 .....65 F5
Clydeview Primary School
MTHW ML1 .....154 A2
Clydeview Shopping Centre
BLTYR/CAMB G72 .....151 G3

Clydeway Business Centre
KVGV G3 .....88 D2
Coatbridge Business Centre
CTBR ML5 .....97 F3
Coatbridge College
CTBR ML5 .....97 G2
Coatbridge Health Centre
CTBR ML5 .....96 D3
Coatbridge High School
CTBR ML5 .....96 D2
Coatbridge Outdoor
Sports Complex Track
CTBR ML5 .....96 C4
Coathill Hospital
CTBR ML5 .....96 D5
Coats Observatory
PSLY PA1 .....84 A4
Cochrane Castle Golf Club
JNSTN PA5 .....121 F1
Cochrane Castle
Primary School
JNSTN PA5 .....121 E1
College of Building & Printing
CGLE G1 .....3 G4
College of Food & Technology
PTCK G11 .....3 G4
Colquhoun Park
Primary School
BSDN G61 .....33 H5
Coltness High School
WISHAW ML2 .....174 C1
Coltness Primary School
WISHAW ML2 .....157 F4
Columba High School
CTBR ML5 .....96 D5
Colville Park Golf Club
MTHW ML1 .....155 E1
Commonhead
Primary School
ESTRH G34 .....94 C1
Condorrat Health Centre
CUMB G67 .....43 H2
Condorrat Primary School
CUMB G67 .....44 A1
Copeland Primary School
GOV/IBX G51 .....88 A2
Corpus Christi Primary School
AIRDRIE ML6 .....118 C1
KNTSWD G13 .....50 D5
Corseford School
HWWD PA9 .....120 C2
Corus Hotel
CGLW G2 .....2 C6
Cotton Street Business Park
DMNK/BRGTN G40 .....110 D2
Cowglen Golf Club
PLKSW/MSWD G43 .....107 G5
Cowglen Hospital
PLK/PH/NH G53 .....107 E5
Craigdhu Primary School
MLNGV G62 .....16 D5
Craighead Primary School
KKNTL G66 .....5 G4
Craighead School
HMLTN ML3 .....152 C3
Craigholme School
PLKSD/SHW G41 .....108 B1
Craigielea Primary School
PSLYN/LNWD PA3 .....83 F3
Craigton Crematorium
CARD/HILL/MSPK G52 .....87 E4
Craigton Primary School
CARD/HILL/MSPK G52 .....87 F4
Croftcroighn School
STPS/GTHM/RID G33 .....71 E5
Crofthead Industrial Estate
BRHD/NEIL G78 .....140 D3
Crookfur Primary School
NMRNS G77 .....144 A3
Crookston Castle NTS
PLK/PH/NH G53 .....106 C2
Cross Arthurlie
Primary School
BRHD/NEIL G78 .....123 H3
Crosshouse Primary School
EKILS G75 .....177 F3
Crowngate Business Centre
DMNK/BRGTN G40 .....90 C4
Crownpoint Sports Complex
DMNK/BRGTN G40 .....90 C3
Crow Wood Golf Club
BAIL/MDB/MHD G69 .....57 H3
Cumbernauld Airport
BALLOCH G68 .....11 E2
Cumbernauld College
CUMB G67 .....26 B4
Cumbernauld High School
CUMB G67 .....27 E4
Cumbernauld Primary School
CUMB G67 .....10 D5
Cumbernauld Shopping Centre
CUMB G67 .....26 D1
Cumbernauld Theatre
CUMB G67 .....26 D1
Cunard Primary School
CLYDBK G81 .....49 F2
Cuthbertson Primary School
PLKSD/SHW G41 .....109 H1
Daily Record & Sunday Mail
Offices
KVGV G3 .....2 A6
Dairsie House School
PLKSW/MSWD G43 .....127 H1
Daldowie Crematorium
UD/BTH/TAN G71 .....114 A4
Dalmarnock Industrial Estate
RUTH G73 .....111 E2
Dalmarnock Primary School
DMNK/BRGTN G40 .....90 D5
Dalmarnock Trading Estate
RUTH G73 .....110 D3
Dalmuir Municipal Golf Club
CLYDBK G81 .....31 F4
Dalreoch Primary School
DMBTN G82 .....12 C2
Dalsholm Industrial Estate
MRYH/FIRH G20 .....52 A4
Dalziel Business Centre
MTHW ML1 .....172 B3
Dalziel High School
MTHW ML1 .....154 C4
Darnley Primary School
PLK/PH/NH G53 .....126 A3
Darrows Estate
UD/BTH/TAN G71 .....135 E1

David Dale College
DMNK/BRGTN G40 .....90 C4
David Livingstone Centre
BLTYR/CAMB G72 .....133 H5
David Livingstone
Primary School
BLTYR/CAMB G72 .....151 G1
David Lloyd Sports Centre
PSLYN/LNWD PA3 .....84 D1
Dean Park Hotel
RNFRW PA4 .....63 H4
Dental Hospital & School
KVGV G3 .....2 C3
The Dollan Aqua Centre
EKILN G74 .....166 B4
The Donald Dewar
Leisure Centre
DRUM G15 .....50 B1
Douglas Academy
MLNGV G15 .....50 B1
Douglas Inch Centre
KVGV G3 .....2 A2
Douglas Park Golf Club
BSDN G61 .....34 D3
Dowanhill Primary School
PTCK G11 .....66 B4
Drumchapel Health Centre
DRUM G15 .....33 E5
Drumchapel High School
DRUM G15 .....33 F4
Drumchapel Hospital
DRUM G15 .....50 B1
Drumchapel Pool
DRUM G15 .....50 A1
Drummore School
DRUM G15 .....33 H4
Drumoyne Industrial Estate
GOV/IBX G51 .....87 F3
Drumoyne Primary School
GOV/IBX G51 .....87 F2
Drumpark Special School
CTBR ML5 .....95 G3
Drumpellier Country Park
CTBR ML5 .....95 H1
Drumpellier Country Park
Visitor Centre
CTBR ML5 .....73 F5
Drumpellier Cricket Club
CTBR ML5 .....96 A3
Drumpellier Golf Club
CTBR ML5 .....96 A3
Drumry Primary School
DRUM G15 .....49 H1
Dry Ski Slopes
BSDN G61 .....16 C5
Duchess Industrial Estate
RUTH G73 .....111 F3
Dullatur Golf Club
BALLOCH G68 .....9 H4
Dumbarton Academy
DMBTN G82 .....13 F3
Dumbarton FC (Strathclyde
Homes Stadium)
DMBTN G82 .....13 E5
Dumbarton Golf Club
DMBTN G82 .....13 E2
Dumbarton Health Centre
DMBTN G82 .....12 D4
Dumbarton Joint Hospital
DMBTN G82 .....12 B3
Dumbarton Peoples Theatre
DMBTN G82 .....13 G5
Dunard Primary School
MRYH/FIRH G20 .....67 E2
Duncanrig Secondary School
EKILS G75 .....165 G4
Duncanrig Sports Centre
EKILS G75 .....165 G5
Dundas Business Centre
COWCAD G4 .....2 D1
Dundyvan Industrial Estate
CTBR ML5 .....96 C4
Dunrobin Primary School
AIRDRIE ML6 .....99 F2
Earnock High School
HMLTN ML3 .....169 F3
Eastbank Academy
CAR/SHTL G32 .....92 C5
Eastbank Primary School
CAR/SHTL G32 .....92 D4
Easterhouse Pool
ESTRH G34 .....93 H1
Easterhouse Sports Centre
ESTRH G34 .....71 G5
Eastfield Primary School
BALLOCH G68 .....25 F4
East Fulton Primary School
PSLYN/LNWD PA3 .....81 G5
Easthall Primary School
STPS/GTHM/RID G33 .....93 G2
East Kilbride Arts Centre
Cinema
EKILN G74 .....166 C2
East Kilbride Golf Club
EKILN G74 .....149 G4
East Kilbride Ice Rink
EKILN G74 .....166 C5
East Kilbride
Shopping Centre
EKILN G74 .....166 B4
East Kilbride Sports Club
EKILN G74 .....179 F2
East Kilbride Stadium
EKILN G74 .....166 D3
East Milton Primary School
EKILS G75 .....165 H4
Eastmuir Special School
STPS/GTHM/RID G33 .....93 E3
East Park Home School
MRYH/FIRH G20 .....66 D1
East Renfrewshire Golf Club
NMRNS G77 .....160 C5
Eastside Industrial Estate
KKNTL G66 .....21 G4
Eastwood High School
NMRNS G77 .....144 B3
Eastwood Recreation Centre
GIF/THBK G46 .....127 E5
Eastwood Theatre
GIF/THBK G46 .....127 E5
Elderpark Clinic
GOV/IBX G51 .....87 G2
Elder Park Primary School
GOV/IBX G51 .....87 F1
Elderslie Cottage Hospital
JNSTN PA5 .....102 A2

Elderslie Golf Club
JNSTN PA5 .....102 D1
Elmvale Primary School
PPK/MIL G22 .....68 B1
Elmwood Medical Centre
NMRNS G77 .....144 C4
Elmwood Special School
DMBTN G82 .....12 D4
The Erskine Bridge Hotel
ERSK PA8 .....46 D2
Erskine Golf Club
BSHPTN PA7 .....29 E3
Erskine Health Centre
BSHPTN PA7 .....30 B5
Erskine Hospital
ERSK PA8 .....29 H3
Erskine Swimming Pool
ERSK PA8 .....47 G1
Erskine View Clinic
OLDK G60 .....30 D2
Esporta, Dougalston Golf Club
MLNGV G62 .....17 H2
The Ewington Hotel
CVH/MTFL G42 .....109 E3
Express by Holiday Inn
BLSH ML4 .....153 E1
CGLE G1 .....3 G7
COWCAD G4 .....2 F3
Failside Secondary School
BSHPTN/TAN G71 .....135 E1
Family Planning Clinic
KVGV G3 .....67 E5
Faraday Retail Park
CTBR ML5 .....96 D3
Farm Castle Industrial Estate
RUTH G73 .....111 F4
Farmeloan Industrial Estate
RUTH G73 .....111 E4
Ferenze Golf Club
BRHD/NEIL G78 .....123 H4
Ferguslie Cricket Club
PSLYS PA2 .....103 H1
Ferguslie Primary School
PSLYN/LNWD PA3 .....83 G3
Fernhill School
RUTH G73 .....130 B4
Festival Business Centre
GOV/IBX G51 .....88 B3
Film Theatre
KVGV G3 .....2 D3
Firhill Business Centre
MRYH/FIRH G20 .....67 F2
Firpark School
MTHW ML1 .....172 A1
Flemington Industrial Estate
BLTYR/CAMB G72 .....132 B3
Florence Street Clinic
GBLS G5 .....89 H4
Flowerhill Industrial Estate
AIRDRIE ML6 .....98 C1
Fordbank Primary School
JNSTN PA5 .....120 D1
Forge Shopping Centre
DEN/PKHD G31 .....91 F3
The Fort Theatre
BSHPBGS G64 .....54 C2
Fountain Business Centre
CTBR ML5 .....96 D2
French Street
Industrial Estate
RNFRW PA4 .....63 G4
Fullwood Health Centre
MTHW ML1 .....137 F5
Fullwood Industrial Estate
HMLTN ML3 .....152 C5
Gadburn Special School
SPRGB/BLRNK G21 .....69 F1
Gallery of Modern Art
CGLE G1 .....3 F5
Gallowgate Market
CGLE G1 .....90 A3
Gallowhill Primary School
PSLYN/LNWD PA3 .....85 E2
Garfield House Hotel
STPS/GTHM/RID G33 .....57 F4
Garnerbank Primary School
KVGV G3 .....2 C2
Garrell Business Centre
KSYTH G65 .....8 A2
Garrion Business Park
WISHAW ML2 .....173 H5
Garrowhill Primary School
BAIL/MDB/MHD G69 .....93 H4
Garscadden Primary School
KNTSWD G13 .....50 A4
Gartconner Primary School
KKNTL G66 .....22 C5
Gartcosh Primary School
BAIL/MDB/MHD G69 .....73 E1
Gartcosh Works Sports Club
BAIL/MDB/MHD G69 .....73 F1
Garthamlock Primary School
STPS/GTHM/RID G33 .....71 E4
Garthamlock
STPS/GTHM/RID G33 .....71 E4
Gartnavel General Hospital
KVD/HLHD G12 .....65 H2
Gartnavel Royal Hospital
KVD/HLHD G12 .....65 H2
Gartsherrie Industrial Estate
CTBR ML5 .....74 C5
Gartsherrie Primary School
CTBR ML5 .....96 B1
Gask House School
BSHPBGS G64 .....54 C4
Gavinburn Primary School
OLDK G60 .....30 A1
Georgian Hotel
CTBR ML5 .....96 B2
GHK RFC
KNTSWD G13 .....51 G5
Giffnock Primary School
GIF/THBK G46 .....127 F4
The Glasgow Academy
KVD/HLHD G12 .....66 D3
Glasgow Airport
PSLYN/LNWD PA3 .....62 A5
Glasgow Botanic Gardens
KVD/HLHD G12 .....66 C2
Glasgow Caledonian University
COWCAD G4 .....3 G2
CGLE G1 .....3 H5
KVGV G3 .....66 D4
Glasgow Cathedral
COWCAD G4 .....3 K4

Glasgow College of
Nautical Studies
GBLS G5 .....89 H4
Glasgow Cross
CGLE G1 .....3 H7
Glasgow Gaelic School
COWCAD G4 .....2 A1
Glasgow Golf Club
BSDN G61 .....52 B1
Glasgow Marriott Hotel
KVGV G3 .....2 B5
Glasgow Moat House
KVGV G3 .....88 C2
Glasgow Museums
Resource Centre
(The Open Museum)
PLK/PH/NH G53 .....125 E2
Glasgow Nuffield Hospital
KVD/HLHD G12 .....66 A1
Glasgow Royal Infirmary
.....3 K3
Glasgow School of Art
COWCAD G4 .....2 D2
Glasgow Science Centre &
IMAX
GOV/IBX G51 .....88 C2
Glasgow Steiner School
KVGV G3 .....88 C1
Glasgow Tower
GOV/IBX G51 .....88 B2
Glasgow Zoopark
UD/BTH/TAN G71 .....114 A2
Glenboig Primary School
.....74 C1
Glenburn Clinic
PSLYS PA2 .....104 A4
Glencairn Primary School
MTHW ML1 .....155 E5
Glencryan School
CUMB G67 .....44 D1
Glendale Primary School
PLKSD/SHW G41 .....89 E5
Glenduffhill Cemetery
CAR/SHTL G32 .....93 E3
Glen Family Centre
GIF/THBK G46 .....126 D5
Glenhead Primary School
CUMB G67 .....126 D5
Gleniffer Braes Country Park
PSLYS PA2 .....122 B1
Gleniffer High School
PSLYS PA2 .....103 F3
Glenlee Primary School
HMLTN ML3 .....152 B5
Glenmanor Primary School
BAIL/MDB/MHD G69 .....152 B5
Glenpark Industrial Estate
DEN/PKHD G31 .....91 E3
Glenvale FC
PSLY PA1 .....83 H5
Glenwood Business Centre
CSMK G45 .....129 F4
Glenwood Business Park
CSMK G45 .....129 F4
Glynhill Hotel
RNFRW PA4 .....63 E5
Goldenhill Primary School
CLYDBK G81 .....32 A2
Golfhill Primary School
AIRDRIE ML6 .....75 H4
DEN/PKHD G31 .....90 C1
Gorbals Health Centre
GBLS G5 .....89 H5
Gorbals Leisure Centre
GBLS G5 .....90 A4
Govan Health Centre
GOV/IBX G51 .....87 F1
Govan High School
GOV/IBX G51 .....87 F2
Govanhill Health Centre
CVH/MTFL G42 .....109 G2
Gowanbank Primary School
PLK/PH/NH G53 .....125 F1
Greenbank Garden (NT)
CRMNK/CLK/EAG G76 .....145 E4
Greenburn Primary School
EKILN G74 .....167 G2
Greenfaulds High School
CUMB G67 .....44 C1
Greenfield Primary School
GOV/IBX G51 .....87 G2
Greenhill Industrial Estate
CTBR ML5 .....74 D5
Greenhill Primary School
CTBR ML5 .....96 D1
Greenhills Health Centre
EKILS G75 .....177 F2
Greenhills Primary School
EKILS G75 .....177 H3
Greenview School
PPK/MIL G22 .....54 A5
Grovewood Business Centre
BAIL/MDB/MHD G69 .....116 B4
Gryffe High School
CRC/CRSL/HOU PA6 .....80 B1
Haggs Castle Golf Club
PLKSW/MSWD G43 .....107 H1
Haghill Primary School
DEN/PKHD G31 .....91 E2
Hairmyres & Stonehouse
Hospitals
EKILS G75 .....165 E4
Halfmerke Primary School
EKILN G74 .....166 D2
Hallside Primary School
BLTYR/CAMB G72 .....132 B3
Hamilton Academical FC
(New Douglas Park)
HMLTN ML3 .....152 D5
Hamilton Business Park
HMLTN ML3 .....153 E5
Hamilton College
HMLTN ML3 .....153 E5
Hamilton Golf Club
HMLTN ML3 .....171 F5
Hamilton Grammar School
HMLTN ML3 .....170 A2
Hamiltonhill Industrial Estate
PPK/MIL G22 .....67 G2
Hamilton Park Racecourse
HMLTN ML3 .....153 E3
Hamilton Public Baths
HMLTN ML3 .....170 A1
Hamilton School for the Deaf
HMLTN ML3 .....169 F3
Hamilton Water Palace
HMLTN ML3 .....153 E5

Hampden Park
GVH/MTFL G42 ....109 H4
Hampden Special School
GVH/MTFL G42 ....110 A4
Harestanes Primary School
KKNTL G66 ....22 A4
Hartfield Clinic
DMBTN G82 ....13 F3
The Harvest Clinic
COWCAD G4 ....2 B1
Hawkhead Cemetery
PSLYS PA2 ....105 F1
Hawkhead Hospital
PSLYS PA2 ....105 F2
Hayston Golf Club
KKNTL G66 ....20 D3
Healthcare International (HCI)
CLYDBK G81 ....48 B1
Heatherbank Museum of
Social Work Trust
KVD/HLHD G12 ....66 D4
Heathery Knowe
Primary School
EKILS G75 ....178 A1
Heriot Primary School
PSLYS PA2 ....103 E4
High Blantyre Primary School
BLTYR/CAMB G72 ....151 E3
High School of Glasgow
BSDN G61 ....34 A4
The High School of Glasgow
KNTSWD G13 ....51 F5
High Street Industrial Estate
KKNTL G66 ....21 E4
Hillhead High School
KVD/HLHD G12 ....66 D4
Hillhead Primary School
KKNTL G66 ....21 G5
KVD/HLHD G12 ....66 D3
Hillhead RFC
KVD/HLHD G12 ....66 A2
Hillington Industrial Estate
CARD/HILL/MSPK G52 ....86 A2
Hillington Park Retail &
Amenities Centre
CARD/HILL/MSPK G52 ....86 B1
Hillington Primary School
CARD/HILL/MSPK G52 ....86 B3
Hillpark Secondary School
PLKSW/MSWD G43 ....127 F2
Hill's Trust Primary School
GOV/IBX G51 ....87 G1
Hilton Strathclyde
BLSH ML4 ....116 C4
HM Prison Barlinnie
STPS/GTHM/RID G33 ....70 A5
HM Prison Low Moss
BSHPBGS G64 ....38 C3
Holiday Inn
CGLW G2 ....2 C5
PSLYN/LNWD PA3 ....62 A5
Hollybrook Special School
GVH/MTFL G42 ....109 G2
Holm Industrial Estate
PSLYS PA2 ....104 C2
Holmlea Primary School
LNPK/KPK G44 ....128 B1
Holmwood House NTS
LNPK/KPK G44 ....128 C3
Holy Cross High School
HMLTN ML3 ....170 B1
Holy Cross Primary School
GVH/MTFL G42 ....109 G2
KSYTH G65 ....24 D1
Holy Family Primary School
BLSH ML4 ....136 B2
KKNTL G66 ....39 G2
Holyrood Secondary School
& Sports Centre
GVH/MTFL G42 ....109 H3
Holytown Primary School
MTHW ML1 ....137 G2
Hotel Ibis
CGLW G2 ....2 C3
House for an Art Lover
CARD/HILL/MSPK G52 ....87 H5
Househillmuir Primary School
PLK/PH/NH G53 ....125 G2
Houston Primary School
CRG/CRSL/HOU PA6 ....80 C2
Howford Special School
PLK/PH/NH G53 ....106 B2
Howwood Primary School
HWWD PA9 ....120 A4
The Hunter Health Centre
EKILN G74 ....166 C4
Hunter High School
EKILN G74 ....167 F3
Hunterhill Tutorial Centre
PSLYS PA2 ....104 D1
Hunterian Museum
KVD/HLHD G12 ....66 C4
Hunter Primary School
EKILN G74 ....167 E3
Hutchesons Grammar
Junior School
KVD/HLHD G12 ....66 C4
Hutchesons Grammar
Prep School
GVH/MTFL G42 ....109 F2
Hutchesons Grammar School
PLKSD/SHW G41 ....108 D2
Hutchesons' Hall
CGLE G1 ....3 G5
Hutchesons St Aloysians RFC
GIF/THBK G46 ....126 D2
Hyndland Primary School
KVD/HLHD G12 ....66 A4
Hyndland Secondary School
KVD/HLHD G12 ....65 H3
Ibrox Industrial Estate
GOV/IBX G51 ....88 A3
Ibrox Primary School
GOV/IBX G51 ....88 A2
Inchinnan Business Park
RNFRW PA4 ....61 H2
Inchinnan Primary School
RNFRW PA4 ....48 A4
International Christian College
COWCAD G4 ....3 J4
IORA Academy
GOV/IBX G51 ....88 B4
Isobel Mair School
CRMNK/CLK/EAG G76 ....145 G1
Italian Centre
CGLE G1 ....3 G6

Jackton Business Centre
EKILS G75 ....176 B1
James Hamilton
Heritage Park
EKILN G74 ....148 C5
John Hillhouse
Industrial Estate
BLTYR/CAMB G72 ....111 C5
John Ogilvie High School
HMLTN ML3 ....168 D1
John Paul Academy
SMSTN G23 ....52 B2
John Smith Memorial
Swimming Pool
AIRDRIE ML6 ....98 B2
Johnstone Health Centre
JNSTN PA5 ....101 C4
Johnstone Hospital
JNSTN PA5 ....101 H2
Johnstone Swimming Pool
JNSTN PA5 ....101 C3
Johnstone High School
JNSTN PA5 ....121 E1
John Wheatley College
SHTL G32 ....92 C4
ESTRH G34 ....72 A5
The John Wright
Sports Centre
EKILN G74 ....166 D3
Jordanhill School
KNTSWD G13 ....65 F1
Jurys Hotel
KVD/HLHD G12 ....65 H1
Keil School
DMBTN G82 ....12 C4
Keir Hardie Mem
Primary School
MTHW ML1 ....138 A4
Keir Hardie Sports Centre
MTHW ML1 ....137 F1
Kelbourne School
MRYH/FIRH G20 ....66 D1
Kelburne Cricket Club
PSLY PA1 ....84 D4
Kelvindale Primary School
KVD/HLHD G12 ....65 H1
Kelvingrove Art Gallery &
Museum
KVD/HLHD G12 ....66 C5
Kelvin Hall International
Sports Arena
KVGV G3 ....66 B5
Kelvinhaugh Primary School
KVGV G3 ....88 B1
The Kelvin Park Lorne Hotel
KVGV G3 ....66 D5
Kelvin School
KVGV G3 ....66 B5
The Kelvinside Academy
KVD/HLHD G12 ....66 C1
Kenilworth Medical Centre
CUMB G67 ....26 A5
Kennyhill School
DEN/PKHD G31 ....91 F1
Kersland School
PSLYS PA2 ....105 F3
Kibble Education &
Care Centre
PSLYN/LNWD PA3 ....83 H1
Kilbarchan Cemetery
KLBCH PA10 ....100 C1
Kilbarchan Primary School
KLBCH PA10 ....100 B2
Kilbowie Cemetery
CLYDBK G81 ....49 F1
Kilbowie Primary School
CLYDBK G81 ....32 A5
Kilbowie Retail Park
CLYDBK G81 ....49 F1
Kildrum Primary School
CUMB G67 ....26 D3
Killermont Primary School
BSDN G61 ....34 D4
Kilpatrick School
CLYDBK G81 ....31 F2
Kilsyth Academy
KSYTH G65 ....8 A1
Kilsyth Health Centre
KSYTH G65 ....8 C2
Kilsyth Primary School
KSYTH G65 ....8 B2
Kilsyth Swimming Pool
KSYTH G65 ....8 A2
Kingsgate Retail Park
EKILN G74 ....149 E4
Kings Park Secondary School
PLSGC/SHW G41 ....128 D2
Kings Theatre
CGLW G2 ....2 B3
Kinning Park Medical Centre
PLKSD/SHW G41 ....88 D3
Kirkhill Golf Club
BLTYR/CAMB G72 ....131 F4
Kirkhill Primary School
NMRNS G77 ....145 E5
Kirkintilloch Foot Clinic
KKNTL G66 ....21 E5
Kirkintilloch Golf Club
KKNTL G66 ....20 C4
Kirkintilloch High School
KKNTL G66 ....40 C1
Kirkintilloch Industrial Estate
KKNTL G66 ....21 F3
Kirklandneuk Primary School
RNFRW PA4 ....63 E3
Kirk Lane Cemetery
PLKSW/MSWD G43 ....108 B5
Kirkriggs School
CSMK G45 ....129 H2
Kirkshaws Primary School
CTBR ML5 ....96 B5
Kirktonholme Primary School
EKILN G74 ....165 H3
Kirkwood Health Clinic
CTBR ML5 ....95 H5
Kittoch School
EKILS G75 ....178 A1
Knightswood
Community Centre
KNTSWD G13 ....50 C5
Knightswood Golf Club
KNTSWD G13 ....50 C4
Knightswood Primary School
KNTSWD G13 ....51 F4
Knightswood
Secondary School
KNTSWD G13 ....51 E5

Knockburn Primary School
SPRGB/BLRNK G21 ....55 F4
Knowetop Primary School
MTHW ML1 ....172 A1
Knoxland Primary School
DMBTN G82 ....13 F4
Ladywell Primary School
MTHW ML1 ....154 C3
Ladywell School
SCOT G14 ....65 E4
Laigh Bent Sports Club
HMLTN ML3 ....170 C1
Laird Business Park
DMNK/BRGTN G40 ....110 D2
Lairdsland Primary School
KKNTL G66 ....21 E5
Lambhill Cemetery
SMSTN G23 ....53 E2
Lamlash Primary School
STPS/GTHM/RID G33 ....92 C1
Lammermoor Primary School
MTHW ML1 ....174 A1
Lanarkshire Ice Rink
HMLTN ML3 ....170 B1
Langcraigs Primary School
PSLYS PA2 ....103 H5
Langfaulds Primary School
DRUM G15 ....33 E4
Langlands School
GOV/IBX G51 ....87 F2
Langloan Primary School
CTBR ML5 ....96 B3
Langs Hotel
CGLE G1 ....3 F3
Langside College
CSMK G45 ....129 G4
GVH/MTFL G42 ....109 F4
Langside Primary School
PLSGC/SHW G41 ....108 C4
Lansdowne Clinic
KVD/HLHD G12 ....65 H1
Lawmuir Primary School
BLSH ML4 ....135 H4
Leithland Primary School
PLK/PH/NH G53 ....106 C4
Lennoxtown Primary School
KKNTL G66 ....4 B2
Lenzie Academy
KKNTL G66 ....39 H2
Lenzie Golf Club
KKNTL G66 ....40 A5
Lenzie Hospital
KKNTL G66 ....40 B5
Lenzie Moss Primary School
KKNTL G66 ....39 G3
Lenzie Primary School
KKNTL G66 ....39 H3
Lethamhill Golf Club
STPS/GTHM/RID G33 ....70 A3
Leverndale Hospital
PLK/PH/NH G53 ....106 A2
Lightburn Hospital
CAR/SHTL G32 ....92 C2
The Lighthouse
CGLE G1 ....2 E6
Linburn Special School
CARD/HILL/MSPK G52 ....86 A3
The Linn Crematorium
CRMNK/CLK/EAG G76 ....146 C1
Linn Park Gardens
LNPK/KPK G44 ....128 B5
Linn Park Golf Club
LNPK/KPK G44 ....128 C3
Linnpark Industrial Estate
CSMK G45 ....128 C5
Linnvale Primary School
CLYDBK G81 ....49 G2
Linwood Health Centre
PSLYN/LNWD PA3 ....82 B4
Linwood High School
PSLYN/LNWD PA3 ....81 G5
Linwood Moss Sports Centre
PSLYN/LNWD PA3 ....81 H4
Littlehill Golf Club
BSHPBGS G64 ....54 D4
Littlehill Primary School
STPS/GTHM/RID G33 ....69 G3
Living Waters
Christian School
PSLYS PA2 ....104 B2
Lochend Community
High School
ESTRH G34 ....94 B1
Lochend Secondary School
ESTRH G34 ....94 B1
Lochfield Primary School
PSLYS PA2 ....104 C3
Lochgoin Primary School
DRUM G15 ....33 E4
Lochinch Playing Fields &
Sports Club
PLKSW/MSWD G43 ....107 G3
Loch Primary School
RUTH G73 ....130 C3
Logans Primary School
MTHW ML1 ....154 A2
London Road Primary School
DMNK/BRGTN G40 ....91 E5
Long Calderwood
Primary School
EKILN G74 ....149 H5
Lorne Street Primary School
GOV/IBX G51 ....88 C3
Lourdes Primary School
CARD/HILL/MSPK G52 ....86 D5
Lourdes Secondary School
CARD/HILL/MSPK G52 ....87 E5
Low Parks Museum
HMLTN ML3 ....153 F5
Low Waters Medical Centre
HMLTN ML3 ....169 H5
Lymnhurst Hotel
JNSTN PA5 ....101 G4
M8 Trading Estate
PLKSD/SHW G41 ....88 D4
Madhok Medical Centre
GVH/MTFL G42 ....109 F5
Maimaison Hotel
CGLW G2 ....2 C4
Manse Road Medical Centre
WISHAW ML2 ....158 B5
Maryhill Crematorium
SMSTN G23 ....52 D3
Maryhill FC
MRYH/FIRH G20 ....52 D5

Maryhill Health Centre
MRYH/FIRH G20 ....52 D5
Maryhill Primary School
MRYH/FIRH G20 ....52 C4
The Mary Russell
Special School
PSLYS PA2 ....105 F2
Mavisbank Special School
AIRDRIE ML6 ....98 A1
Maxwellton Primary School
EKILN G74 ....167 E3
McGill Primary School
PLK/PH/NH G53 ....106 D2
McLellan Galleries
KVGV G3 ....2 C3
Meadowburn Primary School
BSHPBGS G64 ....37 H5
Meadowside Industrial Estate
RNFRW PA4 ....49 G5
Mearns Castle High School
NMRNS G77 ....162 B2
Mearns Cemetery
NMRNS G77 ....162 A3
Merchiston Hospital
JNSTN PA5 ....101 F1
Merkland School
KKNTL G66 ....21 H4
Merrylee Primary School
PLKSW/MSWD G43 ....128 A2
Middlefield Residential School
PTCK G11 ....66 A4
Middlemuir School
CLYDBK G81 ....31 G5
Midlock Medical Centre
GOV/IBX G51 ....88 A4
Millarston Industrial Estate
PSLY PA1 ....103 F1
Millennium Hotel
CGLE G1 ....3 F5
Millersneuk Primary School
KKNTL G66 ....40 B4
Milncroft Primary School
STPS/GTHM/RID G33 ....92 D1
Milngavie & Bearsden
Sports Club
MLNGV G62 ....35 G1
Milngavie Business Centre
MLNGV G62 ....17 E4
Milngavie Primary School
MLNGV G62 ....17 E3
Miltonbank Primary School
PPK/MIL G22 ....53 H3
Milton Clinic
PPK/MIL G22 ....53 H4
Milton Primary School
DMBTN G82 ....14 C3
Milton School
KVGV G3 ....54 B4
Mitchell Theatre & Library
KVGV G3 ....2 A3
Modrvyale Medical Centre
MTHW ML1 ....155 E5
Monklands & Bellshill
Hospitals NHS Trust
BLSH ML4 ....116 D4
Monklands District
General Hospital
CTBR ML5 ....97 G2
Monklands Industrial Estate
CTBR ML5 ....116 C2
Moorpark Primary School
RNFRW PA4 ....63 E4
Morningside Primary School
WISHAW ML2 ....175 G1
Mossedge Industrial Estate
PSLYN/LNWD PA3 ....82 B2
Mossend Primary School
BLSH ML4 ....136 B3
Mosshead Primary School
BSDN G61 ....34 B3
Mossneuk Primary School
EKILS G75 ....177 E1
Mosspark Primary School
CARD/HILL/MSPK G52 ....107 F1
Mossvale Primary School
PSLYN/LNWD PA3 ....84 A2
Motherwell Business Centre
MTHW ML1 ....155 E3
Motherwell Civic Centre
MTHW ML1 ....172 B1
Motherwell College
MTHW ML1 ....172 A2
Motherwell Cricket Club
MTHW ML1 ....172 B2
Motherwell FC (Fir Park)
MTHW ML1 ....172 A1
Motherwell Heritage Centre
MTHW ML1 ....154 C3
Mount Cameron
Primary School
EKILN G74 ....179 E1
Mount Ellen Golf Club
BAIL/MDB/MHD G69 ....59 G5
Mount Florida Medical Centre
GVH/MTFL G42 ....109 F4
Mount Florida Primary School
GVH/MTFL G42 ....109 G5
Mount Manor Business Park
KVGV G3 ....88 C1
Mount Vernon Primary School
CAR/SHTL G32 ....113 E1
Muiredge Primary School
UD/BTH/TAN G71 ....134 B1
Muirhouse Primary School
MTHW ML1 ....172 D3
Muir Street Primary School
MTHW ML1 ....154 C2
Munro Business Centre
KNTSWD G13 ....51 F4
Murano Medical Centre
MRYH/FIRH G20 ....67 E2
Murray Primary School
EKILS G75 ....166 B5
Museum of Scottish
Country Life
CRMNK/CLK/EAG G76 ....165 E1
Museum of Scottish Football
GVH/MTFL G42 ....109 H4
Museum of Transport
PTCK G11 ....66 B5
National Piping Centre
COWCAD G4 ....3 F2
National Swimming Centre at
Tollcross Leisure Centre
CAR/SHTL G32 ....92 A2
Neilsland Primary School
HMLTN ML3 ....169 F4

Neilston Cemetery
BRHD/NEIL G78 ....141 H1
Neilston Primary School
BRHD/NEIL G78 ....141 F3
Neilston Swimming Pool
BRHD/NEIL G78 ....141 F3
Nerston Residential School
EKILN G74 ....149 F3
Nethercommon
Industrial Estate
PSLYN/LNWD PA3 ....84 B2
Nethercraigs Sports Centre
PLK/PH/NH G53 ....107 E2
Netherlee Primary School
LNPK/KPK G44 ....128 A5
Netherton Primary School
WISHAW ML2 ....173 F4
Netherton School
CSMK G45 ....128 D5
New Albion Industrial Estate
KNTSWD G13 ....49 H5
Newarthill Primary School
MTHW ML1 ....138 B4
Newhills School
STPS/GTHM/RID G33 ....93 F2
Newhouse Industrial Estate
AIRDRIE ML6 ....119 E3
MTHW ML1 ....118 D5
MTHW ML1 ....154 C3
Newmains Primary School
RNFRW PA4 ....63 F5
Newmains Primary School
WISHAW ML2 ....175 E1
New Monkland
Primary School
AIRDRIE ML6 ....75 H2
Newspaper Offices
CGLE G1 ....3 H5
New Stevenston
Primary School
MTHW ML1 ....137 E3
Newton Mearns
Primary School
NMRNS G77 ....161 G1
The Nicholas Geraghty Clinic
MTHW ML1 ....155 E3
Nitshill Primary School
PLK/PH/NH G53 ....125 F3
Noble Primary School
BLSH ML4 ....116 C5
North Glasgow College
SPRGB/BLRNK G21 ....68 C2
North Woodside
Swimming Pool
COWCAD G4 ....67 F4
Notre Dame High School
KVD/HLHD G12 ....66 B3
Notre Dame Primary School
KVD/HLHD G12 ....66 B3
Novotel
CGLW G2 ....2 C3
Nuneaton Industrial Estate
DMNK/BRGTN G40 ....110 D1
Oakbank Industrial Estate
MRYH/FIRH G20 ....67 F3
Oakgrove Primary School
COWCAD G4 ....67 F4
Odeon Cinema
CGLW G2 ....2 E4
GOV/IBX G51 ....89 E3
Ogilvie Primary School
STPS/GTHM/RID G33 ....93 C2
Old Aisle Cemetery
KKNTL G66 ....40 C2
Old Kilpatrick Cemetery
OLDK G60 ....30 D1
Old Monkland Cemetery
CTBR ML5 ....116 A1
Old Monkland Primary School
CTBR ML5 ....95 H5
One Devonshire Gardens Hotel
KVD/HLHD G12 ....66 A2
Optimax Laser Eye Clinic
CGLW G2 ....2 A2
Orbiston Business Centre
BLSH ML4 ....135 H4
Our Holy Redeemers
Primary School
CLYDBK G81 ....49 G4
Our Lady of Loretto
Primary School
CLYDBK G81 ....31 E5
Our Lady of Lourdes
Primary School
EKILS G75 ....165 H5
Our Lady of Peace
Primary School
PSLYN/LNWD PA3 ....101 H1
Our Lady of the Annunciation
Primary School
PLKSW/MSWD G43 ....127 H2
Our Lady of the Assumption
Primary School
MRYH/FIRH G20 ....67 F1
Our Lady of the Missions
Primary School
GIF/THBK G46 ....126 D5
Our Lady of the Rosary
Primary School
CARD/HILL/MSPK G52 ....87 E5
Our Lady & St Francis
Primary School
MTHW ML1 ....137 H5
Our Lady & St Josephs
Primary School
CTBR ML5 ....59 H4
Our Lady & St Patricks
High School
DMBTN G82 ....12 B3
Our Ladys High School
CUMB G67 ....25 H4
MTHW ML1 ....172 B2
Outdoor Recreation Centre
BSHPBGS G64 ....54 C3
Oxgang Primary School
KKNTL G66 ....21 H5
Paisley Abbey
PSLY PA1 ....84 C4
Paisley Crematorium
PSLY PA1 ....83 H4
Paisley Golf Club
PSLYS PA2 ....122 C2
Paisley Grammar School
PSLY PA1 ....84 D4
Paisley Maternity Hospital
PSLYS PA2 ....103 F2

Paisley Museum &
Art Galleries
PSLY PA1 ....84 A5
Palacerigg Country Park
CUMB G67 ....27 H5
Palacerigg Golf Club
CUMB G67 ....45 G1
Parkburn Industrial Estate
BLTYR/CAMB G72 ....152 A4
Parkhead Hospital
DEN/PKHD G31 ....91 G4
Park Mains High School
ERSK PA8 ....47 G2
Parkview Business Centre
KVGV G3 ....2 A2
Parkview Primary School
SMSTN G23 ....52 C3
Partick Market
PTCK G11 ....66 B4
Partick Thistle FC
(Firhill Stadium)
MRYH/FIRH G20 ....67 F2
The Pavilion Theatre
CGLW G2 ....2 E5
Peacock Cross
Industrial Estate
HMLTN ML3 ....152 D5
Penilee Secondary School
CARD/HILL/MSPK G52 ....86 A3
Pentagon Business Centre
CGLW G2 ....2 B6
Pentland School
CTBR ML5 ....73 H5
People's Palace
DMNK/BRGTN G40 ....90 B4
Petersburn Primary School
AIRDRIE ML6 ....98 D4
Petershill FC
SPRGB/BLRNK G21 ....68 C3
Petershill Recreation Centre
SPRGB/BLRNK G21 ....69 E3
Phoenix Industrial Estate
PSLYN/LNWD PA3 ....84 B2
Phoenix Retail &
Business Park
PSLYN/LNWD PA3 ....82 D4
Pinewood Primary School
DRUM G15 ....33 H5
Plains Primary School
AIRDRIE ML6 ....77 G4
The Play Drome
CLYDBK G81 ....49 E2
Pollok Country Park
PLKSD/SHW G41 ....107 H3
Pollok Golf Club
PLKSW/MSWD G43 ....107 H5
Pollok House
PLKSW/MSWD G43 ....107 G4
Pollok Leisure Centre
PLK/PH/NH G53 ....106 D5
Pollok Shopping Centre
PLK/PH/NH G53 ....106 D5
Pollokshields Primary School
PLKSD/SHW G41 ....109 E1
Portland High School
CTBR ML5 ....97 E2
Portland Park Medical Centre
HMLTN ML3 ....170 B3
Possil Loch Nature Reserve
SMSTN G23 ....53 G3
Possilpark Health Centre
PPK/MIL G22 ....67 H2
Premier Lodge
CGLW G2 ....2 B3
Priestfield Industrial Estate
BLTYR/CAMB G72 ....151 G5
Prince's Square
Shopping Centre
CGLE G1 ....3 F6
Provand's Lordship
COWCAD G4 ....3 J4
Provan Hall NTS
ESTRH G34 ....71 G5
Provanhall Primary School
ESTRH G34 ....71 H5
Quadrant Shopping Centre
CTBR ML5 ....96 D2
Quality Hotel
CGLW G2 ....2 E6
Quarry Brae Primary School
DEN/PKHD G31 ....91 H4
Quarter Primary School
HMLTN ML3 ....181 F5
Queenslie Industrial Estate
STPS/GTHM/RID G33 ....93 F1
Queen's Park FC
(Hampden Park)
GVH/MTFL G42 ....109 H4
Radisson SAS Glasgow
CGLW G2 ....2 D6
Ralston Golf Club
PSLY PA1 ....85 G5
Ralston Primary School
PSLY PA1 ....85 H4
Ramoy Business Centre
PSLY PA1 ....83 H5
Ramshorn Theatre
CGLE G1 ....3 H5
Ranfurly Castle Golf Club
BRWEIR PA11 ....79 E4
Range Road Industrial Estate
MTHW ML1 ....172 D1
Rangers FC (Ibrox)
GOV/IBX G51 ....87 H3
Rashielea Primary School
ERSK PA8 ....30 C5
Ravenswood Primary School
CUMB G67 ....26 A5
Redburn School
CUMB G67 ....27 E3
Red Deer Day Hospital
EKILS G75 ....165 H5
Regency Medical Clinic
KVGV G3 ....66 D5
Reid Kerr College
PSLYN/LNWD PA3 ....84 B2
Reid Kerr Learning Centre
PSLYN/LNWD PA3 ....83 F3
Renfrew District
Welfare Clinic
PSLYS PA2 ....103 E3
Renfrew Golf Club
RNFRW PA4 ....63 G1
Renfrew Health Centre
RNFRW PA4 ....63 F4

Renfrew High School
RNFRW PA4 ....63 G4
Renfrew-Paisley
Lagoon Ice Rink
PSLY PA1 ....84 C5
Richmond Doctors Surgery
PTCK G11 ....65 H4
Richmond Park School
GBLS G5 ....110 A1
Riddrie Park Cemetery
STPS/GTHM/RID G33 ....69 H3
Righead Industrial Estate
BLSH ML4 ....135 F1
Robertsons Sports Centre
PSLY PA2 ....104 C5
Rob Roy FC
KKNTL G66 ....20 C5
Robslee Primary School
GIF/THBK G46 ....127 E5
Rochsolloch Primary School
AIRDRIE ML6 ....97 H3
Rogerfield Primary School
ESTRH G34 ....94 B1
Rosehall High School
CTBR ML5 ....116 C1
Rosehall Industrial Estate
CTBR ML5 ....116 C1
Rosevale School
PPK/MIL G22 ....54 A4
Rosshall Academy
CARD/HILL/MSPK G52 ....86 B5
Ross Hall Hospital
CARD/HILL/MSPK G52 ....106 B1
Rouken Glen Park
GIF/THBK G46 ....144 C1
Royal Alexandra Hospital
NHS Trust
PSLYS PA2 ....104 A2
Royal College of Nursing
KVGV G3 ....67 E5
Royal Concert Hall
CGLE G1 ....3 F4
Royal Highland Fusiliers
Museum
KVGV G3 ....2 B2
Royal Hospital for Sick Children
& Maternity Hospital
KVGV G3 ....66 B5
Royal Maternity Hospital
COWCAD G4 ....3 H5
Royston Primary School
SPRGB/BLRNK G21 ....68 C5
Royal Scottish Academy of
Music and Drama
CGLW G2 ....2 E3
RSPB Nature Reserve
MTHW ML1 ....171 H3
Ruchazie Primary School
STPS/GTHM/RID G33 ....70 B5
Ruchill Primary School
MRYH/FIRH G20 ....53 E5
Rutherglen Cemetery
RUTH G73 ....129 H1
Rutherglen Health Centre
RUTH G73 ....111 E5
Rutherglen High School
RUTH G73 ....111 E4
Rutherglen Swimming Pool
RUTH G73 ....110 D5
Sacred Heart Primary School
BLSH ML4 ....135 H4
DMNK/BRGTN G40 ....90 C5
SAE Technology College
PLKSD/SHW G41 ....88 D4
St Agnes Primary School
SMSTN G23 ....52 D3
St Aidan's High School
WISHAW ML2 ....174 A1
St Aidans Primary School
CAR/SHTL G32 ....91 G2
St Alberts Primary School
PLKSD/SHW G41 ....88 C5
St Aloysius College
KVGV G3 ....2 C2
St Aloysius Preparatory School
KVGV G3 ....2 C2
St Aloysius Primary School
AIRDRIE ML6 ....119 F2
SPRGB/BLRNK G21 ....68 B1
St Ambrose High School
CTBR ML5 ....96 B1
St Andrews Academy
PSLYS PA2 ....105 F3
St Andrews Cathedral
CGLE G1 ....2 E7
St Andrews Clinics for Children
KVD/HLHD G12 ....66 C3
St Andrews High School
CLYDBK G81 ....49 F5
St Andrew's High School
EKILS G75 ....178 A2
St Andrew's Primary School
AIRDRIE ML6 ....48 H5
St Andrews Primary School
BSDN G61 ....33 H2
St Andrews RC
Secondary School
CAR/SHTL G32 ....92 B2
St Angelas Primary School
PLK/PH/NH G53 ....125 H4
St Annes Primary School
DMNK/BRGTN G40 ....90 D3
ERSK PA8 ....47 H3
HMLTN ML3 ....170 A5
St Anthonys FC
GOV/IBX G51 ....87 H3
St Anthonys Primary School
GOV/IBX G51 ....87 G1
HWWD PA9 ....120 D2
RUTH G73 ....130 B3
St Augustine's
Primary School
CTBR ML5 ....96 C5
PPK/MIL G22 ....53 H4
St Barbaras Primary School
BAIL/MDB/MHD G69 ....58 C4
St Bartholomews
Primary School
CSMK G45 ....129 G3
CTBR ML5 ....73 H5
St Benedict's Primary School
ESTRH G34 ....71 H5

St Bernadette's
Primary School
MTHW ML1 ....154 A2
St Bernards Primary School
CTBR ML5 ....117 E1
PLK/PH/NH G53 ....125 E2
St Blanes Primary School
BLTYR/CAMB G72 ....151 F2
SMSTN G23 ....52 C2
St Brendans High School
LNPK/KPK G44 ....82 B3
St Brendan's Primary School
KNTSWD G13 ....49 H4
MTHW ML1 ....172 C3
St Bride's High School
EKILN G74 ....166 C4
St Bride's Primary School
BLTYR/CAMB G72 ....131 F2
GVH/MTFL G42 ....109 F4
St Brides RC Primary School
UD/BTH/TAN G71 ....134 B3
St Bridgets Primary School
BAIL/MDB/MHD G69 ....94 A4
St Brigid's Primary School
GVH/MTFL G42 ....110 A4
St Brigids Primary School
WISHAW ML2 ....158 A5
St Cadoc's Primary School
BLTYR/CAMB G72 ....131 H5
St Cadocs Primary School
NMRNS G77 ....143 H5
St Catherine's Primary School
PSLYN/LNWD PA3 ....84 C3
St Catherines Primary School
SPRGB/BLRNK G21 ....69 F1
St Charles Primary School
BLTYR/CAMB G72 ....132 C1
St Charles Primary School
MRYH/FIRH G20 ....67 E2
St Charles's Primary School
PSLYS PA2 ....104 C3
St Clare's Primary School
DRUM G15 ....33 F4
St Clare's Primary School
ESTRH G34 ....94 C1
St Columbas High School
CLYDBK G81 ....32 B4
St Columbas Primary School
UD/BTH/TAN G71 ....115 H5
St Columbkilles
Primary School
RUTH G73 ....110 D5
St Convals Primary School
PLKSW/MSWD G43 ....108 C4
St Cuthberts High School
JNSTN PA5 ....120 D2
St Cuthberts Primary School
JNSTN PA5 ....120 D2
HMLTN ML3 ....152 B5
PPK/MIL G22 ....67 G2
St David's Primary School
AIRDRIE ML6 ....77 G4
JNSTN PA5 ....101 E5
St Denis Primary School
DEN/PKHD G31 ....91 E2
St Dominic's Primary School
CSMK G45 ....129 G5
St Dominic's RC
Primary School
AIRDRIE ML6 ....98 D3
St Edmunds Primary School
PLK/PH/NH G53 ....107 E5
St Edwards Primary School
AIRDRIE ML6 ....98 D2
St Elizabeth Seton
Primary School
STPS/GTHM/RID G33 ....92 C1
St Elizabeth's Primary School
HMLTN ML3 ....180 D1
St Enoch Business Centre
CGLE G1 ....2 E7
St Enoch Shopping Centre
CGLE G1 ....3 F7
St Eunans Primary School
CLYDBK G81 ....49 F1
St Fergus Primary School
PSLYN/LNWD PA3 ....83 G4
St Fillan's Primary School
CRG/CRSL/HOU PA6 ....80 C1
St Fillans Primary School
LNPK/KPK G44 ....128 C1
St Flannans Primary School
KKNTL G66 ....21 H4
St Francis of Assisi
Primary School
BAIL/MDB/MHD G69 ....113 G1
BALLOCH G68 ....43 H1
St Francis Primary School
GOV/IBX G51 ....90 A5
St Gabriel's Primary School
UD/BTH/TAN G71 ....116 A4
St Georges Medical Centre
COWCAD G4 ....2 B1
St Georges Primary School
CARD/HILL/MSPK G52 ....86 A4
St Georges School
CARD/HILL/MSPK G52 ....86 B4
St Gerards Primary School
BLSH ML4 ....116 D5
St Gerard's Secondary School
GOV/IBX G51 ....88 A2
St Gilberts Primary School
SPRGB/BLRNK G21 ....69 F3
St Gregorys Primary School
MRYH/FIRH G20 ....67 H4
St Helens Primary School
BSHPBGS G64 ....55 F1
CUMB G67 ....44 A1
St Hilarys Primary School
EKILN G74 ....167 E5
St Ignatius Primary School
WISHAW ML2 ....174 B2
St James Business Park
PSLYN/LNWD PA3 ....82 C5
St James Primary School
CTBR ML5 ....96 B5
DMNK/BRGTN G40 ....90 B4
St James's Primary School
PSLYN/LNWD PA3 ....63 E3
St James's RC Primary School
PSLYN/LNWD PA3 ....84 A4
St James Street Health Centre
PSLY PA1 ....84 B4
St Jerome's Primary School
GOV/IBX G51 ....87 F2
St Joachims RC
Primary School
CAR/SHTL G32 ....112 D3

St Joan of Arc
Secondary School
PPK/MIL G22 ....53 G4
St John Bosco Primary School
ERSK PA8 ....47 E1
St John Ogilvie Primary School
HMLTN ML3 ....85 E5
St Johns Approved School
CAR/SHTL G32 ....93 E2
St John's Primary School
BRHD/NEIL G78 ....124 B3
St Johns Primary School
GBLS G5 ....89 G4
HMLTN ML3 ....170 A2
St John the Baptist
Primary School
UD/BTH/TAN G71 ....134 B1
St Josephs Primary School
BLTYR/CAMB G72 ....151 G2
CLYDBK G81 ....32 C1
COWCAD G4 ....67 F4
CRMNK/CLK/EAG G76 ....145 H4
MLNGV G62 ....16 D4
STPS/GTHM/RID G33 ....71 F1
St Judes Primary School
STPS/GTHM/RID G33 ....93 F3
St Julies Primary School
LNPK/KPK G44 ....129 E3
St Kenneths Primary School
EKILN G74 ....166 A2
St Kevins Special School
RUTH G73 ....130 A2
St Kevin's Primary School
SPRGB/BLRNK G21 ....68 B4
St Kevin's Primary School
BAIL/MDB/MHD G69 ....95 F4
St Leonards Primary School
EKILN G74 ....167 G2
St Louise Primary School
GIF/THBK G46 ....126 A3
St Louises Primary School
EKILS G75 ....178 A1
St Lucys Primary School
CUMB G67 ....27 G1
St Lukes High School
BRHD/NEIL G78 ....142 B2
St Margaret Mary's
Primary School
CSMK G45 ....128 D5
St Margaret Marys
Secondary School
CSMK G45 ....129 E5
St Margaret of Scotland
Primary School
CTBR ML5 ....26 C4
St Margarets Primary School
JNSTN PA5 ....101 F4
St Margarets RC High School
AIRDRIE ML6 ....98 C1
St Mark's Primary School
BRHD/NEIL G78 ....142 B1
CAR/SHTL G32 ....91 H4
St Marks Primary School
RUTH G73 ....130 A2
St Marnock's Primary School
BRHD/NEIL G78 ....106 D3
St Marthas RC Primary School
SPRGB/BLRNK G21 ....69 E1
St Martins Primary School
CSMK G45 ....129 G5
St Marys Cathedral
COWCAD G4 ....67 G4
St Mary's Kenmure School
BSHPBGS G64 ....54 B2
St Marys (Maryhill)
Primary School
MRYH/FIRH G20 ....52 B4
St Marys Primary School
CLYDBK G81 ....31 G2
CTBR ML5 ....96 D4
CUMB G67 ....26 A4
HMLTN ML3 ....170 A1
KKNTL G66 ....20 D5
MTHW ML1 ....157 E1
PSLY PA1 ....83 H5
St Matthews Primary School
BSHPBGS G64 ....55 E1
St Matthew's Primary School
WISHAW ML2 ....173 F1
St Maurices High School
LNPK/KPK G44 ....128 C1
St Michaels Primary School
BAIL/MDB/MHD G69 ....59 F1
St Michael's Primary School
DEN/PKHD G31 ....91 F4
St Mirins High School
PSLY PA1 ....83 G5
St Mirins Primary School
LNPK/KPK G44 ....128 D2
St Mirren FC (St Mirren Park)
PSLYN/LNWD PA3 ....84 B3
St Modans Primary School
STPS/GTHM/RID G33 ....92 B1
St Monicas Primary School
CTBR ML5 ....95 H5
St Monicas Primary School
PLK/PH/NH G53 ....106 B3
St Mungo Museum of
Religious Life & Art
COWCAD G4 ....3 K4
St Mungo's Academy
DMNK/BRGTN G40 ....90 D3
St Mungos Primary School
SPRGB/BLRNK G21 ....3 J5
St Ninians High School
GIF/THBK G46 ....126 C5
KKNTL G66 ....20 D5
St Ninians Primary School
HMLTN ML3 ....168 D1
St Ninian's Primary School
KNTSWD G13 ....50 D2
St Oswald's School
CSMK G45 ....128 B2
St Patrick's Cemetery
MTHW ML1 ....137 E4
St Patricks Primary School
DMTBN G82 ....13 F4
KSYTH G65 ....8 B3
KVGV G3 ....2 B1
St Patrick's Primary School
CTBR ML5 ....97 E2
St Patricks RC High School
CTBR ML5 ....97 G2
St Paul's Primary School
PLK/PH/NH G53 ....107 E4

St Paul's Primary School
CAR/SHTL G32 ....112 B1
St Pauls Primary School
HMLTN ML3 ....152 C4
PSLYS PA2 ....103 E3
St Peters Primary School
DMBTN G82 ....13 G1
St Peter's Primary School
HMLTN ML3 ....169 G4
PSLY PA1 ....103 H4
PTCK G11 ....66 B4
St Philip's Primary School
STPS/GTHM/RID G33 ....70 B5
St Philips School
AIRDRIE ML6 ....77 G5
St Philomena's Primary School
STPS/GTHM/RID G33 ....69 G3
St Pius Primary School
DRUM G15 ....33 F4
St Raymond's Special School
LNPK/KPK G44 ....128 C5
St Robert's Primary School
PLK/PH/NH G53 ....125 H1
St Rochs Primary School
SPRGB/BLRNK G21 ....68 B5
St Rochs Secondary School
SPRGB/BLRNK G21 ....68 B5
St Rose of Lima
Primary School
STPS/GTHM/RID G33 ....70 C4
St Saviour's Primary School
GOV/IBX G51 ....88 A2
St Serfs Primary School
AIRDRIE ML6 ....76 C4
St Stephens Primary School
CLYDBK G81 ....31 G5
St Stephen's Primary School
CTBR ML5 ....97 G4
SPRGB/BLRNK G21 ....68 B4
St Teresas Primary School
MTHW ML1 ....138 A4
St Teresa's Primary School
PPK/MIL G22 ....67 H3
St Thomas Aquinas RC
Secondary School
SCOT G14 ....65 F2
St Thomas Primary School
BRHD/NEIL G78 ....141 E3
STPS/GTHM/RID G33 ....69 H5
St Thomas' Primary School
WISHAW ML2 ....173 G3
St Timothys Primary School
CAR/SHTL G32 ....92 B2
St Vincents Primary School
GBLS G5 ....177 G3
St Vincent's Primary School
GIF/THBK G46 ....126 B3
St Vincents School Tollcross
CAR/SHTL G32 ....112 B2
Sandaig Primary School
STPS/GTHM/RID G33 ....93 F3
Sanderson High School
EKILN G74 ....167 F5
Sandwood Primary School
CARD/HILL/MSPK G52 ....86 B4
Saracen Health Centre
PPK/MIL G22 ....67 G2
Saracen Primary Annexe
PPK/MIL G22 ....67 H3
Saracen Primary School
PPK/MIL G22 ....67 G2
Scotland Street
School Museum
GBLS G5 ....89 E4
Scotstoun Leisure Centre
SCOT G14 ....65 E2
Scotstoun Primary School
SCOT G14 ....64 D2
Scotstoun Stadium
SCOT G14 ....64 D2
Scottish Enterprises
CGLW G2 ....2 B5
Scottish Exhibition &
Conference Centre
KVGV G3 ....88 C2
Scottish Maritime Museum
DMBTN G82 ....13 F4
Scottish TV
CGLW G2 ....2 E5
Scottish Youth Theatre
CGLE G1 ....2 E5
Scotus College
BSDN G61 ....33 H4
Shawbridge Industrial Estate
PLKSW/MSWD G43 ....108 B5
Shawhead Industrial Estate
CTBR ML5 ....117 E2
Shawhead Primary School
CTBR ML5 ....117 E1
Shawlands Academy
PLKSD/SHW G41 ....108 C3
Shawlands Primary School
PLKSD/SHW G41 ....108 C3
Shawlands Surgery
PLKSD/SHW G41 ....108 C4
Sheriff Court
GBLS G5 ....89 G4
Shettleston Day Hospital
CAR/SHTL G32 ....92 A5
Shettleston Health Centre
CAR/SHTL G32 ....92 B4
Showcase Cinema
BAIL/MDB/MHD G69 ....95 G5
PSLYN/LNWD PA3 ....82 D3
Sighthill Cemetery
SPRGB/BLRNK G21 ....68 B3
Sighthill Primary School
SPRGB/BLRNK G21 ....68 A3
Sikeside Primary School
CTBR ML5 ....97 G4
Simshill Primary School
LNPK/KPK G44 ....128 C3
Sir John Maxwell
Primary School
PLKSW/MSWD G43 ....108 D5
Sir Matt Busby
Sports Complex
BLSH ML4 ....135 G2
Smithycroft
Secondary School
STPS/GTHM/RID G33 ....69 H5
Somerset Eye Clinic
KVGV G3 ....88 D1
Southbank Surgery
KKNTL G66 ....21 G5

Southern General Hospital
NHS Trust
GOV/IBX G51 ....87 E1
South Lanarkshire College
EKILN G74 ....166 C3
South Park Primary School
EKILS G75 ....177 H2
South Primary School
PSLYS PA2 ....104 B2
Spectrum Business Centre
RUTH G73 ....110 D4
Spiersbridge Business Park
GIF/THBK G46 ....126 B4
Spittal Primary School
RUTH G73 ....129 G2
Springburn Academy
SPRGB/BLRNK G21 ....68 C1
Springburn Health Centre
SPRGB/BLRNK G21 ....68 C2
Springburn Sports Centre
SPRGB/BLRNK G21 ....68 C2
Springfield Primary School
DMNK/BRGTN G40 ....111 E2
Springhill Primary School
BRHD/NEIL G78 ....142 A1
Stepps Primary School
STPS/GTHM/RID G33 ....57 F5
Stirling Road Industrial Estate
AIRDRIE ML6 ....76 C3
Stirling's Library
CGLE G1 ....3 F6
Stobcross Street
Industrial Estate
CTBR ML5 ....96 D3
Stobhill General Hospital
SPRGB/BLRNK G21 ....54 D5
Stonedyke Primary School
DRUM G15 ....50 C1
Stonelaw High School
RUTH G73 ....111 E5
Stow College
COWCAD G4 ....2 C1
Strathclyde Art Centre
KVGV G3 ....2 B6
Strathclyde Business Centre
GOV/IBX G51 ....88 C3
MTHW ML1 ....137 E3
Strathclyde Country Park
MTHW ML1 ....153 G2
Strathclyde Country Park
Camping & Caravan
MTHW ML1 ....153 H4
Strathclyde Hospital
MTHW ML1 ....154 B5
Strathclyde Park Golf Club
HMLTN ML3 ....155 F5
Strathkelvin Retail Park
EKILN G74 ....38 A4
Summerhill Primary School
DRUM G15 ....33 G4
Summerlee Heritage Park
CTBR ML5 ....96 C2
Sunnyside Primary School
STPS/GTHM/RID G33 ....70 C3
Swinton Primary School
BAIL/MDB/MHD G69 ....94 C3
The Tall Ship at
Glasgow Harbour
GOV/IBX G51 ....88 B1
Tannochside Primary School
UD/BTH/TAN G71 ....115 F4
Taylor High School
MTHW ML1 ....137 F4

Temple Primary School
KNTSWD G13 ....51 G4
Templeton Business Centre
DMNK/BRGTN G40 ....90 B4
Tenement House
KVGV G3 ....2 B2
Tennant Caledonian Breweries
& St Mungo Heritage Centre
COWCAD G4 ....90 B2
Thames Open College
CGLW G2 ....2 D5
Theatre Royal
COWCAD G4 ....2 E2
Theme Park
BLSH ML4 ....153 F1
Thomas Muir High School
BSHPBGS G64 ....55 G2
Thorniewood FC
UD/BTH/TAN G71 ....134 C1
Thornliebank Health Centre
GIF/THBK G46 ....126 C3
Thornliebank Industrial Estate
GIF/THBK G46 ....126 A5
Thornliebank Primary School
GIF/THBK G46 ....126 D3
Thornlie Primary School
WISHAW ML2 ....173 H3
Thorntree Primary School
CAR/SHTL G32 ....92 B3
Thornwood Primary School
PTCK G11 ....65 G4
Tinto Primary School
PLKSW/MSWD G43 ....127 F1
Todholm Primary School
PSLYS PA2 ....105 E2
Tolbooth Steeple
CGLE G1 ....3 H7
Tollbrae Primary School
AIRDRIE ML6 ....98 D2
Tollcross Industrial Estate
CAR/SHTL G32 ....112 B1
The Toonspeak Young
Peoples Theatre
SPRGB/BLRNK G21 ....68 C4
Torrance House Golf Club
EKILN G74 ....179 F2
Torrance Primary School
BSHPBGS G64 ....19 F4
Toryglen Primary School
GVH/MTFL G42 ....110 B4
Toss Theatre
BLSH ML4 ....136 B2
Town Hall Business Centre
MTHW ML1 ....154 C4
Townhead Clinic
CTBR ML5 ....96 B1
KKNTL G66 ....40 A1
Townhead Health Centre
COWCAD G4 ....90 B1
Townhead Primary School
CTBR ML5 ....74 A4
Townhill Primary School
HMLTN ML3 ....168 D3
Travel Inn
BLSH ML4 ....135 F2
CCLE G1 ....3 H5
CUMB G67 ....26 C3
HMLTN ML3 ....153 F4
MTHW ML1 ....119 H5
PSLYN/LNWD PA3 ....84 B1
UD/BTH/TAN G71 ....114 A3

Travelodge
CGLW G2 ....2 D2
DMBTN G82 ....14 C4
GBLS G5 ....89 E5
The Triangle Shopping Centre
BSHPBGS G64 ....54 D2
Trinity High School
BLTYR/CAMB G72 ....111 H5
RNFRW PA4 ....63 G2
Tron Steeple
CGLE G1 ....3 G7
Tron Theatre
CGLE G1 ....3 H7
Tryst Sports Centre
CUMB G67 ....26 C3
Tulip Inn
GBLS G5 ....89 H4
Turnbull High School
BSHPBGS G64 ....54 B1
The Turret Surgery
KKNTL G66 ....21 E5
Turret Theatre
KKNTL G66 ....21 E4
Twechar Primary School
KSYTH G65 ....23 F2
UCI Cinema
CLYDBK G81 ....49 E1
UCI Cinema
EKILN G74 ....166 C5
Uddingston Cricket &
Sports Club
UD/BTH/TAN G71 ....133 H2
Uddingston Grammar School
UD/BTH/TAN G71 ....133 H1
Udston Primary School
HMLTN ML3 ....168 D1
University of Glasgow
BSDN G61 ....34 A1
BSDN G61 ....51 H3
KVD/HLHD G12 ....66 B3
KVD/HLHD G12 ....66 C4
University of Glasgow
Visitor Centre
KVD/HLHD G12 ....66 C4
University of Paisley
PSLY PA1 ....84 A5
University of Strathclyde
COWCAD G4 ....3 H5
KNTSWD G13 ....65 E1
University of Strathclyde RFC
STPS/GTHM/RID G33 ....70 C2
Victoria Buildings
Business Centre
PSLY PA1 ....84 D5
Victoria Infirmary
PLKSD/SHW G41 ....109 E4
Victoria Memorial
Cottage Hospital
KSYTH G65 ....7 H2
Victoria Primary School
AIRDRIE ML6 ....97 H2
GVH/MTFL G42 ....109 G2
Victory Baths
RNFRW PA4 ....63 G2
Viewpark Support Centre
UD/BTH/TAN G71 ....115 G5
Village Theatre
EKILN G74 ....166 C3
Walker Clinic
KVGV G3 ....89 E1

Wallace Primary School
JNSTN PA5 ....102 C2
Waverley Park Day Hospital
KKNTL G66 ....21 F4
Weaver's Cottage
KLBCH PA10 ....100 B3
Welfare Clinic
CUMB G67 ....26 D2
Wellgreen Health Centre
PLKSW/MSWD G43 ....108 B4
Wellhall Medical Centre
HMLTN ML3 ....169 F2
Wellhouse Primary School
STPS/GTHM/RID G33 ....93 F2
Wellshot Primary School
CAR/SHTL G32 ....92 A5
Westburn Cemetery
BLTYR/CAMB G72 ....131 H1
West Cemetery
HMLTN ML3 ....169 F2
West Coats Primary School
BLTYR/CAMB G72 ....131 E2
Wester Cleddens
Primary School
BSHPBGS G64 ....54 D1
Westercommon
Primary School
PPK/MIL G22 ....67 F2
Western Infirmary Accident
& Emergency
PTCK G11 ....66 B4
Westerton Primary School
BSDN G61 ....51 E1
The Westerwood Hotel
BALLOCH G68 ....10 D4
Westfield Health Clinic
CARD/HILL/MSPK G52 ....86 B4
Westfield Industrial Estate
BALLOCH G68 ....42 D2
Westfield Primary School
BALLOCH G68 ....43 G1
West Mains School
EKILN G74 ....166 D5
Westmuir Medical Centre
DEN/PKHD G31 ....91 G4
West of Scotland Cricket Club
PTCK G11 ....66 A4
West of Scotland Science Park
MRYH/FIRH G20 ....51 H2
West Primary School
PSLY PA1 ....83 H5
Westwood Business Centre
ESTRH G34 ....94 A1
Whistleberry Industrial Park
HMLTN ML3 ....152 B3
The Whitecraigs Golf Club
NMRNS G77 ....144 C3
Whitecraigs RFC
NMRNS G77 ....143 F5
Whitecrook Business Centre
CLYDBK G81 ....49 F2
Whitecrook Primary School
CLYDBK G81 ....49 F2
Whitehill Pool
DEN/PKHD G31 ....91 E2
Whitehill Secondary School
DEN/PKHD G31 ....91 E2
Whiteinch Business Park
SCOT G14 ....65 E4
Whiteinch Indoor
Bowling Stadium
SCOT G14 ....65 F4

Whiteinch Primary School
SCOT G14 ....65 F3
Whiteleys Primary School
CUMB G67 ....11 H5
Whitlawburn
Shopping Centre
BLTYR/CAMB G72 ....130 D4
Williamsburgh
Primary School
PSLY PA1 ....84 D4
William Street Clinic
KVGV G3 ....2 A4
Williamwood Golf Club
CRMNK/CLK/EAG G76 ....145 H1
Williamwood High School
CRMNK/CLK/EAG G76 ....145 G2
Williamwood Medical Centre
CRMNK/CLK/EAG G76 ....145 G2
Willowbank Primary School
COWCAD G4 ....67 E4
Willowbank Special School
CSMK G45 ....96 A3
Windlaw Primary School
CSMK G45 ....147 F1
Wishaw Academy
Primary School
WISHAW ML2 ....174 A3
Wishaw Business Centre
WISHAW ML2 ....174 A3
Wishaw General Hospital
WISHAW ML2 ....173 F2
Wishaw Golf Club
WISHAW ML2 ....173 G2
Wishaw Health Centre
WISHAW ML2 ....174 A2
Wishaw Sports Centre
WISHAW ML2 ....173 G3
Woodfarm High School
GIF/THBK G46 ....126 D4
Woodhead Primary School
HMLTN ML3 ....169 F5
Woodhill Primary School
BSHPBGS G64 ....55 F1
Woodilee Industrial Estate
KKNTL G66 ....40 B2
Woodlands Primary School
CUMB G67 ....44 D1
PSLYN/LNWD PA3 ....101 H1
Woodside Place
Business Centre
KVGV G3 ....2 A2
Woodside Primary School
HMLTN ML3 ....170 B3
Woodville Park
Industrial Estate
GOV/IBX G51 ....87 H2
Wyndford Primary School
MRYH/FIRH G20 ....52 C5
Wyndford Recreation Centre
KVD/HLHD G12 ....66 C1
Yoker Primary School
SCOT G14 ....50 A5
Yoker Sports Centre
SCOT G14 ....50 A5
York Place Surgery
KKNTL G66 ....21 E5

Acknowledgements

The Post Office is a registered trademark of Post Office Ltd. in the UK and other countries.

Schools address data provided by Education Direct.

Petrol station information supplied by Johnsons

One-way street data provided by © Tele Atlas N.V.   Tele Atlas

Garden centre information provided by

Garden Centre Association   Britains best garden centres

 **Street by Street** QUESTIONNAIRE

Dear Atlas User
Your comments, opinions and recommendations are very important to us.
So please help us to improve our street atlases by taking a few minutes
to complete this simple questionnaire.

You do not need a stamp (unless posted outside the UK). If you do not want to remove this page from your street atlas, then photocopy it or write your answers on a plain sheet of paper.

Send to: The Editor, AA Street by Street, FREEPOST SCE 4598,
Basingstoke RG21 4GY

ABOUT THE ATLAS...

Which city/town/county did you buy?

Are there any features of the atlas or mapping that you find particularly useful?

Is there anything we could have done better?

Why did you choose an AA Street by Street atlas?

Did it meet your expectations?

Exceeded ☐   **Met all** ☐   **Met most** ☐   **Fell below** ☐

Please give your reasons

ML070z

continued overleaf

Where did you buy it?

For what purpose? (please tick all applicable)

To use in your own local area ☐   To use on business or at work ☐

Visiting a strange place ☐   In the car ☐   On foot ☐

Other (please state)

LOCAL KNOWLEDGE...

Local knowledge is invaluable. Whilst every attempt has been made to make the information contained in this atlas as accurate as possible, should you notice any inaccuracies, please detail them below (if necessary, use a blank piece of paper) or e-mail us at *streetbystreet@theAA.com*

ABOUT YOU...

Name (Mr/Mrs/Ms)

Address

                                                        Postcode

Daytime tel no

E-mail address

Which age group are you in?

Under 25 ☐   25-34 ☐   35-44 ☐   45-54 ☐   55-64 ☐   65+ ☐

Are you an AA member?   YES ☐   NO ☐

Do you have Internet access?   YES ☐   NO ☐

Thank you for taking the time to complete this questionnaire. Please send it to us as soon as possible, and remember, you do not need a stamp (unless posted outside the UK).

We may want to contact you about other products and services provided by us, or our partners (by mail, telephone) but please tick the box if you DO NOT wish to hear about such products and services from us by mail or telephone. ☐

ML070z

Free Car Check worth £9.99 with AA Service Centres

Use yourself or give to a member of your family or a friend.

An AA Car Check could help you steer clear of costly problems by targeting the main causes of breakdown.

- The Car Check includes: tyre check — including spare; charging system/battery; drive belt tension; battery security; cooling system; fluid levels — engine oil and screen wash; lights; brake fluid; windscreen wipers/washers. This doesn't replace the need for regular servicing and maintenance.
- AA Service Centres have a national network of garages that are open 6 days a week, offering servicing, M.O.T., tyre replacement and mechanical repairs.

HOW TO CLAIM YOUR FREE CAR CHECK

- **Simply call 0845 609 0621 to book your car into an AA Service Centre.**
- Cut off the voucher at the bottom of this page and present it when booking your car in.
- **Offer ends 31st December 2005.**

Your FREE
Car Check voucher

(AA Street by Street Atlas 2005)

AASC PLANT NUMBER:

Notes

Notes